D1346492

CABINET GOVERNMENT

CABINET GOVERNMENT

BY

SIR IVOR JENNINGS

THIRD EDITION

CAMBRIDGE
AT THE UNIVERSITY PRESS
1969

Published by the Syndics of the Cambridge University Press
Bentley House, 200 Euston Road, London N.W.1
American Branch: 32 East 57th Street, New York, N.Y. 10022

Standard Book Numbers:
521 05430 3 clothbound
521 09570 0 paperback

First edition 1936
Reprinted 1937 1947
Second edition 1951
Third edition 1959
Reprinted 1961 1965
First paperback edition 1969

Printed in Great Britain
at the University Printing House, Cambridge
(Brooke Crutchley, University Printer)

CONTENTS

CONTENTS

PREFACE

Since the second edition of this book was prepared in 1949 much new material has become available, some of it covering the period before the First War, but most of it dealing with the period between the wars. The present edition brings in such material as was available up to the middle of 1957. The additional material has not required any substantial change in the nature of the book. I have, however, deleted much material from the Appendices in order to avoid making the book unwieldy.

The first edition, which was published in 1936, had two objectives. First, it was a description of the working of an important segment of the British Constitution. Secondly, it was a collection of precedents, as complete as it could be made, regulating the conventions of Cabinet government. Incidentally it fulfilled a third function, of describing the recent development of some British institutions and analysing recent constitutional disputes.

Now that the accumulated precedents of more than twenty years have been added to the Victorian and Edwardian precedents upon which the first edition was largely based, the question has arisen whether to omit some of them in order to make the book more easily read by those who desire examples rather than comprehensive information. Any such change would, I believe, make the book much less useful to the politician and the administrator. It is the accumulation of precedents, each with its different environment, which enables one to say what, in new circumstances, ought to be done; and the precedent which proves most useful is often not the 'leading case' but the case which at first sight seems relatively unimportant. I am reluctant, too, to cut down the historical material. Sir Lewis Namier has put constitutional history out of fashion among the historians, but it is still the servant of the lawyer and the politician, and practical experience leads one to increase rather than to diminish the volume of historical material. In the making and working of political institutions history undoubtedly teaches lessons.

PREFACE

This was intended to be the first of three volumes on the practice of the British Constitution. The second, *Parliament*, was published in 1939 and republished in a much-amended second edition in 1957. The third volume, after many delays, is now in preparation.

W. I. J.

July 1957

CHAPTER I

THE BRITISH CONSTITUTION

§1. *Law and Practice*

The Cabinet is the core of the British constitutional system. It is the supreme directing authority. It integrates what would otherwise be a heterogeneous collection of authorities exercising a vast variety of functions. It provides unity to the British system of government. If, therefore, a constituent assembly were to set out in a written document the present British Constitution, as it is actually operated, the Cabinet would be provided for in a prominent place. In the Cabinet and, still more, out of it, the most important person is the Prime Minister. It is he who is primarily concerned with the formation of a Cabinet, with the subjects which the Cabinet discusses, with the relations between the Queen and the Cabinet and between the Cabinet and Parliament, and with the co-ordination of the machinery of government subject to the control of the Cabinet. He, too, would be given a prominent place in a written constitution.

It is a trite observation that there is no such constitution. With us, 'the law' is not an emanation from authorities set up or provided for by a written and formal document. It consists of the legislation of Parliament and the rules extracted from the decisions of judicial authorities. The powers of these bodies and the relations between them are the product of history. The constitutional authorities have claimed and have exercised law-making functions and the people has acquiesced in their exercise. Revolution has helped to determine constitutional powers; but no revolution has produced a permanent written constitution. It has produced, instead, the recognition of a rule that Parliament can legislate as it pleases and that what Parliament enacts is law. What Parliament has enacted, the courts interpret and apply unless Parliament has otherwise provided. So far as Parliament has not legislated, the law is the body of rules developed and interpreted by the courts in the exercise of a jurisdiction which these courts have secured by the acquiescence of people and Parliament.

Neither the Cabinet nor the office of Prime Minister was established by legislation, nor has either been recognised by the courts of law. Until 1937 the Cabinet was not even mentioned in any Act of Parliament; and the Ministers of the Crown Act, 1937, did no more than provide higher salaries for those ministers who were members of the Cabinet, whereupon it became necessary to define which ministers were of the Cabinet. Until the same Act provided a salary for the Prime Minister and First Lord of the Treasury, there had been only two incidental references to the Prime Minister.[1] Neither the Cabinet nor the Prime Minister, as such, claims to exercise any powers conferred by law. They take the decisions, but the acts which have legal effect are taken by others—the Queen, the Privy Council, a minister, a statutory commission, and the like. These persons are under no legal obligation to obey, but they do obey. There is a whole complex of rules outside 'the law', nowhere inconsistent with it but nowhere recognised by it, which can be stated with almost as much precision as the rules of law. Such rules have been set out by many authorities; they are discussed in Parliament; they are appealed to whenever dispute arises. They are called by various names, but are now commonly referred to as 'constitutional conventions'.[2]

Such conventions develop around most constitutions. The laws provide only a framework; those who put the laws into operation give the framework a meaning and fill in the interstices. Those who take decisions create precedents which others tend to follow, and when they have been followed long enough they acquire the sanctity and the respectability of age. They not only are followed but they have to be followed. The more recent the legal framework, the more likely it is to be in accord with modern conditions. The law will state the practice, and the practice will follow the law. But with us the legal framework is in many respects of ancient origin. Though many changes have been made by legislation, the principles of the law laid down by the courts were established nearly three centuries ago. The change from monarchical to parliamentary government—or, if that be contentious, the

[1] Jennings, *The Law and the Constitution* (4th ed.), p. 70.

[2] Dicey, *Law of the Constitution* (9th ed.), ch. XIV. The term was in constant use in the course of the constitutional difficulties of 1909–14; cf. *Life of Lord Oxford and Asquith*, I, p. 261. See also Jennings, *The Law and the Constitution* (4th ed.), ch. III; and *British Coal Corporation* v. *The King*, [1935] A.C. 500.

recognition of the rights of Parliament—was incorporated into the law. Cabinet government is the consequence of parliamentary government, but this change was not effected by legislation or recognised by the courts. It was an extra-legal development; and though the administrative legislation of Parliament and the administrative decisions of the courts assume a Cabinet system, they neither establish nor formally recognise the rules that govern its operation.

The distinction between laws and conventions is not really of fundamental importance. A constitution necessarily rests on acquiescence, whether it be established by referendum or tacit approval or force. If an organised public opinion regards it as noxious it will be overthrown. If a Louis Napoleon or a Mussolini or a Hitler considers that he can induce or compel acquiescence in a change, he will not hesitate to overturn it merely because it is enacted as law. What is law and what is convention are primarily technical questions. The answers are known only to those whose business it is to know them. For the mass of the people it does not matter whether a rule is recognised by the judicial authorities or not. The technicians of government are primarily concerned. For the technicians, the difference appears to have three aspects.

In the first place, laws commonly have a greater sanctity, and there is greater reluctance to break them. This distinction is largely psychological. A rule of law has no merit merely because it is a rule of law: it is content and not form that matters. The fundamental conventions of Cabinet government are among the bases of the constitutional system; they are as important as the fundamental principles of the law. Their importance is, indeed, recognised. A person who proposed to substitute himself for the Cabinet—to make, that is, a change which could be brought about without any alteration of law—would be regarded as a dangerous revolutionary. Yet it cannot be doubted that, as between laws and conventions of equal constitutional importance, the law has the greater sanctity. Obedience to law is a fundamental duty; it is less frequently realised that obedience to conventions is also among the political virtues.

In the second place, it is the recognised duty of certain persons, especially of judges, to consider whether acts are legally valid and to take such steps as they can to see that the law is obeyed. While it is equally the duty of public authorities to obey the conventions, there is no formal method of determining when they are broken or of setting in motion the train of consequences which this breach should bring. It is commonly said that laws are 'enforced' and that conventions are not. This method of stating the case is a little too simple. It is difficult to conceive of law being enforced on a legislature whose powers of legislation are limited by law; it is difficult, indeed, to conceive of law being enforced against a Government, for the judges do not enforce law, they merely declare it. The so-called enforcement is the application of sanctions by administrative officers who themselves obey law in applying them. Such sanctions might be applied to a subordinate officer or authority; it is difficult to imagine them applying to the central governmental body. In Great Britain, no sanctions could be applied against the Queen, nor, in most cases, against those 'servants of the Queen' who are the principal governors, subject to the Cabinet and to Parliament, of the country. The efficacy of judicial decisions in important governmental matters lies not in enforcement, but in the precision of judgment, the recognised sanctity of law, and the power of public opinion. To break the law is to do something clearly and obviously unconstitutional. Unless there are special circumstances, such as a political or financial emergency, it is the subject of blame; it is possible to rouse public opinion to indignation; the breach would be proclaimed from every platform and blazoned forth in every headline. Breaches of constitutional conventions are less obvious and can be more easily clouded by a fog of misunderstanding. A judicial decision that a law has been broken leaves no room for argument, save as to its political justification; an accusation that a convention has been broken may be met by an accusation of factious and deliberate misrepresentation. The angel who has been formally condemned is no longer an angel; in the absence of formal condemnation he may protest his injured innocence.

In the third place, laws are for the most part precisely formulated. It is usually nobody's business to formulate conventions. They grow out of and are modified by practice, and at any given time it may be difficult to say whether or not a practice has become a convention. This, again, is not true of all conventions. Certain of the conventions governing the relations among the members of the Commonwealth are set out in the preamble to the Statute of Westminster. Others are formally recorded in the reports of Imperial Conferences. Here there is greater precision than with some of the rules of the common law. In any case, a convention that is fortified by a mass of precedents, such as those governing the relations between the Queen and the Government, is at least as closely defined as some of the rules of the common law. The conventional system of the British Constitution is in fact much like the system of the common law.

In short, the conventions are not really very different from laws. Indeed, it is frequently difficult to place a set of rules in one class or the other. For instance, the 'law and custom of Parliament' which are set out in May's *Parliamentary Practice* are, to the strict lawyer, not 'law'; yet they have every characteristic of law—including, in many cases, 'enforcement'. It is not easy to say whether the forms used in government, such as prerogative instruments, are prescribed by law or by convention.[1] From the reign of Edward III to 1921 the Convocations of the Church of England were summoned and dissolved at the same time as Parliament. In 1921 it was decided that this was a matter of practice and not of law and that they could legally be dissolved without a dissolution of Parliament.[2] For at least a century, again, the King's speeches to Parliament were approved in Council. It was at length decided that this, too, was a practice which could be dispensed with.[3] Possibly these practices were neither law nor convention, but at least they showed that the question of what is law and what is convention is not always capable of easy determination. A rule of law may, ultimately, be determined by a court; but until it is so determined it may be a matter of doubt.

§2. *Conventions*

The fact that there is no authoritative tribunal for the determination of conventions does, however, create difficulties. They grow out of practice and their existence is determined by precedents. Such precedents are not authoritative, like the precedents of a court of law. There are precedents which have created no conventions, and there are conven-

[1] Jennings, *The Law and the Constitution* (4th ed.), pp. 108–9.

[2] Fitzroy, *Memoirs*, II, pp. 744, 751.

[3] *Ibid.* II, pp. 756–7.

tions based on precedents which have fallen into desuetude. In discussing the action of the House of Lords on the Franchise Bill, 1883–4, Lord Salisbury said:

> Our constitutional law is built up of precedents. If the House of Lords reverses its course, under threats, because a majority of the House of Commons object to their policy, it will, by that very act, become constitutional law that the House of Lords is bound to submit to the House of Commons.[1]

The argument is a *non sequitur*. Every act is a precedent, but not every precedent creates a rule. It can hardly be contended that if once the House of Lords agrees with the House of Commons it is henceforth bound to agree with the lower House. Again, the fact that George V asked Mr Baldwin and not Lord Curzon to form a Government in 1922 does not of itself imply that the King must never in future appoint a peer as Prime Minister. Similarly, the fact that in 1924 the King granted Mr MacDonald a dissolution does not of itself imply that in future he has no right to refuse. It is more important that there is a course of precedents. The fact that the King assented to the Parliament Bill of 1910–11 and the Home Rule Bill of 1914 does not of itself prove that the King must invariably assent. It is a stronger fact that no monarch since Queen Anne has 'vetoed' a Bill. The facts that no Government has been dismissed since 1783 (regarding the 'dismissal' of Viscount Melbourne in 1834 as not a dismissal), that no peer since the Marquis of Salisbury has been Prime Minister, that a dissolution has not definitely been refused for at least a century, and so on, are important.

Even so, precedents do not definitely prove anything. 'Precedent, like analogy, is rarely conclusive', said Viscount Esher,[2] who was an authority on precedents and the confidential adviser of Edward VII and George V. Precedents create a rule because they have been recognised as creating a rule. It is sometimes enough to show that a rule has received general acceptance. Persons of authority for nearly a century have asserted the right of the Prime Minister to choose his colleagues, while recognising in the monarch the power to offer strong opposition

[1] *Letters of Queen Victoria*, 2nd series, III, pp. 559–60.
[2] *The Influence of King Edward*, p. 67.

to individual nominations. Persons of authority have never, so far as is known, asserted the duty of the monarch to grant a dissolution on request.

But such general recognition cannot always be proved. There can be no sufficient general recognition of a recent precedent. Occasionally, a single precedent will overthrow a long-standing rule. Until Mr Disraeli resigned in 1868, no Government had resigned on defeat at the polls and without meeting Parliament. Until 1932, no modern Government had 'agreed to differ'. Was it possible to say in 1868 that Mr Disraeli's act was unconstitutional, or in 1932 that the Cabinet's act was unconstitutional? The approach to the answer to these questions indicates an important characteristic of conventions. They do not exist for their own sake but because there are good reasons for them. The Reform Act of 1832 and the strict party alignments which had followed from it altered the nature of the Constitution. The power of the Government rested not on its ability to secure a majority of the House of Commons by 'management,' but on the vote of the electorate at the previous election. As Mr Baldwin said in explanation of his resignation in 1929: 'The people of this country had shown plainly that, whether they wanted Hon. Members opposite or not, they certainly did not want me, and I was going to get out as soon as I could.'[1]

The precedent of 1868 was due to the recognition of altered political conditions. The precedent of 1932 was due to exceptional political conditions. There was in existence a Coalition Government, formed of three parties with distinct organisations. It was created for what were alleged at the time to be specific purposes. It was said that the question of general tariffs was not one of the main problems which the Government had been formed to resolve, but was merely incidental. Accordingly it was agreed that members of the Cabinet might speak and vote against the proposal of the majority, which became the proposal of the Government. The precedent did not, therefore, change the ordinary rule of collective responsibility.[2] It provided an exception to it, capable of application only where conditions were similar. For this exception

[1] 261 H.C.Deb. 5 s., 535.

[2] As the Marquis of Lothian said: 'You cannot do it a second time': Thomas Jones, *A Diary with Letters 1831–1950*, p. 53.

special reasons were given; they may not be convincing, but in 1932, as in 1868, there were reasons.

Precedents create conventions because they have reasons of a general nature which relate them to the existing political conditions and because they are generally recognised to be sensible adaptations of existing conventional rules to meet changed or changing political conditions. The Reform Act fundamentally altered the political situation. So far as the older precedents depend upon the unreformed constitutional system, they are worthless. 'It is only within the last fifty years', said Mr Gladstone in 1878, 'that our constitutional system has settled down.'[1] 'The relations of the members of the Cabinet to their chief and to one another', said the Earl of Oxford and Asquith, 'present little resemblance to the practice of the eighteenth century.'[2] The effect of the Reform Act in resting political power upon popular election was not immediately obvious. It was thought necessary even in 1850 to secure from the House of Commons a vote of confidence because the House of Lords had passed a vote of no-confidence. Viscount Melbourne, in 1835, asked whether it was not a serious question for a man with a House of Commons majority to 'engage in political warfare' with the Crown, a majority of the House of Lords, almost the whole of the clergy, and three parts of the 'gentlemen of the country'[3]—the kind of question which no Liberal or Labour Government has since asked itself. In the same year Viscount Melbourne explained to William IV that the confidence of the Crown was essential to the existence of the Government.[4] Sir Robert Peel's refusal of office in 1839 was due to his belief that the dismissal of the Queen's Whig Ladies was necessary as a mark of the confidence of the Crown.[5] At least as late as 1841 a dissolution of Parliament was regarded as an appeal by the Sovereign to the people, and not merely an appeal by the Government.[6] Precedents arising before 1832 must be used in rare cases only, for the Reform Act altered the fundamental assumption of the Constitution. The change was not immediately obvious. The King and his ministers continued to

[1] *Gleanings of Past Years*, I, p. 225.

[2] *Fifty Years of Parliament*, II, p. 190.

[3] *Lord Melbourne's Papers*, p. 239.

[4] *Ibid.* pp. 269–72.

[5] *Peel Papers*, II, p. 392.

[6] See below, pp. 420–7.

make the old assumptions until 1837.[1] For most purposes the new Constitution may be assumed to date from 1841.[2] To say that the accession of the Tory Government in that year marked the acceptance of the principles of democratic government—as was done in earlier editions of this work—is perhaps to over-emphasise the degree of change. There had been a change of emphasis since 1783, and it continued for more than a century after the Battle of Waterloo. There was acceleration after 1832 because a slightly more popular franchise operated in a more representative collection of constituencies. The dependence of the Government upon popular vote—in that very limited sense—became obvious when the Tory Government took office in 1841, though the consequences had not been fully worked out when both the franchise and the distribution of seats were again altered in 1867. Democratic ideas were gradually adopted in the second half of the nineteenth century, though more readily by the Liberals than by the Conservatives. Today these democratic ideas are accepted by all parties and accordingly the normative value of a precedent depends upon its being in accord with those ideas. This is, however, an aspect of a general problem, for some precedents (particularly those of a technical character) have little if any relation with the system of representation; and the question in each case is whether the precedent accords with the principles of the Constitution as now accepted. Most precedents since 1841 are relevant and most precedents before 1841 are not.

This does not mean that earlier precedents are not sometimes quoted. In the debate on Roebuck's motion on the conduct of the Crimean War, Mr Disraeli quoted precedents from Charles II's reign. Mr Gladstone was able to show that they were not exactly in point.[3] Any precedent is good enough to attack an opponent, in spite of Viscount Melbourne's assertion that 'there is nothing so bad as a bad precedent'.[4] But it may be doubted whether the power of Parliament needs support from the actions of the notorious 'Pension Parliament'.

[1] For good examples, see Torrens, *Memoirs of Lord Melbourne*, pp. 378–84; Disraeli, *Lord George Bentinck*, p. 80.

[2] For the period of transition, see Jennings, 'Cabinet Government at the Accession of Queen Victoria', *Economica*, 1932 and 1933.

[3] *Parl. Deb.* House of Commons, 3rd series, vol. 136, col. 1199 *et seq.* (1855).

[4] *Lord Melbourne's Papers*, p. 390.

Another difficulty is that full information about precedents is not always available. Precedents of certain kinds are collected in the Privy Council Office, and precedents of a parliamentary kind are recorded in the Journals of the two Houses: but much of the machinery of government operates in secret. The Cabinet holds firmly to the principle of confidential discussion; the relations between the Crown and the ministers are not conducted openly; much of the work of the parties, too, is conducted in private. A democratic government has to justify itself by its acts, but the process of reaching decisions is conducted in secret. Consequently, many precedents are not known publicly until many years after they have occurred. Most writers have been led astray on the subject of the monarchy, for instance, by Bagehot's exposition. The material now available makes it evident that Bagehot's analysis was in many respects faulty. We all suffer from the same disability. During the twenty years which have elapsed since the first edition of this work was published, much new information about events which took place before 1936 has become available, as a comparison of the first and the third editions will show. In particular, the exposition in the chapter on constitutional monarchy was in many respects inaccurate; even in the present edition it cannot be assumed to be accurate, for no doubt constitutional monarchy has changed its character, in greater or less degree, since the death of George V; and without the use of confidential material it is not always easy to assess the permanent effects of such events as the abdication of Edward VIII or the accession of a young Queen.

Since opinions about constitutionality are as important as facts, the most important material is to be found in 'official' biographies and collections of papers. Such material is rarely published until after the death of the statesman concerned; and even then it is frequently 'edited' in order not to offend susceptibilities. It is also published with the object of 'honouring' the dead. Such material clearly has several defects. In the first place, it is not published until it is stale. The most important source of information is the *Letters of Queen Victoria*, which were not completely published until a generation after the Queen's death. In the second place, no material is available unless it is in writing. In the days when ministers spent most of their time writing letters, this was no great defect. The material now available for the fifty years after the Reform Act is not only abundant but superabundant. But in modern times ministers appear to write fewer letters. They decide matters by personal conversations, telephone communications, departmental minutes, and Cabinet discussions on the basis of memoranda. If records are made, they are usually not published. Indeed, the operations of the Official Secrets Acts have effectively stopped the publication of the most interesting documents. Their application has become stricter since the 'disclosures' of Mr Lloyd George and Mr Winston Churchill.[1]

In the third place, the editors of 'biographical tombstones' are not always competent to select material or to explain it. In some cases, executors have confided papers to relatives whose knowledge is not commensurate with their ambition. Their justification, no doubt, is that they are able to explain the statesman 'as a man'; but in fact the general public is more interested in him as a statesman, and it requires a student of politics to explain politics. The best recent biography, the *Life of Lord Oxford and Asquith*, was produced by the collaboration of a publicist and a relative, the latter himself no mean student of politics.

In the fourth place, the essential material is frequently buried in a mass of general commendation. The reading of Sir Theo. Martin's *Life of the Prince Consort* is like living for six months on a diet of sugar. Some of the sycophancy can be skipped, but it is never possible to be quite certain that the selection of material is not aimed at showing that the deceased was the embodiment of the ultimate good.

Fifthly, much information comes at second hand. There are no 'official' biographies of Lord Derby (the Prime Minister) or Mr Ramsay MacDonald, and some of the judgments of Mr Bonar Law and Lord Baldwin have had to be modified in consequence of the publication of more authentic biographies.[2] Living statesmen have yet to undergo what Mr Gladstone called 'monumental commemoration'. The state-

[1] It should, however, be added that these 'disclosures' were authorised on behalf of the Crown.

[2] The difficulty of the task of the constitutional commentator may, however, be judged by comparing G. M. Young, *Stanley Baldwin*, and A. W. Baldwin, *My Father: The True Story*.

ments of contemporary observers are frequently inaccurate. We need not believe of Greville that

> For fifty years he listened at the door,
> And heard some secrets and invented more.

We may, however, accept the judgment of Sir Alexander Gordon (the fourth son of the Earl of Aberdeen, who became Prime Minister): 'I find that, as regards almost every transaction of which I...happen to know the whole history, he [Greville] knows a great deal about it, but not *all* about it.'[1]

Finally, there are at least two views of the actions of most statesmen. The official biography usually gives one view only. Moreover, the student of the Constitution is necessarily affected by his own bias. If he prefers the view of Mr Gladstone to that of Mr Disraeli, is the preference due to a genuine objective belief that Mr Gladstone understood the way in which the Constitution worked, while Mr Disraeli worked the Constitution to suit his own ends? If he comes to the conclusion that Queen Victoria's relations with the Conservative Opposition were unconstitutional, is his judgment wholly free from unconscious bias? True impartiality is not possible. He can only guard against prejudice, he cannot eradicate it.

For these reasons, the description of a constitution must necessarily be defective. As Mr Baldwin said:

> The historian can tell you probably perfectly clearly what the constitutional practice was at any given period in the past, but it would be very difficult for a living writer to tell you at any given period in his lifetime what the Constitution of the country is in all respects, and for this reason, that almost at any given moment...there may be one practice called 'constitutional' which is falling into desuetude and there may be another practice which is creeping into use but is not yet constitutional.[2]

Even Lord Bryce, whose competence as an expounder of constitutional questions cannot be doubted, says that the British Constitution 'works by a body of understandings which no writer can formulate'.[3] Never-

[1] *Life of Henry Reeve*, II, p. 353.

[2] 261 H.C.Deb. 5 s., 531.

[3] Quoted in Report of the Joint Select Committee on Indian Constitutional Reform (1934), vol. I, part I, p. 7.

theless, these understandings do exist, and the student of the Constitution is able to form some judgment as to their content, though he must recognise that his conclusions are necessarily subject to qualification as more information becomes available. It is not entirely true to say, as Sir Austen Chamberlain said with Mr Baldwin's approval, that '"unconstitutional" is a term applied in politics to the other fellow who does something that you do not like'.[1] That doctrine would justify not merely the 'agreement to differ' that Mr Baldwin was defending, but the use by the Government of its legal means for suppressing the Opposition and so destroying our democratic government, a process which Mr Baldwin would not have sought to justify.

§3. *The Democratic Principle*

Practices turn into conventions and precedents create rules because they are consistent with and are implied in the principles of the Constitution. Of these, there are four of major importance. The British Constitution is democratic; it is parliamentary; it is monarchical; and it is a Cabinet system. It is democratic because it is carried on in the name of the people according to doctrines freely accepted by or acceptable to the people at a general election. It is parliamentary because the people are for the time being represented by the House of Commons, subject always to an appeal to the electorate; because, in consequence, the approval of the House of Commons is necessary for the general policy and, frequently, the specific proposals of the Government; and because all other authorities in the State, including the Sovereign and the House of Lords, must give way to a House of Commons that clearly represents the people. It is monarchical because the titular head of the State is a Sovereign who is the representative for the time being of a dynasty established by law. It is a Cabinet system because responsibility rests, subject to the House of Commons and the people, not in a single individual but on a committee of politicians sitting in Cabinet.

The fundamental principle is that of democracy. The people are all British subjects of full age resident in the United Kingdom and not subject to legal disqualification. The Queen, the Cabinet, the House of Commons and even the House of Lords are the instruments which

[1] 261 H.C.Deb. 5 s., 530 (1932).

history has created as, or political conditions have converted into, instruments for carrying out the democratic principle. It follows that freedom of speech and freedom of association are essential to the Constitution. Without free elections the people cannot make a choice of policies. Without freedom of speech the appeal to reason which is the basis of democracy cannot be made. Without freedom of association, electors and elected representatives cannot band themselves into parties for the formulation of common policies and the attainment of common ends. The extension of the franchise, the attainment of a large measure of freedom of speech, and the organisation of parties, have created the modern Constitution. The House of Commons and the Cabinet are the instruments of democracy. The prerogative of the Crown and, to a less degree, the powers of the aristocracy, have been subordinated to public opinion.

The appeal of the respective parties to the electorate and the choice of the electorate determine the party composition of the House of Commons. The party composition of the House of Commons determines the party origin of the Cabinet. The Revolution of 1688 finally settled that in the last resort the King must give way to Parliament. The Cabinet was the means by which the King on the one hand made certain that his actions had parliamentary approval and on the other hand enabled him to control Parliament through its majority. For many years after 1688 that majority was kept and maintained through 'connection'. Under George I and George II the policy was that of the Cabinet, subject always to royal veto. The 'support' of Parliament was obtained through the system of 'management' which the Duke of Newcastle developed into a fine art. George III adopted his own policy and, until 1784, he was generally able by 'management' to maintain a majority for himself and his Cabinet. From 1784 the policy was primarily that of the Cabinet. 'Management', too, gradually lost its sinister connotation from Burke's Economy Act of 1782 onwards. Parties gradually ceased to be collections of great landlords and their relatives, supported by a motley crew of careerists, and became instead congeries of politicians possessing more or less common ideas. With the accession to power of the Whigs in 1830 government became more dependent on public opinion.

The Reform Act of 1832 not only marked the change, it made it more emphatic. With the almost complete extinction of the 'rotten boroughs' (not entirely complete, as the Churchill borough of Woodstock showed[1]), 'influence' became much less important and candidates began appealing on a policy. Sir Robert Peel's Tamworth manifesto of 1834 showed that Governments must in future appeal to opinion. His accession to office in 1841 demonstrated that opinion could change Governments. Sir Robert Peel was, in the strictest sense, the first of the modern Prime Ministers, and, it has been said, 'the model of all Prime Ministers'.[2]

The changes were not equally obvious to all. Lord George Bentinck, the leader of the Protectionists after their defection from Peel's Government, 'thought that the Constitution of this country required that we should consider what is best for the general good of the country; and that it was not for us to be taught by the constituencies what is best for the interest of the country'.[3] But Disraeli, the apostle of the new age, thought otherwise: 'No one knew better than Sir Robert Peel that, without parliamentary connection, that parliamentary government which he so much admired would be intolerable; it would be at the same time the weakest and the most corrupt in the world.'[4] It would be not only weak, but impossible. The Government rests upon its party support in the House of Commons. Disraeli's criticism of Peel was that he 'seems never to have been conscious that the first duty of an English minister is to be faithful to his party, and that good and honourable government is not only consistent with that tie, but is in reality mainly dependent on its sacred observance'.[5] The statesman's authority rests on his party because his party has successfully appealed to the people. The party supports a policy; the democratic system implies an appeal to the people by contending parties supporting different policies.

Democratic government thus demands not only a parliamentary majority but also a parliamentary minority. The minority attacks the Government because it denies the principles of its policy. The Opposi-

[1] After 1832 there were thirty boroughs with less than 300 electors, seventy-two with less than 500, and 132 with less than one thousand: Seymour, *Electoral Reform in England and Wales*, p. 78.

[2] Rosebery, *Miscellanies*, I, p. 197.

[3] Disraeli, *Lord George Bentinck*, p. 80.

[4] *Ibid.* p. 224.

[5] *Ibid.* p. 282.

tion will, almost certainly, be defeated in the House of Commons because it is a minority. Its appeals are to the electorate. It will, at the next election, ask the people to condemn the Government, and, as a consequence, to give a majority to the Opposition. Because the Government is criticised it has to meet criticism. Because it must in course of time defend itself in the constituencies it must persuade public opinion to move with it. The Opposition is at once the alternative to the Government and a focus for the discontent of the people. Its function is almost as important as that of the Government. If there be no Opposition there is no democracy. 'Her Majesty's Opposition' is no idle phrase. Her Majesty needs an Opposition as well as a Government.

Party warfare is thus essential to the working of the democratic system. Yet it will not function if it is carried to extremes. A Government in control of both Houses could effectively stifle the Opposition. An Opposition which would not accept the majority rule could make the parliamentary system unworkable. In practice, government is by consent and opposition by agreement. In part, no doubt, mutual forbearance is good strategy. Experience has taught the British people that 'fair play' is as necessary in public as in private life. It has taught parties that parliamentary intransigeance and electoral dishonesty brings ultimate retribution at the polls. But the real reason is that the parties, like the people, accept the necessary conditions of democracy. They accept the principle, that is, that the majority may govern but may not oppress the minority. Government and Opposition alike assume the honesty of the other. The British Constitution, said Mr Gladstone, 'presumes, more boldly than any other, the good faith of those who work it'.[1] The 'understandings and habits of mind' by which the Constitution functions are 'bound up with the growth of mutual confidence between the great parties in the State, transcending the political differences of the hour'.[2] Democratic government has its Marquess of Queensberry rules, and public opinion is the referee.

The democratic principle is operated through the medium of the House of Commons. According to the pretty schematisation of the

[1] *Gleanings*, I, p. 245.

[2] Report of the Joint Select Committee on Indian Constitutional Reform (1934), vol. I, part I, p. 7.

textbooks, the member of Parliament represents a majority of the electors; the Government is responsible to a majority of the House of Commons; and the Government thus represents a majority of the electors. The system is, however, more complicated. Though it is convenient, for textbook exposition, to assume the absence of a Government and then to show how the Government is formed, there is in fact always a Government in existence. It is, also, not a group of administrators only but a group of party leaders. Subject to the law as to the termination of Parliament, it chooses for the dissolution of Parliament the moment most propitious to its own party prospects. If, as in 1900, 1918 and 1931, it can seize a moment of international excitement when it has, as it always puts it, 'the nation behind it', it uses its moral authority as a Government to assist its propaganda as a party.

Moreover, the electors do not vote for a candidate but for a party. An unusually feeble candidate may lose some votes; a particularly able candidate may secure some votes on his personality. But the ablest candidate cannot win a seat which is, from the party point of view, 'hopeless'; nor can the feeblest candidate lose a seat which is 'safe'. There is a core of voters who would think it treachery to vote against 'the Party'. Even the so-called 'floating vote', which possesses no fixed party affiliations, is affected more by the reputation of a party than by the reputation of a candidate. Also, though many of the constitutional principles assume the two-party system, whereby one party is 'in' and the other 'out', it frequently happens that there are three or more candidates available for each seat, and since there is no kind of proportional representation, the candidate who is elected may obtain only the largest minority vote and not the votes of a majority. Further, since neither constituency electorates nor majorities are equal, a majority of members of the House of Commons, all of whom secured majorities, would not necessarily represent a majority of the electors. Frequently the size of a majority in the House of Commons has little relation with the size of the majority, if any, of the total votes cast.

Again, though it is true that the Government is responsible to the House of Commons, this must be understood in a peculiar sense. This is not the place to examine the doctrine in detail.[1] Several observations

[1] See ch. xv and Jennings, *Parliament*, ch. v.

must, however, be made. Responsibility does not mean that every governmental act has to be reported to and approved by the House of Commons. The Government needs express parliamentary approval for its legislative proposals and most of its expenditure. It has to seek approval, too, of most of its proposals for taxation. It is called upon to explain and justify its administrative policy. If the House of Commons clearly shows that it does not propose to support the Government—if, that is, the Government has lost the 'confidence' of the House—it must resign, both because of constitutional conventions and because government without constant parliamentary support is legally impossible. But the House of Commons is not composed of individual members, each of whom takes thought about the desirability of each proposal and votes accordingly. The House of Commons consists of parties. The Government, as a party authority, has control over one or more of them. It appoints 'whips' and pays many of them out of public funds. It is their function to see that the members of the party attend the House and support the Government. If the Government has a majority, and so long as that majority holds together, the House does not control the Government but the Government controls the House.

The Government's control over its majority is substantial. To vote against the Government is to vote against the party.[1] To rebel against the Government is to leave the party. To leave the party is to lose party support at the next election; and, since the average elector votes for the party label, this means, probably, that the member will not be re-elected. Membership of the House and accession to office alike depend on party service and party support. Self-interest dictates support even when reason suggests opposition. Moreover, to vote against the Government is to vote with the enemy. To assist in defeating the Government is to risk the coming into office of the Opposition—a result which is, *ex hypothesi*, worse than keeping the Government in

[1] What 'party loyalty' means is perhaps best demonstrated by a letter from Mr Nigel Nicolson, M.P., to the *Spectator*, 30 November 1956, p. 783. 'Most of my Conservative electors feel...strongly that our action (in Egypt in November 1956) was right. But apart from its wisdom and morality, they believe that four separate loyalties, to the Prime Minister, the party, the country and the troops, were simultaneously invoked by it, and in their opinion a Conservative M.P. who disregards these loyalties is a traitor.' Clearly, he is a traitor if he puts wisdom and morality above loyalty.

office. All this does not apply to a Government which possesses no majority, because of the existence of three or more parties. In this case the support of a third party is essential; and, since third parties have difficulty in persuading the electors of the strength of their case, the threat to dissolve is usually effective.

The function of the House of Commons is, therefore, not to control the Government, but to act as a forum for criticism and a focus of outside opinion. The supporter of the Government can make his voice heard in private even when he refrains from acts of opposition. The force of an Opposition's criticism depends on the strength of opinion behind it. Even a dictator must give ear to public opinion. Where, as in the British system, debate is open, argument is public, propaganda has diverse ends and elections are free, and where, again as in our system, elections must occur at regular intervals, opinion has its influence not only at elections but at all times. British Governments are strong Governments, and all the stronger because their power rests on free opinion; but they are not dictators. They can do unpopular things, but retribution follows if popularity is irretrievably lost. Government, with us, is government by opinion; and that is the only kind of 'self-government' that is possible. So there arise 'two familiar British conceptions; that good government is not an acceptable substitute for self-government, and that the only form of self-government worthy of the name is government through ministers responsible to an elected legislature'.[1] There is, indeed, a third British conception, that good government cannot endure unless it is self-government.

[1] Report of the Joint Select Committee on Indian Constitutional Reform (1934), vol. 1, part 1, p. 5.

CHAPTER II

THE CHOICE OF A PRIME MINISTER

The Government is a body of party politicians selected from among the members of that party or group of parties which has a majority or can secure a majority in the House of Commons. By this device the operations of Government and legislature (subject always to the powers of the House of Lords) are integrated. Public opinion controls the Government through the House of Commons; and the Government through its majority controls the House of Commons. But the members of the Government are not elected by the House of Commons. They are nominated by the Prime Minister, subject to what will be said in the next chapter. The choice of a Prime Minister is therefore a function of some importance. It determines, subject to political conditions, the personnel of the Government.

The range of choice is necessarily limited by political conditions. The Prime Minister must be able to secure colleagues and, with his colleagues, he must be able to secure the collaboration of the House of Commons. Frequently there is no choice at all. If a party has a majority no Government can be formed without its support; and if it has a recognised leader that leader must become Prime Minister unless it is, for some special reason, prepared to follow a leader other than its own. At other times, however, the succession is obscure, and then a real choice can be made among several possible candidates.

This choice is made by the Sovereign. It is one of the advantages of constitutional monarchy that the titular head of the State has, so to speak, no party history. Unlike an elected President, he has no party loyalties. He may be, of course, hopelessly incompetent. He will have his prejudices, both political and personal. But the choice of a Prime Minister demands independence of status and familiarity with political conditions; and no method of choice can altogether avoid bias. Monarchy does provide independence of status and it avoids that kind of bias which proceeds from party loyalty. British monarchs, too, usually have a longer period of 'office' than their ministers.

Queen Victoria on one occasion quoted to Mr Gladstone what the Duke of Wellington had told her about William Pitt. George V had twenty-six years' experience of the political situation. George VI had four Prime Ministers. After four years, Elizabeth II had not, as Queen, had experience of a Labour Government, but she had had experience of Prime Ministers as different as Sir Winston Churchill and Sir Anthony Eden.[1]

It is a settled rule that the Prime Minister must be either a peer or a member of the House of Commons. Parliamentary government demands not merely that the Prime Minister shall, with his colleagues, be responsible to the House of Commons, but also that he shall be able to justify his policy in Parliament. Every Prime Minister since Sir Robert Walpole has been in one of the Houses.

As long ago as 1839, the Duke of Wellington stated in the House of Lords: 'I have long entertained the opinion, that the Prime Minister of this country, under existing circumstances, ought to have a seat in the other House of Parliament, and that he would have great advantage in carrying on the business of the Sovereign by being there.'[2] He had already declined the office in 1834, on the ground that the party differences were in the House of Commons.[3] Six of the Prime Ministers between 1837 and 1902 were peers; but experience showed that the Duke exercised unusual foresight. Lord Melbourne had some difficulties with Lord John Russell. Lord Derby had cause to complain that Mr Disraeli accepted amendments of substance in the House of Commons without prior consultation. Lord Aberdeen had the greatest difficulty in collaborating with Lord John Russell. Lord Beaconsfield's overwhelming prestige prevented serious difficulties with so mild a leader of the lower House as Sir Stafford Northcote; but the rise of the 'fourth party' made Lord Salisbury's absence from the House of Commons a source of weakness. Lord Rosebery and Sir William Harcourt found great difficulty in running in harness.

Mr Gladstone in 1894 did not consider that a Prime Minister ought

[1] It is, however, possible to exaggerate the importance of the monarch's experience. Queen Victoria knew less about British politics than she thought she knew. Cf. the remarks of Lord Gladstone, quoted below, p. 342.

[2] *Parl. Deb.* 3rd series, vol. 47, col. 1016.

[3] Peel, *Memoirs*, II, p. 19.

necessarily to be in the House of Commons.[1] But Lord Rosebery told Sir William Harcourt that 'the whole machinery of government was in the House of Commons and that it was next door to an absurdity to conduct it from the House of Lords'.[2] The experience of the 'dark horse in a loose box' accorded with his prophecy. Harcourt's own opinion was that 'the House of Commons makes and unmakes a Government, and has a right to expect that its chief representative should be within its sphere of influence and personally accountable to it'.[3]

Moreover, the relative positions of the two Houses were modified during the nineteenth century. Even after the Reform Act the 'family' system of government continued. Melbourne 'damned the Whigs' because they were 'all cousins'. The possession of great estates was a title to office until quite late in the century. Until 1868 both parties, as well as the Queen, denied the validity of the doctrine of 'democracy'. As late as 1850 the Government regarded a defeat in the House of Lords as serious enough to require a vote of confidence in the House of Commons. The acceptance of democratic principles in 1867 and 1884 gave to the House of Commons an overwhelming preponderance.

Again, there was a real party conflict in the House of Lords for most of the nineteenth century. As the House of Commons became more democratic, however, the House of Lords became more Conservative. Mr Gladstone's many creations did not redress the balance, for the successors of Liberal peers tended to become Conservatives. The introduction of the Home Rule Bill in 1886 turned most of the Liberal peers into opponents of Liberal Governments. Since that time the upper House has been overwhelmingly Conservative. There are now few Liberal peers, and a mere handful of Labour peers—mostly recent creations.[4]

The Parliament Act of 1911, too, considerably reduced the authority of the House of Lords. Though the House contains over 800 members, an attendance of more than 100 is rare. Frequently the 'House of Lords' means little more than the ministers and the other party leaders.

[1] *Letters of Queen Victoria*, 3rd series, II, p. 369.

[2] *Life of Sir William Harcourt*, II, p. 271.

[3] *Ibid.* p. 627.

[4] See Jennings, *Parliament*, ch. XI.

No peer has been Prime Minister since the resignation of Lord Salisbury in 1902. In 1923 the question, whether it was then possible for a peer to become Prime Minister, was definitely raised. The resignation of Mr Bonar Law left George V with a choice between Lord Curzon and Mr Baldwin. Lord Curzon's experience and party standing were greater. It is doubtful if Mr Baldwin would have become prominent in the councils of the Conservative party but for the fact that most of the Coalition Unionists remained faithful to Mr Lloyd George in 1922. The King nevertheless chose Mr Baldwin. Lord Stamfordham on his behalf explained to Lord Curzon that 'since the Labour party constituted the official Opposition in the House of Commons and were unrepresented in the House of Lords, the objections to a Prime Minister in the Upper Chamber were insuperable'.[1]

George V had favoured the decision from the beginning,[2] but his view was supported by Mr Bridgeman and Mr Amery[3] and Lord Balfour.[4] The King believed, too, that he was acting in accordance with the opinion of Mr Bonar Law. As a matter of fact, he was: but Mr Bonar Law's private opinion, which he had carefully refrained from passing on to the King, was based, not on the difficulty of having a Prime Minister in the House of Lords, but on the temperamental unfitness of Lord Curzon for the post.[5] The memorandum handed over by Colonel Waterhouse, Mr Bonar Law's private secretary, was written by Mr J. C. C. Davidson, Chairman of the Conservative Party Organization. This memorandum did mention Lord Curzon's unfitness, but the more convincing argument was that, in the opinion of many members of the House of Commons, 'the time...has passed when the direction of domestic policy can be placed outside the House of Commons'.[6] Mr Bonar Law, so far as is known, had never expressed such an opinion.

Nevertheless, if it was not plain in 1923 that the Prime Minister must necessarily be in the House of Commons—and Lord Salisbury, who

[1] *Life of Lord Curzon*, I, p. 352. [2] Sir Harold Nicolson, *King George V*, p. 376.

[3] Though Sir Harold Nicolson, *loc. cit.* seems to suggest that Messrs Bridgeman and Amery were consulted as Privy Councillors, it appears in fact that they pressed their views upon Lord Stamfordham at an accidental meeting in St James's Park and that they were never summoned by the King. Blake, *The Unknown Prime Minister*, p. 527.

[4] Nicolson, *op. cit.* p. 376; Blake, *op. cit.* p. 526.

[5] Blake, *op. cit.* pp. 511, 521–2. [6] *Ibid.* pp. 520–1.

like Lord Balfour was consulted on Mr Bonar Law's advice,[1] evidently did not think it was—it must be plain now. The Government owes a responsibility to the House of Commons alone. The composition of that House determines the nature of the Government. A vote in that House can compel the Government either to resign or to advise a dissolution. The Prime Minister is not merely chairman of the Cabinet; he is, also, responsible for the party organisation. That organisation matters in the House of Commons and does not matter in the House of Lords. Even when the Government has a majority in the House of Lords, the effective decisions are taken in the lower House. An amendment to legislation is generally accepted in the House of Lords by the Government only *ad referendum*. It is, in practice, essential that the Prime Minister should have his finger on the pulse of Parliament; and that is in the House of Commons. The most important reason is, however, that the Opposition would insist on having the Prime Minister in that House in order that he could be cross-examined and criticised. He, in his turn, would want to be in that House in order that he might defend himself and his Government in the forum in which he was most strongly attacked. If it happened that the Conservative party's most capable leader—or even (though the case is much less likely) the Labour party's most capable leader—was a peer, it would be a pity to exclude him from the succession because he could not lead the House of Commons. The solution seems to be, however, to deprive peers of their hereditary right to sit in the House of Lords and, as a corollary, to allow them to sit in the House of Commons.

The nature of the Queen's choice necessarily depends upon the state of parties in the House of Commons. The simplest case is that in which

[1] There were suggestions in 1940 that Lord Halifax should succeed Mr Neville Chamberlain as Prime Minister, with Mr Churchill as Minister of Defence. The arguments against a peer would be less strong in such an all-party coalition as that of 1940–5. Nevertheless Mr Churchill was appointed. Lord Halifax himself said that 'he felt that his position as a peer, out of the House of Commons, would make it very difficult for him to discharge the duties of Prime Minister in a war like this. He would be held responsible for everything, but would not have the power to guide the assembly upon whose confidence the life of every government depended': Winston Churchill, *The Second World War* (2nd ed.), I, p. 597. There is no evidence that the Labour party would have objected to Lord Halifax: see Dalton, *The Fateful Years*, pp. 307, 309.

a party has a clear majority. The Government must clearly be formed out of that majority and, if it has a recognised leader, he will be the Prime Minister. Such a situation usually arises as the result of a general election. In 1841 the Whigs were defeated at the general election, but met Parliament and were then defeated on a no-confidence amendment to the Address. The Conservatives had a clear majority and recognised Sir Robert Peel as their leader. Thus Queen Victoria had no choice at all. According to the modern practice, the defeated Government would not meet Parliament, but would resign as soon as the result of the general election was known. In 1874, for instance, Mr Gladstone's Government resigned at once, and the Queen sent for Mr Disraeli. In 1924 Mr MacDonald resigned when the Conservatives obtained a majority, and George V sent for Mr Baldwin; in 1945 when the Labour party obtained a majority Mr Churchill resigned and George VI sent for Mr Attlee; and in 1951, when the Labour party lost its majority, the King sent for Mr Churchill.

But the party has not always a recognised leader. In 1868 Queen Victoria might have sent for Lord Russell, though in fact she sent for Mr Gladstone. This step had, however, been expected, and Mr Gladstone had led the Opposition in the previous Parliament. This case is in fact very little different from that of 1874. The general election of 1880 supplies a better example. Mr Gladstone had resigned his leadership in 1874. Lord Granville led the Liberals in the House of Lords and Lord Hartington was leader in the House of Commons. Nevertheless, Mr Gladstone had led the opposition to the Government in the country, and the election was regarded by the ordinary elector as a personal contest between him and Lord Beaconsfield. The Queen sent for Lord Hartington, but he and Lord Granville had already agreed that Mr Gladstone must be Prime Minister. He recognised that no Government could be formed without Mr Gladstone's participation. As soon as he found that Mr Gladstone would not accept subordinate office, he advised the Queen to send for Mr Gladstone, and his arguments were supported by Lord Granville. Accordingly the Queen sent for Mr Gladstone and commissioned him to form a Government. As Lord Morley said:[1] 'It was Mr Gladstone's majority....Whatever liberty of

[1] *Life of Gladstone*, II, p. 618.

choice the theory of our Constitution assigned to the Queen, in practice this choice did not exist.'

Such a situation is not likely to be of frequent occurrence. Normally a party which succeeds in obtaining a majority at an election will have a recognised leader. But the Queen may have an effective choice where a Prime Minister in office offers a personal resignation or dies. The death of Lord Palmerston in 1865 does not provide a very good example because there was little doubt that Lord Russell, who had already been Prime Minister, ought to be his successor. Again, on the resignation of Lord Derby in 1868 there was little doubt that Mr Disraeli must be appointed (although the Government had no majority). The resignation of Mr Gladstone in 1894 provides a better example. He himself informed Mr John Morley that, if asked, he would advise Queen Victoria to send for Lord Spencer. Possibly, Lord Spencer might have secured the support of the Cabinet, for both Lord Rosebery and Sir William Harcourt had opponents as well as supporters. It appears that the great majority of the Cabinet, including Mr Morley himself, favoured Lord Rosebery. It is not clear whether this was known to the Queen. In any case, all her sympathies (so far as she had any sympathies for any Liberal minister) were with Lord Rosebery, and she appointed him to the office.

The Queen has a real discretion only where the retiring or deceased Prime Minister has no accepted second-in-command ready to step into his shoes. In 1923, as we have seen, George V had to choose between Lord Curzon and Mr Baldwin. In 1908, however, Mr Asquith, who had acted as Sir Henry Campbell-Bannerman's deputy during his illness, was the obvious and inevitable successor. In 1935 Mr MacDonald was the leader of a Coalition Government in which the Conservatives had an immense majority. When he resigned (and it appears that he was forced to do so by the pressure of his Conservative colleagues) George V had no alternative but to send for Mr Baldwin, the Conservative leader, who was already in effective control of the Cabinet. In 1937 the Chancellor of the Exchequer, Mr Neville Chamberlain, was Mr Baldwin's principal lieutenant and it had long been 'understood' that he would also be his successor. On the other hand Mr Chamberlain himself had no such second-in-command.[1] His Chancellor of the Exchequer, Sir John

[1] *Life of Neville Chamberlain*, p. 260.

Simon, was a Liberal National who would not have been acceptable to the Conservative party. When Mr Chamberlain resigned in 1940, however, the King's choice was really determined by the Labour party. It was necessary to appoint a Prime Minister who could secure the support of the Labour leaders and form a 'truly National' Government. They were not prepared to serve under Mr Chamberlain or any of the 'men of Munich'. Mr Churchill had attacked the Munich policy, had not been considered responsible for the disaster in Norway (though as First Lord of the Admiralty he had accepted his share of collective responsibility), and was acceptable to the Conservative party as well as to the Labour party. Effectively, the King had no choice.[1] If there is a Deputy Prime Minister he has a sort of claim, not necessarily conclusive but nevertheless strong, to the succession. The office was created by Mr Churchill when the War Cabinet was formed in 1940. It was obviously convenient for Mr Churchill, whose attention was directed mainly to the conduct of the war, and who was sometimes out of the country, to have a deputy, and it cemented the party alliance, without causing jealousy among the Conservatives, to give the office to Mr Attlee. There was, however, no Deputy Prime Minister in Mr Churchill's 'caretaker' Government of 1945, nor in Mr Attlee's Government of the same year, though Mr Herbert Morrison was commonly regarded as his deputy and probable successor if the office of Prime Minister fell vacant while the Labour party retained a majority. On the other hand, Mr Eden was Deputy Prime Minister in Mr Churchill's Government of 1951–5, and during the war Mr Churchill had advised that, in the event of his death, Mr Eden should be summoned. Sir Anthony himself, on taking office, did not appoint a deputy. When, owing to illness or absence, he was unable to preside at Cabinet meetings Mr Butler presided, but without any claim to succeed. It is not the practice in Britain, as it is in some other Commonwealth countries, to appoint an 'Acting Prime Minister'. The Prime Minister remains in effective control of his Government, questions usually addressed to the Prime Minister in the House of Commons are normally answered by the Leader of the House of Commons; and one of the ministers (usually the Leader of the House of Commons but not necessarily—Lord Curzon took the chair during

[1] *Ibid.* pp. 437–42.

Mr Bonar Law's absence in 1923) presides over the Cabinet in the absence of the Prime Minister. Clearly the Leader of the House and the temporary chairman of the Cabinet have claims, but they are far from conclusive, as Lord Curzon discovered. The Queen has a discretionary prerogative, and her selection cannot be forced by action by the Prime Minister. On the other hand, her task is to form a Government which the party majority will follow; and the claims tend to harden into claims of right as the Leader of the House or the acting chairman of the Cabinet becomes more and more clearly acceptable to his party.

In 1957, when Sir Anthony Eden resigned owing to ill-health, the Queen had a genuine choice, though Conservative opinion limited the field to Mr R. A. Butler, Lord Privy Seal and Leader of the House of Commons (who had presided over the Cabinet in Sir Anthony's absence), and Mr Macmillan, Chancellor of the Exchequer. After consulting Sir Winston Churchill and Lord Salisbury, the Queen chose Mr Macmillan, no doubt because he was thought to be more acceptable to the Conservative party. Some Labour members thought that the Queen should wait until the Conservative party had elected a leader, on the ground that Mr Bonar Law refused office in 1922 until he was elected leader. The position in 1922 was, however, entirely different. The Conservative party had split over the issue of support to Mr Lloyd George, and Mr Bonar Law had come out of retirement to lead the opposition to Mr Lloyd George. It was therefore reasonable for him to ask for an election. In 1956 the Conservative party was prepared to follow either Mr Butler or Mr Macmillan and was ready to accept the Queen's choice.

A completely different situation arises where the Government is defeated in the House of Commons and resigns. It may be assumed that such a case as that of 1841, when the Opposition had a clear majority, will not occur again, since, according to the modern practice, if an Opposition party secures a clear majority at a general election the Government does not go through the formality of meeting Parliament. It may be assumed, therefore, that on the defeat of a Government no party will have a majority. Such a situation will arise either because there are three or more parties, none having a majority, as when Whigs and Peelites defeated the Derby Government of 1852; when the Liberals, the Radicals and the Irish defeated the Salisbury Government in 1886 and again in 1892; and when the Labour party and the Liberals defeated the Conservative Government after the general election of 1923; or because the defection of a section of the Government party destroys its majority, as when the Protectionists left Peel in 1846; when Russell 'chalked up "No Popery"' in 1851; when Palmerston had his 'tit for tat' in 1852; when Russell supported Roebuck's motion in 1855; when the Orsini plot destroyed Palmerston's majority in 1858; when Robert Lowe led the Adullamites against the Reform Bill of 1866; when Gladstone was defeated on Home Rule in 1885; and when Rosebery's Government was defeated on the cordite vote in 1895.

In such a case the Queen has to consider three possibilities. The first is that a Coalition Government may be formed. In 1851 Queen Victoria sent for Lord John Russell and Sir James Graham in the hope that a coalition between Whigs and Peelites was possible. The combination was not then possible, but it was effected in 1852, when the Queen sent for Lord Aberdeen and Lord Lansdowne, and the former established a Coalition Government. On the defeat of that Government in 1855, she again tried to form a coalition, after Lord Derby had refused to form a Conservative Government. Lord John Russell failing, Lord Palmerston was invited to re-form, and succeeded in re-forming, the coalition between Whigs and Peelites, though most of the Peelites left the Government shortly afterwards. Lord Derby in 1866 tried to form a Coalition Government, but failed to obtain support outside his own party, and formed a minority Conservative Government instead. The same result followed in 1886, though Lord Salisbury was assured of Liberal Unionist support and a coalition was formed in 1895.

The second possibility is that one party may form a minority Government with the intention of advising a dissolution as soon as it is practicable to do so. Sir Robert Peel undertook to form a Conservative Government in 1839, but the 'Bedchamber question' compelled him to resign his task, and the Whig Government continued in office. In 1851 Lord Stanley tried to form a minority Government but was unable to secure the support of his party. He succeeded (as Lord Derby) in 1852 but was unable to obtain a majority at the ensuing general election.

In 1855 the Queen again sent for Lord Derby, but this time he refused, though he accepted office with the same result in 1858 and in 1866 (though on this ocasion there was no election until 1868). Mr Disraeli refused to accept office in 1873, and thus compelled Mr Gladstone to dissolve in 1874. Lord Salisbury, however, accepted office in 1886 and again in 1895. Sir Henry Campbell-Bannerman and Mr Bonar Law formed Governments in 1905 and 1922 respectively, though in these cases the previous Governments resigned without being defeated.

The third possibility is that a minority Government can be formed which may be able to maintain itself in office in spite of its lack of a majority. This happened in 1846, when Lord John Russell was able to obtain Peelite support; in 1866, when Mr Disraeli's finesse enabled the Conservatives to remain in office until 1868; in 1886, when Lord Salisbury was supported by the Liberal Unionists; in 1892, when the Liberal Government had the support of the Irish so long as Home Rule was in its programme; and in 1924 and 1929, when the Labour party received discriminating Liberal support.

The situation is much the same where political conditions cause the resignation of a Government which has not suffered defeat either in Parliament or at the polls. In 1905, when Mr Balfour decided that he could not continue a Government which was breaking up over Tariff Reform, Edward VII sent for Sir Henry Campbell-Bannerman, who formed a Liberal Government pending an appeal to the people. In 1922, when the Conservative under-secretaries and back-benchers, led by Mr Bonar Law, rebelled against the Coalition, George V sent for Mr Bonar Law, who formed a Conservative Government and advised a dissolution. In 1931 the Labour Government had no majority but was governing with Liberal support. Finding itself unable to agree on measures to deal with the financial crisis, it resigned; and Mr MacDonald was commissioned to form a Coalition Government. In 1940, Mr Neville Chamberlain's majority falling to 81, and the Labour party having withdrawn its general support, the Government resigned and George VI sent for Mr Churchill because he could form a Coalition Government which included members of the Labour party.

Where no party obtains a majority at a general election there are two possibilities only, the formation of a Coalition Government or the formation of a minority Government with Opposition support; for another dissolution is not practicable. This was the position in 1892, when the Liberals had Irish support, and in 1924 and 1929, when the Labour party was supported by the Liberals. In 1892 and 1924, however, the defeated Government met Parliament, partly because the situation was not clear, and partly because it was good tactics to show, in 1892 that the Liberals were dependent on the Irish,[1] and in 1924 that the Liberals intended to support the Socialists.

Apart, therefore, from the conditions which arise when a Prime Minister dies or resigns for personal reasons, the Queen's free choice arises through complications in the political situation. Such complications are of more frequent occurrence than is commonly realised. There were minority Governments from 1839 to 1841, from 1846 to 1852, in 1852, from 1858 to 1859, from 1866 to 1868, from 1885 to 1886, in 1886, from 1886 to 1892, from 1910 to 1915, in 1924, and from 1929 to 1931. There were Coalition Governments from 1852 to 1855, from 1895 to 1905, from 1915 to 1922, and from 1931 to 1945.[2] The exact point at which a coalition becomes a unified party Government is not always clear. There is a tendency for coalitions to lose their party differences. It is not possible to fix the date on which the Peelites were absorbed into the Liberal party, nor that at which the Liberal Unionists were merged into the Conservative party. It would be, for instance, pedantic to refer to the Unionist Governments from 1900 to 1905 as 'coalitions'; and, on the other hand, it is possible to be still more pedantic, and to assert that Palmerston's Government from 1855 to 1858 was a coalition of Liberals and Peelites. Again, the 'National' Governments from 1935 to 1940, if not from 1932 to 1935 also, were really Conservative Governments, since the Conservative party had a majority, the Liberal Nationals were an extremely small party, and the National Labour members (including the Prime Minister from 1932 to 1935) were but

[1] *Life and Letters of Sir Austen Chamberlain*, I, p. 51.

[2] The coalitions of 1915 to 1922 (Asquith and Lloyd George Governments) and 1940 to 1945 (Churchill Government) were peculiar in that one party had a majority but a coalition or 'National' Government representing all parties was considered desirable for the efficient waging of war. Those from 1931 to 1940 (MacDonald, Baldwin and Chamberlain Governments) were peculiar because, though the Conservative party had a majority and the Labour party was in opposition, it was thought desirable to pretend that they were 'National' Governments.

a group. Even in 1956 the Liberal Nationals had not been fully absorbed into the Conservative party.

It must not be thought, however, that the absence of a strict two-party system gives the Queen a discretion to summon as Prime Minister whom she pleases. It is an accepted rule that when a Government is defeated, either in Parliament or at the polls, the Queen should send for the leader of the Opposition. There may be two or more parties in opposition. But the practice of the present century has created an 'official' Opposition whose leader is 'the leader of the Opposition' and since 1937 (except from 1940 to 1945) this post has been officially designated by Mr Speaker in order that the salary provided under the Ministers of the Crown Act, 1937, may be paid to him. That leader is associated with the Prime Minister in non-political matters, such as those connected with the Crown. It is he who asks questions as to parliamentary business, though the conversations 'behind the Speaker's Chair' which enable business to be conducted expeditiously are conducted between the Government and the leaders and whips of all the Opposition parties. The largest party in Opposition is the 'official' Opposition.

The rule is that on the defeat and resignation of the Government the Queen should first send for the leader of the Opposition. This rule is the result of long practice, though it has hardened into a rule comparatively recently. Its basis is the assumption of the impartiality of the Crown. Democratic government involves competing policies and thus the rivalry of parties. The policy to be forwarded is that which secures the approval of the House of Commons, subject to the power of the Government to appeal to the electors. If, therefore, the Government is defeated in the House of Commons and does not appeal to the people, or if, having appealed to the people, it is defeated, a new Government has to be formed. The Queen's task is only to secure a Government, not to try to form a Government which is likely to forward a policy of which she approves. To do so would be to engage in party politics. It is, moreover, essential to the belief in the monarch's impartiality not only that she should in fact act impartially, but that she should appear to act impartially. The only method by which this can be demonstrated clearly is to send at once for the leader of the Opposition.

In 1839 and 1841 Lord Melbourne advised Queen Victoria to send for Sir Robert Peel, as leader of the Conservative Opposition. In 1845 Peel suggested, without formally giving advice, that she should send for Lord John Russell, who was clearly the leader of the Whigs. Lord John Russell was then unable to form a Government, but did so in 1846. In 1851 the Queen decided to send for Lord Stanley; and Lord John Russell and Lord Lansdowne, who were consulted, agreed with the Queen and the Prince Consort that 'Lord Stanley and the Protection Party ought to be appealed to'.[1] Lord Stanley was unable to form a Government, but did so (as Lord Derby) in 1852. The position on his resignation was peculiar, because of the agreement of Whigs and Peelites to serve under Lord Aberdeen. The Queen sent for Lord Aberdeen, but protected herself by sending for Lord Lansdowne as well.

In 1855 Lord Aberdeen agreed with the Queen that 'there remained nothing to be done but to offer the Government to Lord Derby, whose party was numerically the strongest, and had carried the motion'.[2] The Queen sent for Lord Derby 'as the head of the largest party in the House of Commons, and which had by its vote chiefly contributed to the overthrow of the Government'.[3] Lord Derby denied the responsibility, since his party had not proposed the motion and had had no communication with the mover, though their views compelled them to support the motion. Lord Derby, being unable to form a coalition, refused to take office. He was again sent for in 1858, and formed a Government.

In 1859 there was no doubt that the Liberal party must form the Government, and there was doubt only about the leader. On the resignation of Lord Russell's Government in 1866, the Queen sent for Lord Derby. In 1868 she sent for Mr Gladstone 'as the acknowledged leader of the Liberal party'.[4] In 1873 she sent for Mr Disraeli, who refused to form a Government with the existing House of Commons. In 1874 she again sent for him, and this time he accepted office. In 1880 she sent for Lord Hartington 'as leader of the Opposition';[5] though the phrase was

[1] *Letters of Queen Victoria*, 1st series, II, p. 347.
[2] *Ibid.* 1st series, III, p. 101.
[3] *Ibid.* 1st series, III, p. 102.
[4] *Life of Gladstone*, II, p. 252. The phrase is probably not quite accurate.
[5] *Life of the Duke of Devonshire*, II, pp. 272–3.

not accurate, Lord Hartington was certainly leader of the Liberal Opposition in the House of Commons. On the resignation of Mr Gladstone's Government in 1885 she sent for Lord Salisbury, who led the Conservative party in the House of Lords.

The Queen was anxious not to follow this series of precedents on the resignation of Lord Salisbury's Government in 1886. It should first be said in the Queen's favour that it was by no means certain that Mr Gladstone could form a Government. There had been dissensions over Irish policy in his previous Government, and the rumours as to his policy during the election, especially the 'Hawarden Kite' which Mr Herbert Gladstone had flown, had shown clearly that some of the influential Liberal leaders would not follow him. But she had summoned Lord Derby in 1851, 1852, 1855, 1858, and 1866, when it was more difficult for him to form a Government than it was for Mr Gladstone to form a Liberal Government in 1886.[1] Moreover, she had summoned Lord John Russell after Lord Derby's refusal in 1855, when it was obvious to everybody except Lord John Russell that he could not form a Government. The real reason for her hesitation in 1885–6 was that she intensely disliked Mr Gladstone's policy. She was supported, too, by Lord Salisbury, who followed the unconstitutional precedent which Lord Beaconsfield had set in 1880, with the Queen's connivance, of considering the prospects of the Conservative party rather than the necessity of preserving the Queen's impartiality.

When the defeat of the Government at the general election was imminent, the Queen, with Lord Salisbury's consent, opened communications with Mr Goschen, who still called himself a Liberal. 'I appeal to *you*', she said,[2] 'and to all moderate, loyal, and *really patriotic* men, who have the safety and well-being of the Empire and the Throne at heart, and who wish to save them from destruction, with which, if the Government again fall into the reckless hands of Mr Gladstone, they would be threatened, to rise above party and to be true patriots!' The letter went on to explain that it was the duty of moderate Liberals ('who indeed ought to be called "*Constitutionalists*"') 'to prevent Mr Gladstone recklessly upsetting the Government'. She then said that if they did not act the country would be ruined, and explained in a postscript that

[1] Above, p. 29. [2] *Letters of Queen Victoria*, 2nd series, III, pp. 712–14.

the Conservative party 'are very united and strong'.[1] The Marchioness of Ely, on the Queen's behalf, sent a similar but more coherent and less passionate letter to Mr W. E. Forster.[2]

Mr Goschen's reply was, to the Queen, 'very satisfactory' and the replies of Lord Hartington and Mr Forster 'most satisfactory'.[3] Another letter from Mr Goschen explained that 'the most important of Mr Gladstone's late colleagues' would do their utmost to prevent the adoption of any course that might compel the Government to resign.[4] The Queen informed Lord Salisbury of its contents.[5] Another 'very satisfactory' letter from Mr Goschen produced the reply that it was 'now a *duty* of *all true patriots*' to show that 'the moderate leaders of the Liberal party' did *not* lean to Mr Gladstone's way of thinking.[6] But, whatever the 'true patriots' might be thinking or doing, the Government was defeated on the 'three acres and a cow' amendment moved by Mr Jesse Collings. There were, it seems, only about thirteen Liberal patriots true enough to vote with the Conservative Government.

The Queen was reluctant to accept the Government's resignation and suggested that she should talk to Mr Goschen. Lord Salisbury agreed, and suggested that it should be done by his advice in order to relieve her from all responsibility. The Queen satisfied her conscience by considering that 'in former days old Lord Lansdowne and the great Duke of Wellington had been consulted in this way, in '51 and in '55'.[7] Lord Salisbury also expressed the wish that 'the moderate parties should draw together'.[8] He saw the draft of the invitation to Mr Goschen and justified himself by stating that 'the constitutional rule is that your Majesty can never be without a Minister; for, as your Majesty can do no wrong, there must always be somebody whom the House of Commons can impeach. From this Lord Salisbury would deduce that a resignation of a Prime Minister can never be accepted till the successor is definitely suggested.'[9] Mr Goschen, however, telegraphed that his visit would expose the Queen to misconstruction and misinterpretation, and entreated her to send for Mr Gladstone.[10]

[1] *Ibid.* 2nd series, III, pp. 712–14.
[2] *Ibid.* 2nd series, III, p. 714.
[3] *Ibid.* 2nd series, III, pp. 717–18.
[4] *Ibid.* 3rd series, I, pp. 5–6.
[5] *Ibid.* 3rd series, I, p. 8.
[6] *Ibid.* 3rd series, I, pp. 16–17.
[7] *Ibid.* 3rd series, I, p. 24.
[8] *Ibid.* 3rd series, I, p. 25.
[9] *Ibid.* 3rd series, I, p. 26.
[10] *Ibid.* 3rd series, I, p. 26.

Sir Henry Ponsonby then saw Lord Salisbury, and reported that Lord Salisbury had said that 'had Mr Gladstone announced the Irish policy attributed to him, there might have been some grounds for not calling upon him to form a Government. But no public authorised statement had appeared, and he felt compelled to advise that your Majesty should send for Mr Gladstone.' But Lord Salisbury also said that Mr Goschen ought to have gone to Osborne, and that Sir Henry Ponsonby should see Mr Goschen. Mr Goschen was insistent that Sir Henry Ponsonby should see Mr Gladstone at once. Ponsonby then saw Mr Gladstone, and explained that the Queen asked if he could form an administration. He added: 'That your Majesty had understood, from his repeated expressions of a desire to retire from public life, that he would not accept office, and therefore in sending this message she left him free to accept or not.' Mr Gladstone, in accepting, said that he was 'very grateful for your Majesty's gracious consideration for his declining years'.[1]

In the end, therefore, the Queen followed precedent. Her anxiety to see Mr Goschen was due to a hope that a coalition could be formed to keep out Mr Gladstone and to prevent the acceptance of the Home Rule policy which, as she assumed, Mr Gladstone would propose. Her motives were quite unconstitutional. If the Crown accepts a policy and uses its powers to forward that policy, it takes part in party warfare. It is then inevitable that people who disagree with that policy should enter into a contest with the Crown. Lord Salisbury's suggestion that the Queen could have refrained from sending for Mr Gladstone if he had openly declared for Home Rule will not bear examination. The Queen would not have been entitled to use her powers either for or against Home Rule. It was her duty to find a Government which could secure a majority in the House of Commons. The electorate had just returned a substantial Liberal majority which was led by Mr Gladstone. Under his leadership it had supported an amendment to the Address which, as Lord Salisbury rightly saw, compelled the resignation of the Government. But even if the majority in support of the motion had not been a compact group, it would have been out of accord with the precedents not to have applied to Mr Gladstone. The question whether Mr Gladstone could form a Government could be settled as similar

[1] *Letters of Queen Victoria*, 3rd series, I, pp. 27–8.

questions had been settled in the past, by asking Mr Gladstone to make the attempt. We need not, for the moment, ask whether Mr Goschen ought to have given advice.[1]

During the general election of 1886, the Queen asked Mr Goschen if she should not send for Lord Salisbury when Mr Gladstone resigned. He replied in the affirmative.[2] This was a week before Mr Gladstone's resignation, and was quite informal. Immediately on receipt of the resignation, the Queen sent for Lord Salisbury. Before the general election of 1892, the Queen explained to her private secretary that in the event of a change of Government she had intended to send first for Lord Rosebery, though after his recent speech (which was so radical as to be 'almost communistic'), this was impossible.[3] Sir Henry Ponsonby replied that some time before, Lord Rosebery had said that it would be impossible for anyone but Mr Gladstone to form a Government, and that if the Queen sent for any other member of the Liberal party he would refuse. 'If, after refusal, the Queen called on Mr Gladstone, it would do harm to the prestige of the Sovereign, as it would elevate Mr Gladstone into a species of dictator who [*sic*] the Queen was forced to accept.'[4] However, Ponsonby talked to Sir William Harcourt and some minor members of the Opposition. When a Gladstonian majority became evident, Ponsonby again went round collecting the views of minor members of the Liberal party, and especially their views about Mr Gladstone's health.[5] The Queen insisted that if there was an adverse vote in the House of Commons she *must* see Lord Rosebery before anyone else.[6] However, she subsequently thought better of her resolution and sent for Mr Gladstone as soon as Lord Salisbury resigned.[7] On the defeat of the Liberal Government in 1895, the Queen sent at once for Lord Salisbury.

Thus, in every case during Queen Victoria's reign (with the exception of the peculiar case of 1852, when the Opposition had just agreed to coalesce under a new leader), the leader of the Opposition had been sent for. In 1904 Mr Balfour stated to Lord Esher that if a change of

[1] See below, pp. 40–1.
[2] *Letters of Queen Victoria*, 3rd series, I, p. 161.
[3] *Ibid.* 3rd series, II, p. 120.
[4] *Ibid.* 3rd series, II, pp. 121–2.
[5] *Ibid.* 3rd series, II, pp. 130–2.
[6] *Ibid.* 3rd series, II, p. 132.
[7] *Ibid.* 3rd series, II, p. 141.

Government took place he considered 'that the King should send for Campbell-Bannerman, and *not* for Lord Spencer; on the ground that the former *is* the recognised leader of the Liberal party while the latter is only the leader of about 20 peers, and that the question as to whether C. B. could or would form a Government is not one that in its primary stages need concern the Sovereign'.[1] In 1905 Lord Esher noted:

> Great pressure is being put upon the King to send for Spencer and Campbell-Bannerman together and ask their advice. I trust that he will not give way to this temptation, as it would be to give away the most important prerogative of the Sovereign. Although many people think otherwise, there is no precedent for such a step. I have looked through all the precedents for the King in the private archives at Windsor and there is not a single example in the Queen's reign of her asking advice of anyone except the outgoing Minister as to the person upon whom her choice should fall. The obvious duty of the King is to make up his own mind, and the wisest thing he can do is to adhere rigidly to precedent.[2]

These statements are a little too positive. They ignore the fact that Queen Victoria consulted Lord Lansdowne and (informally) the Duke of Wellington in 1851; that she sent for Lord Lansdowne as well as Lord Aberdeen in 1852; that she consulted Mr Goschen in 1885, both by letter and through her private secretary; that she consulted Mr Goschen informally in 1886; and that her private secretary made informal soundings in 1892. Also, if it be accepted that the monarch must send for the leader of the Opposition, he has given away, not retained, a prerogative which the Queen assumed in 1885 that she possessed. A power to consult means a power to choose; absence of a power to consult means a binding obligation to send for the leader of the Opposition. Edward VII did in fact send for Sir Henry Campbell-Bannerman and did not consult (at least formally) any other person. Mr Balfour went through the papers of 1873–4, and Lord Esher provided the King with a memorandum based on the precedents of 1880 and 1895.[3]

The later precedents are those of 1923, 1924, 1929, 1945 and 1951. In each case the King sent for the leader of the Opposition. In 1923 Sir Austen Chamberlain's view was that Mr Baldwin should resign and advise the King to send for Mr MacDonald and Mr Asquith (as leader

[1] *Esher Papers*, II, p. 56. [2] *Ibid.* II, p. 78. [3] *Ibid.* II, pp. 119, 123.

of the Liberal party) together and ask if either of them could form a Government with a parliamentary majority.[1] This would of course have avoided the necessity of the King choosing between a Labour Government and a Liberal Government, and should not be ruled out as a possibility in some conditions; but in the conditions of 1923 such action would have been represented by some Labour politicians as an attempt to keep the Socialists out.

Mr Baldwin's own inclination was to resign forthwith without meeting Parliament, but eventually he agreed with the King that it was his duty to let the House of Commons decide. Moreover, Mr Baldwin made it plain that he would not form an alliance with the Liberals for the sole purpose of keeping Labour out. He had 'killed one coalition and would never join another';[2] nor did he think it fair for the two bourgeois parties to join to keep the Labour party out. Other Conservative leaders were not so complacent, and Lord Stamfordham was deluged with bright ideas:

> Lord Balfour advanced a very tentative opinion that a Conservative Government might still survive under his own leadership or that of Mr Neville Chamberlain; Lord Younger suggested that Mr Baldwin might agree to serve in a coalition under Mr Asquith; Lord Derby felt that Mr Austen Chamberlain ought to succeed Mr Baldwin and might then be able to secure Liberal support; Mr St Loe Strachey, editor of the *Spectator*, made the startling proposal that Mr McKenna (who was not then even a Member of Parliament) should be asked by the King to form a 'Government of National Trustees' who should hold office for two years.[3]

On the other hand, Mr Asquith, when consulted, expressed the opinion that when the Government was defeated in the House of Commons the King should summon the leader of the Labour party. The King himself took the same view. He considered that the Government should meet Parliament and that, if it was defeated, he should send for Mr MacDonald. It was done accordingly.

In 1924, as in 1945 and 1951, there was no difficulty of any kind. In 1924 the Conservative party had a majority, and George V sent for Mr Baldwin; in 1945 the Labour party won the election and George VI

[1] *Life and Letters of Sir Austen Chamberlain*, II, p. 239.
[2] Nicolson, *King George V*, p. 383. [3] *Ibid.*

sent for Mr Attlee; in 1951 the old war-horse, Sir Winston Churchill, came back as leader of the Conservative party. In 1929, when no party obtained a majority but the Conservative party lost its support, Mr Baldwin decided to resign forthwith because the public would think it 'unsporting' of him not to do so and would suspect that he was contemplating a deal with the Liberals.[1] George V agreed with Mr Baldwin and sent for MacDonald.

There is thus a long series of precedents covering more than a century. In each case the monarch has sent for the leader of the Opposition. The precedent of 1852 is quite exceptional. If there was a leader of the Opposition it was Lord Aberdeen. Neither Lord Palmerston nor Lord John Russell could be said to be the Liberal leader, and the Queen had no real information of the coalition under Lord Aberdeen. She therefore sent for the elder statesmen of the two Opposition parties and commissioned Lord Aberdeen as soon as she had information that both parties were prepared to serve under him. The arguments already given[2] appear to be conclusive. The correct rule was stated by Mr Balfour in 1904, and though the statements of Lord Esher in 1905 were not exact, the advice which he gave was correct. Where there is a leader of the Opposition the Queen must send for him.

The rule has for its corollary the rule that before sending for the leader of the Opposition the monarch should consult no one. If he takes advice first, it can only be for the purpose of keeping out the Opposition or its recognised leader. To try to keep out the Opposition is to take sides in a party issue. To try to defeat the claims of the recognised leader is to interfere in the internal affairs of the chief Opposition party. Lord Salisbury's advice in 1885 was quite unsound. The precedents of 1851 and 1855 quoted by Queen Victoria to justify sending for Mr Goschen were not in point. It is true that the Queen saw Lord Lansdowne before she sent for Lord Stanley in 1851. Lord Lansdowne was leader of the House of Lords. He and Lord John Russell discussed the situation with the Queen before Lord John Russell formally resigned. There was no suggestion that he could or would or should assist the Queen to keep out Lord Stanley. Mr Goschen was not a minister of the resigning Government; he was a member of the

[1] *Ibid.* p. 435.

[2] Above, p. 36.

Opposition party. The only purpose of summons to him was to try to discover how a Government of 'patriots' or 'moderate men' could be formed—that is, how Mr Gladstone's majority could be broken up. The Duke of Wellington was seen informally by the Prince Consort after Lord Stanley's first refusal to form a Government. He was formally summoned after further negotiations had proved fruitless. The precedent of 1855 is even less relevant. The Queen sent at once for Lord Derby, and she saw Lord Lansdowne after Lord Derby refused office.

The events of 1885–6 must therefore be taken as constituting a clear precedent against taking advice when the Government resigns after a defeat in the House of Commons or in the country. They constitute a case in which bad arguments were not followed. The informal consultation of Mr Goschen just before Mr Gladstone's resignation in 1886 may be ignored. What the Queen really wanted to know was whether the Liberal Unionists would join a Conservative Government, so as to keep out the enemy and forbid Home Rule. Sir Henry Ponsonby's reconnaissance in 1892 was partly to find out if Mr Gladstone wanted to undertake the ungrateful task once more, and partly to make clear to everyone that Mr Labouchere would not be allowed any office where he had to 'kiss hands'.

This rule does not, of course, prevent the Queen from consulting whom she pleases in other circumstances. Where the Prime Minister dies or resigns personally, the Queen may have the delicate task of choosing a Prime Minister who can keep the Government together. Where a Government resigns owing to internal dissensions it does not necessarily follow that the Opposition must take office. In neither case is the Queen necessarily in the best position for making a choice. She must ascertain the view of the Government party in the first case, and the views of all interested parties in the second case. She is therefore entitled to consult whom she pleases, and the precedents give her full liberty.

In the first place, she need not ask for the advice of the retiring Prime Minister. Lord Melbourne's position as Queen Victoria's mentor gave him privileges which his successors did not possess. In 1845 the Queen and Prince Albert had a long discussion with Sir Robert Peel. In 1852 (when, however, the Government resigned through a defeat in the

House of Commons) Lord Derby advised the Queen that she should send for Lord Lansdowne. Prince Albert interrupted him, saying that, 'constitutionally speaking, it did not rest with him to give advice and become responsible for it'.[1] In 1855 Lord Palmerston refused to give advice after his defeat, but stated his view of the party situation.[2] On the resignation of Lord Derby in 1868, he advised the Queen to send for Mr Disraeli, without being asked for advice.[3] On Mr Gladstone's resignation in 1894 the Queen did not ask his advice, and he refused to give his opinion to Sir Henry Ponsonby except at the Queen's request.[4] It is stated that on the resignation of Lord Salisbury in 1902 Edward VII, 'on his own initiative', sent for Mr Balfour.[5] It is not clear whether Mr Balfour advised the King on the Government's resignation in 1905, but he had previously given his views informally to Lord Esher, who had the ear of the King.[6] Before the resignation of Sir Henry Campbell-Bannerman in 1908, Lord Esher discussed the matter with the King and reported a talk which he had had with Mr John Morley. Lord Esher told Mr Morley that the King would consult no one, but would exercise his prerogative unaided.[7] Later, he notes that Lord Knollys 'is anxious to discover the views of the Cabinet. This is impossible. The King must use his own judgment.'[8] He supplied the King with the papers of 1865, when Lord Palmerston died while in office. It is unlikely that Sir Henry Campbell-Bannerman advised the King, since the King saw Mr Asquith some time before Sir Henry resigned.[9]

The Coalition Government of 1915 was formed on Mr Asquith's advice after the resignation of Lord Fisher; Conservative criticism showed that the Government must be 'reconstructed on a broad and non-party basis'.[10] Mr Asquith thought in 1916 that a minor reconstruction was enough; but when he was informed that Mr Bonar Law and a large part of the Conservative party supported Mr Lloyd George's

[1] *Letters of Queen Victoria*, 1st series, II, p. 501. Contrast Lord Salisbury's statement in 1885, above, p. 36.

[2] *Life of Lord Granville*, I, p. 293.

[3] *Letters of Queen Victoria*, 2nd series, I, p. 497.

[4] *Life of Gladstone*, III, pp. 512, 513.

[5] *Life of the Duke of Devonshire*, II, p. 280.

[6] *Esher Papers*, II, p. 78.

[7] *Ibid.* II, p. 256.

[8] *Ibid.* II, p. 272.

[9] *Life of Lord Oxford and Asquith*, I, p. 194.

[10] Nicolson, *King George V*, p. 264.

proposal for a War Council, he resigned. George V then sent for Mr Bonar Law, according to the biographer,[1] 'in strict accordance with constitutional precedent'. It is not clear, however, what the precedent was. Mr Bonar Law was not leader of the Opposition, but Secretary of State for the Colonies and leader of the Conservative party in temporary alliance with Mr Asquith's party. In any event, the rule that the Sovereign must send for the leader of the Opposition applies only when the Government is defeated by the Opposition either in the House of Commons or at an election. The formation of the Coalition Government in 1852 was not in point, for the Conservative Government was defeated on the budget and Queen Victoria sent for Lord Aberdeen, as one of the Peelite leaders, and Lord Lansdowne, as one of the Whig leaders. For the situation which arose in 1916 there was no precedent, at least since the Reform Act.

Before asking Mr Bonar Law to form a Government, the King informed him, on the advice of Lord Haldane, that, if asked, he would not permit a dissolution.[2] Mr Bonar Law questioned the advisability of such a decision and said that he might succeed in forming a Government if he appealed to the country. He apparently thought that he might be able to form a Government if Mr Asquith was willing to serve; but, Mr Asquith's reply being discouraging, he suggested to the King, on the advice of Lord Balfour, that the King summon a meeting of party leaders. The King agreeing, a conference was held with the King presiding and Messrs Asquith, Lloyd George, Bonar Law, Balfour and Arthur Henderson attending. No decision was reached, but it became clear that the Conservative party would not serve under Mr Asquith, while Mr Asquith was reluctant to serve under Mr Bonar Law.[3] Subsequently Mr Asquith refused to serve under Mr Bonar Law, Mr Bonar Law said that he could not form a Government without Mr Asquith, and the King sent for Mr Lloyd George, who formed a Government.

In 1922 Mr Lloyd George resigned without being defeated in the House of Commons, but because a meeting of the Conservative members at the Carlton Club had resolved, by a large majority, to form an independent party under its own leader. The King sent Lord Stam-

[1] *Ibid.* p. 288. [2] *Ibid.* p. 289.

[3] *Ibid.* pp. 290–1; and see *Life of Lord Oxford and Asquith*, II, p. 274.

fordham to consult Mr Bonar Law, who had moved the resolution. Mr Bonar Law correctly pointed out that he was not leader of the Conservative party, which had broken up. Lord Stamfordham replied that 'it was the King's duty to form a new Government as soon as possible and to send for whoever [*sic*] he considered was the proper person to carry out this great responsibility'. Mr Bonar Law refused, however, to take office until he had been elected leader of the Conservative party. The King insisted that Mr Bonar Law call at Buckingham Palace. A few days later the Conservative party unanimously elected Mr Bonar Law as leader, and he was forthwith commissioned to form a Government.[1] It will be seen that, so far as is known, the King acted without consultation. On the other hand, Mr Bonar Law's refusal to form a Government before being elected leader was unprecedented. It had always been held, both in the Conservative party and in the Liberal party, that the Sovereign should have a free hand in choosing a Prime Minister if the office fell vacant while that party had a majority, and that they should elect as leader the person so chosen. Mr Churchill followed that rule in 1940 though, since Mr Neville Chamberlain was serving under him, he did not ask for immediate election as leader.

When he resigned in 1923, Mr Bonar Law informed Lord Curzon, who had the greatest claims to the succession: 'I understand that it is not customary for the King to ask the Prime Minister to recommend his successor in circumstances like the present, and I presume that he will not do so.'[2] This was perhaps a polite way of telling Lord Curzon that he, Mr Bonar Law, did not wish to take the responsibility of advising Lord Curzon's appointment. The information as to what was customary had come from Lord Crewe, who quoted the precedent of 1894, mentioned above, and also said that Edward VII had appointed Mr Asquith in 1908 without asking for the advice of Sir Henry Campbell-Bannerman.[3] Though Mr Bonar Law would no doubt have given advice if George V had asked for it, he had a verbal message conveyed to the King to the effect that, owing to ill-health, the Prime Minister would prefer not to be consulted and not to take the respon-

[1] Nicolson, *op. cit.* pp. 370–1; Blake, *The Unknown Prime Minister*, pp. 459–61.
[2] *Life of Lord Curzon*, III, p. 350.
[3] Blake, *op. cit.* pp. 514–15.

sibility for any recommendation.[1] This left the King the difficult task of deciding, without the advice of the person best qualified to give it, the very difficult question whether Lord Curzon was temperamentally fitted for the task, and the still more difficult question whether there could be a Prime Minister in the House of Lords with the Labour party forming the main opposition. As we have already seen, what purported to be Mr Bonar Law's views in favour of Mr Baldwin were conveyed to the King, who also consulted the Marquis of Salisbury and Earl Balfour and received indirectly the advice of Mr Bridgeman and Mr Amery.[1] Lord Salisbury—whose father had been the last Prime Minister in the House of Lords—favoured Lord Curzon; but the other advisers strongly supported the appointment of Mr Baldwin. Thus the weightier advice supported the King's own opinion, that it was impracticable to have a Prime Minister in the House of Lords.

The method of forming the National Government in 1931 was peculiar and, in spite of the volume of evidence on the subject, it is difficult to find out exactly what happened.[2] The depression which began in the United States in 1929 had caused a serious financial position in Britain by the end of July 1931, when the report of the May Committee was published. A Cabinet Committee which reported on 19 August suggested drastic economies, which were rejected by the majority of the Cabinet after consultation with the National Council of Labour (i.e. the General Council of the Trades Union Congress, the Executive Committee of the Labour party, and the Consultative Committee of the Parliamentary Labour party). Since the Government had no majority and was dependent upon Opposition support, both the proposals of the Cabinet Committee and the tentative decisions of the majority of the Cabinet had been communicated to the Opposition leaders on 20 and 21 August. The Opposition leaders were thus aware of the division in the Cabinet and, while apparently prepared to support the Government if it carried out the recommendations of the Cabinet Committee, they informed the Prime Minister and the Chancellor of

[1] Above, p. 23; and Blake, *op. cit.* pp. 516–27.

[2] The fullest information is in Nicolson, *King George V*, pp. 453–69; and see Viscount Samuel, *Memoirs*, pp. 207–13; Snowden, *Autobiography*, II, pp. 950–61; Webb, 'What Happened in 1931: A Record', *Political Quarterly* iii, pp. 1–17.

the Exchequer that in their view Parliament would not support the Government if the tentative decisions of the 21st alone were adopted.

This information was before the Cabinet when it met on the 22nd. It was decided at that meeting to seek the views of the Opposition leaders on a compromise solution—put hypothetically because the Cabinet had not agreed upon it. Their reply was that the bankers should be consulted to ascertain whether the economies proposed would be enough to justify the making of the necessary loans. Accordingly the bankers were consulted, and their reply was expected on the evening of the 23rd.

On the morning of the 23rd the Prime Minister had an audience with the King, who had returned to London that morning. After explaining the position, Mr MacDonald

> warned the King that it was possible that certain of his most influential colleagues in the Cabinet, and notably Mr Arthur Henderson and Mr William Graham, would not consent to those economies now tentatively put to New York. If they were to resign from the Government it would not be possible for him to carry on the administration without their assistance. The resignation of the Labour Government as a whole would then become inevitable. The King, on receiving this information, decided that the correct constitutional course was to consult the leaders of the Conservative and Liberal Oppositions.[1]

There is a statement missing here, but it is supplied by the official notification: '*On the Prime Minister's advice* the King has asked Mr Baldwin and Sir Herbert Samuel to see him, because His Majesty wishes to hear from them themselves what the position of their respective parties is.'[2] The clause now italicised is important, for if the King acted on advice it was indeed 'the correct constitutional course'. It would not have been an incorrect constitutional course if the Prime Minister had resigned, for then the King could consult whom he pleased; since there had been no defeat of the Government, the King was not bound to call upon the leader of the Opposition to form a Government.[3] If, however, the King had not received advice to see the Opposition leaders, his decision to do so would have been unconstitutional.[4]

[1] Nicolson, *op. cit.* pp. 460–1.
[2] Snowden, *op. cit.* p. 951.
[3] Above, p. 41.
[4] Below, pp. 380–2.

The point is important, because it was Sir Herbert Samuel who suggested, at his audience on 23 August, that a National Government might be formed. Mr Baldwin was not accessible when he was first summoned, and Sir Herbert Samuel had the first audience. In his view the best solution would be for the economies to be effected either by the Government then in office or by a reconstituted Labour Government. If, however, Mr MacDonald 'failed to secure the support of a sufficient number of his colleagues, then the best alternative would be a National Government composed of members of the three parties. It would be preferable that Mr MacDonald should remain Prime Minister in such a National Government. Sir Herbert made it clear at the same time that such a non-party Government should only be constituted "for the single purpose of overcoming the financial crisis".'[1] Later the King saw Mr Baldwin and asked him whether he would be prepared to serve in a National Government under Mr MacDonald.

Mr Baldwin answered that he would be ready to do anything to assist the country in the present crisis. Even if Mr MacDonald insisted on resigning, he, Mr Baldwin, would be ready to carry on the Government if he could be assured of the support of the Liberal party in effecting the necessary economies. In that event, once the crisis had been surmounted, he would ask His Majesty for a dissolution and go to the country. To this the King agreed.[2]

No information is available as to whether Mr MacDonald knew of these contingent proposals when the Cabinet met at 2 p.m. on the 23rd. Since the reply had not been received from New York, there was an adjournment until 8.45 p.m., when the Prime Minister read the telegram to the Cabinet. Its phrasing was unfortunate; and the specific question which the Prime Minister put to the Cabinet, the reduction of 10 per cent in unemployment relief, was one which the Cabinet as a whole was unlikely to accept. In his report to the King Mr MacDonald stated that eleven members had voted to accept the bankers' terms and eight had voted against; but this vote may have been taken on the proposal to reduce relief. In any case, the Prime Minister stated that he would inform the King and advise him to summon a meeting of party leaders. The Cabinet then authorised the Prime Minister to inform His Majesty that they placed their resignations in his hands.

[1] Nicolson, *op. cit.* p. 461.

[2] *Ibid.* pp. 461–2.

The Prime Minister sought an immediate audience with the King, gave an account of the Cabinet decisions, including the names of the principal opponents of the economies, and tendered the resignation of the Cabinet. 'The King impressed on the Prime Minister that he was the only man to lead the country through the present crisis and hoped he would reconsider the situation. His Majesty told him that the Conservatives and Liberals would support him in restoring the confidence of foreigners in the financial stability of the country.' The Prime Minister then asked if the King would confer with Mr Baldwin, Sir Herbert Samuel and himself on the 24th. The King agreed, and the Prime Minister made the necessary arrangements.[1]

At the conference on the 24th the King pressed for a National Government under Mr MacDonald. Mr Baldwin and Sir Herbert Samuel agreed to serve under him until an Emergency Bill had been passed. After this they would expect the King to grant a dissolution. To this course the King agreed. During the election the National Government would remain in being, each party fighting on its own lines. A memorandum was drawn up, which Mr Baldwin and Sir Herbert Samuel would place before their colleagues. Mr MacDonald would not read it out in the Cabinet but would keep it for those who remained faithful to him.[2]

Mr MacDonald at once informed the Cabinet that it had been decided to form a 'Cabinet of Individuals' to deal with the emergency. He was to be one of these 'individuals', and he invited any who desired to join him. Within 15 minutes he had been deserted by everybody except Mr Thomas, Lord Sankey, and Mr Snowden. In the afternoon he met the junior Ministers and virtually advised them not to join him; with a few exceptions they accepted his advice.

No criticism can be made of the King's action. He might, without impropriety, have gone further in pressing a solution upon the Labour Government itself. He was in Sandringham from 11 to 21 August, when he left for Balmoral on Mr MacDonald's advice in spite of his anxiety to await events. By the time he returned on the 23rd, there was little chance of the Labour Cabinet being able to agree, and it is not at all clear that Mr MacDonald wanted it to agree. Having been informed on the 24th

[1] *Ibid.* pp. 463–4. [2] *Ibid.* pp. 467–8.

of the Cabinet's resignation, the King's seizure of Sir Herbert Samuel's suggestion of a National Government was wholly constitutional.

The temporary expedient of a 'National Government' remained in being, in name, until it was submerged in Mr Winston Churchill's 'truly National' Government in 1940. It was in fact essentially Conservative, if not from the general election of 1931 (when the Conservative party held 471 of the 558 Government seats), then from the resignations of Sir Herbert Samuel and Mr Snowden in 1932. It is not surprising, therefore, that there is no information about the King's action in appointing Mr Baldwin as Prime Minister in 1935. With the prospect of an approaching election, the Conservatives were becoming restive at having to carry the burden of Mr MacDonald. 'It had to be very delicately hinted to MacDonald that by clinging to office he was inviting a revolt which might fatally harm his son's career.'[1] On 7 June 1935, Mr MacDonald resigned 'for reasons of failing health'[2] and was succeeded as Prime Minister by Mr Baldwin. Whether Mr MacDonald advised George V to send for Mr Baldwin is almost irrelevant, for nobody else could have been Prime Minister with so large a Conservative majority.

Nor is there information about advice given to George VI in 1937 and 1940 or to Elizabeth II in 1955. It should be remembered that both monarchs have placed their relations with their Prime Ministers on a more informal basis. When both the Sovereign and the Prime Minister are in London the latter has an audience, usually on Wednesday (the Cabinet usually meets on Tuesday and Thursday) and stays to lunch. It is thus easy for prospective developments to be discussed without the necessity for formal 'advice'. George VI must have been aware in 1937 that Mr Neville Chamberlain was acceptable to the Conservative party as Mr Baldwin's successor, and Elizabeth II must similarly have been aware in 1955 that Sir Anthony Eden was acceptable as Sir Winston Churchill's successor.[3] In 1940 Mr Neville Chamberlain was not defeated, but merely resigned because he had lost the support of the Labour party and felt bound to give way to a Prime Minister who could

[1] G. M. Young, *Stanley Baldwin*, p. 186.

[2] Nicolson, *King George V*, p. 527.

[3] Sir Winston had recommended Sir Anthony as his successor as long ago as 1942: Churchill, *The Second World War*, IV, p. 337.

form a Coalition Government. Accordingly the arrangements for Mr Churchill's succession were made before Mr Chamberlain resigned.

In 1957 Queen Elizabeth was faced with the difficult task of choosing between Mr R. A. Butler, Lord Privy Seal and Leader of the House of Commons, who had presided over the Cabinet in Sir Anthony Eden's absence, and Mr Harold Macmillan, Chancellor of the Exchequer. She sent for Sir Winston Churchill, as an 'elder statesman', and Lord Salisbury, Lord President of the Council and Leader of the House of Lords. What advice they gave her is not known, but she invited Mr Macmillan to form a Government, Mr Butler becoming Home Secretary and Leader of the House of Commons.[1]

It is certain that, where a Cabinet resigns owing to internal dissensions, or where a Prime Minister dies or tenders a personal resignation, or where, on the defeat of a Government, the leader of the Opposition is unable or unwilling to form a Government, the Queen may consult whom she pleases. In 1839 Queen Victoria saw the Duke of Wellington on the 'Bedchamber question'. In 1851, after Lord Stanley's refusal to form a Government, the Queen saw Sir James Graham, Lord Aberdeen, the Duke of Wellington, and Lord Lansdowne. In 1855, after the Earl of Derby's refusal, she saw Lord Lansdowne, Lord John Russell, Lord Palmerston and Lord Clarendon.

A new factor entered with the death of the Prince Consort in 1861 and the appointment (after an interval) of a private secretary. For the private secretary, unlike the Prince, could visit political leaders and ascertain their views informally. The Queen made much use of her private secretaries in this way, and they were able to talk with junior ministers and ex-ministers as well as with the party leaders. Indeed, some of the reports to the Queen (as in 1885–6 and 1892) contain little more than the gossip of the clubs—information which must be even less reliable than that produced by 'our political correspondent' in the leading newspapers. *The Times* under Delane was frequently better informed than the Queen.

There is in fact no further evidence of the consultation of party leaders and 'elder statesmen' in the formation of a Government until

[1] The claim put forward by Sir John Kotelawala in Ceylon in 1952, that the Leader of the House has a claim to the succession, has no warrant in United Kingdom precedents.

1916.[1] The King then saw Mr Bonar Law, Mr Lloyd George, Mr Balfour and Mr Henderson.[2] In 1931, as we have seen, George V consulted Mr Baldwin and Sir Herbert Samuel both before and after Mr MacDonald's resignation, though in the former case on the Prime Minister's advice and in the latter on that of the retiring Cabinet.[3] Except when the Government resigns after a defeat, the Queen has a choice which she must exercise in such a way as to secure the strongest Government in the minimum time. To do this, she must secure the best information available. The best information as to coherent parties can be obtained from the party leaders. The best information as to parties in dissolution can be obtained from the leaders of the respective groups. Sometimes, on the other hand, the 'elder statesmen' who have retired from the political contest can best see the situation as a whole. The Queen may consult any of these, and she needs no formal advice from a Prime Minister.

It is the Queen's primary duty to find a Government. It is no less the duty of political leaders to assist her to find one. In the Duke of Wellington's famous phrase, 'The King's service must be carried on'.[4] This duty is threefold. First, the political leader must, if asked, place his views before the Queen. Mr Gladstone stated to Mr John Morley in 1895, 'it would not be consistent with my view of my duty not to advise if invited';[5] and Mr Bonar Law's biographer makes it plain that, though Mr Bonar Law did not want to have to make a choice between Lord Curzon and Mr Baldwin, he would have felt bound to advise if he had been asked to do so.[6] Secondly, if the official Opposition succeeds in

[1] There are many cases in which the Queen wrote to Opposition leaders, and in 1910–11 the King saw leaders of the Opposition, with the Prime Minister's consent, in order to ascertain the views of the various parties. These form precedents for the summoning of Mr Baldwin and Sir Herbert Samuel before the resignation of the Labour Government in 1931. But they are of a different nature from the formal consultation preliminary to the formation of a Government; in particular, such consultations are undertaken on the advice of the Prime Minister. See below, pp. 380–2, 442–3.

[2] *Life of Lord Oxford and Asquith*, II, pp. 273–5; Addison, *Four-and-a-half Years*, I, pp. 271–2.

[3] Criticisms of the formation of the 1931 coalition rest upon Mr MacDonald's action in relation to his colleagues: Snowden, *Autobiography*, II, p. 954; Laski, *The Crisis and the Constitution*; Jennings, 'The Constitution under Strain', 3 *Political Quarterly*, pp. 194–205.

[4] Duke of Wellington, *Despatches*, new series, IV, p. 209.

[5] Morley, *Recollections*, II, p. 11.

[6] Blake, *The Unknown Prime Minister*, p. 516.

defeating the Government and so causing its resignation, it is the duty of its leaders to form a new Government or to advise the Queen as to an alternative. Thirdly, though this must be stated less positively, it is the duty of the Government to remain in office so long as it can do so without infringing constitutional principles.

The second principle is based upon the assumption that party politics is not just a game. It is not even a mere rivalry of policies. It is a contest between two or more groups for the honour of forwarding their rival policies. There are times when opposition is undesirable—or, as some put it, unpatriotic. There are occasions, as with the Irish Nationalist party, when opposition for the sake of opposition is justifiable. Normally, an opposition party in the House of Commons does not expect to defeat the Government. It hopes that it will persuade enough people outside to give it a majority at an election in the not-too-distant future. Its opposition is part of its propaganda, but it must take the responsibility of its arguments: it must be ready to accept office, if it does succeed in defeating the Government either in the House or in the constituencies. Naturally, it cannot form a Government if it has no prospect of securing sufficient support. Its leaders must in any case assist in the search for a Government that can secure support.

In 1851 the Liberal Government's defeat on Mr Locke King's motion had not been due to the action of the Opposition. It was a Radical motion which was not effectively opposed by the rest of the Liberals. Lord Stanley suggested that Queen Victoria should try a coalition between Whigs and Peelites. But if it was clear that no other Government could be formed, 'he would feel it his duty as a loyal subject to risk everything, except his principles and his honour, to carry on the Government'.[1] Protectionist Opposition assumed, as we may put it, that ultimately there must be a Protectionist Government; and though they had taken no part in defeating the Government, the Protectionist party could not evade the obligations of opposition. The Protectionist Government was accordingly formed in 1852, when the party had supported Lord Palmerston's 'tit for tat'.

The Conservatives supported Mr Roebuck's motion on the Crimean War in 1855, and so became responsible for the defeat of the Govern-

[1] *Letters of Queen Victoria*, 1st series, II, p. 351.

ment. The Queen addressed herself to Lord Derby 'as the head of the largest party in the House of Commons, and which had by its vote chiefly contributed to the overthrow of the Government'.[1] Lord Derby, in the Queen's words, 'threw off this responsibility, saying that there had been no communication with Mr Roebuck...'. He nevertheless tried to form a Government and, on failing to do so, resigned his commission on the ground that 'he would not be able to form such an Administration as could effectively carry on the Government':[2] but he formed a Government on the defeat of Lord Palmerston's Government in 1858. He first asked the Queen to reconsider her offer. The Queen's conclusion was that 'the resignation of the present Government is the result of a conscientious conviction on their part, that, damaged by the censure passed upon them in the House of Commons, they cannot with honour to themselves, or usefulness to the country, carry on public affairs, and Lord Derby is at the head of the only party which affords the material of forming a new Government, is sufficiently organised to secure a certain support, and which the country would accept as an alternative for that hitherto in power'.[3] Lord Derby then accepted the burden.

On its defeat on the Irish University Bill in 1873, the Liberal Government resigned, and the Queen sent for Mr Disraeli. As an immediate dissolution was not possible, he did not want to take office and suffer the indignity and loss of credit involved in winding up the session with a minority Government,[4] and accordingly refused to form a Government. But he added that 'there were instances where a Sovereign had been left without a Government, and in such a case he would, of course, be ready to serve me [the Queen]'.[5] There ensued a controversy between Mr Gladstone and Mr Disraeli, with the Queen as intermediary.[6]

[1] *Ibid.* 3rd series, III, p. 102.

[2] *Ibid.* 1st series, III, p. 106.

[3] *Ibid.* 3rd series, III, p. 340.

[4] *Life of Gathorne-Hardy*, I, p. 323; *Life of Disraeli*, III, p. 340.

[5] *Life of Disraeli*, II, p. 549.

[6] Mr Gladstone's letters are given fully in Guedalla, *The Queen and Mr Gladstone*, I, pp. 395–410, and less fully in *Life of Gladstone*, II, pp. 450–2 and 652–3; Mr Disraeli's letters are given in *Life of Disraeli*, II, pp. 548–57, though the most important are also in Guedalla, *The Queen and Mr Gladstone* (above).

Mr Gladstone objected that Mr Disraeli's refusal was not in accordance with the principles of our parliamentary government:

The vote of the House of Commons...was due to the deliberate and concerted action of the Opposition, with a limited amount of adventitious numerical aid. The division was a party division, and carried the well known symbol of such divisions in the appointment of tellers of the Opposition and Government respectively. The vote was given on the full knowledge, avowed in the speech of the leader of the Opposition, that the Government had formally declared the measure on which the vote was impending to be vital to its existence.

Mr Gladstone humbly conceives that, according to the well known principles of our parliamentary government, an opposition, which has in this manner and degree contributed to bring about what we term a crisis, is bound to use and to show that it has used its utmost efforts of counsel and enquiry to exhaust all practicable means of bringing its resources to the aid of the country in its exigency.[1]

Mr Gladstone then pointed out that in 1830, 1835, 1841, 1852, 1858, 1859, 1866 and 1868 the party in opposition took office. It failed to do this only in 1832, 1851 and 1855. 'But in each of these three cases, the attempt of the Opposition to form a Government was not relinquished until after such efforts had been made by its leaders as to carry the conviction to the world that all its available means of action were exhausted.'[2] Mr Gladstone added:

It is in Mr Gladstone's view of the utmost importance to the public welfare that the nation should be constantly aware that the parliamentary action certain or likely to take effect on the overthrow of a Government; the reception and treatment of a summons from Your Majesty to meet the necessity which such action has powerfully aided in creating; and again the resumption of office by those who have deliberately laid it down,—are

[1] Guedalla, *The Queen and Mr Gladstone*, I, pp. 399–400.

[2] *Ibid.* I, p. 400. Mr Gladstone's statement was not wholly accurate. In 1851 Lord Stanley, on first application, refused to form a Government. He accepted the task only when other applications had failed. Also, there was no such 'conviction' in 1851 and 1855. Many Conservatives, including Mr Disraeli, felt aggrieved at Lord Derby's refusal. Mr Gladstone did not quote the case of 1845, when it could hardly be said that the refusal of Lord Grey to serve with Lord Palmerston under Lord John Russell carried conviction that all available means of action had been exhausted. This case is somewhat different in that the Government was not defeated, but merely resigned.

uniformly viewed as matters of the utmost gravity, requiring time, counsel and deliberation among those who are parties to them, and attended with serious responsibilities.[1]

Mr Disraeli replied that

though, as a general rule, this doctrine may be sound, it cannot be laid down unconditionally, nor otherwise than subject to many exceptions.

It is undoubtedly sound so far as this: that for an Opposition to use its strength for the express purpose of throwing out a Government, which it is at the same time aware that it cannot replace—having that object in view, and no other—would be an act of recklessness and faction, which could not be too strongly condemned. But it may be safely affirmed that no conduct of this kind can be imputed to the Conservative Opposition of 1873.

If the doctrine in question is carried further; if it be contended that, whenever, from any circumstances, a Minister is so situated that it is in his power to prevent any other parliamentary leader from forming an Administration which is likely to stand, he acquires, thereby, the right to call upon Parliament to pass whatever measures he and his colleagues think fit, and is entitled to denounce as factious the resistance to such measures—then the claim is one not warranted by usage, or reconcilable with the freedom of the Legislature.[2]

Finally, Mr Disraeli stated that he had consulted his friends, and that they were unanimously of opinion that it would be prejudicial to the interests of the country for a Conservative Administration to conduct affairs in the then House of Commons. He asked what other means were at his disposal, whether he was to open negotiations with a section of the Liberal Party 'and waste days in barren interviews, vain applications, and the device of impossible combinations', or whether he was to make overtures to the Irish.[3]

Mr Disraeli's reply was, in part, special pleading. The reason why a Government cannot compel the House of Commons to pass any legislation it wishes is that an alternative Government is always possible. What Mr Gladstone asked was not that Mr Disraeli should try 'impossible combinations', but that he should take office. Nevertheless, it was sound in substance. A Government cannot give an Opposition the

[1] *Ibid.* I, p. 402. (The passage has been punctuated in accordance with *Life of Gladstone*, II, p. 451.)

[2] *Life of Disraeli*, II, p. 555.

[3] *Ibid.* II, p. 556.

difficult choice of supporting the Government or of taking office at a stage of the parliamentary time-table when it knows that it cannot advise a dissolution. It cannot turn the rule that an Opposition that opposes must be ready to try to form a Government into a rule that it must take office when it cannot effectively govern.

In 1880 the Queen (with a view to keeping Mr Gladstone out of office) apparently laid great stress upon the duty of Lord Hartington 'as leader of the Opposition' to take office. He asked Mr Gladstone for his opinion upon this doctrine. Mr Gladstone said, according to his own account:[1] 'The leader, if sent for, was in my opinion bound either to serve himself, or to point out some other course to Her Majesty which he might deem to be more for the public advantage, and if that course should fail in consequence of the refusal of the person pointed out, the leader of the party could not leave Her Majesty unprovided with a Government, but would be bound in loyalty to undertake the task.'

In 1885 Lord Salisbury did not refuse to take office, though an immediate dissolution was not possible owing to the recent passage of a Redistribution Bill consequent upon the third Reform Act. Mr Gladstone had stated, however, that he was willing to assist the Government in the interim period. Lord Salisbury desired a formal note to that effect, but the two leaders could not agree upon its terms. Ultimately, a formula was agreed, and Lord Salisbury formed a Government. In 1895 there was no difficulty about a dissolution. Lord Salisbury thought that the constitutional course was for Lord Rosebery's Government to advise a dissolution, but he accepted office and formed a Government.

In 1905 Sir Henry Campbell-Bannerman considered whether he ought not to refuse office, in order to compel Mr Balfour to advise a dissolution. Lord Ripon pointed out to him that 'a refusal on your part to take office on Mr Balfour's resignation would not necessarily involve the resumption of the Government; the King would be perfectly entitled to send not for Balfour, but for Lansdowne or Chamberlain'.[2] Sir Henry came to the same conclusion on different grounds and formed

[1] *Life of Gladstone*, II, pp. 623–4.
[2] *Life of Lord Ripon*, II, pp. 273–4.

a Government. As the Government had not resigned because of a defeat, there was no obligation on him to accept office.

The conclusion seems to be, as Mr Gladstone put it to Lord Hartington in 1880, that it is the duty of the leader of the Opposition to form a Government or to suggest an alternative. But one alternative is that which Mr Disraeli suggested in 1873, namely, the continuance of the existing Government. This alternative does not exist where the House of Commons refuses, by not passing supplies or otherwise, to allow the Government to continue. But a single defeat on a Bill, even if it is made a matter of confidence, does not indicate an intention to follow such a course. Where 'tactics' induce the Government to resign rather than to advise a dissolution, as in 1905, the Opposition, too, may play tactics and refuse to accept office. The real duty of the Opposition is to work the parliamentary system and to see that 'the Queen's service is carried on'. A mere refusal by the Government to carry on the Queen's service is not enough to compel an unwilling Opposition to take office.

Indeed, the case is one of a conflict of rules: for, though it is sometimes the duty of the Opposition to take office, it is sometimes the duty of the Government to continue. There has been less discussion of this point, though it is equally necessary. Government is the duty as well as the right of the majority party. Peel in 1845 had lost his majority (though he had not been defeated) and yet resumed office and repealed the Corn Laws. Lord John Russell in 1851 resumed office. Lord Salisbury in 1885 and 1895, and Sir Henry Campbell-Bannerman in 1905 might have refused office, as Mr Disraeli refused it in 1873. Governments torn by internal dissensions must, if an alternative cannot be found, settle their differences. It is essential to the parliamentary system that a Cabinet should be formed, and the Cabinet must remain until its successors have been appointed.

There was some discussion on these questions in February 1910, when it appeared possible that the Irish, who held the balance of power, would vote with the Conservatives against the Budget, and so defeat the Liberal Government. Mr Austen Chamberlain then advised Mr Balfour that 'in the circumstances and at that time of year, you are not and cannot be bound to take office'. If Mr Asquith resigned without being defeated, he would certainly be compelled to take office again. 'The only thing that would give them a real excuse for resignation and leave you no excuse for refusing to take office, would be your failure or refusal to support them in those purely business measures which are necessary for *any* Government to carry on the business of the nation.' The Budget, he contended, was not such a measure; for, though no Government could continue without Supply, it could continue for a short period at least without the additional taxation imposed under the Budget resolutions.

CHAPTER III

THE FORMATION OF A GOVERNMENT

§1. *The Offices to be Filled*

The offices to be filled when a new Prime Minister takes office are some ninety in number. They are not determined by law, and there is no legal distinction between a political and a non-political office. Some of them, indeed, are survivals of other times and other conditions. A Lord Privy Seal is usually appointed, though there is no Privy Seal office. A Chancellor of the Duchy of Lancaster has about two hours a week of office work. A Lord President of the Council has little more. The chief offices are, however, the key administrative positions. The Chancellor of the Exchequer, the Minister of Defence, the First Lord of the Admiralty, the seven Secretaries of State, the President of the Board of Trade, the Ministers of Labour and National Service, Health, Agriculture, Fisheries and Food, Education, Fuel and Power, Housing and Local Government, Pensions and National Insurance, and Transport and Civil Aviation, and the Postmaster-General, control the main functions of government. Each of them, too, has at least one political subordinate. The Ministers of Works and Supply and the Lord Chancellor also have important departmental duties. There may be five or six Ministers of State assisting the ministers mentioned above. The Attorney-General, the Solicitor-General, the Lord Advocate and the Solicitor-General for Scotland have duties which are, for the most part, not administrative. The Parliamentary Secretary to the Treasury and the Lords of the Treasury have some departmental duties in the Treasury. They have to sign Treasury warrants, but their main function is to control the proceedings of the House of Commons, and keep the majority together, as Government whips under the direction of the Prime Minister or leader of the House. There are about thirty other Parliamentary Secretaries or other persons ranking as assistant ministers. In addition, there are five appointments in the Royal Household which are regarded as political offices.[1] The holders of these offices, too, are whips if they are in the House of Commons, and assist in Government business in the House of Lords if they are peers. The office of Paymaster-General involves no duties except assistance to the Government in the House of Lords. The Lords in Waiting are now Government representatives in the House of Lords.

It is a well-settled convention that these ministers should be either peers or members of the House of Commons. There have been occasional exceptions. Mr Gladstone once held office out of Parliament for nine months. The Scottish law officers sometimes, as in 1923 and 1924, are not in Parliament. General Smuts was minister without portfolio and a member of the War Cabinet from 1916 until 1918. Mr Ramsay MacDonald and Mr Malcolm MacDonald were members of the Cabinet though not in Parliament from the general election of November 1935 until early in 1936.

The House of Commons is, however, critical of such exceptions. In 1923 there was constant criticism of the absence of both Scottish law officers, for whom efforts were made to find seats. Eventually the office of Solicitor-General for Scotland was given to a member of the House, though the Lord Advocate remained out of the House for the whole of the short Parliament of 1922–3. In truth, the conduct of Government business in the House of Commons is such an onerous task that the absence of an important minister places a considerable burden on the rest. Even in the House of Lords the representation of the many departments, the piloting of their legislation, and the explanation of their policy demand the presence of a substantial number of ministers. Practical convenience as well as constitutional convention therefore compel the Prime Minister to confer office only upon members of Parliament or peers. Apart from such exceptions as those of 1924 and

[1] There were more political appointments in the Household before 1924. It was then agreed by George V and Mr MacDonald, after consulting Lord Balfour and Mr Asquith, that the posts of Lord Chamberlain, Lord Steward, Master of the Horse, Captain of the Gentlemen-at-Arms, Captain of the Yeomen of the Guard, and three of the Lords in Waiting, were to be filled at the King's discretion, subject to these peers undertaking to take no part in parliamentary proceedings. The three political Lords in Waiting and the three Household officers in the House of Commons—Treasurer of the Household, Controller and Vice-Chamberlain—were to be political appointments: Nicolson, *King George V*, pp. 390–1.

1929, when the Lord Advocate had a non-political office owing to the paucity of Scots lawyers supporting the Labour Government, ministers are out of Parliament only while they are trying to find seats. If they cannot, and are unwilling to be created peers, they resign.

The nomination of ministers rests with the Prime Minister. This does not mean that the Sovereign may not have considerable influence. Examples will presently be cited where Royal influence has even excluded persons from office. But as against the Queen the Prime Minister has the final word. He must have a Government which can work together and which can secure the support of the House of Commons. If he says that for this reason he must have the assistance of a certain person, the Queen must either give way or find another Prime Minister. The Queen cannot commission another member of the same party; for that is to interfere with the internal affairs of the party and is contrary to precedent. She must, therefore, find another party which can secure the support of the House of Commons, and it must be a strange House that is willing to support alternative Governments.

Nor does the rule mean that the Prime Minister may not consult his friends or that, if he does not, he will not listen to their representations. He, too, has to consider the unity of his Government and the views of the House of Commons. It is unnecessary to quote examples of prior discussions, but cases can be quoted in which the appointment of ministers has been brought before the Cabinet.

Finally, it is necessary to point out, because confusion has arisen on this matter, that though the Prime Minister nominates or, technically, recommends, it is the Queen who appoints. Consequently, though a new Prime Minister may recommend that one minister be superseded by another, it is not necessary for him to recommend that an existing minister be reappointed. That minister remains in office until his appointment is terminated.

§2. *The Influence of the Sovereign*

Speaking in 1850, Sir Robert Peel said: 'The power of a [Prime] Minister to appoint or remove his colleagues is by no means an absolute one.... Speaking generally, the Crown would certainly be influenced by the advice of the Prime Minister in the selection of his colleagues.

The charge of forming a Government is left almost exclusively with the Prime Minister.'[1] This is, perhaps, an understatement. But it is certain that, during Queen Victoria's reign at least, the Crown exercised considerable influence on appointments.

In 1841 Prince Albert's private secretary noted the following advice by Lord Melbourne to the Queen: 'He would advise the Queen to adopt the course which King William did with Lord Melbourne in 1835, viz. desiring Lord Melbourne, before His Majesty approved of any appointments, to send a list of those proposed even to the members of every Board, and the King having them all before him expressed his objections to certain persons, which Lord Melbourne yielded to.'[2] This was the practice followed by the Queen. When Lord Stanley was trying to form a Government in 1851, he stated that he would have to nominate Mr Disraeli as a Secretary of State. The Queen said that 'she had not a very good opinion of Mr Disraeli on account of his conduct to poor Sir Robert Peel, and what had just happened did not tend to diminish that feeling; but she felt so much Lord Stanley's difficulties that she would not aggravate them by passing a sentence of exclusion on him'.[3] The Queen had already said that 'she would herself make it a condition with Lord John [Russell] that [Lord Palmerston] should not be again Foreign Secretary'.[4] When Lord Stanley failed to form a Government, Lord John Russell undertook not to reappoint Lord Palmerston.[5] But later he said that it was quite impossible for him either to expel Lord Palmerston or to quarrel with him, and promised instead to move Lord Palmerston in the Easter recess or to resign himself.[6] Finally, he said that he could not undertake to make any change at the Foreign Office.[7] Palmerston was, however, dismissed for other reasons later in the year, and never again became Foreign Secretary. After his dismissal, the Queen said that 'she must reserve to herself the unfettered right to approve or disapprove the choice of a minister for this office' and declared that she was willing to accept Lord Granville.[8] But the Cabinet decided in favour of Lord Clarendon

[1] Report from the Select Committee on Official Salaries (1850), p. 36.

[2] *Letters of Queen Victoria*, 1st series, I, p. 339.

[3] *Ibid.* 1st series, II, p. 365.

[4] *Ibid.* 1st series, II, p. 354.

[5] *Ibid.* 1st series, II, p. 376.

[6] *Ibid.* 1st series, II, p. 377.

[7] *Ibid.* 1st series, II, p. 381.

[8] *Ibid.* 1st series, II, pp. 415–16.

and, after protests, the Queen acquiesced in Lord Clarendon's being invited, believing that he would refuse, as he did.[1]

In 1852 Lord Derby wished to propose Lord Palmerston as Chancellor of the Exchequer. He would not propose him for the Foreign Office, in view of his dismissal from that post not long before and the 'well-known personal feelings of the Queen'. The Queen replied that she 'would not, by refusing her consent, throw additional difficulties in Lord Derby's way; she warned him, however, of the dangerous qualities of [Lord Palmerston]'.[2]

Later in 1852 the Queen's objection kept Mr Bernal Osborne out of the office of Under-Secretary of State for Foreign Affairs, and he became Secretary of the Admiralty.[3] In 1861 the Queen objected to the appointment of Mr Layard as Under-Secretary of State for Foreign Affairs. Lord Palmerston was insistent, and at last the Queen gave way.[4] In 1866 Lord Russell nominated Mr Goschen as Chancellor of the Duchy of Lancaster with a seat in the Cabinet. The Queen thought that, as Mr Goschen had no ministerial experience, jealousy might be created, and she asked Lord Russell to consult the Cabinet. The Cabinet acquiesced in the proposal.[5] On the formation of Lord Derby's Government later in the same year, she desired to object to Lord Derby's nomination of his son, Lord Stanley, to the Foreign Office, but found difficulty in putting her objection to the father, and Lord Stanley was appointed.[6]

The Queen's personal objections became more frequent after the second Reform Act, by which time she had definitely adopted what she would have called 'anti-democratic' principles and had come under the sway of Mr Disraeli's personality. As soon as Mr Disraeli was defeated in 1868, General Grey saw Dean Wellesley and Lord Halifax in the hope that they would influence Mr Gladstone not to appoint Lord Clarendon to the Foreign Office; and General Grey personally made the same objection when Mr Gladstone took office. Mr Gladstone agreed to try to persuade Clarendon to take some other office, but

[1] *Ibid.* 1st series, II, pp. 419–20.

[2] *Ibid.* 1st series, II, p. 447.

[3] *Ibid.* 1st series, II, p. 514.

[4] *Ibid.* 1st series, III, pp. 567–70.

[5] *Ibid.* 2nd series, I, pp. 294–5.

[6] *Ibid.* 2nd series, I, pp. 352–3.

Clarendon refused the alternative and accordingly was appointed.[1] In 1872 the Queen's objection prevented Mr Gladstone from appointing the Duke of Somerset as Chancellor of the Duchy of Lancaster.[2]

Before Mr Disraeli resigned in 1880, the Queen asked Sir Henry Ponsonby to see Lords Hartington and Granville and to impress upon them that she would have nothing to do with Mr Gladstone, that 'there must be no democratic leaning, no attempt to change the Foreign Policy..., no change in India, no hasty retreat from Afghanistan, and no cutting down of estimates', and that she would not accept Mr Robert Lowe as minister, but that she would allow Sir Charles Dilke to take subordinate office if absolutely necessary.[3] Mr Gladstone became Prime Minister. She accepted Mr Childers at the War Office and Lord Selborne as Lord Chancellor, though with reluctance. She refused to accept Lord Fife as Lord Chamberlain on account of his youth. Before agreeing to the appointment of Mr Joseph Chamberlain she 'would wish to feel *sure* that Mr Chamberlain had never spoken disrespectfully of the Throne or expressed openly Republican speeches'. Before accepting Sir Charles Dilke's appointment as Under-Secretary at the Foreign Office, she insisted 'that he should give a written explanation, or make one in Parliament on the subject of his very offensive speeches on the Civil List and Royal Family'.[4]

On his resignation in 1886, Lord Salisbury told the Queen that she could object to any of Mr Gladstone's appointments, such as Lord Granville.[5] The Queen summoned Mr Gladstone verbally through Sir Henry Ponsonby so that Ponsonby could explain her views. Ponsonby explained that the Queen would not accept Sir Charles Dilke (who had

[1] *Letters of Queen Victoria*, 2nd series, I, pp. 555–66.

[2] Guedalla, *The Queen and Mr Gladstone*, I, p. 348.

[3] *Letters of Queen Victoria*, 2nd series, III, pp. 71–6.

[4] Guedalla, *The Queen and Mr Gladstone*, II, pp. 85–91; *Letters of Queen Victoria*, 2nd series, III, pp. 84–90. In 1882 Mr Gladstone desired to appoint Sir Charles Dilke as Chancellor of the Duchy of Lancaster. The Queen was resigned to his getting into the Cabinet, but objected to the Duchy being given him, since he would be in personal contact with her. Mr Gladstone then suggested that Mr Chamberlain should take the Duchy and Sir C. Dilke go to the Board of Trade. The Queen objected to this, and Dilke became President of the Local Government Board, Mr Dodson taking the Duchy: *Life of Sir Charles Dilke*, I, pp. 492–5.

[5] *Letters of Queen Victoria*, 2nd series, III, p. 709.

been co-respondent in a divorce suit).[1] Mr Gladstone did not nominate him. Mr Gladstone proposed Mr Childers for the War Office, but the Queen 'positively refused' this; and Mr Gladstone appointed him to the Home Office.[2]

In 1892 the Queen told Sir Henry Ponsonby that 'she positively refuses to take either Sir Charles Dilke or... Mr Labouchere. To these, however, she must add Lord Ripon not to have *anything* to do *with India*. Lord Kimberley she is also much against for India, and certainly on no account as Viceroy.'[3] Mr Gladstone did not propose office for Sir Charles Dilke, but he was anxious to appoint Mr Labouchere. The Queen's main objection, apparently, was that Mr Labouchere owned and, in theory, edited *Truth*. The Queen's objection was strong enough to keep him out of office altogether.[4] Lord Ripon went to the Colonial Office, but Lord Kimberley was appointed to the India Office.

If there are more recent precedents they have not been published. Probably there is none. Soon after the first Labour Government (of 1924) was established, George V provided a memorandum on the relations between the King and his ministers. One item was, 'No change is made in the constitution of the Ministry until the King's approval has been obtained'.[5] On the other hand, there is little evidence of that King having any influence on appointments. He raised no objection to the appointment of Mr Lansbury, who had said that 'certain circles' were bringing pressure to bear on the King, and added 'Some centuries ago, a King stood against the common people and he lost his head'.[6] In 1925 the King asked Mr Baldwin to select 'able, efficient and energetic administrators', and added that it would be very welcome to himself if Mr Austen Chamberlain was appointed as Foreign Secretary.[7] In 1929 he suggested (somewhat oddly) that Mr J. H. Thomas 'owing to his close intimacy with Mr MacDonald, might prove an excellent Foreign Secretary'.[8] These few and unimportant examples suggest that the modern practice is to talk over the list of names with the Sovereign, whose advice on personality and efficiency

[1] *Ibid.* 3rd series, I, p. 28.
[2] *Ibid.* 3rd series, I, pp. 38, 42.
[3] *Ibid.* 3rd series, II, p. 120.
[4] *Ibid.* 3rd series, II, p. 150.
[5] Nicolson, *King George V*, p. 388.
[6] *Ibid.* p. 385.
[7] *Ibid.* p. 403.
[8] *Ibid.* p. 435.

may sometimes be useful; but most appointments depend on the political prestige of the persons concerned. Moreover, the Prime Minister, who has studied his colleagues in the Cabinet and in the House of Commons, and who can discuss the capabilities of junior ministers with colleagues who have worked with them, is in a far better position to judge than a monarch who meets them occasionally and, often, casually. It should be noted that Queen Victoria never carried too far any objections on political grounds. No Prime Minister dared after 1851 to suggest Lord Palmerston for the Foreign Office, but probably the Queen would have acquiesced if the political situation had warranted the proposal, or Lord Palmerston had been less good-humoured. Mr Bright was at first kept off the Privy Council by the Queen, but later became a Cabinet minister. Mr Chamberlain was too forceful a politician to be kept out by the Queen. Sir Charles Dilke reached Cabinet rank, but was kept out of further advancement, in spite of his great ability, because of the divorce case in which he was cited. Mr Labouchere was kept out of office altogether, but he had little political following in spite of his very great ability. The objections in the cases both of Dilke and of Labouchere were not placed on political grounds. The Queen, also, had considerable influence on the actual distribution of offices, even more than appears from the above recital. Her successors, it seems, have had very little.

§3. *The Influence of Colleagues*

The influence of the Prime Minister's colleagues is less easy to assess. Mr Gladstone stated positively in 1882 that the Cabinet had no right to be consulted. 'I can affirm with confidence that the notion of a title in the Cabinet to be consulted on the succession to a Cabinet office is absurd. It is a title which Cabinet ministers do not possess. During thirty-eight years since I first entered the Cabinet, I have never known more than a friendly announcement before publicity, and very partial consultations with one or two, especially the leaders in the second House.'[1] This statement was more emphatic than the facts warranted, for examples are not uncommon.

In 1847 the Cabinet was consulted by Lord John Russell on the

[1] *Life of Mr Gladstone*, III, p. 101.

appointment of Lord Clarendon as Lord-Lieutenant of Ireland.[1] When Lord Auckland died at the end of 1848, Lord John Russell asked the views of the Cabinet as to replacing him at the Admiralty by Sir James Graham. The Cabinet agreed, but Sir James Graham refused the offer.[2] On the dismissal of Lord Palmerston from the Foreign Office in 1851, the Cabinet nominated Lord Clarendon as his successor. Lord John Russell, on the Queen's insistence, had proposed Lord Granville. 'The Queen protested against the Cabinet's taking upon itself the appointment of its own members, which rested entirely with the Prime Minister and the Sovereign, under whose approval the former constructed his Government.'[3] Nevertheless, in the belief that Lord Clarendon would refuse, the Queen authorised Lord John to write to Lord Clarendon, who in fact refused.[4]

The Duke of Argyll said that Lord Palmerston always consulted the Cabinet on Cabinet appointments,[5] and there is evidence in support. Mr Gladstone himself suggested, on the formation of Lord Palmerston's Government in 1855, that a certain minor appointment should be considered by the Cabinet.[6] On the resignation of Mr Gladstone and other Peelites in the same year, Lord Palmerston consulted the Cabinet as to whether he should approach Lord John Russell and the Whigs or Lord Derby and the Tories. The Cabinet decided on the former.[7] He also consulted them as to whether Sir George Cornewall Lewis should succeed to Mr Gladstone's office.[8] On the death of Sir William Molesworth in the same year, Lord Palmerston again consulted the Cabinet as to whether he should approach Lord Stanley.[9]

In 1866, on the appointment of Mr Goschen as Chancellor of the Duchy of Lancaster, Lord Russell, on the Queen's suggestion, asked

[1] *Letters of Queen Victoria*, 1st series, II, p. 143.

[2] Greville, *Memoirs*, 2nd series, III, p. 259.

[3] *Letters of Queen Victoria*, 1st series, II, p. 419.

[4] *Ibid.* 1st series, II, pp. 418–22. It would, however, be more accurate to say that Lord John Russell did not offer the post to Lord Clarendon. He wrote to him that he and the Queen thought that Lord Granville should be appointed: *Life of Lord Clarendon*, I, p. 339.

[5] Duke of Argyll, *Autobiography and Memoirs*, II, p. 77.

[6] Guedalla, *Gladstone and Palmerston*, p. 107.

[7] Duke of Argyll, *op. cit.* I, p. 539.

[8] *Life of Lord Clarendon*, II, p. 71.

[9] Duke of Argyll, *op. cit.* I, p. 590.

the Cabinet whether they agreed with the proposal, since Mr Goschen had not held minor office.[1] Finally, just before the general election of 1923, Mr Baldwin consulted the Cabinet as to whether he should appoint Lord Birkenhead and Mr Austen Chamberlain as ministers without portfolio. There being objections, the appointments were not made.[2]

These are all exceptional cases. In most of them the proposed appointment involved going outside the party in power. Also, consultation with the Cabinet is possible only where there is a Cabinet. It is not possible where a Cabinet is being formed. But consultations with other leaders of the Prime Minister's party are, usually, inevitable. The Prime Minister must secure a coherent Cabinet. He must, as far as possible, avoid personal antagonisms. Mr Gladstone and Mr Disraeli were autocrats: they dominated their Cabinets so effectively that they had almost complete power of choice. Even so, Sir Charles Dilke and Mr Chamberlain, by threatening to give independent support (which meant cross-fire from the back benches), forced Mr Chamberlain into the Cabinet in 1880. Sir Robert Peel necessarily consulted the Duke of Wellington; Lord John Russell necessarily consulted Lord Lansdowne; Lord Aberdeen had a long tussle with Lord John Russell. The Liberal Imperialists had much to say in the formation of Sir Henry Campbell-Bannerman's Government; Mr Asquith in 1915 had to consult Mr Bonar Law; Mr Lloyd George and Mr Bonar Law divided the spoils in 1916; in 1929 the major appointments were settled by Mr MacDonald, Mr Snowden, Mr Clynes, Mr Henderson and Mr Thomas. Moreover, an individual minister may demand to know who are to be his colleagues, and to refuse to serve if he disapproves: Lord Grey in 1845 prevented the formation of a Whig Government by refusing to serve with Lord Palmerston at the Foreign Office.

Most of the leading party members, indeed, choose themselves. The nucleus of the Cabinet exists before the Prime Minister begins to draw up lists. His task is to give these leaders appropriate places and they themselves have much to say about their own offices. Lord Palmerston (until 1852) would have nothing but the Foreign Office. Lord Claren-

[1] *Letters of Queen Victoria*, 2nd series, I, pp. 294–5.

[2] *Life of Lord Birkenhead*, II, p. 232.

don in 1868 would have nothing but the Foreign Office. Lord John Russell in 1852 insisted on being minister without portfolio (after a few weeks at the Foreign Office). Consequently, the Prime Minister's free choice applies generally only to the less important Cabinet posts and to minor offices.[1] This depends primarily, however, on the distance which separates the Prime Minister from his colleagues. Mr Asquith never had a free hand because he was merely *primus inter pares* in 1908, and in 1915 he had to consult Mr Bonar Law. In 1916 Mr Lloyd George was dependent on Conservative support and had therefore to consult Mr Bonar Law. On the other hand, Mr Bonar Law in 1922 had such an inexperienced team that he had to do what he could with what he had. In 1924 and 1929 Mr MacDonald had suspicious and politically experienced colleagues at his side; and in 1931 he had to settle every appointment with Mr Baldwin and Sir Herbert Samuel. Mr Baldwin in 1935 could do almost as he pleased, and Mr Neville Chamberlain by 1937 had acquired such prestige that he had an almost free hand. Mr Churchill in 1940 had to consult Mr Attlee about Labour appointments, but for the rest he moved or sacrificed as seemed to him to be appropriate; and in 1951 he could do as he pleased. Mr Attlee in 1945 had less freedom of choice.

In respect of minor offices, however, the Prime Minister has to consider the views of the heads of departments. Speaking of a proposal to appoint an Under-Secretary in 1880, Mr Gladstone said: 'The position of the Crown, and also of the Prime Minister, with regard to these appointments, is peculiar. They are the appointments of the Secretary of State. I learn from Lord Granville that he was sent for by Lord Palmerston, not by Lord Melbourne, when he was made Under-Secre-

[1] But, as an example of the Prime Minister's free choice, see the appointment of Brigadier-General C. B. Thomson as Secretary of State for Air in 1924. He had fought several elections unsuccessfully but had no other political experience. He had considerable ability, but his chief qualification was his personal friendship with Mr MacDonald. On this occasion Mr MacDonald retired to the remote fastness of Lossiemouth and consulted no one, except Thomson, who was unknown to the great majority of the political leaders and really knew little about Parliament, politics, or the Labour party. See *Life of Lord Thomson of Cardington*, pp. 149–51. But see J. H. Thomas, *My Story*, p. 75, where it is said that the principal offices were settled in Mr Thomas' house. They had to send for *Whitaker's Almanack* to find out what places had to be filled. Actually Mr MacDonald drew up several lists.

tary at the Foreign Office.' Sir William Harcourt, as Home Secretary, nominated Mr Leonard Courtney as Under-Secretary, and Mr Gladstone said: 'I should hardly be able to urge on the Secretary of State with due force the withdrawal of this nomination.'[1] Information on this point is meagre. It is clear, however, that Sir Robert Peel and not Lord Aberdeen appointed Mr Gladstone as Under-Secretary of State for the Colonies in 1835.[2] In 1852 the Prime Minister, Lord Derby, appointed his son, the Hon. E. Stanley, to be Under-Secretary at the Foreign Office.[3] In 1859 Lord Palmerston, as Prime Minister, appointed Lord de Grey as Under-Secretary of State for War.[4] The appointment is vested technically in the Secretary of State, but the Queen's pleasure is always taken by the Prime Minister, and the modern practice is the same as for Permanent Under-Secretaries. The Prime Minister in substance makes the appointment, but he consults the minister under whom the junior minister will work. In 1917, however, Mr Lloyd George appointed Mr Cecil Beck to be Parliamentary Secretary to the Ministry of National Service without consulting the Minister, Mr Neville Chamberlain.[5]

§4. *The Allocation of Offices*

The Prime Minister's free choice is further limited by the necessity of allocating offices between the House of Commons and the House of Lords. The Ministers of the Crown Act, 1937, as amended, provides in effect that at least three ministers in addition to the Lord Chancellor and a number of Parliamentary Secretaries must be in the House of Lords. On the other hand, certain offices are usually held by members of the House of Commons. Since the House of Commons has sole responsibility for finance, the Chancellor of the Exchequer, the Financial Secretary to the Treasury and the Financial Secretary to the War Office must be in that House.[6] All the whips must be in the House of

[1] Guedalla, *The Queen and Mr Gladstone*, II, pp. 130–1.

[2] Lady Frances Balfour, *Life of Lord Aberdeen*, II, p. 19.

[3] *Life of Lord Malmesbury*, p. 239.

[4] *Life of Lord Ripon*, I, p. 142.

[5] *Life of Neville Chamberlain*, p. 70.

[6] This did not apply to the First Lord of the Treasury, who was usually the Prime Minister. Under the Ministers of the Crown Act, 1937, the Prime Minister must be First Lord, and this implies (see above, p. 24) that the First Lord must be in the House of Commons.

Commons, so that the Parliamentary Secretary and the Junior Lords of the Treasury must be in that House. Mr Gladstone as Chancellor of the Exchequer insisted in 1860 that the heads of the great spending departments—then the War Office and the Admiralty—should be in the House of Commons, and Lord de Grey was not appointed Secretary of State for War for that reason,[1] but he succeeded to that office on the death of Sir George Cornewall Lewis in 1863.[2] Lord John Russell in 1865 also said that the Secretary of State for War ought to be in the House of Commons, since he was successor to the Secretary at War (who had been concerned with finance and was therefore in the House of Commons). He proposed to replace Lord de Grey by Lord Hartington, but eventually gave way to pressure and allowed Lord de Grey to remain.[3] Two months later, Lord Hartington went to the War Office, and Lord de Grey to the India Office.[4] In 1868 Mr Gladstone again refused to allow Lord de Grey to return to the War Office, and made him Lord President of the Council.[5] In 1885, however, Lord Ripon (as he had now become) became First Lord of the Admiralty.[6]

It is clear from recent experience that no such rule exists. Lord Lansdowne was at the War Office in 1895, Lord Kitchener in 1914–16. Lord Derby succeeded Mr Lloyd George in 1916, and was also at the War Office under Mr Bonar Law and Mr Baldwin. Lord Crewe held the office in 1931, and Lord Hailsham from 1931 to 1935. His successor was Lord Halifax, but only for a few months. The First Lord of the Admiralty has frequently been a peer. Also, these two offices are no longer the only great spending departments. The exclusion, if it were applied, would be equally relevant to the Ministries of Labour, Health, Housing and Local Government, Supply, Works, Agriculture, Fisheries and Food, Transport, Education, Power, National Insurance and Pensions. In large measure the question depends on the attitude of the Opposition in the House of Commons. If the Department is involved in controversial politics, its minister must almost inevitably be in the Commons. During the rearmament programme of 1937, Mr Neville Chamberlain refused to accept the view that the Secretary of State for

[1] *Life of Lord Ripon*, I, p. 180.
[2] *Ibid.* I, p. 191.
[3] *Ibid.* I, p. 212.
[4] *Ibid.* I, p. 215.
[5] *Ibid.* I, pp. 222–3.
[6] *Ibid.* II, p. 180.

Air should be in the House of Commons, but later he moved Lord Swinton to another office. After the resignation of Mr Eden in February 1938, Mr Chamberlain appointed Lord Halifax to be Foreign Secretary, and met the criticism that in the then state of foreign affairs it was necessary to have that minister in the Commons by undertaking to answer Foreign Office questions personally.[1] The Lord Chancellor must, however, be in the House of Lords, whether a peer or not. In practice he is always made a peer.

If the head of a department is in the House of Lords, his Under-Secretary or Secretary must be in the House of Commons. The reverse is not true. The few heads of department in the House of Lords are supported by the Lord President of the Council, the Lord Privy Seal or the Paymaster-General (if any of these is a peer) and by the chief Household officers. The responsibility of answering for the various unrepresented departments is divided among the holders of these offices, the Lords in Waiting, and possibly one or more Ministers of State.

The offices to be filled by the Prime Minister are not precisely defined in number. Those which involve executive action must be provided for, though this can frequently be done by royal warrant transferring functions to other ministers. For instance, the offices of Chancellor of the Duchy of Lancaster and Paymaster-General are sometimes not filled. Neither occupies much time. Accordingly, the former is usually filled by a minister whose advice is required in Cabinet, or who is required to undertake special duties, such as those connected with unemployment or the United Nations. The latter office is generally filled by a peer whose main function is to act for several departments in the House of Lords. Again, there is no legal obligation to appoint seven Secretaries and Under-Secretaries of State. The office of Secretary of State is a single office, and any such Secretary can act for the rest.

Further, the Prime Minister can, subject to certain restrictions, create new offices. He cannot, without legislation, add to the number of Ministers and Parliamentary Secretaries in the House of Commons. But, provided that Parliament will vote the money, he can create other new offices. Whenever the work of a department is particularly heavy, it is now customary to appoint a 'Minister of State' to whom some

[1] 332 H.C.Deb. 5 s., 747 (28 February 1938).

branch of administrative work is delegated by the minister concerned. He can, too, create unpaid offices. But no new office (except that of Secretary of State) carries legal duties without legislation.

The House of Commons has, however, generally shown itself critical of the creation of new offices, especially when such creation has a political motive. It is, for instance, suspicious of ministers without portfolio. The institution is less necessary in the British than in most Cabinets, for the Lord Privy Seal has no administrative duties, the functions of the Lord President of the Council and the Chancellor of the Duchy of Lancaster are light, and a Minister of State can always be appointed. Thus, the Prime Minister has at his disposal three or four offices which can be filled by statesmen whose advice in Cabinet is desired, but who are unwilling or unable to undertake heavy administrative work. Alternatively, these posts can be filled by statesmen undertaking special work. The Lord Privy Seal in the Labour Government of 1929 to 1931 was primarily concerned with the development of schemes for relieving unemployment. In other Governments, either the Lord Privy Seal or the Chancellor of the Duchy has sometimes been concerned with foreign affairs.

Ministers without portfolio are, nevertheless, not uncommon. The Duke of Wellington sat in the Cabinet of 1841–6 and led the House of Lords, without office. In 1852, Lord John Russell refused to take office, and insisted on leading the House of Commons. The chief objection raised to this course was that, as he would not hold an 'office of profit' he would have, as Prince Albert put it, 'slipped into office without having gone through the popular ordeal of a re-election'.[1] He proposed to remove this reproach by accepting the Chiltern Hundreds: but the Prince Consort still held it unconstitutional to lead the House of Commons as 'an irresponsible person' without office.[2] Lord Aberdeen's view was that the Duke of Wellington was 'an exception to all rule; moreover, the Lords are not the Commons, and the principle of popular election being necessary in confirmation of the choice of the Crown where ministers in the House of Commons are concerned does not apply'.[3] Sir James Graham said that, though Russell might accept

[1] *Letters of Queen Victoria*, 1st series, II, p. 511. [2] *Ibid.*

[3] *Life of Sir James Graham*, II, p. 195.

the Chiltern Hundreds, others might not accept the great constitutional principle implied in seeking re-election. 'He will owe nothing to the favour of his Sovereign, while he wields the whole power of the democratic body. He will not be on equal terms with his colleagues. His relations to the country will not be less anomalous. His power will be great, his immediate responsibilities small. He holds no office and presents no assailable front; yet he may sway the Counsels of the State in the most fatal direction.'[1] Lord Palmerston had a more cynical reason. 'Is it not worth while to consider whether it is expedient thus to set the example of gratuitous public service?...If the extensive duties of leader of the House of Commons can be performed without salary, why should any public officer have any?'[2] Lord John Russell yielded to pressure and accepted the Foreign Office until the meeting of Parliament. Within a few weeks he resigned that department, and remained as leader of the House without office until June 1854, when he became Lord President of the Council.

The arguments against Lord John Russell appear specious, and are of no weight now that ministers do not need to seek re-election on appointment. Nevertheless, ministers without portfolio have not been frequent. Lord Lansdowne was leader of the House of Lords, without office, in Lord Palmerston's Government of 1855 to 1858. Mr Spencer Walpole was in the Cabinet without office after his resignation from the Home Office in 1867.[3] Between 1915 and 1921 there were ten ministers without portfolio, and eight of them received salaries. But those who received salaries were appointed after 1917, when a temporary Act suspended the duty to seek re-election.[4] They included the members of the War Cabinet, other than the Prime Minister and the Chancellor of the Exchequer. In 1921 there was a debate on the subject in the House of Commons.[5] After saying that wartime conditions were necessarily exceptional, Mr Lloyd George, then Prime Minister, explained that after the war the pressure of business made it necessary to

[1] *Life of Sir James Graham*, II, p. 196.

[2] *Later Correspondence of Lord John Russell*, II, p. 119.

[3] *Letters of Queen Victoria*, 2nd series, I, p. 145. Mr Gathorne-Hardy sat in the Cabinet in 1866, though his commission as President of the Poor Law Board was not ready: *Life of Gathorne-Hardy*, I, p. 191.

[4] 143 H.C.Deb. 5 s., 596–7.

[5] *Ibid.* 1592–1652.

have an additional minister without departmental responsibilities. He explained that Mr G. Barnes had largely devoted himself to inter-departmental questions which affected the industrial situation, and co-ordinated the work of five or six departments. Sir L. Worthington-Evans had been chairman of many Cabinet committees, and had devoted himself especially to the study of German indemnities, the financial consequences of Home Rule, and unemployment. Dr Addison, who was the then minister without portfolio, was chairman of four Cabinet committees, and a member of six others.

Nevertheless, the sense of the House was clearly that they had had enough of these wartime expedients, and the Prime Minister agreed that Dr Addison's term of office should end with the current session of Parliament. From 1921 to 1935 there was no minister without portfolio. In the third National Government (1935), Lord Eustace Percy and Mr Anthony Eden were ministers without portfolio, the latter being concerned (in collaboration with the Foreign Secretary) with League of Nations affairs:[1] but on the resignation of Sir Samuel Hoare from the Foreign Office in December 1935, Mr Eden was appointed to that post and his own post of 'Minister without Portfolio and for League of Nations Affairs' was left unfilled.

The examples are all exceptional. The Duke of Wellington, as Lord Aberdeen rightly said, was an exception to all rules. The Governments of 1852–4, 1915–21, and 1931–5, were coalitions, in which special provision had to be made for party leaders, and special relations with Parliament were necessary. Lord Lansdowne in 1855 was an elder statesman of great authority, whose age and ill-health unfitted him for anything except occasional consultation, but whose support was a source of political strength to the Government.

Between 1940 and 1945, Mr Winston Churchill appointed many new ministers, but none was described as 'Minister without Portfolio'. No doubt he realised that the name was inappropriate and was in fact a stimulus to criticism. In politics, at least, there is something in a name; and 'Minister of State' has been found to be much less provocative than 'Minister without Portfolio'. There was, however, a minister without portfolio, representing the Government in the House of Lords,

[1] Any legal difficulty was overcome by legislation.

in Sir Anthony Eden's Cabinet of 1955, and the appointment was continued by Mr Macmillan.

§5. *The Cabinet*

The Prime Minister has not merely to determine what posts he shall fill and to find persons to fill them; he must also determine who shall be in the Cabinet. It was formerly the case that in filling the offices he had, for the most part, determined the membership of the Cabinet. The Prime Minister, the Lord President of the Council, the Lord Privy Seal, the Secretaries of State, the Chancellor of the Exchequer, the President of the Board of Trade, the First Lord of the Admiralty, and the Ministers in charge of Education, Labour, Health and Agriculture were almost always in the Cabinet. The holders of other offices might be included if their personal counsel or their political prestige warranted inclusion. The difficulty was that, in the last quarter of the nineteenth century and in the present century, the number of departments increased with the expansion of the functions of government. Disraeli in 1874 was able to govern with a Cabinet of twelve. Between the wars the number was seldom less than twenty: in 1935, for instance, there were twenty-two.

The problem of size is, of course, associated with the problem of function. The Cabinet is responsible for all the activities of the Government, whether settled by civil servants, by ministers, or by the Cabinet itself. There was accordingly a temptation to refer to the Cabinet all questions which had or might have political implications, or in other words all questions on which there ought to be discussion in the House of Commons. Since at any meeting the business of any minister might be under discussion, particularly before 1916 when there was no formal agenda and nobody save the Prime Minister—and not always he—knew what questions were to be raised, it was desirable to have all the ministers present. With the increase in the functions of government, civil servants and ministers had to take greater responsibility and to refrain from submitting to the Cabinet such questions as could with reasonable safety be disposed of departmentally. Even then it was thought desirable to have all the busy departmental ministers in the Cabinet, so that they might know the Cabinet's collective 'mind' and be able to take decisions which the Cabinet would be prepared to support if they were challenged.

It was also necessary to have a few ministers, such as the Lord President of the Council, the Lord Privy Seal, the Chancellor of the Duchy of Lancaster, and perhaps a minister without portfolio, who had no departmental duties or extremely light ones. Such ministers could devote their time to Cabinet business, would be reasonably certain (unlike departmental ministers) to have read their agenda papers and could be appointed to serve on committees without producing protests that departmental business was being held up. Besides, there were ministers—often the most active and articulate of the ministers—who were ineffective as administrators but wise as counsellors. Mr John Bright, for instance, was inefficient at the Board of Trade, but he could do no harm to the Duchy of Lancaster, he was helpful in Cabinet, and it was in any case politically necessary to include him in any Liberal Cabinet which claimed to speak for what is now known as 'the common man'. There were also 'elder statesmen' like the first Duke of Wellington, the Marquis of Lansdowne in Lord Aberdeen's Government, his successor in Mr Balfour's Government, Lord Balfour after 1918, and Mr Ramsay MacDonald after 1935. Sometimes they were wise in counsel, sometimes they had the prestige of age, and sometimes they were politically useful so long as they could do no harm.

The experience of Mr Lloyd George's War Cabinet did not suggest that in peacetime a select Cabinet was practicable, and indeed Mr Bonar Law returned to the older methods in 1922. Though the War Cabinet contained only five or six members its sessions tended to resemble public meetings. Departmental ministers and their advisers were summoned to all meetings at which their affairs were under discussion, and as many as thirty-five persons are known to have been present, some sitting on tables and improvised chairs in odd corners. Though the War Cabinet alone was collectively responsible in the widest sense, every minister (and his adviser) wanted to see that his department got fair play, especially with Mr Lloyd George in the chair.

The solution was found by a progressive diminution in the variety of Cabinet business. The circulation of agenda, the insistence on memoranda, the requirement that inter-departmental questions should be settled outside the Cabinet, the delegation to committees of all controversial issues except those of the highest political importance, and generally the procedure described in the first edition of this work, enabled the Cabinet to deal with an increasing volume of business without increasing the time devoted to it. The process of delegation proceeded much further during the war of 1939–45, and Mr Churchill's Cabinets seem to have discussed only major issues of policy. All other questions were referred to Cabinet committees for whose work a member of the War Cabinet assumed responsibility.

Mr Attlee found it necessary to appoint a larger number of departmental ministers than his pre-war predecessors. Though the Burma Office and the India Office (which were occupied by the same Secretary of State in 1936) had disappeared, there were new Departments of Civil Aviation, Defence, Food, Fuel and Power, National Insurance, Supply, and Town and Country Planning. If these had been added to the pre-war Cabinet, it would have contained twenty-eight or twenty-nine members. The experience of Mr Churchill's War Cabinet of 1940–5 had, however, enabled Mr Attlee to change the tradition. In the first place, the three Service Ministers could be replaced by the Minister of Defence, since he and not they was responsible for the major decisions on policy. Secondly, only the older and larger Civil Departments were represented in the Cabinet. Thus in January 1949 the Foreign Office, the Treasury, the Home Office, the Colonial Office, the Office of Commonwealth Relations, the Scottish Office, the Board of Trade, and the Ministries of Labour, Health, Agriculture, and Education were included, while the Ministries of Transport, Food, Town and Country Planning, National Insurance, Supply, Fuel and Power, Civil Aviation, Works and Pensions, and the Post Office, were excluded.

When Mr Churchill returned to office in 1951, he sought to carry this arrangement still further. Three ministers—all, as it happened, peers—were given light departmental duties but were made responsible for the co-ordination of various parts of governmental policy. Lord Cherwell, who held the titular office of Paymaster-General, was charged with the co-ordination of scientific research and development; Lord Woolton as Lord President of the Council was to co-ordinate food and agricultural policies; and Lord Leathers was given the grand title of

Secretary of State for the Co-ordination of Transport, Fuel and Power. A sceptical press dubbed them 'the overlords'. They were members of the Cabinet, which contained only sixteen members. The Ministers of Agriculture and Fisheries, Food, Transport and Civil Aviation, and Fuel and Power were not in the Cabinet.

Mr Churchill's Cabinet was smaller than Mr Attlee's by two members. The Ministers of Food, Transport, Civil Aviation, and Fuel and Power were not in either Cabinet, so that Lord Leathers' appointment did not reduce the size of the Cabinet but increased it by one. Lord Woolton's assignment, on the other hand, enabled Mr Churchill to deprive the Minister of Agriculture and Fisheries of membership of the Cabinet. The reduction in the size of the Cabinet was therefore due not to the creation of the 'overlords', but to the fact that Mr Churchill himself took the office of Minister of Defence and that the Chancellor of the Duchy of Lancaster was not in the Cabinet.

Lord Cherwell was really assistant to the Prime Minister in respect of scientific matters, about which the Prime Minister himself was profoundly ignorant; and no doubt he drafted, or helped to draft, some of those secret and terse minutes which, as *The Second World War* revealed, Sir Winston Churchill was in the habit of addressing to his colleagues and subordinates. Lord Cherwell had no departments to co-ordinate; and indeed most scientific research in civil matters was, in so far as it was the business of the Government at all, the business of his peer, the Lord President of the Council. In a sense, therefore, Lord Cherwell was the overlord of an overlord. There is no evidence what the other 'overlords' did as 'overlords'. Lord Woolton had some departmental duties and some ceremonial duties as Lord President of the Council, and he also had the responsible, but not strictly governmental, task of looking after the Conservative party. His functions as 'overlord' could therefore fade away inconspicuously, and they did. Lord Leathers' office disappeared after twenty-three months; and during those months he was probably a minister without portfolio charged with the responsibility of knowing a little more about Transport, Fuel and Power than the ordinary Cabinet ministers.

The experiment of appointing a Minister for the Co-ordination of Defence between the wars had proved that an 'overlord' could not co-ordinate defence. As we shall see,[1] the minister was mainly a chairman of committees and sub-committees of the Committee of Imperial Defence. The solution to the problem of co-ordinating defence (other than civil defence), which had become more acute when so many warlike actions required the co-operation of all three armed forces, was found during the war by creating the Ministry of Defence; and this arrangement continued after the war.[2] The difference between a Minister of Defence and a Minister for the Co-ordination of Defence was that the latter had no departmental powers; all the powers were vested in the Defence Departments, and his task was to co-ordinate them through inter-departmental committees.

The appointment of the new 'overlords' was criticised in the House of Commons,[3] mainly on the ground that they took away responsibility from the departmental ministers without being answerable to the House of Commons. This criticism was reinforced when Lord Woolton announced in the House of Lords that the 'overlords' were responsible not to Parliament but to the Cabinet: under the previous Government co-ordination had been effected by a committee, which had not been reappointed. 'Instead, ministers are good enough to confer with me, bringing their departmental staff with them.'[4] Lord Salisbury explained next day[5] that the responsibility to Parliament rested with the departmental ministers, and the co-ordination was a mere matter of administrative convenience.

A few days later Mr Churchill claimed[6] that the arrangements were a development of the system of Cabinet committees established during the war and continued by the Labour Government. The 'overlords' were not in the same position as the Minister of Defence, who was not a 'co-ordinating minister' but a departmental minister exercising statutory powers:

> The co-ordinating ministers have no statutory powers. They have, in particular, no power to give orders or directions to a departmental minister. A departmental minister who is invited by a co-ordinating minister to adjust a departmental policy to accord with the wider interests of the Government

[1] Below, pp. 136.
[2] Below, pp. 313–15
[3] 493 H.C.Deb. 5 s.
[4] 176 H.L.Deb. 5 s., 476.
[5] *Ibid.* 523.
[6] 500 H.C.Deb. 5 s., 188.

as a whole always has access to the Cabinet; and, if he then finds that he cannot win the support of his ministerial colleagues, he should accept their decision....

Thus, the existence and activities of these co-ordinating ministers do not impair or diminish the responsibility to Parliament of the departmental ministers whose policies they co-ordinate. Those ministers are fully accountable to Parliament for any act of policy or administration within their departmental jurisdiction. It does not follow that the co-ordinating ministers are 'non-responsible'. Having no statutory powers as co-ordinating ministers, they perform in that capacity no formal acts. But they share in the collective responsibility of the Government as a whole, and, as Ministers of the Crown, they are accountable to Parliament.

The problem of reducing the size of the Cabinet while increasing the number of ministries was met by keeping a number of ministries out of the Cabinet and by using the War Cabinet technique of having departmental ministers attend Cabinet meetings while matters affecting their departments are under discussion. The departments whose ministers were not in the Cabinet have been:

1945	1951	1955
Admiralty	Admiralty	Admiralty
Air Ministry	Agriculture and Fisheries	Air Ministry
Civil Aviation	Air Ministry	Fuel and Power
Food	Duchy of Lancaster	Post Office
Fuel and Power	Education	Supply
Health	Food	Transport and Civil Aviation
National Insurance	Fuel and Power	War Office
Pensions	National Insurance	Works
Post Office	Pensions	—
Supply	Post Office	—
Transport	Supply	—
War Office	Transport and Civil Aviation	—
Works	War Office	—
—	Works	—

Sir Anthony Eden in fact reverted to the pre-war scheme of a Cabinet containing the ministers of all the important departments, except that the Defence Departments were represented by the Minister of Defence. His Cabinet had eighteen members; and outside there were eight departmental ministers, five Ministers of State, and a Minister without Portfolio who assisted with Government business in the House of Lords. There were no 'overlords'. Mr Macmillan followed his example in 1957.

It is not necessary to take the Queen's pleasure as to the promotion of a minister to Cabinet rank. Formerly there was a legal distinction between ministers inside the Cabinet and those outside because the former were sworn of the Privy Council in order to apply to them the Privy Councillor's oath. When the King was 'advised' to admit a minister to the Privy Council he was of course informed that it was proposed to summon the minister to the Cabinet. Nowadays, however, it is the practice to admit to the Council all ministers in charge of departments and Ministers of State, whether members of the Cabinet or not. Consequently, there is no longer any question of taking the Queen's pleasure, though no doubt the Queen is informed, informally, as a matter of courtesy. A minister is made a member of the Cabinet by a note from the Prime Minister requesting him to attend. It is, however, necessary to notify the appointment of a minister, whether to the Cabinet or not, in the *London Gazette*, in order that he may have the salary prescribed by the Ministers of the Crown Act, 1937.

§6. *The Change of a Prime Minister*

So far as the law is concerned there is no office of Prime Minister, though he has occasionally been mentioned in statutes. There was and is no salary attached to the office. It was, however, customary for the Prime Minister to take some other office, usually that of First Lord of the Treasury. It gave him the Treasury patronage and enabled him to reside in one of the three Treasury houses in Downing Street, Whitehall.[1] The First Lord occupied No. 10, the Chancellor of the Exchequer No. 11.[2] This arrangement was in effect perpetuated by the Ministers of the Crown Act, 1937, which provided a salary of £10,000 a year for the

[1] He occupies Chequers as Prime Minister: see Chequers Estate Act, 1917.

[2] The third house, No. 12, is the whips' office, i.e. the office of the Junior Lords of the Treasury.

'Prime Minister and First Lord of the Treasury'. The office of First Lord is not quite a sinecure. The Treasury always speaks through 'the Lords Commissioners' or 'their Lordships', though official documents are usually signed by Junior Lords. Nor will the Treasury admit that the Chancellor of the Exchequer is head of the Treasury. Even informally it speaks of 'the Treasury Ministers'.

The Cabinet depends on the Prime Minister because it is, technically, a meeting of 'Her Majesty's confidential advisers' summoned by the Prime Minister to consider what advice shall be given to the Queen; but legally the ministers as such do not depend on the Prime Minister for their offices. They are appointed by the Queen and they hold office during Her Majesty's pleasure. Until they are allowed to resign or are dismissed, therefore, they remain in office. In fact, however, their offices are always considered to be held at the Prime Minister's disposal. If he desires to replace a minister by another, he simply informs the two persons concerned. The minister then surrenders his seal, if he has one, and the Queen gives it to the other person; or, if there is no seal, the new minister kisses hands. Whether the retiring minister is said to have resigned or to have been dismissed is therefore a matter of no importance. Frequently he writes to the Prime Minister saying that he is glad to place his office at the Prime Minister's disposal in order to facilitate the reconstitution of his Government; but it makes not the slightest difference if he does not, for it is no longer Her Majesty's pleasure that he be employed in that office.

This applies *a fortiori* where the Prime Minister formally resigns (whether on his own behalf, or on that of his Government) and is commissioned to form a new Government. This usually happens only when it has been decided to reconstitute the Government on a different political basis. For instance, Mr Asquith formally resigned in 1915 in order to form a Coalition Government. Again, Mr MacDonald resigned in 1931 in order to form the 'National' Government. In such a case it is assumed that all the offices are potentially vacant. It is, however, not always easy to determine when a new Government is formed and when an existing Government is reconstituted. Whenever there is a change of Prime Minister there must be a new Government even if most of the ministers retain their offices—this happened, for instance, in 1937 when

Mr Neville Chamberlain replaced Mr Baldwin, in 1955 when Sir Anthony Eden replaced Sir Winston Churchill, and in 1957 when Mr Macmillan replaced Sir Anthony. When, however, the same Prime Minister continues in office it is not easy to decide. In Appendix I it is assumed that a new Government was formed by Mr MacDonald after the General Election of 1932 and by Mr Churchill when the Labour ministers resigned in 1945, but that the numerous changes made by Mr Churchill between 1940 and 1945 did not result in a change of Government.

The formal procedure may be illustrated by the formation of Mr Churchill's 'Caretaker Government' after the resignation of the Labour ministers in May 1945. On the morning of 24 May Mr Churchill 'tendered his resignation as Prime Minister and First Lord of the Treasury and Minister of Defence'. The same afternoon the King 'was graciously pleased to accept his resignation' of these offices and invited him 'to form a new Administration'. Mr Churchill, according to the official statement, 'accepted His Majesty's offer of the post of Prime Minister [*sic*] and kissed hands upon his appointment'. All political offices were then deemed to be at his disposal and he formed a new Administration, though many of the former ministers were confirmed in their offices, so that new formal appointments were unnecessary.

The offices are similarly at the new Prime Minister's disposal when the former Prime Minister dies or resigns. Usually, the new Prime Minister requests most of his colleagues to remain in their existing offices. But, subject to all the limitations on his freedom of choice set out above, he can alter or reconstruct the Government as he pleases. On the death of Lord Palmerston in 1865, the Cabinet met and Lord Russell asked for their support, but he made some modification in the distribution of offices.[1] On the resignation of Lord Derby in 1868, Mr Disraeli treated all the offices as at his disposal, refused to recommend the continuation of Lord Chelmsford in office as Lord Chancellor, and recommended Lord Cairns.[2] (That is why Lord Chelmsford said that the old Government was the Derby and the new the Hoax.) Similarly, on the resignation of Sir Henry Campbell-Bannerman in 1908, Mr

[1] *Letters of Queen Victoria*, 2nd series, I, pp. 281–3.
[2] *Life of Disraeli*, II, pp. 326–9.

notably Mr Philip Snowden, occupied a high place in that class list which civil servants draw up in assessing the competence of their respective ministers.

There is, too, another difficulty for the inexperienced. Decisions are taken on the basis of memoranda. The ability to seize the gist of a long statement by a single reading is acquired only by experience. The untrained minister may be compelled to read and re-read before he feels that he has mastered the problem that is put before him. Some ministers never acquire the art of rapid digestion. Few acquire it without previous experience. The parliamentary private secretary and the junior minister acquire the practice without having the responsibility for decision. Sir Robert Peel and Mr Gladstone were correct in their inference, though their conclusion is not always practicable in our political system.

Nor is the progression of a minister from office to office always a disadvantage. Rapid changes are deprecated because it takes some time for a minister to grasp the implications of the questions submitted to him: but there is little harm and some good in transfers at intervals. The minister is not an expert, nor can he ever hope to compete with his advisers on their own subjects. Sir Edward Carson put the matter admirably when he was appointed First Lord of the Admiralty in 1916. He explained to his senior officers that he was not appointed because he was a lawyer of some eminence but because 'he knew nothing at all about the job'. As he said, 'my only qualification for being put at the head of the Navy is that I am very much at sea'.[1] The minister's task is to bring an independent mind to the questions put before him, to be convinced by his experts that they are right, or to settle in the light of common sense the disputes between the experts. The wider his vision, the easier it becomes to grasp the implications. The dangerous minister is he who fails to see consequences, not merely in relation to his own department, but in relation to the process of government as a whole, and especially in relation to its impact on the House of Commons and upon public opinion. 'The value of the political heads of departments', said Sir William Harcourt, 'is to tell the permanent officials what the public will not stand.'[2] It must, however, be confessed

[1] Colvin, *Life of Lord Carson*, III, p. 217.

[2] *Life of Sir William Harcourt*, II, p. 587.

that there are occasions when the permanent officials have to tell the politicians what the public will not stand.

It follows that a narrow departmental experience is a disadvantage, and that, within limits, variety of office is desirable. That result is obtained whenever a party has been able to serve a substantial period, or a number of periods, of office. Sir Robert Morant is believed to have said that the differences in the salaries of Cabinet offices made for rapid transition of ministers. In fact, however, these differences had small effect and in any case the anomalies have been removed by the Ministers of the Crown Act, 1937, which gives all Cabinet ministers except the Prime Minister and the Lord Chancellor £5000 a year. A minister is usually concerned primarily with his reputation. He cannot make a personal reputation unless he has time to take effective control of his department. There are, of course, certain offices, especially the Ministry of Labour and the Board of Trade, where it is difficult to make any reputation except a bad one. But even in such offices, as Sir Kingsley Wood showed at the Post Office, an energetic and imaginative minister can (by fighting his permanent officials if necessary) add to his parliamentary authority. An ambitious minister will prefer to stay long enough to do this, rather than to accept the kind of 'promotion' which is an admission of defeat.

The real reason for having ministers at the heads of departments is, however, that this is an effective method of bringing government under public control. As Sir William Harcourt said with conscious exaggeration, if the country were governed by permanent officials it would be extremely well governed for twelve or eighteen months, and then the public would hang all the heads of the civil service to the nearest lamp-posts.[1] It was no doubt this idea, and not merely a suspicion of military experts, which impelled a French Prime Minister to say that war was too serious a matter to be carried on by generals and admirals. The same idea, expressed with more decorum and a greater sense of responsibility, was behind the recommendation of the Hartington Commission in 1890, that the office of Commander-in-Chief should be placed under a Secretary of State. 'Under our Constitution, it is impossible to place any direct control over the army, over army organisation, in the hands

[1] *Life of Sir William Harcourt*, II, p. 587.

of any man except one who shall be directly responsible to the House of Commons.'[1]

There is no doubt that an able minister can have great influence on a department. It is true that he can take only a few of the decisions taken in his department every day. Indeed, his value to his department will be greater if he does not try to deal with everything; for his essential function is to relate the policy of the department to the general policy of the Government and if he immerses himself in departmental duties he becomes not a minister but a very senior administrator. He must know what is going on in the world around him and study the reactions or ideas that filter through public opinion, the House of Commons and the Cabinet. He must, therefore, travel around the country a little, read widely in the newspapers, study his Cabinet papers, attend regularly in Parliament and be accessible to those who can give him ideas. In his department he must concentrate on the matters which he deems important, especially those raising general issues of policy. After a short experience the senior officials will know his mind and be able to take decisions which he would approve if he had time to deal with them.

As Sir Oliver Franks has said:

Two things struck me [in the Ministry of Supply] about the relation of a minister to his department. They are at first sight a little incongruous. The first was how limited in number, in a large department like the Ministry of Supply, were the topics on which a minister could keep himself regularly informed and take the important decisions. It was not a question of energy or will. All the ministers under whom I served worked long hours and worked hard. It was the result of the sheer volume of business and the extreme variety of matters it concerned. In consequence while the minister was responsible for all that was done, most things were done without his knowledge. Secondly, the effect of a change of ministers on headquarters was considerable. It went beyond the circle of those who advised the minister. The two phenomena are connected. No man's tastes and methods of work are identical with another's. Precisely because the minister knew of and decided relatively few of the matters for which he was responsible, it was important that the officials who made decisions on his behalf should know his mind and conduct their business in that knowledge. The speed with which

[1] *Life of the Duke of Devonshire*, II, p. 219.

the wishes and views of an incoming minister became known reflects the desire of the good official to construct the necessary concept of the minister's mind on his business.[1]

This system has the disadvantage that the downfall of a Government may replace an able minister by a less able, and that the able minister has to try to convert himself into an Opposition leader whose main function is to 'swear horrible'.

> One result of a great electoral reverse is to invert the functions of most members of Parliament, and in particular of the two Front Benches.... [In 1880] the interchange of functions consequent on the change of Government was disastrous to the Conservative Party. Sir Stafford Northcote, Sir Richard Cross, Mr W. H. Smith, were excellent heads of great departments and able Cabinet ministers. But when the Cabinet ceased to exist, and the great departments fell to their opponents, they were transferred, through no fault of their own, from duties which they performed with credit, to duties which they could not perform at all.[2]

These eminent men might have retorted that a detached member of the 'Fourth Party' was in no position to judge impartially the leadership of the Conservative party; and Liberals might have suggested that the chief effects were to supersede an unscrupulous adventurer by 'the Grand Old Man' and to substitute for a set of amiable old gentlemen, who were incapable of restraining the adventures of their leader, a team of virile and energetic statesmen with minds of their own. The debate, indeed, continues; for this is the party system, and the judgments of one side are not accepted by the other.

§2. *Ministers and Civil Servants*

The check upon incompetence arises not merely from the reaction of parliamentary and public opinion, but also from the competence of the civil service. The minister has at hand the best opinion available. A First Lord of the Admiralty will hesitate to overrule a unanimous judgment of the rest of the Board of Admiralty; and the Secretaries of State for War and Air must similarly approach with deference the

[1] Sir Oliver Franks, *The Experience of a University Teacher in the Civil Service* (1947), p. 13.

[2] Balfour, *Chapters of Autobiography*, pp. 140–1.

united opinion of their Councils. They are certainly not always united or unanimous. The greatest capacity which experts possess is to differ among themselves. 'It is the common belief that when naval or military questions arise, a Prime Minister has nothing to do but deliver himself into the hands of experts who will decide for him, but much more often he finds himself called upon to decide between rival experts advancing contradictory propositions on equal authority.'[1] The task is by no means easy. Lord Morley once quoted as the minister's main function Lord Bowen's famous definition of hard work—'answering yes or no, on imperfect information'.[2]

There is, indeed, a peculiar problem of the service departments. There is a certain 'discipline' or 'loyalty' which prevents a military or naval officer from differing from his superior officer. During the war of 1914–18 both Mr Asquith and Mr Lloyd George found it necessary to call in other advice. Mr Asquith called in Lord Roberts, General Haig and Sir Henry Wilson to offset the advice of Sir John French and the Chief of the Imperial General Staff. Similarly, after the Battle of Passchendaele Mr Lloyd George called in Lord Ypres and Sir Henry Wilson to offset the advice of Sir Douglas Haig and Sir William Robertson.[3] On the other hand, there seems to have been no such problem in the war of 1939–45. There was apparently no conflict between the services and the 'frocks' (perhaps they ought now to be called 'sirens'), in spite of disasters far greater than those of 1914 and 1915. Possibly both those in uniform and those out of it had learned that the art of war, like the arts of peace, depends more on wisdom and common sense than on technical training.

The problem of a Prime Minister in time of war is more difficult than that of an ordinary minister in time of peace. Questions which depend on *expertise* are usually settled by experts. In any department there must be a substantial measure of delegation; questions which come to the minister are usually of some political importance; and upon them his own opinion is better than that of his advisers. Moreover, the minister has at his hand the services of the permanent head of his department

[1] *Life of Lord Oxford and Asquith*, I, p. 346.
[2] Sir Austen Chamberlain, *Politics from Inside*, p. 69.
[3] Lloyd George, *War Memoirs*, IV, p. 2367.

who 'is not (except by accident) a specialist in anything, but rather the general adviser of the minister, the general manager and controller under the minister, with the *ultimate* responsibility to the minister for *all* the activities of the department (and of its officials)'.[1] This distinguished civil servant has usually had experience outside his present department. He has, usually, none of that deference to experts which most ministers possess. He is able to put before the minister the possible alternatives, to select the weak points in the specialist's case, and to give his own opinion of rival theses.

Sometimes, it is true, the permanent head acts as a selective filter which allows to pass only those things of which it approves. Yet a strong minister can always open up the stream. Mr Lloyd George has stated his own practice.

I have never taken the view that the head of a Government Department is forbidden by any rule of honour or etiquette from sending for any person either inside or outside his office, whatever his rank, to seek enlightenment on any subject affecting his administration. If a minister learns that any subordinate in his department possesses exceptional knowledge or special aptitude on any question, it is essential he should establish direct contact with him....Freedom of access to independent information is quite compatible with order and due respect for the hierarchy, if that liberty is tactfully and judiciously exercised by the minister and wisely acquiesced in by the service.[2]

Not all those who worked with Mr Lloyd George would give such a rosy picture of his relations with his departments. The opposite view may be judged from the following:

The Prime Minister [Lloyd George]...was accustomed to boast that he had his own sources of information from the Admiralty, and it was discovered that some of his secretaries were in the habit of going down to the canteen in the Admiralty basement, where the Second Division clerks had their lunch, and gathering there for the delectation of the Chief information more surprising than authoritative of what went on upstairs. Little wonder if with such encouragement tittle-tattle grew until the First Lord [Carson] issued an order that if officers were found to be gossiping about the affairs of the Admiralty he would take a serious view of their conduct.[3]

[1] From a memorandum by Sir Warren Fisher (Permanent Secretary to the Treasury): Royal Commission on the Civil Service (1929), Minutes of Evidence, p. 1272.

[2] Lloyd George, *War Memoirs*, III, pp. 1171–2.

[3] Colvin, *Life of Lord Carson*, III, pp. 262–3.

This is an allegation of a sort of espionage conducted by the Prime Minister against a departmental minister and it may not be true; but Mr Lloyd George was known to have personal friends among public servants, some of whom would certainly have behaved with complete rectitude while the motives of others were sometimes questioned. There is danger in a modification of the usual channels. Public servants are much like other people; they may have axes to grind and ambitions to achieve. The traditions of the public service do their best to encourage honest opinion and fearless criticism, but so long as politicians can influence promotions and the distribution of honours there is risk of toadying, flattery and self-seeking. If the minister reads his papers thoroughly (and Mr Lloyd George rarely did) and listens at departmental committees, he will soon discover whether his officials are agreed; and if he has any reason to believe that a point of view is being inadequately expressed to him, he can ask for a memorandum from a specified officer, on which, of course, others will be allowed to comment, or a personal discussion at which the opposing theses can be confronted. Only if he suspected that a point of view was being suppressed or played down and that loyalty to or fear of a superior officer was preventing an adequate case being made, would a minister be justified in going behind his principal advisers; and such cases would happen extremely rarely.

In an ordinary department a minister who has the time or the patience to read minutes can easily make use of the collective wisdom of his department. For whether the question is so important that the file goes down from the permanent head to the officer most intimately concerned, or whether the file comes up from an assistant principal to the minister, it passes through several hands. In passing, it grows like a stream, and if the currents are not all in one direction the minister knows what they are. If they flow together the minister may be sure that, political considerations apart, it is safe to act.[1]

[1] In spite of all this, the minister may run counter to his departmental opinion. When Mr Arnold-Forster succeeded Mr Brodrick at the War Office in 1902, 'Bromley-Davenport, who only came in as Financial Secretary on Friday, opened his tenure of office by writing "I don't agree" across the completed and approved papers of the War Office Journal scheme. How can good work be done with such fools?' *Diaries of Field-Marshal Sir Henry Wilson*, I, p. 53.

Nor must it be forgotten that the minister can always add to the wisdom of his department by calling in outside advice. The tradition that the citizen with expert knowledge can always be called upon to place it at the disposal of the Government is one of the happiest features of our civic life. In many departments there are advisory committees meeting at regular intervals. In others experts of special eminence are considered to be 'on tap', so that a senior official or a minister feels able at all times to ask for advice. These civic duties are in all cases carried out gratuitously. Indeed, it rarely happens that a person is not out of pocket when he is summoned to London to attend a meeting or to give personal assistance, for a grateful country pays a subsistence allowance which is carefully assessed to avoid the possibility of profit. It is, nevertheless, very desirable that the principle of gratuitous service should be maintained, for it enables the State to call for advice whenever it is needed; and though it is very necessary that departments should have their permanent and paid advisers, it is equally necessary that they should call on outside opinion. The Adviser is the person who most needs advice; and indeed if he is good at his job he will be the first to recognise that fact.

When the minister has taken his decision, he has at hand the expert staff to carry it out. He may generally assume that his assistants will loyally carry out his decision even if they do not approve of it. To give the example of Sir Robert Morant is, perhaps, rather like appealing to the practice of an archangel.[1] Yet the Education Bill of 1906 supplies a good instance. It was in many respects the exact converse of the Bill of 1902, which might justly be described as Morant's 'baby'. Nevertheless, the Minister acknowledged that in assisting with the Bill of 1906 Morant did his 'very best and utmost to make it a workable measure'.[2] A more cynical and, perhaps, more typical example is that of a Colonial Office official who was informed that Sir Michael Hicks Beach had given notice of his intention to raise the question of the salaries of officers on the west coast of Africa. The official replied that as soon as he could learn what it was that Hicks Beach proposed—

[1] For a different opinion on Morant's place of abode, see Michael Sadleir, *Michael Ernest Sadler*, especially pp. 169 and 219–21.

[2] *Life of Sir Robert Morant.*

whether to raise or lower—he would send 'in either event, a perfect case'.[1]

Sir Warren Fisher has stated the principles upon which civil servants act.

> Determination of policy is the function of ministers, and once a policy is determined it is the unquestioned and unquestionable business of the civil servant to strive to carry out that policy with precisely the same good will whether he agrees with it or not. That is axiomatic and will never be in dispute. At the same time it is the traditional duty of civil servants, while decisions are being formulated, to make available to their political chiefs all the information and experience at their disposal, and to do this without fear or favour, irrespective of whether the advice thus tendered may accord or not with the minister's initial view. The presentation to the minister of relevant facts, the ascertainment and marshalling of which may often call into play the whole organisation of the department, demands of the civil servant the greatest care. The presentation of inferences from the facts equally demands from him all the wisdom and all the detachment he can command.[2]

Some other aspects were brought out in 1929 by a memorandum submitted by the association representing the administrative class of the civil service:

> The civil servant has so to act as not to embarrass his minister and the Government of the day in their relations with Parliament and with organisations having political power. The volume of official work which calls for decisions affecting the public is nowadays such that it is physically impossible for the minister himself to give the decision except in the most important cases. And further, even when the issue is one which can and must be submitted for the minister's personal decision, it has to be fully and fairly presented to him so that all the material facts and considerations are before him. The need for services of this kind is present in every department which has a political head.
>
> There is another common feature of all work which is strictly administrative in character. It is usually described—for instance by the Reorganisation Committee of 1920—by the somewhat general expression 'the formation of policy'. What is meant is, we think, this. The business of government, if it is to be well done, calls for the steady application of wide and long views to

[1] *Life of Sir Charles Dilke*, I, pp. 288–9. It has been pointed out to me by a former official who knew Sir Robert Herbert that the observation may not have been cynical at all. What he probably meant was that he could supply a complete statement of the facts of the case and suggest arguments which the minister might find useful in debate.

[2] Royal Commission on the Civil Service (1929), Minutes of Evidence, p. 1268.

complex problems, for the pursuit, as regards each and every subject-matter, of definite lines of action, mutually consistent, conformed to public opinion and capable of being followed continuously while conditions so permit and of being readily adjusted when they do not. Almost any administrative decision may be expected to have consequences which will endure or emerge long after the period of office of the Government by which or under whose authority it is taken. It is the peculiar function of the Civil Service, and the special duty of the Administrative Class of that Service, in their day-to-day work to set these wider and more enduring considerations against the exigencies of the moment, in order that the Parliamentary convenience of today may not become the Parliamentary embarrassment of tomorrow. This is the primary justification of a permanent administrative service. Vacillation, uncertainty and inconsistency are conspicuous symptoms of bad administration. The formation of policy in this limited sense—subject always to the control of the minister and to the supreme authority of Parliament—is typical of administrative work in all departments and in relation to all subject-matters whether of greater or of lesser importance.[1]

The civil servant's function is thus to advise, to warn, to draft memoranda and speeches in which the Government's policy is expressed and explained, to take the consequential decisions which flow from a decision on policy, to draw attention to difficulties which are arising or are likely to arise through the execution of policy, and generally to see that the process of government is carried on in conformity with the policy laid down. It is inevitable that he should develop and give expression to views of his own and that the department as a whole should adopt and seek to give effect to principles of action which arise out of the common experience of its senior members. It would be difficult to give specific examples because any such principles would not be expressed in writing; they would be the sum of the 'inarticulate major premises' of the officials concerned, and would be imperfectly known to the officials themselves. They would appear as the basis of minutes and memoranda and could be traced only by a careful comparison of the action recommended and taken with the conditions in which the recommendations were made. Such examples as may be cited are mere allegations, insusceptible of proof.

[1] Royal Commission on the Civil Service (1929): Statement submitted by the Association of First Division Civil Servants, p. 5.

It was assumed before the depression of 1929–33 that the Treasury was dominated by the principles of 'Gladstonian finance', which attributed the highest virtue to balancing the Budget and would have scorned such a policy as President Franklin D. Roosevelt's 'New Deal'.[1] It was assumed, too, that the Treasury and even more the Board of Trade (because it was concerned primarily with the encouragement of exports) was until 1932 (at least) convinced of the validity of the free trade doctrine. It was alleged that the Foreign Office under Sir Robert Vansittart was Germanophobe and Francophile; and the policies publicly advocated by Lord Vansittart since his emancipation from office do not tend to deny the allegation. Nor can more personal bias be excluded. Sir Arthur Nicolson, the Permanent Under-Secretary at the Foreign Office before the war, was a strong Ulsterman, and as a result of the Government's policy on Ireland (which had nothing to do with the Foreign Office) there grew up in 1914 a certain constraint between him and Sir Edward Grey.[2] Senior civil servants are, however, intelligent persons, and intelligent persons recognise their bias and do their best to articulate their premises.

Nevertheless, the tradition is firm that when the Government changes the policy, the departmental policy must change. When at last, in 1932, the United Kingdom went protectionist, there was no change in the personnel of the Treasury and the Board of Trade, but the officials of those departments did their best to produce the most efficient protective system that their ingenuity could devise. By a somewhat remarkable coincidence, Sir Robert Vansittart was promoted to be Chief Diplomatic Adviser to the Foreign Secretary on 1 January 1938; and Mr Anthony Eden resigned in February 1938 because he did not agree with the Prime Minister's foreign policy, while Mr Neville Chamberlain in his subsequent discussions with the dictators was advised by the Chief Economic Adviser, not the Chief Diplomatic Adviser.[3] The interpre-

[1] 'No school of thought is so strong or so enduring as that founded on the great traditions of Gladstonian and Peelite finance.' Sir Winston Churchill in *Life of Lord Randolph Churchill*, II, p. 180. 'The Gladstonian garrison for free trade': *Life of Joseph Chamberlain*, IV, p. 23.

[2] Nicolson, *Lord Carnock*, pp. 401–2.

[3] There was indeed a conflict between the Prime Minister and the Foreign Office: see Viscount Templewood, *Nine Troubled Years*, pp. 259–61. Sir Horace Wilson was 'in every respect the orthodox, conscientious and efficient civil servant'. He would have

tation that Sir Robert Vansittart was out of sympathy with the new foreign policy is irresistible.[1] It is to be noted, too, that in December 1937, when the rearmament programme was in full swing, the Chief of the Imperial General Staff and the Adjutant-General resigned 'in order to facilitate the promotion of younger officers', while the Master-General of the Ordnance relinquished his post 'to facilitate a reorganisation'.[2]

Thus, while the 'spoils' system is not in operation, it is not always possible for ministers to continue to work with senior civil servants who have strong views on policy. Such changes as occur do not, however, arise through a change of Government. As a sympathetic American has observed:

> The accession of the Labour party to power in 1924 marked a political revolution in British history. Yet the break with the past involved in a Government committed to the principle of socialism was accomplished with a shift of less than one hundred persons. In large matters of foreign policy one can hardly conceive of more contrasting types than Lord Curzon and Mr Ramsay MacDonald. Yet when Mr MacDonald succeeded Lord Curzon at the Foreign Office, the official who had served Lord Curzon continued as Mr MacDonald's private secretary.[3]

The Labour party was, of course, in the particular difficulty that the social environment which gave birth to the party was outside the experience of most members of the administrative class of the civil service, and the view had been expressed by some Labour publicists that it would be necessary to change the occupants of some of the key positions in the public service. No such step was, however, taken in 1924, in 1929 or in 1945. On the contrary, the Labour ministers of 1924 spoke emphatically of the assistance which they had received from the civil service. To prevent any possible difficulty in foreign policy, Mr Arthur Henderson, who became Foreign Secretary in 1929, circu-

preferred to continue with his own work at the Treasury, but he was particularly skilful in preparing difficult questions for ministerial decision, and Mr Chamberlain had found this sort of help useful in the Ministry of Health and the Treasury and sent for Sir Horace to help him find his way through the unfamiliar problems of foreign affairs. The world, especially the official world, thought that a new Foreign Office, like the notorious 'garden suburb' of Mr Lloyd George, was being set up at No. 10 Downing Street.

[1] Sir Winston Churchill, *The Second World War*, I, p. 217.

[2] *The Times*, 3 December 1937.

[3] Frankfurter, *The Public and its Government*, p. 139.

lated in the Foreign Office copies of the official Labour party programme, *Labour and the Nation*.[1] By 1945, however, the views of Labour politicians were sufficiently well understood to make such a precaution unnecessary: and the principal Labour ministers had had lengthy official experience under Mr Churchill.

There is certainly no evidence of any kind of intrigue between civil servants and the Opposition. One may, sometimes, suspect their impartiality; but one never suspects their honesty. There is evidence that senior military officers, on the other hand, cannot always be trusted. Their 'discipline' may stop short at the highest military rank, and their 'loyalty' may not extend to the politicians who are in control. As long ago as 1893 Admiral (Lord) Fisher, then Third Sea Lord, wrote to Mr Austen Chamberlain, who was then in Opposition, to say that Sir William Harcourt, Leader of the House of Commons, had 'told an unmitigated lie' and to thank Mr Joseph Chamberlain for his speech.[2] General Wilson, who was in 1912 Director of Military Operations, and therefore a member of the War Office staff, had many meetings with Opposition leaders to further the campaign for conscription, though this was contrary to Government policy;[3] and in 1913 and 1914 he had many meetings with Mr Bonar Law about the relation of the Army to an Ulster rebellion.[4] On 1 August 1914 Sir Henry Wilson got into touch with the Opposition leaders to bring pressure upon the Government to declare war. As a result, a semi-minatory letter was sent to the Government by Mr Bonar Law.[5] On 4 August he had further discussions with the Conservatives in order to induce the Government to send the Expeditionary Force to France.[6] Nor did these unconstitutional activities cease on his appointment to a staff post in the field. When he was on leave at the beginning of 1915, he saw the representative of the American press, Lord Milner, Mr Bonar Law, Mr Austen Chamberlain and the Editor of the *Morning Post*.[7]

His superior officer, Sir John French, was more circumspect but not wholly averse from the use of extra-constitutional methods. As

[1] *Life of Arthur Henderson*, p. 348.
[2] *Life and Letters of Sir Austen Chamberlain*, I, p. 61.
[3] *Diaries of Field-Marshal Sir Henry Wilson*, I, pp. 114, 116, 126.
[4] *Ibid.* I, pp. 131, 138, 140, 141, 143, 144, 147.
[5] *Ibid.* I, p. 154. [6] *Ibid.* I, p. 156. [7] *Ibid.* I, pp. 200–1.

General Officer-in-Chief at Aldershot he used his friendship with Lord Esher, who had influence with the King, to secure the acceptance of his views by the Secretary of State against those of the Army Council.[1] Above all, when he was Commander-in-Chief in France after the second Battle of Ypres, he gave information to *The Times* military correspondent and sent two staff officers to interview Conservative leaders and others.[2] Whether this was due to his belief that the attack had failed because of the neglect of the Government to supply the necessary ammunition, as he and Mr Lloyd George suggested, or to his recognition of the principle of strategy that the best means of defence from attack by politicians is to attack politicians on their own ground, as Lord Beaverbrook suggests, is immaterial. The fact is that he took steps which might have resulted (and were thought at one time to have resulted) in the overthrow of the Government. His colleague, Sir Henry Wilson, was by no means backward in the intrigues which resulted in the fall of the first Coalition Government in 1916.[3]

These are probably exceptional cases, but they illustrate one difficulty of political control. Another difficulty arises through the scattered nature of the British dependencies. The 'man on the spot' must be allowed a large measure of discretion; and he does not always possess either the sense of political realities or the recognition of his own position in the scheme of things which he needs to form a satisfactory judgment. Sir Bartle Frere brought on the Zulu War in 1878 without the consent of the Secretary of State.[4] The electric telegraph has reduced the power of 'prancing proconsuls'; but even in present conditions a British representative can misconceive the nature of his instructions or interpret them in a spirit alien to the Government's

[1] *Life of Lord Ypres*, p. 140.

[2] *Life of Lord Oxford and Asquith*, II, p. 141; Lloyd George, *War Memoirs*, I, pp. 199–200; *Diaries of Field-Marshal Sir Henry Wilson*, I, p. 226; Beaverbrook, *Politicians and the War*, I, pp. 90–4; Sir Austen Chamberlain, *Politics from Inside*, pp. 626, 630. What is sauce for the goose is sauce for the gander. Sir Douglas Haig, in command of the First Army under Sir John French, was in correspondence with Buckingham Palace, whence pressure was being brought for the removal of Sir John French: *Private Papers of Douglas Haig, 1914–19*, pp. 97, 113, 138. For communications between officers of the Royal Air Force and Opposition leaders in 1939, see Dalton, *The Fateful Years*, p. 165.

[3] *Diaries of Field-Marshal Sir Henry Wilson*, I, pp. 298–9, 304.

[4] *Life of Sir Michael Hicks Beach*, I, ch. V.

intentions. It is possible to argue that British relations with Egypt in 1923–4 would have been easier if the High Commissioner had not been Lord Lloyd.[1] One of the first acts of the Labour Government was to recall him.

One difficulty has certainly been overcome. The 'spoils' system does not exist in Great Britain. An independent body, the Civil Service Commission, has powers of control over nearly all admissions to the civil service. By an Order in Council of 1920 it is provided that, subject to certain exceptions, 'the qualifications of all persons proposed to be appointed, whether permanently or temporarily, to any situation or employment in any of His Majesty's Civil Establishments shall, before they are appointed, be approved by the Commissioners, and no person shall be so appointed until a certificate of his qualification has been issued by the Commissioners'.[2] The exceptions are: (i) persons to whom a certificate has already been issued, (ii) persons who are appointed to certain senior positions directly by the Crown (usually these are filled by promotion), (iii) persons transferred by or under an Act of Parliament (as when a local or commercial service is transferred to the Crown), (iv) persons appointed to certain unestablished offices.[3]

Again, though every civil servant (subject to a few isolated exceptions) is legally dismissible at the pleasure of the Crown, in fact a person who holds a pensionable post is not dismissed without pension except for misconduct. Even such power of dismissal is hedged about with restrictions designed to protect the officer.[4] He may retire with an allowance before he attains the age of sixty if he shows that he is permanently incapacitated by ill-health, or if his office is abolished. He may be asked to retire with an allowance on account of his 'inability to discharge efficiently the duties of his office'; but in such a case a Minute must be laid before Parliament.[5]

Above all, there is the ultimate control of Parliament exercised both directly and through the Select Committee of Public Accounts. Any

[1] It is also said that Lord Allenby's ultimatum to Egypt after the murder of Sir Lee Stack would not have received Foreign Office sanction as to some of its terms.

[2] Royal Commission on the Civil Service (1929), Minutes of Evidence, Appendix I, p. 43.

[3] *Ibid.* pp. 44–6.

[4] *Ibid.* pp. 29–30.

[5] *Ibid.* p. 64; Royal Commission on the Civil Service (1929), Minutes of Evidence, p. 1269.

misuse of departmental patronage which became known to the Comptroller and Auditor-General would be reported to Parliament and would be the subject of investigation by the Select Committee.[1] Any suspicion of 'jobbery' would form the subject of an attack in Parliament. As Mr Disraeli said in 1858, 'the interests of the party can never require an improper appointment: an improper appointment is a job, and nothing injures a party more than a job'.[2] It is true that he added: 'At the same time, there is nothing more ruinous to a political connection than the fear of justly rewarding your friends, and the promotion of ordinary men of opposite opinions in preference to qualified adherents.'[3] But there are few appointments now available by which 'qualified adherents' can be 'rewarded'. The appointments in question were naval lordships, which are now purely professional appointments. Similarly, though Sir Charles Dilke said that Sclater-Booth (1874–80), Dodson (1880–82) and Goschen (1868–71) at the Local Government Board had appointed 'political partisans or supporters',[4] the tightening up of Orders in Council and the psychological effects of the reforms of 1855 have, as far as can be judged, removed the political element from all appointments save those of some judgeships and colonial governorships. Nothing delights an Opposition more than a suspicion of a 'job'. It is as anxious for the chase as a hound that has scented the fox.

There is, however, a new problem arising from the creation of numerous autonomous boards in recent years. Generally speaking, technical knowledge is not required for appointments to these boards, since technical officers are employed by the boards. There is thus a great temptation, which has not always been resisted, to appoint to them defeated parliamentary candidates who have done good party service, parliamentary secretaries and others whose parliamentary service has been honest but inconspicuous, wives of ministers because they are vaguely 'interested' and public opinion thinks that there is something called 'the women's point of view', and generally the hangers-on of the party machine. These are, of course, the principles upon which directors

[1] Cf. Epitome of the Reports from the Committee of Public Accounts, pp. 97, 235, 312–13, 316.

[2] *Life of Disraeli*, I, p. 1658.

[3] *Ibid.*

[4] *Life of Sir Charles Dilke*, I, p. 504.

of public companies are often appointed, but the tendency shows the development of a new 'spoils' system.

These are, however, exceptional illustrations of exceptional problems. The essential feature of the British system is on the one hand the clear division between politicians and public servants and on the other hand the close relationship between policy and administration. This feat is achieved through ministerial responsibility and the efficient organisation of parliamentary Opposition. The minister being responsible for everything done in his department, everything that is done may be the subject of parliamentary scrutiny. Sir Oliver Franks has again borne testimony:

> Even in war, when the executive was so strong, the reality of parliamentary control was an impressive fact. It was exercised through visits and letters from members of Parliament, parliamentary questions, and the investigations of the Select Committee on National Expenditure[1] and of the Public Accounts Committee. No matter what the state of the war or the urgency of business the drafting of replies to letters or parliamentary questions or of memoranda at the request of one or other committee was given a considerable degree of priority. High standards of thoroughness and accuracy were observed and a considerable amount of the time of many officials was diverted from their ordinary work. The influence of these manifestations of parliamentary control went far beyond the particular subjects on which inquiries or investigations were made. It amounted to a continuous element of discipline in the minds of officials. The knowledge that any hesitation might become the subject of parliamentary scrutiny gradually sank into the minds of temporary civil servants until it became as habitual to them as to their permanent colleagues. It made necessary the keeping of records of what was done, in detail otherwise unnecessary. But more important it made an official in the moment of decision almost automatically ask himself how he could justify it in Parliament if called upon directly or through his superiors.[2]

[1] This Committee replaced the Select Committee on Estimates during the war.

[2] Sir Oliver Franks, *op. cit.* pp. 13–14.

CHAPTER VI

INTER-DEPARTMENTAL RELATIONS

In the British Constitution no reform is ever so radical that all relics of the superseded system are removed. According to the theory of the eighteenth century, the King appointed a minister to administer certain services on his behalf; the minister alone was responsible for the administration of those services, the appointment and dismissal of the staff, the handling of the funds placed at his (or the King's) disposal for those services, and the general control of the establishments under his charge. This idea has never completely disappeared. A department is a separate unit in which, in principle, the minister is responsible for providing the staff out of moneys provided by Parliament, for maintaining efficiency among that staff, and for advising the Queen about the decisions to be taken or, if necessary, for taking the decisions himself in the Queen's name. The reforms of two centuries have in some degree provided for co-ordination, have caused general principles to be laid down for all of 'Her Majesty's Civil Establishments', and have enabled the Treasury Ministers to intervene in matters which departmental ministers would have regarded as within their competence.

The King consulted some or all of his 'confidential advisers' in Cabinet Council, and gradually the power of decision passed from the King to the Cabinet, which thus obtained a power of co-ordination of policy. In particular, since the King was compelled to rely on his Cabinet because of their ability to secure supplies from Parliament, and since Parliament insisted on appropriating supplies for particular purposes, the Cabinet could effectually control departmental policy by asking for supplies in the King's name. Since it proved possible to obtain regular supplies only by means of a party majority or a combination of parties, there developed a close relation between the Cabinet and the House of Commons which created the principle of collective responsibility not merely to the King but also to Parliament; and the minister's individual responsibility was subordinated to the Cabinet's collective responsibility. Generally speaking, the link between the Cabinet and the King and also between the Cabinet and the House of Commons was the First Lord of the Treasury, whose Financial Secretary looked after supplies to the departments and whose Parliamentary Secretary—or Patronage Secretary—looked after the majority in the House of Commons. Clearly the Treasury occupied a central position, and the First Lord was usually Prime Minister. Mr Pitt's financial reforms strengthened the hands of the Treasury and the Prime Minister; but though the Treasury secured the funds it did not control the departments. Sir Robert Peel exercised a degree of supervision which secured co-ordination at the highest administrative level. Also, Mr Gladstone's reforms, the creation of the Civil Service Commission and the introduction of the competitive examination, provided a single civil service for Her Majesty's Civil Establishments: but it was still true at the end of the nineteenth century that the departments, now becoming more numerous, were independent units controlled at the political level by the Cabinet and the Prime Minister and administratively co-ordinated, at least in some measure, by the Treasury through the power of the purse.

The expansion of the functions of Government rendered the problem of co-ordination more acute. The disasters of the Boer War and the growing danger in Europe drew attention to the need for securing joint action by the Admiralty, the War Office, the Foreign Office, the Colonial Office and the India Office. The examination of this problem in 1903 and 1904 resulted in the creation of the Committee of Imperial Defence—now the Defence Committee—and in due course the joint staffs working under the Chiefs of Staff Committee exercised what became in effect an administrative as well as a political control over the Defence Services. Theoretically, the responsibilities of the First Lord of the Admiralty and the Secretary of State for War—to whom was added in 1917 the Secretary of State for Air—remained unimpaired. The Chiefs of Staff Committee reported to the Committee of Imperial Defence, which reported to the Cabinet. In fact, however, numerous decisions were taken even before 1914, under the authority of the Prime Minister, in matters of administration.

The creation of the Air Arm added to the complication by producing a new source of controversy between the Admiralty and the War Office. In 1915 an Air Board was created under Lord Curzon to act as a co-ordinating committee. This proving ineffective owing to the opposition of the Admiralty, Lord Curzon brought the matter before the War Cabinet, where there ensued a long debate between Lord Curzon and Mr Balfour. Heads of a settlement were agreed by the Cabinet, but the change of Government in 1916 enabled the question to be reopened. Mr Lloyd George refused to go back on the arrangement, and the Air Board was reconstituted with enlarged terms of reference. The success of the German air raids led the Cabinet to believe that a much more energetic policy had to be followed. A Cabinet committee recommended a separate Air Ministry and Air Force. The Admiralty objected, but the War Cabinet accepted the report and the necessary legislation was introduced and passed.[1] Henceforward three Service Departments had to be co-ordinated.

The rearmament programme of 1936–9 again raised the problem of co-ordination. Mr Baldwin's solution, which was followed by Mr Neville Chamberlain, was to appoint a Minister for the Co-ordination of Defence who, *inter alia*, presided over the Chiefs of Staff Committee in the absence of the Prime Minister.[2] In fact, however, he made little attempt to co-ordinate general administration, and his real task was to co-ordinate production, a branch of administration which, as will presently be seen, has a separate history. The office disappeared in 1940 and late in the same year Mr Winston Churchill, on becoming Prime Minister, assumed also the functions of Minister of Defence. The office added nothing to the powers which he might have exercised as Prime Minister, but the title made plain that he proposed to take personal control of strategy, subject of course to the War Cabinet, which in fact left him a very large element of discretion.[3] Mr Attlee followed his example for a short period, but in 1946 a separate Minister of Defence was appointed, to preside over the Chiefs of Staff Committee when required, and to take decisions on matters of strategy common to all three Services. In this instance, accordingly, the problem of co-ordination was solved by the creation of a separate ministry.

One of the essential tasks of the Committee of Imperial Defence

[1] Lloyd George, *War Memoirs*, IV, ch. LVII; see also *Life of Lord Curzon*, III, pp. 145–7.

[2] See below, pp. 302–4.

[3] See below, pp. 310–13.

between the wars was the co-ordination of supplies to the three Services. This was done through a body set up in 1924 and known as the Principal Supply Officer's Committee, with the President of the Board of Trade in the chair. It had a system of committees and sub-committees. On the supply side (it dealt also with raw materials) the administrative body was the Supply Board.[1] Though originally provided to co-ordinate supplies for the Service Departments, it was found to be so useful as a means of securing economy that, on the advice of the Select Committee on Estimates,[2] its jurisdiction was extended to cover numerous supplies for civil departments like the Post Office, the Stationery Office, the Office of Works and the Home Office. It worked through numerous sub-committees and sub-sub-committees, each concerned with a product, or a group of products, in demand by two or more departments. In relation to each it was able to adopt some method for reducing cost—by securing common specifications, the synchronisation or spreading of orders, the purchase of articles by one department as agent for another, and so on. These functions became so important when the rearmament programme was drawn up in 1936 that there were insistent demands for a Ministry of Supply. Mr Baldwin sought to meet this demand, as well as that for a Ministry of Defence, by his appointment of a Minister for the Co-ordination of Defence; and in fact the Minister was more concerned with supply than with strategy. Mr Neville Chamberlain continued to resist the appointment of a Minister of Supply until April 1939, when a Ministry was established by legislation to take over the supply functions of the War Office. This was made easier by the fact that, as a result of reorganisation at the War Office from 1936, the responsibility for supply was vested in a Director-General of Munitions Production.[3] Power was taken to add other functions, but the Admiralty and the Air Ministry continued to accept responsibility for their own supplies. In 1938, however, a reorganisation of the Air Ministry vested vast supply functions in the Air Member for Development and Production. Accordingly, it was not difficult for

[1] Chester and Willson, *The Organization of British Central Government, 1914–1956*, pp. 228–9.

[2] Reports from the Select Committee on Public Accounts, 1931, pp. 420–1.

[3] Chester and Willson, *op. cit.* p. 229.

Mr Churchill in 1940 to transfer the production of aircraft to a new Ministry of Aircraft Production. Thus by 1940 supply for the Navy was undertaken by the Admiralty, supply for the Army by the Ministry of Supply, and supply for the Air Force by the Ministry of Aircraft Production, though with some common arrangements, for the most part on an agency basis. This created a new problem of co-ordination, which had to be effected mainly by the Prime Minister as Minister of Defence. Mr Churchill at first refused to delegate, but the need to co-ordinate supplies from the United States led in 1942 to the creation of the Ministry of Production.[1]

After the war the Ministries of Aircraft Production and of Production were abolished by Mr Attlee. Their functions were transferred to the Ministry of Supply, which thus took over the main functions of the Supply Board.

The practice is to provide for the requirements of the Army in the Army Estimates and for those of the Royal Air Force in the Air Estimates, but the materials are in fact supplied by the Ministry of Supply, which also supplies stores and other materials to the other departments, including the Admiralty, the Ministry of Civil Aviation, and to other civil departments where that is the most convenient method. For instance, the 1949–50 Estimates enabled the War Office to purchase stores to the value of over £66 million, the Air Ministry to purchase stores and aircraft to the value of over £71½ million, and the Admiralty to purchase stores to the value of nearly £21 million, through the Ministry of Supply. This does not prevent the practice of agency buying through other departments, but the amounts are comparatively small—just over £1 million in the case of the War Office and rather more than £2 million in the case of the Air Ministry. The problem of co-ordination has therefore been much simplified by the establishment of the Ministry of Supply, but it remains as a problem; for clearly there must be close collaboration between the Ministry of Supply, as the supplying authority, and the various consuming authorities.

Other pre-war problems of co-ordination have been solved, or solved partially, by the creation of new ministries. Thus, social security was the concern of the Ministry of Health (health and other forms of

[1] Chester and Willson, *op. cit.* pp. 232–5.

insurance), the Ministry of Labour (unemployment insurance), the Board of Customs and Excise (non-contributory old age pensions) and the Assistance Board (unemployment assistance). Now all these functions are exercised in respect of a unified social security scheme by the Ministry of Pensions and National Insurance, though clearly there are problems of co-ordination between this Ministry on the one hand and the Ministry of Health (in respect of the National Health Service and the health functions of local authorities) and the Ministry of Labour (in respect of employment) on the other.

Another series of problems arises from the fact that many functions of government are exercised by different authorities in England and Wales, Scotland, and Northern Ireland respectively. Northern Ireland is in a peculiar position because many functions are vested in the Parliament of Northern Ireland, so that the problem is one not merely of co-ordinating administration but also of co-ordinating legislation; but this problem of course arises only where the Government of Northern Ireland wishes to follow a precedent set by the Government of the United Kingdom or where some interchange of availability (as in respect of social security) is desired by the two Governments. In Great Britain, on the other hand, there is a single Parliament but different laws and systems of administration in respect of the matters covered (in England and Wales) by the Ministries of Education, Health, and Agriculture and Fisheries and by the Home Office. In part this problem is met by empowering 'the Ministers' (i.e. the Minister in England and Wales and the Secretary of State in Scotland) to act in unison or by having joint advisory committees. Even then, of course, the problem of consultation and joint action remains. There is, however, an opposite tendency in Great Britain, arising from the development of a local nationalism in Wales and Scotland. The Scottish Office has a Minister of State and three Parliamentary Under-Secretaries, in addition to the Secretary of State; before 1939 there was one Parliamentary Under-Secretary. Also, one Minister has exercised the additional functions of Minister for Welsh Affairs and a Minister of State has been appointed for Wales.

Again, it is possible to have a joint body acting on behalf of two ministries. Owing to a difference of opinion between the Foreign Office and the Board of Trade, the Cabinet found it difficult to decide whether the Department of Overseas Trade, which acted mainly through commercial attachés in the embassies, should be controlled by the Foreign Secretary or the President of the Board of Trade, and it was eventually agreed that the Department should be controlled by a Secretary responsible to both. This arrangement did not survive the war, and the Secretary for Overseas Trade became a Parliamentary Secretary to the Board of Trade. Even that arrangement has been allowed to disappear, and the Department of Overseas Trade has been absorbed into the Board of Trade. The State Management Districts Council, which controlled the State-owned licensed premises in a few areas of England and Scotland, was a joint body responsible to the Home Secretary and the Secretary of State for Scotland. This body has now disappeared. There are, however, two other examples of co-ordination between England (and Wales) and Scotland.[1] The Forestry Commission has functions in both countries but is required to comply with directions given by the Secretary of State (for Scotland) and the Ministry of Agriculture, Fisheries and Food (for England and Wales). It has separate National Committees for England, Wales and Scotland. The Commissioners of Crown Lands consisted of the same Ministers, plus a permanent Commissioner—though this arrangement was altered in 1956. The Central Land Board is appointed jointly by the Secretary of State and the Minister of Housing and Local Government.

Finally, it has to be noted that the complex problems of modern government require close co-ordination of departments in economic matters. This raises wider questions, however, which are discussed in ch. XI.

Though the extensions of the field of government before the war of 1939–45, during that war, and under the Government which took office in 1945, have made the whole problem of government organisation much more difficult, there has been a considerable improvement in inter-departmental relations. The reader of the first edition of this work may have noticed that most of the examples of inter-departmental conflict dated from the early years of the century and from the 'twenties. The explanation might have been the usual efficient secrecy of the civil service, which allows no information to escape until ministers write

[1] Royal Commission on Scottish Affairs, 1952–54 (Cmd. 9212), pp. 61–3.

their memoirs. It seems to have been due in fact, however, to a change in the practice of administration, which had rendered the problem less acute. Emphasis has already been laid upon the historic separateness of the government departments, due to the personal responsibility of ministers, and this persisted into the 'twenties. Though few of the specific recommendations of Lord Haldane's Committee on the Machinery of Government were carried out, it is evident that a good deal of thought was given to the problems there raised and that between the wars the civil service itself was not at all complacent about its own procedure. The Treasury took the lead and the creation—or re-creation—of the office of 'Head of the Civil Service'[1] was one aspect of it. In fact, however, several of the Permanent Secretaries were involved: and it seems that, gradually, a new tradition of consultation with 'opposite numbers' grew up.

Partly, no doubt, this was due to insistence by the Cabinet that all interested departments be consulted before a matter came to the Cabinet. This was necessary to enable the Cabinet to get through its business, and if a department had to brief its minister to oppose or modify a proposal on which it had not been consulted, the Permanent Secretary who had had the proposal put up without prior consultation would get rapped over the knuckles. What is more, the way to get a proposal through without opposition was to satisfy the possible opponents beforehand that it was quite innocuous. This is not, however, the whole explanation. The growing use of departmental committees to settle questions by personal consultation necessarily led to consultation with other departments. If the matter under discussion infringed upon the field of another department or if it was a problem in which another department could help, it was both easy and convenient to get the department to send somebody over.

We may note, too, the development of 'informal' correspondence. Mr Jones, can, no doubt, write to Mr Brown to say that the Secretary of State would welcome the views of the Minister on such and such a subject and that he is, Sir, his obedient Servant; but he does not, for, if he has to write—and he prefers to telephone—he much prefers a 'demi-official letter' asking what about it, and would Brown like to

[1] Below, pp. 149–50.

see the file. For purposes of practical administration, the theory of the separateness of the departments is dead, and at all levels civil servants are only too glad to get what help they can from each other and to lighten their loads by consulting each other. The Principal tries to settle with the Principal, the Assistant Secretary with the Assistant Secretary, the Deputy Secretary with the Deputy Secretary; and if disputes have to go to the Permanent Secretaries or the Ministers there must be some important principle at stake or some very severe difference of opinion, like the old problem (often referred to in the first edition of this work) of the Fleet Air Arm.

In the long run, however, effective co-ordination must come at the top. The system of co-ordinating Cabinet Committees arose out of the Committee of Imperial Defence, and was developed by the War Cabinet of 1940–5; the experience of both is discussed in ch. XII. The Labour Government of 1945–51 inherited this committee system and applied it to the diverse problems of post-war reconstruction under a socialist programme.[1] As we have seen,[2] Mr Churchill made a short and unsuccessful experiment with co-ordinating ministers, or 'overlords'. It might have been longer and more successful if 'the overlords' had not been peers or even if they had been peers with House of Commons experience; from the political point of view, the Prime Minister could hardly have made a worse choice than Lords Cherwell, Leathers and Woolton, for the experiment was necessarily attacked in the House of Commons. In fact, however, the 'overlords' did little more than had been done for more than a decade by the chairmen of co-ordinating committees of the Cabinet.[3]

There was, too, a further development during the period of Hitler's rise and fall which seems to have persisted. This was to organise, officially or demi-officially, committees of civil servants parallel with the Cabinet committees. These committees, which originated with

[1] Morrison, *Government and Parliament*, pp. 18–23.

[2] Above, pp. 80–1.

[3] Mr Morrison, *op. cit.* pp. 45–56, criticises the 'overlords', but describes the same function as having been performed by chairmen of Cabinet committees under the Labour Government, *op. cit.* pp. 24–5. For a departmental minister there is, of course, a psychological difference between putting one's case to a co-ordinating minister and putting the same case to a Cabinet committee of which one is a member.

Sir Warren Fisher and were developed by Sir Horace Wilson,[1] prepared the ground for the Cabinet committees by setting out clearly the issues which could be settled out of hand and those which required discussion and decision. They stopped the committees from ranging over the whole field in discursive talk and enabled the chairmen to put the alternatives with clarity and precision. Probably there are still inter-departmental battles, but they must be fewer and less important than they were a generation ago.

[1] Viscount Templewood, *Nine Troubled Years*, pp. 260–1.

CHAPTER VII

TREASURY CONTROL

§1. *Treasury Control of the Civil Service*

It is not entirely an accident of history that the Prime Minister is also the First Lord of the Treasury. In the days when majorities were swayed by the exercise of patronage and the patronage of the Treasury was the most valuable, the principal politician was necessarily the First Lord or, to put it equally truly, the First Lord was the principal politician. Even now the Chief Whip, whose official title is 'Parliamentary Secretary to the Treasury' is sometimes called by his old name, which was 'Patronage Secretary'. Though all the Treasury Ministers were technically responsible, the financial business was left to the Chancellor of the Exchequer, while the political business—the distribution of patronage and the management of Parliament—was undertaken by the First Lord with the assistance of the Patronage Secretary and the Junior Lords of the Treasury, who became the Government whips.

With the disappearance of patronage as a political weapon, the Prime Minister's responsibility for appointments to the public service and his responsibility for the management of the House of Commons became quite distinct, and the Parliamentary Secretary ceased to deal with patronage, except the minor patronage involved in the distribution of honours to Members of Parliament and their principal supporters in the constituencies. Nevertheless, it was desirable that the Treasury should retain a general control of the public service, not merely for financial reasons, but also because it was necessary to create a unified service with such departmental variations as the functions of government made necessary. Though departmental ministers have particular responsibilities for their departmental officials, the civil service as a whole is controlled by the Treasury under the direction of the Prime Minister as First Lord.

This means, for example, that the consent of the Prime Minister is required for the appointment of permanent heads of departments, their deputies, principal financial officers and principal establishment officers.[1] As a result, the senior posts in the civil service have not a purely departmental character, but are frequently filled by transfer from other departments. This, in its turn, assists in creating the notion of the unity of the civil service. The service estimate of the capacities of individual officers for higher appointments is obtained and collated by informal discussions between the Permanent Secretary to the Treasury and his senior service colleagues, and it is the duty of the former, when a vacancy occurs of a kind requiring the Prime Minister's sanction, to submit advice for the consideration of the Prime Minister and the departmental minister concerned.

In the second place, Treasury control of the civil service means that the general regulations by which the civil service is governed are laid down by the Treasury.

The post-war theory of the control of civil service organisation rests on active co-operation and goodwill between the Treasury on one hand and the department on the other. They are jointly trustees for the efficient and economical administration of the service. In the Treasury there has been since 1919 an Establishments Department which has specialised in questions of organisation of departments, personnel, superannuation and so on. In the departments, responsible officers have been appointed directly answerable to the head of the department on questions of office management. For a number of years now there has been going on a regular overhaul of staffs and establishment officers, aided by advice and assistance from the expert Department of the Treasury.... We are satisfied that the method of control adopted is well calculated to maintain a high standard of administration.[2]

'Advice and assistance' means more today than it meant when this was written in 1931. There is a fist inside the velvet glove, attached to the body of financial power presently to be described. It involves complete control of establishments and some control of the organisation and methods of work of the departments. During the inter-war period, and still more during the post-war period, the Treasury has done its best, not merely to keep down the cost of administration, but also to get the best value out of the administration, by helping in the training

[1] Royal Commission on the Civil Service (1929), Minutes of Evidence, p. 1269 (evidence of Sir Warren Fisher, Permanent Secretary to the Treasury). This was laid down in a Treasury minute in 1920, regularising and extending the then existing practice: see 149 H.C.Deb. 5 s., 1565–6.

[2] Report of the Committee on Public Expenditure (1931), p. 22.

of probationers and other assistant principals, by encouraging departments to reorganise themselves, and by advising them about methods of work generally. This is now organised under a Director of Organisation and Methods with the rank of under-secretary. His sub-department, if it may be so called, is organised in four divisions, dealing respectively with training and education, the machinery of government, and organisation and methods (two). Unlike those of the rest of the Treasury, their functions are purely advisory, though there is always ultimate recourse to the Cabinet. Their task is threefold, to make suggestions for altering the departmental structure, to find out the best methods of carrying out office work at all levels, and to provide the junior officials with a broader understanding of the process of government than can be obtained from mere departmental training.[1]

These advisory functions, as has been said, need four divisions. Five divisions deal with other aspects of 'establishments'. Civil servants are servants of the Crown. Speaking legally, the Crown in its discretion can lay down what regulations it pleases for the conduct of its officers. Yet the Crown has annually to seek from Parliament the means for the payment of its officers; and this means, in practice, that the Treasury has to approve departmental Estimates and submit them, or agree to their submission, to the House of Commons. The only statutes applying to civil servants are the Superannuation Acts and certain statutes prohibiting some civil servants from being elected to the House of Commons. But even the grant of superannuation is wholly discretionary, and is therefore under the control of the Treasury. Apart from these

[1] Establishments were formerly dealt with incidentally by the Supply divisions of the Treasury. In the reforms of 1919–20 a separate Establishment division was created at the Treasury and establishments officers appointed in the other departments. There were also a few investigating officers with special knowledge of office methods. From this nucleus grew 'O. & M.' during the war of 1939–45. Training and education were started in consequence of the Committee on the Training of Civil Servants (Cmd. 6525 of 1944). Meanwhile a Cabinet Committee on the Machinery of Government, appointed in 1942, recommended that the Treasury should assume responsibility for questions relating to the machinery of Government. The Machinery of Government branch was established in 1946, and its work was expanded in consequence of the Fifth Report from the Select Committee on Estimates, H.C. 143 of 1946–7. The post-war changes in administration were due to a Government Organization Committee appointed in 1947, an official committee working under and parallel with the Cabinet Committee. See Chester and Willson, *The Organization of British Central Government*, pp. 291–4, 309–10, 333–8.

statutes, the civil service is governed by formal and informal rules issued under the prerogative powers of the Crown indicating, in law, not the rights of civil servants (for their legal rights differ from those of ordinary citizens only in minor matters) but the practices which the Crown intends to follow and to have followed in the government of the civil service.

The major principles are contained in Orders in Council. The earlier Orders, beginning with that of 1855, regulated admission to the service. The Civil Service Commission was set up under these Orders. Later, they were extended to deal with the remuneration, hours of duty and other conditions of service of the classes of civil servants common to the departments. Later still they were applied to the conditions of service of 'all permanent officers in His Majesty's Civil Establishments'. These Orders were consolidated in 1910, and the consolidated Order has been amended by other later Orders. Since conditions of service are, primarily, questions of finance, any such amending Orders are necessarily issued at the request of the Treasury. But the later Orders have left many matters to be dealt with by regulations issued by the Civil Service Commissioners and the Treasury. In substance, therefore, conditions of service are dealt with by Treasury regulations.[1]

The matters dealt with in Orders or in formal regulations are, however, comparatively simple in character and few in number.

Decisions affecting the civil service generally are normally promulgated by Treasury circulars addressed to the permanent heads of all departments. Thus, when a decision is reached (whether by an agreed settlement with the association concerned, or by an award of the Industrial Court, or in any other manner) involving some change in the remuneration or terms of employment of civil servants as a whole or of a class of civil servants common to the service, authority to give effect to the change is conveyed to departments by Treasury circular.[2]

[1] Royal Commission on the Civil Service (1929), Minutes of Evidence, Appendix I, pp. 23–7. For the history up to 1910, see Royal Commission on the Civil Service (1912–15), 4th Report, pp. 7–24. The powers of the Treasury are in practice limited by the extensive machinery for the negotiation and submission to arbitration of civil service conditions. Though there is nothing to prevent the Treasury from refusing to accept the decision of, for example, the Industrial Court, it invariably accepts it.

[2] Royal Commission on the Civil Service (1929), Minutes of Evidence, Appendix I, p. 27.

All this is implicit in the 'power of the purse'. The administrative *cadre* of each department is recommended by the department but the decision rests with the Treasury. In the event of any dispute the matter could in theory go to the Cabinet, but the Cabinet would not welcome such a reference and, if the minister insisted, it is probable that it would support the Treasury. Effectively, therefore, the *cadre* is under Treasury control. Salary scales and other conditions of service are obviously Treasury matters. Indeed, the number of officers in each class and the scales of salary are included in the Estimates, which require Treasury approval according to the procedure presently to be described. Nevertheless, Treasury control is not dependent on its financial powers, for it arises from the Prime Minister's general responsibility as First Lord. The fact that a reorganisation promised to reduce costs would be a persuasive argument in the Treasury, but it would not take the matter out of Treasury control. No increase of staff, no change of classification, and no alteration of the conditions of service, can be effected without treasury sanction. On the other hand, the meticulous control of establishments which was practised before the war is no longer possible. Though before 1939 it was necessary to secure express Treasury authority for every alteration in the *cadre*, since 1940 departments have been allowed to vary establishments within limits fixed by the Treasury. Each department is required to have an organisation—generally its Establishments Branch—for keeping watch on the economy of its structure, and staff inspectors from the Treasury make inspections from time to time to assist Establishment Officers in their work. Thus, the principle of Treasury control of establishments is maintained, but it is operated with some elasticity.[1]

Moreover, Treasury control of civil service conditions is by no means limited to appointments and salaries.

> Treasury circulars or minutes are sometimes issued on matters of discipline. It is no part of the function of the Treasury to issue instructions which would derogate in any way from a minister's responsibility to Parliament for the conduct of his department, or would interfere with the necessary control of the staff of the department by those responsible for its immediate management and direction. Apart from the constitutional aspect of the

[1] See S. H. Beer, *Treasury Control*, pp. 10–11.

matter the different conditions prevailing in different departments and the nature of the duties to be performed make special departmental rules or instructions necessary. But from time to time it has been found necessary, particularly in cases where diversity of practice would be indefensible, to lay down general regulations applicable to the whole civil service.[1]

In short, 'as a result of its special constitutional position the Treasury ...has come to be charged with the duty of acting on behalf of His Majesty's Government in matters affecting the civil service as a whole and with responsibility for the general supervision and control of the civil service'.[2] Consequently, though until recently the civil service was only a series of departments which did not think of themselves as merely units of a complete and correlated whole, the situation has now changed. Status, remuneration, prestige and organisation have been assimilated.[3]

The general supervision and control of the civil service is vested in the Lords of the Treasury, among whom the Prime Minister as First Lord takes the major share of responsibility, while the Chancellor of the Exchequer is primarily concerned with financial and economic policy. In Mr Churchill's Government of 1951 there was also a Minister of State for Economic Affairs, but later the post was stepped down to one equivalent to that of Parliamentary Secretary.[4] Accordingly, there is now a Financial Secretary to deal, mainly, with the Estimates, and an Economic Secretary to deal with economic affairs. Until recently (except during the war of 1914–18)[5] there was a single Permanent Secretary, serving both the Treasury Ministers, who held the title of 'official Head of the Civil Service'.[6] Since 1 October 1956, however,

[1] Royal Commission on the Civil Service (1929), Minutes of Evidence, Appendix I, p. 27.

[2] *Ibid.* p. 23.

[3] Royal Commission on the Civil Service (1929), Minutes of Evidence, p. 1267.

[4] The Parliamentary Secretary to the Treasury is, however, the Government Chief Whip.

[5] When there were Joint Permanent Secretaries: see Mr Austen Chamberlain in 120 H.C.Deb. 5 s., 743 (1919).

[6] The post is said to have been created by Treasury minute in 1867, but the minute has been lost (194 H.C.Deb. 5 s., 295). It has also been stated that the post originated in 1872 (105 H.L.Deb. 5 s., 851). The title was, however, recognised in 1919 (120 H.C.Deb. 5 s., 743 and 125 H.L.Deb. 5 s., 244) and in 1937 Mr Neville Chamberlain said that it was a 'convenient and businesslike arrangement'. (326 H.C.Deb. 5 s., 1479.) See also the debate in the House of Lords in 1942 (125 H.L.Deb. 5 s., 224 *et seq.* and 275 *et seq.*).

there have been two Joint Permanent Secretaries. The one deals with financial and economic matters and is wholly responsible to the Chancellor of the Exchequer. The other, who is also Secretary to the Cabinet, has charge of other Treasury work, including that which falls within the responsibility of the Prime Minister as First Lord of the Treasury; and he is called 'official Head of the Home Civil Service'. This division of functions implies, apparently, that for purposes of control the Establishments divisions of the Treasury have been separated from the other divisions; while the insertion of the word 'Home' indicates the separation of the Foreign Service from the Home Civil Service which took place in 1943.[1]

§2. *Financial Control in General*

Control over the civil service is, however, merely one aspect of Treasury control. The most effective power of that department lies in its control over finance, exercised by or under the direction of the Chancellor of the Exchequer in consultation—as all ministers consult—with the Prime Minister and under the control of the Cabinet. This power dates from the great financial reforms of Sir Robert Peel[2] and arises out of the responsibility of the Chancellor of the Exchequer, under Cabinet control, for the financial policy of the Government.

The major functions of the Treasury were summarised by the Machinery of Government Committee:[3]

(*a*) Subject to Parliament it is responsible for the imposition and regulation of taxation and the collection of the revenue, for which purpose it has the assistance of the Revenue Departments.[4]

(*b*) It controls public expenditure in various degrees and various ways, chiefly through the preparation or supervision of the estimates for Parliament.

(*c*) It arranges for the provision of the funds required from day to day to

[1] *The Times*, 21 July 1956.

[2] 194 H.C.Deb. 5 s., 322.

[3] Report of the Machinery of Government Committee (1918), p. 16.

[4] The Board of Inland Revenue, the Board of Customs and Excise, and the Post Office. But, though the Post Office Estimates are included in the Estimates for Revenue Departments, it is no longer a Revenue Department strictly, for the Treasury takes only a fixed contribution from the Post Office: see Finance Act, 1933, Part IV. For the inapplicability of the term see 298 H.C.Deb. 5 s., 1564. For the arrangement between the Post Office and the Treasury, see 280 H.C.Deb. 5 s., 2255–6.

meet the necessities of the public service, for which purpose it is entrusted with extensive borrowing powers.

(*d*) It initiates and carries out measures affecting the public debt, currency and banking.

(*e*) It prescribes the manner in which the public accounts should be kept.[1]

This list has something of an early Georgian, or even Edwardian look; none of these functions has been lost since paper replaced golden sovereigns, but new responsibilities have been added. The listed functions, or most of them, are now the concern of the Second Secretary concerned with Supply and Home Finance. There are, however, two other Second Secretaries within the jurisdiction of the Chancellor of the Exchequer. One of these is concerned with Economic Policy, a subject of government which had the adventurous life described in ch. XI, but which found a home at last in the Treasury. The other Second Secretary is concerned with overseas finance. The explanation of these changes is twofold. First, we have a managed currency which is not freely convertible, but which has to be managed in relation to the sterling area, the European Payments Union, and currencies not included in either. Secondly, finance is no longer merely a problem of raising revenue to meet expenditure or even of borrowing to meet capital expenditure: it is also an instrument of politics designed, whether called 'economic planning' or by some less pretentious name, to effect political and social changes by altering the distribution of wealth.

This chapter is concerned, however, not with financial and economic policy, which must be a matter for the Cabinet, even when the Treasury is the instrument of administration, but with the Treasury as an instrument of departmental co-ordination. One method of such co-ordination, Treasury control over establishments, has already been discussed. The other methods, which continue the traditions, and even in some respect the methods, established by Sir Robert Peel and Mr Gladstone, are control over Supply or Estimates and control over accounts or expenditure.

The control over expenditure involves far more than a mere concern for the financial stability of the nation's finance during the current or the

[1] See also a note by Sir R. (Lord) Welby as to the functions of the Chancellor of the Exchequer, *Life of Childers*, II, pp. 148–9.

ensuing year. Though, as will be explained, Treasury control is merely the control of the Chancellor of the Exchequer, subject to the power of the Cabinet, no efficient Chancellor is concerned only with immediate expenditure or the balancing of his own budgets. He would not be exercising his function properly if he assumed that future expenditure was the concern of his successors. It is his business to safeguard the revenue as far into the future as it is possible to foresee. Accordingly, the Treasury is as concerned with future contingencies as it is with immediate expenditure. The 'policy of the Treasury' in relation to technical matters is not subject to variation from year to year or from Government to Government. It is, therefore, not 'Treasury policy' but 'Treasury practice'. That practice is, in part, laid down in Treasury minutes; in part, it is to be found in the resolutions and recommendations of the Select Committee of Public Accounts and the Select Committee on Estimates; in part, however, it is just practice, developed over a long period since the reforms of Sir Robert Peel and Mr Gladstone.

Proposals which involve substantial increases in expenditure, immediately or contingently, are obviously of such an order of magnitude that they require Cabinet sanction. A Cabinet decision is binding on the Chancellor of the Exchequer and therefore upon the Treasury. But care is taken to ensure that no decision is taken before the financial aspects of the proposal have been fully considered by the Treasury and placed before the Cabinet by the Chancellor of the Exchequer. The details are set out in a subsequent chapter;[1] but it should be said here that no proposal is circulated to the Cabinet until all interested departments have been consulted, and that if the proposal involves financial implications this rule requires consultation with the Treasury. If the Treasury is unable to agree it will brief the Chancellor of the Exchequer to oppose it in the Cabinet, and if this is done the proposal is not likely to be accepted. Moreover, Cabinet approval of expenditure does not render unnecessary the departmental sanction of the Treasury. The policy is binding on the Treasury, but the details and the execution are still subject to Treasury control.[2]

[1] Below, pp. 247–8.

[2] See Epitome of the Reports from the Public Accounts Committee, pp. 587–8, and Exchequer and Audit Departments Act, s. 1 (3).

Proposals of a more departmental nature do not need Cabinet sanction. But if they contain financial implications, they need the approval of the Treasury. Any changes in the number (outside limits laid down by the Treasury) or classification or conditions of service of the staff necessarily require Treasury consent, for reasons already explained. Any expenditure on works above £1000, even if already sanctioned by the Treasury, or by the Cabinet, or by Parliament, also needs express Treasury approval. If, for instance, the War Office desired to acquire a piece of land on Salisbury Plain, or to provide additional barrack accommodation at Aldershot, Treasury sanction for the proposal and the price would have to be obtained. Provision would also have to be made in the Army Estimates, which again need Treasury sanction. The Estimates would be presented to Parliament and the expenditure authorised in the Appropriation Act. Moreover, in making the contracts the War Office must abide by general Treasury regulations.[1] Indeed, Treasury sanction would be necessary even if additional expenditure was not required. If, for instance, the War Office desired to sell one piece of land and to acquire another, Treasury sanction would be necessary. Nor would it matter that a profit would be made on the transaction: for, if a profit can be made, it must be the largest possible profit. It is the business of the Treasury to see that Her Majesty, like a good householder, buys in the cheapest market and sells in the dearest.

This principle can be applied to works but cannot be applied in its full rigour to all the activities of the departments. The Treasury cannot supervise every contract, though it can, and does, lay down the general principles upon which contracts should be made. In particular, it cannot control the specifications laid down by the Service Departments; indeed, those departments possess in this respect a somewhat greater independence than is possessed by the Civil and Revenue Departments. But the Treasury expects to be consulted whenever a new kind of contract is proposed, or where it is proposed to limit the field of tender or to substitute contracts by private negotiation for contracts by public tender. Above all, 'any proposal involving an increase in expenditure or any new service, whether or not involving an increase in the total

[1] First and Second Reports from the Select Committee on Estimates (1926), App. II.

expenditure of the Department, would require Treasury sanction'.[1] Or, as the Treasury put it seventy years ago: 'Before any proposal involving serious increase in expenditure is adopted...it should be submitted to my Lords [of the Treasury], with a statement of which it might be convenient to receive several copies, in print, showing at length....'[2]

Moreover, though the phrase 'Treasury control' is used, it must not be thought that it means that someone is told 'to see what Johnny is doing and tell him to stop it'. Treasury control, like parental control, has changed its connotation in recent years. Every department is anxious to increase its expenditure, but only because it desires to increase its services. It is as much interested as the Treasury in the economical administration of its existing services; for the Treasury is concerned primarily in the almost constant increase in the total of the budget. It will look askance at any proposal which will involve an increase of expenditure, immediately or contingently. It is likely to be more complaisant if a service can be extended without an increase in cost. Consequently a department welcomes, within limits, the collaboration of Treasury officials. In any case, both the minister and the permanent head feel a personal responsibility for the efficiency of their department.

This collaboration is the more effective because each of the large departments has its own financial staff. It is the business of that staff to perform within the department the function which the Treasury performs throughout the administrative system. Though the dog inside the house has to protect the people inside against the dog outside, it has also to see that the people inside do not provoke the dog outside. For that dog is rather a big one; and the dog inside knows which dog will bite which if a fight ensues. Consequently, if one may leave the metaphor, collaboration between the financial staff of the department and the appropriate staff of the Treasury is close.

In the result, the Treasury is frequently consulted before the need for formal sanction arises, especially on large schemes and establishment

[1] A statement accepted by Sir R. R. Scott, for the Treasury, Royal Commission on the Civil Service (1929), Minutes of Evidence, p. 2.

[2] Second Report from the Select Committee of Public Accounts (1884), Epitome of the Reports of the Committees of Public Accounts, p. 160; repeated in Second Report (1885), *ibid.* p. 169; see also the Third Report (1920), *ibid.* pp. 608–9.

matters. The appropriate departmental officer works out a scheme and there comes a point at which he says: 'It's no use going any further till we know what so-and-so at the Treasury thinks about it.' Accordingly, he crosses to Treasury Chambers to see 'so-and-so'. Possibly he takes with him the technical expert. In the result the Treasury is seised of all the facts and gets in on the ground floor. Then, when the scheme is elaborated, it is formally submitted to the Treasury and as formally approved. Moreover, any large scheme would be worked out by a departmental committee, on which it would be common sense to have Treasury representation: and, according to the modern technique, the Treasury official is there not as watchdog but in order to help the department produce the best possible scheme. Even more certainly would he be there if the scheme affected several departments and was devised by an inter-departmental committee.

All this is quite independent of control over the Estimates. It arises before the Estimates or the Supplementary Estimates are submitted. It is the normal and, as will be seen, the more effective part of Treasury control.

§3. *Control over Estimates*

Certain items of expenditure are authorised by Parliament by permanent statutes and therefore do not appear in the Estimates. They are said to be 'charged on the Consolidated Fund', and are referred to as 'Consolidated Fund Services'. The most important of them are the management and service of the National Debt, the grants to Northern Ireland, the Queen's Civil List and other grants to the Royal Family, and the salaries of judges, the Comptroller and the Auditor-General, and the members of the National Assistance Board. With these we are not here concerned, since they involve no Treasury control over Estimates. The rest of the public expenditure is voted annually by means of the Appropriation Act and Consolidated Fund Acts, and the services are known as 'Supply Services'. The amounts required are approved by the House of Commons in Committee of Supply after consideration of the Estimates or Supplementary Estimates submitted to the House. Consideration of Treasury functions in relation to Supplementary Estimates may for the moment be postponed.

The Estimates are presented in five volumes,[1] dealing respectively with the Army, the Navy, the Air Force, the three Revenue Departments (the Board of Inland Revenue, the Board of Customs and Excise and the Post Office),[2] and the rest of the Supply Services (referred to as the 'Civil Estimates'). The first three are presented by their respective ministers (or the junior minister when the heads of the departments are in the House of Lords); the last two are presented by the Financial Secretary to the Treasury. This difference does not mean that there is any substantial difference of Treasury control.[3] The Treasury exercises the same functions in respect of these Estimates as it exercises in respect of the Estimates which it presents. It is obvious that its control must be less effective where it is dealing with a highly technical service. If the Admiralty says that more expensive guns are necessary, the Treasury usually has not such means for denial as it would have if, for instance, the Ministry of Education suggested that more expensive schools were required and that accordingly the Education grants should be increased.[4] This is a difference of efficiency, not a difference of authority.

The Estimates are submitted to the Treasury by the departments. Since they are to be discussed in Parliament before the end of the current financial year (ending on 31 March) and in the early months of the financial year for which they are prepared, they are submitted, usually, in November. They are thus framed on the basis of the previous year's experience; and, since the accounts of the previous financial year have not yet been completed and the prospects of the coming financial year are as yet unknown, they can hardly be wholly accurate.

The Treasury is not without knowledge of the trends of expenditure in the departments. As has been mentioned, its approval will have been obtained for every development which will involve a substantial increase of expenditure. In so far as the sums voted for the previous year

[1] Actually, the Civil Estimates are presented in sections, but are paged and indexed as a single volume. The Estimates of the Ministry of Defence are published in a separate leaflet.

[2] But see the note, above, p. 150.

[3] See 287 H.C.Deb. 5 s., 1232. Broadly speaking, while control for new services is the same, the control over detailed expenditure provided under a particular sub-head is less in the case of the Defence Departments.

[4] Cf. Third Report of the Committee on National Expenditure (1922), p. 166.

proved to be inadequate, the departments will have submitted Supplementary Estimates to the Treasury, and these will subsequently have been submitted to the House of Commons. If there was likely to be a surplus on one item and over-expenditure on another, the consent of the Treasury to the transfer may already have been obtained, in accordance with the practice presently to be explained. Moreover, the accounts for the last full year will already have been presented and audited. In considering the Estimates for 1956–7, the Treasury will have had the complete experience of the year 1954–5. By reason of Supplementary Estimates and requests for transfers, it will have some experience of the expenditure of 1955–6. It will, finally, have given its consent to increased expenditure for 1956–7.

The older procedure for the consideration of Defence Estimates has thus been explained:

> The procedure, as explained to us by experienced Treasury officials, was broadly that the estimates of the previous year were taken to form a base line, and that the deviations from that line were arrived at by consultation between the Chancellor of the Exchequer and the minister at the head of the department. As a result of the consultation, the minister would know that the Chancellor of the Exchequer was prepared to budget for estimates representing a certain sum of money, and would tell his department the amount available for the following year's estimates. The essence of this system was to take the previous year's normal expenditure from which to measure departures.[1]

This statement is not quite exact in relation to the Civil Estimates. It has already been explained that proposals for increases of expenditure come to the Treasury before the Estimates are submitted. The fact that the total of the department's expenditure will be increased is an important factor to be considered when those proposals are first made. But approval or disapproval of increased expenditure is not left to be given when the Estimates are presented. If a new service or an expansion of an existing service is provided for the first time in the Estimates without previous consultation, the Treasury will want to know why. It will suggest that the proposal be taken out until it has been fully considered. Consequently, the increases in the Estimates are due either

[1] First Report of the Committee on National Expenditure (1922), p. 4.

to automatic increases on services provided for by statute or by Treasury regulations, such as the normal increases on pensions, teachers' superannuation and civil service salaries, or to the creation of new services or the expansion of existing services for which Treasury approval has already been obtained.

This does not mean that approval of the Estimates is automatic. The Treasury considers the Estimates with two factors in mind. The first is that the department's estimate may be faulty. The Treasury cannot, without securing legislative authority, cut down expenditure on pensions. It can assert, however, that the Estimates of the department concerned with the expenditure are faulty. It can suggest that in forecasting the number of deaths among pensioners the department has been too pessimistic—or, from the point of view of the pensioners, optimistic—and that the proportion of deaths is likely to be higher. In the second place, when the Chancellor of the Exchequer sees the total of the Estimates, he may be appalled at the task which faces him, and may desire the Treasury to find means for reducing the total.

It may well be asked whether the Treasury has the means for criticising the Estimates made by the department; the department possesses the expert knowledge, the Treasury does not. In part, this observation is true: if the Admiralty asserts that the cost of moving a fleet to the Mediterranean will be so much, the Treasury has not the necessary knowledge to make a completely different estimate. The statement is not, however, wholly true. In the first place, fleets have been moved before, and the Treasury knows what they cost and has some idea whether they could not have been moved more economically. In the second place, it does not accept the *ipse dixit* of the Secretary's Department of the Admiralty. Though the cost will appear in the Estimates merely as increases in allowances, stores, etc., the Treasury requires far more information than the Admiralty proposes to put before Parliament. If the Admiralty does not spontaneously give the information, the Treasury will ask, in the legal phrase, for 'further and better particulars'. It must be remembered, too, that most expenditure is not brought about by abnormal conditions. The total of an item varies from year to year in a more or less regular sequence. Every item has its history and its trend of development. Expenditure on war pensions, for instance, is necessarily decreasing. The trend of that decrease and the factors which cause the decrease are almost as well known to the Treasury as to the Ministry of Pensions. Information is kept up to date. Each vote has its 'blue note' which sets out the history of the vote, the changes in the vote, the cost of administration, the method of administration, and so on. This blue note is kept in type; it is altered from year to year; it is used by the Treasury when the vote comes up for consideration. Each vote thus has a pamphlet attached to it which is of some assistance in checking the departmental Estimates.

This power of control necessarily operates within narrow limits. Control over the total is more effective. Any sanction which the Treasury has given is subject to the overriding power of the Chancellor of the Exchequer to protect his budget. If he finds that the total expenditure will be excessive, he will ask for it to be cut down. If, after consulting his officials, he decides that ten million pounds must be saved, then that sum has to be apportioned among the departments. Possibly, the Treasury may be able to indicate what new services or extensions of existing services may be postponed. The department concerned is informed to that effect. The minister will, no doubt, object. The departmental official will argue with the Treasury official; a higher departmental official will argue with a higher Treasury official; the minister will plead with the Chancellor. If necessary, the minister can appeal to the Cabinet. Alternatively, the Chancellor of the Exchequer may decide that, say, the Ministry of Education must reduce its estimates by £50,000. If the same process of protest and argument proves unavailing, the department must itself determine in what branch or branches of its administration the saving is to be effected. On the other hand, the procedure may begin at the other end, and nowadays often does. At an early stage of the process of Estimate-making, the Chancellor may be able to indicate the limits within which Estimates should be framed. This is particularly true of the Defence Estimates, for the real question to be decided is not what expenditure is needed for the adequate defence of the country but what expenditure the country can afford towards meeting, in some degree, the needs of defence. Since the establishment of the Ministry of Defence, it has become easier to give a total, because that Ministry can be relied upon to decide how the total can be so distributed as to secure the best possible defence system within the financial limit laid down.

It should be added that the Treasury is not concerned only with expenditure. It is concerned also with income. It may assert that the Board of Inland Revenue ought to have fewer bad debts, or that not enough profit is being made out of the Crown lands, or that the appropriations-in-aid of any other department ought to be larger.

There are, however, cases where the Treasury has no effective control. Where, for instance, a department is given control of a grant-in-aid with no obligation to surrender any unexpended balance, the Treasury in some cases finds difficulty in suggesting that the grant should be reduced.[1] Strictly speaking, the Treasury has no control over Estimates where a vote of credit is sought for emergency expenditure such as the conduct of a war,[2] for in such a case no detailed Estimates are presented to Parliament. But the Treasury can criticise the total; and the practice between 1914 and 1918 and from 1939 to 1945 was to ask the departments to submit Estimates to the Treasury, though not to Parliament.[3] Also, the vote is usually given to the Treasury, which can thus exercise some control over expenditure. Finally, there are cases where a department, in the exercise of its statutory functions, undertakes services which will ultimately result in expenditure. For instance, no Treasury sanction is necessary before the Ministry of Works takes over ancient monuments on which expenditure will be required.[4]

[1] See Epitome of the Reports from the Committees of Public Accounts, pp. 390–5, 428–9; but see Reports from the Select Committee of Public Accounts (1929), p. vi.

[2] Epitome of the Reports from the Committees of Public Accounts, pp. 93–5, 100–2, 564–7, 568–74, 575–8. See also Cd. 9031/1918. The extent of the control depends on the case and the conditions laid down. In the case of grants-in-aid to colonies and many other cases there is no difference of control.

[3] Report from the Select Committee on Estimates (1932–3), p. xii. In 1940–5 the ordinary Estimates for the Navy, Army and Air Force were confined to nominal sums, which afforded opportunities for discussion in Supply and provided a statutory basis for appropriation accounts. Substantive provision was drawn, as required, from votes of credit. Vote A (numbers of officers and men) was drawn in a vague form, 'such numbers as His Majesty may deem necessary'. The civil departments, also, drew such sums as were due to conditions of war from the votes of credit, and a special vote, containing nominal amounts only, was created for this purpose. The special wartime departments (Food, Economic Warfare, Information, etc.) were wholly financed in this way, though the ordinary expenditure of the permanent civil departments was financed as usual through Estimates.

[4] Report from the Select Committee on Estimates (1932–3), p. xii.

These methods of financial control are probably now as efficient, subject to minor defects, as they could be made. In the last resort, all expenditure must depend either on policy, which is the province of the Cabinet, or on the good faith of the department concerned. The Treasury does not know, and has no means of knowing, whether expenditure on a technical service is justified or not. If the Cabinet decides that the Navy shall be as strong as the strongest fleet afloat, and the Admiralty puts forward a programme on that basis, the Treasury cannot effectively balance ship against ship and gun against gun. It is true that in 1913 the Admiralty put forward claims based upon the numbers of ships in the various fleets (comparing on the two-power standard), and the Treasury, 'which was not without information from expert naval sources', replied with an Estimate which was qualitative, based on speed, weight of guns, and age.[1] It needs little imagination to suggest that these 'expert naval sources' were the opponents of the policy (and personality) of the then First Sea Lord. It is not the function of the Treasury to take sides in a contest between experts: nor, in any event, can it set up its own judgment on technical issues against that of the Board of Admiralty. In greater or less degree, this consideration affects every technical branch of government. For this reason, both Mr Gladstone and Lord Randolph Churchill admitted that the Chancellor of the Exchequer could not under the pre-war system control the details of expenditure, but could only reduce aggregate sums.[2]

This was the opinion, also, of Sir Michael Hicks Beach. 'I have found by experience that detailed criticism by the Chancellor of the Exchequer of estimates already prepared in the departments rarely produces any result worth the labour and friction which it involves.'[3] Nor is the method of reducing an aggregate necessarily effective. When Lord George Hamilton went to the Education Department, he cut down Estimates as much as he could. The Treasury then reduced the aggregate by £10,000. Hamilton pointed out that he had already reduced by more than that amount, and asked for reasons. 'In reply I was informed that it always had been the practice of the Treasury to cut

[1] Lloyd George, *War Memoirs*, I, p. 9.

[2] Lord George Hamilton, *Parliamentary Reminiscences*, I, pp. 303–4.

[3] *Life of Sir Michael Hicks Beach*, II, p. 151.

down education estimates by £10,000, and to that rule they intended to adhere.' Accordingly, he put up the Estimates in the following year so as to give the Treasury the pleasure of cutting them down.[1] The method of reducing an aggregate is effective, however, where the Treasury decides to make *pro rata* cuts in order to avoid increased taxation, or, in furtherance of the Government's deliberate policy, it decides to economise on one group of services in order to spend more on another group. The Estimates for a department then suffer an aggregate reduction and it is left to the department to determine under which sub-heads expenditure can be restricted by abolishing or reducing existing services or postponing developments.

The most effective method is the close scrutiny of all proposals involving increased expenditure. According to Sir Edward Hamilton, Permanent Secretary to the Treasury, this was the method which Hicks Beach used. 'With him Treasury control was a reality. It is probably true to say that this control has never been a reality since. With him it was not interference with small detail. It was exercised at the really effective point, that is to say by a close scrutiny of any proposals to be put before Parliament which involved the expenditure of public money. His colleagues and their departments had to make a very good case for schemes necessitating a charge on the revenue.'[2] This is the method now universally adopted. It must also be remembered that the Treasury, unlike the other departments, is concerned with the indirect as well as with the direct consequences of public expenditure. The departments may be encouraged to spend more in order to reduce deflation or to spend less in order to reduce inflation; or, what is much the same thing, they may be encouraged to spend more in order to reduce unemployment or to spend less to relieve a shortage of man-power. In other words, the Treasury is concerned with the economic structure of the country, and not merely with the problem of raising money to meet public expenditure.

If the Treasury and a minister cannot agree, the question must be submitted to the Prime Minister[3] or to the Cabinet. For instance, the

[1] Lord George Hamilton, *Parliamentary Reminiscences*, I, p. 304.

[2] *Life of Sir Michael Hicks Beach*, II, p. 178.

[3] E.g. Sir William Harcourt in 1886: *Life of Sir William Harcourt*, I, pp. 570–1.

Admiralty Estimates for 1913 were defended in a memorandum of eighty pages. The Treasury would not agree to the great increases proposed, and the matter was submitted to the Cabinet. It formed the main and often the sole topic of conversation at fourteen full meetings of the Cabinet. Though the First Lord of the Admiralty was originally in a minority of one, the Cabinet ultimately overruled the Treasury.[1] It is in the Cabinet that the Chancellor of the Exchequer really exercises his influence. He can go so far as to threaten resignation. 'Though he has no right to demand the concurrence of his colleagues in his view of the estimates,' said Mr Gladstone, 'he has a rather special right, because these do so much towards determining budget and taxation, to indicate his own views by resignation. I have repeatedly fought estimates to the extremity, with an intention of resigning in case.'[2] Yet others, too, can fight to the last ditch. Mr Gladstone himself, as Prime Minister, resigned in 1894 because he agreed with his Chancellor that the Estimates were inflated. Lord Randolph Churchill had his bluff called in 1886. Sir William Harcourt, Sir Michael Hicks Beach and Mr Lloyd George all suffered defeat. Treasury control has no basis save the authority in Cabinet of the Chancellor of the Exchequer. If his authority is overborne the Treasury must comply.[3]

It should be added that the acceptance of collectivist principles by all political parties has much reduced the area of Treasury control. Most of the expenditure on social services is automatic. The principles upon which expenditure on social security, children's allowances, and the like, are based are settled in Cabinet and by Parliament. The cost changes automatically with the size and composition of the population and the condition of trade. Treasury control is thus capable of being exercised only in relation to costs of administration.[4] This is true also of grant-aided services such as education, police and housing. Once the principle of the grant has been accepted the Treasury can bring little influence to

[1] Churchill, *World Crisis*, I, pp. 172, 178. It has been said that the Admiralty wanted six dreadnoughts, the Treasury suggested four, and the Cabinet compromised on eight. In fact, however, the keels of the eight ships were to be laid over two years.

[2] *Life of Gladstone*, III, p. 365.

[3] Cf. evidence of Sir Warren Fisher, Royal Commission on the Civil Service (1929), Minutes of Evidence, p. 1270.

[4] Cf. Mr Baldwin in 1919: 116 H.C.Deb. 5 s., 481–3.

bear. The difficulty is even greater where subsidies are given to industry. For here there is no control at all. The terms of subsidy are laid down in legislation. Though sometimes conditions are attached subject to Treasury sanction, once the general principles have been approved by the Cabinet, the Treasury has little authority.

§4. *Control over Expenditure*

The sums asked for by the Treasury and the Service Departments are voted to the Queen by Parliament in Consolidated Fund Acts and the Appropriation Act. For the benefit of those accustomed to other systems it is necessary to emphasise that the sums voted to the Queen for the services which she specifies in the Estimates are submitted by her ministers. The Acts give her and them authority to spend the money on the services specified in the Appropriation Act. They do not indicate any decision by Parliament as to what money shall be spent—though such decisions are often included in other legislation, such as Acts dealing with social security—they indicate the maximum amounts which the Queen may spend if she so desires. Provided that the provisions of other Acts are satisfied, the Government may decide not to spend the whole or any part of a vote. All the sums so voted are appropriated to the specific services by the Appropriation Act, which therefore determines the maximum that may be spent on each service. Section 3 of that Act incorporates Schedules A and B of the Act. Schedule A sets out all the sums voted since the previous Appropriation Act. It sets out, therefore, (*a*) the sums voted by way of Supplementary Estimates for the expenditure of the previous year, (*b*) the sum voted as a vote on account to provide for the period of the current year between the beginning of the financial year and the passing of the Appropriation Act, and (*c*) the sums granted towards making good votes in Supply. These sums are allocated to the specific services by Schedule B. Parts I to IV of that Schedule allocate the Supplementary Estimates of the previous year, and the rest of the Schedule allocates the total voted for the service of the current year. Accordingly, the legal authority for the various departments to spend money on their respective services is to be found in section 3 and Schedule B of the Appropriation Act.

Schedule B is based on the Estimates, but does not contain the same detail. For instance, the services provided by the Ministry of Supply are set out in Class IX, Vote 1, of the Civil Estimates, which deals with that vote in three sections. First, the total of the Estimate is set out. Secondly, the Estimate sets out the sixteen sub-heads 'under which this Vote will be accounted for by the Ministry of Supply' and the sub-head for 'Appropriations in aid'. Thirdly, the Estimate sets out the details of each sub-head. This is a case in which almost the whole expenditure of a department falls within a single vote. It is not always so. In particular, it is not so in the Service Departments. The expenditure of the War Office, for instance, falls into ten different votes, each of them having separate sub-heads. For instance, the cost of the Territorial Army and Reserve Forces falls under Vote 2 of the Army Estimates. The cost of the Combined Cadet Force falls under sub-head D of that vote.

The Appropriation Act sets out neither the detail of the sub-heads nor the sub-heads themselves. Parliament, accordingly, appropriates expenditure only to specific votes. It follows that it is illegal for a department to spend money beyond the amount allocated to a vote, though it is perfectly legal to transfer sums from one sub-head to another. If, for instance, the Ministry of Supply were able to save £100 on sub-head B of Class IX, Vote 1 of the Civil Estimates, it would not be committing an illegal act in spending that £100 on sub-head A of the same vote. Similarly, the Army Council could spend less money on the Combined Cadet Force and more money on the Territorial Army without committing an illegal act. On the other hand, it could not without parliamentary sanction spend less on the Territorial Army and more on the Regular Army, since these appear in separate votes.

But a transfer between sub-heads, though legal, would be a breach of faith with the House of Commons, for that House has voted the sums in the Appropriation Act after considering the details in the Estimates. Accordingly, it has been laid down by the Treasury, and emphatically endorsed by the Select Committee of Public Accounts, that no such transfer can be permitted except with Treasury consent, and then only subject to specific limitations. 'The good faith of government is pledged by the details of an estimate on the strength of which Parliament grants the vote.'[1] Nor is this the only reason. If a department receives a specific grant, there is naturally a tendency for it to spend all of it. Accordingly, if there were a specific saving on one item, it might look round to see if there was another item on which expenditure might profitably be made. In the result, therefore, the Treasury has a control over expenditure even within the legal limits.

Moreover, the Treasury has legal authority to authorise transfer between votes in the Navy, Army and Air Force respectively. Section 4 of the Appropriation Act provides that so long as the aggregate expenditure on naval, military and air services respectively is not made to exceed the aggregate sums appropriated for those services, any surplus arising on any vote for those services may, with the sanction of the Treasury, be applied either to making up a deficiency in appropriations in aid or in defraying expenditure in the same department which is not provided for in the sums appropriated and which 'it may be detrimental to the public service to postpone until provision can be made for it by Parliament in the usual course'. The power is in any case strictly temporary. The Treasury has to report each case to Parliament, and parliamentary sanction in a subsequent Appropriation Act is necessary. This sanction is given by section 5 and Schedule C of the Appropriation Act.

Whether the transfer is between sub-heads or between votes, it is spoken of as a 'virement'. Virement is thus of two kinds, according as it is between sub-heads or between votes.[2] The former is the more common and, given the difficulty of forecasting expenditure four months before the beginning of the financial year, it is the only means by which the system of presenting detailed Estimates to Parliament can be worked.[3] It is recognised that, where parliamentary as well as Treasury control is required, the service should be provided for in a separate vote.[4] The Treasury does not consider that it is so bound by the Estimates that it cannot sanction a new service or a development of a service not contemplated by Parliament provided that the department keeps within its vote;[5] but it does so only subject to the criticisms of the Comptroller and Auditor-General and of the Select Committee of

[1] Epitome of the Reports from the Select Committees of Public Accounts, p. 347.
[2] *Ibid.* p. 90.
[3] *Ibid.* pp. 90, 348.
[4] *Ibid.* p. 253.
[5] *Ibid.* p. 350.

Public Accounts, and therefore exercises its power with care.[1] 'The Treasury would not be prepared to allow an old sub-head to be exceeded or a new sub-head to be opened if they thought the expenditure in question either from its amount or from its nature was such that Parliament ought to have cognizance of it before it was spent', and for a large item, especially a new work, sanction in advance of parliamentary sanction would be given 'very sparingly indeed'.[2] It insists that sanction should be obtained before the expenditure is incurred;[3] and it has, on occasion, withheld sanction until the matter has been considered by the Select Committee of Public Accounts.[4]

Virement between votes of a Service Department is a more serious matter[5] and its desirability has frequently been discussed.[6] It is usually exercised in cases where the excess is not deliberate, as for instance where it is due to expenditure by outlying spending departments whose total is not known until the accounts come in.[7] In wartime, if detailed Estimates are not replaced by votes of credit, it is more often used.[8] The application for sanction must be in writing and must give reasons.[9] Where the over-expenditure is deliberate, sanction must be applied for before it is incurred;[10] and where it is automatic, sanction must be sought as soon as the excess is known.[11] There must in either case be urgent necessity for the expenditure.[12]

Since this kind of virement requires subsequent parliamentary approval, statements are attached to the Appropriation Accounts, a resolution is passed in Committee, and sanction is given by the next Appropriation Act. In addition, the Select Committee of Public Accounts gives consideration to the material attached to the Appropriation Accounts and the reports of the Comptroller and Auditor-General thereon. It may ask the department, the Treasury, and the Comptroller and Auditor-General to give further explanations and will report to the House of Commons if it is not satisfied.

[1] *Ibid.* pp. 352–3.
[2] *Ibid.* p. 261.
[3] *Ibid.* pp. 65, 622, 640.
[4] *Ibid.* pp. 77–8, 556.
[5] For the history of this power, see *ibid.* pp. 10–11.
[6] *Ibid.* pp. 13–15, 89, 252, etc.
[7] *Ibid.* p. 91.
[8] *Ibid.* p. 460. See the figures for 1892–1902.
[9] *Ibid.* pp. 14, 224–5, 227.
[10] *Ibid.* pp. 17, 54, 89–90, 226–7.
[11] *Ibid.* pp. 14, 91.
[12] *Ibid.* pp. 224, 328–9, 487–8.

It has been mentioned above[1] that, in addition to the sub-heads, the details of expenditure under those sub-heads are given in the Estimates. It is considered, however, that the department is not bound as closely by these details as it is by the sub-heads. Consequently, the Treasury does not control in detail the expenditure of a department within a sub-head. As it explained in 1868:

> It appears to my Lords that it would be beyond the functions of this Board to control the ordinary expenditure placed under the charge of the several departments, within the limits of the sums set forth under the sub-heads of the several grants of Parliament, and that it is only in exceptional cases that the special sanction of the Treasury should be held to be necessary. My Lords consider that such sanction should be required for any increase of establishment, of salary, or of cost of a service, or for any additional works or new services which have not been specifically provided for in the grants of Parliament.[2]

In fact, however, the exceptions cover much of the detail set out in the Estimates. This is particularly true of the Civil Estimates, where most of the detail is concerned with the number of the establishment and the salaries paid to it. These are necessarily under the control of the Treasury on account of the general civil service control mentioned at the beginning of this chapter.

Any expenditure beyond the limits of a vote, or in the cases of the Service Departments the total of its votes, is illegal, and the department has to seek express parliamentary approval. It is one of the Treasury's duties to see that illegal expenditure is not incurred, though its functions in this connection are not so important as those of the Comptroller and Auditor-General, and the Select Committee of Public Accounts. The Queen by royal order places the total parliamentary grant at the disposal of the Treasury.[3] The departments obtain their funds from the Paymaster-General (the Revenue Departments excepted, since they defray their expenses in the first instance out of the revenues which they collect), and, in so far as he has no adequate balance from other sources, he applies to the Treasury from day to day for issues from the Conso-

[1] Above, p. 165.
[2] Epitome of the Reports from the Committees of Public Accounts, pp. 20–1.
[3] *Ibid.* p. 348.

lidated Fund. The Treasury and the Comptroller and Auditor-General authorise issues from the Consolidated Fund Account at the Bank of England.[1]

An adjustment of accounts of a general character takes place monthly, a fairly accurate adjustment takes place at the end of each quarter, and at the close of the financial year all possible precautions are taken to make issues from the Consolidated Fund correspond with what will be the final audited expenditure of the year. These issues are taken by the Chancellor of the Exchequer in his budget speech to be the 'expenditure' of the previous year: it is, however, only an approximation, since the actual expenditure will not be known until the Appropriation Accounts have been made up and audited.[2]

In each department there is an 'accounting officer', being either the permanent head of the department or the chief financial officer, who is appointed by the Treasury, and is responsible through the minister to Parliament, for departmental expenditure.[3] In 1920 the Public Accounts Committee decided, on the recommendation of the Treasury, that the official head of the department should normally be the accounting officer, but left open the application of this principle to the fighting services.[4] In 1925 the Committee reconsidered the question and advised that the principle should apply also to the fighting services.[5] By 1935, only the Foreign Office, the India Office and the Post Office were exceptions. The Committee then considered that a case under consideration, in which the accounting officer was not consulted because the officer concerned with action did not realise that there were financial implications, would not have arisen if the Permanent Under-Secretary of State had been the accounting officer, and accordingly they advised strict adherence to the principle.[6] He is personally and pecuniarily liable for irregular or unauthorised expenditure unless he has made a written protest to and received authority from the minister;[7] and even when he is overruled he can communicate his protest to the Treasury and the Comptroller and Auditor-General.[8] When he finally

[1] *Ibid.* pp. 175–6.
[2] *Ibid.* pp. 176–7.
[3] See *ibid.* pp. 610–20, 686.
[4] *Ibid.* pp. 610–20.
[5] *Ibid.* p. 686.
[6] *Ibid.* p. 748.
[7] *Ibid.* pp. 28, 30–2, 46–7, 68–9, 199, 605–11.
[8] *Ibid.* p. 635.

produces his Appropriation Account he will be made to answer to the Treasury, the Comptroller and Auditor-General, and the Select Committee of Public Accounts, for any kind of irregularity.[1]

If the department finds that it will exceed its appropriation and virement is not possible or, in the opinion of the Treasury, undesirable, a Supplementary Estimate will become necessary. The responsibility for making such proposals rests with the Treasury. Accordingly, the Treasury insists that when departments consider that a Supplementary Vote is necessary, and in all cases of doubt, a full statement of the condition of the votes shall be submitted.[2] It exercises the same powers of scrutiny over Supplementary Estimates as it exercises over Estimates, and with the knowledge that an increase of expenditure may show a deficit on the year's working owing to revenue being so arranged as to meet only the Estimates and the Consolidated Fund Services, and that Parliament regards Supplementary Estimates with suspicion. The Select Committee of Public Accounts has laid down the rule that the practice of Estimates should be followed for Supplementary Estimates. Consequently, provision should be made under every sub-head where there is an anticipated deficit, whether it is covered or not by savings on other sub-heads, unless the amount is trivial and the subject appears to be uncontentious.[3] This rule was, however, laid down primarily to permit of full debate in Parliament and not for financial reasons.

If the excess is discovered too late for a Supplementary Estimate, an excess vote, incorporated in the Appropriation Act, will be required. The Treasury has under its control a Civil Contingencies Fund out of

[1] In the Epitome of the Reports from the Committees of Public Accounts, pp. 767–8, the duty of the accounting officer was thus defined:

'The accounting officer is personally responsible for the correctness of the Appropriation Account which he renders on behalf of his department, for the proper conduct of its financial business and for the balance in the custody of the department. If he takes office during the period of an account and subsequently signs the account for the whole year, he thereby accepts responsibility for the whole of that account. He is not required to possess technical knowledge of accounts, but it is his duty to see that proper supervision and control are exercised over the persons executing the detailed business of account and book-keeping in the department, and to satisfy himself by appropriate means of the correctness and propriety of the transactions embodied in the accounts, as well as to represent his department before the Public Accounts Committee.'

[2] Epitome of the Reports from the Committees of Public Accounts, p. 165.

[3] *Ibid.* p. 733.

which payments can be made. But the amount of the advance must be repaid to the Fund, and in any case parliamentary sanction to the excess is legally necessary. Excesses are scrutinised by the Select Committee of Public Accounts, and parliamentary sanction is not regarded as a mere formality.[1]

§5. *The Results of Financial Control*

The sum of these various legal and customary requirements is that the Treasury has control, subject to the Cabinet, of the financial aspects of departmental proposals and of the accounting systems of the departments, and is one of the chief instruments by which departmental expenditure is kept not only within the law, but, subject to virement, within the Estimates. The powers and their exercise give the Treasury a preponderance which the finance department of any economical system of government must necessarily provide. In so far as it is ineffective, its failure is due not to defects in the system but to the necessary consequences of that division of labour which requires that one authority shall raise money and other authorities spend it. It has been said that Treasury control involves too much accounting and too little control; but the survey above—necessarily elementary though it is—indicates that it is largely through accounting that control is exercised. It has also been said that boards of directors allow their managers to spend money subject only to audit. Even if this be so, there is an obvious difference between a board of directors and the Cabinet. The directors' measure of efficiency is the percentage of profit. In no part of government—not even in the Post Office—can there be any such test.

On the whole, experience seems to show that the interests of the tax-payer cannot be left to the spending departments; that those interests require the careful consideration of each item of public expenditure in its relation to other items and to the available resources of the State, as well as the vigilant supervision of some authority not directly concerned in the expenditure itself; and that such supervision can be most naturally and effectively exercised by the department which is responsible for raising the revenue required.[2]

[1] Reports from the Select Committee of Public Accounts (1933), pp. 123–4.

[2] Report of the Royal Commission on the Civil Service (1929), Minutes of Evidence, p. 1270.

But Treasury control is not a fifth wheel in the coach; it is not a wheel at all. It rests only on the authority which the Chancellor of the Exchequer wields in the Cabinet. He himself discusses with other ministers the more important questions at issue: and if it is convenient to speak of 'the Treasury' and if it frequently happens that questions are discussed between and decided by officials, the reason is only that the Chancellor cannot do everything and that delegation is the art of government. Treasury control is nothing more than the Chancellor's control of finance. He himself and, through him, his officials, are subject to the Cabinet. He and they advise the Cabinet on the financial implications of a policy; but the Cabinet decides.

CHAPTER VIII

THE PRIME MINISTER

§1. *The Prime Minister's Position*

'The Prime Minister', said Mr John Morley, 'is the keystone of the Cabinet arch.'[1] If that were all, it would be necessary first to examine the working of the Cabinet and then to consider the functions of its chairman. It would, however, be more accurate to describe the Prime Minister as the keystone of the Constitution.

He is, in the first place, the leader of his party. He will usually have been chosen as Prime Minister because he is the leader of the largest party in the House of Commons; and in other cases he will be elected leader as soon as he is appointed Prime Minister. Leadership of the party inside Parliament does not necessarily imply office in the party outside. The chairman of the Labour party is elected annually and for one year only. Nevertheless, the Prime Minister has to give effective leadership, particularly during a general election, when much depends on his personality, prestige, and even strategy; for though electioneering effects few conversions, it forces the waverers to decide whether to vote or not. There is, however, always an election round the corner, and the Prime Minister has to pay special attention to the popularity of his Government and the moods of public opinion. If it seems to be losing support, he has to consider whether to reverse the policy, to change its emphasis by starting a new and more popular line, or to send out his golden-voiced orators to prove to the electorate that it has been mistaken.

The Prime Minister has thus to be not only a close student of public opinion but also an expert in propaganda. He must know what to say, when to say it, and when not to say anything. He must give close attention to the newspapers while realising that the views of journalists or of newspaper proprietors, though having some influence on public opinion, probably give a false impression of it. He must also study the reports which the party managers receive from the constituencies and the views

[1] Morley, *Walpole*, p. 157.

which his supporters in Parliament express in the lobbies, realising that the views of committee men and others who collect the votes are not necessarily the views of the voters themselves. Since his personality and prestige play a considerable part in moulding public opinion, he ought to have something of the popular appeal of a film actor and he must take some care over his make-up—like Mr Gladstone with his collars, Mr Lloyd George with his hair, Mr Baldwin with his pipes, and Sir Winston Churchill with his cigars. Unlike a film actor, however, he ought to be a good inventor of speeches as well as a good orator. Even more important, perhaps, are his microphone and camera manner, for few attend meetings but millions listen to broadcasts. These, however, are the more general attributes. There are all kinds of problems, mostly personal, connected with what Mr Bonar Law's biographer happily calls 'the backstairs of politics'.[1] In the Conservative party the leader is responsible for party organisation, which in turn depends upon party funds and the personalities of all those who work for the party either because they believe in it or because they want to get something out of it. In the early years of the century there were still 'pocket boroughs', dependent not on bribery or 'influence' as in the previous century, but on the financial support of a rich man who provided the party funds and therefore expected to nominate the Conservative candidate[2]—they seem to have disappeared only with the reforms which followed the Conservative defeat of 1945. Even so, there are persons of influence in a party who expect the support of the leader for obtaining seats in Parliament or honours. Anybody who has to handle staff knows how difficult personal problems can be. They can be even more difficult where the whole staff is voluntary.

None of our recent Prime Ministers has had all the required qualities and it is unlikely that all of them will ever be concentrated in one person. Messrs Bonar Law and Neville Chamberlain were lacking in most of them, though Mr Chamberlain was a most efficient party manager behind the scenes. Mr MacDonald in his younger days was a most persuasive orator, but he was out of sympathy with his party long before 1931 and as Prime Minister of the National Government and

[1] Blake, *The Unknown Prime Minister*, p. 99.

[2] *Ibid.* p. 101. Mr Bonar Law was then leader of the Opposition.

'the prisoner of the Tories' he was a pathetic figure. Mr Baldwin was not a very efficient party manager,[1] though when he roused himself he knew how to fight the 'press barons' who tried to run the Conservative party. His personality, however, proved singularly attractive. He built up his character as that of a plain, honest man who could smoke a pipe with anyone and whose ambition was to tickle the pigs in Worcestershire. As his biographer wrote:[2] 'No Prime Minister, it was said, spent so much time in attendance on the House of Commons. And no Prime Minister ever spent so much in neglecting the other duties of his office.' Mr Lloyd George had many of the qualities required, though he had never to manage a party and indeed had no party after 1922. Mr Churchill had had a curiously variegated experience before 1940; his work as a national leader during the war was magnificent; but his management of the general election of 1945 showed lack of appreciation of popular feeling. He was better advised in 1951, but he won the election by reaction against wartime controls, which the Labour party wished to continue as part of the controls required by economic planning, while the electors wanted to get back to freedom as they understood it. Mr Butler, not Sir Winston, provided the policy.

Secondly, the Prime Minister is leader of the House of Commons. It is true that, in order to relieve himself of part of his burden, he may delegate the day-to-day management to another minister, who is designated Leader of the House, but nothing can deprive him of the ultimate responsibility. The Leader of the House arranges business with the Chief Whip, settles procedure and the distribution of time with the Opposition, and gives assistance to the Speaker and the Chairman in the maintenance of order and decorum. But ultimately the management of the Government's majority and the maintenance of smooth relations with the Opposition must depend on the Prime Minister.

It would be impossible adequately to compare Prime Ministers in

[1] Mr Churchill nevertheless called Mr Baldwin 'the greatest party manager the Conservatives ever had. He fought, as their leader, five general elections, of which he won three.' He lost in 1923; he won in 1924 on the 'Red Letter' and the reaction against the first Labour Government; he lost in 1929; he won in 1931 in the midst of a financial crisis which made the whole world (except six million solid Labour voters) Conservative; and he won in 1935, when the reaction had not gone far. The conclusion seems to be that he was not a good party manager, but that he was very, very lucky.

[2] G. M. Young, *Stanley Baldwin*, p. 57.

this respect, because each Parliament has a quality of its own. The Conservative party has a strong, and perhaps exaggerated, notion of loyalty which makes it easy to lead, though it has a curious habit of suddenly repudiating its leaders; the Labour party has more eccentrics and rebels. A Conservative Opposition led by a Lord Randolph Churchill or an F. E. Smith can be a highly effective political instrument, though it is usually solid and uninspiring, whereas a Labour Opposition contains too many guerrillas to make an effective army. It follows that a Conservative Prime Minister has an easy task, while a Labour one may find it difficult. Wartime experience is peculiar, and so little can be said about Mr Lloyd George. Of Mr Bonar Law it has been said that he 'conducted business in the House with an ease and smoothness which gained him universal praise. He remained till his final illness master of the House of Commons to an extent seldom rivalled in modern times.'[1] He was, of course, very experienced. He had led the Conservative party from 1911 to 1921; he had led the House of Commons from 1916 to 1921; while Prime Minister he was the only member of the Government in the House of Commons with lengthy experience. He was therefore able to do the job competently, but he could hardly be said to be inspiring. Mr MacDonald had too difficult a task, with an inexperienced party which lacked general agreement, a strong and reasonably united Opposition and a secretive and tortuous mind which left him remote from his own party, to be an effective leader of the House. Mr Baldwin, on the other hand, was notable for his calm and effective if somewhat careless management of the House. He had great respect for the House and showed it in his handling of its affairs. What is more, he, like Sir Winston Churchill, could rise to full stature when he was called upon, as a Prime Minister often is, to speak not for his party but for the nation. Mr Amery's request to Mr Greenwood, at the outbreak of war, to 'speak for England' was proof that there are occasions when a political leader must shed his party character and become the spokesman for a united people. Mr Amery's request was an indication that Mr Chamberlain had failed. On such occasions Mr Baldwin was at his best; and, of course, Sir Winston Churchill's wartime speeches will echo down the corridors of time. Mr Neville Chamberlain,

[1] Blake, *The Unknown Prime Minister*, p. 498.

like all the Chamberlains, was essentially a shy man and had none of the easy mastery which Mr Baldwin could display when he exerted himself and often when he did not. Mr Chamberlain was the maker of cold, efficient speeches, who rarely said anything wrong and hardly ever said anything exactly right. Mr Attlee was quiet and efficient, but modest and full of platitudes. Sir Winston Churchill, after 1951, was the popular elder statesman, whom even the ranks of Tuscany could scarce forbear to cheer.

Finally, the Prime Minister is chairman of the Cabinet and co-ordinator of policy. The two functions are quite distinct. He may be a good chairman and a wise counsellor, like Mr Balfour, and yet be unable to secure fundamental agreement, though it must be confessed that after Mr Joseph Chamberlain raised the standard of tariff reform Mr Balfour's task was infinitely difficult. He may be an excellent leader, like Mr Lloyd George and Mr Churchill, and therefore an excellent wartime Prime Minister, but too impulsive and too lacking in committee sense to guide the nation's destinies in peace. No doubt there were many reasons for the defeat of Mr Churchill in 1945; but if among them was the realisation that he would have made a bad chairman of a Cabinet the electorate must be congratulated on its perspicuity. In studying the judgments of contemporaries, it must be remembered that the diverse requirements are not always brought out, that most ministers were concerned with their Prime Ministers mainly as chairmen of Cabinets and advisers, and that all their opinions were based on personal experience.

According to Lord Rosebery, Sir Robert Peel was the 'model of all Prime Ministers'.[1]

It is more than doubtful [he added] if it be possible in this generation, when the burdens of empire and of office have so incalculably grown, for any Prime Minister to discharge the duties of his high post with the same thoroughness or in the same spirit as Peel. To do so would demand more time and strength than any man has at his command. For Peel kept a strict supervision over every department: he seems to have been master of the business of each and all of them. He was conversant with all departmental questions, and formed and enforced opinions on them. And, though he had

[1] Rosebery, *Miscellanies*, I, p. 197.

an able Chancellor of the Exchequer, in whom he had full confidence, he himself introduced the great Budget of 1842 and that of 1845. The War Office, the Admiralty, the Foreign Office, the administration of India and of Ireland felt his personal influence as much as the Treasury or the Board of Trade.[1]

The emphasis of this passage is fully justified by the documents printed in the *Peel Papers*. Yet Peel's pre-eminence was exceptional; and none of his successors, not even Mr Disraeli and Mr Gladstone, attained to the same measure of control. One element in his predominance, as Lord Rosebery suggested, was the narrow range of administrative activity. The State had not, in 1846, entered upon the interference in social and economic life that the industrial revolution had made necessary. The finance of government was comparatively simple. The practical administration of the Army was primarily in the hands of the Commander-in-Chief, not in those of the Secretary of State. The Navy was, by modern standards, a small affair. Foreign and colonial policy involved a leisurely consideration of despatches, not a feverish interchange of telegraphic messages. The 'man on the spot' in the colonies was a local dictator. India was governed primarily by the local agents of the East India Company. Even the government of Ireland was, in the main, a matter of police. Above all, Peel's personality impressed itself upon his colleagues. His Cabinet contained some able members. Sir James Graham's qualities as a politician were, perhaps, not attractive; his capacity as an administrator could not be denied. Lord Aberdeen as Foreign Secretary might be accused of pro-French bias, and his relations with *The Times* are not to be defended; yet his appointment to office smoothed all the feathers that Lord Palmerston had ruffled. The Duke of Wellington, in spite of the broken windows of 1832, held an unassailable position in public esteem. When Mr Gladstone was moved into the Cabinet his capacity was already evident. In spite of all this, Peel dominated his Cabinet. The 'principles of Sir Robert Peel' were an important element in policy long after his death. For Mr Gladstone he remained the oracle of the Constitution.

Peel's own views as to a Prime Minister's functions were put by him to a Select Committee in 1850.

[1] Rosebery, *Miscellanies*, I, p. 197.

You must presume that he reads every important despatch from every Foreign Court. He cannot consult with the Secretary of State for Foreign Affairs and exercise the influence which he ought to have with respect to foreign affairs, unless he be master of everything of importance passing in that department. It is the same with respect to India.... In the case of Ireland and the Home Department it is the same. Then the Prime Minister has the patronage of the Crown to exercise...; he has to make inquiries into the qualifications of persons who are candidates; he has to conduct the whole of the communications with the Sovereign; he has to write...the letters in reply to all persons of station who address themselves to him; he has to receive deputations on public business; during the sitting of Parliament he is expected to attend six or seven hours a day, while Parliament is sitting, for five or six days a week; at least, he is blamed if he is absent.[1]

Mr Gladstone's explanation differs but slightly.

The Head of the British Government is not a Grand Vizier. He has no powers, properly so-called, over his colleagues: on the rare occasions when a Cabinet determines its course by the votes of its members, his vote counts only as one of theirs. But they are appointed and dismissed by the Sovereign on his advice. In a perfectly organised administration, such for example as was that of Sir Robert Peel in 1841–6, nothing of great importance is matured, or would even be projected, in any department without his personal cognisance; and any weighty business would commonly go to him before being submitted to the Cabinet. He reports to the Sovereign its proceedings, and he also has many audiences of the august occupant of the Throne.[2]

Lord Morley's account is said to have been the work of Mr Gladstone.[3] 'Although in Cabinet all its members stand on an equal footing, speak with equal voice, and, on the rare occasions when a division is taken, are counted on the fraternal principle of one man one vote, yet the head of the Cabinet is *primus inter pares*, and occupies a position which, so long as its lasts, is one of exceptional and peculiar authority.'[4] He then points out that, though the monarch chooses the Prime Minister, 'the Crown could hardly exercise any real power either of selection or exclusion against the marked wishes of the constituencies',[5] and that,

[1] Report from the Select Committee on Official Salaries (1850), pp. 40–1.
[2] Gladstone, *Gleanings*, I, pp. 242–3.
[3] Oxford and Asquith, *Fifty Years of Parliament*, II, p. 183.
[4] Morley, *Walpole*, p. 157.
[5] *Ibid.*; see above, ch. II.

though his colleagues are in some cases designated to him by public opinion and parliamentary position, and the predilections of the Sovereign have some influence, 'there is more than a margin for his free exercise of choice in the persons admitted to his Cabinet, and in all cases it is for him alone to settle the distribution of posts'.[1]

Lord Morley continued:

The flexibility of the Cabinet system allows the Prime Minister to take upon himself a power not inferior to that of a dictator, provided always that the House of Commons will stand by him. In ordinary circumstances he leaves the heads of departments to do their work in their own way. It is their duty freely and voluntarily to call him into council, on business of a certain order of importance. With the Foreign Secretary alone he is in close and continuous communication as to the business of his office. Foreign affairs must always be the matter of continuous thought in the mind of the Prime Minister. They are not continuously before the Cabinet; it has not therefore the same fulness of information as the Prime Minister; and consequently in this important department of public action, the Cabinet must for the most part, unless there be some special cause of excitement, depend upon the prudence and watchfulness of its head.[2]

Lord Morley added that the Prime Minister settled differences between departments,[3] that he could, with the Sovereign's assent, call for a colleague's resignation, and that he was consulted on the appointment of all the highest posts in the service of the Crown.

Sir William Harcourt thought that Lord Morley's estimate of the powers of the Prime Minister was exaggerated. He agreed that 'though theoretically he is *primus inter pares*, he should in reality be *inter stellas luna minores*'.[4] But he said that 'in practice the thing depends very much upon the character of the man'.[5] Lord Oxford and Asquith said the same: 'the office of Prime Minister is what its holder chooses to make it'.[6]

Personality undoubtedly plays a great part in determining the power of a Prime Minister. Peel's predominance has already been mentioned. Sir James Graham said of him: 'We never had a Minister who was so

[1] Morley, *Walpole*, p. 158; see above, ch. III.
[2] *Ibid.* p. 158.
[3] See above, ch. IV.
[4] *Life of Sir William Harcourt*, II, p. 612.
[5] *Ibid.* p. 610.
[6] *Fifty Years of Parliament*, II, p. 185.

truly a first Minister as he is. He makes himself felt in every department, and is really cognisant of the affairs of each. Lord Grey could not master such an amount of business. Canning could not do it. Now he is an actual Minister, and is indeed, *capax imperii*.'[1] It may be added that neither Lord Melbourne nor Lord John Russell obtained such a supremacy. Lord Melbourne was too lazy and Lord John Russell too impetuous. Each of them, too, had in Lord Palmerston a leading subordinate whose exuberance could not be controlled. The influence of personality rests not merely on the force of character of its possessor, but also on the force of character of those with whom he is in relation.

Palmerston himself, according to Mr Gladstone, was a weak Prime Minister. 'He said that in Peel's Cabinet, a Cabinet minister if he had a measure to bring forward consulted Peel and then the Cabinet. Nobody thought of consulting Palmerston first, but brought his measure at once to the Cabinet.'[2] This statement must be taken with some reserve, because it was made after Gladstone's conflict with Palmerston over the budget of 1860. Palmerston told the Queen that if the Lords destroyed the Paper Duties Bill 'they would perform a good public service'.[3] It is, nevertheless, instructive to compare the budget of 1841 with that of 1860. The proposal to impose the income tax and to relax some of the import duties came from Peel. It was worked out in a series of communications between Peel and his ministers, and the resources of the several departments were utilised. The budget of 1860, which completed the work of the budget of 1841 and the Corn Laws Act of 1846, was drawn up by Mr Gladstone alone and was carried through the Cabinet in spite of the Prime Minister's strenuous opposition. It must again be remembered, however, that the difference was at least as much the consequence of the difference between Goulburn and Gladstone as of the difference between Peel and Palmerston.

Of Disraeli, there are different views. Lord Salisbury was a hostile witness, but his evidence is important.

As the head of a Cabinet his fault was want of firmness. The chiefs of departments got their own way too much. The Cabinet as a whole got it too little, and this necessarily followed from having at the head of affairs a states-

[1] *Life of Gladstone*, I, p. 248. [2] *Ibid.* II, p. 35.
[3] *Life of the Prince Consort*, V, p. 100.

man whose only final political principle was that the Party must on no account be broken up, and who shrank therefore from exercising coercion on any of his subordinates. Thus it became possible that the Transvaal should be annexed—not indeed against the wish of the Cabinet, but actually without its knowledge. Lord Carnarvon wished to do it. Lord Beaconsfield was persuaded that it was an excellent thing to do; i.e., the responsible head of the Department told him, and he believed, that it was an excellent thing to do, and it was done. Again, Bartle Frere should have been recalled....So thought the majority of the Cabinet, so thought Dizzy himself. But the Queen was strongly opposed to it, and Hicks Beach was strongly opposed to it; and the Prime Minister was unable to resist his Sovereign and the Colonial Secretary together. Again, it was decided in Cabinet that the invasion of Afghanistan should take place through one Pass. Lytton objected. Because Lytton did, Hardy did. Because Hardy did, Dizzy did; for was not Hardy at the head of the India Office? And so the plans were altered.[1]

It would seem that the examples do not support the generalisation. Disraeli certainly did not keep in touch with the affairs of each department, as Peel had done. No Prime Minister since Peel has been able to do so. He was therefore disposed to support the view of the head of a department against the combined wisdom of his colleagues. So great was his influence that he was able to support Lord Carnarvon, Hicks Beach and Gathorne-Hardy against the rest of the Cabinet. In respect of Bartle Frere, Hicks Beach himself regarded Lord Beaconsfield's action as indicating strength, not weakness.[2]

Hicks Beach, indeed, contrasted Lord Salisbury and Lord Beaconsfield.

As Prime Minister [Lord Salisbury] did not exercise the control over his colleagues, either in or out of the Cabinet, that Lord Beaconsfield did. I have known Lord Beaconsfield enforce his view on the Cabinet after all its members but one had expressed a different opinion;[3] Lord Salisbury frequently allowed important matters to be decided by a small majority of votes, even against his own opinion. Lord Beaconsfield kept a very watchful eye on the proceedings of all his colleagues. When I was Irish Secretary in 1874, the *Daily News* had an article charging me with a new departure in Irish

[1] Balfour, *Chapters of Autobiography*, pp. 113–14.

[2] *Life of Sir Michael Hicks Beach*, I, p. 130.

[3] This refers apparently to 1879, when Lord Beaconsfield supported Hicks Beach over the proposal to recall Bartle Frere.

Education. On the next morning a letter came to Dublin from Mr Disraeli asking me for an explanation. Lord Salisbury left his colleagues very much to themselves, unless they consulted him.[1]

That Disraeli could, if necessary, support his colleagues against the head of a department is shown conclusively by Lord Derby's tenure of the Foreign Office at the period of the Russo-Turkish War. Before his resignation in 1878 Lord Derby was opposed to the Government's 'forward' policy, and Lord Beaconsfield was, for practical purposes, his own Foreign Secretary.[2] In truth, the policy was the Prime Minister's. He persuaded the Cabinet to agree, and he overruled his own Foreign Secretary. Whatever be thought of the policy and of its execution, it must be agreed that the method bears no trace of weakness.

Apart from his Palmerstonian beliefs in force and prestige, supported as they were by an almost childish delight in the colour of the Orient, Disraeli had no policy and no desire (or, indeed, capacity) to form one.[3] He was an arbiter, a strong judge, who, as Mr Dooley said of the judges of the Supreme Court of the United States, kept his eye on the election returns. Lord Salisbury had a foreign policy, but nothing else, and did not watch public opinion. Both differed in this respect from Mr Gladstone. He, too, interfered little in ordinary administration after 1880, and was not much concerned with foreign policy (as the Gordon episode shows). Like Disraeli, he kept his ear to the ground. But, unlike Disraeli, he considered that 'heroic' measures were necessary to rally his party and to give it a majority. He therefore followed Peel's practice of initiating such measures and working them out in detail. The Irish Church Bill and the two Home Rule Bills, above all, bore the impress of his personality. While these measures were on the anvil, sparks might fly in other directions almost without his noticing them. Neither Disraeli nor Lord Salisbury was a legislator. It is true that, according to his biographer, 'there are among [Lord Salisbury's] papers initialled memoranda dealing with Bills under discussion; draft clauses in his handwriting; suggestions for legislation which he is circulating

[1] *Life of Sir Michael Hicks Beach*, II, pp. 360–1.

[2] *Life of Disraeli*, II, pp. 997 *et seq.*

[3] I do not forget '*sanitas sanitatum, omnia sanitas*': the origin of the fantastic belief of the Primrose League that Disraeli was a great social reformer is set out in the *Life of Lord Norton*.

for his colleagues' opinion'.[1] But there is no evidence that either he or Disraeli actually initiated legislation.[2] Moreover, Lord Salisbury did not regard it as his duty to supervise the work of his colleagues.[3]

Mr Gladstone's practice in respect of administration was much the same. In 1868–74, it is true, he attempted to follow Peel's example;[4] but he gave up the attempt in his later periods of office. His control over his Cabinet was, however, considerable. Between 1868 and 1874 his power was almost absolute. The forceful and truculent ambition of Mr Chamberlain and the gradual realisation of the Whigs that Liberalism and Radicalism were becoming almost synonymous converted his function into one of conciliation and arbitration. The purge caused by the acceptance of the principle of Home Rule would, no doubt, have restored his hegemony: but by the time he returned to power in 1892 new fissures had opened in the Liberal landscape, and only the 'Grand Old Man' prevented disruption. These fissures widened while Lord Rosebery was Prime Minister. The opposition between the 'Imperialist' and the 'Little England' sections of the Liberal party became acute. The leader of the one was Prime Minister, the leader of the other the leader of the House of Commons. Rosebery, too, was concerned primarily with foreign affairs. The conditions did not enable him to control his Cabinet.

Mr Balfour accepted a *damnosa hereditas*. His primary task was to prevent the question of tariff reform from creating an open rupture. But, after 1903, the resignations of so many of those who had led the Unionists in the earlier period of their hegemony left him with a comparatively young and inexperienced body of ministers. His predominance was then undoubted. His skill as chairman was immense. He was able to draw out the elements of agreement. His intellectual capacity enabled him, not to control ministers in their departmental work, but to give them valuable assistance whenever they consulted him. He was, therefore, consulted frequently. Sir Austen Chamberlain, who had held office under five Prime Ministers, told the present writer in 1935 that he considered Mr Balfour to have been the ablest of them. He was of

[1] *Life of Robert, Marquis of Salisbury*, III, p. 167.

[2] *Ibid.* III, p. 168.

[3] *Ibid.* III, p. 169.

[4] Oxford and Asquith, *Fifty Years of Parliament*, II, p. 185, footnote.

course thinking of Mr Balfour as chairman of the Cabinet and leader of his Government, not as leader of his party. As he has said in writing:

> He was not a successful party leader, but on a calm review of the obstacles which beset his path from the first, and of his achievement, who shall deny him title to be named among our great Prime Ministers?[1]

As party leader, Mr Balfour had the impossible task of trying to keep Mr Joseph Chamberlain and the Conservative free traders in the same Government, during a period, too, when the Liberal Party was gaining from the reaction to the Boer War. Sir Austen was referring to Mr Balfour as a colleague, while his biographer was concerned with him as a party leader:

> It is difficult to resist the conclusion that he was an admirable second-in-command but a bad leader. He was constitutionally incapable of looking at any question as the ordinary man in the street looked at it, and he could not understand the other's point of view. He was incapable of working up crowd emotion in his favour. He could only state issues as he saw them, not as they might appeal to the average man, which is the secret of successful propaganda. In this lay one of the principal causes of his failure as a leader.[2]

There is no doubt much truth in this analysis, but the concept of the Prime Minister as a combination of a film-star and a successful criminal lawyer, though based on the experiments of Mr Gladstone, was introduced by Mr Lloyd George. Judged by the test applicable to Sir Robert Peel, Mr Balfour was an excellent Prime Minister.[3]

According to Lord Esher—who was prejudiced—Sir Henry Campbell-Bannerman had no effective control, and the work of the departments was carried on practically without reference to the Prime Minister.[4] In truth, his health did not permit him to accept Peel's task, even if more modern conditions had not prevented it. His primary purpose was to prevent the 'Pro-Boers' and the Liberal Imperialists from seizing each others' throats. In this he was largely successful; but

[1] *Life and Letters of Sir Austen Chamberlain*, I, p. 156. [2] *Ibid.* I, p. 104.

[3] Mr Balfour worked on some of the clauses of the Education Bill of 1902. The draftsman said of his work: 'You have written a good popular account of the Bill': *Life of A. J. Balfour*, I, 324. His most successful effort as a draftsman was in the Balfour Report on Inter-Imperial Relations in 1926, long after he had ceased to be Prime Minister.

[4] *Esher Papers*, II, pp. 160–1.

he could not, at the same time, intervene in departmental matters. His sound judgment was available to any minister who sought it, and it may be assumed that his comparatively inexperienced team of ministers took advantage of it.

Mr Asquith not only had no taste for interference in administration, but also believed that it was impracticable.[1] As chairman of the Cabinet, it has been generally agreed—and not merely stated by Mr Lloyd George—that in his later years of office he had no real control. This was particularly true after 1915, when the burden of the war and above all the personal loss which he suffered caused him to lose interest. His Coalition Government was necessarily both large and influential, since it contained the most important and experienced Conservative leaders as well as his own political subordinates, some of whom had had nine years' continuous experience of office. It is said that, when a discussion in which he was not interested was proceeding, he would proceed to write letters until the discussion appeared to have worn itself out. He would then remark, 'Well, gentlemen, as we are now agreed, shall we pass on?'—whereupon it would be asked on what they were agreed, and a new discussion would arise over this question. On occasions, indeed, there would be a discussion at each end of the table, Mr Asquith imperturbably writing his letters in the middle. This weakness was the ostensible reason for the intrigue by which he was ousted in 1915; but it is unlikely that the Conservative ministers would have assented to Mr Lloyd George's leadership if there were no substance in the complaint.

Indeed, Mr Austen Chamberlain's contemporary account shows this to be true:

> Asquith lacks the power to drive. Whether he was always deficient in it, or whether the habit of waiting on events and on colleagues has grown upon him in these later years, I cannot say. In any case the result is the same. Any Committee—call it War Council or Cabinet or what you will—is apt to dissolve in talk unless the chairman keeps them steadily to the point at issue, and makes it his business to secure from them a decision on each question as it is raised. Asquith never so understood his duties. He waited on others. He no doubt often averted conflict, but he never contributed a suggestion. He only once in my experience directly helped us to a rapid decision.[2]

[1] Oxford and Asquith, *Fifty Years of Parliament*, II, p. 186.

[2] *Life and Letters of Sir Austen Chamberlain*, II, pp. 55–6.

It must nevertheless be remembered that Mr Asquith was one of our most fluent speakers and able debaters. Lord Rosebery thought him

> the greatest Parliamentarian that ever lived. Much greater than Gladstone or Dizzy or Palmerston or Peel. A cultured scholar of amazing power of parliamentary speech: never a word wrong and never a word too much; wholly unlike Gladstone whose exuberance of oratory marred its effectiveness.[1]

The problems which faced Mr Lloyd George's Government were of a peculiar nature, and the institution of the War Cabinet necessarily modified ordinary methods of government. It is admitted even by his opponents that he was quick to seize the point of a difficulty, especially if it were put to him orally. (The common statement that Mr Lloyd George never read anything is untrue, but it is certain that he preferred to have the points put to him shortly and succinctly by word of mouth.) As Lord Esher said in 1916:

> Mr Lloyd George possesses two essential qualities...at such a crisis as that through which we are now passing. He has the invaluable gift of concentrating the attention of his fellow-countrymen upon any issue vital at the moment. And secondly, he is an administrator, in the sense that he can get things done where other people cannot. His gifts as an administrator are not of the ordinary peace kind. He does not attempt to exercise minute supervision over detail. He is not content to apply with added force the principles of sanction and careful audit that ever since the days of Sir Robert Peel have rightly obtained throughout our administrative system. He has adopted with marked success the plan of cutting away red-tape and of placing reliance upon personal responsibility by bestowing extended powers upon individuals selected for their capacity, vigour and courage. This is the only method in wartime that is conducive to success.[2]

In the Cabinet he was in complete control, bringing out the elements of agreement in competing proposals and, naturally, emphasising those with which he himself agreed. More than any recent Prime Minister except Mr Chamberlain he intervened in departmental business. He reduced his Foreign Secretary almost to the position of an Under-Secretary. His private secretariat in the 'garden suburb' was almost a second Foreign Office. He himself saw foreign ambassadors, sometimes without notifying the real Foreign Office. So obvious was this

[1] *Life of Randall Davidson*, I, p. 868. [2] *Esher Papers*, IV, pp. 68–9.

that in 1920 a deputation of back-benchers called on him in order to complain of his absence from the House of Commons and of his extra-parliamentary pronouncements. Mr Neville Chamberlain, who was one of the deputation, thought that there was a real danger of our sliding into a big change in the Constitution, under which the Prime Minister would deal with 'trade unions, employers, and interests of various kinds, direct'.[1] The Prime Minister, in short, was becoming an extra-parliamentary governor like the President of the United States, the management of the House of Commons being left to a subordinate as 'floor leader'.

Mr Bonar Law's short Government of 1922–3 was not a very successful reaction. Not only was the full-sized Cabinet restored and the 'garden suburb' brought under a clearance order but also proposals were made for abolishing the Cabinet Office. Fortunately wiser counsel prevailed. Nevertheless Mr Bonar Law was a 'strong' Prime Minister:

> Bonar Law under his diffident manner was much more of an autocrat than Lloyd George and much more set in his ways. He was a business man for whom an agenda was something on which decisions were to be got as soon as possible, not a series of starting points for a general discussion. Sooner than let discussion roam afield or controversy be raised, he would cut things short by suggesting a compromise.[2]

Lord Lee of Fareham, by giving Chequers to the nation as a country house for the Prime Minister, has perhaps changed the Constitution more emphatically than he anticipated. Mr Baldwin was the first to make constant use of it, and Mr MacDonald, Mr Neville Chamberlain, Mr Churchill and Sir Anthony Eden followed his example. Even when the war was at its height, Mr Harry Hopkins complained to the President of the United States about the 'English week-end'. His complaint was no doubt unjustified. There were senior civil servants and service officers in Whitehall ready to take instant decisions if they were needed, while Mr Churchill could be fetched in an hour. It is nevertheless true that Chequers can be not only a rest for tired statesmen but also an excuse for a harassed Prime Minister to get away from his colleagues. Mr Baldwin not only favoured the long week-end but refused to have

[1] *Life of Neville Chamberlain*, p. 84.

[2] L. S. Amery, *My Political Life*, II, p. 246.

papers sent to him there. Though, as we have seen, he had many of the qualities of a good party leader and excelled in the House of Commons on non-party issues, he made no attempt to control his colleagues. So long as he was in Downing Street he was always accessible to his ministers and was on terms of easy familiarity with them. What is more, he was intensely loyal to them and they could always be sure of his support. On the other hand, he was rarely of much assistance to them when they needed advice. A Prime Minister like Mr Balfour would listen carefully to a long exposition of a problem, pick on the weak points on each side of it, and produce a masterly summary which usually led the departmental minister to the right conclusion. Mr Baldwin had no such capacity. Sir Austen Chamberlain explained to the present writer that when the preliminaries of the Locarno Pact were under discussion at the Foreign Office he took the whole problem to the Prime Minister, since any further steps in the negotiations would necessarily bind His Majesty's Government to take some steps, at least, to meet the German point of view. Mr Baldwin listened carefully, but at the end his remark was: 'Well, Austen, do what you think fit and I will support you.' This was no doubt gratifying to Sir Austen, but what he wanted was a second opinion on the scheme which was being worked out by the Foreign Ministries; and this Mr Baldwin was unable or unwilling to give him. Sir Austen's biographer has made the same point, though somewhat less emphatically:

> It was always the custom of Mr Baldwin to allow his Ministers a free hand, and a Foreign Secretary in his Cabinet was particularly favoured in this respect, for the Prime Minister had little knowledge of, or interest in, international affairs. Austen enjoyed, for example, far more freedom both in the initiation and execution of his policy than had been allowed to Sir Edward Grey by Mr Asquith, but he could also count, as experience was to prove, on Mr Baldwin's loyal support in a crisis.[1]

It must not be thought, however, that Mr Baldwin exercised any greater control in home affairs. A less easy-going Conservative leader would quietly have ejected Mr Ramsay MacDonald from the National Government before 1935; but when he again became Prime Minister internal policy, especially economic policy, was stimulated more by

[1] *Life and Letters of Sir Austen Chamberlain*, II, p. 246.

Mr Neville Chamberlain than by the Prime Minister.[1] Lord Samuel has given a picture:

> Reticent in Cabinet, one might almost say taciturn, Baldwin rarely, if ever, initiated a proposal; but often, when a discussion was taking an awkward turn, he would intervene at the end with some brief observations, full of common sense, that helped to an agreement.[2]

It must be remembered, however, that Lord Samuel had no experience of Mr Baldwin as Prime Minister. His observations apply to the National Government of 1931–2, when the word 'National' was not entirely a pretence and the task of the Cabinet, as its members saw it, was to keep the Government together in order to pull through the economic crisis. In such conditions Mr Baldwin's task was to keep the Cabinet cool, calm and collected. His function changed when he again became Prime Minister in 1935 and the adjective 'National' had become a fiction. Mr Neville Chamberlain criticised him for lack of leadership,[3] and for failing to give firm guidance to his Cabinet.[4] In fact he drew a picture of him in Cabinet, letting the discussion range, robbing his countenance of expression, and meditatively stabbing at the table with his pencil.[5] Even so, it seems clear that he steered the Cabinet, the House of Commons and the country through the Abdication crisis in December 1936 with admirable skill.

From Lord Samuel we have an excellent description of Mr Ramsay MacDonald as Prime Minister in his later years:

> He was a good chairman of the Cabinet, carefully preparing his material beforehand, conciliatory in manner and resourceful. In the conduct of a Cabinet, when a knot or a tangle begins to appear, the important thing is for the Prime Minister not to let it be drawn tight; so long as it is kept loose it may still be unravelled. MacDonald was skilful in such a situation—and there were many. In statesmanship his chief fault was a tendency to evasion. Not seldom he was like the man who said, 'I will look my difficulties firmly in the face, and pass on'. But it must be recognised that with so few supporters of his own, either in Parliament or in the country, he was rarely in a position to take a strong line.[6]

[1] Lord Samuel, *Memoirs*, p. 216. This, however, relates to the Government of 1931–2.

[2] *Ibid.* p. 215.

[3] *Life of Neville Chamberlain*, p. 164.

[4] *Ibid.* p. 111.

[5] *Ibid.* p. 164.

[6] Lord Samuel, *Memoirs*, p. 214.

Mr MacDonald's behaviour between 1914 and 1918, when he was falsely[1] accused of being a pro-German and a pacifist and was one of the most unpopular men in the country, shows that he was capable of taking a strong line in his early days, and alone. Yet he was always alone, for he had a tortuous mind which often made it impossible for his colleagues to follow his line of thought. When he was prominent both in the Fabian Society and in the Independent Labour party, which were then at issue over policy, he was thought by each to be hostile to it and a supporter of the other. He managed to work with both Mr Henderson and Mr Snowden, but he was liked by neither, and his relationships with them were official and strained. In the Labour party he trod the middle path very dexterously, so that he was the inevitable leader; and yet neither the trade union leaders nor the intellectuals trusted him. Accordingly, the usual confidence of Cabinet ministers in their chairman did not apply to the Labour Cabinets of 1924 and 1929 to 1931, and though he kept an eye on what was going on in the departments, the subtle influence which can be exercised through mutual confidence and esteem did not arise. His enormous capacity for reading papers, his businesslike practice of marking them with coloured pencils, and the sense of order which had developed while he was the inevitable secretary of every progressive society, meant that he was always well-informed: but he had not the capacity of Mr Balfour to mould a discussion as he intended. He could draft a compromise, but he could not persuade. While it is clear that his intellectual qualities have been underestimated, his personality prevented him from being a good Prime Minister.[2]

Sir Winston Churchill has drawn a comparison between Mr Baldwin and Mr Neville Chamberlain:

> Baldwin was the wiser, more comprehending personality, but without detailed executive capacity. He was largely detached from foreign and

[1] Lord Elton, *James Ramsay MacDonald*, I, ch. IX.

[2] He had eliminated all his political 'friends' long before 1931 and his formation of the National Government turned them into bitter enemies. His continuance in office after 1932 did not gain him friends among the Conservatives. He is once said to have reported that he had converted Lord Rothermere by threatening to resign. Mr Neville Chamberlain commented: 'I have always heard that Rothermere was easily frightened, but I confess I find it difficult to believe that the thing was as simply done as that': *Life of Neville Chamberlain*, p. 228. This being the atmosphere it is not easy to take a balanced view of his capacity.

military affairs. He knew little of Europe and disliked what he knew. He had deep knowledge of British party politics, and represented in a broad way some of the strengths and many of the infirmities of our Island race. He had fought five general elections as leader of the Conservative party and had won three of them. He had a genius for waiting upon events and an imperturbability under adverse criticism. He was singularly adroit in letting events work for him, and capable of seizing the ripe moment when it came. He seemed to me to revive the impressions history gives us of Sir Robert Walpole, without of course the eighteenth-century corruption, and he was master of British politics for nearly as long.

Neville Chamberlain, on the other hand, was alert, businesslike, opinionated and self-confident in a very high degree. Unlike Baldwin, he conceived himself able to comprehend the whole field of Europe, and indeed the world. Instead of a vague but none the less deep-seated intuition, we had now a narrow, sharp-edged efficiency within the limits of the policy in which he believed. Both as Chancellor of the Exchequer and as Prime Minister he kept the tightest and most rigid control upon military expenditure. He was throughout this period the masterful opponent of all emergency measures. He had formed decided judgments about all the political figures of the day, both at home and abroad, and felt himself capable of dealing with them. His all-pervading hope was to go down to history as the great Peace-maker, and for this he was prepared to strive continually in the teeth of facts, and face great risks for himself and his country.[1]

Every man is the prisoner of his environment; and history, so far as it has been written, has dealt hardly with the reputations of Lord Baldwin and Mr Neville Chamberlain because they directed affairs during the rise of Hitler. They were the leaders of a group known to their opponents as 'The Guilty Men',[2] though that phrase is sometimes limited to the 'Men of Munich', who pressed the policy of appeasement after Lord Baldwin's resignation in 1937. Lord Baldwin himself has found an able defender in his son; clearly he was a sympathetic person, but his direction was weak and his control lax. So far, the most that has been said in favour of Mr Neville Chamberlain is that, in a well-worn groove, he was a most efficient administrator. He was much less of a politician and much more of an administrator than any of his immediate predecessors. At the Ministry of Health he brought order into

[1] Winston Churchill, *The Second World War* (2nd ed.), I, pp. 199–200.

[2] Cato, *Guilty Men* (over 200,000 copies were sold).

what had been a chaotic department and solved some of the problems which had been held over for twenty years. As Chancellor of the Exchequer he carried out his father's tariff policy and introduced a system which, whatever the economists may think of its principles, has worked with astonishingly little friction in practice. His methods in the Cabinet of 1931–2 have been thus described by Lord Samuel:

> Neville Chamberlain...was always ready to take the lead, particularly on the economic questions which then held the field and which had always been his special province. His ideas were positive and clear-cut; he was tenacious in pursuit of them, whether in the Cabinet itself, or in committee, or in the conversations that, as in all Governments, were continually proceeding among its members. Courteous and agreeable in manner, Chamberlain was always willing to listen to arguments with a friendly spirit—but a closed mind.[1]

The sting at the end might perhaps be regarded as a reflection of the controversy, which all the Chamberlains had had with all the Liberals for thirty years, over free trade: but Lord Samuel's analysis is in fact supported by Mr Chamberlain's biographer:

> Masterful, confident, and ruled by an instinct for order, he would give a lead, and perhaps impart an edge, on every question. His approach was arduously careful but his mind, once made up, hard to change; he would make relevance a fundamental and have the future mapped out, thus asking his departmental ministers to envisage two-year programmes. His preparation for business was, no doubt, complete. When he fell, his file was filled with thanks from colleagues for the weight and volume of his assistance; 'you cannot know', wrote Ernest Brown, 'what a comfort it was to hard-pressed departmental ministers to know, that, when their subjects have to be discussed, whoever else had not read their papers and digested them, one man had—the Prime Minister'.[2]

A more comprehensive and even more favourable picture has been drawn by another of the 'Men of Munich', Viscount Templewood (in Chamberlain's Cabinet as Sir Samuel Hoare):

> His personal influence was due to his mastery of facts, his clear head and his inherited gift of incisive speech. As Prime Minister, he took the closest possible interest not only in the Foreign Office, but in all the Departments

[1] Lord Samuel, *Memoirs*, p. 215. [2] *Life of Neville Chamberlain*, p. 303.

of State. Being a remarkably quick worker, he was able to keep in touch with every important question, domestic as well as foreign, that concerned the Government. Ministers constantly visited Downing Street to discuss their affairs with him. His relations with the Foreign Office and the Foreign Secretary in no way differed from his relations with other Departments. With the Foreign Secretary, the meetings became particularly frequent in the days of Eden. With Halifax, the coming and going between the two sides of the street never slackened. From time to time, with the full approval of the Foreign Secretary, he would send for Cadogan, the Permanent Under-Secretary of State, just as he would send for the Permanent heads of other offices, also with the full approval of the departmental minister, and discuss with him in detail some urgent question. The civil servants would invariably find that he had already read and mastered any papers that had been circulated on the subject, and that he clearly wished to test and, if necessary, modify his provisional conclusions with the help of their expert knowledge. His reputation in Whitehall was of a Prime Minister who kept abreast of everything that was happening, and was always available to give his personal help in any departmental difficulty. His private secretaries were amazed at his command of intricate detail, and compared the atmosphere of perpetual movement that pervaded Downing Street with the peaceful quiet of his predecessor's regime.

In the Conservative party, his qualities had much the same influence as they had in Whitehall. Like his father before him, he always kept his hand on the party machine. When the party's fortunes were at a low ebb in the days of MacDonald's second administration, he reconditioned the organisation and appointed new men to manage it. The party's policy was constantly in his mind, and no Conservative minister ever took a more detailed interest in election programmes. It was not, therefore, surprising that his position in the party was unassailable.

In the House of Commons, where it was no less secure, it was further strengthened by his talent for debate. A party expects fighting qualities in its leader. Chamberlain delighted his followers not only with his gifts of clear statement and keen argument, but still more, with the evident pleasure that he showed in routing his enemies. Every offensive that the Opposition launched against him he repelled with a devastating counter-attack. Even Churchill's stirring eloquence he was able to meet with close-knit arguments and ready retorts that justified the Government policy and encouraged his followers. Whenever he met the Conservative members of the House of Commons in the party meeting known as the 1922 Committee, and explained to them his line of policy, he invariably received an overwhelming vote of confidence. In the autumn of 1938, for instance, he described to them in detail the steps that he intended to take to reach an agreement, first with Mussolini, and next, with Hitler. I was at the meeting, and I well remember the cheers that greeted his speech. In 1939 there were similar demonstrations of support. Perhaps the most significant was in March 1939, when the party was clamouring for conscription. Nothing could have better proved his hold upon his followers than their acceptance with scarcely a murmur of his plea for further delay, on the ground that it would be dangerous to disturb organised labour until the crisis became more serious. The Government whips and his intimate friends repeatedly assured him that no Conservative Prime Minister had ever had so strong a hold on his party in the House of Commons.[1]

It would seem then that, of all the seventeen Prime Ministers of the last hundred years, Mr Neville Chamberlain approached the nearest to the Peelite tradition, with perhaps the single exception of Mr Gladstone in the Government of 1868 to 1874. Indeed, he had many of the personal characteristics of Sir Robert Peel. But whereas Sir Robert Peel's major decisions were in a field which he had made his own, and where he was so sure of himself that he was prepared to commit the politician's deadliest sin, and to break his party in order to carry them out, Mr Chamberlain's were in a field where he was neither learned nor experienced. Though it is important to give no countenance to the theory that foreign policy is an occult science revealed only to the initiated, and though it is true that the Foreign Office is not necessarily right, it would seem essentially dangerous for a Prime Minister to force his own policy not merely on the Foreign Secretary but also on his departmental advisers. It may fairly be argued that the Peelite tradition does not require a Prime Minister to be a second and superior Foreign Minister: it requires him to keep track of foreign policy, to suggest caution when he is not convinced, to draw attention to internal difficulties that may arise from any particular line of policy, to give judicious advice where it is sought by the Foreign Secretary, to make suggestions that might be departmentally examined, and generally to act as sympathetic critic and helpful adviser. In other words, Mr Disraeli was nearer the Peelite tradition than Mr Chamberlain.

Mr Churchill's task was fundamentally different. The methods that succeed in peace are not suited to war. Happy is the country that can

[1] Viscount Templewood, *Nine Troubled Years*, pp. 375–7.

call out its Palmerstons, its Lloyd Georges and its Churchills in time of war and send them packing when the war is over. In wartime there is one supreme governmental function, which must inevitably be the Prime Minister's personal concern, and all else must be subordinated to it. The items of the Cabinet agenda have a central theme; proposals from the departments which have no close connection with the winning of the war are not irrelevant but subordinate. Mr Asquith and Mr Neville Chamberlain both made the mistake of not putting the Government itself on a war footing.

Mr Churchill made no such mistake. He had himself appointed Minister of Defence by way of a gesture, for his effective power lay in his position as chairman of the Chiefs of Staff Committee. Through the Chiefs of the Staffs orders went direct to the commanders of the armed forces. Nevertheless, matters of policy had still to be settled by the Cabinet, and Mr Churchill's strength lay in the fact that, backed by the advice of the Chiefs of the Staffs, he had the confidence of his colleagues in the Cabinet. He has himself described the situation:

> As confidence grew the War Cabinet intervened less actively in operational matters, though they watched them with close attention and full knowledge. They took almost the whole weight of home and party affairs off my shoulders, thus setting me free to concentrate upon the main theme. With regard to all future operations of importance I always consulted them in good time; but, while they gave careful consideration to the issues involved, they frequently asked not to be informed of dates and details, and indeed on several occasions stopped me when I was about to unfold these to them.[1]

He mentions particularly that some of his messages to President Franklin D. Roosevelt were circulated to the War Cabinet after they had been sent.

> Never did a British Prime Minister receive from Cabinet colleagues the loyal and true aid which I enjoyed during the next five years from these men of all parties in the State. Parliament, while maintaining free and active criticism, gave continuous, overwhelming support to all measures proposed by the Government, and the nation was united and ardent as never before.[2]

[1] Winston Churchill, *The Second World War*, II, p. 18.
[2] *Ibid.* p. 24.

A report by Mr Harry Hopkins to the President of the United States indicates the strength of Mr Churchill's position:

Your 'former Naval person' is not only the Prime Minister, he is the directing force behind the strategy and the conduct of the war in all its essentials. He has an amazing hold on the British people of all classes and groups. He has particular strength both with the military establishments and the working people.[1]

Even so, Mr Churchill was not a dictator. He had not even the personal power of the President of the United States. Anything that was physically possible was politically practicable to him, but only because he had a united War Cabinet, a united Parliament, and a united people behind him. He had therefore to observe the constitutional forms: he needed the consent of his colleagues in Cabinet, and the Cabinet was dependent upon the unswerving support of the House of Commons. As Prime Minister he had not the constitutional power of the President; but equally as Prime Minister he had greater strength, for there were no checks and balances to deter him. It is important to remember that though Mr Churchill had such effective power as no British Prime Minister had had before, he was turned out by the people as soon as the war in Europe was won. The War Cabinet or Parliament could have ejected him at any moment during the preceding five years. Sir Winston Churchill has himself drawn attention to the fact in his story of the dinner at Teheran when President Roosevelt and Mr Stalin were present.[2] Mr Harry Hopkins, in an after-dinner speech, said that 'the provisions of the British Constitution and the powers of the War Cabinet are just whatever Winston Churchill wants them to be at any given moment'. Without taking the joke too seriously, Sir Winston comments that on more than one occasion 'it was with some pride that I reminded my two great comrades...that I was the only one of our trinity who could at any moment be dismissed from power by the vote of a House of Commons freely elected on universal franchise, or could be controlled from day to day by the opinion of a War Cabinet representing all parties in the State'.

[1] Robert E. Sherwood, *The White House Papers of Harry L. Hopkins*, I, p. 257.

[2] Winston Churchill, *The Second World War*, V, pp. 340–1.

If this be remembered, and if it be remembered that Mr Churchill almost always carried his policy in the War Cabinet and invariably in Parliament, the comparison made by Mr Harry Hopkins' biographer of the methods used on H.M.S. *Prince of Wales*, when the Atlantic Charter was agreed, will be illuminating:

The Atlantic Conference gave Hopkins an opportunity to observe more clearly than ever the difference between the American and British systems of democracy. This was the first time he had seen both the President and Prime Minister in operation away from their bases. He remarked on the fact that whereas Roosevelt was completely on his own, subject only to the advice of his immediate and self-selected entourage, which advice he could accept or reject, Churchill was constantly reporting to and consulting the War Cabinet in London, addressing his communications to the Lord Privy Seal, who was then Clement Attlee. During three days more than thirty communications passed between the *Prince of Wales* and Whitehall, and the speed of communication and of action thereon was astonishing to the Americans. For example, on Monday, August 11th at 1.50 p.m. (Argentia time), Churchill filed a cable to London containing the agreed text of the Atlantic Charter, which was then seven points, and describing in detail all the changes suggested and the reasons therefor. Due to the time necessary for coding and decoding and the difference in time between Newfoundland and the United Kingdom, the message did not reach Attlee until shortly after midnight. However, the War Cabinet was ready to go into session at that late hour. At 4.10 a.m. (London time) it cabled its approval of the document word by word and suggested the addition of an eighth point, which Roosevelt heartily approved (it was in line with Freedom from Want) and which was incorporated as Number Five in the Charter.[1]

It must not be thought that speed of this character is always advantageous. It may be that a delay of 24 hours, to enable the Colonial Office to consider the effect of the Charter on the dependent peoples of the Commonwealth, would have been helpful. The point is, however, that the President (holding that the Charter was not a treaty which required ratification by the Senate) pledged the United States, while the War Cabinet, not the Prime Minister, pledged the United Kingdom.

History has still to tell us about the methods of Mr Attlee and Sir Anthony Eden. Lord Attlee's autobiography, *As it Happened*, tells very

[1] Robert E. Sherwood, *The White House Papers of Harry L. Hopkins*, I, p. 362.

little. He was in office continuously, as Deputy Prime Minister and Prime Minister, for the unusual span of eleven years; and as Deputy to Mr Churchill he took the major responsibility for domestic affairs. The fact that he was able to continue for so long shows a capacity for rapid, orderly and efficient work, without fuss or bother, which is rare. That he lacked imagination was, in the Labour party, no disadvantage, for that party usually has too much of it. That he was not a prima donna was also an advantage, for a plain, simple man (but not consciously plain and simple like Mr Baldwin) helped to keep down the incipient conflicts among the 'stars'. There was only one 'split' in the Labour party while Mr Attlee was Prime Minister, and that began while he was in hospital.

It will be seen from this examination of the methods of our Prime Ministers that much depends on the personality of the man himself, the support that he enjoys in his Cabinet, the personalities of the other members of the Cabinet, the strength of its party in the House of Commons and the country, and the political conditions of the time. Given a solid party backing and confidence among party leaders, a Prime Minister wields an authority that a Roman Emperor might envy or a modern dictator strive in vain to emulate; he can indeed 'speak for England', although he must also remember Wales and Scotland. The field of government has, however, grown too vast for Peel's methods to be applied in every department.

As Lord Rosebery said: 'A Prime Minister who is the senior partner in every department as well as president of the whole, who aspires and vibrates through every part, is almost, if not quite, an impossibility. A First Minister is the most that can be hoped for, the chairman and, on most occasions, the spokesman of that Board of Directors which is called the Cabinet; who has the initiation and guidance of large courses of public policy; but who does not, unless specifically invoked, interfere departmentally.'[1] Lord Oxford and Asquith not only quoted this statement with approval, but added: 'No Prime Minister could find time or energy for such a departmental autocracy as Peel appears to have exercised. Lord Palmerston's authority in his Cabinet (though he was to the last one of the most industrious of men) was maintained by

[1] Quoted by Lord Oxford and Asquith, *Fifty Years of Parliament*, II, pp. 185–6.

widely different faculties and methods.'[1] Peel himself, it should be added, had arrived at the same conclusion by the end of his last Government.[2] Peel, too, never had to look after a popular constituency. As Disraeli said in his remarkable character sketch: 'Although forty years in Parliament, it is remarkable that Sir Robert Peel never represented a popular constituency or stood a contested election.'[3]

Nevertheless, the Prime Minister's actual authority has tended to increase. He is not merely *primus inter pares*. He is not even, as Harcourt said, *inter stellas luna minores*. He is, rather, a sun around which planets revolve. Though he may rise to office because of the Queen's choice or the election of his parliamentary colleagues, he owes his majority to the choice of the electorate. Generally, a party obtains office because of a general election. A general election is, primarily, an election of a Prime Minister. The wavering voters who decide elections support neither a party nor a policy, they support a leader. Peel, with unusual prescience, realised in 1834 that this was an inevitable consequence of the first Reform Act. His famous Tamworth Manifesto was, technically, his address to the electors of Tamworth. It was, in substance, an appeal to the people. It failed in 1834, but it succeeded in 1841. Croker said that the election of 1841 was the first that was fought on the principle of voting for a Prime Minister.[4] It was, in fact, a contest between Queen Victoria and Lord Melbourne on the one hand, and Sir Robert Peel on the other.

With the passage of the years, the fact became more obvious. Gladstone said of the election of 1857 that 'it was not an election like that of 1784, when Pitt appealed on the question whether the Crown should be the slave of an oligarchic faction, nor like that of 1831, when Grey sought a judgment on reform, nor like that of 1852, when the issue was the expiring controversy of protection. The country was to decide not upon the Canton river, but whether it would or would not have Palmerston for Prime Minister.'[5] The election of 1859 was again a contest between statesmen, between 'those terrible old men' (to use

[1] Lord Oxford and Asquith, *Fifty Years of Parliament*, II, p. 186.

[2] See a letter to Mr Arbuthnot in 1845 (*Peel Papers*, III, p. 219) and a conversation with Mr Gladstone in 1846 (*Life of Gladstone*, I, pp. 298–300).

[3] Disraeli, *Lord George Bentinck*, p. 225.

[4] *Peel Papers*, II, p. 475.

[5] *Life of Gladstone*, I, p. 564.

Queen Victoria's words), Lord Palmerston and Lord John Russell, on the one hand, and Lord Derby and Mr Disraeli on the other.[1] Palmerston went to the country in 1865, it was said, on the cry of 'Palmerston and no Politics' or 'Palmerston and no Principles'.[2]

With the death or retirement of the old men, elections became a personal contest between Gladstone and Disraeli. Even Lord Russell noted the change, and the Duke of Bedford observed that neither of them was fit for government.[3] Disraeli in 1868 realised that his election address was a manifesto to the nation, and secured Hardy's approval of it.[4] Gladstone in 1874 justified his announcing a new policy in his election address by referring to the Tamworth Manifesto, and secured the Cabinet's approval of large portions of it.[5] In 1880 he was no longer leader, but the Midlothian campaign was an onslaught on Lord Beaconsfield, and the question which electors asked themselves was whether they wished to be governed by Lord Beaconsfield or by Mr Gladstone. Lord Beaconsfield had appealed to them through his election address. Mr Gladstone replied in his election address and from numerous platforms.[6] Mr Gladstone was preferred and became Prime Minister by choice of the people.[7]

It was a necessary consequence that the Prime Minister should tour the country, setting forth his policy, and asking the electors to support his candidates. Queen Victoria, as might be expected, objected to the innovation, and reproved Mr Gladstone in 1886 for speaking outside his constituency, especially at the railway stations.[8] Mr Gladstone replied that he could willingly do without it: but since 1880 the leaders of the Opposition 'have established a rule of what may be called popular agitation by addressing public meetings from time to time at places with which they were not connected. This method was peculiarly marked in the case of Lord Salisbury, as a peer, and this change on the part of the leader of the Opposition has induced Mr Gladstone to deviate on this critical occasion from the rule which he had (he believes) generally or uniformly observed

[1] *Ibid.* I, p. 622.
[2] *Life of the Duke of Devonshire*, I, p. 61. [3] *Life of Gladstone*, II, p. 229.
[4] *Life of Gathorne-Hardy*, I, p. 282.
[5] Guedalla, *The Queen and Mr Gladstone*, I, p. 442; *Life of Gladstone*, II, pp. 485–7.
[6] *Life of Gladstone*, II, pp. 605–6 and 618.
[7] Above, ch. II, p. 25. [8] *Letters of Queen Victoria*, 3rd series, I, p. 149.

in former years'.[1] Mr Gladstone's accusation was literally correct, but, in substance, the 'pilgrimages of passion' began with his own Midlothian campaign in 1880. It may be added that the Queen took a very different view of Mr Joseph Chamberlain's 'pilgrimage of passion' in 1900.[2]

Today, it is not only part of the Prime Minister's duty to his party to set out his policy in his election manifesto and to speak to vast concourses at party meetings; it is his duty, also, to send a letter in support of his candidate at every by-election and, at a general election, to speak to the electorate through the broadcasting system. The general election of 1945 was in fact a personal appeal to the electors by Mr Churchill to re-elect him as Prime Minister, bringing his tail behind him. The Conservative party hoped to 'cash in' on his personal popularity. Every hoarding had a picture of the Prime Minister, headed by the slogan 'Help him finish the job'. Underneath in comparatively small letters was the almost irrelevant injunction to 'Vote for Bloggs'. There was no Conservative party manifesto, because Mr Churchill issued one of his own, beginning very appropriately with the word 'I'. The Prime Minister gave four of the ten broadcasts allowed to supporters of the Government. He conducted what Mr Gladstone had called 'popular agitation' on a large scale, travelling from Chequers to Edinburgh (mostly through carefully chosen marginal constituencies) by car and special train making party speeches. Back in London he took three drives through the inner and outer suburbs, speaking on several occasions each evening. Two days before the election he spoke to an audience of 20,000 in Walthamstow Stadium. Candidates sometimes went so far as to ignore their party labels and to call themselves 'Churchill candidates'. The newspapers said that the issue lay between 'Churchill and Chaos', or 'Churchill and Laski', Mr Harold Laski being the current bogyman. The electorate was, in other words, asked to choose for or against the Prime Minister. They chose against.

It is possible that the Conservatives overplayed their hand, though subsequent reflection suggests that they would have lost in any event, because opinion, especially among the young men and women in the armed forces, was moving against them. The Labour party had no

[1] *Letters of Queen Victoria*, 3rd series, I, pp. 149–50.

[2] *Life of Joseph Chamberlain*, III, p. 508.

comparable star and therefore played up 'the Party', with Mr Attlee being driven round by Mrs Attlee in the family four-seater like any other common man. In 1951 the 'cult of personality' was less in evidence even among the Conservatives; and in 1955 the election was so tame that many forgot to vote and many more could not be bothered. Nevertheless, those who did vote knew that they were voting for a Prime Minister and cared very little about Bloggs.

The result of this sort of electioneering, necessarily, is to strengthen the hands of the Prime Minister against his colleagues in the Government and in Parliament. Since he has so much personal support, he is perhaps essential, and certainly useful, to the Government. As such, he is able, within limits, to dictate policy. Even Mr MacDonald in 1935, though without a party, was able to secure terms from his successor that his personal parliamentary support could not alone justify. Yet, in the last resort, his power depends upon his party: for he goes to the country not as an individual but as the leader of his party. His personal prestige is one of the elements that make for party cohesion. Loyalty is one of the political virtues. His prestige is, too, one of the elements that make for party success. But without his party he is nothing. When Peel lost his party in 1845 he reigned on sufferance till he had passed the Corn Laws Bill, and was then immediately ejected. Mr Gladstone returned in 1892 because he had kept his party. Mr Lloyd George, in spite of his great abilities, was never, after 1921, a likely Prime Minister. Mr MacDonald remained in office after 1932 only because it was considered necessary to retain, not his personal prestige, but the fiction of non-party government.

The Prime Minister's power in office depends in part on his personality, in part on his personal prestige, and in part upon his party support. But his relations with his colleagues depend also upon the substantial powers that appertain to his office. With the Queen's consent, he appoints and dismisses ministers. With the like consent, he exercises a wide patronage; and he has a right to be consulted on the more important appointments made by other ministers. He is constantly consulted by ministers on the major problems of their departments; and he is, usually, in particularly close contact with the Foreign Office.[1] Subject

[1] Cf. Winston Churchill, *The Second World War*, I, p. 215; Viscount Templewood, *Nine Troubled Years*, p. 375; etc.

to appeal to the Cabinet, he settles disputes between departments. He convenes and presides over the informal meetings of ministers which decide common action by their departments. He sets up bodies, like the pre-war Committee of Imperial Defence and Economic Advisory Council, which determine the common action of departments within their terms of reference. In particular, he presides over the Defence Committee, which prepares plans for the co-ordination of departmental activity in the event of a war. He controls the Cabinet Secretariat and is consulted by ministers as to the matters which ought to be brought before the Cabinet. He is responsible for seeing that the departments carry out Cabinet decisions. In matters of emergency, he authorises the departments to take action on matters which ought, if there were time, to be brought before the Cabinet. He is the channel of communication between the Queen and the Cabinet, though other ministers communicate with the Queen on matters affecting their departments, and the minister in attendance, if any, expresses general opinions. He is in direct communication with the other Prime Ministers of the Commonwealth, and presides at their meetings. He sometimes receives foreign ambassadors, and sometimes represents the British Government at international conferences. He receives deputations on matters of general political importance. He is leader of his own parliamentary party and must therefore maintain contact with his supporters in Parliament. If, as is no longer usual, he is Leader of the House of Commons, he is, subject to the determination of priority of proposals by the Cabinet, in control of the business of the House, through the Government whips. He answers questions in Parliament on matters of general policy. He is expected to speak in general policy debates in the House of Commons. As leader of the parliamentary party he is, generally, leader of the party outside. In that capacity, he is in charge of the central party machine and takes a prominent part in political propaganda. Some of these functions are discussed elsewhere in this book;[1] others are discussed in the present chapter.

[1] For the appointment of ministers, see above, ch. III; for the patronage, see below, ch. XIV; for the Cabinet, see below, ch. IX; for the Cabinet Secretariat, see below, ch. IX; for the Defence Committee, see below, ch. X; for his relations with the Queen, see below, ch. XII; for his relations with Parliament, see below, ch. XV.

It is obvious that these manifold functions make the office of Prime Minister a full-time occupation. The Prime Minister is usually First Lord of the Treasury, and must hold that office if he wishes to draw the £10,000 provided by the Ministers of the Crown Act, 1937. If he is not First Lord but holds another office, or if he is merely Prime Minister, he draws £5000 a year like other Cabinet Ministers. Some Prime Ministers have taken executive office either in substitution for or in addition to the office of First Lord. Pitt, Perceval and Canning provide early precedents of Prime Ministers who were also Chancellors of the Exchequer. Peel was also Chancellor of the Exchequer in 1834–5. Disraeli said in 1868 that the pressure of work made the junction of the two offices impossible,[1] but Mr Gladstone became Chancellor of the Exchequer after the resignation of Mr Robert Lowe in consequence of the Post Office scandals in 1873 and he again held the office between 1880 and 1882. Mr Baldwin retained the office for a short time after he became Prime Minister in 1923. In each case the Prime Minister was also First Lord of the Treasury.[2]

In 1885 Lord Salisbury was Foreign Secretary as well as Prime Minister. He proposed that Sir Stafford Northcote, as the Leader of the House of Commons, should become First Lord of the Treasury. But Lord Randolph Churchill objected to having Northcote as leader, and the latter went to the House of Lords with an earldom and was placated by being made First Lord and the second minister in the Government.[3] Lord Salisbury's original intention was carried out when Lord Randolph Churchill resigned in 1886. Lord Salisbury again became Foreign Secretary, and Mr W. H. Smith became First Lord of the Treasury and Leader of the House of Commons. The same arrangement was made in 1895, Lord Salisbury being at the Foreign Office and Mr Balfour being First Lord of the Treasury.[4] Mr MacDonald was both First Lord of the

[1] *Letters of Queen Victoria*, 2nd series, I, p. 500.

[2] Since both the First Lord and the Chancellor of the Exchequer are Lords Commissioners of the Treasury, there was an interesting discussion in 1873 as to whether Mr Gladstone had accepted a new office involving re-election. See *Life of Gladstone*, II, pp. 465–72.

[3] *Life of Robert, Marquis of Salisbury*, III, pp. 139–40; for the difficulties of distribution of functions which the original scheme might have caused see *Life of Sir Stafford Northcote*, p. 358.

[4] *Life of Robert, Marquis of Salisbury*, III, p. 339.

Treasury and Foreign Secretary in 1924, but the example was not one to be followed. He was without governmental experience and, at his initial audience, George V declared himself

> inclined to wonder whether Mr Ramsay MacDonald had fully considered the heavy responsibilities and duties incurred by undertaking the office of Secretary of State for Foreign Affairs, in addition to that of Prime Minister. The King referred to the case of Lord Salisbury who, in spite of his great knowledge of foreign affairs, found it difficult to carry on the duties of both offices: indeed he did very little of the work of the Prime Minister, whereas nowadays the latter's position in itself and its heavy responsibilities must be a serious tax upon anyone holding that office.[1]

The King's warning proved to be justified. As the King's biographer has said:

> Mr MacDonald's achievements as Foreign Secretary were quick, startling and beneficial. It is improbable that any man could so rapidly have altered the whole tone of international relations. But for these achievements he paid a formidable price. The effort of those nine months was so gigantic that it damaged his health; his powers of assimilation, memory and concentration were seriously overstrained. The pressure of external affairs prevented him, moreover, from devoting to internal politics the close attention that they merited; mistakes were made. Above all, the cloud of overwork that hid the Prime Minister from his colleagues and supporters produced an impression of misty and even conceited aloofness—an impression which, as it hardened into a grievance, created an ever-widening rift between Mr MacDonald and the rank and file of his own party.[2]

In 1931–5 Mr Baldwin was both First Lord of the Treasury and Lord Privy Seal, but the latter office imposes no duties. From 1940 to 1945 Mr Churchill was both First Lord and Minister of Defence, but there are no serious party troubles in wartime; nor was there an Opposition to answer; and Mr Churchill could leave most questions of internal politics to his colleagues. Mr Attlee was Minister of Defence until 1946 and Mr Churchill again took that office in 1951 and held it until his retirement.

Charles James Fox declared that the man who held the headship of the Treasury must be the most important minister because he controlled the patronage of the Crown and the Secret Service money. But

[1] Nicolson, *King George V*, p. 385. [2] *Ibid.* p. 388.

that statement referred to a time when the House of Commons was controlled by bribes, pensions and 'honours'. The Prime Minister's control over his colleagues is derived, not from any office known to the law at all, but from the office of Prime Minister, which is not so known. It is true that Lord Beaconsfield signed the Treaty of Berlin as Prime Minister, that letters patent of 1905 confer a precedence upon the Prime Minister as such, and that the Chequers Estate Act, 1917, refers to 'the person holding the office popularly known as Prime Minister'. But these are casual recognitions of a constitutional situation, not the legalisation of that situation. His powers derive from, and are limited by, constitutional conventions.

§2. *The Dismissal of Ministers*

The Prime Minister's power of appointing ministers with the consent of the Queen and his power to dissolve a Government by a personal resignation are referred to in ch. III. He possesses also the power to advise the Sovereign to dismiss a minister. According to law, the minister holds his office at the pleasure of the Crown. He can, therefore, be dismissed, according to law, at any moment: and this prerogative is exercised solely on the advice of the Prime Minister. Such advice would be required only in the most extreme cases, where the minister insisted on retaining office and would not allow the Prime Minister to say that he had resigned. A dismissal is a declaration of weakness which necessarily has repercussions in the House of Commons and in the constituencies. The minister dismissed may have support in the House or even in the Cabinet. If a sufficient section of the House supports him, the Government will be defeated. If a sufficient section of the Cabinet supports him, the Cabinet will be broken up. In all normal cases the ministers concerned would resign when asked to do so, and in many they would offer their resignations without being asked. Particularly would this be so when some embarrassment had been caused to the Government by a decision for which the minister was actually or technically responsible, like Mr Lowe and Mr Ayrton in 1873, Colonel Seely in 1914, Mr Montagu in 1917, Mr Austen Chamberlain in 1917, Sir Samuel Hoare in 1935 and Sir Thomas Dugdale in 1954. It must be remembered, too, that the Prime Minister's decision to bring about a change of ministers is not necessarily an accusation of incompetence or bad administration: it may be due to political conditions. A minister always holds his office 'at the disposal of' the Prime Minister, so that he may be said to have resigned—and the newspapers will announce that he has resigned—when he knows nothing whatever about it. There are parts of the world where no public servant is ever 'dismissed' because 'discontinued' is not so harsh a term; similarly in Britain a minister is not dismissed, he 'resigns in order to facilitate a reconstruction of the Government'.

The classic precedent for the dismissal of a minister occurred in 1851. As early as 1848 Queen Victoria was anxious for the removal of Lord Palmerston from the Foreign Office to some other department because of her fundamental disagreement with his policy. Lord John Russell explained that the Cabinet was in general agreement with that policy, although he frequently disagreed with Palmerston's mode of expression, and that in any case they could not afford to risk Palmerston's hostility.[1] The Queen's complaints, first, that she could not agree with many of Palmerston's drafts and, secondly, that frequently they were sent without her prior approval, continued throughout 1849, 1850, and the early months of 1851. Early in 1850, Baron Stockmar[2] advised the Queen that 'having given once her sanction to a measure, the minister who, in the execution of such measure alters or modifies it arbitrarily, commits an act of dishonesty towards the Crown which the Queen has an undoubted constitutional right to visit with the dismissal of that minister'.[3] Later in the same year the question of removing Lord Palmerston from the Foreign Office was considered by Lord John Russell and Lord Lansdowne in consultation with the Queen and Prince Albert.[4] Palmerston refused to move to another office unless there were some reason for it, such as his taking the lead in the House of Commons. He added that 'if the Queen or the Cabinet were dissatisfied with his management of the Foreign Affairs, they had a right to demand his

[1] *Letters of Queen Victoria*, 1st series, II, pp. 231–3.

[2] The views of Baron Stockmar on British constitutional questions are of no value, except as indicating what the Queen and Prince Albert believed to be the constitutional position. See below, pp. 343–4.

[3] *Letters of Queen Victoria*, 1st series, II, p. 282.

[4] *Ibid.* 1st series, II, pp. 289–90, 309–12.

resignation, and he would give it, but they could not ask him to lower himself in public estimation'.[1] As Palmerston had just defended his foreign policy triumphantly in the House of Commons, this was the last thing that Lord John wanted. Accordingly, Palmerston remained at the Foreign Office, but the Queen laid down in a memorandum the duty of the Foreign Secretary to keep her informed, to send the drafts for her approval, and to state distinctly to what her sanction was required. If a draft was arbitrarily altered or modified, she would be entitled to exercise her right of dismissing the minister.[2] The central part of this memorandum was copied almost word for word from Baron Stockmar's memorandum. Lord John Russell sent the Queen's memorandum to Lord Palmerston, who agreed to abide by it.[3]

There was little further difficulty until the arrival of Kossuth in England in the autumn of 1851. The Queen asked Lord John Russell to try to prevent Lord Palmerston from receiving Kossuth. This Russell refused to do,[4] but he appears to have changed his mind and 'positively requested' Palmerston not to receive Kossuth.[5] Palmerston at once replied: 'I do not choose to be dictated to as to who I may or may not receive in my own house; and...I shall use my own discretion in this matter. You will, of course, use yours as to the composition of your Government.'[6] In consequence Russell advised the Queen 'to command Lord Palmerston not to receive M. Kossuth'.[7] But he thought better of it, decided to consult the Cabinet first, and wrote to Lord Palmerston that the matter would be brought before the Cabinet.[8] The Cabinet agreed with Russell and Palmerston gave way.[9] Nevertheless, he consented to receive at the Foreign Office some deputations with addresses which spoke of the Emperors of Austria and Russia as 'odious and detestable assassins'. At the Queen's request the matter was brought before the Cabinet, who expressed regret that Palmerston had

[1] *Ibid.* 1st series, II, pp. 313–14.
[2] *Ibid.* 1st series, II, p. 315; the actual terms are set out below, p. 365.
[3] *Ibid.* 1st series, II, pp. 315–16.
[4] *Ibid.* 1st series, II, pp. 392–3.
[5] *Life of Lord John Russell*, II, p. 133.
[6] *Ibid.*
[7] *Letters of Queen Victoria*, 1st series, II, p. 393.
[8] *Ibid.* 1st series, II, pp. 394–5; *Life of Lord John Russell*, II, p. 134.
[9] *Life of Lord John Russell*, II, p. 134.

not ascertained the terms of the addresses, but declined to come to any formal resolution.[1]

Almost immediately the decisive event happened. When the news of Louis Napoleon's *coup d'état* reached England, the Queen at once said that the British Government should stand aloof and express no opinion. Russell and the Cabinet agreed, and Palmerston sent a despatch accordingly. But when the ambassador communicated its terms to the French minister, he received the reply that Lord Palmerston had already expressed approval of the *coup d'état* in a conversation with the French ambassador. The British ambassador reported this in a despatch which came before the Queen,[2] and she at once asked Lord John Russell for information.[3] After five days Lord Palmerston gave an explanation of his views of events in France.[4] Lord John Russell replied that the question was not as to events in France, but as to the action of the Foreign Secretary in expressing an opinion, which would be taken as the opinion of the British Government, in direct contradiction to a Cabinet decision. He said, therefore, that he had come to the conclusion 'that the conduct of foreign affairs can be left no longer in your hands with advantage to the country', and offered Lord Palmerston the Lord-Lieutenancy of Ireland, with or without a peerage.[5] Palmerston declined the offer and stated: 'I... shall be prepared to give up the seals of the Foreign Office whenever you inform me that my successor is ready to receive them.'[6] The Queen accepted Russell's advice and Palmerston's resignation.[7] The Cabinet also approved Russell's action.[8]

According to a footnote in the *Letters of Queen Victoria*,[9] Prince Albert wrote to Lord John Russell when the Prime Minister communicated his advice to the Queen, saying that the Queen 'had contemplated dismissing Lord Palmerston herself, but naturally shrank from using the power of the Crown, as her action would have been criticised without the possibility of making a public defence'. This

[1] *Life of Lord John Russell*, II, p. 137.

[2] The despatches are in Ashley, *Life of Viscount Palmerston*, I, pp. 289–99.

[3] *Letters of Queen Victoria*, 1st series, II, p. 412.

[4] Ashley, *Life of Viscount Palmerston*, I, pp. 300–306.

[5] *Life of Lord John Russell*, II, p. 139.

[6] *Ibid.* II, p. 140.

[7] *Letters of Queen Victoria*, 1st series, II, p. 415.

[8] *Ibid.* 1st series, II, p. 418.

[9] *Ibid.* 1st series, II, p. 416.

passage was omitted from the letter as published in the *Life of the Prince Consort*.[1] The notion that the Sovereign could, without the consent of the Prime Minister, dismiss a minister, is without foundation. In this instance such action would at once have brought the Crown into conflict with the House of Commons, if not with the Government. The idea is probably the product of Baron Stockmar's unqualified statement in the previous year. Baron Stockmar, as is shown elsewhere, was a dangerous adviser.[2]

Lord Palmerston himself stated the correct doctrine in the House of Commons. 'I do not dispute', he said, 'the right of the noble Lord [John Russell] to remove any Members of the Government whom he may think it better to remove than to retain in the Cabinet.'[3] He criticised Lord John Russell not for his dismissal, but for assuming that every act of the Foreign Secretary must be previously approved by the Cabinet.[4]

This precedent certainly established the right of the Prime Minister, with the Sovereign's assent, to dismiss a minister (or, what comes to the same thing, to demand his resignation). But it also shows the difficulty of exercising the right. Lord John Russell took the final step only after a long series of incidents. Each time he hesitated because he believed that Palmerston's secession would split the Cabinet. The resignation was, in the end, the death-warrant of the Government, for Palmerston had his 'tit for tat' within three weeks of the meeting of Parliament; the Government was defeated and resigned.

It is not surprising that subsequent precedents are few. There was certainly a case for the removal of Mr Ayrton from the Office of Works in 1870, and the Queen suggested it.[5] In 1872 Mr Gladstone himself considered dismissal. But he reminded the Queen that 'before a public servant of this class can properly be dismissed, there must be not only a sufficient case against him, but a case of which the sufficiency can be made intelligible and palpable [to] the world'.[6] The motive force behind

[1] *Life of the Prince Consort*, II, pp. 418–19.

[2] See below, pp. 343–4.

[3] *Parl. Deb.* 3rd series, vol. 119, col. 112.

[4] For Palmerston's defence, see Ashley, *Life of Viscount Palmerston*, I, ch. VII, where a better defence was made than in the House of Commons.

[5] Guedalla, *The Queen and Mr Gladstone*, I, pp. 229–30.

[6] *Letters of Queen Victoria*, 2nd series, II, p. 225.

the changes consequent upon the Post Office scandals of 1873 is not clear, but it seems that Mr Gladstone himself decided the transfer of Mr Lowe to the Home Office and of Mr Ayrton to the office of Judge-Advocate-General and accepted the resignation of Mr Monsell.[1]

In 1875 Mr Disraeli decided to dismiss Sir Charles Adderley from the Presidency of the Board of Trade but, finding rearrangement difficult, did not do so.[2] In 1884 Mr Gladstone desired to remove Lord Carlingford from the office of Lord Privy Seal, not because of any misconduct or disagreement, but in order to make way for Lord Rosebery. Lord Carlingford, however, refused to resign. Sir William Harcourt then stated the constitutional position:

> I confess I have never doubted that Cabinet offices were held *durante bene placito* of a Prime Minister. No doubt when it comes to an open breach as between Pitt and Thurlow the direct interposition of the Crown may have to be invoked, and the removal would be at the Sovereign's command. But in the ordinary working of a Cabinet I have always supposed that the Prime Minister had the same authority to modify it as he has to construct it....
>
> In my opinion it is no more open to the head of a department in the Cabinet to say to the potter that he will be an *urceus* or an *amphora* than it is to the Commander of a Division to say to the Commander in Chief that he will not be superseded in the command by another officer. The interests at stake are far too serious to admit of the doctrine of fixity of tenure.
>
> That this must be so is obvious because the First Minister can always say to any other of the Administration, 'if you don't go, I will'. But it is incredible that things should ever be pushed to such a point as that. Good feeling as well as good sense forbids it. And a man must be pachydermatous indeed who is incapable of accepting the first hint that his room is wanted whether he is on a visit or in a Cabinet....[3]

It was in connection with this case that Harcourt wrote to Morley that Mr Gladstone 'entertains great doubts as to the right of a Prime Minister to require a Cabinet Minister to resign. I know that he tried it in one case for convenience of reconstruction; he was point blank refused, and acquiesced.'[4] Lord Carlingford remained in office until the end of the year, when he resigned.

[1] *Life of Gladstone*, II, pp. 460–4; *Letters of Queen Victoria*, 2nd series, II, pp. 270–6; Guedalla, *The Queen and Mr Gladstone*, I, pp. 420–6.

[2] *Life of Lord Norton*, p. 222.

[3] *Life of Sir William Harcourt*, I, pp. 508–9.

[4] *Ibid.* II, p. 610.

Lord Salisbury in 1886 in effect dismissed Lord Iddesleigh from his post as Foreign Secretary. Lord Randolph Churchill having resigned, it became desirable to bring in Mr Goschen as Chancellor of the Exchequer. But Mr Goschen very strongly urged that Lord Iddesleigh should not stay at the Foreign Office. Lord Salisbury decided to take the Foreign Office himself, and he justified his supersession of Iddesleigh, both to Iddesleigh and to the Queen, by asserting that it was necessary to give Mr W. H. Smith, as Leader of the House of Commons, an office without administrative duties, and the office of First Lord of the Treasury was the only office available. Actually, Lord Iddesleigh first learned of his supersession through a newspaper report.[1]

In 1890 Lord Salisbury desired the resignation of Mr Matthews from the Home Office. He spoke to the Lord Chancellor, who was the Home Secretary's personal friend. In communicating with the Queen, he said:

> At present Lord Salisbury does not think that a bare dismissal would be admissible. It would be looked upon as very harsh, and would beget numberless intrigues. When Mr Gladstone got rid of Mr Bruce, who was also an unsuccessful Home Secretary, he put him into another office, the Presidency of the Council. Mr Walpole resigned in 1867, at a time when he was very unpopular on account of the mistakes he had made; but his resignation, to all appearances, was quite voluntary. There is no instance of dismissal;[2] and it would require some open and palpable error to justify it.[3]

The tactics by which Mr Balfour rid himself of some of his free trade colleagues in 1903 produced from Lord George Hamilton, one of the sufferers, the comment that: 'A Prime Minister has an undoubted right to request any of his colleagues, whose presence in his Cabinet is, in his opinion or judgment, prejudicial to the efficiency or policy of the Government, to resign his office.'[4]

In 1911 the reluctance of the Admiralty to accept reforms on the lines of the War Office decided Mr Asquith to transfer Mr McKenna from the Admiralty to the Home Office and Mr Churchill from the Board of Trade to the Admiralty.[5] How Mr Lloyd George regarded

[1] *Life of Robert, Marquis of Salisbury*, III, pp. 339–42.

[2] Technically, Lord Palmerston resigned in 1851; but it is difficult not to call it a 'dismissal'.

[3] *Letters of Queen Victoria*, 3rd series, I, p. 646.

[4] *Life of the Duke of Devonshire*, II, p. 351.

[5] *Life of Lord Oxford and Asquith*, I, p. 347.

his powers can be judged from the draft of a letter, never sent because Mr Bonar Law censored it, to Mr Hayes Fisher:

I regret that I have been forced to the conclusion that in the conduct of your office you have shown such lack of judgment and want of efficiency that I can no longer accept your services as a member of the Government. I am advising the King to this effect and as to the appointment of a successor in your office. I should be greatly obliged, therefore, if you would place your resignation in my hands for submission to His Majesty as soon as possible, as I wish your successor to begin work tomorrow at latest.[1]

Mr Hayes Fisher being a Conservative, Mr Bonar Law intervened; Mr Lloyd George minuted: 'The P.M. doesn't mind if he [Hayes Fisher] is drowned in Malmsey wine, but he must be a dead chicken tonight.' A less peremptory letter was sent; Mr Hayes Fisher was raised to the peerage and made a director of the Suez Canal Company.[2]

Mr Churchill records that he attended a committee meeting over which the Secretary of State for Air presided. A note came from Downing Street for the Air Minister. 'He desired us to continue our discussions, and left at once. He never returned. He had been dismissed by Mr Chamberlain.'[3] Five years later, probably, Mr Churchill himself would have telephoned the dismissal or sent a messenger. Sir John Reith was asked by letter, delivered by motor cycle, to place his office at the Prime Minister's disposal, which he did, and joined the Royal Navy instead.[4] Mr Attlee, on the other hand, had a conscience:

On a number of occasions I had to tell ministers that the time had come when they must give place to younger men and, in one or two instances, to tell them that I thought they were not quite up to their job. I should like to record that, with the exception of one person who was clearly unfit, all my colleagues took my decision with complete loyalty and never displayed the least resentment. Nevertheless, it is a distasteful thing to have to say to an old friend and colleague that it is time for him to make room for a younger man and I am eternally grateful to my colleagues for their magnanimity.[5]

The conclusion seems to be that the Prime Minister possesses the right to ask a minister to resign or to accept another office. This right

[1] Blake, *The Unknown Prime Minister*, p. 382. [2] *Ibid.* p. 383.

[3] Winston Churchill, *The Second World War*, I, p. 208.

[4] Lord Reith, *Into the Wind*, pp. 442–5.

[5] Attlee, *As It Happened*, p. 155.

arises from the necessary pre-eminence of the Prime Minister in his Cabinet. It is, usually, not necessary to use the Crown's power of dismissal. There is a tradition—a kind of public-school fiction—that no minister desires office, but that he is prepared to carry on for the public good. That tradition implies a duty to resign when a hint is given. But, in the last resort, the Prime Minister could advise the Queen to dismiss any recalcitrant minister. As Sir Robert Peel said: 'Under all ordinary circumstances, if there were a serious difference of opinion between the Prime Minister and one of his colleagues, and that difference could not be reconciled by an amicable understanding, the result would be the retirement of the colleague, not of the Prime Minister.'[1]

Conflict between the Prime Minister and a colleague is, however, a rare occurrence. There is, usually, on the one hand confidence in the colleague and on the other hand loyalty to the Prime Minister. The Prime Minister rarely has either the time or the desire to interfere in departmental matters. If a colleague cannot be trusted, he will not be appointed. If he proves inefficient, a hint is usually enough to produce a resignation. If he proves ineffective in a particular office, it is usually possible to obtain his consent to a transfer, provided that it is possible to make it appear a promotion or that some good reason can be assigned for it. The offices of Lord President of the Council and Lord Privy Seal are very useful for this purpose. They give the holder a high precedence, and they involve no contact with major administration. In the last resort there is always the House of Lords.

§3. *The Control of Administration*

The function of the Prime Minister is primarily one of giving advice when it is asked. Plans are discussed with him long before the stage at which they can be brought before the Cabinet. 'There are two persons with whom a Minister ought to be able to toss his thoughts and policy', said Sir Edward Grey.[2] 'One is his chief private secretary, and the other is the Prime Minister.'

In particular the Foreign Secretary is usually in close touch with the Prime Minister. The Foreign Office differs from other departments in

[1] Report from the Select Committee on Official Salaries (1850), p. 36.
[2] Grey, *Twenty-five Years*, I, p. 119.

that matters of political importance are of almost daily occurrence. It is impracticable to bring every item before the Cabinet.[1] That body can do no more than lay down the general lines of action and trust to the Foreign Secretary and the Prime Minister to conform. As Sir Charles Wood wrote to Lord John Russell, with reference to Lord Palmerston's action in 1846, 'the Cabinet cannot interfere, for the mischief is done before we hear of anything; and a Cabinet is too cumbersome a machine for such work'. Therefore he wrote to impress upon Lord John Russell the necessity of taking more into his own hands 'the direction of the *detailed steps* of foreign matters with France'.[2]

Lord Grey, according to the same minister, had exercised a close control over Palmerston.[3] Lord John Russell was compelled to do the same. He frequently amended Lord Palmerston's despatches.[4] Sometimes, even, he directed Lord Palmerston as to what he was to say.[5] In 1850 he informed Lord Palmerston that all drafts should have his concurrence before they were submitted to the Queen.[6] In the same year he ordered Lord Palmerston to withdraw a note which Palmerston had already sent off without consultation.[7]

The arrangement by which despatches went to the Prime Minister before submission to the Queen was mentioned to Lord Derby in 1852.[8] But after the fall of Lord Palmerston the practice became one of consultation rather than of control. The Duke of Argyll, who was in Lord Aberdeen's and Lord Palmerston's Cabinets, said: 'It is the system of all Cabinets to which I have belonged that the Secretary for Foreign Affairs is in close personal relations with the Prime Minister, and that a great deal of the Foreign Office business is settled between them, without its being referred to the Cabinet at all.'[9] During the Russo-Turkish War, the lack of sympathy between Lord Derby at the

[1] The important telegrams are circulated to the Cabinet, but prior sanction is obtained only for major developments of policy.

[2] *Life of Lord John Russell*, II, p. 4.

[3] *Ibid.*

[4] For examples, see *Later Correspondence of Lord John Russell*, I, pp. 357–8; *Letters of Queen Victoria*, 1st series, II, pp. 221–2; *ibid.* p. 262; *ibid.* pp. 276–7; *ibid.* pp. 277–8; *ibid.* pp. 398–9.

[5] *Letters of Queen Victoria*, 1st series, II, pp. 212–15.

[6] *Ibid.* 1st series, II, pp. 263–4.

[7] *Ibid.* 1st series, II, p. 322.

[8] *Ibid.* 1st series, II, p. 453.

[9] Duke of Argyll, *Autobiography and Memoirs*, I, p. 445.

Foreign Office and the rest of the Cabinet compelled Lord Beaconsfield to interfere widely in foreign affairs and, after January 1878, Lord Derby became 'almost an under-secretary'.[1]

Mr Gladstone's practice may be stated in his own words. To Sir William Harcourt he said in 1894: 'I was made habitually privy in the time of Clarendon and Granville to the ideas as well as the business of the Foreign Minister, and in consequence the business of that department, if and when introduced to the Cabinet, came before it with a joint support as a general rule.'[2] With Lord Rosebery at the Foreign Office the same practice was followed. He was 'in almost daily communication with the Prime Minister, often by brief notes, oftener still by stepping across Downing Street to secure five minutes of advice'.[3]

Lord Salisbury held a different view. 'The Prime Minister', he said, 'may lay down the broad principles of foreign policy, but those principles can only be carried out by the judicious execution of a number of details, and if the Prime Minister attempts to interfere in these latter, the only result is confusion.'[4] This statement was made in 1886 when, for a short time, Lord Salisbury was not his own Foreign Secretary. It may be doubted whether it is consistent with experience. Obviously the Prime Minister has not the same control of foreign policy as the Foreign Secretary. It is the latter who distinguishes between principles and details and he consults the Prime Minister on the former only. Lord Salisbury himself pointed to the importance of the Prime Minister's control when, early in the same year, he told Queen Victoria that Lord Rosebery ought to bring as little as possible before the Cabinet and settle it with Mr Gladstone and the Queen. 'Nothing', he said, 'was ever settled satisfactorily in the Cabinet.'[5] The Queen adopted his advice and, almost, his language.[6] Later in the year, indeed, she reminded Lord Salisbury, who was again Prime Minister, of his former advice.[7]

The Queen, of course, trusted Lord Salisbury and (with qualifica-

[1] *Life of Disraeli*, II, p. 1119.

[2] *Life of Sir William Harcourt*, II, p. 270; see also *Life of Sir Edward Cook*, pp. 148–9.

[3] *Life of Lord Rosebery*, I, p. 277.

[4] *Life of Robert, Marquis of Salisbury*, III, pp. 313–14.

[5] *Letters of Queen Victoria*, 3rd series, I, p. 45.

[6] *Ibid.* 3rd series, I, p. 48.

[7] *Ibid.* 3rd series, I, p. 211.

tions) Lord Rosebery. She distrusted the foreign policy of Cabinets, especially Liberal Cabinets. The Cabinet can and does lay down the general tendency of foreign policy, but for matters of urgency the Foreign Secretary must rely on consultation with the Prime Minister.[1] He can also consult the Prime Minister on semi-technical matters which do not appear to be of sufficient importance to demand Cabinet sanction. The most notorious example is that of the 'conversations' between French and British military advisers which began in 1905 under the Conservative Government. They were renewed by the Liberal Government by agreement between the Prime Minister, the Foreign Secretary and the Secretary of State for War.[2] Though of a purely technical nature they involved political issues, for their assumption was that Germany would attack France and that Great Britain would support France. The fact of consultation did not imply a promise of support to France, but it necessarily led French ministers to assume that such support would be forthcoming. Lord Grey therefore considered, in 1925, that they ought to have been brought before the Cabinet.[3] But neither the Prime Minister nor Lord Ripon, who represented the Foreign Office in the House of Lords, and who was informed of them, suggested a Cabinet discussion.[4] They must have become known to the members of the Committee of Imperial Defence, but Mr Asquith did not hear of them until 1911, and they then seemed to him to be 'rather dangerous'.[5] They became known to other members of the Cabinet in 1912 and it was then agreed to secure a statement from France that Great Britain was not pledged to action by them.[6] In 1914 further conversations took place with Russian military officers, and this time Cabinet approval was obtained.[7] There can be no doubt that the conversations were one of the elements that compelled the majority of the Cabinet to agree in 1914 that Great Britain was 'pledged in honour' to France, though the actual *casus belli*, which was accepted by all but

[1] A standing Cabinet Committee is another method: see below, p. 241.

[2] Grey, *Twenty-five Years*, I, pp. 74–6.

[3] It is said in the *Life of Lord Oxford and Asquith*, I, pp. 348–9, that the Cabinet was always consulted, but that ministers absorbed in their own departments paid little attention to memoranda until the Agadir crisis frightened them. The evidence of Lord Grey, Lord Morley and Mr Lloyd George is to the contrary.

[4] *Ibid.* I, pp. 86–7.

[5] *Ibid.* I, pp. 94–5.

[6] *Ibid.* I, pp. 96–9.

[7] *Ibid.* I, p. 285.

two of the Cabinet as compelling British intervention, was the infringement by Germany of Belgian neutrality.[1]

The telegram by which, on 30 July 1914, Sir Edward Grey refused to bind Great Britain to neutrality on terms suggested by Bethmann-Hollweg was sent off with Mr Asquith's sanction, but was not submitted beforehand to the Cabinet. It was approved by the Cabinet the same afternoon.[2] The ultimatum to Germany in 1914 was sent also without prior Cabinet approval, though with the consent of the Prime Minister:[3] but it was necessarily consequent upon previous Cabinet decisions.[4] Thus, the Prime Minister's function here was to see that the action of the Foreign Secretary was consistent with the Cabinet decisions. His action was subsequently approved by the Cabinet, though two ministers resigned. As soon as war broke out, foreign policy was subservient to war policy. The dilatory nature of the Cabinet system compelled a much greater freedom of action by the two war ministers and the Foreign Secretary in consultation with the Prime Minister. Such informal consultations became canalised in formal channels with the setting up of the War Committee; but the necessity of bringing the decisions of the Committee before the Cabinet produced, in the opinion of some, delay and hesitation. The demand made by Mr Lloyd George and supported by Mr Bonar Law for a War Committee with ample executive powers was the main cause of the resignation of Mr Asquith in 1916. Henceforth the Cabinet was superseded by a small War Cabinet which, in substance, controlled foreign policy as one of the aspects of war government.[5]

In the War Cabinet the Prime Minister was pre-eminent. He became, in substance, an administrator. Indeed, he created a special secretariat—known as the 'garden suburb' because it was housed in temporary buildings in the garden of 10 Downing Street—with whose assistance he was able to intervene in the various departments. The Foreign Secretary was not a member of the War Cabinet and became, like Lord Derby in 1878, almost an under-secretary. Nor was the inter-

[1] For the consultations with France, see also *Life of Sir Henry Campbell-Bannerman*, II, pp. 252, 256, 266.

[2] Grey, *Twenty-five Years*, II, p. 339.

[3] Churchill, *World Crisis*, I, p. 220.

[4] *Life of Lord Oxford and Asquith*, II, p. 93.

[5] On the Cabinet in wartime, see below, ch. X.

vention ended at the armistice in 1918. Mr Lloyd George was necessarily the chief British representative at the Peace Conference, and questions were settled by him as one of the 'Big Five', frequently without reference to the Foreign Secretary or his officials.[1]

Subsequently, nearly all questions of foreign policy arose out of Peace Conference decisions and were settled by the Prime Minister.

In the large private secretariat which he built up for himself in Downing Street, he found a convenient and ever ready agency for carrying into effect any orders which he felt moved to give. In the pressure of the times the necessity for consulting or even informing the Foreign Secretary was sometimes overlooked. Interviews would be granted to the representatives of foreign Governments without the knowledge of the Foreign Minister; and in these circumstances it is not surprising that occasions arose on which it seemed to other Powers that the British Government spoke with two discordant voices.[2]

The Treaty of Sèvres was negotiated by Mr Lloyd George at the Supreme War Council in London and settled at San Remo in April 1921. It contained two outstanding provisions to which the Foreign Secretary had always been opposed. The subsequent negotiations between Greeks and Turks were presided over by the Prime Minister.[3] Lord Curzon finally drafted a protest which was not sent owing to the resignation of Mr Lloyd George.

There has grown up a system under which there are in reality two Foreign Offices: the one for which I am for the time being responsible, and the other at No. 10—with the essential difference between them that whereas I report not only to you but to all my colleagues everything that I say or do, every telegram that I receive or send, every communication of importance that reaches me, it is often only by accident that I hear what is being done by the other Foreign Office.[4]

Mr Lloyd George's account gives a different impression. He assumes as axiomatic that it was for the Prime Minister to play the major part in the peace negotiations and the subsequent discussions and considers

[1] *Life of Lord Curzon*, III, pp. 259–60.

[2] *Ibid.* III, p. 261.

[3] *Ibid.* III, pp. 271–4; for further examples, see *ibid.* III, p. 314; Fitzroy, *Memoirs*, II, p. 699; Nicolson, *Curzon, The Last Phase*, p. 173.

[4] *Life of Lord Curzon*, III, p. 316.

that the difficulty was due to Lord Curzon's inability to work with Mr Philip Kerr (afterwards Marquess of Lothian) who was in charge of the 'garden suburb':

> The arrangement worked well as long as Mr Balfour remained at the Foreign Office, for they were in complete harmony. Mr Balfour welcomed Philip Kerr's assistance. There is no office upon which it is more necessary that the Prime Minister of the day should keep a constant oversight than the Foreign Office. With the multifarious duties which fell upon me in clearing up the veritable chaos of transferring the activities of Government and nation from war to peace, I could not have kept fully in touch with events abroad without Mr Kerr's intelligent and informed vigilance. Some friction arose when Mr Balfour resigned and Lord Curzon became his successor He resented Kerr's intervention. That is what one might expect from one who never got over the autocratic experiences of his Viceregal days.[1]

That is what one might expect from one who never got over the autocratic experiences of his War Cabinet days. In wartime foreign policy is merely a slice of war policy and the Foreign Office is one of the 'Service' Departments. After the war the essential problems were those of foreign policy and inevitably the Prime Minister was drawn into them. Also, foreign policy had ceased to be a matter for negotiation through ambassadors, but became (largely under Mr Lloyd George's influence) a matter for direct discussion between heads of Governments. The era of 'Diplomacy by Conference'[2] had begun, and Mr Lloyd George, having taken control of the peace negotiations in Paris, continued to exercise that control until the under-secretaries, led by Mr Bonar Law, rebelled in the Carlton Club in 1922.

Mr Bonar Law tried to restore the pre-war system, and the 'garden suburb' was pulled down. Mr Baldwin had no great interest in foreign policy and complete faith in Mr Austen Chamberlain, who was much senior to the Prime Minister in party and government service, and who might himself have been Prime Minister had he not supported the continuation of the Lloyd George coalition. Mr Baldwin attended no conferences and the Locarno policy was worked out by Mr Chamberlain and the Foreign Office. Mr MacDonald took the office of Foreign Secretary in 1924, but from 1929 to 1931 Mr Henderson as Foreign

[1] Lloyd George, *The Truth about the Peace Treaties*, I, p. 265.

[2] Lord Hankey, *Diplomacy by Conference*, ch. I.

Secretary would have brooked no interference by a Prime Minister whom he disliked and distrusted. From 1931 to 1937, too, foreign policy was under the control of Sir John Simon, Sir Samuel Hoare and Mr Anthony Eden. Sir Samuel Hoare negotiated the Hoare-Laval Pact in 1935 without prior Cabinet approval, though he had had a preliminary discussion with the Prime Minister and the agreement was made conditional on approval by the Cabinet.[1] Leakage from the French Government and a rousing public opinion compelled the Cabinet to disown the Foreign Secretary, who resigned in preference to disavowing the whole transaction.

Mr Neville Chamberlain reverted almost to Mr Lloyd George's practice. There was no 'garden suburb', but the Economic Adviser to the Government, Sir Horace Wilson, supplied personal advice. The situation had of course altered through the development of personal government by the dictators. It was common experience in the dictatorships, including the Soviet Union, that negotiations at the Foreign Secretary level produced no conclusions. Mr Neville Chamberlain believed—or perhaps 'hoped' is more accurate—that he could maintain peace by direct contact with Mussolini and Hitler. With this policy, as worked out in relation to Spain and Italy, Mr Eden did not agree. A letter from Mr Chamberlain to Signor Mussolini in 1937 was not shown to Mr Eden 'for I had the feeling that he would object to it'.[2] After Mr Eden's resignation, Mr Chamberlain was urged to take the Foreign Office himself.[3] However, he appointed Lord Halifax and met Opposition criticisms by undertaking to answer Foreign Office questions personally. The telegram to Hitler in September 1938 was sent without prior Cabinet approval.[4] The only evidence of disagreement between the Foreign Office and the Prime Minister was in March 1939, when Lord Halifax protested that a talk to journalists by the Prime Minister did not accord with Foreign Office policy.[5] On the other hand, Mr Chamberlain was always careful to take the Cabinet with him, and up to 1938 all the principles of his policy were discussed in the Foreign

[1] Viscount Templewood, *Nine Troubled Years*, p. 178. 'Looking back, I am certain that I should have insisted upon the summoning of a special Cabinet, and a clear agreement as to how far I could go with Laval.'

[2] *Life of Neville Chamberlain*, p. 330.

[3] *Ibid.* p. 339.

[4] *Ibid.* p. 363.

[5] *Ibid.* p. 396.

Policy Committee of the Cabinet.[1] The practice changed in 1938, when the Committee tended to be replaced by an 'Inner Cabinet' consisting of the Prime Minister, the Foreign Secretary, Sir John Simon and Sir Samuel Hoare. 'The critical situation was then changing so constantly that the summoning of a large committee became practically impossible.'[2] At the time of Munich this 'Inner Cabinet' was in almost continuous conference.[3]

As has already been explained,[4] Mr Churchill concentrated on war strategy and left the War Cabinet to settle ordinary policy. It was, however, clear that foreign policy, especially in relation to France and the Low Countries up to 1940, the United States, and the Soviet Union, was part of the war strategy. At an early stage he opened direct communications as 'former Naval person' with President Roosevelt, and all the major Anglo-American problems were discussed at this high level, the Foreign Office dealing with the State Department on matters of less importance. Mr Churchill has said that he was 'hand-in-glove with the Foreign Secretary and his department, and any differences of view were settled together'.[5]

Though the Prime Minister's relations are closest with the Foreign Office, he is available for consultation by other ministers. Such consultation is especially necessary where preliminary steps are taken which may have important political consequences. For instance, Lord Carnarvon received Lord Salisbury's consent before he entered into communication with Mr Parnell.[6] Apparently the decision to reinforce the troops at the Cape in April 1897, the first step towards acceptance of the idea that war with the Boers might break out, was taken by Lord Salisbury on the recommendation of Mr Joseph Chamberlain as Colonial Secretary. Mr Chamberlain had had a meeting with Lord Lansdowne, Mr Balfour, Lord Goschen and Sir Michael Hicks Beach, but the Cabinet had not been consulted.[7] Lord Milner's letter of 23 February 1898, saying that we ought 'to work up to a crisis' was answered by Mr Chamberlain without consultation with the whole Cabinet, though he did consult Lord Lansdowne, Mr Balfour,

[1] Viscount Templewood, *Nine Troubled Years*, p. 290. [2] *Ibid.* p. 291.
[3] *Ibid.* p. 375. [4] Above, pp. 195–8. [5] *The Second World War*, II, p. 21.
[6] *Life of Lord Randolph Churchill*, I, p. 447.
[7] *Life of Joseph Chamberlain*, III, pp. 140–1.

Sir Michael Hicks Beach, the First Lord of the Admiralty, and the Secretary of State for War. Lord Salisbury was ill.[1] Such consultations are also important where emergency action is necessary and there is no time to secure Cabinet approval. Thus, the Bank Charter Act was suspended in 1847, 1857, 1866 and 1914 by a letter to the Bank of England signed by the Prime Minister and the Chancellor of the Exchequer.[2] Numerous other technically illegal acts were done in 1914 with the Prime Minister's sanction and were subsequently ratified by Parliament.[3]

Sometimes, indeed, the Prime Minister interferes without being asked. Mr Gladstone said that 'the Prime Minister has no title to override any one of the departments. So far as he governs them, unless it is done by trick, which is not to be supposed, he governs them by influence only.'[4] But the right of the Cabinet to override a minister cannot be contested, and a Prime Minister who is sure of obtaining support if necessary can in practice override a colleague's decision. This is done, usually, at the request of another minister, and particularly where a dispute arises between two departments. A good example was the contest in 1915 between the Ministry of Munitions and the War Office over the design of shells. Design was the function of the Ordnance Board, which was subject to the War Office. But Mr Lloyd George, as Minister of Munitions, claimed that as he was responsible for the quality of munitions, he must be responsible for their design. He appealed to the Prime Minister, who decided in his favour, and the function was transferred to the Ministry of Munitions.[5] In 1907 the Admiralty refused to allow a certain paper to be submitted to the Committee of Imperial Defence. Mr Haldane appealed to the Prime Minister, who overruled the Admiralty.[6] In 1915 the War Office proposed to remove an intelligence officer who was sending 'discouraging' reports from Russia. When Mr Lloyd George 'heard this on good authority', he went to the Prime Minister, who 'promptly interposed his authority and the distinguished officer remained at his post'.[7] An even stronger case

[1] *Life of Joseph Chamberlain*, III, p. 365.

[2] Lloyd George, *War Memoirs*, I, p. 103.

[3] *Ibid.* I, pp. 105–11.

[4] Gladstone, *Gleanings*, I, p. 244.

[5] Addison, *Four and a Half Years*, pp. 146 *et seq.*

[6] *Esher Papers*, II, pp. 246–7.

[7] Lloyd George, *War Memoirs*, I, p. 457.

of intervention was provided by Mr Lloyd George in 1921. He sent for the Officer Commanding the Home District in order to obtain some information. He came to the conclusion that the officer was 'no use' and asked the Secretary of State to remove him. The Secretary of State objected, on the advice of Sir Henry Wilson, and ultimately a compromise was reached.[1]

In order to exercise this authority, the Prime Minister must be able to obtain adequate information. He can, of course, ask for papers. Lord Palmerston indicated to Lord Panmure, during the Crimean War, the kind of despatches to the army that he wished to see.[2] There are cases, too, in which the Prime Minister has not hesitated to communicate with subordinates of the ministers. Peel was in constant communication with Gladstone when the latter was Vice-President of the Board of Trade.[3] Lord Granville said in 1870: 'I imagine that the Prime Minister has an undoubted right to communicate directly either with our representatives abroad or with Foreign Ministers in London. But I think it is in his interest as much as in that of the Foreign Secretary that he should only appear as the *deus ex machina*.'[4] Mr Lloyd George imposed no such self-limitation during the war and afterwards.[5] Lord Randolph Churchill, however, objected to the intervention of the Prime Minister in 1885. Queen Victoria was extremely anxious that the Duke of Connaught should be appointed to the command at Bombay. Churchill, as Secretary of State for India, did not desire to appoint him. The Queen asked Lord Salisbury to ask the opinion of the Viceroy. The reply was communicated by Salisbury to Churchill, who at once tendered his resignation. Salisbury did not claim any right to intervene, but merely said that he telegraphed on behalf of the Queen because the Viceroy did not possess the Queen's cipher. The dispute was settled by Salisbury's informing the Viceroy that his message had been from the Queen, that the Cabinet had not yet considered the question, and that the matter was still open.[6] The conclusion seems to be that it is wise for the Prime Minister not to intervene except in extreme cases.

[1] *Diaries of Sir Henry Wilson*, II, p. 285.
[2] *Panmure Papers*, I, p. 150.
[3] Hyde, *Mr Gladstone at the Board of Trade*, p. 34.
[4] *Life of Lord Granville*, II, p. 64.
[5] See above, pp. 219–21.
[6] *Life of Lord Randolph Churchill*, I, pp. 504–16.

§4. *Action without Cabinet Approval*

There is, finally, one aspect of the Prime Minister's pre-eminence which, to some extent, indicates the Cabinet's dependence upon him. New policies are, in theory, the concern of the Cabinet: but the Prime Minister can, within limits, compel the acceptance of policies by announcing them publicly. The Cabinet then has either to accept the policy or lose its leader. Frequently the first is the better alternative. Lord John Russell's letter on the Corn Laws was written while the Whigs were in Opposition: but effectively it bound them to a programme which they must have put in force if they had accepted office when Sir Robert Peel resigned. In 1850 Lord John Russell's famous letter in denunciation of the new Catholic hierarchy was sent without Cabinet consultation, and it bound them to acceptance of a Bill which many of them disliked.[1] Lord John Russell was particularly liable to 'upset the coach', but other examples are not wanting. Mr Gladstone in effect decided to dis-establish the Irish Church and to introduce Home Rule—though in both cases he was in Opposition. Mr Disraeli, even when not Prime Minister, sometimes accepted amendments of substance without consultation. In accepting a motion for a committee of inquiry on the 'Kilmainham Treaty' in 1882, Mr Gladstone ran counter to a previous Cabinet decision. He subsequently apologised to the Cabinet for having been carried away by temper.[2] In the debate on the Education Bill, 1896, Sir John Gorst refused to allow non-county boroughs to become local education authorities. Mr Balfour, who was then Leader of the House of Commons, was not present for the whole debate, but after listening to part of it he accepted an amendment to confer educational functions on non-county boroughs of more than 20,000 inhabitants.[3] Sir Henry Campbell-Bannerman's personal decision exempted trade unions from liability for torts and included domestic servants within the Workmen's Compensation Bill.[4] In respect of the former he reversed a decision of the Cabinet; in respect of the latter he decided against the publicly expressed intentions of the minister in

[1] *Later Correspondence of Lord John Russell*, I, p. 46.

[2] *Life of Sir Charles Dilke*, I, p. 489. [3] *Life of Arthur James Balfour*, I, p. 244.

[4] *Life of Sir Henry Campbell-Bannerman*, II, pp. 278, 280

charge of the Bill. Sir Austen Chamberlain said that Mr Asquith's statement of the Government's intention to introduce adult suffrage was made without consulting the Cabinet.[1]

In 1916 Mr Lloyd George apparently decided to summon the Imperial War Conference on his own responsibility. He consulted the Colonial Secretary. A week later he announced his intention in Parliament. The first the War Cabinet heard of the matter officially was on the following day, when he reported his speech. The War Cabinet was evidently doubtful of the proposal, but ultimately agreed not to a formal conference, but to a series of enlarged meetings of the War Cabinet.[2] Mr Lloyd George, with the consent of Sir Eric Geddes, First Lord of the Admiralty, dismissed Admiral Sir John Jellicoe in 1918. This did not require Cabinet sanction, but the King was apparently informed that there had been a Cabinet decision. There was no such decision.[3] It is even said that Mr Baldwin publicly raised the standard of 'protection' in 1923 without consulting the Cabinet.[4] Mr Neville Chamberlain's telegram to Hitler in September 1938 was sent without discussion with the Cabinet.[5]

But it appears that in general Mr Baldwin placed more reliance on his departmental ministers than did any of his predecessors. It must be emphasised once more that the office of Prime Minister, like every other office in the Government, is very largely what its occupant chooses to make it.

[1] Sir Austen Chamberlain, *Politics from Inside*, p. 413.
[2] Lloyd George, *War Memoirs*, IV, pp. 1731–5.
[3] Sir Roger Bacon, *Earl Jellicoe*, pp. 378–85.
[4] *Life of Lord Cave*, p. 264.
[5] *Life of Neville Chamberlain*, p. 396.

CHAPTER IX

THE CABINET

§1. *The Nature of the Cabinet*

The Cabinet has been described as 'such of Her Majesty's confidential servants as are of the Privy Council'. Like some of Dr Johnson's definitions, this raises more questions than it solves. When Lord Melbourne used the phrase in one of his letters to Queen Victoria, the editors of the Queen's *Letters* thought it necessary to insert a footnote to explain what it meant.[1] The nature of the Cabinet is more easily explained by analogy than by definition. It is the board of directors for Great Britain and all those parts of the Commonwealth which do not possess self-government. It is said to be a body of servants of the Crown because, usually, its members hold office under the Crown, though, as has been explained in ch. III, members without portfolio are not uncommon. They are said to be confidential servants because they determine the main issues of the 'Queen's' policy. They belong to the Privy Council because, historically, the Cabinet is a private meeting of those Privy Councillors in whom the Sovereign has particular 'confidence' for the time being.

The definition is, in short, a relic of history. In substance, the Cabinet is the directing body of the national policy. Consisting of the principal leaders of the party in power, it is able to forward that policy by reason of its control of the House of Commons. Consisting, too, of the heads of the more important Government departments, it is able to forward its policy by laying down the principles to be followed by the central administrative machine. Their service under the Crown is the legal explanation of the political fact that ministers hold important Government offices. Membership of the Privy Council is a historical survival. It is said that the Privy Councillor's oath restrains those who take it from publishing information obtained in the service of the Crown. It is difficult to believe that it is the oath alone and not the weight of

[1] *Letters of Queen Victoria*, 1st series, I, p. 285. It is in fact no longer accurate. Usually all 'Ministers', even Ministers of State, are sworn of the Council.

tradition, the insistence of the Prime Minister, or the disapproval of colleagues, that makes the secrecy of the British Cabinet more effective than is common in most governmental systems. In spite of the oath, close relations between ministers and the press have not been unknown at various times in the history of the Cabinet. The Official Secrets Acts now provide legal penalties for the disclosure of Cabinet secrets.

It was formerly the practice to include in the Cabinet the heads of all important departments as well as a number of ministers, like the Lord President of the Council, the Lord Privy Seal, and sometimes the Paymaster-General or the Chancellor of the Duchy of Lancaster, whose departmental duties were either non-existent or not heavy.[1] The application of this principle to a governmental system whose powers were increasing necessarily brought about an increase in the size of the Cabinet. During most of the nineteenth century, the Cabinet contained from twelve to fifteen members. Disraeli's Cabinet of 1874 contained twelve members only. He excluded, for instance, the President of the Board of Trade. The experiment was not a success, for one of the most important legislative proposals was a Merchant Shipping Bill which was promoted by the President and withdrawn by the Cabinet. The session was not propitious for the Government, and Sir Stafford Northcote said that the Government's misfortunes were largely due to the fact that the President had not been able 'to make himself disagreeable in Cabinet'.[2] It may indeed be said that Peel's Cabinet of thirteen in 1841 was the smallest possible even at that date. During the present century the number of Secretaries of State increased from five to eight and has now become seven. The Department of Education was separated from the Privy Council in 1899 and its functions have immensely increased, first as the Board of Education and now as a Ministry. The Board of Agriculture and Fisheries was converted into a Ministry with substantially increased functions.[3] In the present century many new depart-

[1] See above, ch. III; and as to the War Cabinet, see below, ch. X. In the post-war period there has been some increase in the work of the Lord President of the Council, who is mainly responsible for scientific research. The office now falls into the class occupied by the Lord Chancellor and the Commonwealth Relations Office; the duties are important, but light.

[2] *Life of Lord Norton*, p. 220.

[3] It was practically laid down in 1895 that the President of the Board of Agriculture should be in the Cabinet; cf. Fitzroy, *Memoirs*, I, p. 236.

ments have been created, some more or less permanently and some temporarily. Among those which have survived are the Ministries of Labour, National Service (generally combined with Labour), Health, Transport, Civil Aviation (generally combined with Transport), Defence, Supply, Power, Pensions, National Insurance (often combined with Pensions), and Welsh Affairs (generally combined with another Ministry).

Even before 1939, however, it was the practice to omit some of the ministers from the Cabinet. Selection of those to be omitted depended partly on their political importance and partly on the political importance of their departments—not always the same things, though there is a close relation. Generally the Postmaster-General, the First Commissioner (now the Minister) of Works, the Minister of Pensions, the Paymaster-General (whose functions are nominal) and, less often, the Minister of Transport, were excluded. This kept the size of the Cabinet down to twenty-one or twenty-two members, though there were occasions under Mr Asquith and Mr Neville Chamberlain when the number rose to twenty-three.

It is well known that a large committee cannot function as a committee, but resembles a small debating assembly; and a large part of the success of the Cabinet system has lain in the ability of ministers to reach an agreed conclusion by informal discussion. The difficulty was met by a system of Cabinet committees, which discussed and virtually settled nearly all contentious matters. Even so, the work of the Cabinet itself has increased—the Cabinet meets twice a week whereas before the war one meeting a week generally sufficed.

Mr Attlee therefore reduced the Cabinet to seventeen members. The creation of the Ministry of Defence enabled the First Lord of the Admiralty and the Secretaries of State for War and Air to be excluded. He also excluded the Ministers of Transport, Food, Town and Country Planning, National Insurance, Supply, Fuel and Power, and Civil Aviation. Mr Churchill's youthful flirtation with 'overlords'[1] would have increased the size of the Cabinet. He was, however, able to reduce it from seventeen to sixteen by excluding the Ministers of Education and Agriculture and Fisheries, and both exclusions were criticised.

[1] Above, pp. 78–80.

Sir Anthony Eden restored both and also brought in the Minister of Pensions and National Insurance. These and other changes brought the number up to eighteen. Mr Macmillan made some changes, but kept the number at eighteen.

In substance, therefore, the size of the Cabinet has been reduced since 1939 by combining some offices and excluding the holders of others. Outside the Cabinet there are now nine heads of departments (excluding the Attorney-General), five Ministers of State, and one minister without portfolio (who helps with Government business in the House of Lords). These are all 'Ministers of Cabinet Rank'. If the Law Officers be included among them, only about half 'the Government' is now in the Cabinet, though no doubt it is the better half.[1]

The reduction in the size of the Cabinet and the increase in the number of Cabinet meetings have not affected the tendency, noticeable before 1939, for matters to be discussed and (often) settled outside the Cabinet by informal discussions or for the delegation of matters to committees. Though the number of Cabinet committees is not disclosed, the volume of committee work is, for some ministers, very heavy. Though ministers without heavy departmental duties, like the Lord President of the Council, the Lord Privy Seal, and the Chancellor of the Duchy of Lancaster, can do useful work as chairmen of committees, the burden must always fall mainly on the departmental ministers. Ministers of State and parliamentary secretaries can effectively deputise for the departmental ministers only when they have themselves assumed the responsibility (subject to the control of the departmental ministers) for the branch of administration under discussion.

Though, as has been said, the Cabinet is chosen when the Government is formed,[2] and though certain offices are recognised as carrying Cabinet rank, there is nothing to prevent the Prime Minister from promoting a junior minister to the Cabinet without changing his office. Thus, Sir Rufus Isaacs and Sir Douglas Hogg, while holding the office of Attorney-General, were brought into the Cabinet; and Mr Herbert Morrison was similarly promoted while Minister of Transport. Ministers not in the Cabinet are entitled to attend to discuss matters

[1] For the present Cabinet, see Appendix II, below, p. 538.

[2] Above, pp. 76–82.

affecting their departments. Also, the Prime Minister may request the attendance of any person, whether a minister or not, to give advice on a particular matter. For instance, the Attorney-General would be summoned if some legal question were involved and the Lord Chancellor desired assistance; a parliamentary secretary might be asked to attend if a departmental matter was under discussion and the Minister was not available; the Chiefs of Staff frequently attend; and so on. The old rule that only Cabinet ministers might attend has thus been relaxed.

The Cabinet consists of party leaders with parliamentary experience. For the most part, they will have borne the burden of Opposition, itself a training for government. Generally, they have had experience of office in previous Governments. Occasionally, as in 1852 (when Derby's 'who? who?' ministry of untried men came into office), in 1905 (when the Liberals came in after eleven years of Opposition), and in 1924 (when the Labour party first secured office), a large proportion of members inexperienced in government has entered the Cabinet. Generally, however, it is energy and not experience that is lacking. Sometimes, indeed, one is reminded of the reply of M. Clemenceau at the age of eighty, to the question why he was not in M. Briand's Government. 'Je suis trop jeune', he said. Lord Derby, the Prime Minister, once remarked that he was often urged to bring in 'new blood', but that, as often as he followed this advice, he heard complaints about 'raw recruits'.

§2. *Functions*

The main functions of the Cabinet were set out in the Report of the Machinery of Government Committee[1] (1918) as:

(*a*) the final determination of the policy to be submitted to Parliament;

(*b*) the supreme control of the national executive in accordance with the policy prescribed by Parliament; and

(*c*) the continuous co-ordination and delimitation of the authorities of the several Departments of State.

This statement rightly makes no distinction between legislation and administration. In the modern State, most legislation is directed

[1] Report of the Machinery of Government Committee, Cd. 9230/1918, p. 5.

towards the creation or modification of administrative powers. The importance of private law cannot be denied; and one of the purposes of a constitution is to provide a means by which disputes as to private rights can be settled. It is, further, one of the functions of government to provide for modifications in the judicial system and the law which it administers as between subject and subject. In most countries it is a principal task of the Ministry of Justice to secure improvements in the civil law and its administration. Even in England, where there is no such Ministry, the Lord Chancellor has as one of his numerous duties the supervision of the civil law. But in most highly developed communities, and above all in Great Britain, the main function of government is the provision of services, including the maintenance of external relations and the defence of the country, for the welfare of the people. Legislation is thus the handmaid of administration, and Parliament's legislative powers are part of the means by which it controls administration.

Whether legislation is required to carry out an administrative policy is a technical question. The Cabinet has to decide on the policy. The technician explains that to carry it out legislation is required. Since parliamentary time is limited and parliamentary control over an alteration of law is far greater than it is over an alteration of administration within the law, this fact has to be taken into account in determining the policy.[1] But otherwise no distinction is made between a policy that requires legislation and a policy that does not. The Cabinet is not an 'executive' instrument in the sense that it possesses any legal powers; it is a policy-formulating body. When it has determined on a policy, the appropriate department carries it out, either by administrative action within the law or by drafting a Bill to be submitted to Parliament so as to change the law.

The Cabinet is a general controlling body. It usually meets twice a week only and for 2 hours at a time. Many of its members are departmental ministers, with important departmental duties to perform. It neither desires nor is able to deal with all the numerous details of

[1] At the beginning of each session a committee of the Cabinet discusses what Bills shall be promoted in the session. Of the Bills proposed (frequently enough for a whole Parliament) at least 90 per cent are 'departmental'.

government. It expects a minister to take all decisions which are not of real political importance. Every minister must therefore exercise his own discretion as to what matters arising in his department ought to receive Cabinet sanction.[1] The minister who refers too much is weak; he who refers too little is dangerous. Lord Palmerston was among the latter. While he was Foreign Secretary his colleagues went in perpetual fear of trouble. A revealing anecdote by Lord Clarendon suggests that, as Prime Minister, he suffered from the same belief in the soundness of his judgment. 'I remember once his agreeing with me that Vera Cruz ought to be blockaded, and desiring me to write accordingly in the Queen's name to the Admiralty. I said, "Surely not without bringing it before the Cabinet?"—"Oh, ah! the Cabinet," was his answer, "very well, call them then, if you think it necessary."'[2] Mr Joseph Chamberlain, as Colonial Secretary, was inclined to be Palmerstonian.[3] Mr Baldwin, surprisingly enough, settled the American debt payments in 1923, when he was Chancellor of the Exchequer, without consulting the Cabinet.[4]

Certain matters are, however, regarded as being normally outside the Cabinet's competence. Lord Oxford and Asquith said that, speaking generally, the exercise of the prerogative of mercy, the personnel of the Cabinet, and the making of appointments, are not discussed in Cabinet.[5] The question of the reprieve of Sir Roger Casement in 1916 was brought before the Cabinet.[6] But normally the exercise of the prerogative of mercy is left to the Home Secretary; the function is as 'judicial' a function as any that goes by that name. The personnel of the Cabinet, on the other hand, has frequently been discussed by the Cabinet in the past, though usually in exceptional circumstances.[7] Other appointments are still regarded primarily as matters of 'patronage' which are left to

[1] See Gladstone, *Gleanings*, I, p. 242; and Mr Gladstone's statement reported in *Life of Sir Edward Cook*, pp. 148–9.

[2] *Life of the Earl of Clarendon*, II, p. 240. For other examples of decisions by the Prime Minister without Cabinet sanction, see above, pp. 226–7.

[3] For a good example see *Life of Joseph Chamberlain*, II, pp. 440–1: and see Joseph Chamberlain, *A Political Memoir*, pp. 73, 83.

[4] Blake, *The Unknown Prime Minister*, p. 491.

[5] Oxford and Asquith, *Fifty Years of Parliament*, II, p. 194.

[6] *Life of Randall Davidson*, II, p. 789.

[7] See above, ch. III.

the Prime Minister for the time being, or to a minister in consultation with the Prime Minister, or to a minister acting on his own responsibility. But it is clear that, where a real political issue is involved, Cabinet authority would be obtained.

Another matter which is rarely, if ever, discussed in Cabinet is the conferment of honours.[1] Queen Victoria assumed that the question of granting a dukedom to the Marquess of Lansdowne, on his retirement from the Viceroyalty of India, had been considered by the Cabinet in 1894. Accordingly she protested, 'as the fountain of honour', that such matters are not discussed by ministers.[2] Mr Gladstone replied that the Cabinet might be consulted as to both the conduct and the appointment of a Viceroy and added:

> Mr Gladstone has never known a case where the Cabinet have interfered in a question of honour purely titular, or honour connected with an office lying beyond the established circle of political administration. But, in the public mind, and in ordinary practice, the Cabinet is viewed as the seat of ultimate responsibility; and, in view of the precedents he has quoted [relating only to conduct and appointment], Mr Gladstone owns himself unable to exclude from all concern in the honours bestowed upon a Viceroy those who have been and may be consulted upon his retirement, and who are ultimately responsible for his administrative acts. It is true indeed, as your Majesty observes, that the Sovereign is the fountain of honour; but it is also true that the Sovereign is the fountain of law. That Mr Gladstone did not consult the Cabinet (to which every minister is as a rule entitled to appeal in matters concerning him) was due to the absence of Lord Kimberley [Secretary of State for India] but also to a sentiment of deference to your Majesty.[3]

Mr Gladstone, it may be suggested, laid down the correct doctrine in this passage. The Cabinet is regarded as having, and accepts, ultimate responsibility for all political acts. If an act of a minister involves, or may involve, political issues of some magnitude, he ought to bring it before the Cabinet. Normally, the prerogative of mercy involves the exercise of a judicial function, yet it is not impossible to imagine

[1] 'The Prime Minister may consult anybody he pleases, and very often does, but the idea that he should bring before the Cabinet the question of honours is one utterly foreign to our whole constitutional procedure.' Marquess Curzon of Kedleston in the House of Lords, 7 March 1923: 53 H.L. Deb. 5 s., 286–7.

[2] *Letters of Queen Victoria*, 3rd series, II, p. 347.

[3] *Ibid.* 3rd series, II, pp. 349–50.

circumstances in which it would be of major political importance. The pardon of the perpetrator of a political crime, such as political assassination, treason,[1] riot, unlawful assembly, or seditious libel, might involve political questions of the first order of magnitude. It would not be, in substance, different from the release of Mr Parnell in 1885. A somewhat similar question is raised by the discretion of the Attorney-General, through his control of the Director of Public Prosecutions, as to public prosecutions. It is unthinkable that the desirability or otherwise of such a prosecution should in ordinary circumstances be brought before the Cabinet. But it is clear that a prosecution for a political offence may raise political issues. The breadth of the offence of sedition, for example, is such that the law is much stricter than the practice.[2] Accordingly, it is not uncommon for the question of prosecution to be considered by the Cabinet. Thus, the War Cabinet appears to have given instructions to Sir Frederick Smith (afterwards Earl of Birkenhead) as to certain prosecutions, though Sir Frederick protested.[3] In 1919 Sir Gordon Hewart (afterwards Lord Chief Justice) consulted the Home Secretary, who brought the matter before the Cabinet, as to a prosecution for sedition.[4] In 1924 Sir Patrick Hastings gave instructions for a prosecution against the editor of *The Workers' Weekly* for an offence under the Incitement to Mutiny Act. Questions were asked in the House of Commons, the Prime Minister intervened, the question was discussed by the Cabinet, and thereupon the Attorney-General gave instructions to ask the magistrate's leave to withdraw the prosecution. These proceedings led to the moving of a vote of censure in the House of Commons. An amendment for a Select Committee, moved on behalf of the Liberal party, was passed against the Labour Government.[5] The Government thereupon advised a dissolution and was defeated at the ensuing general election. The Attorney-General and the Prime Minister defended themselves on the ground that a political prosecution may

[1] As in 1916, when the proposed reprieve of Sir R. Casement, convicted of treason for inciting Irish soldiers to fight on the German side, was brought before the Cabinet: *Life of Randall Davidson*, II, p. 789. The exercise of the prerogative would have had political repercussions.

[2] See Jennings, *The Law and the Constitution* (4th ed.), pp. 251–2.

[3] 177 H.C.Deb. 5 s., 614–15.

[4] *Ibid.* 598–9.

[5] See the debate: 177 H.C.Deb. 5 s., 581–704.

involve political questions. 'Where the public interest may conflict with the strict exercise of his duty', it is, said Sir Patrick Hastings, not only the right but the duty of the Attorney-General to consult the Cabinet.[1] 'Every Law Officer who is undertaking a prosecution in the interests of the State must possess himself not only of guidance on technical law', said the Prime Minister, 'but must possess himself of guidance on this question, whether if a prosecution is instituted the effect of the prosecution will be harmful or beneficial to the State in whose interests it has been undertaken.'[2] The Liberal members did not specifically dissent from these propositions, but contented themselves with a demand for inquiry. Whatever be the merits of their application to Mr Campbell's case, it seems that the propositions themselves cannot seriously be controverted.

Again, most appointments are determined by the qualifications of the available personnel; yet certain key positions like the Permanent Secretaryship to the Treasury, or the office of Chief Planning Officer, might be, in some political conditions, major political questions.[3] Similarly, though the grant of honours is too unimportant a matter to occupy the time of the Cabinet, it is conceivable that with a Labour majority in the House of Commons it might assume larger proportions.

The annual Budget statement occupies a peculiar position. Though of major political importance, and therefore always brought before the Cabinet, it is not circulated, but is disclosed orally to the Cabinet a few days before it is made in the House of Commons.[4] It therefore does not follow the usual procedure whereby the principles are discussed in Cabinet, the details worked out in committee, and the full proposals circulated and debated. The reason is the fundamental importance of secrecy[5]—though it may be doubted whether the need for secrecy is

[1] 177 H.C.Deb. 5 s., 599.

[2] *Ibid.* 629.

[3] In 1918 the resignation of Major-General Sir Hugh Trenchard was considered by the War Cabinet, and the Secretary of State did not accept the resignation until it had been so considered: 105 H.C.Deb. 5 s., 972. The office of Chief Planning Officer, instituted by the Labour Government of 1945–51, has since been abolished.

[4] See the evidence of Sir Maurice Hankey before the tribunal of inquiry in 1936: Budget Disclosure Inquiry (1936), Minutes of Evidence, p. 25. The average period was four or five days, but it was twelve days in 1933 and twenty-one days in 1936, in both cases because of the Easter recess.

[5] Snowden, *Autobiography*, II, p. 617.

any greater in this case than in many other matters—but its effect is to give the Chancellor of the Exchequer a much greater personal control over his Budget than is the case with most other departmental proposals. The rule is in any case one of convenience only, and the Cabinet may ask for longer notice and more effective discussion. In 1860 the Cabinet asked for nearly a month's notice of Mr Gladstone's famous Budget of that year. Owing to the fact that the financial year had not then closed, Mr Gladstone was unable to agree, but he gave a week's notice.[1] The Budget must be distinguished from the Estimates. Occasions on which disputes over Estimates have been brought before the Cabinet are frequent. As a result of Cabinet decisions on such disputes, Lord Randolph Churchill resigned in 1886 and Mr Gladstone in 1894. Again, it is inconceivable that fundamental changes will be made without the Prime Minister's prior consent. Further, the Cabinet can always insist on modifications after the Budget statement has been made. (They can be camouflaged as 'concessions' to public or parliamentary opinion.) Finally, the Cabinet can overthrow a Budget altogether if it is prepared to risk the resignation of the Chancellor of the Exchequer.

It has also to be noted that, although the Budget as a whole may not be brought before the Cabinet until the last minute, any major change of taxation policy may be considered at length before the Budget is produced. Mr Winston Churchill said in 1937[2] that

> although the general layout of financial policy should emanate from the Chancellor of the Exchequer personally, and should be submitted to the Cabinet only in its final form, there ought to be, and there nearly always has been, a special procedure in respect of new and novel imposts. I remember, for instance, that we sat for five months and had at least a dozen Cabinet Councils on the Land Tax and Mineral Royalty duties. That was in 1909, and for five months these matters were continuously argued out.... When the Betting Bill, of inglorious memory was being considered, a strong Cabinet Committee was appointed in November and sat for over four months before they reported, wrongly, that, on the whole, it was worth trying. It would be, in my opinion, a departure from custom, for any Chancellor of the Exchequer to present to a Cabinet, only a few days before the opening of the Budget, some great scheme of new taxation, which had not been examined. When I say 'examined' I mean by people who have the right

[1] Guedalla, *Gladstone and Palmerston*, p. 162.

[2] 324 H.C.Deb. 5 s., 890–2.

and the mood, and are encouraged to criticise and pick holes in the plan. It is in the last degree imprudent to go into action upon a political or financial scheme which has not first of all had a good deal of knocking about behind the scenes. It is only by that process that you can find out whether it can stand up to the battery to which it will, and ought to be exposed when it comes to the House of Commons.

Another matter which is now never discussed in Cabinet is the exercise of the prerogative of dissolving Parliament.[1] This is, however, a development since 1918; and if the Prime Minister desires the advice of the Cabinet there is nothing to prevent him from raising the question.

It is not only the right of a minister to consult the Cabinet on major matters; it is his duty to do so. Sometimes, however, the urgency of the matter makes prior consultation impossible. In such circumstances, the Prime Minister's authorisation is enough. Examples have already been cited.[2] The situation most frequently occurs in respect of foreign affairs, where most matters are of political importance and yet have frequently to be decided out of hand. Sometimes, indeed, it is necessary for the Foreign Secretary to refuse to give an answer until the Cabinet, and occasionally Parliament also, have been consulted. For instance, Sir Edward Grey in 1906 refused to give an assurance that if France were attacked by Germany Great Britain would support France, and said that such an assurance would require both Cabinet and parliamentary authority.[3]

The difficulty that most Foreign Office action is of political importance, but that prior consultation is not always possible, is overcome by circulating important Foreign Office telegrams and despatches daily to each member of the Cabinet, whose members can then raise any question they think fit—provided that they read the daily print.[4] The Duke of Argyll emphasised the duty of the Foreign Secretary in 1891.[5] Nevertheless, some Foreign Secretaries have been inclined towards

[1] See below, pp. 412–28. [2] Above, ch. VIII, pp. 226–7.

[3] *Life of Sir Henry Campbell-Bannerman*, II, p. 255.

[4] Important telegrams and despatches are also circulated by the Commonwealth Relations Office and the Colonial Office.

[5] *Life of Lord Granville*, II, pp. 506–7, quoting a letter by the Duke to *The Times*, 16 April 1891.

secretiveness. Lord Palmerston frequently failed to consult not only the Cabinet, but also the Prime Minister and the Queen.[1] In 1886, when the Queen and Lord Salisbury were in alliance against the Liberal party, Lord Salisbury advised the Queen that Lord Rosebery ought to bring as little as possible before the Cabinet, and to settle everything with the Queen and Mr Gladstone, as nothing was ever settled satisfactorily in the Cabinet.[2] The Queen advised Lord Rosebery accordingly, using almost Lord Salisbury's own words.[3] The Queen was sufficiently impartial to consider that what was sauce for a Liberal was also sauce for a Conservative; and later in the same year she reminded Lord Salisbury, now both Prime Minister and Foreign Secretary, of his advice.[4] Lord Salisbury agreed, but pointed out that it was necessary to discuss the Bulgarian question in the Cabinet because some of the members desired to criticise a Foreign Office telegram.[5]

Lord Rosebery, at least, seemed to agree with Lord Salisbury's advice. In 1893 he extended British influence in Uganda without Cabinet sanction, and marked the document in question 'not to be printed'. This fact was discovered by Sir William Harcourt nine months later, and he wrote: 'The claim therefore is that the Foreign Secretary may set aside the judgment of the Prime Minister and the Cabinet, and give without their knowledge instructions of the gravest consequence which are contrary to their opinion. I believe such a pretension to be absolutely inconsistent with the traditions of English administration, and it was finally condemned in the well-known case of Lord Palmerston in 1851.'[6]

Nevertheless, when Lord Rosebery was Prime Minister in 1895, he refused to accede to Sir William Harcourt's request, which was supported by Lord Kimberley, the Foreign Secretary, to submit the Nicaraguan dispute to the Cabinet, alleging that it was impossible to collect the Cabinet together. Sir William Harcourt said that 'the refusal of Lord Rosebery to reserve a question for the Cabinet on the request of the Foreign Secretary and the remonstrance of the

[1] Above, pp. 208–11.
[2] *Letters of Queen Victoria*, 3rd series, I, p. 45.
[3] *Ibid.* 3rd series, I, p. 48. [4] *Ibid.* 3rd series, I, p. 211. [5] *Ibid.*
[6] *Life of Sir William Harcourt*, II, pp. 315–16; see also *ibid.* II, p. 319.

leader of the House of Commons is, according to my experience, without precedent'.[1]

Mr Lloyd George alleges that from 1906 to 1914 'there was a reticence and a secrecy which practically ruled out three-fourths of the Cabinet from the chance of making any genuine contribution to the momentous questions then impending [in foreign policy].... Direct questions were answered with civility, but were not encouraged....We were not privileged to know any more of the essential facts than those which the ordinary newspaper readers could gather.'[2]

A comparison of accounts does not suggest that there was any deliberate concealment. Mr Lloyd George's impression was probably derived from Sir Edward Grey's excessive departmentalism and his lack of interest in internal questions. There is no adequate evidence on Mr Lloyd George's assertion that there was deliberate suppression and distortion of information by the military authorities later in the war. Mr Lloyd George says that Sir Henry Wilson, at Sir Douglas Haig's instigation, misled the Cabinet on the subject of the morale of the French troops and suppressed the facts that the French generals were against the Passchendaele plan, that the battlefield was unsuitable for the plan, and that some of the British generals were against the plan.[3] Later on, the Cabinet was not told that the generals actually fighting advised stopping the offensive nor informed of the defeat at Cambrai.[4]

There is also a tendency to 'short circuit' the Cabinet when a strong Cabinet Committee has been set up. This was so in 1938, when the Foreign Policy Committee set up by Mr Baldwin's Government was used by Mr Neville Chamberlain for the taking of urgent decisions, though Lord Templewood says that the full Cabinet always had the last word upon the more important questions after hearing the explanations and recommendations of the Foreign Secretary and the Prime Minister.[5] Later in 1938 the Foreign Policy Committee was virtually superseded by an 'Inner Cabinet', consisting of Mr Chamberlain, Lord Halifax, Sir John Simon and Sir Samuel Hoare: 'The critical situation was then changing so rapidly that the summoning of a large committee was

[1] *Ibid.* II, pp. 331–2.
[2] Lloyd George, *War Memoirs*, I, pp. 46–51.
[3] *Ibid.* IV, pp. 2140–8, 2191–2204.
[4] *Ibid.* IV, pp. 2216, 2257.
[5] Lord Templewood, *Nine Troubled Years*, p. 290.

practically impossible.'[1] The Munich declaration was signed by Mr Chamberlain without consultation with the Cabinet, and in consequence Mr Duff Cooper resigned:

I would suggest that for the Prime Minister of England [*sic*] to sign, without consulting with his colleagues and without, so far as I am aware, any reference to his Allies, obviously without consultation with the Dominions and without the assistance of any expert diplomatic adviser, such a declaration with the dictator of a great State, is not the way in which the foreign affairs of the British Empire [*sic*] should be conducted.[2]

§3. *The Cabinet Secretariat*

Until 1916 the business of the Cabinet was run on lines which would seem peculiar to the present generation of ministers. There was no Cabinet Office and no Secretary.[3] There was, therefore, no formal agenda. A minister who desired to raise a matter for decision circulated a memorandum if he thought fit, and informed the Prime Minister, whether or not a memorandum had been circulated, that he proposed to bring a certain matter before the Cabinet. The Prime Minister was thus able to compile an informal agenda. As a rule the meeting began with any items of foreign affairs which the Foreign Secretary desired to raise, or which any minister desired to bring up in consequence of the telegrams and despatches which had been circulated. Then the Prime Minister would call in turn upon those ministers who had indicated to him their desire to raise questions of home or imperial affairs. There was, therefore, some order in the discussion. Indeed, it was rare for a minister to raise a matter without informing the Prime Minister beforehand. For if a minister, finding that time was being taken over other subjects, tried to 'jump a claim' or interpose some item which the Prime Minister had not put down, the Prime Minister would gently suggest that the question might be postponed until certain other questions had been disposed of. Then, while the discussion was proceeding, he might pass a note suggesting that perhaps it would be well to postpone the matter until next time, when it could be taken earlier in the

[1] Lord Templewood, *Nine Troubled Years*, p. 291.

[2] Quoted Joel, *Britain and Europe*, p. 346.

[3] See Lord Curzon in 30 H.L.Deb. 253, and Lord Hankey, *Diplomacy by Conference*, p. 53.

sitting and perhaps discussed with that close attention and at that length that its importance obviously warranted.

The discussion on any item having terminated, the Prime Minister would make a note in order to convey the result to the Sovereign, and the Cabinet would proceed to the next business. The minister concerned would then indicate to his department what the decision was—that is, if he could remember it. With some Prime Ministers, the Cabinet was never in doubt what the decision was. Mr Balfour, for instance, always made the point abundantly clear. With other Prime Ministers, however, the Cabinet might break up convinced that it had come to a conclusion, but not knowing what that conclusion was. While Mr Asquith was Prime Minister, for instance, it was quite common for a minister's private secretary to telephone to the Prime Minister's private secretary to ask what the decision had been, for there was no record of the Cabinet's decision save the letter sent to the King, of which the Prime Minister would keep a copy.[1]

This unbusinesslike system completely broke down under the stress of war. One of the first acts of Mr Lloyd George was to institute a Cabinet Secretariat to organise the business of the War Cabinet. This Secretariat was in fact the Secretariat of the Committee of Imperial Defence. When the former War Committee was reconstituted by Mr Balfour in 1903, a Foreign Office clerk was assigned to keep the minutes. With the increase of the Committee's work and the setting up of sub-committees under Sir Henry Campbell-Bannerman, the Secretariat necessarily increased both in size and in importance. It not only prepared the agenda and kept the minutes of the Committee and its sub-committees, but also acted as the link connecting the Service Departments, the Foreign Office, and the other departments concerned with the development of war plans. Those plans were put into execution on the outbreak of war. The War Council set up in November, 1914, was developed out of the Committee and used its Secretariat. It was replaced by the Dardanelles Committee in 1915, and the functions of the latter were gradually extended so that it became the War Committee. It used the same Secretariat, and 'Colonel Hankey [the

[1] See some examples, below, pp. 270–1, and Lord Hankey, *Diplomacy by Conference*, pp. 52 and 62–9.

Secretary] sat between the Prime Minister and the door, ready to attend to either, as might be required'.[1]

On the formation of the War Cabinet in 1916,[2] Mr Lloyd George attached the War Committee's Secretariat to the Cabinet. Thus, the Secretariat of the Committee of Imperial Defence became the Secretariat of the Cabinet; and Colonel (now Lord) Hankey, the Secretary to the Committee, became the first Secretary to the Cabinet.[3] Lord Hankey records that 'Mr Lloyd George...had, with Mr Asquith's knowledge, often discussed with me academically the possible evolution of some such system, and on Sunday, 17 December 1916, after about a week with the new War Cabinet, I sat up half the night drafting the new administrative arrangements for the War Cabinet Office and to this day they are based on that system'.[4] The new department appeared in the Estimates in 1917 (on a Supplementary Estimate). The Machinery of Government Committee in 1918 recommended that the Secretariat should be permanently maintained 'for the purpose of collecting and putting into shape [the Cabinet] agenda, of providing the information and the material necessary for its deliberations, and of drawing up the results for communication to the departments concerned'.[5] In 1922 Mr Bonar Law regarded it as one of the undesirable relics of the War Cabinet and proposed to abolish it. Its utility had, however, been so clearly proved that it was decided to continue it, though its functions were narrowly defined.

Sir Maurice Hankey was not only Secretary to the Cabinet, but also Secretary to the Committee of Imperial Defence and Clerk of the Privy Council. This last office was apparently assigned to him to meet the criticism to which the institution of the Cabinet Office was at one time subject.[6] On his retirement in 1938 a change was made. A unified Office under the title 'Offices of the Cabinet, Committee of Imperial Defence, Economic Advisory Council and Minister for Co-ordination

[1] Clement Jones, *Empire Review*, XIX, p. 1410, and see Lord Hankey, *Diplomacy by Conference*, p. 55.

[2] See below, pp. 297–9.

[3] Lloyd George, *War Memoirs*, III, pp. 1080, 1081, and Lord Hankey, *Diplomacy by Conference*, pp. 55–7.

[4] Lord Hankey, *Diplomacy by Conference*, p. 58.

[5] Report of the Machinery of Government Committee, p. 6.

[6] Lord Hankey, *op. cit.* p. 60.

of Defence' was erected. The official head, who was made a member of the Committee of Imperial Defence, was styled 'Permanent Secretary and Secretary of the Cabinet'. He was assisted by two other officers, styled respectively 'Clerk of the Privy Council and Deputy Secretary of the Cabinet' and 'Secretary of the Committee of Imperial Defence'.[1] In 1956 the Secretary to the Cabinet also became Joint Secretary to the Treasury, but this was no doubt a personal arrangement, not an attempt by the Treasury to absorb the Cabinet Office.

In the first War Cabinet, the Secretary and two Assistant Secretaries were usually present. The practice was afterwards altered and between the wars only the Secretary was present. Now the Deputy Secretary and sometimes an Under-Secretary also attend. During the war of 1914–18, also, the Cabinet Office transmitted to the departments the decisions of the War Cabinet.[2] This practice too has been altered; each minister, whether or not in the Cabinet, now receives the Cabinet Conclusions and it is his responsibility to instruct his department as to the decisions taken, in so far as they need departmental action.

The functions of the Cabinet Office are, therefore:

(*a*) to circulate the memoranda and other documents required for the business of the Cabinet and its committees;

(*b*) to compile under the direction of the Prime Minister the agenda of the Cabinet and, under the direction of the chairman, the agenda of a Cabinet committee;

(*c*) to issue summons of meetings of the Cabinet and its committees;

(*d*) to take down and circulate the conclusions of the Cabinet and its committees and to prepare the reports of Cabinet committees; and

(*e*) to keep, subject to the instructions of the Cabinet, the Cabinet papers and conclusions.

§4. *The Cabinet Agenda*

In the eighteenth century it was the practice of any minister who desired to lay a matter before the Cabinet to summon it for that purpose. The regularisation of business made for regular Cabinets, and for many years the Cabinet met weekly during the parliamentary session. Since

[1] *The Times*, 2 June 1938.

[2] See *The War Cabinet*: Report for the Year 1917, Cd. 9005/1918, pp. 3–4. For a defence of this practice, see 155 H.C.Deb. 5 s., 223.

1945 it has usually met twice a week. Additional meetings are summoned by the Prime Minister when they are necessary. The question of the right of the Prime Minister to refuse to summon a Cabinet is perhaps of some theoretical interest. As a matter of practice, it never arises. If a matter is of great urgency, it is inconceivable that the Prime Minister will not recognise it as such. If a dispute has arisen between the Prime Minister and a minister, that alone is a question of urgency upon which the Prime Minister himself will desire an immediate decision.

Normally, a proposal is submitted to the Cabinet by the minister concerned in the form of a written memorandum.[1] Copies of these memoranda are produced, usually by the Cabinet Office, and are circulated by that Office. If a memorandum is of any considerable length it generally concludes with a summary prepared in order that ministers who are not specially conversant with the subject may readily inform themselves of what is proposed. But the insistence on memoranda, which is an elementary rule of business, does not prevent an item being placed, with the Prime Minister's approval, on the agenda without a memorandum. Moreover, it is of course open to the Prime Minister to allow questions not mentioned on the agenda to be raised as matters of urgency.

Before the war of 1939–45 there was a Cabinet instruction, renewed by each Cabinet, that memoranda, draft Bills and other constituents of Cabinet agenda were not to be circulated until after their subject-matter had been fully examined between the departments from which they emanated, the Treasury, the Law Officers where contentious Bills were involved,[2] and any other departments concerned. The post-war rule is apparently not so detailed, but it is still the rule that proposals affecting other departments must not be submitted to the Cabinet until they have been thoroughly discussed with those departments at the official

[1] In 1932 Mr MacDonald wished to protest against the number of Cabinet memoranda and to suggest that no memorandum be sent without his first reading and approving it. His note 'was sent to Hankey who told him, politely, that it was nonsense': Thomas Jones, *A Diary with Letters*, p. 69.

[2] It is believed that this requirement and indeed much of the present procedure was originated by the Labour Cabinet in 1924 as a result of complaints by Sir Patrick Hastings, then Attorney-General. When an important and contentious Bill is on the agenda, the Attorney-General may be summoned.

level and, if necessary, between ministers. Where there is a conflict of interest between departments, it should never come to the Cabinet until the possibilities of securing agreement at lower levels have been fully explored and exhausted.

As a result of attempts made in 1919 to secure proper financial control it was also laid down that no proposal involving finance should be circulated until the sanction of the Chancellor of the Exchequer had been obtained: but this rule disappeared during the war and has been replaced by the rule, already quoted, requiring preliminary consultation, which necessarily applies *a fortiori* to the Treasury. Moreover, the general practice of consultation, to which reference has already been made,[1] makes formal instructions less necessary.

The Prime Minister can always refuse to have a question discussed until, in his opinion, it is ripe. In January 1919 Mr Churchill, as Secretary of State for War, concocted a scheme for the armies of occupation with Field-Marshal Sir Henry Wilson. It was based on the continuance of compulsory service, and was strongly objected to by Mr Lloyd George, who was in Paris. Mr Lloyd George refused to have it brought before the War Cabinet in his absence, and Mr Bonar Law, who presided over the Cabinet, refused to allow a decision to be taken. But next day Churchill, Wilson and Haig saw Lloyd George, who then allowed it to be brought before the Cabinet.[2]

It is an instruction to the Secretary, subject to the power of the Prime Minister to waive the requirement, that no proposal shall be placed upon the Cabinet agenda until a period of two clear days has elapsed since the circulation of the appropriate memoranda.[3] These memoranda are circulated daily, and more often if necessary. At the end of each week a programme of Cabinet business for the following week is issued, with the sanction of the Prime Minister, for the guidance of the departments, so that they may have advance notice of the subjects likely to be raised. The final agenda papers are issued later, though still a day or two in advance of the meeting. These name the ministers other than members

[1] Above, pp. 140–3.

[2] *Diaries of Field-Marshal Sir Henry Wilson*, II, pp. 165–6.

[3] In 1924 a rule requiring five days' notice was laid down; but owing to the pressure on departments it was impracticable to restore this rule in 1945.

of the Cabinet who are invited to be present for particular items, and specify the time at which they are to attend. At the first of the weekly meetings the traditional order of business is followed and the first item is 'Foreign Affairs (if any)'. This enables the Secretary of State to give any general explanation that he thinks fit, and enables any minister to call attention to any matter of importance set out in the Foreign Office despatches and telegrams of the week. At the second meeting of the week it is usual to discuss the parliamentary business for the next week, which is announced in the House of Commons that afternoon. The agenda is, however, invariably submitted to the Prime Minister, and he can change the order, or direct the deletion of items, or add new items. The agenda, in short, is as much under the control of the Prime Minister as it was when there was no formal circulated agenda. Each item refers, however, to the relevant Cabinet papers. Thus, a minister's private secretary can gather together the necessary documents, attach them to the agenda, and so enable the minister to prepare himself for the Cabinet discussions.

If, after the agenda has been circulated, questions of urgency arise, the Prime Minister can always authorise a supplementary agenda paper. This is circulated as quickly as possible and is, if necessary, laid on the table. It is the recognised right of a minister to have circulated as a Cabinet document any remarks which he may desire to make on a Cabinet proposal.[1] When Mr Balfour circulated his memorandum on fiscal reform in 1903, for instance, Mr Ritchie and Lord Balfour of Burleigh circulated reasoned statements against its conclusions.[2] But it appears that normally, and apart from departmental memoranda, ministers may prefer to make orally such statements on general policy. It has to be remembered, in this connection, that the Cabinet minutes will contain a reference to the memorandum and the memorandum itself will be preserved in the Cabinet Office, unless the Cabinet otherwise directs. If, on the other hand, the minister states his case orally, the minutes will not as a rule indicate which minister put forward these arguments. In other words, the minister who circulates a memorandum is putting his views on record.

[1] *Life of the Eighth Duke of Devonshire*, II, p. 339.

[2] *Ibid.*

The items on the agenda are usually concerned with questions of departmental policy upon which the ministerial head of a department desires a Cabinet decision. Wider political questions, not of a departmental nature, would normally be raised by the Prime Minister. It is generally understood by the departments that their documents should be as complete as possible, and should contain the various arguments in favour of the proposal and the criticisms which might be brought against it. But, probably, the purpose of this rule is effectively secured by the requirement, already mentioned, that no proposal should be circulated until it has been submitted to the interested departments, especially the Treasury in respect of financial matters, or to the Law Officers in respect of legislative proposals. In any case, the Cabinet does not like to be confronted with technical inter-departmental questions of minor importance. It considers that the ministers concerned should themselves settle such matters.

§5. *Procedure in Cabinet*

When Lord Balfour became Lord President of the Council in 1925 he told Mr Baldwin that Cabinet business was three or four times as great as when he first took Cabinet office in 1886. The amount of business necessarily depends on political conditions. There have been periods of overwhelming pressure, as between 1914 and 1919, between 1930 and 1932, between 1935 and the outbreak of war, under the Labour Government of 1945–51, during the Suez dispute of 1956–7, and so forth. During the intervals, the Cabinet as such has not been heavily overburdened. In 1934 there were less than fifty meetings, though this was below the average, which between the wars was between sixty and seventy a year and has now risen to between eighty and one hundred. Certainly the length of Cabinet meetings has not expanded in proportion to the increase in business. For this there are several reasons. The first is that Cabinet instructions since 1919 have made clear, and have repeated at intervals, that no question is to be brought before the Cabinet until it has been submitted to all the departments concerned. Inter-departmental questions must therefore be settled inter-departmentally so far as is possible. The institution of the Cabinet Secretariat has enabled this rule to be effectively enforced. Secondly, the practice of consultation between leading ministers[1] has enabled agreement to be reached before it becomes a matter of Cabinet debate.[2] This development is neither so recent nor so important as is commonly alleged.[3] Thirdly, the better distribution of memoranda through the Cabinet Office and insistence upon the rule that, so far as possible, every proposal should be accompanied by a memorandum, and every memorandum circulated for two clear days before it is discussed, together with the circulation of a formal agenda, have enabled ministers to come to a meeting much better prepared. Fourthly, the Cabinet now makes much greater use of committees. Finally, the Defence Committee has relieved the Cabinet of the necessity for discussing problems of defence except so far as they involve questions of principle.

But for these developments, the Cabinet would be quite unable to dispose of the growing number of public questions with which the Government is concerned. The Cabinet may contain sixteen or more ministers. Most of them have long political experience. Most of them have important departmental duties which, in their turn, have grown in number and importance. Most of them have popular constituencies to nurse. Most of them, too, have to attend to business in or near the House of Commons while it is sitting—and the House sits more frequently than it used to sit. Some of them, further, are concerned with the general management of their party machines.

If the work is to be done, however, ministers must refrain from talking too much. Mr Lloyd George has stated in evidence before a Select Committee: 'A man who makes a five minutes' speech in a Cabinet is voted a bore straight away.'[4] A minister explaining a budget or a Bill is necessarily allowed some latitude, but even then it never approximates to 'the limits of Parliamentary indulgence'.[5]

Even now, complaints are sometimes made that the Cabinet is overworked. Careful examination of these complaints suggests, first, that

[1] Sometimes referred to as 'the inner Cabinet', but erroneously, for it is purely informal and bears no relation to the 'inner Cabinet' of the eighteenth century.

[2] 304 H.C.Deb. 5 s., 363 (1935).

[3] But see for the 'Inner Cabinet' which produced Munich, Lord Templewood, *Nine Troubled Years*, pp. 291–2.

[4] H.C. 161 of 1931, Q. 1010.

[5] Lloyd George, *The Truth about the Peace Treaties*, I, p. 113.

those who complain do not distinguish between the Cabinet work of ministers and their work in other capacities, and, secondly, that they usually arise during periods of political pressure. An agenda of fifteen items, every one of which has been carefully prepared, is not usually too long for a committee meeting of 2 hours. Experienced ministers are accustomed to rapid decisions. If the subject-matter is really controversial and has not been properly discussed beforehand, reference to a committee is an obvious expedient, and it is an expedient which is often adopted. But where there has been a full exploration of the ground, either inter-departmentally or in committee, a long debate ought not to be necessary. Where the point is one of real political importance, it may have been discussed informally by the leading ministers. The complaints arose chiefly immediately after the war of 1914–18, when the scope and variety of problems were alike enormous, during the Labour Governments, and between 1935 and 1939.

We may put aside as wholly exceptional the problems of the two post-war periods. Also, no system of government can cope adequately with a situation such as that of 1935–6, when the Italo-Abyssinian conflict, the denunciation of the Locarno Treaty, the expansion of the defence services, the settlement of the Dardanelles question, the negotiations with Egypt, and the approval of Unemployment Assistance Regulations, all had to be settled almost at the same time. It is more instructive to consider the experience of the earlier Labour Governments. Undoubtedly, a party which comes newly to power, with a mass of general proposals for social reform, must necessarily be called upon to do more work than a party which has been in power, with short intervals, for a long period, and which does not propose radical reforms. Also, the social and economic difficulties which the Labour Government of 1929–31 had to face were greater than those of any Government since 1922. That Government came into power just after the top of the boom had been reached, and world economic and, therefore, political conditions were rapidly deteriorating. Further, the Labour Governments had no majority in the House of Commons, and they had to face the opposition of the House of Lords to all their more important legislative proposals. Possibly, too, the difficulties of the Labour ministers were aggravated by their own inexperience. Few of them had had much departmental experience. They had, for the most part, been unable to pass through the regular progression from parliamentary private secretary to junior minister, and from junior minister to the Cabinet. Some of them were, in consequence, unable to make the fullest use of their official advisers. For all these reasons, the position of the Labour Governments was exceptional. Whatever happens, a Labour Government must be more hard pressed than a Conservative Government or a coalition which contains a substantial Conservative element. But a Labour Government with a majority, and composed mainly of persons with previous ministerial experience, would, as that which took office in 1945 demonstrated, be able to carry out reforms at a reasonable pace. It is certainly the impression that the Conservative Government of 1924–9 and the National Governments between 1932 and 1935 (omitting, therefore, the difficult period of the first National Government) were able to cope with their Cabinet business without difficulty. The Labour ministers were undoubtedly heavily burdened between 1945 and 1950; but once more it was the weight of departmental decisions rather than the burden of Cabinet business which caused them to age noticeably. They had to put through an immense programme in difficult world conditions, and with a majority which, while large, tended like all left-wing majorities to become restive on slight provocation.

It is true that sometimes decisions are not taken until too late. The Cabinet of 1884, and Mr Gladstone in particular, was so concerned with the prospect of obtaining an international conference to discuss the problem of Egypt that there was no time to discuss the rescue of General Gordon.[1] Sometimes the appropriate minister has to take action with the Prime Minister's sanction and without consulting the Cabinet.[2] Sometimes the minister himself takes action in the hope that his action will be ratified. Thus, in 1915 there was a dispute between Lord Kitchener at the War Office and Mr Lloyd George at the Ministry of Munitions as to the provision of guns. Lord Kitchener appealed to the Cabinet, which set up a committee to determine whether the guns

[1] *Life of Sir Charles Dilke*, II, p. 57; *Life of the Eighth Duke of Devonshire*, I, pp. 465–6; *Life of Joseph Chamberlain*, I, p. 524.

[2] See above, pp. 226–7.

were necessary. The committee met and adjourned. But Mr Lloyd George deemed the matter urgent and provided the guns without Cabinet sanction.[1]

The minister can always protect himself by consulting the leading ministers. Though in theory all Cabinet ministers are equal, in practice a few ministers dominate discussions by reason of their personality, their political support, and the importance of their offices. 'In most Governments', said Mr Lloyd George, 'there are four or five outstanding figures who by exceptional talent, experience, and personality, constitute the inner council which gives direction to the policy of a ministry. An administration that is not fortunate enough to possess such a group may pull through without mishap in tranquil season, but in an emergency it is hopelessly lost.'[2]

Many examples could be cited;[3] but a few are of outstanding importance. In 1853, when the question was raised of sending ships for the protection of Constantinople, Lord Aberdeen summoned a meeting of five ministers. Lord John Russell attended as Secretary of State for Foreign Affairs. Sir James Graham, as First Lord of the Admiralty, was technically responsible and necessarily present. Lord Palmerston who, as Home Secretary, was not departmentally concerned, was summoned so as to prevent his opposing the step when Cabinet sanction was sought.[4]

In 1878, when the defence of Constantinople again became a question of policy, 'an inner Cabinet was formed to direct the activities of the rest. It consisted of the Prime Minister, Lord Salisbury and Lord Cairns.... These three men met together constantly, went through the messages which had been received from abroad since their last consultation, and decided upon the action to be recommended to their colleagues.'[5] The situation here was peculiar, for the Foreign Secretary, Lord Derby, was not in agreement with the Cabinet's policy. Thus, the

[1] Lloyd George, *War Memoirs*, II, pp. 559–61.

[2] *Ibid.* III, p. 1042.

[3] One of the earliest examples occurred in 1832. The Prime Minister (Lord Grey), the Lord Chancellor (Lord Brougham), and the Home Secretary (Lord Melbourne) decided an Irish question because the dispersion of ministers made a Cabinet impossible: *Melbourne Papers*, p. 190.

[4] *Life of the Earl of Clarendon*, II, p. 3; *Life of Henry Reeve*, I, p. 295.

[5] *Life of Robert, Marquis of Salisbury*, II, p. 209.

inner Cabinet was actually in departmental control. It reported to the whole Cabinet, where the policy agreed upon was forced upon the Cabinet and sometimes telegrams were actually drafted in the Cabinet.[1]

In 1898 Lord Milner's letter from South Africa, which in effect contemplated war with the Transvaal, was circulated by Mr Joseph Chamberlain, as Colonial Secretary, only to Mr Balfour (acting Prime Minister), the Duke of Devonshire, the Chancellor of the Exchequer, the First Lord of the Admiralty, and the Secretary of State for War. Mr Chamberlain answered without consulting the Cabinet.[2]

The steps leading to the outbreak of war in 1914 were taken by the Foreign Secretary in consultation with the Prime Minister.[3] The consequential steps, such as the carrying out by the departments of the plans of the Committee of Imperial Defence, were authorised by the ministers concerned after informal consultations.[4] Subsequently, the conduct of the war fell largely into the hands of committees of the Cabinet, until it became necessary to supersede the ordinary Cabinet altogether by the War Cabinet of five members.[5]

In 1930 the Prime Minister, Mr Henderson (Foreign Secretary), Mr Thomas (Lord Privy Seal) Mr Snowden (Chancellor of the Exchequer), and Mr Clynes (Home Secretary) were in the habit of meeting once a week for a general conversation about the parliamentary situation and the state of the Labour party.[6] In Mr MacDonald's coalition Cabinet of 1932–5 there was an inner group known as 'the Six' composed (after the resignation of Lord Samuel) of Messrs MacDonald and Thomas (Labour), Sir John Simon and Mr Runciman (Liberal National), and Messrs Baldwin and Neville Chamberlain (Conservative).[7] Mr Baldwin in 1936 reported his conversations with Edward VIII about his marriage to 'about four' of his colleagues.[8] In Mr Neville Chamberlain's

[1] *Life of Robert, Marquis of Salisbury*, II, p. 209.

[2] *Life of Joseph Chamberlain*, II, p. 365.

[3] Above, p. 219.

[4] Churchill, *World Crisis*, I, pp. 217–30. The decision to order Sir John French not to retire beyond the Seine after the retreat from Mons was taken by 'a few ministers', who sent Lord Kitchener to France with 'Cabinet instructions'. Sir Edward Grey, Lord Kitchener and Mr Churchill decided (in the absence of the Prime Minister) to send the Naval Brigade to the defence of Antwerp. See *Life of Lord Oxford and Asquith*, II, p. 125.

[5] Below, ch. x.

[6] Snowden, *Autobiography*, II, pp. 924–5.

[7] *Life of Neville Chamberlain*, p. 199.

[8] 318 H.C.Deb. 5 s., 290.

Government the decisions which led to Munich and eventually to the war of 1939–45 were taken initially by the Foreign Policy Committee of the Cabinet, which met over fifty times between 1937 and 1939 and which consisted of nine or ten ministers. In the late summer of 1938 even this body became too large, and it was virtually succeeded by an 'Inner Cabinet' consisting of the Prime Minister, the Chancellor of the Exchequer (Sir John Simon), the Foreign Secretary (Lord Halifax) and the Home Secretary (Sir Samuel Hoare), known as 'the Big Four'. These were, for those who disliked Munich, 'the Guilty Men'.[1] In Mr Churchill's War Cabinet there was a formal Defence Committee, which consisted initially of the Prime Minister, Mr Neville Chamberlain, Mr Attlee, and the three Service Ministers, with the Chiefs of the Staffs in attendance.[2]

The committee system is now an essential part of Cabinet procedure. Such committees were not unknown even in the first half of the nineteenth century. The Reform Bill of 1832 was drafted by a committee of four persons, not all of whom were members of the Cabinet.[3] That of 1851 was referred to a committee of three persons.[4] Committees were used during the Crimean War; and those on military affairs and coast defences were reconstituted in 1856.[5] The War Cabinet of 1916–19 developed the committee system considerably. Indeed, the War Cabinet discussed only general issues and its normal method of operation was through committees.[6] Though this vast network disappeared after 1919 and above all after 1922, the committee system continued to be used. Between the wars there were in an average year some twenty Cabinet committees in existence.[7] Usually they were *ad hoc* committees, established to deal with particular problems and expiring when reports had been made to the Cabinet or, if the Cabinet so ordered, when consequential decisions had been taken by the Committee. It is not easy, however, to distinguish precisely between an *ad hoc* committee and a standing committee. Except by deliberate decision of the new Cabinet,

[1] Lord Templewood, *Nine Troubled Years*, p. 290 *et seq.*

[2] Churchill, *The Second World War*, II, p. 18.

[3] *Memoirs of Earl Spencer*, p. 292; *Creevey Papers*, II, p. 264.

[4] Greville, *Memoirs*, 2nd series, III, p. 418.

[5] *Panmure Papers*, II, p. 317.

[6] Below, pp. 299–301.

[7] W. K. Hancock and M. M. Goring, *British War Economy*, p. 42.

no Cabinet committee can survive the disappearance of the Cabinet which appointed it. The Finance Committee set up in October 1919[1] might have continued as a standing committee but did not. The Home Affairs Committee,[2] which was originally an *ad hoc* committee, became a standing committee.

The War Cabinet of 1940–5 again made use of committees[3] and some of these continued under the Labour Government of 1945–51. The most important was the Defence Committee, which replaced both the wartime Defence (Operations) Committee and the pre-war Committee of Imperial Defence.[4] The Lord President's or Steering Committee continued until September 1945, when Sir Stafford Cripps became Minister for Economic Affairs. The Lord President's Committee was then replaced by an Economic Policy Committee under the Prime Minister and a Production Committee under Sir Stafford Cripps.[5] The Legislation Committee[6] was another wartime committee which was continued, and to it was added the Future Legislation Committee.[7] Other standing committees are listed by Mr Herbert Morrison,[8] though it was evident that there was a considerable shuffle in 1947. Information about subsequent developments is lacking, probably because of the operation of the rule that, speaking generally, information should not be given about existing Cabinet committees lest the responsibility of the departmental ministers be undermined. Under the system developed by Sir John Anderson in Mr Churchill's War Cabinet, and continued by Mr Attlee, a Cabinet committee generally co-ordinates a group of departments concerned with a common field of government, and functions under one of the Cabinet ministers. If it is known in the House of Commons that a particular committee is functioning under a particular chairman, there is a danger that the chairman, and not the departmental minister, will be regarded as the expositor of Government policy. That the danger is real was shown by Mr Churchill's experiment

[1] 120 H.C.Deb. 50, 744–5; and *Cabinet Government* (2nd ed.), p. 237.

[2] Below, p. 258; and Addison, *Four and a Half Years*, II, p. 542.

[3] Below, pp. 309–11.

[4] Below, p. 313.

[5] H. Morrison, *Government and Parliament*, pp. 20–7; Chester and Willson, *The Organization of British Central Government, 1914–1956*, pp. 310–14.

[6] Below, pp. 258–9.

[7] Below, p. 259.

[8] *Government and Parliament*, pp. 18–23.

with 'overlords' in 1951. It had to be explained that these overlords were *not* responsible to Parliament, and this the Opposition in the House of Commons considered to be adding an insult to an injury.

Cabinet committees, like committees appointed by other bodies, fulfil two functions. First, they debate and report on matters which must ultimately be decided by the Cabinet. A Cabinet committee brings the problem down to its elements, enables the contestants (if the matter is controversial) to debate the issue and, perhaps, reach some kind of compromise and, in short, saves the time of the Cabinet by settling the point, or the several points, which require Cabinet decision. Secondly, in matters of less importance they exercise functions delegated by the Cabinet and decide matters which would otherwise take up Cabinet time. For instance, some Bills go direct to the Cabinet, some are examined and reported on by Cabinet committees, and some are disposed of by Cabinet committees without reference to the Cabinet because they are not of major political importance. The time of Cabinet ministers is economised because a committee is always smaller than the Cabinet and may contain ministers who are not members of the Cabinet or even parliamentary secretaries. Also, it is not uncommon for senior civil servants to attend as advisers to their ministers, who are thus enabled to save the time involved in an adjournment for consultation. There are even Cabinet committees, usually not of political importance, of which officials are made full members with the right to speak. Generally, however, the responsibility of the ministers for policy is maintained, and officials speak only when they are asked for advice.[1]

As mentioned above, Cabinet committees are of two kinds, standing committees and *ad hoc* committees. The standing committee provides a regular means of handling, below Cabinet level, problems of a Cabinet nature which arise regularly during the course of a year. Whenever there is a considerable bulk of homogeneous questions which can reasonably be discussed below Cabinet level, a standing committee is appointed, and all such questions stand referred to the committee.

[1] The difficulty of generalisation may be illustrated by the experience of the present writer in another Commonwealth country. While advising one minister, he was frequently summoned to Cabinet meetings and expected to speak freely. While advising another minister he was summoned only to meetings of Cabinet committees, and only for the purpose of advising the minister: he was not allowed to speak.

The *ad hoc* committees are set up by the Cabinet or the Prime Minister to settle, or to report on, problems of transient importance. They may be required to report on a particular problem, or to solve a problem which has already been debated in Cabinet, or to work out the consequences of a decision already taken in Cabinet. They have usually completed their work when they have reported, but sometimes they are kept in existence in order to take consequential decisions or to make successive reports. Usually, they are smaller than standing committees and may contain only three or four members, who are not necessarily Cabinet ministers.

The Cabinet committees function much like the Cabinet itself though, as has been mentioned, officials attend more frequently and the committees are smaller. A member of the Cabinet Secretariat is assigned to act as secretary, and memoranda are circulated as for a Cabinet meeting. Minutes are kept, and they are circulated to the departments. If, however, the function of the committee is to report to the Cabinet, it is generally possible for the chairman's report to supersede the separate memoranda furnished by the departmental minister. By this means the amount of 'paper' to be read by a Cabinet minister may be diminished; and this is an important consideration; for Cabinet ministers agree that their fundamental problem is to reduce the volume of 'paper'—a fact which enthusiastic civil servants and even more the 'experts' outside often fail to realise.

As an example of the working of Cabinet committees it may be convenient to explain how the legislative programme for a parliamentary session is settled.

Between the wars there was a Home Affairs Committee charged with two functions. First, it considered the technical aspects of Government Bills. Secondly, it kept under review the work of the session. After the formation of the War Cabinet in 1940 these functions were taken over by the Home Policy Committee, which had much wider and more important functions; but in due course these functions passed to the Lord President's Committee or Steering Committee,[1] leaving the function of looking after legislation to the Legislation Committee. Its task is not to plan future legislation but to control the legislative pro-

[1] Below, pp. 312–13.

gramme in the current session. Every month it reviews the progress of all Bills and regulates the flow of instructions to Parliamentary Counsel and the flow of Bills to Parliament accordingly. It also admits new Bills to the list or withdraws Bills from the list. Secondly, it considers the drafts of all Bills. For this reason its members include, in addition to the Leaders of the two Houses and the Chief Whip, the Lord Chancellor and the Law Officers.[1] Ministers whose Bills are under discussion attend to discuss their Bills, and papers for the Committee are circulated to all departments, so that ministers not expressly invited may know which Bills will be under discussion and decide whether they ought to be present. Criticisms of the draft are made by the members, and the appropriate minister or Parliamentary Counsel replies. It should, however, be added that the same rule applies to the Committee as to the Cabinet itself, that as far as possible the draft should have been agreed beforehand by the departments concerned. The Committee has power to act, and therefore to decide the date of introduction and the House in which the Bill is to be introduced. If there is disagreement on major issues of policy, however, it must be referred to the Cabinet.

The Legislation Committee is not concerned with the planning of the work of a new session. This work has been undertaken since the post-war Labour Government, by the Future Legislation Committee. It is a small committee consisting of ministers who are not in charge of 'legislating' departments, but including the Leaders of both Houses and the Chief Whip. Before it the departmental ministers 'fight for time' on the floor of the House. It plans the work of the next session on the basis of the annual legislation which must be passed (e.g. the financial legislation, the Public Works Loan Bill and the Expiring Laws Continuance Bill), the major Government Bills, the departmental Bills of no great political importance which are to be given priority, the departmental Bills which may be put forward if there is time, and a reserve of time for unanticipated legislation.[2]

The Secretary to the Cabinet or, as is in fact usually the case, one of

[1] Report from the Select Committee on Delegated Legislation, H.C. 310, p. x. The Committee also considers statutory instruments if the chairman thinks it necessary.

[2] H. Morrison, *Government and Parliament*, pp. 223–4.

his assistants, acts as secretary to all Cabinet committees. Where, however, the question involved is of a technical nature, an official from the department most concerned will act as joint secretary. Documents are circulated to the committee as to the Cabinet, and minutes are kept. These minutes are rather fuller than are the minutes of the Cabinet. The report containing the committee's recommendations, when approved by the chairman of the committee, is circulated to the Cabinet as a Cabinet paper. It is for the Cabinet itself to reach decisions on the recommendations so submitted.

At every committee which considers serious departmental issues the ministerial heads of the departments concerned must necessarily be present. They alone are fully informed of the nature of the problem; they will have the responsibility of carrying out the decision to which the Cabinet may come on the recommendation of the committee. Since most questions of government involve financial considerations, it follows that the Chancellor of the Exchequer usually has more committee work than any other minister.

Again, when foreign affairs are disturbed, the Foreign Secretary will necessarily have much committee work in spite of the pressing demands of his own departmental questions. The Prime Minister himself will be chairman of many of the most important committees. One result of the Cabinet system is, therefore, that the burden of committee discussion falls primarily on ministers who are already oppressed with much departmental work. Also, they cannot substantially be relieved by the appointment to committees of ministers with less urgent departmental work, Ministers of State or ministers without portfolio. There are no doubt in every Cabinet ministers of wide experience possessing the ability to seize the issues of a complicated question of whose background they have no official knowledge. A minister without heavy departmental duties may be useful as chairman of a committee to consider an intractable interdepartmental question. Sometimes, too, a junior minister can take the place of the ministerial head of a department. But, speaking generally, Cabinet committees require the assistance of the members familiar with the questions to be discussed. Consequently, when a minister's departmental duties become heaviest his work on Cabinet committees also becomes heavy. Since a Cabinet may at a given time have as many as thirty committees in existence, and since as many as fifteen of these may involve financial questions and necessitate the presence of the Chancellor of the Exchequer or of the Financial Secretary to the Treasury, it can readily be understood that committee work may be largely the cause of that pressure of Cabinet business which is so obvious in times of emergency or political difficulty.

The results of the committee system can be stated in general terms only. It can be assumed, however, that if a committee produces an agreed report, subsequent Cabinet discussion is rarely necessary. If, on the other hand, the committee cannot reach agreement, the whole question is thrown open to the Cabinet. On one occasion before 1939 a committee was agreed except for the chairman. The chairman, having stated the view of the committee, proceeded to state his own view. Thereupon the Prime Minister emphatically asserted his agreement with the chairman, and after little more discussion the Cabinet accepted his point of view. It appears, however, that committee disagreements are rare. The committee contains the ministers primarily concerned. If they cannot find a compromise in committee, it is unlikely that they will be able to reach a compromise in Cabinet. But the whole process of Cabinet government implies compromise, and it is the purpose of a committee to find the formula in which that compromise can be stated.

The Cabinet takes decisions by a majority whenever it cannot reach an agreed conclusion. It appears that the practice of taking votes and deciding by a majority did not originate until 1880. The decision to arrest Dillon in 1881 was carried by Mr Gladstone's casting vote. Lord Granville, who was not present, later said that 'he never knew numbers counted in the Cabinet before, and that it was absurd to count heads in assemblies in which there was such a difference in the contents of the heads'.[1] (A criticism that applies to all counting of heads.) The question of the removal of the Duke of Wellington's statue from Hyde Park Corner in 1883 was decided by a show of hands. Sir Charles Dilke said that 'it was the only subject upon which, while I was a member of it, I ever knew the Cabinet to take a show of hands'.[2] This appears not to

[1] *Life of Sir Charles Dilke*, I, p. 370.

[2] *Ibid.* I, p. 528. Dilke was not in the Cabinet of 1881.

be correct, for Lord Granville told Mr Gladstone in 1886, 'I think you too often counted noses in your last Cabinet',[1] and Lord Morley gives examples.[2]

In any case, the taking of votes is exceptional. It is said that on the Education Bill in 1901 the Cabinet divided several times, 'a practice which large Cabinets have rendered unavoidable'.[3] It was decided to restrict the Bill to secondary education by a vote of ten to eight.[4] Nevertheless, Lord Oxford and Asquith wrote: 'It is not, or was not in any other Cabinets in which I have sat, the custom (unless in exceptional cases not always of the first importance) to take a division.'[5] It may be assumed that fewer divisions of opinion appeared in Conservative than in Liberal Cabinets. It is the general experience, however, that votes are rare. The debate is continued until agreement is reached. The Naval Estimates of 1913 were the main and often the sole topic of discussion at fourteen full meetings of the Cabinet.[6] If, however, the 'voices' have to be taken, the practice is for each member of the Cabinet to express his views. The Secretary notes the number for and against, and the Prime Minister announces the decision of the Cabinet without mentioning numbers, thus avoiding the appearance of a division.[7]

The Cabinet itself is a committee, and it comes to its conclusions in much the same way as other committees. That is, it talks around a subject until some compromise suggests itself. Only when there are fundamental divergencies does the majority override the minority. The problem of securing agreement is greater in the Cabinet, partly because of the fundamental importance of its decisions, and partly because, as will be explained presently, it is the duty of the dissenting minority either to resign or to support the decision of the majority. Resignations may entail the breaking up of the Cabinet and, in addition, a party split. Great efforts are therefore made to secure agreement. Compromise is the first and last order of the day.

Disraeli once said that in his Cabinet of twelve members there were seven different opinions.[8] The problem is not merely that there may be

[1] *Life of Gladstone*, III, p. 5.
[2] *Ibid.*
[3] Fitzroy, *Memoirs*, I, p. 63.
[4] *Ibid.* I, p. 67.
[5] *Fifty Years of Parliament*, II, p. 196.
[6] Churchill, *World Crisis*, I, p. 172.
[7] H. Morrison, *Government and Parliament*, pp. 5–6.
[8] This was on the Russo-Turkish War in 1877: *Life of Disraeli*, II, p. 1066.

divergent views of general public policy or of the effect of that policy on public opinion; frequently the Cabinet has to choose between rival experts.

From beginning to end [of the war of 1914–18] civilian ministers found themselves compelled to choose between rival and competing military plans, each of which had highly expert authority behind it, and to adjust whatever plan was chosen to the policy and strategy of Allies.... In whatever way the ministerial pack might be shuffled, it was not to be supposed that active and conscientious men who accepted responsibility for the results would remain mere spectators of the conflict, or refrain from expressing opinions which they held with conviction. Lord Kitchener is reported to have said after one of his differences with the Cabinet that it was 'repugnant to him to have to reveal military secrets to twenty-three gentlemen with whom he was barely acquainted', but the twenty-three being charged with the ultimate responsibility could not reasonably be asked to accept the plea of military necessity as a ground for keeping them in ignorance of the facts.[1]

Yet the task of securing agreement is not so difficult as it sounds. A difference between two ministers or two departments can usually be settled by a private consultation or by arbitration by the Prime Minister. In the Cabinet the Prime Minister occupies a position of pre-eminence, varying in strength according to the weight of personality, which frequently enables him to impose a decision.[2] If, as may sometimes happen, agreement is reached among the more prominent Cabinet ministers, it may be assumed that the agreement of the Cabinet will, as a rule, follow.[3]

Above all, the Cabinet is usually composed of leaders of a single party. The Prime Minister is the leader of that party, and his fifteen or more colleagues owe him a personal as well as a party allegiance.[4] They are at various stages of their political careers, and only a few have

[1] *Life of Lord Oxford and Asquith*, II, pp. 123–4.

[2] See above, ch. VIII, p. 203.

[3] Another method of securing agreement is indicated in the following passage: 'What really happens in the Cabinet is that...the Secretary of State for War brings forward his Estimates and then his right hon. friends bring forward their Estimates. They never criticise each other. There is a tacit understanding that they will always vote for each other's Estimates': 215 H.C.Deb. 5 s., 1039.

[4] For instance, most of his colleagues supported Peel in 1845 and 1846 though they had strong views about the Corn Laws. Cf. Greville, *Memoirs*, 2nd series, II, p. 364.

substantial personal prestige. They have a common party loyalty and, generally, a common political faith. It may be true, as Mr Lloyd George has said, that there is 'no generosity at the top'. There is, however, a tradition of appearing to be generous, partly at least because it is good policy. Moreover, it is difficult for an ambitious politician—and the most obstreperous minister is usually the most ambitious—to separate himself from his party. A dissenting minister who threatens to resign has to consider whether his presence is necessary to the Government. A minister who miscalculates—as when Lord Randolph Churchill 'forgot Goschen'—may send himself into the political wilderness. A minister who resigns on the ground of disagreement must, if his political ambition is to be further realised, either form a new party or join the Opposition. Lord John Russell's resignation in 1855 prevented him from again becoming Prime Minister until after Palmerston's death. Lord Derby, Disraeli's Foreign Secretary, became a Liberal. The Liberal Unionists struggled back into office under a Conservative Prime Minister. Mr Winston Churchill, after each tergiversation, had to wait for office. Other less eminent men have undergone political extinction.

In any case, office has its attractions. It is natural for a politician to hesitate before he consigns himself to the back benches. He must choose between his opinions and his prospects; usually, he forgoes the former. So, Tories who supported Peel against Catholic Relief and the repeal of the Corn Laws supported him in effecting both. Conservatives who cheered Disraeli's attacks on Gladstone's Reform Bill cheered him also when he 'dished the Whigs'. Whigs who were Conservative in all but name supported Radical measures until Home Rule became the order of the day. Free-trade Liberals found special circumstances to justify protective duties. And we are all Socialists now that the franchise has been extended to the common man—and his wife. We need not always assume motives; but motives are commonly mixed.

§6. *Coalitions*

No such considerations strengthen a Coalition Government. Here there may be little personal and no party loyalty. The Cabinet has a plethora of eminence. There are rival policies as well as rival ambitions.

'England', said Disraeli, 'does not love Coalitions.' The truth is that Coalitions do not love each other. Both Mr Gladstone[1] and the Duke of Argyll[2] have testified to the smoothness with which Lord Aberdeen's Cabinet of 1852–5 functioned. The latter said: 'I have been a member of every Liberal Cabinet that succeeded it for twenty-nine years, and I never saw any of them which worked more smoothly or with less individual friction.' It may be noticed that it produced an amalgamation of Whigs and Peelites which had only been prevented before by Lord John Russell's 'chalking "No-Popery"' and running away. In any event, the Duke could not have been aware of the broadsides which Lord John Russell fired at Lord Aberdeen or the discussions between these two and Lord Clarendon.[3] Great Britain muddled into the Crimean War because the Cabinet was divided; and because it was divided it accepted compromises which led it inevitably nearer and nearer to war. The fleet was sent to the Dardanelles because some wanted offensive operations and some wanted no operations at all. The compromise was necessary to prevent the break-up of the Cabinet. It inevitably led to war, though it did not itself denote war.

The coalition of 1895 was not really a coalition at all. The Conservative Party was renewing its youth by an infusion of Whig men. Of the coalition of 1915 we have some graphic descriptions. Its members 'were constantly looking over their shoulders to see whether they could carry their parties with them'.[4] On the question of conscription, Mr Bonar Law informed Mr Asquith: 'I believe that it is easier for you to obtain the consent of your party to general compulsion than for me to obtain the consent of my party to its not being adopted.'[5] Mr Asquith could not closure debate in the Dardanelles Committee because some members did not belong to his party.[6] Mr Winston Churchill was, no doubt, a prejudiced observer, but his remarks bear the stamp of credibility.

[1] *English Historical Review*, II, p. 288; *Life of Gladstone*, p. 495.

[2] *Autobiography and Memoirs*, I, p. 388.

[3] Cf. *Life of Gladstone*, I, p. 495, and Gladstone, 'The History of 1852–60 and Greville's Latest Journals', *English Historical Review*, II, pp. 288–9. In any case, those who approved of the war approved on very different grounds: *ibid.* p. 289. See also Gordon, *Life of Lord Aberdeen*, ch. x.

[4] *Life of Lord Oxford and Asquith*, II, p. 211.

[5] *Ibid.*

[6] *Ibid.* II, p. 188.

> Whereas practically all the important matters connected with the war had been dealt with in the late Government by four or five ministers, at least a dozen powerful, capable, distinguished personalities who were in a position to assert themselves had to be consulted. The progress of business therefore became cumbrous and laborious in the last degree, and though all these evils were corrected by earnest patriotism and loyalty, the general result was bound to be disappointing. Those who had knowledge had pasts to defend; those free from war commitments were also free from war experience. At least five or six different opinions prevailed on every great topic, and every operative decision was obtained only by prolonged, discursive and exhaustive discussions. Far more often we laboured through long delays to unsatisfactory compromises.[1]

Again, 'from the moment of the formation of the Coalition power was dispersed and councils were divided, and every military decision had to be carried out by the same sort of process of tact, temporising, and exhaustion which occurs over a clause in a keenly contested Bill in the House of Commons in time of peace'.[2] Finally, 'I was, and am, strongly of opinion that it would have been better to break up the Cabinet, and let one section or the other carry out their view in its integrity, than to preserve what was called the "national unity" at the expense of vital executive action.'[3]

Mr Lloyd George solved the problem by putting the Cabinet out of action for the remainder of the war.[4] Though by 1919 the party lines of five years before had been all but obliterated, the revived Cabinet did not long survive the tumults of peace. But the 'national unity' was restored in 1931 and a Coalition Government—this time called 'National'—was again formed. Of this we know little save that on a most vital point its unity was maintained by an agreement not to be united. After the defection of the 'independent' Liberals and Lord Snowden, there was nobody of outstanding personality who was not, in sympathy if not in affiliation, a Conservative.

Curiously enough the coalition which saved civilisation between

[1] Churchill, *World Crisis*, II, p. 384.

[2] *Ibid.* II, p. 393.

[3] *Ibid.* II, p. 477. Cf. Lord Stanley in 1834: 'Confidence in public men has been more shaken by coalitions than by all the acts of personal misconduct taken together': *Peel Memoirs*, II, p. 40. But this is a conclusion drawn from a completely different Constitution, that of George III.

[4] Below, pp. 297–301.

1940 and 1945 seems to have been at least as united as the ordinary party government. It is true that we hear of disputes between Mr Bevin and Lord Beaverbrook; but this was probably a conflict more of personality than of party. Probably the explanation lies in several factors. First, the fear of invasion and defeat was a remarkable stimulus towards agreement. Secondly, the Labour ministers had every confidence in Mr Churchill as war-leader and gave him a virtually free hand to plan strategy in consultation with President Roosevelt and with the advice of the Chiefs of Staffs. Thirdly, Mr Churchill left the management of home affairs to his colleagues, among whom the Labour ministers played the most significant part. There were no doubt differences of opinion and clashes of personality which have not yet been disclosed; but it seems that the wartime coalition was a remarkable success. Even so, the Labour ministers decided, as soon as the Germans had been defeated, that the problems of reconstruction demanded a return to party government.

§7. *Cabinet Secrecy and Cabinet Minutes*

The Cabinet deliberates in secret; its proceedings are confidential. The Privy Councillor's oath imposes an obligation not to disclose information; and the Official Secrets Acts forbid the publication of Cabinet as well as other official documents.[1] But the effective sanction is neither of these. The rule is, primarily, one of practice. Its theoretical basis is that a Cabinet decision is advice to the Queen, whose consent is necessary to its publication. Its practical foundation is the necessity of securing free discussion by which a compromise can be reached, without the risk of publicity for every statement made and every point given away.

A minister who resigns from the Cabinet usually desires to make an explanation in Parliament. Since this involves an explanation of Cabinet discussions, he must secure the Queen's consent. For this purpose he asks permission through the Prime Minister. Lord Melbourne objected in 1834 to the King's giving consent without consultation with the

[1] Mr Edgar Lansbury was fined in 1934 for publishing a memorandum submitted to the Labour Cabinet of 1929–31 by his father, Mr George Lansbury: Anson, *Law and Custom of the Constitution* (4th ed.), II (1), p. 122.

Prime Minister as 'subversive...of all the principles upon which the Government of this country has hitherto been conducted'.[1] When Lord Derby resigned, he asked permission to state his reasons, and permission was given. But four months later he returned to the subject. This, Queen Victoria said, 'is a most unusual and, she cannot but think, hardly constitutional course'.[2] In reply to Lord Derby's explanation, General Ponsonby wrote: 'Her Majesty expects that, whenever a Privy Councillor makes any statement in Parliament respecting proceedings in her Majesty's Council, the Queen's permission to do so should first be solicited, and the object of the statement made clear; and that the permission thus given should only serve for the particular instance, and not be considered as an open licence.'[3] Lord Salisbury described this statement as 'a valuable addition to constitutional law'.[4]

The rule was explained to the Cabinet by Mr Gladstone in 1880.[5] In 1886 Mr Gladstone interrupted Mr Joseph Chamberlain, who was indicating his reasons for resigning, by observing that he had not received the Queen's permission to disclose information on the matters then under discussion. Mr Chamberlain subsequently asked the Queen's permission, through Mr Gladstone. The Queen replied that in her opinion he had received ample permission before, and that he had not exceeded the permitted limits.[6]

Nevertheless, the rule is not always obeyed. In the first place, there comes a time when Cabinet proceedings pass into history. Full information is now available as to the proceedings of the nineteenth-century Cabinets, and only the absence of biographies of leading statesmen prevents us from having detailed knowledge of the Cabinet from 1900 to 1905. The particular importance of the events leading up to the outbreak of war, and the assumed necessity of showing that the British Government did not contemplate any 'encirclement' of Germany and did its best to prevent war, have enabled the principal actors to state their

[1] *Melbourne Papers*, pp. 215–16.

[2] *Letters of Queen Victoria*, 2nd series, II, pp. 631–2.

[3] *Ibid.* II, p. 634.

[4] *Ibid.*

[5] *Ibid.* III, p. 96; see also *Life of Gladstone*, III, p. 114.

[6] *Letters of Queen Victoria*, 3rd series, I, pp. 100–5. Lord Salisbury in 1886 refused to allow Lord Randolph Churchill to publish his letters of resignation: *Life of Lord Randolph Churchill*, II, pp. 256–7.

versions of the progress of discussion of foreign affairs in the Cabinets of 1906 to 1914. Some have continued the story until 1918, though Mr Lloyd George's use of Cabinet memoranda has been criticised in Parliament.[1] For the inter-war period the material is rather scanty, chiefly because the leading ministers left few papers. Sir Austen Chamberlain, Lord Samuel and the biographers of George V, Mr Bonar Law, Lord Baldwin and Mr Neville Chamberlain have, nevertheless, given some information. Mr Winston Churchill's *The Second World War* contains some material about the working of the War Cabinet, based on official documents, but for the present we lack information about home affairs. The *Official History* is concerned mainly with operations at administrative level.

Secondly, the press is not always left entirely without guidance. It is known that during the war of 1914–18 the representatives of the press were able to secure information from the Prime Minister's secretariat in the 'garden suburb'; and it seems that on occasions since then the press has been enabled to 'understand' the nature of the subject under discussion. There have in the past been periods when the press had its contributors or correspondents in the Cabinet.

Thirdly, it is difficult to prevent revelations of Cabinet discussions when they are matters of political controversy. After the resignation of the Labour Government and the formation of the National Government in 1931, both ministers and ex-ministers disclosed the proposals upon which they had tentatively agreed and those upon which they had not been able to agree.

The taking of notes by any minister other than the Prime Minister was for long forbidden. Sir William Molesworth took notes in the Cabinet of Lord Aberdeen, and on one occasion Lord Granville refused to continue a statement until Molesworth laid down his note-book.[2] Lord Derby took notes in Lord Beaconsfield's Government, asserting that he saw no objection to temporary notes that were subsequently destroyed.[3] Both Lord Salisbury[4] and Mr Asquith[5] forbade the taking

[1] See the practice stated by Mr Baldwin: 238 H.C.Deb. 5 s., 2205–12. See also 83 H.L.Deb. 5 s., 551–2. Mr Lloyd George had the King's permission.

[2] Duke of Argyll, *Autobiography and Memoirs*, I, p. 460.

[3] *Life of Disraeli*, II, p. 1136.

[4] *Life of Robert, Marquis of Salisbury*, II, p. 223.

[5] Oxford and Asquith, *Fifty Years of Parliament*, II, p. 197.

of notes. The result was that normally there was no record of Cabinet decisions except the Prime Minister's letter to the Sovereign.[1] Though a minister might have to order his department to put a Cabinet decision into action, he had no record of what the decision was. Sometimes, indeed, it was by no means certain what the Cabinet had decided. In 1876 it was not certain whether instructions for the Constantinople Conference had been approved.[2] In 1877 it was not certain whether it had been agreed that in certain circumstances no opposition should be offered to the Russian advance towards Constantinople.[3] In 1878 there was misunderstanding as to the effect of the discussion on the occupation of Cyprus.[4] In 1900 the publication of the Spion Kop despatches was due to a misunderstanding in the Cabinet. Some ministers, including Lord Salisbury, were under the impression that no action was to be taken. In consequence, Lord Salisbury expressed a doubt whether 'our traditional practice of not recording Cabinet decisions is a wise one'.[5] Lord Lansdowne said, 'our decisions are not always very distinctly intimated to those who have to carry them out'.[6] There was another dispute as to a Cabinet decision in 1903.[7]

On important occasions, however, the Cabinet has drafted a formal minute. This was, apparently, a frequent practice under George III and George IV,[8] but it has been adopted only occasionally since 1832.[9] In 1840 the Cabinet drafted a formal minute of advice to Queen Victoria on the Eastern question, and minutes of dissent by Lords Clarendon and Holland were attached.[10] The purpose of this was, apparently, the same

[1] See below, ch. XII, pp. 354–6.

[2] *Life of Disraeli*, II, p. 967.

[3] *Ibid.* II, p. 1070.

[4] *Ibid.* II, pp. 1145–9.

[5] *Life of Lord Lansdowne*, p. 184.

[6] *Letters of Queen Victoria*, 3rd series, III, pp. 541–2.

[7] *Life of the Duke of Devonshire*, II, p. 298. See also Sir Austen Chamberlain, 155 H.C.Deb. 5 s., 224. The following amusing letter was written by Lord Hartington's private secretary to Mr Gladstone's private secretary in 1882: 'Harcourt and Chamberlain have both been here this morning and *at* my Chief about yesterday's Cabinet proceedings. They cannot agree about what occurred. There must have been some decision, as Bright's resignation shows. My Chief has told me to ask you what the devil *was* decided, for he be damned if he knows. Will you ask Mr G. in more conventional and less pungent terms?' quoted 86 H.L.Deb. 5 s., 529.

[8] *Peel Papers*, III, pp. 496–8; see also *Melbourne Papers*, p. 247, and Lord Hankey, *Diplomacy by Conference*, pp. 46–51.

[9] For the Cabinet minutes of 1832 advising the creation of peers, see *Taylor Papers*, pp. 342, 355.

[10] *Life of the Earl of Clarendon*, I, pp. 195–7.

as the 'agreement to differ' of 1932, namely, to keep the Cabinet together and yet to allow the dissentients to dissociate themselves from the treaty.[1] In 1871 the Queen insisted on a formal minute advising her to issue an order abolishing the purchase of Army commissions. The abolition had been provided for in a Bill in order that compensation might be given, but the House of Lords had struck out this provision. There was, however, power for the purpose in an Act of George III, and the Cabinet advised the Queen to exercise this power. Since such exercise involved overruling the House of Lords, the Cabinet recognised that the Queen was entitled to more formal advice than could be given in the usual letter from the Prime Minister.[2] In 1877 the Cabinet put into writing the answer to be given to Mr Gladstone's question on the Russo-Turkish War in the House of Commons.[3] In 1878 a formal minute, agreeing to the acquisition of a naval base in the Eastern Mediterranean, was drawn up by the Lord Chancellor and agreed by the Cabinet.[4] In 1910 the Cabinet, at the King's request, drafted a minute stating that advice would not be tendered for the creation of peers to overcome the opposition of the House of Lords unless the actual necessity arose.[5] The request for an undertaking from the Crown for a promise to create peers was embodied in a minute later in the same year.[6]

Since 1916, however, there have been formal Cabinet minutes. Unless the Cabinet otherwise directs—and there have been one or two occasions on which the Cabinet has so directed—the Secretary to the Cabinet or his Deputy is present at every Cabinet meeting. He takes no part in the discussion unless his opinion is asked on a particular point (such as a point of procedure), but merely makes a note of the Cabinet's decisions. The note is known officially as the Cabinet 'Conclusions', though more popularly as the Cabinet 'minutes'. Under the War Cabinet of 1916–19, the minutes contained a full summary of the discussion; but this practice is no longer followed, and the minutes contain only enough information to enable the reader to understand the nature of the conclusions. It is, in fact, said to be an instruction to

[1] Greville, *Memoirs*, 2nd series, I, p. 304.
[2] *Life of Gladstone*, II, p. 363; *Letters of Queen Victoria*, 2nd series, II, pp. 152–4.
[3] *Life of Disraeli*, II, p. 1018.
[4] *Ibid.* II, pp. 1127–8.
[5] *Life of Lord Oxford and Asquith*, I, p. 273.
[6] *Ibid.* I, pp. 296–7.

the Secretary in drafting Cabinet minutes to avoid any reference to opinions expressed by any individual and to limit the minutes as narrowly as possible to the actual decision agreed to. This is done by referring to and summarising the document or documents on which the Cabinet is asked to make a decision, by setting out the substance of any statement of fact made by a minister, by indicating the general nature of the arguments urged in the course of the discussion (without mentioning any names), and by setting out in full the decisions. Thus, the minute of a discussion as to the attitude of the British Government to a dispute between Arcadia and Ruritania might be in the following form:

6. *Arcado-Ruritanian Dispute*

The Cabinet considered a memorandum on the Arcado-Ruritanian Dispute by the Secretary of State for Foreign Affairs and a memorandum by the Secretary of State for Commonwealth Relations on the attitude of the other members of the Commonwealth, from which it appeared that:

1. ...
2. ...

The Minister of Defence stated that.... It was argued on the one hand that...; and on the other that....

It was agreed that:

1. ...
2. ...

These minutes are drafted by the Secretary on the basis of notes which he personally takes in the Cabinet. There can no longer be any doubt as to what the decisions are because, as Mr Austen Chamberlain said in 1922, if the decision were not clear the Secretary would ask, 'What have I to record?' The minutes are drafted as soon as possible after the conclusion of the meeting. One copy is sent to the Queen and other copies go to the ministers, whether they are members of the Cabinet or not. The Law Officers receive copies of such conclusions as concern them.[1]

[1] Occasionally the Queen's permission may be obtained for Cabinet minutes to be sent to other persons: e.g. to Mr Neville Chamberlain after his resignation owing to ill-health in 1940.

Great care is taken to ensure the secrecy of the Cabinet minutes. The minimum staff is employed on their reproduction and all notes are destroyed as soon as they are transcribed. The copies are sealed at once in special envelopes addressed to the ministers entitled to receive them. These envelopes are locked in the Cabinet boxes, which are then delivered by messengers to the ministers to whom they are addressed. A record copy is kept in the Cabinet Office under the immediate control of the Secretary.

It was formerly open to Cabinet ministers to take away with them, on their resignation, their copies of Cabinet minutes and memoranda. The Cabinet decided in 1934 that they would return their documents, and they asked former ministers to do the same. If this precedent is followed, the only Cabinet minutes available for future historians, if any, will be the set kept in the Cabinet Office. Mr Lloyd George suggested in 1932 that where a minister or ex-minister published a one-sided account of a transaction, other ministers ought to be able to publish the whole; and he gave as one example the partial disclosures of 1931.[1] He admitted that it was open to the minister or ex-minister to ask the King's permission, but he added: 'As anyone who knows the Constitution will understand, that really means going to the Prime Minister. The Sovereign is constitutionally bound to take the advice of his chief Minister, and therefore if the chief Minister, who is—I will not say more or less implicated—he is bound to be more or less partial in the matter—gives advice to the contrary, then the person who is damnified, as it were, by the partial disclosure has no remedy at all.'[2] The suggestion was not approved, and the obligation of secrecy continues to apply to Cabinet documents. In a minute of 30 April 1945, however, Mr Winston Churchill slightly modified the rule:

> Ministers are entitled to keep all telegrams, minutes or documents circulated to the Cabinet which they wrote and signed themselves. Many of the Ministers have copies of these documents, of which usually a good many were struck. These must be regarded as their personal property, except that they will be bound by the rules governing the use of official papers, which are well established. To these should be added, in the case of the Prime Minister, correspondence with heads of Governments. All other papers

[1] Above, p. 269.

[2] 273 H.C.Deb. 5 s., 1301 (1932).

should be available to the departmental Ministers concerned, and they should have free access to them, although they must be deposited in the Government strong room.[1]

Mr Churchill of course meant the retiring ministers; the ministers of one Government are not entitled to examine the Cabinet documents of their predecessors, though some of those documents (without the minutes) will be in the secret departmental files.

The presence of the Secretary in the Cabinet has involved a definite breach in the old tradition that only Privy Councillors ought to be present in the Cabinet.[2] Lord Oxford and Asquith has described the formality of Cabinet sessions. 'No stranger (unless specially summoned to give information on a particular matter) was ever admitted; and when a message came from outside the door was always opened and shut by a minister. No food or drink was allowed, except some hard biscuits which were believed to date from the time of Pitt, and some plain water. Smoking was strictly tabooed. In the matter of seating there was no order of precedence, but each minister always occupied the same place.'[3] It is stated in the 1935 edition of a standard text-book: 'It might be questioned whether a meeting can be regarded as a meeting of the Cabinet while a person is present who is under no obligation to secrecy.'[4] Perhaps civil servants are regarded as under an obligation to secrecy;[5] but it is certain that ministers who are not Privy Councillors sometimes attend. Naval and military officers, civil servants, junior ministers, and others, were frequently present at the meetings of the War Cabinets. From December 1916 to December 1917 no less than 248 persons other than members of the War Cabinet or its Secretariat attended the meetings of the War Cabinet.[6] 'Almost all its meetings are attended by the ministers [i.e. of the departments] and their chief departmental officials concerned. The majority of the sessions of the War Cabinet consist, therefore, of a series of meetings between members

[1] Churchill, *The Second World War*, VI, p. 644. See also a correspondence in *The Times*, reproduced in *The Times Weekly Review*, 21 August 1952.

[2] For the old practice, see 143 Parl. Deb. 4 s., 863.

[3] Oxford and Asquith, *Fifty Years of Parliament*, II, p. 196.

[4] Anson, *Law and Custom of the Constitution* (4th ed.), II (1), p. 123.

[5] Civil servants as well as ministers are of course within the Official Secrets Acts.

[6] *The War Cabinet*, Report for the Year 1917, C. 9005/1918, p. 1.

of the War Cabinet and those responsible for executive action.... Ministers have full discretion to bring with them any experts, either from their own departments, or from outside.'[1] This practice is not followed by peacetime Cabinets, but there is no reason whatever why the Cabinet should not discuss a question with any person who may be able to render assistance. Sometimes the Chiefs of the Staffs are invited to advise on strategic questions, and ministers not in the Cabinet are always summoned when matters affecting their departments are under discussion. The pre-war precedents were not conclusive,[2] and the question may now be regarded as settled. The rule was correctly stated in 1915 by Sir Almeric Fitzroy: 'It is no doubt true that the Prime Minister can command the attendance of anyone whose advice is required by the Cabinet, but no one attends as a Cabinet Minister except as one of His Majesty's servants, whose advice is needed by the Sovereign.'[3]

The Secretariat is not in any sense an advisory body. It is not a planning commission. It does not make recommendations. It does not interfere with departmental responsibility. A member of the Secretariat of the first War Cabinet has said: 'It has been suggested that the Secretariat interfered with the responsibility of the departments; that the Secretariat issued statements which should have been issued by departments; that the Secretariat put forward and used their position to push forward ideas of their own; that, in fact, they usurped whatever they could in the way of departmental powers. Nothing could be further from the truth.'[4] One of the three rules[5] laid down by Colonel Hankey was that the Secretariat was not to interfere with the responsibility of the departments. 'If, in the course of our secretarial work, ideas occurred to us, we were to communicate them to the responsible departments. In no case, as far as I can remember, was independent action taken by the Secretariat.'[6]

[1] *Ibid.*

[2] *Peel Memoirs*, II, p. 51; 143 Parl. Deb. 4 s., 863; Fitzroy, *Memoirs*, I, p. 242.

[3] Fitzroy, *Memoirs*, I, p. 600.

[4] Clement Jones in 'The War Cabinet Secretariat', *Empire Review*, January 1924, p. 71.

[5] The others were: (1) not to issue statements to the press or to give interviews to journalists; and (2) not to laugh at the jokes made by ministers, though a smile was permissible: *ibid.*

[6] 'The War Cabinet Secretariat', *Empire Review*, January 1924, p. 71.

§8. *The Execution of Cabinet Decisions*

On the basis of the documents submitted, and as a result of the discussions among its members, the Cabinet comes to a conclusion. Two things follow. First, the decision is carried out by the departments. Secondly, the members of the Cabinet, and the ministers and junior ministers outside the Cabinet who accept the decision, may be called upon to defend it.

The decisions of the War Cabinet were communicated by the Cabinet Office to the departments affected. This practice is no longer followed. Each minister concerned is reminded of the Cabinet decision by the receipt of the Conclusions. No other intimation is given, and ministers are personally responsible for making such communications as they deem necessary to their respective departments. But the decision of the Cabinet is binding upon all persons concerned in government and it is the duty of the Cabinet Secretariat to verify that action has been taken by the departments to give effect to the Cabinet's conclusions.

Even a Commander-in-Chief in the field is subject to orders; he can, for instance, be ordered to supersede a general.[1] Similarly, the proconsuls are as subject to Cabinet instructions as the youngest official. As Lord Morley wrote to the Viceroy of India: 'The Government of India is no absolute or independent branch of Imperial Government. It is in every respect answerable to the Cabinet, as every other department is, and if the Cabinet decides . . . that ends the matter.'[2] And again: 'His Majesty's Government have determined on their course, and it is for their agents and officers all over the world to accept it.'[3]

Sometimes, however, a change of circumstances or some other reason may make it necessary for a minister, preferably in consultation with the Prime Minister, to modify the application of a Cabinet decision. In 1880 the Cabinet approved draft instructions to the ambassador at Constantinople. Sir Charles Dilke persuaded Lord Granville to strike out a paragraph on his own responsibility.[4] The action of the Foreign Office in 1914 was constantly in advance of the Cabinet. But a minister

[1] *Letters of Queen Victoria*, 3rd series, III, pp. 525–6.
[2] Morley, *Recollections*, II, p. 308.
[3] *Ibid.* II, p. 178.
[4] *Life of Sir Charles Dilke*, I, p. 327.

must not exercise this power to defeat the policy of the Cabinet. Such an act led to the dismissal of Palmerston in 1851.[1] Nevertheless, a minister cannot be expected to carry out enthusiastically a policy adopted against what he thinks to be his better judgment. As Lord Goschen said of Lord Salisbury, as Prime Minister in 1900: 'If some policy is forced on Salisbury, which he disapproves of, it breaks down in the execution.'[2]

§9. *Collective Responsibility*

> For all that passes in Cabinet [said Lord Salisbury in 1878] each member of it who does not resign is absolutely and irretrievably responsible, and has no right afterwards to say that he agreed in one case to a compromise, while in another he was persuaded by his colleagues....It is only on the principle that absolute responsibility is undertaken by every member of the Cabinet who, after a decision is arrived at, remains a member of it, that the joint responsibility of Ministers to Parliament can be upheld, and one of the most essential principles of parliamentary responsibility established.[3]

Perhaps Mr Joseph Chamberlain's definition is better, for he had occasion to study the matter both as *enfant terrible* under Mr Gladstone and in his middle age under Lord Salisbury:

> Absolute frankness in our private relations and full discussion of all matters of common interest...the decisions freely arrived at should be loyally supported and considered as the decisions of the whole of the Government. Of course there may be occasions in which the difference is of so vital a character that it is impossible for the minority...to continue their support, and in this case the Ministry breaks up or the minority member or members resigns.[4]

A minister who is not prepared to defend a Cabinet decision must, therefore, resign. Of such resignations there are many examples. Lord Palmerston resigned in 1853 because he could not agree to Lord John Russell's Reform Bill, though he afterwards withdrew his resignation. Lord John Russell resigned in 1855 because he agreed with Roebuck's motion and was not prepared to join with the Cabinet in resisting it.

[1] Above, pp. 208–11. [2] *Life of Joseph Chamberlain*, IV, p. 138.

[3] *Life of Robert, Marquis of Salisbury*, II, pp. 219–20.

[4] *Life of Joseph Chamberlain*, IV, p. 118.

Mr Gladstone and other Peelites resigned in the same year because they would not accept Roebuck's adjourned motion. General Peel and three others resigned in 1867 because they could not support Disraeli's Reform Bill. Sir Herbert Samuel and other Liberals, and Viscount Snowden, resigned in 1932 because they could not support the Ottawa Agreements. Mr Eden resigned in 1938 because he was unable to agree with the foreign policy adopted by Mr Neville Chamberlain and the Cabinet. Lord Salisbury resigned in 1957 after the release of Archbishop Makarios.

If a minister does not resign he is 'responsible'. The nature of that responsibility is studied elsewhere.[1] From the minister's point of view it means only that he must vote with the Government, speak in defence of it if the Prime Minister insists, and that he cannot afterwards reject criticism of his act, either in Parliament or in the constituencies, on the ground that he did not agree with the decision. The story is told of Lord Melbourne that after his Cabinet had come to a conclusion on the Corn Laws he said, 'By the bye, there is one thing we haven't agreed upon, which is, what are we to say? Is it to make our corn dearer, or cheaper, or to make the price steady? I don't care *which*: but we had better all be in the same story.'[2] That puts the matter precisely; they must all tell the same story.

Questions are sometimes left as 'open questions', so that any minister may vote or speak as he pleases. Thus, the question of the repeal of the Corn Laws was regarded as an open question by the Cabinet of 1831–4, though subsequently this was disputed.[3] Lord John Russell declared in 1839 that though it might be convenient for a Government to have many open questions, it was not 'for their honour and glory'. Nevertheless, honour and glory had to give way to convenience, and on Mr Grote's motion in favour of the ballot Lord John Russell, the leader of the House, spoke against, and seven ministers voted for it.[4] In 1841, with the same Government, Lord Melbourne 'declared before God that he considered leaving the whole agricultural interest without protection the wildest and maddest scheme that had ever entered into the imagi-

[1] See below, ch. XV.
[2] *Life of Lord John Russell*, I, p. 369.
[3] *Parl. Deb.* 3rd series, vol. 45, cols. 585–6.
[4] *Life of Lord John Russell*, I, pp. 324–6. (See also *Lord Melbourne's Papers*, p. 399.)

nation of man', but the leader of the House of Commons and nine other ministers voted for the repeal of the Corn Laws.[1]

The Whig Government of 1839 to 1841 was particularly weak, and was in office only because the Queen had objected to changing her Ladies in 1839. It would be impossible for any modern Government to leave open such a question as that of the Corn Laws. It is not a question merely of 'honour and glory'; it is, rather, a question of public opinion. A Government that cannot make up its mind on a fundamental issue ought not to be the Government and will be so regarded in the constituencies. Its fall may be regarded as imminent.

In 1873 the extension of the county franchise was regarded as an open question,[2] but at the dissolution not long afterwards the Opposition party secured a majority for the first time since 1846. In 1905 the Cabinet could not agree on Mr Arnold-Forster's scheme for dealing with the militia, and the Minister was allowed to explain his views to the House of Commons as being only his personal opinions.[3] But the majority that supported this Government was wiped out at the general election shortly afterwards. In the Liberal Government of 1908 to 1914 the enfranchisement of women was an open question;[4] and it was again left open in 1917.[5] In 1928 the revision of the Prayer Book was regarded as a non-political question, which did not require decision by the Cabinet.[6] It is not unusual for the House of Commons to be left to a 'free vote' on private members' Bills and resolutions which do not raise political issues. A distinction must however be drawn between 'free votes' and 'open questions'. The Government may have a collective opinion about a question, like the abolition of the death penalty in 1956, and yet decide to take off the whips in order that its supporters may vote as they please. The reform of the Prayer Book in 1927 was, however, an 'open question', because there was no Cabinet decision.

In 1932 the Cabinet adopted the strange device of an 'agreement to differ'. The financial difficulties of 1931 led to the formation of a coalition or 'National' Government supported by the Conservative

[1] *Ibid.* I, p. 367.
[2] *Life of Lord Ripon*, II, pp. 376–8.
[3] *Memoirs of Arnold-Forster*, pp. 262–3; Lee, *King Edward VII*, II, p. 205.
[4] *Ibid.* II, p. 653.
[5] *Life of Lord Curzon*, III, pp. 191–3.
[6] Taylor, *Jix—Viscount Brentford*, p. 253.

and Liberal parties and a few members of the Labour party.[1] An electoral arrangement was made at the ensuing general election, as a result of which, with a few exceptions, supporters of the National Government were not opposed by other supporters of that Government. The Conservative party asserted that tariff duties were a solution of the difficulties; but as the members of other parties would not agree, each candidate was left to advocate his own remedies, and the Government as a whole adopted no policy, but asked for a 'doctor's mandate' to make a diagnosis and prescribe such remedies as it thought fit. After the election, a Cabinet committee proposed a general tariff. Four members of the Cabinet disagreed and proposed to resign. The Prime Minister saw them privately and pleaded that their resignation would make his position 'embarrassing and humiliating'. He suggested that their resignation might be averted by conceding to them the liberty to express their dissent publicly. 'This was considered, but dismissed as impracticable and Gilbertian.' But when the suggestion was made at the Cabinet the dissenting ministers, after some hesitation, agreed on condition that they were to be free to vote and speak against any tariff proposals, that members of Parliament were to have the same liberty, and that the whips were not to exert influence to persuade members to vote for tariff proposals.

The official announcement was then made in the following terms:

> The Cabinet had had before it the Report of its Committee on the Balance of Trade, and after prolonged discussion it had been found impossible to reach a unanimous conclusion on the Committee's recommendations.
>
> The Cabinet, however, is deeply impressed with the paramount importance of maintaining national unity in the presence of the grave problems now confronting this country and the whole world.
>
> It has accordingly determined that some modification of usual ministerial practice is required, and has decided that ministers who find themselves unable to support the conclusions arrived at by the majority of their colleagues on the subject of import duties and cognate matters are to be at liberty to express their views by speech and vote.
>
> The Cabinet being essentially united in all other matters of policy believe that by this special provision it is best interpreting the will of the nation and the needs of the time.[2]

[1] Above, pp. 45–9.

[2] Snowden, *Autobiography*, II, pp. 1010–12.

This decision was attacked in both Houses, but, being supported by the Government majorities, it was acquiesced in, and the dissentient ministers and their supporters spoke and voted against the Government. The question was not left open. It was decided by the Cabinet, and the whips were put on. The procedure was not, therefore, in accordance with precedent. Logically, there is something to be said in its favour. It cannot be expected that a body of able ministers can agree about all questions all the time. Particularly is this so with a Coalition Government.[1] Frequent resignations involve frequent party splits, and party splits lead to short and weak Governments which in turn lead to distrust of the democratic system. Yet this argument, logical as it seems, is fallacious. Both logic and experience show that, under the party system, resignations need not be frequent. A Cabinet that is agreed upon fundamentals can compromise upon incidentals. A party Cabinet is normally agreed on fundamentals; if it is not, as in 1845 and 1885, the time has come for a new alignment of parties. Coalitions, unless they are merely part of the process of remoulding party alignments, are necessarily unprincipled. The party system is the real protection of democracy. Party Governments are strong Governments. An 'agreement to differ' in order to maintain a coalition is an attempt to break down the party system and to substitute government by individuals for government by political principles. No harm was done by the precedent of 1932 provided that it is not regarded as a precedent.[2] The dissenting ministers, having swallowed the camel of a general tariff, strained at the gnat of imperial preference and resigned within eight months.[3] The position of the Prime Minister, presumably, was no longer 'embarrassing and humiliating', for he held it for nearly three years longer.

Cabinet ministers are expected not merely not to oppose a Cabinet decision but also to support it. Mr Gladstone in the Cabinet of 1868–74

[1] See above, pp. 264–7.

[2] Lord Hailsham, who is believed to have proposed the 'agreement to differ', said: 'I justify it to myself and, I hope, your Lordship's House, as an exception to a very sound constitutional principle which can only be justified by exceptional circumstances': 83 H.L.Deb. 5 s., 551–2.

[3] For the reasons, see Thomas Jones, *A Diary with Letters*, p. 53. It was felt that they 'could not do it a second time', that many Liberals would oppose, and that in any case it was necessary to keep alive the Liberal party and its organisation in order to provide the electors with an alternative to the Labour party.

strongly criticised the absence of a minister from a division. 'I should not act frankly by you if I did not state it, without hesitation, as a general and prospective proposition, that, without reference to the likelihood or unlikelihood of defeat, upon motions which must from their nature be votes of confidence, [there can] be but one rule for the members of the Government, and that is to give the votes themselves which at the same time the Government with less strong title is asking from the members of their party.'[1] This does not imply, of course, that a minister may not 'pair' with a member of the Opposition in accordance with the usual practice.

The obligation on ministers not in the Cabinet is not, apparently, so strong. They have, as Mr Gladstone said, 'only a secondary and derivative share in the higher responsibilities'.[2] In 1838 Lord Charles Fitzroy, the Vice-Chamberlain, was dismissed from his post for voting against the Government.[3] In 1856 Queen Victoria asked Lord Palmerston to 'make it quite clear to the subordinate members of the Government that they cannot be allowed to vote against the Government proposal about the National Gallery to-morrow, as she fears that several fancy themselves at liberty to do so'.[4] Mr Stanley Evans, Parliamentary Secretary to the Ministry of Food, was required to resign his office in 1950 after making a public statement on agriculture which conflicted with Government policy.[5]

But failing to vote in favour of a proposal is not so heinous an offence as voting against a proposal. In 1881 Mr Gladstone wrote to the Queen, in connection with the failure of Mr Bright, Mr Chamberlain and Sir Charles Dilke to vote for the Government's proposal for a memorial for Lord Beaconsfield, 'as regards members of the Government not in the Cabinet, I think a single case of absence, in circumstances where individual votes were unimportant, would not according to usual practice be taken account of. *In strictness*, however, leave ought to be asked. Undoubtedly members of the Cabinet are bound to vote in every case—apart from accidental absences'.[6]

[1] *Life of Gladstone*, II, p. 418; see also *ibid.* II, p. 419.

[2] Gladstone, *Gleanings*, I, p. 224.

[3] Greville, *Memoirs*, 2nd series, I, p. 86.

[4] *Letters of Queen Victoria*, 1st series, III, p. 249.

[5] H. Morrison, *Government and Parliament*, p. 60.

[6] Guedalla, *The Queen and Mr Gladstone*, II, p. 156.

In 1882 Sir Charles Dilke (Under-Secretary at the Foreign Office) and Mr Fawcett (Postmaster-General) did not vote for the proposal to grant Prince Leopold an annuity on his marriage. Mr Gladstone then wrote:

> Questions relating directly to the Sovereign, and involving money, are questions of importance, and still more of delicacy; and of risk: for on these questions serious opposition might entail consequences worse than defeat. This being so, it is necessary on all such subjects for the Government to rally its independent supporters to the best of its ability. But no call can be forcibly made upon the independent supporters of a Government in such a case, unless the official servants of the Crown vote uniformly and steadily for the grant proposed. The Queen is therefore entitled to require their votes: and her Majesty is believed by Mr Gladstone to take her stand upon this unquestionable title.[1]

He also wrote that if there was any reason to apprehend repetition of the act, 'precautions ought to be taken on a future occasion'.[2] Lord Granville wrote to Dilke on the same occasion: 'The Queen appears to me to have a *prima facie* right to complain of any of her servants refusing to support a Government measure which she and the administration think necessary for her comfort and position. But if you stated to the Prime Minister on taking office that you did not intend to vote for these grants, your responsibility ceases.'[3]

In 1883 Sir Charles Dilke, who was now in the Cabinet, Mr Fawcett and Mr L. Courtney abstained from voting with the Government and against a women's suffrage amendment to the Reform Bill. Lord Hartington told Dilke that his position was different because he was a party to the decisions of the Cabinet, and 'custom binds the minority in the collective decisions of her Majesty's servants'.[4] But Dilke remained in the Cabinet.

The strict party discipline of the present century and the practice of 'refusing the whip' to party members who consistently oppose the Government have perhaps weakened the position of a junior minister who does not agree with Cabinet policy. Though there must clearly be

[1] *Letters of Queen Victoria*, 2nd series, III, p. 291.

[2] Guedalla, *The Queen and Mr Gladstone*, II, p. 183.

[3] *Life of Sir Charles Dilke*, I, pp. 423–4.

[4] *Ibid.* II, p. 9.

exceptions, it seems that a Prime Minister would normally require a junior minister to vote or pair with the Government. The case is not so strong where the minister is a peer and is not at the moment called upon for a decision. When Lord Cork proposed to resign over Home Rule in 1886, Mr Gladstone said that he did not conceive it to be 'sound political doctrine that members of a Government, not in the Cabinet, and not in the House where action has been taken, should give effect to their views by resignation'.[1]

The duty of a minister is not merely to support the Government but to refrain from making any speech or to do any act which may appear to implicate the Government. The Prime Minister or the leader of the House of Commons, or even an individual minister, must on occasions take decisions without Cabinet sanction.[2] But this does not mean that he may reverse a Cabinet decision without just cause or branch out into new lines of policy without prior Cabinet consent. Lord Derby reproved Mr Disraeli in 1858 for altering the India resolutions without the Cabinet's consent.[3] In 1878 Mr Disraeli, in his turn, reproved the next Lord Derby for making a speech contrary to Cabinet policy.[4]

The duty of the minister in respect of speeches was stated by Lord Palmerston in a letter to Mr Gladstone in 1864:

> A member of the Government when he takes office necessarily divests himself of that perfect freedom of action which belongs to a private and independent member of Parliament, and the reason is this, that what a member of the Government does and says upon public matters must to a certain degree commit his colleagues, and the body to which he belongs if they by their silence appear to acquiesce; and if any of them follow his example and express as publicly opposite opinions, which in particular cases they might feel obliged to do, differences of opinion between members of the same Government are necessarily brought out into prominence and the strength of the Government is thereby impaired.[5]

Mr Gladstone gave the same reason in 1883.[6]

Nevertheless, ministers, and especially Prime Ministers, have sometimes claimed or exercised a wider liberty. Lord John Russell in 1839

[1] *Letters of Queen Victoria*, 3rd series, I, p. 103. [2] See above, pp. 226–7.
[3] *Life of Disraeli*, I, pp. 1538–9. [4] *Ibid.* II, p. 1885.
[5] Guedalla, *Gladstone and Palmerston*, p. 288; see also *ibid.* pp. 326, 327.
[6] *Life of Gladstone*, III, pp. 113–14.

announced his views on the Corn Laws before the Cabinet decision; though ultimately the Cabinet left it as an 'open question'.[1] In 1850 Lord John Russell, as Prime Minister, issued his letter to the Bishop of Durham on the Catholic hierarchy without consulting the Cabinet.[2] In 1852 Sir William Molesworth retained the right to advocate the ballot, though he was in the Cabinet.[3] In 1867 Mr Disraeli, as leader of the House of Commons, agreed to introduce a Reform Bill instead of resolutions without consulting the Cabinet, and subsequently accepted without consultation the Liberal amendment to abolish compounding for rates.[4]

Mr Chamberlain in the Government of 1880 to 1885 demanded a greater liberty than Mr Gladstone was prepared to grant. In 1883 Mr Gladstone wrote: 'Though speech cannot universally be confined by a minister within the limits of action to which he has conformed, yet declarations tending to place him markedly in advance or in arrear of his colleagues on subjects of high politics, or otherwise delicate, should be made as rarely and reservedly and, if I may say so, as reluctantly as possible.'[5] In reply to a complaint by Queen Victoria in the following year, Mr Gladstone said: 'As all Cabinet ministers are in an important sense equals, and all members of the House of Commons have a representative as well as an official character to sustain, it is but a limited and rare power that Mr Gladstone's office allows him to claim.'[6] Later he said: 'I have no general jurisdiction over the speeches of my colleagues, and no right to prescribe their tone and colour. When they offend against an assurance which with their authority I have given to the Queen, they then afford me a title to interfere upon which I have been, I hope, not unduly slow to act.'[7] To this the Queen replied: 'The Queen thinks, and maintains that the Prime Minister has and ought to

[1] *Peel Papers*, II, pp. 380–2; *Life of Lord John Russell*, I, pp. 324–6; and see above, p. 226.

[2] *Later Correspondence of Lord John Russell*, I, p. 46.

[3] *Life of Sir James Graham*, II, p. 204.

[4] *Life of Robert, Marquis of Salisbury*, I, pp. 227, 268; *Life of Disraeli*, II, pp. 275–6.

[5] *Letters of Queen Victoria*, 2nd series, III, pp. 433–5. See also the letter to Mr Chamberlain in Joseph Chamberlain, *A Political Memoir*, p. 88, and Mr Chamberlain's reply, *ibid.* p. 89.

[6] Guedalla, *The Queen and Mr Gladstone*, II, p. 292.

[7] *Ibid.* II, p. 294; see also *Letters of Queen Victoria*, 2nd series, III, pp. 526–8.

have that power, and that former Prime Ministers did exercise it.' Mr Gladstone's answer was, in substance, an acceptance of the obligation:

Your Majesty is well aware that there is no code on record from which he [Mr Gladstone] may learn the powers of his office in such matters, and he has formed his estimate simply according to such knowledge as he has gathered under the heads of the Cabinets in which he has served. As he would be very sorry to exaggerate the rights appertaining to his office, so he would deem it a serious offence knowingly to allow any of them to fall into abeyance. He does not doubt that there are many cases in which the Prime Minister can interfere, both as to acts and language: for instance cases which affect duty to the Crown, or cases where a minister undertakes to commit his colleagues.

In the case then under discussion, however, he did not think he could intervene.[1]

Mr Chamberlain and Sir Charles Dilke agreed in 1885 on the right of ministers to say what they pleased on issues of the future as distinct from current Cabinet questions,[2] and the former inspired the famous *Radical Programme* which was considerably in advance of the programme of the Cabinet, in which the Whigs were still strong.[3] Mr Chamberlain explained to Mr Gladstone his reasons:

Popular government is inconsistent with the reticence official etiquette formerly imposed on speakers and which was easily borne as long as the electorate was a comparatively small and privileged class, and the necessity of consulting it at meetings infrequent and limited. Now the platform has

[1] *Letters of Queen Victoria*, 2nd series, III, pp. 526–8.

[2] 'I have proceeded on the assumption that with regard to questions of the future, which were not immediately before the constituencies but which were properly matters for discussion, each Minister was free to express an individual opinion without committing his colleagues or the Government to its acceptance. On the other hand in regard to questions which form part of the Government Programme, or which have been matters of discussion and argument in the Cabinet, I have always endeavoured, to the best of my ability, loyally and without reserve, to defend the conclusions arrived at': Joseph Chamberlain, *A Political Memoir*, pp. 112–13. Mr Gladstone's characteristic reply was: 'I do not go so far as to meet this proposition, or rather this opinion...by an absolute assertion of its opposite, but I think it cannot safely be admitted as a practical guide': *ibid.* p. 114.

[3] *Life of Joseph Chamberlain*, I, pp. 559–62.

become one of the most powerful and indispensable instruments of government, and any ministry which neglected the opportunities offered by it would speedily lose the confidence of the people.[1]

The necessity for securing his colleagues' agreement was a restriction too heavy for Mr Chamberlain. So long as he expected the reversion of the Conservative leadership he kept his ideas to himself. After Mr Balfour's appointment, however, he again decided to force the pace and raised the question of tariff reform. No conclusions being reached, Mr Chamberlain began a platform campaign. The Cabinet thereupon agreed upon an inquiry, and it was decided that while it was proceeding no public speeches should be made. Mr Balfour stated that though a Prime Minister was responsible for the action of the Cabinet, he was not responsible for the expression of individual opinions.[2]

In 1896 Mr Balfour in the House of Commons accepted an amendment to the Education Bill. Sir John Gorst, who had been in charge of the measure, had already opposed the amendment, and when the Cabinet came to discuss the position, it was realised that the amendment would make the Bill unworkable, and it was withdrawn.[3] Sir Henry Campbell-Bannerman followed Mr Balfour's example. He accepted the principle of a Labour party Bill to exempt trade unions from liability for torts although the Cabinet had already decided against it.[4] Similarly, he accepted an amendment to include domestic servants within the scope of the Workmen's Compensation Bill although ministers and Law Officers had resisted the Bill up to the Report stage.[5]

Mr Lloyd George made his famous Mansion House speech on the Algeciras crisis in 1911 after consulting the Prime Minister and the Foreign Secretary, though without consulting the Cabinet. In 1916, however, he laid down the policy of 'the Knock-out Blow' in an interview with an American journalist without consulting anybody,

[1] *Ibid.* I, p. 563. The letter is given in full in Joseph Chamberlain, *A Political Memoir*, pp. 115–19. It also includes the statement 'I admit that no minister has a right to advocate opinions which are contrary to any principle laid down or acted upon by the Government as a whole; and I will go further and say that he should endeavour to avoid raising questions which might place his colleagues under the absolute necessity of repudiating his conclusions': *ibid.* p. 117.

[2] *Life of the Duke of Devonshire*, II, pp. 301 *et seq.*

[3] *Life of Sir Robert Morant*, p. 109.

[4] *Life of Sir Henry Campbell-Bannerman*, II, p. 278.

[5] *Ibid.* II, p. 280.

and Sir Edward Grey protested.[1] It appears that Mr Baldwin, as Prime Minister, raised the question of protection without consulting the Cabinet.[2] In 1927 Sir William Joynson-Hicks, speaking on a private member's Bill with the Prime Minister beside him, startled the House by stating that the Cabinet would introduce a Bill to reduce the age at which women were entitled to the franchise. The Cabinet had taken no such decision, and it is said that most of its members were against the proposal. Nevertheless, the Cabinet felt bound to support the Home Secretary.[3]

These precedents are inconclusive. It may be said, first, that the Prime Minister is frequently in a position to pledge his colleagues' support, because the only alternative is his own resignation. Secondly, a minister should not announce a new policy without Cabinet consent; but, if he does, the Cabinet must either support him or accept his resignation. Thirdly, a minister ought to be chary about expressing personal opinions about future policy except after consultation; and if the circumstances are such as to pledge the Government, the Prime Minister has real cause for complaint. Any statement in advance of a Cabinet decision is dangerous to the stability of the Government.

The question of public controversies between ministers seems never to have arisen in the United Kingdom, though it has arisen elsewhere in the Commonwealth. The agreement to differ of 1932[4] necessarily involved a decision to allow ministers to express different views, but the liberty thus accorded was exercised discreetly, so as not to threaten the stability of the Government. In normal conditions controversies between ministers in the House of Commons—except when a free vote was allowed—would be so obviously an infringement of the principle of collective responsibility that it is extremely unlikely that it would happen. It is far more likely to occur on public platforms, when ministers sometimes say more than they should, especially when they are heckled by an unsympathetic audience. When the Labour party was in Opposition one of its leaders was particularly liable to make indiscreet comments; and of him another Labour leader said that 'every time he opens his mouth he loses twenty thousand votes'. Clearly adverse

[1] Lloyd George, *War Memoirs*, II, pp. 856–7.
[2] *Life of Lord Cave*, p. 264.
[3] *Life of the First Earl of Birkenhead*, II, pp. 291–2.
[4] Above, pp. 279–81.

comments by a minister on the policy or administration of another ministry would be a breach of the rules of collective responsibility, for he would be responsible for the policy or administration which he criticised. The more likely case, which has happened outside the United Kingdom, is that in which one minister was led to emulate Mr Joseph Chamberlain by propagating a policy of his own, thus leading another minister to criticise him. Since the Government ought to be responsible for both policy and criticism it would be inconsistent with the rules. The fact that such controversy is likely is a good reason for not allowing a minister to go off on a frolic of his own. In any event, a Government in which such controversies developed would be riding for a fall.

CHAPTER X

WAR AND DEFENCE

§1. *The Committee of Imperial Defence before 1914*

The defence of the country against possible invasion, the protection of the far-flung boundaries of the Commonwealth overseas, the maintenance of order in colonies, protectorates and trust territories, and the use of armed forces for the fulfilment of treaty obligations, are among the most important functions which the Government has or may have to exercise. For these purposes there are three armed forces in a state of preparation for war; and, if war breaks out, they are rapidly expanded by voluntary enlistment or conscription. Indeed, in such a war as that of 1914 to 1918 or 1939 to 1945 all the energies of the Government may be directed towards bringing the war to a successful conclusion.

The three forces are under the control of separate ministers. From 1936 to 1940 there was a Minister for the Co-ordination of Defence, and since 1940 there has been a Minister of Defence. Since 1946 he has been charged with specific functions under the defence scheme mentioned later. There are, however, many other departments concerned with defence problems, and when war breaks out the whole policy of the Government must be attuned to war. In January 1904 Lord Esher's War Office (Reconstitution) Committee, in its first report, set out the nature of the administrative problem of defence:

> There are...no means of co-ordinating defence problems, for dealing with them as a whole, for defining the proper functions of the various elements, and for ensuring that, on the one hand, peace preparations are carried out upon a consistent plan, and, on the other hand, that in times of emergency a definite war policy, based upon solid data, can be formulated.[1]

The means were found in the Committee of Imperial Defence, which is now called the Defence Committee.

The genesis of the Committee of Imperial Defence may be traced to the Hartington Commission of 1890.[2] In the same year Lord Salisbury

[1] Quoted in Lord Hankey, *Diplomacy by Conference*, p. 84.

[2] C. 5979, p. viii. For the details, see N. H. Gibbs, *The Origins of Imperial Defence*, p. 8, where reference is made to a Colonial Defence Committee of 1878.

set up a naval and military committee of the Cabinet under the presidency of Lord Hartington to study strategy. It had the services of a Foreign Office clerk, but it had no regular meetings and no records. It was reconstituted in December 1902, on the proposal of Mr Balfour based on a memorandum by Lord Middleton and Lord Selborne.[1] The War Office (Reconstitution) Committee in 1904 recommended that the Committee should be made permanent and that it should have a secretariat. This recommendation was accepted by Mr Balfour, who reconstituted the Committee as the Committee of Imperial Defence. The Prime Minister was to be the only permanent member. But the persons regularly summoned were the Prime Minister, the Lord President of the Council, the Secretary of State for War, the First Lord of the Admiralty, the First Sea Lord, and the Commander-in-Chief, with the heads of the Naval and Military Intelligence Departments as joint Secretaries and a Foreign Office clerk to keep the minutes.[2] The Committee was to meet only when summoned. As Lord Esher said, the true inwardness of the Committee of Imperial Defence was that 'the Prime Minister should be the Minister for Defence, for he only can co-ordinate all the departments concerned in the immense business of providing for the defence of the Empire'.[3]

Sir Henry Campbell-Bannerman continued Mr Balfour's system, but it seems that he recognised the necessity for full collaboration with the Foreign Office. Under his direction, the Committee began the process of setting up sub-committees to inquire into and report upon strategic questions, with power to call witnesses and to take evidence.[4] Thus the work of preparing for the war which was clearly not far off was undertaken in a scientific manner. Above all, the agreement with France in 1904 was followed by technical discussions between French and British military experts. As a result of these discussions, the Committee authorised

[1] Lord Hankey, *Diplomacy by Conference*, p. 85. For Mr Balfour's memorandum see *Life of Arthur James Balfour*, I, pp. 366–7.

[2] Lord Hankey, *op. cit.* pp. 85–7; Fitzroy, *Memoirs*, I, p. 118. A somewhat different list is given in W. K. Hancock and M. M. Gowing, *British War Economy*, p. 33.

[3] *Esher Papers*, III, p. 14.

[4] Some of these were standing sub-committees, viz. the Overseas Defence Committee, the Home Ports Defence Committee, Co-ordination Committee, and Air Committee: Lord Hankey, *op. cit.* p. 88. Thirty such committees were set up between July 1909 and August 1914: *British War Economy*, p. 34.

and approved plans for the support of French troops by a British expeditionary force in the event—which happened in 1914—of an attack by Germany upon Belgium.[1] Mr Asquith saw that other departments, besides the Service Departments, were concerned, and he set up a Standing Sub-Committee, to be presided over alternately by the First Lord of the Admiralty and the Secretary of State for War, and composed of representatives of all the departments likely to have urgent problems on the outbreak of war.

Lord Esher explained in 1912 that the Committee had considered the following matters, among others: aerial navigation, the strategical aspects of the Forth and Clyde Canal, oversea transportation of reinforcements in time of war, the treatment of aliens in time of war, press censorship in war, postal censorship in war, trading with the enemy, wireless stations, local transportation and distribution of food supplies in wartime.[2] But these were obvious subjects. He did not reveal the complete—or almost complete—plans for assembling, transporting and reassembling at a fixed spot in northern Europe six divisions of the British Army, nor the plan for passing a Defence of the Realm Act and the issue of Regulations thereunder so as to give immense powers to the Government on the outbreak of war. All these matters were included in the famous 'War Book' which was prepared and from time to time revised and which was put into immediate operation as soon as the war broke out in 1914.[3]

The object of the pre-war Committee was precise and definite. It was to provide the plans necessary to defend the country and the Empire and to check the German invasion of Belgium which the British military experts (unlike the French) had foreseen with remarkable accuracy. General Henry Wilson, at the famous meeting of the Imperial Conference on 23 August 1911, gave the assembled statesmen a complete exposition of the probable German line of attack.[4]

The association of certain ministers with the work of the Committee raised a new problem, for it involved a formal 'inner Cabinet' which alone was aware of the detailed plans being prepared. The Cabinet was only theoretically in control, and there were among the ministers some

[1] *Esher Papers*, III, p. 58. [2] Esher, *The Influence of King Edward*, p. 146.

[3] See Asquith, *The Genesis of the War*; and Lord Hankey, *op. cit.* pp. 88–9.

[4] *Diaries of Field-Marshal Sir Henry Wilson*, I, pp. 99–102.

jealousy and suspicion of the Committee's activities. Sir Almeric Fitzroy says that at the Lord President's dinner in March 1914,

> there was evidently some jealousy on the part of those Cabinet Ministers, who were not on the Committee, of the preponderant influence which membership gave to certain members in council....Lord Morley had to admit that the Committee was virtually supreme upon the issues with which it dealt. It had not made a war yet, but the experience of 1911 showed that it easily might. At that time [the Algeciras crisis] no Cabinets met, Lord Morley was in Scotland, and I received and acted upon instructions conveyed by the Secretary of State for War, with the assumed concurrence of the Prime Minister.[1]

It 'made a war' five months later. Though it is unlikely that Great Britain would have kept out of the struggle if there had been no Committee of Imperial Defence, the fact of the 'conversations' with the French military authorities, and above all the arrangements whereby the French Atlantic fleet was transferred to the Mediterranean, were important elements in the decision. Also, the military authorities having prepared plans were anxious to use them, and were even willing to use the Opposition to put pressure on the Government.[2]

On the other hand, when war broke out, the machinery of government was very different from what it had been in previous wars. It 'worked with an amazing celerity, precision and completeness'.[3] In spite of some changes of plan, four divisions (later increased to six) were moved across the Channel and assembled in France to meet the advance which the General Staff had foreseen. In England, the Defence of the Realm Act was passed, the Regulations drawn from their pigeon-holes and put into force, and the nation organised for war. Defects appeared only when the plans of the Committee had been carried out and the next steps had to be taken.

[1] Fitzroy, *Memoirs*, II, p. 539.

[2] For the proof that the 'conversations' were regarded by France as committing Great Britain to war in 1914, see the statement of the French Ambassador to (Lord) Lloyd on 1 August 1914: Chamberlain, *Down the Years*, p. 94. These 'conversations' were mentioned in the original draft of the Unionist leaders' communication to the Government pressing the Government to declare war, though they were left out of the final draft: *ibid.* pp. 95, 99.

[3] Fitzroy, *Memoirs*, II, p. 560; see also Lord Hankey, *op. cit.* pp. 260–1. Sir Almeric Fitzroy's eulogy must, however, be read with some qualification in the light of the even greater efficiency of 1939.

§2. *The Cabinet, 1914–19*

On the outbreak of war, the ordinary departmental and Cabinet system continued. Mr Winston Churchill at the Admiralty and Lord Kitchener at the War Office, in consultation with the Prime Minister, accepted responsibility for day-to-day operations. Mr Lloyd George at the Treasury, Mr Walter Runciman at the Board of Trade, and other ministers in a less degree, took the measures necessary for fitting the ordinary peace mechanism to a state of war. There was no established Council, but there were sporadic consultations between the ministers concerned with inter-departmental questions.[1] The Government was engaged, in the main, in working out the plans of the Committee of Imperial Defence, and Cabinet consultation was necessary only for new departures. The Committee was available for 'serious questions involving new departures in policy or joint strategic operations'; but no attempt was made in the early months of the war to draw a hard-and-fast line between an inner and an outer Cabinet.[2] Sir John French's announcement that he proposed to withdraw behind the Seine on 1 September was dealt with by a few members of the Cabinet, who agreed that Lord Kitchener should go to France with 'Cabinet instructions'.[3] So, on 2 October, Sir Edward Grey, Lord Kitchener and Mr Churchill (the Prime Minister being away) decided to send the Naval Division to assist in the defence of Antwerp.[4] The Cabinet met at intervals of three to seven days and received a general survey of the position from Lord Kitchener, but the effective decisions had already been taken, and it could do no more than approve.

The Committee of Imperial Defence had necessarily restricted itself to the preparation of plans for the outbreak of war. Subsequent developments depended upon the military and naval situation. As soon, therefore, as the preliminary plans had been worked out, the need for closer central control and the preparation of plans for emergencies became evident. In October, Mr Asquith decided to convert the Committee of Imperial Defence into a 'War Council', consisting of the Prime Minister, the Secretaries of State for War, India and Foreign

[1] Lloyd George, *War Memoirs*, I, p. 389.

[2] *Life of Lord Oxford and Asquith*, II, pp. 123–4. [3] *Ibid.* II, p. 125. [4] *Ibid.*

Affairs, the Chancellor of the Exchequer, and the First Lord of the Admiralty, together with Mr Balfour (who had assisted the Committee of Imperial Defence) and the necessary experts. Lord Haldane and Sir Arthur Wilson were added in January 1915. This Council took over the Committee's Secretariat, minutes were taken and, for the first time, formal notes of decisions were circulated to the departments concerned.[1] It was in fact the Committee of Imperial Defence under another name, the main difference being that it had more executive authority.[2]

'Broadly speaking the Cabinet kept under its own control all large decisions relating to the choice of objectives, finance, domestic questions arising out of raising men and munitions and supplies. Quite early in the day it decided that its own numbers were too big for some of these, and appointed small committees to take charge of them.'[3] It rarely intervened in military matters, though on 8 September it rejected the suggestion to send 20,000 to 30,000 troops to hold the road from Ostend to Antwerp.[4] After the battle of the Marne this decision was reversed by the ministers concerned, when Mr Churchill was sent to see to the defence of Antwerp and the maintenance of the line of retreat.[5] But the line between military and domestic questions was not easily drawn. The need for man-power and munitions depended on the military position; and the Cabinet complained that Lord Kitchener did not give them enough information.[6] A Munitions Committee of the Cabinet was set up on 12 October 1914, and consisted of Lord Haldane, the Secretary of State for War, the Chancellor of the Exchequer, the First Lord of the Admiralty, the Home Secretary, the President of the Board of Trade and the President of the Board of Agriculture.[7] It met only six times between 12 October 1914 and 1 January 1915, and was dissolved on the latter date. A new Committee consisting of the Chancellor of the Exchequer, Mr Balfour, Mr Edwin Montagu, a business-man, and representatives of the departments was set up in April 1915, but shortly

[1] *Life of Lord Oxford and Asquith*, II, p. 126; Oxford and Asquith, *Memoirs and Reflections*, II, pp. 87–8; Lord Hankey, *op. cit.* p. 262.

[2] Lord Hankey, *op. cit.* p. 262.

[3] *Life of Lord Oxford and Asquith*, II, p. 127.

[4] *Ibid.* II, p. 125.

[5] *Ibid.*; and see Churchill, *World Crisis*, I, pp. 338–40.

[6] *Life of Lord Oxford and Asquith*, II, p. 128.

[7] *Ibid.* II, p. 136; Lloyd George, *War Memoirs*, I, pp. 146–7.

afterwards its functions were taken over by the new Ministry of Munitions, and Mr Lloyd George left the Treasury to become head of the new department.[1] According to Mr Lloyd George, the incessant demands of the Commander-in-Chief for munitions were never brought before the Cabinet[2] nor even before the Munitions Committee.[3]

The decision to force the Dardanelles was taken, for effective purposes, in the War Council. The Cabinet dealt with matters of foreign policy, such as the Balkan situation, the bringing in of Italy, and maritime questions touching the rights of neutrals.[4] The lack of central direction in respect of military questions is shown by the fact that from 6 April to 14 May 1915 the War Council did not meet.[5] In the meantime, the 'Opposition'—which had ceased to oppose—was becoming more and more restive as news came from the Western Front of the shortage of shells, and as dispute about the Dardanelles campaign became more acute. The resignation of Lord Fisher from the post of First Sea Lord produced a demand for coalition, and the Coalition Government was formed in May 1915.

Mr Asquith had sometimes expressed the wish that he had 'more Greys and Crewes' and not quite so many 'very clever men'.[6] He wanted, that is, ministers immersed in their own departmental work who would not raise inconvenient questions in the Cabinet. Whether it can be said that the number of 'clever men' was increased by the coalition or not, it is certain that the number of ministers who thought they had a right to take part in the general control was at least doubled. The War Council was converted into the Dardanelles Committee. It now consisted of the Prime Minister, Lord Kitchener, Mr Lloyd George, Mr Balfour (Admiralty), Mr Churchill, Sir Edward Carson, Mr Bonar Law, Lord Lansdowne, Lord Crewe, Lord Curzon and Lord Selborne. In spite of its size, there were enough other ministers in the Cabinet to compel rediscussion of every issue when its proceedings were reported to the Cabinet.[7]

[1] Lloyd George, *War Memoirs*, I, pp. 186–7; *Life of Lord Oxford and Asquith*, II, p. 140.

[2] Lloyd George, *War Memoirs*, I, p. 195.

[3] *Ibid.* I, pp. 202–3.

[4] *Life of Lord Oxford and Asquith*, II, p. 130.

[5] Lloyd George, *War Memoirs*, I, p. 224.

[6] *Life of Lord Oxford and Asquith*, II, p. 131.

[7] *Ibid.* II, p. 180.

In 1916 Mr Asquith himself indicated the defects of the War Committee:[1] (1) Its membership was too large. (2) There was delay, evasion, and often obstruction, on the part of the departments in giving effect to its decisions. (3) It was often kept in ignorance by the departments of information which was essential and even vital, though of a technical kind. (4) It was overcharged with duties, many of them of a kind suitable for subordinate bodies.[2] This was in reply to a memorandum by Lloyd George advocating the setting up of a War Committee with full executive powers, subject to the right of the Prime Minister to refer any matter to the Cabinet.[3] The plan involved the suspension of the Prime Minister from the direct control of the war and led ultimately to the resignation of Mr Asquith and the formation of the second War Coalition under Mr Lloyd George.

The new Prime Minister decided to supersede the ordinary Cabinet by a War Cabinet of five members, none of whom, except the Chancellor of the Exchequer, should possess departmental duties. Mr Lloyd George has explained his motives:

> I had long come to the conclusion that a body of twenty members was a futile instrument for the conduct of any business which required immediate action. I ultimately resolved to set up a Cabinet of five to whom the whole control of the War should be entrusted. I felt that they must remain in almost constant session to review events from day to day. Ministers who were in charge of departments could rarely be available for purposes of consultation, and their minds would naturally be taken up with the innumerable petty details of their respective offices. The War Cabinet must therefore consist of men who were free from all departmental cares and who could devote the whole of their time and thought to the momentous questions which were involved in the successful direction of a world war. When matters arose which affected any particular department, the head of that department could be summoned to attend the Cabinet bringing with him appropriate experts. It was made quite clear that the Cabinet would have the same direct access to those experts as their departmental chiefs, that questions could be addressed to them directly, and that they were to speak their minds freely without awaiting the permission or opinion of their political chiefs.[4]

[1] The Dardanelles Committee became the War Committee in November 1915

[2] Lloyd George, *War Memoirs*, II, p. 984.

[3] *Ibid.* II, pp. 982–3.

[4] *Ibid.* III, pp. 1063–4.

It was agreed at the outset that collective responsibility in the strict sense would attach only to the members of the War Cabinet.[1] The Secretariat of the War Council became the Secretariat of the War Cabinet,[2] and exercised the functions which the Cabinet Secretariat now performs.[3] The War Cabinet met daily in the morning and sometimes in the afternoon and evening as well.[4] Its procedure was thus described:

At each meeting the Cabinet begins by hearing reports as to the progress of the war since the preceding day. Unless it wishes to confine its deliberations to questions of policy, it then proceeds to deal with questions awaiting its decision. As these questions in the vast majority of cases affect one or more of the administrative departments, almost all its meetings are attended by the ministers and their chief departmental officials concerned. The majority of the sessions of the War Cabinet consist, therefore, of a series of meetings between members of the War Cabinet and those responsible for executive action at which questions of policy concerning those departments are discussed and settled. Questions of overlapping or conflict between departments are determined, and the general lines of policy throughout every branch of the administration co-ordinated so as to form part of a consistent war plan. Ministers have full discretion to bring with them any experts, either from their own departments or from outside.[5]

From 9 December 1916 to December 1917, 248 persons other than members of the War Cabinet and its Secretariat attended the War Cabinet. The Secretary of State for Foreign Affairs, the First Sea Lord and the Chief of the Imperial General Staff attended every meeting to communicate the latest information and to consult on questions of policy. In 1917 the War Cabinet held over 300 meetings.[6]

A considerable number of less important, but often highly complex, questions are referred to individual members of the War Cabinet or to committees of ministers or others. In some cases the minister or committee has power to decide, in others the instruction is to carry out a detailed investigation such as the War Cabinet itself could not usefully undertake and

[1] Beaverbrook, *Politicians and the War*, p. 323. A. Birrell, *Things Past Redress*, p. 228.
[2] *The War Cabinet*, Report for the Year 1917, Cd. 9005/1918, pp. 2–3.
[3] See above, pp. 243–5.
[4] *Life of Lord Curzon*, III, p. 148.
[5] *The War Cabinet*, Report for the Year 1917, Cd. 9005/1918, p. 2.
[6] *Ibid.* Cd. 9055/1918, p. 2.

submit a report for final decision to the Cabinet. By this means the War Cabinet is enabled to carry out exhaustive investigations without the whole of its members being overburdened with the details of every question.[1]

To the Cabinet of five persons was added in 1918 General Smuts, who was, of course, neither a peer nor a member of the House of Commons.[2] The procedure established in 1916 was continued until 1919. Much more use was made, however, of standing committees. Usually, a member of the War Cabinet was in the chair, but, except in a few cases, the other members were ministers outside the Cabinet and departmental experts. The most interesting of these committees was the War Priorities Committee. The three services wanted men for the forces. The Ministry of Munitions wanted men at home for the production of munitions. Industry, including agriculture, required men and women for the maintenance of production and distribution. The Ministry of National Service was concerned to see that the men and women were provided. The problem was, therefore, to secure a constantly changing scheme of priorities in which the respective needs in personnel—and, through personnel, of material—could be met. Until the Committee was appointed the scramble among the departments was usually settled by the prestige or the persistence of the ministers concerned. General Smuts, who suggested the formation of the Committee in 1917, wished to have each question decided on its merits.[3] The Committee consisted of General Smuts, the First Lord of the Admiralty, the Secretaries of State for War and Air, and the Ministers of Munitions and National Service.

The Committee set up seventeen sub-committees to deal with each subject or commodity of which there was an excess of demand over supply. These reported to the Committee, which decided any question or disagreement. In addition, the Committee set up a Permanent Sub-Committee of departmental officials to act as an intermediate court between the sub-committees and the War Priorities Committee; a Permanent Labour Sub-Committee to co-ordinate departmental methods of dealing with labour dilution, release of men for war-service, etc.; a Works Construction Sub-Committee to deal with the priority of

[1] *Ibid.*
[2] S. G. Millin, *General Smuts*, II, pp. 56–7.
[3] *Ibid.* II, pp. 74–5.

building schemes; and an Industries Sub-Committee to provide for the needs of non-essential industries under governmental control.[1]

The War Cabinet had also an Eastern Committee, with Lord Curzon of the War Cabinet in the chair. It co-ordinated military and diplomatic policy in the Near East and Central Asia, and thus was concerned primarily with the work of the Foreign, India and War Offices, of the Admiralty, of the Ministry of Shipping, and of the Treasury. This committee was dissolved at the opening of the Peace Conference, though its work was continued by a departmental committee.[2] In addition there were an Economic Defence and Development Committee, a Home Affairs Committee and a Demobilisation Committee.[3]

The War Cabinet held 187 meetings in 1918, and 278 persons, besides members of the War Cabinet and the Secretariat, attended its sessions.[4]

The sittings of the War Cabinet were enlarged, both in 1917 and in 1918, by the attendance of Dominion ministers. Mr Lloyd George had announced in 1917 that a special Imperial Conference would be summoned. Not all the Prime Ministers were able to attend, and the sittings were more informal than at the regular Imperial Conferences. The opportunity was taken to hold special sessions of the War Cabinet at which the general Imperial contribution to the war was examined.[5] Including these sessions, the War Cabinet met 524 times between December 1916 and December 1918.[6]

The experience of the war taught several lessons. First, the ordinary Cabinet system provides insufficient control where day-to-day decisions of outstanding importance have to be taken. The Cabinet system assumes that the main lines of departmental policy can be laid down well in advance, so that the departments can take consequential decisions without constant reference to the Cabinet. Where the pace of national activity has to be speeded up, as in war or in time of financial crisis, the Cabinet system has to be modified.

Secondly, the experience of the War Cabinet shows that, normally,

[1] *The War Cabinet*, Report for the Year 1918, Cmd. 325/1919, p. 2.

[2] *Ibid.* p. 3. [3] *Ibid.* p. 4. [4] *Ibid.* p. 5.

[5] *The War Cabinet*, Report for the Year 1917, Cd. 9005/1918, pp. 6–7; Report for the Year 1918, Cmd. 325/1919, p. 8.

[6] Cmd. 325/1919, p. 5.

the Cabinet must contain the chief departmental ministers. The conduct of war implies the subordination of governmental activity to the attainment of a single objective. As soon as the demands of the war became less insistent and the demands of peace became obvious, there arose complaints that departmental ministers were deprived of an effective voice in the determination of questions that affected their departments. Evidence to this effect was given before the Machinery of Government Committee in 1918. Also, the matters for determination became wider in their variety and hardly less wide in their scope. Conflicts between the Prime Minister and the Foreign Secretary (who was not in the War Cabinet) became common.[1] A Cabinet of departmental ministers was necessary to control the whole.

Finally, the war showed the imperative necessity of greater co-ordination of the three Service Departments. There was indeed after 1922 a substantial body of opinion which favoured the unity of the services under a single Cabinet minister, with a minister outside the Cabinet at the head of each. Mr Winston Churchill defended his dual position as Secretary of State for War and for Air in 1921 by pointing to the necessity of co-ordination. The Geddes Committee in 1922 recommended the creation of a Ministry of Defence.[2] A Cabinet Committee accepted the proposal in principle, but considered that the time was not then appropriate. It recommended instead that the Committee of Imperial Defence should be in constant session in order to consider and advise on matters of policy affecting the three fighting services.[3]

§3. *The Committee of Imperial Defence, 1919–39*

The development of the Committee along these lines was discussed by a sub-committee of the Committee of Imperial Defence (the Salisbury Committee) in 1923,[4] and its proposals were for the most part accepted and put into force. From 1920 to 1924 the Committee of Imperial Defence was presided over not by the Prime Minister but by a nominee of his. Lord Balfour presided in place of Mr Lloyd George,

[1] Above, pp. 219–21.

[2] Report of the Committee on National Expenditure.

[3] Report of the Committee of the Committee of Imperial Defence on National and Imperial Defence, Cmd. 2029/1924, p. 9.

[4] *Ibid.*

Lord Salisbury in place of Mr Bonar Law, Lord Curzon in place of Mr Baldwin in his first year of office, and Lord Haldane in place of Mr MacDonald in 1924.[1] The Salisbury Committee recommended that this practice should be continued, but on resuming office in 1924 Mr Baldwin decided that he ought to exercise the function personally, and Mr MacDonald followed his example from 1931 to 1935.[2] Mr Baldwin in 1928 gave three reasons for his decision—first, that the Prime Minister ought to be familiar with the matters which are going to be brought before the Cabinet; secondly, that he ought to be aware of developments in case war breaks out; and thirdly, that he could not exercise his function of deciding questions as to the Estimates unless he was familiar with the problems of defence.

When the rearmament of Europe in 1936 induced the Government to propose substantial increases in the British defence forces, the practice which Mr Baldwin and Mr MacDonald had followed came in for criticism. Suggestions for a Ministry of Defence to co-ordinate the Defence Departments were renewed. Alternatively, it was suggested that some person other than the Prime Minister should act as chairman of the Committee of Imperial Defence. The Government decided not to accept either proposal, but agreed to the appointment of a Minister for the Co-ordination of Defence. The Government's decision was thus announced to Parliament:

It has been decided that, while the Prime Minister will retain, as he clearly must, the Chairmanship of the Committee of Imperial Defence and of the Defence Policy and Requirements Committee [see below], a Minister will be appointed as Deputy-Chairman of these Committees to whom the Prime Minister will delegate the following duties:

(i) The general day-to-day supervision and control on the Prime Minister's behalf of the whole organisation and activity of the Committee of Imperial Defence; the co-ordination of executive action and of monthly progress reports to the Cabinet, or of any Committee appointed by them, on the execution of the re-conditioning plans; discernment of any points which either have not been taken up or are being pursued too slowly, and (in consultation with the Prime Minister or other Ministers or Committees as required) of appropriate measures for their rectification;

(ii) In the Prime Minister's absence, taking the Chair at the Committee

[1] 287 H.C.Deb. 5 s., 1321. [2] *Ibid.*

of Imperial Defence and the Defence Policy and Requirements Committee;

(iii) Personal consultation with the Chiefs of Staff together, including the right to convene under his chairmanship the Chiefs of Staff Committee [see below] whenever he or they think desirable;

(iv) The chairmanship of the Principal Supply Officers' Committee [see below].

It will be the duty of the Deputy-Chairman to make such recommendations as he thinks necessary for improving the organisation of the Committee of Imperial Defence.[1]

The Salisbury Committee recommended that the chairman, when not the Prime Minister, should have powers of initiative under the general direction of the Cabinet. He would then have the four functions of presiding over the Committee, reporting to the Prime Minister and the Cabinet the recommendations of the Committee, interpreting the decisions of the Prime Minister and the Cabinet to the departments in matters of detail, and keeping the defence situation constantly in view.[2] These functions are more precisely delineated in the decision of 1936 set out above.

The Committee also recommended a greater permanency in the membership of the Committee. This was in fact done, though the theory of its composition remained unaltered. The Treasury minute of 4 May 1904 still governed its membership and provided that the Committee should consist of 'the Prime Minister with such other members as, having regard to the nature of the subject discussed, he may from time to time summon to assist him'.[3] But in fact its nucleus was more or less permanently fixed because the ministers at the head of the important departments concerned had necessarily to be summoned. In 1936 it consisted of the Prime Minister, the Deputy Chairman, the Lord President of the Council, the Chancellor of the Exchequer, the Secretaries of State for Foreign Affairs, Home Affairs, the Dominions, the Colonies, India, War and Air, the First Lord of the Admiralty, the Parliamentary Under-Secretary of State for Foreign Affairs, the three Chiefs of Staff, and the Permanent Secretary to the Treasury as head

[1] 309 H.C.Deb. 5 s., 659; see also Cmd. 5107/1936, p. 14.

[2] Report, pp. 16–18.

[3] Treasury minute of 4 May 1904, quoted, 191 H.C.Deb. 5 s., 1527.

of the Civil Service. Its composition was, however, at the discretion of the Prime Minister.

Mr Balfour appointed two 'permanent' members, who were intended not to change with the Government; but this practice was not followed after 1915.[1] Sometimes Opposition leaders were summoned. The Labour Government in 1930 and 1931 invited members of the Opposition to attend on special occasions.[2] In 1931 a 'Three-Party Committee' of the Committee of Imperial Defence was set up 'to advise as to the policy to be adopted at the forthcoming Disarmament Conference'. It consisted of the Prime Minister, Mr Snowden as Chancellor of the Exchequer, Mr Henderson as Foreign Secretary, Mr Thomas as Dominions Secretary and the Ministers of the Defence Departments; Lord Robert Cecil, Sir Austen Chamberlain, Sir Thomas Inskip, Mr Eden and Sir Samuel Hoare to represent the Conservative party; and Lord Lothian, Mr Lloyd George and Sir Herbert Samuel to represent the Liberal party. It held ten meetings and reached agreed conclusions, which formed the basis of British policy until the Disarmament Conference failed in 1935.[3] Representatives of the Dominions were summoned when the business of a meeting affected the Dominions.[4] Also, as will be explained, the Committee operated through sub-committees with their separate sub-sub-committees, and a considerable number of ministers, officials and outside experts was associated with their work.

The Committee dealt only with general policy, for it had 'a regular warren of committees, all breeding a numerous progeny of sub-committees'.[5] Of these the most important after 1924 was the Chiefs of Staff Committee, consisting of the Chiefs of Staff of the Navy, Army and Air Force with the Prime Minister (or in his absence the Minister for the Co-ordination of Defence) as chairman. It dealt with all the

[1] 191 H.C.Deb. 5 s., 1029, 1528. Mr Balfour and Lord Esher continued until 1915: *Esher Papers*, III, p. 215.

[2] 299 H.C.Deb. 5 s., 998.

[3] Lord Templewood, *Nine Troubled Years*, pp. 117–19.

[4] It was so resolved at the Imperial Conference of 1911: see Dawson, *The Development of Dominion Status*, p. 159; and the decision was reaffirmed in 1926. In reply to a question in the Canadian House of Commons in 1937 it was stated that there was no record of attendance by a Canadian representative for nine years.

[5] 215 H.C.Deb. 5 s., 1039.

technical problems of defence, and it was responsible, subject to the Committee of Imperial Defence and the Cabinet, for the consideration and investigation[1] of Imperial defence as a whole, and for co-ordinating the functions and requirements of the three Defence services. It was described as 'an Imperial General Staff in Commission'. In 1927 a Joint Planning Committee, consisting of the Directors of Plans of the three Services, was formed so as to provide the Chiefs of Staff Committee with a planning staff; and in 1936 a Joint Intelligence Committee, consisting of the Directors of Intelligence of the three Services with a representative of the Foreign Office (who took the chair after 1939). Another important Committee was the Principal Supply Officers' Committee, whose task was the co-ordination of service supplies, and which was considered so important that in 1936 the Minister for the Co-ordination of Defence superseded the President of the Board of Trade as its chairman. There was also a Man-Power Committee to decide priorities among the available personnel.[2]

In July 1935 the Cabinet decided to set up a standing Committee called the Defence Policy and Requirements Committee 'to keep the defensive situation as a whole constantly under review so as to ensure that our defence arrangements and our foreign policy are in line and to advise the Cabinet and the Committee of Imperial Defence in the light of the international and financial situation as to any necessary changes in policy or in the defence proposals'.[3] This Committee was an ordinary Cabinet committee consisting of the Prime Minister, the Foreign Secretary, the heads of the three Service Departments, and certain other ministers. It developed the rearmament plans which were published in 1936,[4] but it is not clear that it survived afterwards. It was not mentioned in February 1939 when Lord Chatfield became Minister for the Co-ordination of Defence.[5]

In the memorandum published in 1946[6] it was stated that in those respects of defence preparations which required collaboration between

[1] It had powers of initiation: 215 H.C.Deb. 5 s., 1030.

[2] See the chart in *British War Economy*, p. 43.

[3] Cmd. 5107/1936, p. 14. It had been preceded by a Defence Requirement Committee constituted in 1932: *British War Economy*, p. 63.

[4] Cmd. 5107/1936, p. 14.

[5] 343 H.C.Deb. 5 s., 1365 (13 February 1939).

[6] Central Organisation for Defence, Cmd. 6923/1946.

military and civil agencies of government the country was fully prepared in 1939, and the transition from peace to war was smoothly made. Qualitatively the Navy and Air Force were not badly equipped, but there were serious gaps. The Army was small and badly equipped. This was mainly due to the political and economic circumstances of the decade before 1939, which had the result of postponing until far too late the start of an effective programme of rearmament.[1] There was also a defect of organisation, the absence of a guiding hand to formulate a unified defence policy.

For lack of such a unifying influence separate aspects of our defence tended to be examined one by one. Thus, the Admiralty building programme, the strength of the Metropolitan Air Force, the number of guns and searchlights to be deployed in the air defence of Great Britain, the equipment of the field force—each of these subjects came up for review separately. There was no provision within the central organisation for the regular examination of Service programmes to ensure that, if war came, we should be ready in all important respects to meet it. This weakness was not remedied by the appointment of a Minister for the Co-ordination of Defence. His duties were strictly limited to co-ordinating, and he had no power to take executive action. He was not given responsibility to Parliament, nor did he have any jurisdiction over the apportionment of the available resources between [*sic*] the three Services.[2]

§4. *The War Cabinet, 1939–45*

On the outbreak of war on 3 September 1939, Mr Neville Chamberlain formed a War Cabinet consisting of Mr Chamberlain as Prime Minister, Sir John Simon as Chancellor of the Exchequer, Lord Halifax as Foreign Secretary, Sir Samuel Hoare as Lord Privy Seal, Admiral of the Fleet Lord Chatfield as Minister for the Co-ordination of Defence, Mr Winston Churchill as First Lord of the Admiralty, Mr Hore-Belisha as War Secretary, Sir Kingsley Wood as Air Minister, and Lord Hankey

[1] The use of the word 'decade' was no doubt intended to avoid political controversy. It can hardly be contended that a policy of 'collective security' should have been superseded, or even supported, by a policy of rearmament until at the earliest the Japanese assault on Manchuria in 1931, and a more reasonable date would be 1933, when Hitler seized power, or 1934, when his intentions first became manifest. The use of one of these dates would, however, have placed the blame on the Conservative party. For Mr Baldwin's personal responsibility, see below, pp. 506–9.

[2] Cmd. 6923, p. 3.

as Minister without Portfolio.[1] Thus six of the nine members had heavy departmental duties. Apparently Mr Churchill's wish to return to the Admiralty compelled Mr Chamberlain to bring all the Service Ministers into the Cabinet.[2]

Mr Chamberlain considered that the joint planning machinery centred on the Chiefs of Staff Committee had fundamentally altered the position since 1918 and accordingly that a War Cabinet on Mr Lloyd George's model was unnecessary,[3] but in October 1939 the War Cabinet set up a Military Co-ordination Committee consisting of the Minister for the Co-ordination of Defence and the Service Ministers, with the Chiefs of Staff as advisers.[4] The office of Minister for the Co-ordination of Defence was retained until April 1940, but in fact the Minister had been more concerned with supplies than with strategy, and even in that respect his functions had diminished through the creation of the Ministry of Supply in April 1939. Though the Ministry was given wide legal powers potentially, its essential task when first created was to provide supplies for the Army, those for the Navy and Air Force being still provided by the Admiralty and the Air Ministry respectively. Accordingly there was still a problem of establishing priorities. This problem was not dealt with until August 1939, when a Ministerial Priority Committee, consisting of the Minister for the Co-ordination of Defence as Chairman, Sir Samuel Hoare (Lord Privy Seal) and 'the Ministers likely to be concerned' was set up. This Committee may never have functioned in fact, because the work was undertaken by five sub-committees, each with a Parliamentary Secretary as chairman, concerned with Labour, Materials, Production, Transport, and Building Labour. There was a secretariat in the Ministry of Supply known as the Central Priority Department, whose duty was 'to secure the submission by departmental representatives of any matters which they desire to be considered by the Priority Committees, to take note of the decisions made by the Priority Committees and to notify all decisions through the whole of the machinery of departments interested'. In addition to

[1] But several ministers, the Permanent Secretary to the Treasury and one at least of the Chiefs of Staff were usually summoned. Generally about fifteen persons attended. *British War Economy*, p. 91.

[2] J. R. M. Butler, *Grand Strategy*, II, p. 5.

[3] *Life of Neville Chamberlain*, p. 425.

[4] *British War Economy*, p. 91. Mr Churchill became chairman in April 1940.

their secretarial functions the Central Priority Department continued the function previously exercised by the Supply Board (the official committee subordinate to the Principal Supply Officers' Committee of the Committee of Imperial Defence) and the Supply Committee of the co-ordination of demands for production capacity. This allocation had for one of its objects the avoidance of wasteful changes in production programmes in individual factories and was performed by six allocation sections. This machinery, in turn, was connected with the departments by Priority Officers in the Admiralty, Air Ministry, Board of Trade, British Broadcasting Corporation (whose overseas broadcasts were under Government control), Colonial Office, Home Office, India Office, Mines Department, Office of Works, Post Office, War Office, the Ministries of Agriculture, Food, Health, Labour, Supply and Transport, and the Scottish Departments of Health and Agriculture.[1]

There was also a Ministerial Committee on Economic Co-ordination under the Chancellor of the Exchequer, which had Lord Stamp, (Sir) Henry Clay and (Sir) Hubert Henderson as advisers. Lord Stamp presided over the subordinate committee of officials, composed of the permanent heads of the departments concerned with economic policy.[2] There was a Civil Defence Committee under the Minister of Home Security, numerous *ad hoc* committees, and a Home Policy Committee under the Lord Privy Seal which dealt with all domestic questions not referred to other committees, Government legislation, Regulations under the Emergency Powers (Defence) Act, 1939, and so on.[3]

As the war developed, however, the Chiefs of Staff Committee became the most important body beneath the War Cabinet. Its terms of reference were 'to hear reports and consider the situation, to decide day-to-day problems concerning operations, and to consider any matters specially remitted to them by the War Cabinet'.[4] In effect they advised the Cabinet on grand strategy and took decisions on other matters of war which were sent as instructions to the commanders in the field. They were served by two sub-committees, the Joint Planning Sub-Committee consisting of executive officers in each of the three Service Departments, and the Joint Intelligence

[1] 352 H.C.Deb. 5 s., 865–8. [2] *Ibid.* 27–31. [3] *Ibid.* 871.
[4] J. R. M. Butler, *Grand Strategy*, II, p. 6.

Sub-Committee, also consisting of executive officers in each of the three Service Departments, but with a representative of the Foreign Office as chairman.[1] Under Mr Chamberlain this machine was not as effective as it became under Mr Churchill, partly for reasons of personnel, but partly also because the War Cabinet itself was badly composed. It not only had two leaders, Mr Chamberlain and Mr Churchill, but also several others who were prepared to run the war. The situation was very much better under Mr Churchill, because he had a much less talkative Cabinet which allowed him to win the war. Mr Chamberlain was not prepared to appoint Mr Churchill as Minister of Defence and thus to give him authority over the War Office and the Air Ministry.[2] Perhaps the Norwegian campaign would have been less of a catastrophe if he had: but though the House of Commons did not know exactly how the war was being mismanaged, it had no doubt that it was. Fortunately His Majesty still had an Opposition.

When Mr Winston Churchill became Prime Minister in May 1940 he appointed a Cabinet of eight members, five from the Conservative party and three from the Labour party. Three ministers, Mr Attlee as Lord Privy Seal, Sir John Anderson as Lord President of the Council, and Mr Greenwood as Minister without Portfolio, had no substantial departmental duties. They were in effect chairmen of Cabinet committees, which were reorganised by Sir John Anderson. Mr Churchill considered, however, that 'War Cabinet members should also be the holders of responsible offices and not mere advisers at large with nothing to do but think and talk and take decisions by compromise or majority'[3] —though that perhaps was a little unfair to Mr Attlee and Sir John Anderson, who spent their days as chairmen of committees. When he reconstructed the War Cabinet in 1942, Mr Churchill promoted Mr Attlee to the post of Deputy Prime Minister and also gave him the Dominions Office to keep him out of mischief. Sir Stafford Cripps was Lord Privy Seal, but was also charged with the leadership of the House of Commons. Sir John Anderson remained Lord President of the Council. The other ministers had heavy departmental duties, and the size of the Cabinet was reduced to seven members.

[1] *Ibid.* II, p. 7. [2] *Ibid.* II, p. 131.
[3] Winston Churchill, *The Second World War*, IV, pp. 75–6.

Mr Churchill's most important change, however, was to have himself appointed Minister of Defence. The office of Minister for the Co-ordination of Defence had already been abolished, because his position had been anomalous. 'He could not control the mobilisation and direction of the whole resources of the nation for total war, a task which of necessity falls to the Prime Minister, nor had he any specific responsibility for knitting together the activities of the three Services.'[1] Mr Churchill set up a Defence Committee (Operations) which for the greater part of the war consisted of the Prime Minister as chairman, the Deputy Prime Minister, the Foreign Secretary, the Minister of Production, the Service Ministers and the Chiefs of Staff, other ministers attending when matters affecting their departmental responsibilities were under consideration. This Committee examined the military plans prepared by the Chiefs of Staff and the Joint Staff and took decisions on behalf of the War Cabinet. A parallel body, the Defence Committee (Supply), dealt with the main lines of the production programmes.[2] The Home Policy Committee under Mr Attlee assumed responsibility for domestic policy.

Mr Churchill's functions as Minister of Defence were deliberately left undefined. He was able to assume in effect the supreme direction of the war because he established confidence among the authorities concerned, the War Cabinet, the officials, the Service leaders, and the House of Commons. As he himself has said, if definition had been attempted, 'all the delicate adjustments... most of which settled themselves by personal goodwill, would have had to be thrashed out in a process of ill-timed constitution-making'.[3] What others thought of the situation is indicated by Lord Hankey's reported remark that it was 'in theory and practice a "one man show"'.[4] This must be understood, however, as referring to the conduct of the war. Mr Churchill was punctilious about constitutional forms, and no major changes were made without Cabinet sanction. The Prime Minister waged war as Minister of Defence. His merits have thus been summarised by Sir James Butler: 'his constancy in subordinating minor points to

[1] Cmd. 6923, p. 3. [2] *Ibid.*

[3] Winston Churchill, *The Second World War*, II, p. 19.

[4] Lord Beveridge, *Power and Influence*, p. 404.

those of permanent and supreme importance (such as the need of a good understanding with the United States of America); his fertility in suggesting, and his readiness to entertain, new ideas; and his refusal to tolerate obstruction and delay'.[1] Considering Mr Churchill's astonishing methods of work,[2] the system worked extraordinarily well. The British Constitution, perhaps surprisingly, became Britain's best weapon —and there was no need to keep it secret.

There was, however, no Ministry of Defence. Mr Churchill's secretariat was the secretariat of the War Cabinet and his principal instrument was the Chiefs of Staff Committee. This association produced a change in the position of the Service Departments.

The Service Ministers continued to be associated with the operational conduct of the war through their membership of the Defence Committee; but the Chiefs of Staff in their corporate capacity became the authority which issued to Commanders-in-Chief unified operational instructions and strategical guidance on the conduct of the war. The responsibility for the day-to-day administration of the Services remained with the Service Departments, who followed up the central directives issued by the Chiefs of Staff with detailed instructions to their own Commanders-in-Chief on such matters as the composition, equipment and movement of the forces under their command, and the provision of reinforcements and supplies.[3]

The chain of responsibility was thus made up of the Chiefs of Staff Committee, the Defence Committee (Operations), and the War Cabinet, the Prime Minister being chairman of all three. Formal meetings of the Defence Committee became fewer as the war proceeded and confidence in Mr Churchill's management developed.[4] Nor was it necessary for the War Cabinet to meet daily with the Chiefs of Staff. As the machine began to work smoothly he substituted a weekly meeting known as the 'General Parade'.

Every Monday there was a considerable gathering—all the War Cabinet, the Service Ministers and the Minister of Home Security, the Chancellor of the Exchequer, the Secretaries of State for the Dominions and for India, the Minister of Information, the Chiefs of Staff, and the official head of the

[1] J. R. M. Butler, *Grand Strategy*, II, p. 249.

[2] See Sir Arthur Bryant, *The Turn of the Tide*.

[3] Cmd. 6923, p. 3.

[4] Churchill, *op. cit.* p. 18. It met forty times in 1940, seventy-six in 1941, twenty in 1942, fourteen in 1943, and ten in 1944.

Foreign Office. At these meetings each Chief of Staff in turn unfolded his account of all that had happened during the previous seven days; and the Foreign Secretary followed them with his story of any important developments in foreign affairs.[1]

It will be seen that these were meetings for information, not for decision, and Mr Churchill adds that there was the fullest circulation of all papers affecting the war and of all important telegrams sent by him. Thus the War Cabinet, while retaining control in principle, in fact delegated the ordinary conduct of the war to the Prime Minister.[2]

Mr Churchill has given us the programme for the first week in March 1942.[3] In a shortened form it was as follows:

1. Monday, 5.30 p.m. at No. 10: General Parade.

Business: general war situation, without reference to special secret matters such as forthcoming operations; and any other appropriate topics.

2. Tuesday, 6 p.m. at No. 10: Pacific Council.
3. Wednesday, 12 noon at House of Commons: War Cabinet only.
4. Wednesday, 10 p.m.: Defence Committee.
5. Thursday, 12 noon at House of Commons: War Cabinet.

Additional meetings of the War Cabinet were to be held on Wednesday and Thursday at 6 p.m., if the business required it.

On the civil side there were five Standing Committees of the Cabinet, each under the chairmanship of a member of the War Cabinet. These were the Production Council, the Economic Policy Committee, the Food Policy Committee, the Home Policy Committee and the Civil Defence Committee. These were 'concerted and directed' by the Home Policy Committee or Lord President's Committee or Steering Committee (its name was changed from time to time), which consisted of the Lord President of the Council, the chairmen of the five committees,

[1] *Ibid.* The ministers who were not members of the War Cabinet, but who were summoned to the 'General Parade', were known as the 'Constant Attenders'. Lord Cranborne, as leader of the House of Lords, thought that he ought to be a member of the War Cabinet, or at least have an absolute right to attend meetings. Mr Churchill did not wish to enlarge the War Cabinet, or have too many people present when secret matters were discussed. Hence, the 'General Parade' was an exposition of the previous week's military operations. See Winston Churchill, *The Second World War*, IV, pp. 76–7.

[2] Above, p. 196.

[3] Winston Churchill, *op. cit.* IV, p. 78.

and the Chancellor of the Exchequer. It relieved the War Cabinet of a great deal of its work.[1]

The system worked, and worked well, because of the personal qualities of Mr Churchill. The House of Commons and the War Cabinet did not abdicate their functions; they insisted on being informed and they would have intervened if things had gone wrong. The fact that there was so little change of personnel, political or official, at the top, bears witness to the mutual confidence which was established and to the adaptability of the British constitutional machine.

§5. *After the War*

The difficulties of the post-war world compelled the Labour Government to re-examine defence organisation with a view to assessing its ability to change to a war footing should the need arise. The scheme elaborated in 1946[2] was based on wartime experience. Supreme responsibility was vested in the Prime Minister, but it was decided to establish a Ministry of Defence. The Committee of Imperial Defence was replaced by a Defence Committee with the Prime Minister as chairman and the Minister of Defence as deputy chairman. Its composition was to be flexible, the Lord President of the Council, the Foreign Secretary, the Chancellor of the Exchequer, the Service Ministers and the Ministers of Labour and Supply would be regular members, and the Chiefs of Staff would be in attendance. Such other ministers, officers and officials as might be required would be invited to attend meetings, according to the subjects under discussion. The Committee would have a system of sub-committees, constituted mainly of officials, to prepare plans for mobilising the national resources and to secure the collaboration of most of the Government departments to that end.

In 1951 Mr Churchill, as Prime Minister, again took the portfolio of Minister of Defence, but his example was not followed by Sir Anthony Eden or Mr Macmillan. Sir Anthony made arrangements, however, for an increase in the functions of the Ministry of Defence.[3] By reason of the transfer to the Board of Trade of certain functions of the Ministry

[1] J. R. M. Butler, *Grand Strategy*, II, p. 250; and above, pp. 256, 258.

[2] Central Organisation for Defence, Cmd. 6923/1946.

[3] H.C.Deb., 5 s. (25 October 1955).

of Supply, the latter Ministry had virtually become a fourth Defence Department, and accordingly the Ministry of Defence was empowered to co-ordinate the activities of the Ministry of Supply with those of the other Defence Departments. Moreover, the Ministry of Defence was empowered not merely to apportion resources among the three Service Departments, but also to see that the composition and balance of forces within the Services met the strategic policy laid down by the Defence Committee.

The Chiefs of Staff Committee was retained in 1946 as during the war. It was apparently contemplated that, in the event of a war, the Prime Minister would assume the chairmanship, but that in practice the Minister of Defence would preside if and when he or the Chiefs of Staff so desired. In practice, the senior of the Chiefs of Staff presided until 1955, when Sir Anthony Eden provided for a permanent Service chairman because of the increase of work involved in international defence organisations like N.A.T.O. The Chiefs of Staff Committee prepares strategic military plans and submits them to the Defence Committee directly, not through the Minister of Defence. The Chiefs of Staff organisation is within the Ministry of Defence and the Minister discusses any strategic plan before it is submitted to the Defence Committee, but he is not their mouthpiece in the Committee. Nor has the appointment of a chairman to the Chiefs of Staff Committee altered the collective responsibility of that Committee for the tendering of military advice. Where, however, any member differs from his colleagues, he may tender his personal advice.

Within the resources allotted to them, the Service Ministers are responsible to Parliament for the maintenance and administration of their Services. Their demands and operations are co-ordinated by a Standing Committee of Service Ministers over which the Minister of Defence presides. It is assisted by the Consultative Committees of Principal Personnel Officers and Principal Supply Officers, both of which are linked with the Chiefs of Staff Committee. Thus, the Chiefs of Staff indicate the strategy and the Service Departments the needs of the Services in personnel and material in the light of that strategy. These needs can be discussed in the sub-committee and settled for submission to the Defence Committee, which thus has a comprehensive and coherent scheme of expenditure which, after examination, it can submit to the Cabinet.

This is of course subject to the problem of production, which is the concern of another committee of ministers, the Defence Production Committee, consisting of the Service Ministers and the Ministers of Supply and Labour, with the Minister of Defence as chairman. Under it is the Joint War Production Staff, composed of serving officers and representatives of the Service and Civil Departments concerned, under a permanent chairman on the staff of the Minister of Defence. This Committee's task, among others, is to study all aspects of war potential, and for this purpose it is a sub-committee of the Defence Committee. The President of the Board of Trade and such other ministers as may be concerned from time to time are co-opted to the Ministerial Committee.

The war showed the fundamental importance of scientific research. In order that there may be 'continued and complete integration of military and scientific thought', there is a Committee on Defence Research Policy, with an independent scientist on the staff of the Minister of Defence as chairman and containing those responsible, both from the operational and from the scientific angle, for research and development in the Service Departments and the Ministry of Defence. It should be noted, however, that this is a committee of the Ministry of Defence, not a sub-committee of the Defence Committee.

The functions of the Minister of Defence do not include what was known during the war as 'home security'. This embraces a large number of activities apart from air raid precautions and fire services and includes the maintenance of food supplies for the civil population, transport, hospitals, and so on, which fall within the scope of the civil ministries. Accordingly, the Civil Defence Committee has been reconstituted as a sub-committee of the Defence Committee.

The functions of the Ministry of Defence have been thus defined:

(*a*) The apportionment, in broad outline, of available resources among the three Services in accordance with the strategic policy laid down by the Defence Committee. This includes the framing of general policy to govern research and development, and the correlation of production programmes; (and since 1955 it also includes the composition and balance of forces within the individual Services).

(*b*) The settlement of questions of general administration on which a common policy for the three Services is desirable.

(*c*) The administration of inter-Service organisations, such as Combined Operations Headquarters, the Joint Intelligence Bureau, and the Imperial Staff College.

The Minister's proposals under the first of these heads go to the Defence Committee and the Cabinet. He is not, however, responsible for the execution of Cabinet decisions in this field, since this function belongs to the Service Departments and the Ministry of Supply.

CHAPTER XI

ECONOMIC POLICY

The co-ordination of economic policy has been a growing problem as the State has intervened more actively in economic affairs, and machinery has had to be devised to meet it. Until 1906 the economic problem was thought of primarily as a fiscal one and, since free trade was the policy adopted, the functions of the State were almost entirely regulatory except for the 'gas and water socialism' which developed in the second half of the nineteenth century through controlled or publicly owned monopolies, and except for the provisions of the poor laws, which had remained unchanged in principle since 1834. The Liberal Governments of 1906 to 1914 did not go much further, though they began to re-distribute income by increasing taxation and developing social services. Between the wars, however, unemployment became the major political problem, while the growth of the Labour party and world conditions generally focused attention upon economic problems and compelled Governments to intervene more actively in industry. The fiscal policy was changed in 1932, but it had already become a question of relatively minor importance, since tariffs are only one of the methods for controlling economic development.

The first effect of the changed attitude was an increase in the number of departments concerned with economic matters. In 1906 there were only the Treasury, the Board of Trade, the Board of Agriculture and Fisheries, the Local Government Board (in respect of the poor law), and the counterparts in Scotland and Ireland of the Board of Agriculture and Fisheries and the Local Government Board. Four Insurance Commissions were added for the administration of the health insurance scheme. The war of 1914–18 did not at once change the administrative arrangements, though the functions of the Board of Trade were changed considerably, and the Ministry of Munitions, established in 1915, began the process of State intervention in industry. In the Lloyd George Government, however, the Ministries of Labour, National Service, Pensions, Food and Shipping were established, mainly by the transfer of functions from the Board of Trade. Also, a Department of Overseas Trade was established in 1917, the respective claims of the Foreign Office and the Board of Trade being compromised by its being made a joint department of the two Ministries.

Many of the wartime functions were continued after the war, and accordingly a reorganisation of departments took place. The remaining functions of the Ministry of National Service were transferred to the Ministry of Labour. The functions of the Local Government Board and the Insurance Commissions for England and Wales were transferred to a new Ministry of Health, and corresponding changes were made in Scotland and Ireland, but without creating new Ministries. The functions of the Board of Trade relating to transport and electricity, and also the functions of the Ministry of Shipping, were transferred to a new Ministry of Transport, but that Ministry did not deal with civil aviation, the responsibility for it having already been vested in the Air Ministry. There was much argument over the establishment of a Ministry of Mines, but it was eventually decided to create a Department of Mines under the Board of Trade. Thus in 1921 the departments concerned with economic problems were the Treasury, the Board of Trade, the Ministry of Agriculture and Fisheries (so-called from 1919), the Ministry of Labour, the Ministry of Pensions, the Ministry of Health and the Scottish Office (in relation to agriculture, fisheries, poor law and health insurance).

Meanwhile there had been a reorganisation at the Board of Trade in 1917, and in particular there had been established a General Economic Department designed to assist the Permanent Secretary in relation to questions involving economic policy, especially those extending beyond the sphere of any particular department. It was to have no executive functions but would be charged with the duty of systematically studying the general economic position of the country and the problems arising therefrom.[1] The department was combined with another department in 1919 and disappeared completely in 1922, all that was left being the post of Chief Economic Adviser, which had been created in 1919.[2]

[1] Memorandum with respect to the reorganization of the Board of Trade, Cmd. 8922 of 1918.

[2] Chester and Willson, *The Organization of British Central Government, 1914–1956*, pp. 295–6.

The need for economic research had been explained by the Haldane Committee (the Machinery of Government Committee), which reported in December 1918. Attention was naturally directed to the success of the Committee of Imperial Defence in planning the steps to be taken in the event of war breaking out and also to the valuable research carried out through the Department of Scientific and Industrial Research attached to the Privy Council Office. The Haldane Committee thought that there should be a similar department charged with economic research, working under the control of the Lord President of the Council, and if these functions grew it might be necessary to appoint a separate minister to preside over the department.[1]

No action was taken on this recommendation, and Sir John Anderson says[2] that Lord Haldane's own opinion changed later to the view that an organisation like the Committee of Imperial Defence was more appropriate. He stimulated Mr Ramsay MacDonald to produce a memorandum, during the Labour Government of 1924 (of which Lord Haldane was a member), advocating the establishment of a Committee of Economic Inquiry based on the analogy of the Committee of Imperial Defence. The Prime Minister would be chairman, though in his absence the chair would be taken by a minister nominated by him. The membership would be fluid, so that the Prime Minister would from time to time summon such ministers as were specially concerned with the subjects under discussion. He would also summon such economic and statistical experts as he might think fit. It was believed that this Committee would achieve three objects:[3]

(*a*) to ensure that national problems were actually being faced and thought out in advance on a basis of fact;

(*b*) to assist the Government of the day with an organisation—stable but not rigid—for exploring the problems in which it is interested without the need of improvising co-ordination; and

(*c*) to utilise to the greatest advantage the existing facilities of the Government departments under conditions most likely to command the ready co-operation of their officials.

[1] Report of the Machinery of Government Committee, Cd. 9230.

[2] Sir John Anderson, *The Organization of Economic Studies in relation to the Problems of Government*, p. 80.

[3] *Ibid.* pp. 9–10.

The Labour Government fell before action could be taken on this memorandum. In June 1925 Mr Baldwin established a Committee of Civil Research which examined a number of minor problems like industrial fatigue and the distribution of tsetse fly in East Africa[1] but can hardly be said to have solved any major problems, and in January 1930 its functions were taken over by the Economic Advisory Council established by Mr MacDonald more or less on the basis of his memorandum of 1924.[2] The Council was a standing body reporting to the Cabinet. Its functions were to advise the Government in economic matters, and to make continuous study of developments in trade and industry and in the use of national and imperial resources, of the effect of legislation and fiscal policy at home and abroad, and of all aspects of national, imperial and international economy with a bearing on the prosperity of the country. It was subject to the directions of the Prime Minister, and its expenses were borne on the Treasury vote. It was directed to keep in close touch with the departments affected by its work, with a view to a concerted study of economic problems of national interest. It was, however, forbidden to interfere with the functions or responsibilities of ministers or of the departments over which they presided. It was a purely advisory body and had no executive or administrative power.

The Prime Minister was chairman, and the Chancellor of the Exchequer, the Secretary of State for the Dominions, the President of the Board of Trade, and the Minister of Agriculture and Fisheries were members. The Prime Minister might summon other ministers from time to time, and outside experts were chosen as members because of their special knowledge and experience in industrial and economic matters. Of these outside experts there were originally fifteen. The Council had a secretary holding the rank of assistant secretary in the civil service, a number of assistant secretaries, and other staff.

Provided that it acted after receiving the approval of the Prime Minister, the Council might initiate inquiries into, and advise upon, any subject within its terms of reference, including proposals for legislation. It was directed to consult departments and outside authorities as to work in hand or projected, and to collate such statistical or other

[1] Sir John Anderson, *op. cit.* p. 10.

[2] See Cmd. 3478/1930.

information as might be required for the performance of its work. The meetings of the Council were mainly directed to a review of the state of trade and to consideration of reports from committees. These committees, like the sub-committees of the Committee of Imperial Defence, were not necessarily composed entirely of members of the Council. Indeed, the Council was directed to prepare a list of persons with industrial, commercial, financial and working-class experience, and of persons who had made a special study of social, economic and other scientific problems, who were able to assist by serving on committees or in other ways. The Council had two standing committees, the Committee on Economic Information and the Committee on Scientific Research, and a varying number of *ad hoc* committees.

It may be noted that when the problem of unemployment became acute, Mr MacDonald did not rely on the Economic Advisory Council, but set up a 'panel' of civil servants, under the supervision of the Permanent Under-Secretary of State at the Home Office. The panel was to examine every expedient likely to reduce unemployment and to report to the Cabinet through the Lord Privy Seal. The secretariat of the Economic Advisory Council was placed at the panel's disposal. This panel disappeared when the National Government was formed in 1931.[1] The Economic Advisory Council remained in existence, but it played no part in solving the problems created by the economic crisis. It did not in fact meet after 1931, but its two standing committees, the one for economic information and the other for scientific research, continued to meet until 1939.[2]

The Council's failure was believed at the time to be due to the widely differing views held by its members, who were in any case not all professional economists. Sir John Anderson considers that there were two other factors.[3] In the first place, it was not effectively integrated with the departments affected: 'It bears the appearance of an auxiliary engine not geared to the main shaft.' In the second place, ministerial responsibility was too diffuse. The Prime Minister had a host of other functions and there was no minister in charge. Sir John added that he

[1] Sir John Anderson, *op. cit.* pp. 11–12.

[2] Chester and Willson, *The Organization of British Central Government, 1914–1956*, pp. 322–3.

[3] Sir John Anderson, *op. cit.* pp. 16–17.

would predict failure for any organisation that was deficient in these respects.

The threat of war in 1939 again brought attention to bear on the problem of economic planning, since the rearmament programme was taking a large slice of the national income and the outbreak of war would cause an economic disturbance greater even than that experienced after 1914. Suggestions for an Economic General Staff or a Department of Economic Planning were made but not approved. Instead, Lord Stamp, who was assisted by Professor (Sir) Henry Clay and Professor (Sir) Hubert Henderson, was given the task of running an 'Economic Survey'. When war broke out Lord Stamp was given the title of 'Adviser on Economic Co-operation' and appointed to preside over an Inter-departmental Committee on Economic Co-ordination. In little more than a year the Survey produced 'a very large number of most valuable studies'; though, as Sir John Anderson adds, 'whether full use was made of them is another matter'.[1] Sir John also points out that the Survey, like the Economic Advisory Council, was deficient in that it had no responsible minister.[2] There was, however, a standing committee of the Cabinet concerned with economic policy.[3]

Partly to meet the requirements of the Survey, and partly for other purposes, a number of economists and statisticians was recruited to the temporary staff of the Cabinet Office to serve as a 'Central Economic Information Service'. When at the end of 1940 the Survey came to an end, the statisticians of the Central Economic Information Service were separated from the economists to form the Central Statistical Office, which is still a branch of the Cabinet Office and has been mainly responsible for the vast improvement in the Government's statistical service since the war. The economists, with the remains of the Stamp Survey, became the Economic Section working under the Lord President of the Council, which was charged by Mr Churchill in February 1941 with a 'special responsibility for the economic side of the Home Front'.[4] The Cabinet Committee on Economic Policy was then discharged.[5]

At this stage of the war the economic organisation at Cabinet level

[1] Sir John Anderson, *op. cit.* pp. 12–14.

[2] *Ibid.* p. 17.

[3] Chester and Willson, *op. cit.* p. 323.

[4] Sir John Anderson, *op. cit.* p. 15.

[5] Chester and Willson, *op. cit.* p. 324.

was as follows.[1] There was a Production Executive consisting of the four ministers responsible for production (apparently the First Lord of the Admiralty and the Ministers of Supply, Aircraft Production and Works) with the Minister of Labour and National Service as chairman, and an Import Executive consisting of the five ministers mainly responsible for imports (apparently the First Lord of the Admiralty, the President of the Board of Trade, and the Ministers of Supply, Aircraft Production and Food). Sir John Anderson, as Lord President of the Council, was chairman of a committee known sometimes as the Lord President's Committee and sometimes as the Steering Committee. It consisted of the chairmen of the Executives and of the other main Cabinet committees, and its function was 'to knit together the work of all those bodies, to settle any differences that may arise in the course of their work, to deal with any residual problems, and finally to consider the larger economic issues which the Government must keep constantly under review but which do not fall directly or completely within the scope of any one of the other executives or committees'.[2] Mr Churchill later explained that the Steering Committee was created to avoid frequent recourse to the War Cabinet.[3]

Except in respect of the Steering Committee, this arrangement proved to be unsatisfactory.

The Production Executive never took charge of the main production plans, which in this period were substantially determined in the Defence Committee (Supply). In the last half of 1941, it met only five times. Meanwhile, there had been insistent public demands for a Minister of Production to co-ordinate the activities of the three Supply Departments. Early in 1942 the Prime Minister decided that a Ministry of Production had become necessary, not for the reasons hitherto advanced, but to handle the new problems of international coordination arising from America's entry into the war. The Production Executive then finally lapsed. The Import Executive had been only a little more successful. After all, the whole import situation was governed by the allocation of shipping between military and civil uses, and this was a matter which could hardly be settled below Cabinet level. Moreover, one of the specific difficulties which the Import Executive had been instructed to tackle—the co-ordination of port management and inland transport—was tackled in another way when the Ministries of Shipping and

[1] 368 H.C.Deb. 5 s., 81–3 (Mr Bevin). [2] *Ibid.* 82. [3] *Ibid.* 264.

Transport were fused together in May 1941 as the Ministry of War Transport. Meanwhile, in March 1941, the Prime Minister had begun meetings of a Battle of the Atlantic Committee, which at the beginning concerned itself chiefly with operational matters but soon went on to consider anything to do with imports. The Import Executive continued its rather attenuated existence until May 1942. It then gave place to a Shipping Committee which was instituted at the official level, not to decide, but to report.[1]

The Steering Committee, on the other hand, became 'the most important focus of civil government under the War Cabinet, handling and settling a great deal of the business which the War Cabinet itself would otherwise have had to carry on as additional burden'.[2] It dealt especially with the 'large issues of economic policy' and had settled the main lines of economic policy by the end of 1941. It then began to tackle the more general problems of the 'home front' and virtually superseded the Home Policy Committee and the Food Policy Committee, though the legislation functions of the Home Policy Committee continued to be exercised by the Legislation Committee.[3]

The Economic Staff assisted the Lord President in the exercise of his functions as chairman of the Steering Committee, and this arrangement continued virtually unaltered until it was changed by the Labour Government in 1947. In the White Paper on Employment Policy in 1944[4] it was stated that the Economic Section of the Cabinet Office would remain as a permanent piece of government machinery. Sir John Anderson described its functions in 1943 in the following terms:[5]

The Economic Section of the War Cabinet Secretariat consists of a Director and eight assistants recruited from academic life. Each member is allotted a particular sphere of work which is not covered exclusively by the activities of a single administrative department, e.g. man-power, shipping, national income and expenditure. It is his duty (i) to be acquainted with departmental activities in his allotted sphere and (ii) to keep *au courant* with any scientific developments in that sphere and with the work which his colleagues are doing. Stress is laid by the Director of the Section on this duality of functions. The routine duties of the Section are dictated by the week-to-week business of the Lord President's Committee, the Section being

[1] *British War Economy*, pp. 219–20. [2] *Ibid.* p. 220. [3] *Ibid.*
[4] Cmd. 6527 of 1944. [5] Sir John Anderson, *op. cit.* pp. 15–16.

responsible for 'briefing' the Lord President on the various items appearing on the agenda and providing technical assistance in connexion with the many special inquiries and investigations which the Lord President undertakes in his function as co-ordinator of the Home Front. Members of the Section maintain touch with departmental activities mainly by a variety of informal contacts, particularly with expert economists working within the departments, but, in addition, they sit on various standing and *ad hoc* official committees (e.g. the Shipping Committee, the Man-power Committee, the Materials Committee, etc.) which deal with matters of general economic interest.

The Economic Section issues few papers for general circulation apart from a Quarterly Survey of the General Economic Position, which attempts in the light of all the information available to present a concise picture of recent developments and some analogies of present tendencies and future problems. In general, the Section prefers that the opinions arrived at as a result of its studies should either be embodied in its reports to the Lord President, or that they should simply become part and parcel of the general consensus of opinion which emerges through committee discussions or through informal conversations with the departments.

It is generally agreed that the country's economic problems were well handled both during the war and in the immediate post-war years, a fact which suggests that the economic advice tendered to the Government was good. The aims of our policy were, of course, simple: to find means for winning the war and, after the war, to increase exports (especially to dollar countries) so as to produce a balance of payments and dispense with American aid. This may perhaps explain, in part at least, the continuation of 'this impressive wartime harmony of economists'.[1] The Labour Government had, however, far wider aims. Moreover, though the wartime system of economic controls functioned reasonably successfully until 1947, there then developed an acute shortage of fuel and acute danger to sterling. The policy of the Labour Government led to the appointment of a Chief Planning Officer who was 'to develop the long-term plan for the use of the country's man-power and resources'. He was to work directly under the Lord President and to have access to all the ministers concerned with production.[2] In October 1947, however, the urgency of economic problems led to the appoint-

[1] Sir John Anderson, *op. cit.* p. 17.

[2] 435 H.C.Deb. 5 s., 1412–13.

ment of Sir Stafford Cripps as Minister of Economic Affairs, whose function was, with the Chancellor of the Exchequer 'to co-ordinate the economic effort both at home and abroad in all its various ramifications'.[1] This was, of course, the function which had hitherto been exercised by the Lord President. When Dr Dalton unexpectedly resigned his office over the budget leakage late in 1947, Sir Stafford Cripps was appointed Chancellor of the Exchequer and took with him to the Treasury his functions as Minister of Economic Affairs. He was provided with an additional Parliamentary Secretary known as the Economic Secretary to the Treasury, who was to be concerned with 'general economic policy and planning, including the economic aspects of Treasury supply work, overseas financial negotiations, and internal financial planning'. The Central Planning Staff retained its identity, but was transferred to the Treasury. It was stated that the Central Planning Staff maintained close relations with the Economic Section of the Cabinet Office and would continue to provide a service for ministers generally.[2] The Cabinet Office therefore continued to assume responsibility for the Economic Section and the Central Statistical Office.

Treasury control over 'planning' and economic policy generally was consolidated under the succeeding Conservative Governments. The 'Chief Planning Officer' resigned and was replaced by an 'Economic Adviser to the Government', who is a Treasury official with a larger salary than that of a Third Secretary, but a smaller salary than that of a Second Secretary. The Economic Section of the Cabinet Office has become the Economic Section of the Treasury under a Deputy Director, whose salary is slightly lower than that of an Under-Secretary. Only the Central Statistical Office remains in the Cabinet Office. Accordingly, the Chancellor of the Exchequer—or perhaps more accurately 'the Treasury Ministers', i.e. the First Lord or Prime Minister and the Chancellor of the Exchequer—is in charge of economic policy. He is assisted in this task by the Economic Secretary to the Treasury and his principal adviser, presumably, is the Economic Adviser to the Government, who has at his service the Economic Section of the Treasury, consisting of a Deputy Director and six Economic Advisers. The 'Economic General Staff' has been fully integrated with the depart-

[1] 443 H.C.Deb. 5 s., 40.

[2] 445 H.C.Deb. 5 s., 1861–2.

mental machinery. Perhaps this was inevitable. Though the older view of the Treasury's function was 'go and see what Johnny is doing and tell him not to do it', the Cambridge economists have in fact persuaded it to use the instruments of government, especially taxation, exchange control, the bank rate, the issue of Treasury bills and Government stock to produce a 'managed economy'. Whether the economy would be better if it were not managed is a question over which politicians and others dispute: but the main instruments of management are in the hands of the Treasury and the Bank of England, a nationalised institution closely related to the Treasury. If the economy has to be managed, therefore, it is logical and convenient to let the Treasury do it under the control of the Chancellor of the Exchequer and the Cabinet. It is a day-to-day affair, like the running of the Service Departments, not a problem of producing economic strategy.

CHAPTER XII

CONSTITUTIONAL MONARCHY

§1. *The Position of the Sovereign*

The existence or absence of a monarch does not in itself make a fundamental distinction in a Constitution. In a Cabinet system the Cabinet governs. The functions of the head of the State, be he King or President, are ancillary.[1] It would be wrong, however, to underestimate the influence of the monarch in British politics. The documents now available show that the Whig view of monarchy[2] which prevailed in the middle of last century and which was expounded by Bagehot was not wholly in accordance with the facts. The Sovereign must, in the last resort, accept the decisions of the Government, but he may have considerable influence on those decisions.

The advantage of constitutional monarchy is that the head of the State is free of party ties. A promoted politician cannot forget his past; and, even if he can, others cannot. Impartiality is not to be expected in any person. The liberal tradition, which is the basis of the democratic system, does not assume the existence of impartiality. It assumes only that different opinions may be honestly held and that the person who occupies a judicial position, whether he be King, Speaker of the House of Commons, or judge of the High Court, will try to exclude his bias from any decision that he may take in the exercise of the functions of his office.

Association with particular parties or particular classes, however, renders the task of the arbiter more difficult. The Sovereign, unlike an elected President, has no party associations. He is bred in a highly selective atmosphere and he does not form party loyalties. As a result,

[1] Cf. the Constitutions of India and Pakistan, which take nearly all their leading ideas from the British Constitution.

[2] In a pamphlet published by 'Verax' in 1878—a document which had a certain success in its day—it was said: 'The Crown we only know as the ceremonial device on the Great Seal by which the nation's resolves are determined, and the moment we are forced to know it in any other capacity danger commences for one party, though hardly for both': quoted, *Quarterly Review*, CLVIII, p. 28.

not only is he in a position to act more impartially but also, what is of more importance, he is believed by others to be impartial. Yet until the reign of Queen Victoria, the British monarchy had not attained this position of independence. The political sympathies of all the monarchs from Anne to George IV were well known. William IV had not, before his accession, associated himself with any party: he had led the life of a worthy burgess. Even so, he was assumed in fact to be a supporter of the Whig party. Queen Victoria, too, was assumed to be partisan. Her accession gave a new lease of life to the Whig Government.[1] The King of the Belgians said that she was the only one of the whole family, except the Duke of Sussex, who would keep them in office; consequently, they were bound to serve her with sincerity and attachment.[2]

The lesson of the Reform Act had not yet been learned. It was still not understood that the power of the Government rested on the vote of the electorate, not on the 'confidence' of the Queen. There had formerly been no distinction between the two. From 1714 to 1782 no Government lost a general election, nor did any Government ever fail to sway Parliament so long as it possessed the King's confidence.[3] It was therefore not surprising that the Queen herself did not understand the situation. She invited Lord Melbourne to dinner once a week 'as I think it right to show publicly that I esteem him and have confidence in him, as he has behaved so well'.[4] The dispute over the Ladies of the Bedchamber in 1839 was due to the fact, not that Peel feared that the Whig Ladies would whisper Whig ideas into the Queen's ears,[5] but that he thought that some demonstration of confidence in him was necessary. The Whigs had great difficulty in 1841 in drafting a Queen's Speech which did not appear to make the Queen side with them;[6] and

[1] G. Kitson Clark, *Peel and the Conservative Party*, p. 361. 'Nobody can deny that [the accession of Queen Victoria] has given the Whig Government an advantage over the Tories. Hitherto the Government have been working against the stream, inasmuch as they had the influence of the Crown dead against them': Greville, *Memoirs*, 2nd series, I, p. 5.

[2] *Letters of Queen Victoria*, 1st series, I, pp. 92–3.

[3] Keir, *Constitutional History of Modern Britain*, p. 297.

[4] *Letters of Queen Victoria*, 1st series, I, p. 110.

[5] Though at a later stage Conservative Ladies certainly whispered Conservative ideas: A. Ponsonby, *Henry Ponsonby*, p. 154. General Ponsonby thought that the Ladies of the Bedchamber ought to change with the Government.

[6] *Annual Register*, 1841, p. 198.

Lord John Russell had to explain to the House of Commons that the ministers and they alone were responsible for it.[1] Melbourne's desire not to dissolve in that year had been due to his belief that an unsuccessful appeal to the people by the Whigs would be an affront to the Crown.[2] When the Government was defeated he advised her to say 'that your Majesty's present servants possessed your Majesty's confidence, and that you only parted with them in deference to the will of Parliament'.[3] As late as 1855 the Queen offered Lord Aberdeen the Garter because she 'wishes to give a public testimony of her continued confidence in Lord Aberdeen's administration'.[4]

Until 1841 the Queen completely identified herself with the Whig party. In 1837 she wrote to the King of the Belgians: 'With respect to the Elections, they are, I am thankful to say, rather favourable, though not so as we could wish. But upon the whole we shall have as good a House as we had.... The Irish Elections are very favourable to us; we have gained six in the English boroughs, and lost, I grieve to say, several in the counties.'[5] In 1840 she wrote: 'The Tories really are very astonishing; *as they cannot and dare not attack us in Parliament, they do everything that they can to be personally rude to me.... The Whigs are the only safe and loyal people, and the Radicals will also rally round their Queen to protect her from the Tories.*'[6] In 1841 she told Lord Clarendon that she had not seen an article in *The Times* 'for she only read the papers on *our own* side'.[7]

The Prince Consort, however, effected a change. Baron Stockmar, for once, gave him advice which was almost correct.[8] In any case, his native intelligence was enough to show him that the fundamental principle of constitutional monarchy is that in party politics the Crown should not take sides. It can have real influence on policy, but it should never be brought into political controversy. When the Duke of Wellington could speak, not incorrectly, of 'being governed by a

[1] *Annual Register*, 1841, 198.
[2] *Letters of Queen Victoria*, 1st series, I, p. 348.
[3] *Ibid.* 1st series, I, p. 385.
[4] *Ibid.* 1st series, III, p. 84. The Garter was then given on the advice of the Prime Minister.
[5] *Ibid.* 1st series, I, p. 116.
[6] *Ibid.* 1st series, I, p. 268 (italics in the original).
[7] *Life of the Earl of Clarendon*, I, p. 221.
[8] *Life of the Prince Consort*, I, p. 110; for Baron Stockmar, see below, pp. 343–4.

Sovereign who is the head of an adverse party',[1] the Crown's position was fundamentally weak. After 1841 that accusation could not be levelled against the Queen during the Prince's lifetime.

It was indeed the aim of ministers from Sir Robert Peel onward to keep the Sovereign's name out of political controversy. Though Mr Gladstone, as will presently be seen, had more cause to complain even than the Tories of 1839, no word of public criticism passed his lips. Prince Albert committed a *faux pas* in attending the debate on the Repeal of the Corn Laws, and was duly criticised by Lord George Bentinck;[2] personal criticism of the Queen—as distinct from criticism of monarchy as such—ceased to be a feature of English public life. Matters affecting the monarch personally were, with the exception of the Queen's assumption of the title of 'Queen-Empress of India', settled by agreement between the Government and the Opposition. Lord Granville's criticism of Mr Disraeli's neglect in the excepted case was fully justified.[3] Enormous care was taken in 1910 and 1911 to prevent any discussion of the King's actions and to ensure that criticism should be aimed at the Government.[4]

Nevertheless, the Queen became definitely a partisan after 1868. She was apt to take violent dislike to individual ministers. Sir Robert Peel became an enemy by opposing the Prince's grant in 1840, though personal acquaintance removed feelings of antipathy. Lord George Bentinck and 'that detestable Mr D'Israeli' became the subjects of royal disfavour by their consistency to Tory policy when the (by now) favourite minister ate his words. But Mr Disraeli knew how to make the most of his opportunities once he was given personal access. Mr Gladstone had been in high favour as a follower of Sir Robert Peel, but as he progressed further to the left in his political opinions, and became more and more antagonistic to Mr Disraeli, antipathy grew. Mr Disraeli's flattery,[5] the Queen's growing conservatism, the new spirit that necessarily pervaded the Constitution after Disraeli's Reform Act, and Mr Gladstone's complete acceptance of the new conditions and the

[1] *Peel Papers*, II, p. 426. [2] Disraeli, *Lord George Bentinck*, p. 75.

[3] *Life of Lord Granville*, II, pp. 160–2. [4] Below, pp. 435–44.

[5] E.g. *Letters of Queen Victoria*, 2nd series, II, pp. 624–5. For another example, see *ibid.* 2nd series, I, p. 551.

Radical principles that they implied, produced an antagonism in the Queen. Mr Gladstone before 1868 received lessons in Court behaviour from the Dean of Windsor.[1] They availed him nothing. In 1897 Mr Gladstone spoke privately of the Queen's attitude as one of 'armed neutrality'.[2] 'Neutrality', even armed, is not the word. The documents now available show that she was using more formidable weapons against him from 1885 onwards. Sir Charles Dilke was more correct in saying, even in 1879, that she was a Conservative.[3] It should be added, however, that she was a Conservative only in private; in public the fiction of impartiality was maintained—except when the death of Gordon moved her to commit the indiscretion of telegraphing *en clair* what she thought of Mr Gladstone.[4]

During the Parliament of 1874–80, as Lord Oxford and Asquith has said, the Queen 'entered heart and soul' into partnership with Mr Disraeli.[5] Of the Opposition's attitude to the Eastern Question in 1876 she wrote: 'The Queen has never made any secret of her disapproval and indignation at Mr Gladstone's conduct and that of his followers, and General Ponsonby may repeat it to anyone—as it is totally different to Home Affairs and thus future interests of this country are imperilled by his conduct.'[6] On receiving news of the defeat of the Government in 1880 she wrote: 'This is a terrible telegram....The Queen cannot deny (Liberal as she has ever been but never Radical or democratic) she thinks it a great calamity for the country and the peace of Europe.'[7] In a letter to General Ponsonby she said that she 'would sooner *abdicate* than send for or have any *communication* with *that half-mad firebrand* who would soon ruin everything and be a *Dictator*'.[8] She did not carry out her threat, but she began at once to raise objections to Liberal policy.[9] She refused to answer one of Mr Gladstone's letters, but wrote to Lord Granville (himself falling out of favour as a 'weak reed')[10] to

[1] Guedalla, *The Queen and Mr Gladstone*, I, pp. 44–5.
[2] *Life of Gladstone*, III, p. 291. [3] *Life of Sir Charles Dilke*, I, p. 286.
[4] *Letters of Queen Victoria*, 2nd series, III, p. 597.
[5] Oxford and Asquith, *Fifty Years of Parliament*, I, p. 48.
[6] A. Ponsonby, *Henry Ponsonby*, p. 161.
[7] *Letters of Queen Victoria*, 2nd series, III, p. 73.
[8] A. Ponsonby, *Henry Ponsonby*, p. 184.
[9] *Letters of Queen Victoria*, 2nd series, III, pp. 117, 121, 122, 135.
[10] *Life of Lord Granville*, II, p. 5; *Letters of Queen Victoria*, 2nd series, III, pp. 508–9.

make it plain that 'silence does not mean assent.... She deeply grieves to see us [in the Eastern Question] on what she *must* call the wrong side.'[1] She asked Lord Granville to read to the Cabinet a letter full of attacks on Radicalism;[2] she objected strongly to a statement by Mr Childers that the House was 'pledged to administrative reform';[3] she said that the House of Commons was becoming like one of the Assemblies of a Republic. But 'The House of Lords [where there was now a Conservative majority] has shown every disposition to be conciliatory, while the House of Commons only becomes more presumptuous'.[4] She refused to agree to the evacuation of Candahar[5] or to the reversal of Lord Beaconsfield's policy in the Near East[6] (which had nevertheless been the main subject of attack by the Liberals at the election of that year). She stated that she *never* wrote to Mr Gladstone except on formal official matters:[7] but she found it necessary to invite him to Windsor chiefly because of rumours that she would not.[8] She appealed to Lord Hartington to stand up to the Radicals ('*Let* them *go*')[9] and to Mr Forster to deal with Ireland without worrying about the Radicals.[10] She had a long controversy with the Cabinet on the Queen's speech and, being successful, communicated her triumph to Lord Beaconsfield.[11] Nor was this the only communication with Lord Beaconsfield.[12]

In 1882, in a letter sprinkled with underlinings, she complains to the Prince of Wales about 'this dreadfully Radical Government which contains many thinly-veiled *Republicans*' and about 'this most dangerous man' who led it. 'How differently do the leaders of Opposition in the House behave.'[13] Yet Mr Joseph Chamberlain earned a stern reproof when he said that 'there were no royalties in Birmingham and that no one had missed them'.[14]

When, after more of this kind of controversy, the Government fell, the Queen proceeded at once to try to drive a wedge between Whigs

[1] *Letters of Queen Victoria*, 2nd series, III, p. 122.
[2] *Ibid.* 2nd series, III, pp. 130–1.
[3] *Ibid.*
[4] *Ibid.* 2nd series, III, p. 136.
[5] *Ibid.* 2nd series, III, pp. 137–8.
[6] *Ibid.* 2nd series, III, p. 141.
[7] *Ibid.* 2nd series, III, p. 143.
[8] *Ibid.* 2nd series, III, pp. 159–60.
[9] *Ibid.* 2nd series, III, pp. 163–4.
[10] *Ibid.* 2nd series, III, pp. 165–6.
[11] *Ibid.* 2nd series, III, pp. 178–81.
[12] See especially, *ibid.* 2nd series, III, pp. 146–7.
[13] *Ibid.* 2nd series, III, pp. 298–9.
[14] *Ibid.* 2nd series, III, pp. 429–31, 433–7.

and other Liberals, and asked Mr Gladstone to make a speech affirming that 'liberalism is not socialism and that progress does not mean revolution'.[1] It is not surprising that at the general election of 1885 the Queen identified herself with the Conservative party. 'The elections are not good, though there are some striking Conservative victories.'[2] The elections certainly were not good, for in spite of the Queen's manœuvres[3] the Liberals came back into office. The Queen now became a kind of external leader of the Opposition caucus. She discussed with Mr Goschen the possibility of defeating Home Rule,[4] and suggested to Lord Salisbury a coalition of Conservatives and Liberal Unionists.[5] 'As this is no party question, but one which concerns the safety, honour, and welfare of her dominions' she expressed her admiration of and thanks for a speech by the leader of the Liberal Unionists in opposition.[6] She was informed by telegram of the proceedings of a great anti-Home Rule demonstration.[7] She again urged fusion of the Opposition, and Mr Goschen informed her that the best chance of success was a Conservative Government supported by the Liberal Unionists.[8] This letter was communicated to Lord Salisbury; but he, referring to a hint that the Queen might dissolve Parliament without advice, recommended that such a dissolution should be resorted to only on the advice of Mr Gladstone.[9]

However, it appearing likely that the Government would be defeated, Lord Salisbury wrote a long memorandum discussing what the Queen should do if Mr Gladstone advised a dissolution. This memorandum considered only the advantages which might accrue to the 'party of resistance', and did not consider whether the Queen owed any duty to the Constitution.[10] This was followed by a conversation on the same subject between the Queen and Mr Goschen.[11] Lord Salisbury, in another letter, discussed motives quite openly. He spoke of 'a decided probability that the Unionists will gain on a dissolution'; and accord-

[1] *Ibid.* 2nd series, III, pp. 695–703.

[2] *Ibid.* 2nd series, III, p. 706.

[3] Above, pp. 34–7.

[4] *Letters of Queen Victoria*, 3rd series, I, pp. 83, 90–1.

[5] *Ibid.* 3rd series, I, p. 98.

[6] *Ibid.* 3rd series, I, p. 102.

[7] *Ibid.* 3rd series, I, p. 105.

[8] *Ibid.* 3rd series, I, pp. 111–14.

[9] *Ibid.* 3rd series, I, pp. 116–17.

[10] *Ibid.* 3rd series, I, pp. 128–30.

[11] *Ibid.* 3rd series, I, pp. 131–2.

ingly he offered advice 'at your Majesty's gracious invitation' to grant Mr Gladstone a dissolution.[1] When Mr Gladstone said that, if defeated, the Cabinet would probably advise a dissolution, the Queen at once said that she would sanction it.[2] This being done, the Government was defeated and the Queen, anxious for the return of her own party, asked Lord Rosebery to persuade Mr Gladstone to resign at once.[3] The Queen's party thus came into office once more, and her efforts for the next few years were directed to the cementing of the Unionist alliance and the keeping out of the Liberals.[4]

The Queen's judgment of the Gladstone period of office is summed up in language which Lord Beaconsfield himself might have used. 'Lord Beaconsfield raised up the position of Great Britain from '74 to '80 in a marvellous manner. Mr Gladstone and Lord Granville pulled it down again during the five years of their mischievous and fatal mis-rule.'[5]

On no constitutional principles can the Queen's conduct be defended. It cannot be expected that a monarch of strong views will be impartial, given the atmosphere in which he is bred and in which he lives; it is to be expected that, normally, he will be more in sympathy with conservative than with other opinions. A progressive Government, in the political sense, cannot expect to have its proposals approved so readily as a Conservative Government. The monarch, on his side, is entitled to put his own views before the Government and to ask the Government to weigh them thoroughly. But if ministers insist, he must give way. He is not entitled to identify himself with a particular set of measures or a particular set of party politicians, for, if he does, he himself becomes a politician, entitled to be criticised and attacked like other politicians. The justification for his high position and the principles which have been established to keep his acts out of controversy will then have disappeared, and he must expect that steps will be taken to limit his powers.

Queen Victoria offended against these principles. She tried to thwart the policy which the Liberal party had put before the electors in 1880

[1] *Ibid.* 3rd series, I, pp. 134–5.
[2] *Ibid.* 3rd series, I, pp. 140–1.
[3] *Ibid.* 3rd series, I, pp. 159–61.
[4] *Ibid.* 3rd series, I, pp. 172–4, 234–6, 617, 619.
[5] *Ibid.* 3rd series, I, p. 196.

and which had secured for that party a large majority. She used her power to try to prevent the formation of a Liberal Government when the same party secured a majority in 1886. She intrigued with the leaders of the Opposition in an attempt to secure the defeat of the Government later in the same year. She acted as broker in the alliance between Conservatives and Liberal Unionists.

The subsequent monarchs appear to have taken a constitutional view of their functions. A phrase from a letter from the private secretary to the Prime Minister, referring to the Army reforms of 1905, is worth quoting. 'The King cannot withhold his consent from the proposals which he is advised by the Cabinet to approve, but he cannot conceal his strong misgiving....'[1] Though George V insisted on seeing the leaders of the Opposition in 1910, he did so with the Prime Minister's consent, and he sought information, not assistance in defeating the Government.[2] In 1918, when George V tried to persuade the Prime Minister to retain Sir William Robertson as Chief of the Imperial General Staff, Mr Lloyd George threatened resignation if the King insisted. Lord Stamfordham replied that the King had no idea of insisting.[3] In 1929, apparently, George V raised objections to receiving an ambassador from the Soviet Union. 'The Foreign Secretary had to put it to his Sovereign that here was a Cabinet decision. Politely but firmly, he did so put it':[4] and the King received the ambassador.

Mr Asquith in 1913 wrote a long memorandum on the rights and obligations of the Crown.[5]

> We have now a well-established tradition of two hundred years, that, in the last resort, the occupant of the Throne accepts and acts on the advice of his ministers....He is entitled and bound to give his ministers all relevant information which comes to him; to point out objections which seem to him valid against the course which they advise; to suggest (if he thinks fit) an alternative policy. Such intimations are always received by ministers with the utmost respect and considered with more respect and deference than if they proceeded from any other quarter. But, in the end, the Sovereign always acts upon the advice which ministers, after (if need be) recon-

[1] Lee, *King Edward VII*, II, p. 206. [2] Below, pp. 442–3.

[3] Nicolson, *King George V*, pp. 321–2.

[4] *Life of Arthur Henderson*, p. 312.

[5] *Life of Lord Oxford and Asquith*, II, pp. 29–31.

sideration, feel it their duty to offer. They give that advice well knowing that they can, and probably will, be called upon to account for it by Parliament.[1]

The dispute over Home Rule, which produced this memorandum, also produced one from Lord Esher, who was advising George V:

Every constitutional monarch possesses a dual personality. He may hold and express opinions upon the conduct of his ministers and their measures. He may endeavour to influence their actions. He may delay decisions in order to give more time for reflection. He may refuse assent to their advice up to the point where he is obliged to choose between accepting it and losing their services.

If the Sovereign believes advice to him to be wrong, he may refuse to take it, and if his minister yields the Sovereign is justified. If the minister persists, feeling that he has behind him a majority of the people's representatives, a constitutional Sovereign must give way.

It is precisely at this point that the dual personality of the Monarch becomes clear. Hitherto he has exercised free volition, he has used his prerogatives of criticism and delay, of personal influence and remonstrance. At a given moment, however, when he is forced to choose between acquiescence and the loss of his minister, the Sovereign automatically, under the Constitution which by the Constitution Oath he has sworn to maintain, ceases to have any opinion.

The King can do no wrong. This cannot be said of anyone who is a free agent. Within certain limits, and under certain circumstances, the King ceases, constitutionally, to be a free agent. Hence the meaning of the pregnant phrase, the King can do no wrong. With due regard to the security of the Throne, the Sovereign cannot retain the final right of private judgment.

Has the King then no prerogatives?

Yes, he has many, but when translated into action they must be exercised on the advice of a minister responsible to Parliament. In no case can the Sovereign take political action unless he is screened by a minister responsible to Parliament.

This proposition is fundamental, and differentiates a constitutional monarchy based upon the principles of 1688 from all other forms of government.

No one acquainted with the inner working of the Constitution can doubt the enormous powers retained and exercised by the Sovereign. In the domain

[1] The rest of the memorandum deals with the dismissal of ministers, and is discussed in the next chapter, below, p. 408. For the King's acceptance of Mr Asquith's quoted principle, and his qualification to it in the circumstances of the case, see Nicolson, *King George V*, pp. 225–6.

of patronage and appointment, naval, military, ecclesiastical and civil, he wields great influence and power. Over foreign policy his personality exercises a sway commensurate with his intimate knowledge of foreign courts, and his sustained relations with foreign potentates. In the distribution of honours and rewards, the impartiality of the Sovereign renders his decision final.

Even within the doubtful land of legislation the King's influence and power of suggesting compromise, and sometimes effecting it, are invaluable assets in the difficult business of government.

It is irrational to contend that because under our constitutional rules and practice the Sovereign has now and then to act automatically, he is therefore an automaton without influence or power....

What then is the King to do, if he is asked by his minister to violate the Constitution?

The answer is that the Sovereign cannot act unconstitutionally so long as he acts on the advice of a minister supported by a majority in the House of Commons. Ministerial responsibility is the safeguard of the monarchy. Without it, the throne could not stand for long, amid the gusts of political conflict and the storm of political passion.

What, however, is the King to do if he is asked to support his ministers in putting a strain upon the Constitution, which in his view is improper and dangerous to the welfare of the state?...

In the last resort the King has no option. If the constitutional doctrines of ministerial responsibility mean anything at all, the King would have to sign his own death-warrant, if it was presented to him for signature by a minister commanding a majority in Parliament. If there is any tampering with this fundamental principle, the end of the monarchy is in sight....

Even if it is true that the King has no power to act upon his private judgment and to override the will of the ministers, he has, however, the unquestioned right of remonstrance. This right should be used for the double purpose of safeguarding the King's conscience and of placing beyond all risk of misconception the whole responsibility for the advice they tender upon the shoulders of the Ministry....[1]

This statement must be read with some qualification. The legal rule that 'the King can do no wrong' has no application to the matter. Since an act of the King could not give a private citizen a legal remedy at common law it was no doubt desirable that executive acts should be

[1] *Esher Papers*, III, pp. 126–9. Other portions of this memorandum, relating more specifically to the events of 1913, are quoted below, pp. 397–8.

done by ministers and other servants of the Crown; but this has no relevance to the duty or otherwise of the King to act on the advice of his ministers. Nor is much help obtained by an appeal to the 'principles of 1688'. For a century after 1688 the King was by no means bound to accept the advice of ministers. The change came about not because Whig principles were accepted but because after 1832 Governments rested not on the favour of the Crown but on the vote of the people. Unless the King could appeal to the people against his Government he had to accept its advice; and if he appealed to the people against the Government he must expect the Government to appeal to the people against the King. In other words, he had inevitably in such a case to enter into a party conflict which he stood every chance of losing, if not immediately, at least in the future. Lord Esher rightly based his memorandum on the principle that if the King exercised his own judgment 'the throne could not stand for long'.

By way of further qualification it should also be noted that the King's influence on foreign policy cannot now be greater than his influence on domestic policy, for knowledge of foreign courts and relations with foreign potentates gives no help in a world most of which has decided to abolish courts and dispense with potentates. On the other hand, there are functions which the King does not, or may be claimed not to exercise, on ministerial advice. The most important of them is the appointment of a Prime Minister.[1] In addition, it is sometimes said that the dismissal of ministers and the dissolution of Parliament may be undertaken without the consent of the Government.[2] In relation to patronage and honours, too, the Sovereign exercises a substantial element of discretion.[3]

In relation to ordinary policy, the King's influence may be substantial, though it is rarely the determining factor. It is advisory and not decisive. Whether the monarch has the ability to give effective advice is largely an accident of birth. There is no presumption that the lineal descendant of Princess Sophia of Hanover possesses greater intelligence than the foremost statesmen of the day, but frequently the Sovereign has more practical experience of affairs than the statesmen in control

[1] Above, ch. II.
[2] See below, ch. XIII.
[3] See below, ch. XIV.

of the governmental machine. Disraeli, for once, was not exaggerating when he wrote:

For more than forty years your Majesty has been acquainted with the secret springs of every important event that has happened in the world, and, during that time, have [*sic*] been in constant communication with all the most eminent men of your Kingdom. There must, necessarily, have accrued to a Sovereign, so placed, such a knowledge of affairs and of human character that the most gifted must profit by an intercourse with your Majesty, and the realm suffer by your Majesty's reserve.[1]

On one occasion Queen Victoria gave Mr Gladstone information which the Duke of Wellington had given her about Mr Pitt. By the end of her reign she had been in public life for over sixty years. Edward VII might, as Prince of Wales, have studied governmental problems for twenty years, had he been so minded, before he came to the throne. Lord Esher could say of George V in 1913 that he was better informed than his ministers about the prospects of rebellion in Ireland.[2] At the end of his reign he had had twenty-five years' experience. George VI knew four Prime Ministers; even Elizabeth II has known three.

Moreover, the divinity that hedges a King places him in a strong position. 'It is not for a subject to bandy civilities with his Sovereign', said Dr Johnson. 'You cannot argue on your knees', it has been remarked. Far greater deference must therefore be accorded to the views of a King than would be given to similar views by other persons. Lord Salisbury said that he had four departments, the Prime Ministership, the Foreign Office, the Queen, and Randolph Churchill—'and the burden of them increases in that order'.[3] When Sir William Harcourt remarked that he was going to have a tooth out, Mr Asquith said that he was in a similar plight, for he was going to see the King.[4] George V certainly knew what he could do. Writing of the Home Rule controversy in 1914 he said in a letter to Lord Stamfordham:

I am not discouraged, and, with your kind help, common sense, good judgment and advice, I think I shall come out on top; at least I mean to try

[1] *Letters of Queen Victoria*, 2nd series, III, pp. 146–7; cf. *Life of Disraeli*, II, p. 325.
[2] *Esher Papers*, III, p. 145.
[3] *Life of Robert, Marquis of Salisbury*, III, p. 180.
[4] Fitzroy, *Memoirs*, II, p. 524.

to!...If you think it necessary later, I shall certainly ask the P.M. to come here to see me for one night;...I shall keep on bothering him as much as possible.[1]

Yet there are disadvantages in the royal position. The first is that the King never takes responsibility. He is carefully shielded from it; for responsibility implies criticism, and criticism must detract from impartiality. Yet opinion divorced from responsibility may well be theoretical and extravagant. That Queen Victoria felt responsibility cannot be doubted; but, if she had been compelled to defend herself in Parliament, to carry public opinion with her, and to have attributed to her the death of those who were compelled to fight in 'side shows', she might have been less prone to think of Great Britain as a fine fellow strutting up and down Europe like a peacock on the terrace at Hughenden.

Secondly, his position is fundamentally weak because he cannot take positive action without involving himself in political controversy. King George V felt this strongly in 1913 and 1914. One half of his people expected him to refuse assent to the Home Rule Bill and would be annoyed if he did not. The other half expected him to assent and would be annoyed if he did not.[2]

Above all, a monarch must live in a remote if not highly artificial world. He is compelled by his people to live in a Palace surrounded by deferential servants and cannot mix with his subjects with the freedom of a private citizen. He cannot be treated as a colleague of higher rank. There has to be an air of formality even about his social contacts; and the experience of Edward VIII showed, even before there was any question of his marriage, that a wise monarch cannot be catholic in his choice of friends. With ordinary people, the men and women who live ordinary lives, there can be no contact except on formal occasions. Nor, indeed, do ordinary people want it: the King would not be a King if he were not the prize exhibit in the national show. Edward VIII may, as has sometimes been alleged, have appreciated the point of view of the great mass of his people; but if he did it was due to excellent powers of intuition, for he could never have had the opportunity of hearing them

[1] Nicolson, *King George V*, p. 233.

[2] See opinion of Mr Bonar Law, *ibid.* p. 201; and of the King himself, *ibid.* pp. 223, 228 and 236.

express their opinions in the club, the bus or the factory. It is inevitable that the King should be expected to be not merely *bon père de famille* but also *bon roi.*

Writing of Queen Victoria, Lord Gladstone said:

> Prince Albert and Lord Beaconsfield alike had made her believe that continuity of high responsibility gave her knowledge and experience to which no passing minister could attain.... But in fact this continuity on the heights cut her off from all personal contact with the ideas of the people, and relieved her from the necessity of ever going to the roots of big questions by reason and argument. Politicians had to fight these things out in principle and detail on the platform, in the press, and in the House of Commons. They were in the continuity, not of the throne, but of arduous public life.... Discussion and inquiry produced stages in their minds and in the minds of the people, which were steps to progress. Continuity such as the Queen experienced, was a great disadvantage because in its constitutional irresponsibility it was out of touch with forward movements.[1]

Mr W. S. Blunt, whose judgment is not to be taken too seriously, said that the Queen was 'easy to flatter and mislead, the only paper she read was the *Morning Post* and the people about her did not dare tell her the real truth of things'.[2] However much a caricature, this statement represents a view which was widely held but rarely expressed. Sir Charles Dilke said on one occasion that as *The Times* had said that a speech of Mr Chamberlain's was too violent, the Queen would say so too.[3] When Mr Gladstone's private secretary was told by General Ponsonby that 'we don't like Joe's speeches here', he replied: 'It is possible...that H.M. has not read the speeches, but only goes by what she is told by friends on the other side, who see High Treason in the Prime Minister's shirt collar.' Nor is it unlikely that the private secretary made a choice of suitable reading-matter. On one occasion, certainly, General Grey told the Queen that she need not read a debate, but only the summary in *The Times*.[4] Yet *The Times* summary, like Dr Johnson, takes care that the Whig dogs do not have the best of it.

In this respect, certainly, the position has now much altered.

[1] Lord Gladstone, *After Thirty Years*, p. 375.

[2] W. S. Blunt, *My Diaries, 1888–1914*, p. 415.

[3] *Life of Sir Charles Dilke*, II, p. 65. (She did say so.)

[4] *Letters of Queen Victoria*, 2nd series, I, pp. 395–6.

Buckingham Palace has as many newspapers as a London club, and the private secretary would be failing in his duty if he did not mark, for the Queen's perusal, all items of news, whatever their political flavour, which raised political issues of some importance.[1] Whether the Queen reads them depends on the Queen herself, but none of the more recent monarchs would have dared to express an opinion on a political issue without having read the papers, public and confidential, as if he were himself concerned with the matters in hand.

§2. *Irresponsible Advisers*

The Sovereign must necessarily rely on what Lord Palmerston once called 'Her Majesty's irresponsible advisers'. 'I do not know much of the interior side of court gossip,' said Mr Gladstone, 'but I have a very bad opinion of it, and especially on this ground, that while absolutely irresponsible it appears to be uniformly admitted to be infallible.'[2] Goaded to unusual bluntness by Queen Victoria's telegram *en clair* on the news of the fall of Khartoum, Mr Gladstone said that he 'does not presume to estimate the means of judgment possessed by your Majesty'.[3]

Those 'irresponsible advisers' who have held official positions appear, so far as the means available permit of a judgment, to have uniformly acted with honesty and discretion. Sir Henry Ponsonby, on occasions, modified the consequence of the Queen's bias. Exactly what part Baroness Lehzen played is not clear. Baron Stockmar had some doubts about her influence.[4] Stockmar himself posed as an authority on the British Constitution, but frequently wrote nonsense.[5] One such statement[6] was said by Mr Gladstone, with unnecessary under-emphasis, to be based 'mainly upon misconception and confusion, such as we

[1] 'There is no Socialist newspaper, no libellous rag, that is not read and marked and shown to the King if they contain any criticism friendly or unfriendly to His Majesty and the Royal Family.' So wrote Lord Stamfordham in 1917. It will, however, be noted that 'Socialist newspapers' and 'libellous rags' were associated in Lord Stamfordham's mind, though a Socialist was in the War Cabinet. See Nicolson, *King George V*, p. 309.

[2] *Life of Gladstone*, II, p. 254.

[3] *Letters of Queen Victoria*, 2nd series, III, p. 603. [4] *Ibid.* 1st series, I, p. 283.

[5] The best example is in the *Life of the Prince Consort*, I, pp. 314–15; see also the passage referred to in the next footnote.

[6] *Life of the Prince Consort*, II, pp. 545–57.

should not have expected from a man of the Baron's long British experience, and acute perceptions'.[1] Later on, he said with even greater truth, that 'his constitutional knowledge was, after all, only an English top-dressing on a German soil'.[2]

So long as Prince Albert lived, the Queen possessed an adviser of sagacity and discretion. The sycophancy of Sir Theodore Martin's *Life* has, by reaction, caused his judgment to be underestimated. From the resignation of Lord Melbourne in 1841 to the death of the Prince in 1861, Prince Albert was, in substance, the monarch. After his death, the appointment of a private secretary became necessary, though it was not until 1867 that General Grey, who had been private secretary to the Prince Consort and continued to act for the Queen, was formally gazetted to the post. There is no evidence that he, or any of his successors, failed to exercise his office with due discretion. Indeed, there is ample evidence to the contrary. Yet the views which they presented must necessarily have been clouded with personal bias. They were nearly all military officers. Several of them were closely related.[3] Occasionally their personal views have been allowed to appear. General Ponsonby, who was appointed in 1870 and held office until 1895, was considered to have 'extreme Radical tendencies'[4] and, what was worse, a wife who was thought to be 'clever'—'a very undesirable quality in Court circles'.[5]

Actually, General Ponsonby was a very moderate Liberal, though that no doubt was extremely Radical for Buckingham Palace in the Victorian era. The Queen often quizzed him on what she believed to be his Whig, Liberal or even Radical sympathies and thought that his wife was in correspondence with Liberal friends.[6] There was indeed advantage in his Liberalism, for whenever he was goaded to reply to the Queen's attacks on the Liberals in her private correspondence with him, he did at least give the impression that there was one person, in other respects apparently sane, who sometimes agreed with Mr Gladstone.[7] Unlike the rest of the Household, too, he realised

[1] Gladstone, *Gleanings*, I, p. 75.
[2] *Ibid.* I, p. 84.
[3] See the remarkable genealogical table in Emden, *Behind the Throne*, p. 274.
[4] A. Ponsonby, *Henry Ponsonby*, p. 35.
[5] *Ibid.* p. 154.
[6] *Ibid.*
[7] *Ibid.* pp. 155 *et seq.*

the dangers into which the Queen's antagonism to Mr Gladstone was leading her:

His refusal to recant politically... quite definitely prevented a real conflict between the Queen and her Liberal Governments, which might have taken place if her animosity had not been occasionally curbed. Unrestrained, with a Private Secretary who encouraged her in expressions of indignation; she might have found herself confronted with resignations, full reasons being given for them, and a first-class constitutional crisis would certainly have arisen.[1]

Lord Ponsonby of Shulbrede has thus described General Ponsonby's methods:

The difficulties and obstacles he had constantly to overcome can now be shown as not only consisting in sometimes redrafting or toning down the Queen's first impetuous expressions of opinion, in fact, to use a modern metaphor, acting as a shock-absorber, but in actually reaching her, in penetrating the atmosphere which surrounded her, in threading his way through the official tangles, in counteracting what he deemed to be objectionable influences and in preventing her seclusion becoming an excuse for forcing her into a backwater. Further it can be noticed that in the longer political communications, while the Queen's general style is skilfully retained, the arguments, the protests and the queries are set out with a clarity and sequence of thought of which, unaided she would have been quite incapable. The pepper and mustard are retained as light seasoning but not intruded as potent ingredients.[2]

The documents make plain that General Ponsonby had a very definite theory of royal duty. The Queen was to be an adviser, a brake, an arbiter, but not a protagonist. She was impetuous in her judgments, obstinate in her opinions, and sweeping in her expressions, while she was remote from the influences which made nineteenth-century Radicalism and did not appreciate the sources from which they had sprung. His task was not to make her a Liberal but to prevent her Toryism from leading her into a conflict inappropriate to a monarch. It is difficult for us, in these days, to appreciate the virulence of Society's opposition to Mr Gladstone and therefore to understand and excuse the behaviour of the Queen. The Radical Movement was slowly but nevertheless inevitably destroying the foundations on which Victorian privilege rested,

[1] *Ibid.* p. 172.

[2] *Ibid.* p. 173.

and Society found itself caught up in a lava stream which it was powerless to resist. The kind of language which it used is exhibited by a letter from Sir Dighton Probyn, of the Prince of Wales' Household, written to General Ponsonby in 1886:

> Don't talk to me about Gladstone. I pray to God that he may be shut up as a lunatic at once, and thus save the Empire from the Destruction which he is leading her to. If he is not mad, he is a *Traitor*.[1]

This was written from Marlborough House and illustrates the environment in which the Queen lived. Yet there never was a breach and indeed the world knew little of the dangers that beset the monarchy just when, as the Jubilee approached, it appeared to be at its strongest. Much is owed to the restraint and patriotism of Mr Gladstone, whose statue ought to stand in the Mall; but much also is owed to Sir Henry Ponsonby. The gale blew itself out and the 'little old lady' carried her bonnet triumphantly at the head of the wave of patriotic emotion which swept Great Britain in 1887 and 1897—not, be it noted, without assistance from the Conservative Government.

Sir Henry Ponsonby's successors, Lord Stamfordham, Lord Wigram and Sir Alan Lascelles, had a much easier task in the political field, though the work has grown in quantity as the functions of government have broadened and become better organised. Edward VII's interest in politics was intermittent. George V had a number of difficult problems to face but took great care to be impartial and for this purpose relied heavily on Lord Stamfordham, who became his private secretary in 1901. Of him the King said, 'He taught me how to be a King'.[2] It is reasonably accurate to say that, throughout the Home Rule debates, George V never made a mistake. George VI, though the most conscientious King of the century, had not to face serious constitutional issues. There was gossip in 1914 that Lord Stamfordham was against the Home Rule Bill[3] and in 1923 he was said to favour Lord Curzon.[4] Otherwise the private secretaries have hidden their quite brilliant lights.

Private secretaries, however irresponsible in theory, occupy what they recognise to be a responsible position. They are aware that their

[1] A. Ponsonby, *Henry Ponsonby*, p. 355.
[2] Nicolson, *King George V*, p. 64.
[3] Addison, *Four-and-a-half Years*, I, 28.
[4] Sylvester, *The Real Lloyd George*.

office calls for discretion and impartiality. No such knowledge is possessed by the private persons who, for social reasons, may have the ear of the King. King Edward VII, as Prince of Wales, ascribed part of Queen Victoria's antipathy to Mr Gladstone to Prince Leopold's Toryism.[1] There are several examples where criticism by the Queen of governmental action was based on private and obviously biased information.[2] We are told[3] that King Edward VII usually relied for his views on any subject on one person. Thus, Sir John Fisher was made principal naval aide-de-camp in order that he might have direct access to the King. Yet the Navy at this time was divided into two camps, for and against Fisher. Lord Esher had the ear of the King on military as well as on constitutional matters, so that the King's principal military adviser was a Conservative while his Government was Liberal.[4] His views on constitutional questions were usually sound and he had excellent judgment as to what it was fit that a king should do; but the bias of his opinion is sufficiently indicated by his own statement: 'I am the last imaginable person to approve of "democracy", which I frankly detest.'[5]

The general atmosphere at Osborne in 1873 was thus described by General Ponsonby:

> There seems to be a general Tory atmospheric disturbance. Whether it be that when the pot is boiling the scum comes to the top, or that they are doing their best to discredit the Government, or that here we are enveloped in Tory density, I don't know. But not a day passes without some crime being attributed to the Government—some sneer uttered about them or some denigreing [*sic*] remark most of which go to the Queen and set her against the Ministers. Perhaps now it does not really matter whether the Queen dislikes them or not, but I think Sir R. Peel was right in insisting that the ladies of the bedchamber should change with the Government. Incessant sneers or conversation against a policy always damages. I must say the Queen says as little as possible, but one can't help seeing that she is impressed by it.[6]

Mr Gladstone in 1892 made a general complaint. 'At the present juncture, the views of your Majesty's actual advisers, although now

[1] Lee, *King Edward VII*, I, p. 514.

[2] See, e.g. *Letters of Queen Victoria*, 2nd series, III, pp. 257–8, 267–8; and *ibid.* 3rd series, I, pp. 465–6.

[3] Lee, *King Edward VII*, II, pp. 327–9.

[4] See *Esher Papers*, *passim*, especially vol. II.

[5] *Ibid.* III, p. 146.

[6] A. Ponsonby, *Henry Ponsonby*, p. 154.

supported by a majority of the people...are hardly at all represented, and as Mr Gladstone believes, are imperfectly known, in the powerful circles with which your Majesty has personal intercourse.'[1] This was the inevitable result of 1885. When the Whigs joined with the Conservatives, the old division of Society, as it is called, disappeared. Henceforth, with a few exceptions, the upper classes supported the Conservative Party.[2] The Sovereign is necessarily more closely associated with those classes than with the poorer section of the population. In 1945 visitors to Britain remarked that they had failed to meet anybody who had voted Labour; like the King, they had not met the right people.

The balance can, to some extent, be redressed by a close association between the King and his ministers. For Queen Victoria, such an association was impossible. 'The dignity of the Crown', said Mr Gladstone,[3] 'requires that it should never come into contact with the public, or with the Cabinet, in mental deshabille.' Of the Queen, Lord Esher wrote: 'Her interviews with her most prominent and most powerful servants were of rare occurrence. Nearly the whole of the State business, with which she was so largely identified, was carried on by correspondence.'[4] Even with her personal friends—Lord Melbourne, Sir Robert Peel, Lord Aberdeen, and Lord Beaconsfield—her relationships contained a substantial element of formality.

The methods of King Edward VII were different.

> He was always accessible to his ministers, and far more than half of the business transacted by the King was transacted orally, by personal interview. He enjoyed putting questions to his ministers, and he liked to state his own views, not in a formal document, but face to face with whom the matter concerned. It is true that he fortified himself for these interviews by frequently instructing his private secretaries to make enquiries, or to remonstrate against public acts or speeches of which he disapproved. But, in the long run, the King himself had his say, and unlike Queen Victoria, he had his say verbally.[5]

[1] *Letters of Queen Victoria*, 3rd series, II, p. 172.

[2] Note the difficulty which Mr Gladstone and other Liberal and, above all, Labour ministers have had in finding Household officers.

[3] *Gleanings*, I, p. 73.

[4] Esher, *The Influence of King Edward*, p. 42.

[5] *Ibid.* p. 43.

Moreover, much business was done by communications between the King and the Prime Minister's private secretaries. The institution of the telephone, too, has tended to make personal contacts less frequent.[1]

George V was a competent and conscientious naval officer, of a conservative cast of mind, though not a party politician, and lacking in imagination. He was, it has been said,[2] 'sensitive to criticism, essentially diffident and prone to discouragement. The phrases of some impatient intellectual, the jokes of some weary commentator, rankled unduly.' He relied heavily on Lord Stamfordham, who did not betray his trust; but inevitably he was remote even from the circles in which Mrs Asquith moved, and far removed from the Liberal voters of Bethnal Green or Caernarvon. On the other hand, it is probable that the King had a better understanding of the man from Balham than he had of Mrs Asquith.

> He was in constant communication with such people as Mr St Loe Strachey, Colonel Unsworth of the Salvation Army, Mr Hagberg Wright, the Bishop of Chelmsford or Canon Woodward, Rector of Southwark, whose activities brought them into touch with different sections of the community.[3]

He was sensitive to the criticism that he was surrounded by a 'complacent phalanx of courtiers',[4] and the phrase is far from accurate. George V was in many ways a typical grouse-shooting squire, interested in people, and therefore possessing an instinctive knowledge of ordinary people which neither the intellectuals nor the curious collection into which 'Society' was developing could have acquired. Neither Mr Asquith nor Mr Lloyd George was on terms of intimacy with him, and it is significant that Mr Balfour and Mr Bonar Law handled him better.

George VI, however, established a new relationship with his Prime Minister. It should be emphasised that his relationship necessarily depends on the attitude not only of the Sovereign himself but also of the Prime Minister. Queen Victoria, as has been mentioned, did most

[1] See Lee, *King Edward VII*, pp. 48–9. King George's first contact with his future Labour ministers (other than those in the War Cabinet) was, apparently, in 1923. Mr MacDonald was invited to Buckingham Palace, and Messrs Clynes, Thomas and Snowden were invited to dine at Lady Astor's to meet the King and Queen: Snowden, *Autobiography*, II, pp. 661–2.

[2] Nicolson, *King George V*, p. 309.

[3] *Ibid.*

[4] *Ibid.* p. 142.

of her work in writing even within the confines of the Household. Consequently, there were long periods when even Mr Disraeli, anxious as he was to establish personal relations, and welcome though he was on all personal and political grounds, did not see the Queen. Mr Gladstone was unwelcome not only because she disliked his policy but also because he 'addressed her like a public meeting'. In any case the Queen like many administrators thought through her pen. Edward VII, on the other hand, liked to see and talk to people; but, naturally, he preferred to talk to people who knew how to talk. Of the three Prime Ministers with whom he was associated, only Mr Balfour was an easy talker, and it was therefore with him that the King's relations were closest. The fact that there are masses of documents from the Queen's reign and few from those of Edward VII must not lead to the conclusion that the latter was without influence, though it is true that he had not the sustained and absorbing interest in politics that his mother had exhibited.

George V was a homely and conscientious monarch who followed his father's practice of developing the 'dignified' part of his functions, which Queen Victoria had neglected. He attached importance to ceremonial: it had to be not merely splendid, but meticulously efficient.[1] The popularity of the Royal Family is partly stimulated by the popular newspapers, which follow the principle that everybody loves a princess and gets excited about a palace: but George V, with the magnificent support of his Queen, deliberately set about the process of seeing and being seen. Speaking generally, he allowed politics to take their course. He reigned, however, over an uneasy United Kingdom. Home Rule until 1914, the war of 1914–18 (so less efficiently managed than the war of 1939–45, in spite of the shocks of the latter), the post-war depression, the financial crisis of 1931, created a series of problems in which the King was necessarily involved. Having as a boy made a précis of Bagehot's *English Constitution*[2], he knew all about his right to warn, and he had the sort of mind which lowered the temperature even when Mr Lloyd George was involved in a short circuit. His influence was not profound but he did insist that from time to time common sense creep into the process of party government. The innovation due to George VI and Mr Winston Churchill was obviously a product of

[1] Nicolson, *King George V*, p. 142.

[2] *Ibid.* p. 62.

that genius for personal relationships which made Mr Churchill such a great wartime Prime Minister. Every week while the King was in London Mr Churchill had an audience and stayed to lunch. Since the King had received all, or nearly all, the documents seen by the Prime Minister, the events of the week could be fully discussed. It would be impossible for an outside observer to assess the importance of a free and easy conversation of this character; one can say only that it is potentially important. Most Prime Ministers are lonely folk: if they develop the practice of tossing their thoughts in Buckingham Palace the royal influence may become profound. It should also be pointed out that on a number of occasions the King and Queen dined with the War Cabinet and the Chiefs of the Staffs at Downing Street. Consequently George VI was more closely in touch with his ministers than any of the more recent monarchs, not excluding Queen Victoria.

Under Elizabeth II there have been signs of a change at Buckingham Palace, though they are probably not of great significance. The heavy round of ceremonial duties has been made heavier by frequent tours abroad. It is improbable that the Queen can spend much time on political questions, nor would her influence have been substantial while Sir Winston Churchill was Prime Minister. The Duke of Edinburgh evidently relieves the Queen of much of her work, particularly the mastering of the 'brief' which every tour, internal or external, requires. The signs of a change indicate a desire to get closer to ordinary people, though the task is formidable. It is, however, unlikely that at this stage of her reign the Queen will have much influence on political developments.

§3. *The Sovereign and the Cabinet*

Nowhere in the governmental machine is there a place for the ordinary man. Civil servants prepare memoranda for their ministers; ministers discuss in Cabinet; proposals are debated in the House of Commons. All the persons involved are peculiar people, and nobody knows what the man in the back street thinks of it all—though the politician often thinks he does. The Queen is an even more peculiar person, but she is outside the forcing environment of Whitehall and she has no political axe to grind. Apart from a handful of private secretaries she alone has the means for knowing everything about everything. At some stage in the proceedings, and often at several stages, a proposal comes to her for her 'pleasure' to be indicated. Even if no formal action on her part is required, she is informed and can insist that she be, if not convinced, at least consulted. Strange though it may seem, she is the nearest approach to the ordinary man provided by the British constitutional machine. She is not a politician; she is not controlled by politicians; she is just the daughter of her father. True, she lives in an environment of her own, but it cannot altogether destroy the plain common sense upon which, in the last resort, all government plans have to be judged. Indeed, it would be easy, if the Queen had the time and was prepared to take the trouble, for the effects of the environment to be set off. Not only in theory but in fact she can 'command' any advice that she thinks fit to summon—certain kinds of political advice excepted. She would not be justified in discussing official secrets with any person outside the official hierarchy, but there is no reason why she should not discuss ordinary matters with ordinary people, except that there is a risk of indiscretion and some danger of adding to the number of irresponsible advisers. It does not in fact appear that there has been any substantial attempt to broaden the sources of the Queen's information, but we shall see that they are already numerous and indeed almost overwhelming in quantity.

Naturally, her closest contacts are with the Prime Minister and, through him, with the Cabinet. She sees all Cabinet papers, whether they are circulated by the Cabinet Office or by the departments. Most papers, other than those relating to purely party matters, which go to the Prime Minister, go to her. She receives the Cabinet agenda in advance. She can discuss memoranda with the ministers responsible for them. She can ask for information on the items (rare though they are) which are not supported by memoranda. If she requires information from a department she can ask for it. If other information would be helpful, she can ask her private secretary to obtain it. She receives copies of all important Foreign Office telegrams and despatches and can draw the attention of the Foreign Secretary or the Prime Minister to anything in them which she dislikes or about which she is doubtful. Like a Cabinet minister, again, she receives the reports of the Defence

Committee and, like the Prime Minister, she is provided with copies of reports from its sub-committees, including the Chiefs of Staffs Committee. She is furnished with the summary of the Commonwealth press circulated by the Office of Commonwealth Relations. She has personal contacts and conducts a regular correspondence with the Governors-General, the Governors of the more important Colonies, and the British Ambassadors to foreign countries. Whenever a person is appointed to any of these posts he has an audience with the Queen and is invited to communicate anything of importance with which he may meet during his term of office.

In short, the Queen is better informed than the average Cabinet minister on the matters which are brought before the Cabinet. In some respects, notably on foreign affairs and on matters dealing with the Commonwealth, she may be better informed than the Prime Minister. What is more, though a minister has a department to administer and the Prime Minister has to run the parliamentary and party machines, the Queen could devote a large part of her time to what may be called Cabinet business. Also, while Prime Ministers and ministers change, the Queen goes on until she dies. Cabinet business is thus continuous for her and a change of Government is merely a change of personnel. Apart from all this, her views may be particularly valuable precisely because they are not clouded by political controversy. The parliamentary and party aspects of any question are, of course, fundamentally important and are matters of primary consideration for every Government: but it may be extremely useful to have an outside opinion, which has no party objective at all, on proposals which the party politicians must ultimately settle. The whips may advise that a decision will be popular or unpopular in the House of Commons or in the constituencies: that is one aspect, and a very important aspect: but the Queen may advise that the decision will cause difficulties in Burma or Patagonia or will create trouble for her next Government.

Thus the Queen may be said to be almost a member of the Cabinet, and the only non-party member. She is, too, the best-informed member and the only one who cannot be forced to keep silent. Her status gives her power to press her views upon the minister making a proposal and (what is sometimes even more important) to press them on the minister who is not making proposals. She can do more, she can press those views on the Prime Minister, the weight of whose authority may in the end produce the Cabinet decision. She can, if she likes to press her point, insist that her views be laid before the Cabinet and considered by them. In other words, she can be as helpful or as obstreperous as she pleases: and she is the only member of the Cabinet who cannot be informed that her resignation would assist the speedy dispatch of business. Naturally, the extent to which she uses these powers depends upon the extent to which she is prepared to study Cabinet questions and the extent to which she forms opinions of her own. It depends, too, on the manner in which she is 'managed' by the Prime Minister.

In the end, of course, she is bound by a Cabinet decision, but she may play a considerable part in the process by which it is reached. She could not carry her point so far as to threaten the stability of her Government, partly because it has a majority in the House of Commons, but mainly because, if the Cabinet resigns, it must state why, and the Queen's action immediately enters into political controversy. She could, however, go a long way towards preventing a decision which she believed to be profoundly mistaken. Nor need her influence be ended with the Cabinet decision. She receives a copy of the Cabinet minutes and can follow the decision through the departments responsible for carrying it out. She could play the same part in the determination of consequential questions as in the original decision. Thus, the heads of proposals for legislation designed to carry out the decision would reach her as they would reach a Cabinet minister, and she could take up any point which appeared to her to be arguable. She would then receive the draft Bill when it was circulated to the Cabinet and drafts of any amendments laid on the table in the House of Commons or brought before the Cabinet for decision.

In short, the creation of the Cabinet Office and the organisation of Cabinet procedure has enabled her to keep more closely in touch with the formulation of decisions than was the case before 1916. The information supplied to Queen Victoria and Edward VII depended on the industry of the Prime Minister and the ministers concerned with the proposals. There was no formal Cabinet agenda and the monarch did not know what was going to be discussed unless memoranda had been circulated or the Prime Minister informed him. Nor was the practice of circulating memoranda fully developed until the Cabinet Office came into existence. There was no record of Cabinet decisions except the Prime Minister's letter to the Sovereign. Queen Victoria often complained of being inadequately informed, though she was so obviously the third House to the Legislature that most Prime Ministers took as much trouble with her as with the House of Commons. Edward VII, on the other hand, was not very interested in public business and had little aptitude for it. The result was that he soon had cause to complain of neglect. He once desired of Mr Balfour that, 'as of old, the length should run to four sides of a quarto sheet'.[1] He also complained of Sir Henry Campbell-Bannerman's neglect.[2] On one such occasion, Lord Esher wrote:

> According to the ancient usage which has prevailed for 60 years,[3] the fullest statement should have been placed before the King, anterior to any final decision. As it is, the King will know nothing until the decisions of the Cabinet are irrevocable, because to upset them would mean a change of ministers. The practice which now governs the relations between the King and his ministers, if allowed to continue, must inevitably end in weakening the authority of the Crown.... The only solution is to get the King to write or dictate regularly and openly to his Prime Minister.[4]

Similarly in 1912 George V complained that he was not adequately informed of events in Parliament:

> I quite appreciate all your difficulties and sympathise with you accordingly, but I do look to my Prime Minister for that confidence which will ensure his

[1] Lee, *King Edward VII*, II, p. 47. [2] *Ibid.* II, pp. 454, 466–7.

[3] It is apparently to be inferred that the practice of sending a Cabinet report originated with Sir Robert Peel. This is not the case, however. The practice is much older. Perhaps Lord Esher confused the Cabinet letter with the letter describing parliamentary debates. The latter was first sent by Sir Robert Peel, at the Queen's request (*Letters of Queen Victoria*, 1st series, I, p. 405), and was continued by his successors until 1893 (Guedalla, *The Queen and Mr Gladstone*, II, p. 459), when Mr Gladstone delegated the task to Sir William Harcourt. (*Letters of Queen Victoria*, 3rd series, II, p. 216). After Mr Gladstone's retirement, the Prime Minister again sent a letter. King Edward VII allowed the Home Secretary to send the parliamentary letter, and King George allowed the practice to lapse: Lee, *King Edward VII*, II, p. 47. Since the *Official Report* is available within a few hours, the letter is no longer necessary. If, however, there was anything in the debate of which the King ought to have immediate information (such as a possible resignation of the Cabinet), the Vice-Chamberlain of the Household would send a note to Buckingham Palace immediately. [4] *Esher Papers*, II, pp. 265–6.

keeping me fully informed on all matters, especially those which affect questions of such grave importance to the State, and indeed to the Constitution.[1]

The task of informing the Queen is no longer left to the personal initiative of the appropriate minister and the Prime Minister. The Cabinet agenda and papers are forwarded to the Queen by the appropriate official in the normal course of business. If any item of the agenda required the Queen's preliminary sanction, and her pleasure had not been taken, the private secretary would point out the omission to the appropriate department. Anything which goes to the Cabinet is reported to the Queen both before and afterwards; and if it is desired to keep anything from her (as in the discussions about the marriage of Edward VIII) it is necessary to have an informal meeting of ministers instead of a Cabinet. Further, the Queen knows from the Cabinet minutes whether there has been any difference of opinion, though she does not know what opinions are held by whom. If the differences were of such a nature that a political crisis was likely to follow, the Secretary to the Cabinet would inform the private secretary, without disclosing details, so that the Queen could be warned to be available. The result of all this is not only that the Queen is much better informed, but also that some of the sources of controversy in Queen Victoria's reign have been removed.

It used to be a matter of controversy whether the Prime Minister ought to disclose to the Sovereign the divisions of opinion among Cabinet ministers. The question has for most purposes been resolved by sending the Cabinet minutes. The principle involved is nevertheless of some importance. Mr Gladstone stated that in his reports and audiences the Prime Minister is bound 'not to counter-work the Cabinet; not to divide it; not to undermine the position of his colleagues in the Royal favour. If he departs in any degree from strict adherence to these rules, and uses his great opportunities to increase his own influence, or pursue aims not shared by his colleagues, then, unless he is prepared to advise their dismissal, he not only departs from rule, but commits an act of treachery and baseness.'[2] Elsewhere he said: 'The Sovereign is to know no more of any differing views of different

[1] Nicolson, *King George V*, p. 203. [2] Gladstone, *Gleanings*, I, p. 243.

ministers than they are to know of any collateral of the monarchical office; they are an unity before the Sovereign; and the Sovereign is an unity before them.'[1]

In so far as this suggests that the Prime Minister may not disclose that some members of the Cabinet are opposed to the desire or decision of the majority, it can hardly be said to be altogether consistent with practice. While some Prime Ministers, including Mr Gladstone himself, have generally refrained from such disclosures, others have not been so reticent.

Lord Melbourne discussed his colleagues' opinions with great freedom. In 1837, for instance, he told Queen Victoria that Lord Howick, among others, held peculiar opinions on the policy to be followed in Canada.[2] In 1839, he described the 'atmosphere' of a Cabinet, and again mentioned opposition by Lord Howick.[3] In 1840 minutes of dissent by Lord Clarendon and Lord Holland were attached to the formal Cabinet minute on the Egyptian Question.[4]

Sir Robert Peel and Sir James Graham had a discussion on the subject of formal minutes; the latter mentioned that William IV was aware of differences of opinion in the Cabinet, and when an important step was taken he sometimes required proof of Cabinet agreement. Prince Albert remarked that this practice ought to be revived, since it was a great weakness of the Crown not to be able to follow the course of argument in the Cabinet.[5] Peel himself usually did not disclose Cabinet divisions.[6] For instance, he did not explain the lines of opinion on the Corn Laws in 1845.[7] Actually, the chief dissentient, Lord Stanley, personally explained his opinions.[8] Later, when the Cabinet met again, after the failure of Lord John Russell to form a Government, Peel stated how far there was any dissent; but this was necessary in order to explain that Lord Stanley, and Lord Stanley only, would resign.

Lord John Russell generally did not disclose the names of ministers holding minority opinions; but occasionally he made an exception.[9]

[1] *Ibid.* I, pp. 74–5.

[2] *Letters of Queen Victoria*, 1st series, I, p. 127.

[3] *Ibid.* 1st series, I, pp. 184–5.

[4] *Life of Lord Clarendon*, I, pp. 195–7.

[5] *Peel Papers*, III, pp. 496–8.

[6] *Life of Sir James Graham*, II, p. 25.

[7] *Peel Papers*, III, pp. 234 *et seq.*; *Letters of Queen Victoria*, 1st series, II, pp. 62–3.

[8] *Letters of Queen Victoria*, 1st series, II, p. 64.

[9] E.g. *Life of Lord John Russell*, II, p. 137.

Of Lord Aberdeen's Government, Mr Gladstone has said: 'From near presence, and close and constant intercourse, reaching far beyond established forms, they [the Queen and Prince Albert] knew not only the resolutions of the... Cabinet, but the interior mind of all those members of it who had special titles to exercise an influence on its foreign policy.'[1]

Lord Aberdeen was almost 'a friend of the family'.[2] Lord John Russell addressed his complaints to the Queen as well as to others.[3] Sir James Graham was always available to give yet another account.[4] Lord Palmerston was usually more reticent. Mr Gladstone on one occasion asked him if names had been disclosed. Lord Palmerston replied: 'No mention has ever been made, nor any allusion, to particular members of the Cabinet. The Cabinet has always been mentioned as an aggregate body.'[5] But on one occasion at least, he departed from this practice.[6] Once, too, he committed the more serious offence of saying to the Queen that if the House of Lords destroyed Mr Gladstone's Paper Duties Bill 'they would perform a good public service'.[7] The Queen, however, was able to secure details of Cabinet discussions from Lord Granville[8] and Sir Charles Wood.[9] Lord Granville again acted as private informer in the Cabinet of 1868–74[10] though perhaps with more justification, since he was trying to prevent the development of the growing hostility between the Queen and Mr Gladstone. Mr Gladstone in this Cabinet followed his own rule; for instance, he did not explain that the dissolution of 1874 was due to internal dissensions.[11]

Mr Disraeli, even as Chancellor of the Exchequer, gave the Queen full information.[12] As Prime Minister, he occasionally neglected to or

[1] Gladstone, *Gleanings*, I, p. 101.

[2] E.g. *Letters of Queen Victoria*, 1st series, II, pp. 573–5; III, p. 27.

[3] E.g. *Ibid.* 1st series, III, p. 26.

[4] *Life of Sir James Graham*, II, p. 208; *Letters of Queen Victoria*, 1st series, II, pp. 552–4.

[5] Guedalla, *Gladstone and Palmerston*, pp. 258–9.

[6] *Letters of Queen Victoria*, 2nd series, I, p. 248.

[7] *Life of the Prince Consort*, V, p. 100.

[8] *Life of Lord Granville*, I, pp. 349–52, 469–70, 477; II, p. 123; *Letters of Queen Victoria*, 2nd series, I, pp. 67–8, 69.

[9] *Letters of Queen Victoria*, 2nd series, I, p. 228.

[10] E.g. *Ibid.* 2nd series, I, p. 622; III, pp. 246–7.

[11] *Ibid.* 2nd series, III, p. 305.

[12] *Life of Disraeli*, II, pp. 229–31; *Letters of Queen Victoria*, 2nd series, I, pp. 396–9, 413.

refrained from doing so.[1] But this was contrary to his usual practice.[2] This was, no doubt, one of the many elements of his popularity at Court. The Queen could not fail to be annoyed at the change when his rival came into office in 1880. She complained at once that she had no information. In 1880 she telegraphed to Lord Granville making this complaint, and informing Lord Granville that she 'must request Lord Granville either to tell her what truth there is in the statement [in the newspapers] as to dissensions or to induce Mr Gladstone to do so'.[3] According to Sir Charles Dilke:

> Mr Gladstone always held that the Queen ought not to be told about dissensions in the Cabinet, that Cabinets existed for the purpose of differing —that is, for the purpose of enabling ministers who differed to thresh out their differences—and that the Queen was only concerned with the results which were presented to her by, or in the name of, the Cabinet as a whole. This seems reasonable and ought, I think, to be the constitutional view; but the Queen naturally...hates to have personal differences going on of which she is not informed.[4]

After the death of General Gordon, General Ponsonby took a verbal complaint to Mr Gladstone, and then explained the latter's view to the Queen.

> She listened carefully to all I repeated respecting the reporting of the opinions of members of the Cabinet but insisted that most Prime Ministers had fully informed her on the points. When I told her about Lord Palmerston she said it was true that he had never given her this information or if he ever did it had never been very accurate. Her Majesty still maintains that Lord Melbourne, Sir Robert Peel, Lord John Russell and Lord Beaconsfield always gave her an insight into the opinions of her ministers.[5]

As a result, Mr Gladstone gave her some indication of the shades of opinion in the Cabinet on the Irish question.[6]

But when Mr Gladstone proposed withdrawal from the Sudan, the Queen again complained to Lord Granville. 'He is so reserved and writes such unsatisfactory letters, that the Queen never knows where

[1] *Letters of Queen Victoria*, 2nd series, II, pp. 332–3, 335–6, 340.

[2] *Life of Disraeli*, II, pp. 1024, 1027, 1043–4, 1056, 1065–7, and many other references.

[3] *Life of Sir Charles Dilke*, I, pp. 346–7.

[4] *Ibid.*

[5] Guedalla, *The Queen and Mr Gladstone*, II, p. 352.

[6] *Letters of Queen Victoria*, 2nd series, III, pp. 652–6.

she is. She does not know *who* takes his or other views (which all her predecessors kept her informed of)[1] and she is left powerless to *judge* the state of affairs.'[2] As usual, the Queen sought an informer, and Sir Henry Ponsonby wrote to Lord Rosebery, who had just joined the Cabinet as Lord Privy Seal, for his personal opinion.[3] In April 1885 she again complained that Mr Gladstone always kept her in the dark:

> In Lord Melbourne's time she knew *everything* that *passed* in the Cabinet and different views that were entertained by the different ministers and there was no concealment. Sir Robert Peel who was completely *master* of his Cabinet (and the Prime Minister *ought* to be) was, after the first strangeness for her [who] hardly knew him, also very open. Lord Russell less communicative but still far more than Mr Gladstone and Lord Palmerston too. They mentioned the names of ministers and their views. Lord Palmerston again kept his Cabinet in great order. Lord Derby was also entirely master of his Cabinet. Lord Aberdeen most confidential and open and kind—Lord Beaconsfield was like Lord Melbourne. He told the Queen everything (he often did not *see* her for months) and said: 'I wish you to know everything so that you may be able to judge.' Mr Gladstone never once has told her the different views of his colleagues. She is kept completely in the dark—and when they have quarrelled over it and decided amongst themselves he comes and tries to *force* this on her.[4]

What she wanted, clearly, was to know the strength of the minority in order that she could press her own view. In 1892 Lord Rosebery informed the Queen that he did not entirely agree with some of his colleagues, but asked her to keep the letter secret.[5] In 1893 he told her that he disagreed with his colleagues, whom he mentioned by name, and agreed with her.[6] In 1893 he wrote to the Queen to secure her assistance in pressing upon the Cabinet a more active policy in Egypt, and the Queen wrote to Mr Gladstone accordingly.[7] In 1892 Mr Gladstone himself informed the Queen that Lord Rosebery differed in opinion, but Lord Rosebery had already written to the Queen to that effect.[8]

[1] The list has lengthened; presumably it now includes Lord Palmerston as well as Sir Robert Peel, neither of whom usually disclosed divisions.

[2] *Letters of Queen Victoria*, 2nd series, III, pp. 642–3.

[3] *Ibid.* 2nd series, III, p. 640.

[4] A. Ponsonby, *Henry Ponsonby*, p. 195.

[5] *Letters of Queen Victoria*, 3rd series, II, pp. 159–60, 162.

[6] *Ibid.* 3rd series, II, p. 211.

[7] *Ibid.* 3rd series, II, pp. 216–17.

[8] *Ibid.* 3rd series, II, p. 160.

With such occasional exceptions, Mr Gladstone followed his own rule to the end of his official career. He did not, for instance, give the Queen any hint that the Cabinet was divided on the Home Rule Bill in 1893.[1] Lord Rosebery, as Prime Minister, appears to have followed the same rule.

Lord Salisbury, on the other hand, appears to have followed Lord Beaconsfield's practice, though with greater discretion and with greater loyalty to his colleagues. In one of his earliest reports in 1885 he mentioned that Lord Randolph Churchill dissented from the Cabinet decision on one point.[2] Sometimes he mentioned that there was dissent without quoting names.[3] Sometimes, as on the Parnell Commission Bill, he did not mention divisions.[4] But usually he gave full information.[5]

On the practice of later Prime Ministers, little information is available. Mr Asquith quoted divisions and the names of those who differed on the Naval Estimates in 1909.[6] In 1910, Lord Morley informed Lord Esher that he did not agree with the Cabinet proposals, and Lord Esher informed the King.[7] In 1914, Mr Asquith did not inform the King (at least in writing) that four members contemplated resignation, until two had actually resigned.[8] But he mentioned the divisions on the subject of the use of reprisals at sea[9] and on Home Rule.[10] The question is now much less important because the Queen receives the Cabinet minutes, which indicate the competing opinions without stating who hold them.

The only conclusion which results from practice is that the extent of communication depends on the Prime Minister's discretion. The Sovereign naturally desires to know whether her point of view is represented in the Cabinet, and the strength of the contemporary parties. She can urge her arguments with greater persistence if she knows that they are also being put in Cabinet. At the same time, there are several possible dangers. In the first place, it would be undesirable for the

[1] *Ibid.* 3rd series, III, p. 385.
[2] *Ibid.* 2nd series, III, p. 685. See also p. 690.
[3] *Ibid.* 2nd series, III, p. 711.
[4] *Ibid.* 3rd series, I, pp. 433–4.
[5] *Ibid.* 3rd series, I, pp. 10, 201–3, 211, 229.
[6] Lee, *King Edward VII*, II, p. 679.
[7] *Esher Papers*, II, pp. 453–5.
[8] *Life of Lord Oxford and Asquith*, II, pp. 81–3.
[9] *Ibid.* II, p. 131.
[10] *Ibid.* II p. 219.

Sovereign to identify herself with a Cabinet minority. An identity of opinion would probably lead to an alliance, and the monarch would then be a disruptive element in the Cabinet and, if a secession took place, her position *vis-à-vis* the Cabinet would be difficult. Secondly, a Sovereign who supported the majority would probably take an unfavourable view of the minority. Queen Victoria's opinion of Lord Randolph Churchill became immediately unfavourable because of his opposition on a point in the 'Government of Caretakers' in 1885.[1] An even better example occurred in connection with the discussions about the deposition of Alexander of Bulgaria in 1886. The Queen was violently anti-Russian, 'poor dear young Sandro' being a Coburg. Lord Salisbury mentioned that there was opposition in the Cabinet. The Queen, in reply, expressed the hope that Lord Salisbury would 'not allow the two young men, comparatively ignorant and inexperienced in these affairs, to pretend to oppose what older, wiser heads understand and know is the only true policy for their country'.[2] Knowing that there was opposition to her policy, the Queen a few days later reminded Lord Salisbury of his (wholly unconstitutional) advice to Lord Rosebery to bring as few Foreign Office matters before the Cabinet as possible.[3]

The best example of an alliance between the Sovereign and the Prime Minister against a minority of the Cabinet occurred during the Russo-Turkish War. The Queen was extremely belligerent.[4] In a letter full of underlinings and double underlinings, she announced that 'Lord Derby *must* be overruled...as also Sir Stafford Northcote'.[5] While the pressure of opposition in the Cabinet compelled the majority to consider each step carefully, a stream of emphatic letters poured out of Balmoral urging prompt and bellicose action.[6] She was even willing to allow Lord Beaconsfield to make such use of her name as he desired.[7]

Even if Queen Victoria's policy were right, such intervention in Cabinet discussions, especially with a Prime Minister so unscrupulous as Lord Beaconsfield, would be undesirable. It would lead necessarily

[1] *Letters of Queen Victoria*, 2nd series, III, p. 687.
[2] *Ibid.* 3rd series, I, p. 202.
[3] *Ibid.* 3rd series, I, p. 211.
[4] *Ibid.* 2nd series, II, pp. 559, 561–2, 567–8.
[5] *Ibid.* 2nd series, II, p. 570.
[6] See especially *Letters of Queen Victoria*, 2nd series, II, pp. 573–4.
[7] *Ibid.* 2nd series, II, p. 576.

to the attachment of a party label to the monarchy. The Crown possesses the advantage of remoteness from party strife. The Queen can study a question freed from the limitations imposed by public opinion and parliamentary conditions. She is thus in a position to give a calm and judicial opinion on any policy which is put before her. To descend into the cockpit is to lose the advantage of independence and to arouse opposition to the monarchy itself among those who are unable to agree. Lord Derby, who led the Opposition in the Cabinet, subsequently joined the Liberal Party. It is certain that the knowledge that Queen Victoria was an extreme jingo (as the Liberals would naturally put it) did not assist the smooth functioning of a Liberal Government.

It seems, therefore, that Mr Gladstone took a logically correct view in refraining from disclosing the details of Cabinet differences, but it cannot be said that the practice supports his rule. It supports, rather, the opposite rule. Lord Palmerston's practice and Mr Gladstone's rule led to communications between the Queen and other members of the Cabinet. Such communications were obviously unjustifiable. Lord Rosebery once said that 'he conceives that it is the right of the Prime Minister to inform your Majesty with respect to what passes at Cabinet Councils, and he cannot be too careful of trenching on that privilege'.[1] To have various sections of the Cabinet angling for the Sovereign's support would destroy all Cabinet order and decorum. The Cabinet is a committee where matters are discussed freely and privately in order that agreed solutions may be reached. Lord Melbourne in 1834 objected to a communication by Lord John Russell to William IV as 'subversive of all the principles upon which the Government of this country has hitherto been conducted'. The King replied that he 'had never contemplated for a moment holding correspondence with any of your colleagues, or with anyone, on questions affecting the Government, of the nature and extent of which the individual at the head of the Government should be ignorant'.[2] The only recent example known to have occurred was in 1912 when Mr Haldane informed Lord Esher, who informed George V, of the dispute between Mr Lloyd George and Mr Winston Churchill over the Admiralty Estimates.[3]

[1] *Ibid.* 3rd series, II, p. 162.
[2] *Lord Melbourne's Papers*, pp. 215–17.
[3] *Esher Papers*, III, p. 151.

Sometimes the influence of the Sovereign can be used to mitigate Cabinet differences. In 1840, Lord Melbourne asked Queen Victoria to use her influence with Lord Palmerston.[1] In 1855 the Queen and Prince Albert tried to induce the Peelites to support Lord Palmerston's Government;[2] and there are several similar examples. In 1867 she succeeded, by means of a personal request, in preventing General Peel from resigning from the Cabinet on account of the Reform Bill.[3]

Again, the Sovereign's influence is not limited to the consideration of matters put before her by the Prime Minister. She can herself raise questions. Queen Victoria frequently asked for Foreign Office despatches to be submitted to the Cabinet.[4] In 1858, and on many other occasions, she asked the Prime Minister to bring before the Cabinet the question of the national defences.[5] The Instructions for the new Volunteer Corps were drawn up by Prince Albert, submitted to the Cabinet, and approved without alteration.[6] In 1872 the Queen raised the question of punctuality and safety on the railways.[7] In 1893 the Duke of Argyll asked the Queen to submit a memorandum to the Cabinet on the changes made in the Home Rule Bill.[8]

The Sovereign has, at least according to Queen Victoria's practice, a right to be consulted on every major change of policy before it is publicly announced. In 1835 Lord Melbourne apologised for not having submitted the Irish Municipal Corporations Bill to William IV before its introduction.[9] In 1859 the Queen was 'shocked' to see that the Government moved for a Select Committee on Military Departments without having previously communicated with her.[10] Lord Palmerston replied that it was merely the reappointment of a Committee set up in the previous Parliament.[11] In 1863 Lord Granville found that a Bill which touched the prerogative was about to be introduced

[1] *Letters of Queen Victoria*, 1st series, I, p. 304.

[2] *Ibid.* 1st series, III, p. 125.

[3] *Ibid.* 2nd series, I, p. 399.

[4] Below, pp. 367–9.

[5] *Letters of Queen Victoria*, 1st series, III, p. 349.

[6] *Life of the Prince Consort*, IV, p. 437. So was a plan for the command of the Crimean Army in 1855: *Life of the Prince Consort*, III, pp. 381–4.

[7] *Letters of Queen Victoria*, 2nd series, II, pp. 229–30.

[8] *Ibid.* 3rd series, II, pp. 279–80.

[9] *Lord Melbourne's Papers*, pp. 307–8.

[10] *Letters of Queen Victoria*, 1st series, III, p. 448.

[11] *Ibid.* 1st series, III, pp. 448–9.

without the Queen's sanction, and asked the Lord Chancellor to postpone it.[1]

In 1864 the Queen complained of Mr Gladstone's famous speech, in which he stated that every man was within the pale of the Constitution, as being imprudent and unconstitutional.[2] In 1890 she was so perturbed about the recommendation of the Hartington Commission to abolish the office of the Commander-in-Chief that she tried to prevent it from being discussed in Cabinet.[3] In 1894 she was so concerned with Lord Rosebery's attack on the House of Lords that she (unconstitutionally)[4] consulted Lord Salisbury. He advised that 'on a matter of this vital importance he [Lord Rosebery] has no right to announce a totally new policy without first ascertaining your Majesty's pleasure on the subject, and if he is unable to convince your Majesty, it is his duty to tender his resignation'.[5] The Queen thereupon complained to Lord Rosebery,[6] who replied that he

> would never dream of proposing a constitutional revolution to the House of Commons without submitting it after mature consideration by the Cabinet, to your Majesty. But he would humbly deprecate the view that it is necessary for a minister, before laying a question before a popular audience, to receive the approval of the Crown. Such a principle would tend to make the Sovereign a party in all the controversies of the hour, and would hazardously compromise the neutrality of the Sovereign. But should a Ministry desire to present to Parliament a resolution of this kind, they would certainly be ignorant of the first elements of their duty, did they neglect to obtain the sanction of the Sovereign to its being presented to the decision of Parliament.[7]

The answer to Lord Rosebery was that a fundamental change of policy ought not to be announced without the consent of the Cabinet. Before the decision is finally reached, the Sovereign should have the

[1] *Ibid.* 2nd series, I, pp. 77–8. This is, however, a special case, since the Bill affected the royal prerogative. As to this, see Mr Gladstone's resolution on the Irish Church (1868), *Letters of Queen Victoria*, 2nd series, I, p. 517; *Life of Lord Granville*, I, pp. 523–5; and Lord Lansdowne's motion for restricting the prerogative of creating peers (1911), Asquith, *Fifty Years of Parliament*, II, p. 95.

[2] *Letters of Queen Victoria*, 2nd series, I, pp. 189–90.

[3] *Ibid.* 3rd series, I, p. 577; see also pp. 582–4, 589, 594–5, 597–602.

[4] See below, pp. 384–5.

[5] *Letters of Queen Victoria*, 3rd series, II, p. 433.

[6] *Ibid.* 3rd series, II, pp. 437–8.

[7] *Ibid.* 3rd series, II, p. 440.

opportunity of expressing views and, if necessary, of trying to convince the Cabinet that the policy is wrong. The problem could now arise only if there was no Cabinet decision or the matter was brought up in Cabinet without notice. If it were on the agenda the Queen would necessarily have knowledge of it. On the other hand, Lord Salisbury's notion that if the Sovereign is not convinced the Cabinet should resign, is grotesque. If that were the case, there would never have been a Liberal Government after 1868. His letters show the danger of private communication with Opposition leaders, for Lord Salisbury desired the Liberals to resign in order that the Conservatives might hold a general election at which, as they rightly believed, they would obtain a majority.[1]

In 1901 Edward VII complained that the Report of a Committee on the Royal Declaration against Transubstantiation had been published without his consent.[2] In 1905 the Government published the Curzon-Brodrick correspondence without his consent. Lord Esher said that such a thing would not have been possible 'even under ministers as headstrong as Palmerston, or as truculent as Lord John Russell'.[3] When, in 1906, Mr Lloyd George made a speech which seemed to promise a new 'minister for Wales', the King protested that he had not been consulted.[4] Mr Lloyd George also attacked the House of Lords, and again the King protested.[5] When, in 1908, the King protested against a speech by Mr Lloyd George in favour of women's suffrage, Mr Asquith pointed out that the question was an open one in the Cabinet.[6]

The duty of the Prime Minister in relation to the Sovereign is summarised in a memorandum sent by George V to Mr MacDonald on his appointment in 1924.[7] It deals especially with ecclesiastical preferment and honours, which are dealt with hereafter,[8] but it also mentions the duty of the Leader of the House of Commons to send a letter every day during the session, the duty of one of the whips to send a telegram 'briefly reporting any outstanding particulars in the proceedings', and the rule about matters discussed in Cabinet.

[1] See below, pp. 414–15.

[2] Lee, *King Edward VII*, II, pp. 23–4.

[3] *Esher Papers*, II, p. 103.

[4] Lee, *King Edward VII*, II, pp. 455–6; *Life of Sir Henry Campbell-Bannerman*, II, pp. 313–14.

[5] Lee, *King Edward VII*, II, p. 456.

[6] *Ibid.* II, p. 653.

[7] Nicolson, *King George V*, pp. 388–9.

[8] Below, ch. XIV.

§4. *The Sovereign and the Departments*

New policies are hardly distinguishable from matters discussed in Cabinet and matters decided by the departments. Of the former, it has been said already that the Queen receives full information. Of the latter, it has now to be explained that she is, or may be, in close touch with some of the departments and that where an act has to be done in her name and is of real importance, her pleasure must be taken before the act is done. The acts which are done in her name are, with a few exceptions, acts authorised by the 'prerogative powers' vested in her by common law. They are exercised, in the main, by the Foreign Office, the Commonwealth Relations Office, the Colonial Office, the War Office, the Air Ministry and the Admiralty. With these, and to a less extent the Home Office, the Queen may be in close touch. But, on the one hand, the extent of her active interest in their work must necessarily depend on her personality, and, on the other hand, there is nothing to prevent her from asking for information from any department in respect of any branch of its administration, and from criticising proposals and actions.

All Foreign Office despatches which bore the Sovereign's name were formerly approved by him, and no despatch bore his name unless his pleasure had been taken.[1] The obligation to secure prior approval was laid down in 1850 and 1851 in the dispute between Queen Victoria and Lord Palmerston. The Queen made complaints of Palmerston's failure to submit despatches from 1847 onwards.[2] In 1849 Lord John Russell suggested that drafts should be sent to him, as Prime Minister, before they were submitted to the Queen, so that the Queen might have his views on them. The Queen agreed, and the practice was adopted.[3] In 1850, acting on Stockmar's advice,[4] the Queen stated exactly what she expected from the Foreign Secretary.

She requires: (1) That he will distinctly state what he proposes in a given case, in order that the Queen may know as distinctly to *what* she has given her Royal sanction; (2) Having *once given* her sanction to a measure, that it be not arbitrarily altered or modified by the Minister; such an act she must

[1] *Letters of Queen Victoria*, 2nd series, II, pp. 293–4.
[2] *Ibid.* 1st series, II, pp. 132, 143, 153, 202.
[3] *Ibid.* 1st series, II, pp. 262–4.
[4] *Ibid.* 1st series, II, p. 282.

consider as failing in sincerity towards the Crown, and justly to be visited by the exercise of her constitutional right of dismissing that Minister; She expects to be kept informed of what passes between him and Foreign Ministers before important decisions are taken, based upon that intercourse; to receive the foreign despatches in good time, and to have the drafts for her approval sent to her in sufficient time to make herself acquainted with their contents before they must be sent off.[1]

Lord Palmerston agreed to these rules.[2]

Nevertheless, the Queen had cause to complain again almost at once;[3] and his unauthorised communication to the French Ambassador, in defiance of a Cabinet decision approved by the Queen in a despatch, compelled Lord John Russell to ask for Lord Palmerston's resignation.[4] In the ensuing debate, Lord John Russell said: 'I think that when, on the one hand, the Crown, in consequence of a vote of the House of Commons, places its constitutional confidence in a minister, that minister is bound, on the other hand, to the Crown, to the most frank and full detail of every measure that is taken, and is bound either to obey the sanction of the Crown, or to leave to the Crown that full liberty which the Crown must possess, of no longer continuing that minister in office.'[5] The Foreign Secretary, he added, 'can only act with the sanction of the Crown in matters of very great importance. In matters of small importance, I am ready to admit that the Secretary of State must be allowed to take a course which to him seems best, without a continual reference to the Crown'.[6]

The practice of passing drafts through the Prime Minister's hands was criticised by Mr Gladstone[7] and appears not to have been followed.[8] But the Queen was careful to insist on the rule that all decisions should be submitted to her before they were acted upon. In 1852 she complained because a Protocol was signed without previous consultation with her.[9] In 1854 she complained that Lord Clarendon had not submitted despatches for approval before sending them off.[10] In 1862 she

[1] *Letters of Queen Victoria*, 1st series, II, p. 315.

[2] *Ibid.* 1st series, II, pp. 315–16.

[3] *Ibid.* 1st series, II, p. 321.

[4] Above, pp. 210–11.

[5] *Parl. Deb.* 3rd s., vol. 119, cols. 89–90.

[6] *Ibid.* col. 97.

[7] *Gleanings*, I, pp. 86–7.

[8] It was, however, explained to Lord Derby in 1852: *Letters of Queen Victoria*, 1st series, II, p. 453.

[9] *Ibid.* 1st series, II, p. 495.

[10] Balfour, *Life of the Earl of Aberdeen*, II, pp. 219, 226.

reminded Lord Russell of the rule that no drafts should be sent without the Queen's having first seen them.[1] Later complaints are numerous.[2] Even in 1924 George V said that all important Foreign Office despatches were submitted to him before being sent.[3]

These rules are for practicable purposes obsolete. Life moves more quickly than it did in Victorian days, and the important Foreign Office documents are not the despatches but the telegrams, which cannot be submitted to the Queen before they are sent off. The Queen is, however, much better informed than under the old practice. All important telegrams are marked 'Queen, Dominions, Cabinet' and are circulated to the Queen and to the Cabinet, in the daily print. They are, however, either preliminary to a Cabinet decision or consequential upon it, and the Queen's influence can be brought to bear before the Cabinet decision. There are of course occasions when a decision has to be taken as a matter of urgency, without a Cabinet decision, but with the sanction of the Prime Minister or a Cabinet committee. The Queen has thus the same opportunity for raising issues as an ordinary Cabinet minister.

Queen Victoria used to sign every commission appointing an officer, but an Order in Council of 1862 provided that only the first commission should be under the sign manual.[4] She had previously requested the Commander-in-Chief (whose functions are now exercised by the War Office) to submit a descriptive list showing at a glance the purport of documents to be signed, 'as is done with papers from other Government offices'.[5] In 1899 the Queen protested against decisions being taken in relation to the Boer War without her sanction. She received no account of the proceedings of the Defence Committee at which it had been decided to send Lord Roberts and Lord Kitchener to South Africa, and Lord Roberts had been appointed Commander-in-Chief without her opinion being asked. On this point Mr Balfour had no defence. When, however, the Queen protested that she had not been consulted before General Buller was ordered to relieve Ladysmith, Mr Balfour said that 'this represented a theory of constitutional government which I could

[1] *Letters of Queen Victoria*, 2nd series, I, p. 10.

[2] *Ibid.* 2nd series, I, pp. 472, 476; 2nd series, II, pp. 625–8, 649; 3rd series, II, pp. 205, 207.

[3] Nicolson, *King George V*, p. 388. [4] *Letters of Queen Victoria*, 2nd series, I, p. 33.

[5] *Ibid.* 1st series, III, p. 50.

not accept. The Queen's advisers must be permitted to issue important military orders without her previous sanction.'[1] Edward VII was much interested in military matters, and complained in 1904 that Mr Arnold-Forster had made changes in the War Office without discussing them with him.[2] Accordingly, the subsequent changes were submitted to and criticised by the King in great detail.[3] The King insisted that he receive the reports of the Army Council as well as of the Committee of Imperial Defence.[4] In the following year he complained that army proposals were submitted informally by letter from private secretary to private secretary, and that not enough time was allowed for consultation.[5]

King George V took an active interest in the conduct of the war of 1914–18. He told General Haig in 1914 that he got reports from 'a large number of officers of all ranks'.[6] In July 1915 he told him that he had lost confidence in Haig's superior officer, Sir John French, and Haig mentioned a suitable time for his removal. The King asked Haig to write to the Private Secretary and said that nobody else would know what he had written.[7] Some months later Field-Marshal Robertson was asked over the telephone whether the time had not come for Sir John French to be replaced.[8] According to the King's own account, he insisted on the Prime Minister removing Sir John French.[9]

Since all this happened while Mr Asquith was Prime Minister, it is not clear how far these Buckingham Palace influences were known to Mr Lloyd George. Probably the Prime Minister realised, however, that the King was a strong supporter of Sir Douglas Haig. In February 1917 the War Cabinet decided to put Haig under General Nivelle's orders for the purpose of the coming offensive. Haig described the proposal as 'madness'[10]. A compromise proposal was, nevertheless, agreed, and Haig wrote a full explanation to the King.[11] Lord Stamfordham replied[12] that the King was unaware that the question of command was discussed at the War Cabinet meeting, and that he did

[1] *Life of Arthur James Balfour*, I, p. 296.

[2] Lee, *King Edward VII*, II, p. 200.

[3] *Ibid.* II, pp. 200–3.

[4] *Ibid.* II, p. 200.

[5] *Ibid.* II, pp. 213–14.

[6] Robert Blake, *The Private Papers of Douglas Haig*, p. 78.

[7] *Ibid.* p. 97.

[8] *Ibid.* p. 108.

[9] *Ibid.* p. 138.

[10] *Ibid.* p. 201.

[11] *Ibid.* p. 203.

[12] Nicolson, *King George V*, p. 305.

not receive the minutes until four days later. 'Had the ordinary procedure been followed and the King informed of this momentous change in the conduct of the campaign His Majesty would have unquestionably demanded further explanation before giving his consent to the proposal.' It will be seen that Mr Lloyd George did not play the game according to the rules, but it is a little difficult to do so when the other side has private access to the referee. The Queen now receives the minutes of the Defence Committee and the Chiefs of Staff Committee as a matter of routine and is thus kept in close touch with defence policy. During the war of 1939–45 the King received all the important documents sent to the Prime Minister as Minister of Defence, and his contact with the Prime Minister and the Chiefs of the Staffs was particularly close. In fact, it may be said that the much more efficient arrangement of business enabled George VI to be much better informed in 1939–45 even than George V was in 1914–18. The whole procedure has been taken out of its rather casual atmosphere and has become a matter of ordinary official routine.

Queen Victoria complained in 1854 that decisions as to the placing of statues of royal personages were being taken by the Office of Works without her consent.[1] In 1862 she pointed out that Admiralty Regulations had been changed without her sanction. In 1904 the King complained that a decision as to Chinese labour had been taken by the Colonial Office without his authority;[2] and when under the new Government the Colonial Office abolished Chinese labour, his private secretary wrote: 'His Majesty directs me to point out to you that it is his constitutional right to have any despatches of any importance, especially those initiating or relating to a change of policy, laid before him prior to it being finally decided upon.'[3] In 1906 he insisted that the Colonial Secretary should be summoned to the Privy Council in order that a Transvaal Order in Council should be explained to him.[4] The practice as to the Sovereign's consent to the exercise of the prerogative of mercy was explained in 1903. 'The usual routine in such cases was for the Home Secretary's decision to be communicated to the King in

[1] Frances Balfour, *Life of the Earl of Aberdeen*, II, p. 200.
[2] Lee, *King Edward VII*, II, pp. 279–80.
[3] *Ibid.* II, p. 479.
[4] Fitzroy, *Memoirs*, I, p. 297.

order that the royal pleasure might be taken, though the minister's decision took effect as soon as it was reached.'[1] The slight difference here is due to the necessity of keeping the Sovereign's name out of the question.

§5. *The Influence of the Sovereign*

Though papers be submitted and 'pleasure' be taken, the influence of the Crown depends upon the wearer. The impress of Queen Victoria's personality is evident on every page of the political history of England during her long reign. She was a clog on the activity of every Liberal Government after 1841 and a stimulus to every Conservative Government after 1868. Whether her influence was, on the whole, for good or ill must be left to historians; and historians will come to their conclusions according to their initial assumptions.

Of her methods, many examples could be given. She induced ministers to alter despatches[2] and referred or compelled them to refer matters to the Prime Minister[3] or to the Cabinet.[4] She wrote long memoranda.[5] She once tried to persuade Sir William Harcourt, as minister in attendance, to alter the Queen's Speech, though without effect.[6] King Edward's influence was much smaller. He rarely criticised or made suggestions,[7] though a few cases are known.[8] His personality proved to be useful, however, in helping to settle some of the diplomatic problems of his reign. Sir Harold Nicolson has said that, though too superficial to be a statesman, he was a supreme diplomatist. His visit

[1] Lee, *King Edward VII*, II, p. 39. For cases in which George VI differed from the Home Secretary, but eventually accepted advice 'with every good grace', see H. Morrison, *Government and Parliament*, p. 81.

[2] *Letters of Queen Victoria*, 1st series, II, pp. 161, 221, 276, 277; 2nd series, I, pp. 15–16, 83; 3rd series, II, pp. 367–8.

[3] *Ibid.* 1st series, II, pp. 160, 212, 221, 230, 235, 277, 308, 397, 412; 1st series, III, pp. 470, 494, 496; 2nd series, I, pp. 143–4.

[4] *Ibid.* 1st series, II, pp. 298, 397; 1st series, III, pp. 451, 453, 461, 464, 523, 562; 2nd series, I, pp. 51, 83, 150; 2nd series, II, pp. 642–4; 2nd series, III, pp. 508–9.

[5] *Ibid.* 1st series, II, p. 425; 2nd series, I, p. 138.

[6] *Life of Sir William Harcourt*, I, pp. 598–600. This does not mean that verbal and other amendments may not be made in agreement with the Government: cf. H. Morrison, *Government and Parliament*, p. 81.

[7] *Life of Lord Lansdowne*, p. 293; Grey, *Twenty-five Years*, I, pp. 204–5.

[8] Lee, *King Edward VII*, II, pp. 205–7, 210–12, 699, etc.

to Paris in 1904 provided the atmosphere in which Anglo-French negotiations could fruitfully be initiated. It was followed in 1908 by a visit to Reval which was a fitting prelude to the formation of the Entente Cordiale. His influence in both can easily be exaggerated. The German Emperor and not Edward VII was responsible for the Entente Cordiale; the ground had been well prepared by diplomatic exchanges; the King himself did not take part in negotiations, though he knew enough about them and was skilled enough in diplomacy to say the right things. What was needed at the moment was that the Entente should be made cordiale; Edward VII was temperamentally suited to the task of persuading French public opinion that Great Britain was neither barbarous nor perfidious and of persuading British opinion that there was something to be said even for a despotic Czar. In other words, the Government used the King's social gifts to popularise a foreign policy which it believed to be necessary.

George V's opportunities related mainly to Ireland. From his accession in 1910 he was caught up in the heated, and to a later generation incredible, party conflict over Home Rule; and the role of mediator was, as we shall see,[1] cast upon him. His interest and activity in the conduct of the war of 1914–18 have already been mentioned.[2] In 1921, on the suggestion of General Smuts, he seized the opportunity of his speech at the opening of the Parliament of Northern Ireland to make an appeal for a settlement of the Irish problem. On Lord Stamfordham's advice, General Smuts' draft was forwarded to the Prime Minister. Three days later Lord Stamfordham called on Mr Lloyd George, complained that the King had been kept in the dark about the nature of his speech, and said that the King wished to be acquainted with the views of the Cabinet. Thereupon the drafts prepared by the Irish Office were scrapped and a new draft, written by Sir Edward Grigg, was approved by the King. General Smuts believed that a promise of Dominion status *by the King*[3] would create a new situation. The speech as delivered did not go so far, but its terms were broad enough to enable the Government of the United Kingdom to found on it an appeal to the Irish

[1] Below, pp. 387–9.
[2] Above, pp. 370–1.
[3] Italics in General Smuts' letter to the Prime Minister: Nicolson, *King George V*, p. 350.

leaders, and the proposal laid before the ensuing conference was indeed Dominion status. Mr de Valera refused the proposal as framed, and submitted a counter-proposal. The British Government's draft reply was aggressive, but it was seen by the King and on his advice redrafted in a much more conciliatory tone. This new draft, which was approved by the Cabinet, was the prelude to final and successful negotiations which led to the establishment of the Irish Free State.[1]

The experience of George V suggests that there is some danger in the free use of the Sovereign's name and personality, for it may result in the association of the monarch with a party policy. In the Home Rule dispute of 1912–14 one party urged the King to assent to the Bill and the other wanted him to refuse assent. In the ridiculous speech made by Sir Arthur Paget at the Curragh in 1914 he said that his instructions were 'the direct orders of the Sovereign' and not merely the commands of 'those dirty swine, the politicians'; in fact, however, the King learned about the incident from the newspapers.[2] There was less danger in Ulster in 1921, because the Government of the United Kingdom was a coalition: but when the removal of the Indian capital to Delhi was announced by the King, Mr Austen Chamberlain suggested that it was unconstitutional for an announcement to be made in this manner, since it was impossible for the Opposition to attack and defeat the Government on this issue without lowering the King-Emperor's prestige in India.[3]

The wide social sympathies which Edward VIII was believed by many to possess have been alleged to have been the determining factor in the attitude adopted by the Baldwin Government to the proposal that the King should marry the present Duchess of Windsor. There is, of course, no evidence that this was so. On the contrary the attitude of the Labour Opposition, if nothing else, shows the allegation to be completely false. The fact that it could be made shows, however, a general recognition that the monarch need not be a cipher and that he is in a position to press any views that he may form. The survey given

[1] *Ibid.* pp. 348–62. The text of the King's Speech is on pp. 352–4, and see especially Major Hardinge's note on p. 359.

[2] *Ibid.* p. 238.

[3] Sir Austen Chamberlain, *Politics from Inside*, pp. 409–10.

in the preceding sections of this chapter show that the impression is indeed correct. It must be emphasised that we are at present concerned with the normal working of the political machine. The special functions which the Sovereign may be called upon to perform in relation to acute political troubles or on special occasions are discussed later. In respect of the matters now under discussion the Cabinet takes full political responsibility, and the decisions are in fact Cabinet decisions. It will have been seen, however, that the Queen can be politically the best-informed person in her dominions. That is to say, the volume of political information which pours into Buckingham Palace is greater and of more immediate importance even than the volume which pours into 10 Downing Street. Indeed, the volume is so great that the difficulty is not to keep the Queen fully informed but to sort it out and arrange it in such a manner that she is not completely overwhelmed with paper. Nor is it wholly official. We have seen that the Governors-General, the Governors of some of the colonies, Her Majesty's ambassadors and ministers abroad, and other persons are encouraged to send more or less demi-officially their comments on affairs in the territories to which they have been posted. There is a constant stream of official and demi-official visitors being received by the Queen and explaining themselves if not the policies with which they are concerned. Only those with experience of official correspondence, especially with persons overseas, can appreciate the importance of actually meeting and talking to one's correspondents. If, for instance, the Governor-General of Ceylon sends an account of his relations with his ministers, it is important for the proper understanding of the issues involved that the person reading it shall know something of the personality of the Governor-General and of the ministers concerned. Treated as a mere description of relations between two unknown persons, it may bear one meaning: to a person who knows the personalities involved the implications may be quite different.

It is of course true that the trappings of royalty, its formality and remoteness from ordinary life, impose limitations upon the Queen to which others are not subject. There are aspects of politics, those concerned with the ideas and aspirations of ordinary people, which the Queen will invariably find difficulty in understanding, simply because she is a Queen and has always been a princess. She mixes with all classes except the real people, those in the back-streets of the great cities and their suburbs, and those who live in the villages. This remoteness is, however, relative. Mr Macmillan does not normally order tea and a bun at the Corner House, nor has he been seen recently at a Palais de Danse. He could not do either without upsetting temporarily the ordinary social machine. The social contacts of high station are necessarily limited, and it is probable that George V, for instance, had a more accurate impression of public opinion than Mr Ramsay MacDonald after 1929. Undoubtedly there is this weakness in the royal status, but it is offset by the fact that the Cabinet, which is presumably in close touch with the constituencies, takes the responsibility. All that it means, in fact, is that when a monarch states that a line of action (such as a coalition) will be popular, he may mean that it will be popular in Mayfair and the Brigade of Guards. It will be for the Prime Minister to submit, with humble duty, that it will be regarded with less favour in Huddersfield or Gorbals.

The influence that the Sovereign may bring to bear will depend, in the first instance, on his capacity for hard work, his powers of perception, and his personality. It must be emphasised that the work is indeed hard and unremitting. The social functions which are an essential part of his work, and which are explained in a later section, are exceedingly wearing. It looks easy to drive through the streets of Liverpool or Birmingham, waving and smiling: in fact, however, it is extremely hard work simply because it requires concentration. It also looks easy to shake hands with a string of aldermen, but to find the right word at the right moment, to pose in the right place at the right time, to smile when smiling is called for and to look sad when sadness is appropriate, again require complete concentration on the job in hand.[1] Yet all this is incidental. While it is going on there is at least one courier on his way with another red box full of documents which have to be sorted and digested and, in many cases, signed. When the royal party has shaken hands with the mayor, bowed to the aldermen, waved to the school-children, and smiled at the faces in the crowd, the real work begins, and it goes on the whole time, in Balmoral or Windsor as in Buckingham

[1] Especially when the Sovereign, and a woman at that, is appearing on television.

Palace. When Queen Victoria said that she was physically unfit to open Parliament in person, there were some who disbelieved her. In fact, as we now know, there was some justification for her frequent and prolonged periods of residence at Balmoral. The volume of reading and writing which her normal work required was immense and imposed a considerable strain upon her constitution. The kind of tamasha appropriate to a State opening of Parliament would have required an additional tax upon her powers which she might not have been able to bear. Under subsequent monarchs the social or 'dignified' section of the work has much increased, while the volume of paper pouring in has immensely increased. It is true that the organisation of the work has been much improved, that people write short memoranda and not long letters, that Household affairs are no longer regulated by notes passing to and from the Sovereign, and that Queen Victoria's successors have been sufficiently revolutionary to introduce typewriters. Nevertheless, he will be an unusual monarch who undertakes one-quarter of the ceremonies that he is asked to attend, who reads sufficient of his official papers to keep himself fully informed on all questions that may be submitted to him, who reads a sufficient selection of daily newspapers and periodicals to gather some idea of what people are thinking, and who maintains all the personal contacts that his office requires. Edward VII has been described as 'lazy', but that means only that he did not read as much as his mother and disliked writing. George V covered most of the field of work. Edward VIII evidently disliked the formal side of his duties. George VI was, however, undoubtedly the most persistent worker of this generation.

Powers of perception are necessary because, if the Queen's assistance is to be of any value, it is not enough for her to read everything of importance. She must be able to appreciate the principles underlying a memorandum in order that she may be able to foresee the implications of the policy proposed. A student of government may be able to recite the organisation and powers of all Government Departments, to quote every document issued in the last quarter of a century, and to remember the name of every senior official in every part of the Commonwealth, and yet not understand how the machine works: and the Queen is, or ought to be, the most learned student of government in her dominions.

A person who is really expert in affairs can find far more in a newspaper than the casual reader and learn far more from a casual discussion than the ordinary man could obtain from all the lectures of the London School of Economics. It is particularly desirable that the Queen should have these qualities because there are, as we shall see, special occasions on which robust common sense and an understanding of the political situation may help her to enable political leaders to find their way out of acute difficulties. They are, however, necessary also in normal times. Her remoteness from the lives of ordinary people renders it particularly difficult to see the motives behind political movements. Queen Victoria, for instance, obviously did not understand the Radical movement and the forces which gave Mr Gladstone such strength.

The Queen's influence depends, finally, on her personality and on the personalities of those with whom she is in contact. In ordinary political matters she possesses influence and not power. She cannot give instructions; she can only advise. It is true that her position gives her advice a force which that of no ordinary woman could give. A Prime Minister is bound to listen deferentially to a Queen and to give an answer to the most stupid proposal. Nevertheless, the advice will not be accepted unless it is not only good but also put persuasively. On the other hand, the acceptance depends on the willingness of the minister concerned to take advice. If the documents be carefully examined, it will be found that Queen Victoria had more influence on the policy of Mr Gladstone than on that of Mr Disraeli, not because her advice was better or more attuned to his political conditions, but because Mr Gladstone, in spite of his stiffness, took her less violent remarks far more seriously than Mr Disraeli did. Mr Gladstone may have treated her as a public meeting, but public meetings have a way of influencing the speaker. Mr Disraeli, on the other hand, tended to treat her as a charming woman who had to be flattered but whose views were not to be regarded with much seriousness.

The Queen's function is, however, advisory only. She can press her opinions as hard as she likes, but in the last resort she must give way. Queen Victoria's last resort was sometimes rather far away. As Dr Sidney Herbert pointed out to Lord Granville in 1859, when the missionary zeal of the 'two dreadful old men' in the cause of liberty was meeting strong opposition from Osborne, the position of a monarch when parties are evenly balanced is strong. '"If we differ your opinion must give way to mine" is not an agreeable statement to hear, nor a prudent one to make to a person who has a good deal of indirect power and the spirit to use it if *poussée à bout*.'[1] Lord Derby, on one occasion, made a delicate suggestion that he ought to resign.[2] Occasionally a hint appears that the ministers' resignation is the alternative to acceptance by the Queen of the tendered advice.[3] It is stated in a standard work that Queen Victoria 'repeatedly had to yield on reminders that the alternative was the resignation of her ministers'.[4] The published documents do not warrant such a sweeping statement. The Queen needed no such reminders. She was aware that, so long as a policy was supported by the Cabinet, she had no remedy. She was able to appeal from Lord Palmerston to Lord John Russell in 1850 and 1851. She appealed to the Cabinet, sometimes successfully, against Lord Russell and Lord Palmerston in the struggle for Italian independence in 1859 and in the Schleswig-Holstein question in 1864. Against Mr Gladstone there was no appeal, for the Cabinet was with him. Mr Gladstone never deigned to threaten resignation. He recognised no right in the Crown to assume 'independent power'.[5] He was aware, and the Queen was aware, that, no matter how frequently the Queen said that she would '*never* consent', she was bound to give way. A refusal to consent would be tantamount to a dismissal of ministers, the exercise of a power which, if it existed,[6] would be fraught with consequences dangerous to the stability of the monarchy. King Edward's repeated assertions that, though he disagreed, he was bound to assent, were in accord with constitutional facts.[7] The fear that a decision by George V might cause the resignation of the Government is implicit, and sometimes explicit, in the long controversy over Home Rule;[8] and even Mr Lloyd George once threatened resignation.[9]

[1] *Life of Lord Granville*, I, pp. 354–5.

[2] *Letters of Queen Victoria*, 1st series, III, p. 406.

[3] *Ibid.* 1st series, III, p. 472 (Lord John Russell—but the suggestion is very remote); *ibid.* 1st series, III, p. 474 (Lord Palmerston).

[4] Anson, *Law and Custom of the Constitution*, vol. II, part I (4th ed.), p. 54. The references do not bear out the statement.

[5] Gladstone, *Gleanings*, I, p. 233.

[6] See below, pp. 403–12.

[7] Morley, *Recollections*, II, p. 302; Lee, *King Edward VII*, II, pp. 42, 91–2, 385.

[8] See, e.g. Nicolson, *King George V*, p. 118.

[9] *Ibid.* p. 321.

The Sovereign's power to warn and advise is, nevertheless, important. Of even more importance is her power to render less acute the controversies of political life and secure agreements 'behind the Speaker's chair'. For mediation demands tact, a quality which most monarchs possess, rather than ability and specialised knowledge, which they do not necessarily possess. This power has been exercised repeatedly during the past six reigns.

Queen Victoria's communications with the Opposition followed no rule. She created an unfortunate precedent when she continued writing to Lord Melbourne after his resignation in 1841. Even Baron Stockmar, who was given to exaltation of royal functions, thought that such a correspondence was 'productive of the greatest possible danger'.[1] This gloomy prophecy was not fulfilled. Lord Melbourne had the good sense to restrict his correspondence to gossip and general constitutional instruction, and gradually the correspondence became less frequent until it ceased altogether. At no time was Lord Melbourne guilty of any intrigue against the Conservative Government.

This cannot be said of the Queen's correspondence with Lord Beaconsfield after 1880.[2] It began fairly tactfully, with only a little mild sarcasm at Mr Gladstone's expense. Within five months the Queen confided her anxieties over the Government's Eastern policy, sent an extract from a letter by Lord Granville on the state of parties, and explained that she looked to Lord Beaconsfield for ultimate help.[3] Lord Beaconsfield naturally seized the opportunity to expound his own policy, and gave his own views on the state of parties. With these incursions into unconstitutional advice was mixed much clever flattery.[4] Such a letter could have no other result than to stimulate the Queen's opposition to the Government. A fortnight later the Queen communicated confidential information of the Government's plans.[5]

Disraeli's biographers called this correspondence 'a dangerous experiment'.[6] It was far more: it was a constitutional innovation which went contrary to fundamental principles of constitutional monarchy.

[1] *Letters of Queen Victoria*, 1st series, I, p. 415.

[2] *Ibid.* 2nd series, III, pp. 127 *et seq.*; *Life of Disraeli*, II, pp. 1414 *et seq.*

[3] *Letters of Queen Victoria*, 2nd series, III, pp. 143–4.

[4] *Ibid.* 2nd series, III, pp. 144–7.

[5] *Life of Disraeli*, II, p. 1415.

[6] *Ibid.* II, p. 1414.

The Constitution assumes that, even if the Sovereign is not impartial, at least he will try to behave as if he were. If he is to become a definite supporter of a particular party, then the Constitution must provide alternate monarchs as it provides alternate Governments. This complete acceptance of Conservative principles led inevitably to the attempt to keep out the Liberals in 1885.[1]

Queen Victoria relied much upon the advice of 'elder statesmen' like the Duke of Wellington, Lord Lansdowne and Lord Aberdeen when there was difficulty in forming a new Government.[2] This was clearly unobjectionable, for though technically a retiring Government remains in office until its successor is appointed, the Sovereign does not act upon its advice, but takes a personal decision. That decision must depend on parliamentary conditions, and advice from experienced statesmen is useful to the Sovereign and a check upon his personal prejudices.

The Queen occasionally asked Opposition leaders to support non-political proposals by the Government. Thus, in 1856, Lord Derby and Lord Lyndhurst agreed to support a Bill for settling the precedence of Prince Albert.[3] In 1863 she urged Derby to support the proposal to purchase the site and buildings of the Prince Consort's Exhibition of 1851.[4] The Government was nevertheless defeated. In neither case did she act upon the advice of the Government or with its consent.

There are other ways in which the prestige of the monarch may sometimes be utilised for public purposes. There is a well-established tradition, of infinite value for the successful working of political institutions, that where a person is asked to undertake some task as a matter of public duty he should do his best to accept, even at considerable inconvenience to himself, and without haggling about remuneration. There are, of course, occasions on which the inconvenience is so considerable that the person hesitates to accept. In such a case the expression of a personal wish of the Sovereign may tip the scale. In 1931 Sir Herbert Samuel, as Home Secretary, wished to secure the appointment of Lord Trenchard as Commissioner of the Metropolitan Police, but Lord Trenchard declined because he had accepted another post outside the

[1] Above, pp. 34–5.

[2] See above, ch. II, pp. 41–50.

[3] *Letters of Queen Victoria*, 1st series, III, pp. 249–50.

[4] *Ibid.* 2nd series, I, p. 89.

public service. The Home Secretary mentioned the matter to George V, who concurred in the opinion that Lord Trenchard should be pressed to accept the post. The Home Secretary reported this to Lord Trenchard and put the matter to him as a public duty. Thereupon Lord Trenchard accepted the appointment and secured his release from his prior commitment.[1]

§6. *The Queen as Mediator*

The Queen may also use her prestige to settle political conflict or diminish the virulence of opposition. In 1866 Queen Victoria wrote to Lord Derby to try to modify the opposition to Lord Russell's Reform Bill.[2] This effort failing, and a Conservative Government taking office as a result of the defeat of the Government, she tried to persuade Lord Granville to support the Conservative Bill of 1867.[3] In 1869 she tried to mitigate Conservative opposition to the Irish Church Bill in order to prevent a collision between the two Houses.[4] None of these steps was advised by the Government, though Mr Gladstone was subsequently informed of the last.[5] Also, while the Queen urged moderation on the Opposition, she at the same time urged moderation on the Government.[6]

In 1869 the Queen had previously, at Mr Gladstone's request, arranged an interview between the Prime Minister and Archbishop Tait.[7] But the Archbishop had been Mr Disraeli's nominee, and it was arranged that he should lead the Opposition in the House of Lords.[8] The Queen made further efforts to arrange a compromise.[9] The Archbishops did not vote on the second reading, which was accordingly passed. Archbishop Tait, however, had decided that substantial amendment was necessay, and the Queen again urged moderation.[10] The Bill was substantially modified. The Archbishop continued to mediate and 'was in almost hourly communication with the Queen'.[11] Ultimately,

[1] Lord Samuel, *Memoirs*, p. 220.
[2] *Letters of Queen Victoria*, 2nd series, I, pp. 330–1.
[3] *Ibid.* 2nd series, I, pp. 411–12.
[4] *Ibid.* 2nd series, I, p. 603.
[5] *Ibid.* 2nd series, I, p. 604.
[6] *Ibid.* 2nd series, I, pp. 605–16.
[7] *Life of Archbishop Tait*, II, pp. 8–11.
[8] *Ibid.* II, pp. 18–20.
[9] *Ibid.* II, pp. 20–8.
[10] *Ibid.* II, pp. 34–6.
[11] *Ibid.* II, p. 39; see also *ibid.* pp. 41–2.

an agreement was reached, the Bill passed, and a collision between the two Houses avoided. There has been some tendency to exaggerate the Queen's influence. The successful termination of the negotiations was largely due to Lord Cairns. Yet it is probable that the Queen's constant interventions played a large part in minimising the hostility of the contestants. In any event, her intervention created a precedent which has since been followed on several occasions.

In 1872 the Queen wrote to Lord Russell, without Mr Gladstone's knowledge, to urge him not to move for papers on the Alabama question, so that the Government should not be embarrassed.[1] In 1877 she suggested to Lord Beaconsfield that she should appeal to the Opposition 'to desist from constant questions as to what the Government is going to do'.[2] Lord Beaconsfield's reply was made orally, but it appears to have been in the affirmative, for the Queen communicated through Lady Ely to Mr Forster and, through him, to Lord Hartington;[3] she also communicated directly with the Duke of Argyll.[4] In 1881 she asked General Ponsonby to see Sir Stafford Northcote and Lord Beaconsfield to secure agreement about the Government's proposals to meet Irish obstruction.[5] This step was apparently taken on her own initiative, but the Government had already been in communication with the Opposition. In the following year the Queen, again without Mr Gladstone's knowledge, appealed to Lord Salisbury and the Duke of Abercorn not to insist on an amendment to the Arrears Bill which, in Mr Gladstone's opinion, went to the root of the Bill. Lord Salisbury gave way.[6] Later in the same year she wrote to Sir Richard Cross regretting that the Conservatives moved a motion criticising the Government's action in handing over Arabi Pasha to the Egyptian authorities.[7]

The Queen's mediation was again very useful in the dispute between the two Houses over the Reform Bill of 1884. With Mr Gladstone's consent, she wrote to Lord Salisbury to urge a compromise.[8] This

[1] *Letters of Queen Victoria*, 2nd series, II, p. 212. Lord Russell was not, however, in opposition.

[2] *Ibid.* 2nd series, II, p. 532

[3] *Ibid.* 2nd series, II, p. 534.

[4] *Ibid.* 2nd series, II, p. 538.

[5] *Ibid.* 2nd series, III, p. 187.

[6] *Ibid.* 2nd series, III, pp. 320, 325, 326.

[7] *Ibid.* 2nd series, III, pp. 358–9.

[8] *Ibid.* 2nd series, III, pp. 515, 518–19; for what follows, see also *Life of Gladstone*, III, pp. 130 *et seq.*

failing, she urged the Duke of Argyll to see Mr Gladstone, and ordered Sir Henry Ponsonby to read to Mr Goschen a memorandum written by Mr Gladstone.[1] Again with Mr Gladstone's consent, she saw the Duke of Richmond, who saw Lord Cairns.[2] Lord Cairns made suggestions which were submitted to Mr Gladstone, the Duke of Richmond consulted Lord Salisbury, and in a long correspondence between Lord Salisbury and Mr Gladstone Sir Henry Ponsonby acted as intermediary.[3] Agreement was ultimately reached, and Lord Granville said that the Queen 'must feel rather proud of the powerful influence which your Majesty has brought to bear upon the probable settlement of this burning question'.[4] The Queen had in fact stimulated both sides to accept terms which would lead to a settlement.

In 1885 the Queen's mediation was again very useful in assisting in finding terms for an agreement by which Lord Salisbury could take office and remain in office until the Redistribution Act could take effect.[5]

The efficacy of these efforts obviously depended on the independent and, comparatively, impartial position of the Queen. That position had, however, already been undermined by her correspondence with Lord Beaconsfield after 1880. The efforts which she made to keep Mr Gladstone out after the election of 1885 demonstrated her complete partiality and therefore threatened her independence and her utility as a mediator. She appealed to the Whigs not to support Mr Gladstone.[6] After Mr Gladstone took office without them she continued her communications with Mr Goschen, urging the Whigs not to support Mr Gladstone, and sending his letters to Lord Salisbury.[7] Though the Government had been formed, she continued to communicate with Lord Salisbury and Mr Goschen.[8] In particular, she was aiming at a union between Conservatives and Whigs to defeat Home Rule, the major item of the Government's policy. This she urged upon Mr Goschen[9] and upon Lord Salisbury.[10] She expressed admiration of a speech by Lord Hart-

[1] *Letters of Queen Victoria*, 2nd series, III, pp. 520–2, 531.

[2] *Ibid.* 2nd series, III, pp. 537, 539.

[3] *Ibid.* 2nd series, III, pp. 542, 548 *et seq.*

[4] *Ibid.* 2nd series, III, p. 577.

[5] *Ibid.* 2nd series, III, pp. 670 *et seq.*

[6] *Ibid.* 2nd series, III, pp. 709–18; 3rd series, I, pp. 5–29.

[7] *Ibid.* 2nd series, I, pp. 32–4.

[8] *Ibid.* 3rd series, I, pp. 37, 41, 45, 49–50, 79, 90–1, 98, 101, 111–12, 116–17, 128–30, 131–2, 134–5, 138.

[9] *Ibid.* 3rd series, I, p. 91.

[10] *Ibid.* 3rd series, I, p. 98.

ington and trusted 'that these dangerous and ill-judged measures for unhappy Ireland will be defeated'.[1] She wrote to Mr Goschen that 'we must *not* mind this narrow view (which is, moreover, NOT shared by the Conservatives!) and organise the opposition to these dangerous Bills separately, and then act together. That once effected, we shall see more clearly what can be done'.[2] Mr Goschen explained in reply how the Liberals were trying to 'sink party differences'.[3] This letter was sent to Lord Salisbury, who proceeded to discuss whether the Queen could dissolve Parliament without Mr Gladstone's consent.[4] This reply was later elaborated into a full memorandum, which discussed whether the Queen should grant a dissolution if Mr Gladstone asked for one. This was discussed, not from the constitutional point of view, but simply as to the effect of a dissolution on the 'party of resistance'. Accordingly, he advised that the Queen should grant a dissolution.[5] Mr Goschen was of the same opinion.[6] Both agreed, on further reflection, 'that the Unionists will gain on a dissolution'.[7] Mr Gladstone did ask for a dissolution and mentioned, with unconscious irony, that the Opposition leader had very strongly urged it.[8]

Thus, the Queen was in league with the Opposition. She did not, it is true, communicate information about Mr Gladstone's plans. But she was engaged in negotiations with the Opposition. She was urging the union of the two wings of the Opposition and took advice from the leader of the Opposition as to whether she should dissolve without advice or refuse a dissolution in spite of the Government's advice. She was, in short, a member of the Unionist parties. These events are the best illustration of the remark made by Mr Joseph Chamberlain (before he became a Unionist) that she was, after all, the granddaughter of George III.

The Queen's position was much less strong in 1893. She had no hope of organising an effective Opposition in the House of Commons, and she could rely only on the House of Lords. She asked Lord Hartington to write to Sir Henry Ponsonby if there was 'anything

[1] *Letters of Queen Victoria*, 3rd series, I, p. 102.
[2] *Ibid.* 3rd series, I, p. 112.
[3] *Ibid.* 3rd series, I, p. 113.
[4] *Ibid.* 3rd series, I, pp. 116–17.
[5] *Ibid.* 3rd series, I, pp. 128–30.
[6] *Ibid.* 3rd series, I, pp. 131–2.
[7] *Ibid.* 3rd series, I, pp. 134–5.
[8] *Ibid.* 3rd series, I, p. 143.

going on' about the Home Rule Bill, and when she was told that the Opposition desired to postpone the Bill, she wrote to Mr Gladstone suggesting postponement.[1]

Her successors took a more constitutional view of their duties. In the dispute between the House of Commons and the House of Lords over the Education Bill of 1906, Edward VII drew attention to the precedent of 1869 and advised Sir Henry Campbell-Bannerman to get into touch with the Archbishop. Though the negotiations failed, he continued to press the Government to make concessions.[2]

In 1908, at Mr Asquith's suggestion, the King urged Lord Roberts not to raise a debate on the question of invasion.[3] In the dispute over the Finance Bill of 1909, the King asked Mr Asquith whether he would be acting within constitutional lines in taking it upon himself to give advice to and, if necessary, put pressure upon the Conservative leaders. 'I replied that I thought what he was doing and proposing to do perfectly correct, from a constitutional point of view; that the nearest analogy was the situation and action of William IV, at the time of the Reform Bill; in both cases the country was threatened with a revolution at the hands of the House of Lords. He said that, in that case, he should not hesitate to see both Balfour and Lansdowne on his return to London.'[4] The King saw both leaders, and found that no decision had yet been taken by them. He then apparently asked Lord Cawdor, who was prominent in Opposition, to write him a memorandum.[5]

Mr Asquith, it will be seen, justified the King's action by the precedent of 1832. Lord Esher advised the King similarly, but he mentioned also the precedents of 1869 and 1884.[6] None of them was directly in point, for the Bill had not at this time passed the House of Commons. In 1832, 1869 and 1884 the Bills had already been substantially amended in the House of Lords. Nevertheless, opposition between the two Houses was to be apprehended, and there seems nothing objectionable

[1] *Letters of Queen Victoria*, 3rd series, II, pp. 236–7.

[2] *Life of Sir Henry Campbell-Bannerman*, II, pp. 301–5; Lee, *King Edward VII*, II, pp. 461–2; *Life of Randall Davidson*, I, pp. 524–9.

[3] *Esher Papers*, II, pp. 360–1.

[4] *Life of Lord Oxford and Asquith*, I, p. 257.

[5] Lee, *King Edward VII*, II, pp. 667–8.

[6] *Esher Papers*, II, pp. 413–16, 418–20. It is not always clear whether Lord Esher was referring to 1884 or 1885. The former provides the nearer analogy.

in the King offering his mediation before the crisis became acute, for, when once contestants have publicly announced their decisions, they frequently consider that they cannot withdraw without loss of prestige.[1] Mr Balfour, in private, expressed approval of the King's action.[2] After the rejection of the Bill by the House of Lords, and the moderate success of the Government at the first general election of 1910, the King again tried to secure some measure of agreement for passing the Bill, but without effect.[3]

After the second general election of 1910 and the introduction of the Parliament Bill, King George V desired to see the Opposition leaders. Mr Asquith objected. He had already placed his views on record in a memorandum in which he wrote:

It is not the function of a Constitutional Sovereign to act as arbiter or mediator between rival parties and policies; still less to take advice from the leaders on both sides, with the view to forming a conclusion of his own.[4] George III in the early years of his reign tried to rule after this fashion, with the worst results, and with the accession of Mr Pitt to power he practically abandoned the attempt. The growth and development of our representative system, and the clear establishment at the core of our Constitution of the doctrine of ministerial responsibility, have since placed the position of the Sovereign beyond the region of doubt or controversy.[5]

The King insisted, however, that he was not seeking advice, but desired to obtain knowledge at first hand of the views of the Opposition; and Mr Asquith reluctantly agreed. Lord Lansdowne expressed his agreement with the King's action. 'I said that I could not conceive that there should be any impropriety in such conversations. As a constitutional Sovereign, his Majesty was no doubt obliged to be guided by his ministers, but the obligation did not seem to me in any way to preclude him from seeking information either as to questions of fact or as to matters of opinion.'[6]

This was clearly a different case from that of 1909. It cannot be

[1] *Esher Papers*, II, pp. 418–20.
[2] *Ibid.* II, p. 421.
[3] *Life of Lord Lansdowne*, pp. 388–9.
[4] This is reminiscent of Mr Gladstone's language: *Gleanings*, I, p. 233.
[5] *Life of Lord Oxford and Asquith*, I, p. 306.
[6] *Life of Lord Lansdowne*, p. 409.

doubted that, where opposition had arisen between the two Houses and was likely to lead to a deadlock, the King might, in spite of Mr Asquith's statement, act as mediator between the two sides. Exactly at what point he should ask to be allowed to intervene must be a question of doubt. If he can intervene when the dispute has broken out, he can surely intervene, as in 1909, when a controversy is to be expected. To be able to intervene effectively he must know the opinions of both sides. His mediation will be ineffectual if it is too late. If it is too early he runs the risk of appearing to take sides in a purely party controversy. Mr Asquith's reluctance in 1911 was justified by the fact that the House of Lords had not yet indicated its decision on the Parliament Bill, and by the fact that suggestions were being made that the King should refuse his assent to the Bill. On the other hand, no harm could be done by an interview which was limited to facts and opinions and was not directed towards the undermining of the Government's position.

The King had in any case already been in touch with the Opposition leaders through his private secretary, Lord Knollys, and Lord Esher. In January 1911 the two of them had dinner with Mr Balfour to discuss the King's action and Mr Balfour expressed opinions which contemplated the possibility of forcing the Government to resign.[1]

In 1913 and 1914 the King made efforts to secure agreement on the Home Rule Bill.[2] In 1913 his efforts were directed mainly to the securing of a conference of party leaders, so that a settlement by consent might be obtained. He urged this solution first on Mr Asquith[3] and then on Mr Bonar Law.[4] Mr Asquith thought that a conference would prove to be 'either a tea party or a bear garden'.[5] What he did was to enter into secret conversations with Mr Bonar Law. Though there was a tentative agreement for the exclusion of Ulster from the Home Rule Bill, opinion on both sides began to settle against a compromise, and the King went so far as to say that it would be his duty to intervene to prevent bloodshed.[6] The King's Speech of February 1914 included an appeal for a 'lasting settlement'. Lord Stamfordham sought an interview with Mr Bonar Law and urged that the violence of Conservative

[1] *Esher Papers*, III, pp. 40–4.
[2] *Life of Lord Oxford and Asquith*, II, p. 28.
[3] Nicolson, *King George V*, pp. 223, 228.
[4] *Ibid.* p. 231.
[5] *Ibid.* p. 232.
[6] *Ibid.* p. 233.

speeches was rendering a peaceful settlement impossible.[1] Lord Stamfordham also visited Sir Edward Carson to ask him not to make a violent speech when the Home Rule Bill was again introduced.[2] Mr Asquith's proposals for a temporary exclusion of Ulster did not satisfy Sir Edward Carson; and the King again pressed Mr Asquith. The latter said that 'he was deeply grateful to the King, without whose help he could not have achieved as much as had been done. Throughout the King had, he thought, behaved in exactly the manner a Constitutional Sovereign should act.'[3] After the 'Curragh revolt' Mr Bonar Law telephoned to Lord Stamfordham to say how grave he thought the situation, asserting that nothing could stop the ruin of the Army and civil war but an immediate settlement between the Government and the Opposition.[4] The King intensified his efforts, pressing Mr Asquith to put his foot down. Mr Asquith resumed his private discussions.[5] It was largely due to the King's initiative that the controversy was narrowed down to the area and conditions of exclusion of Ulster. As early as May he secured the Speaker's approval to a suggestion that Mr Lowther should preside over a conference, but he was not able to secure Mr Asquith's consent until July, Mr Asquith emphasising that the invitation must come from the King in order that the Irish leaders could 'save their faces with their more extreme supporters'.[6] He then summoned the Home Rule Conference of July 1914.[7] His speech to the Conference was sent to and approved by the Prime Minister, and was published by the Conference.[8] The Conference failed, but the King nevertheless played a part in the settlement of the Irish question. The speech from the Throne on the opening of the Parliament of Northern Ireland was the first step towards the negotiations between the British and Irish leaders which led to the 'Articles of Agreement for a Treaty between Great Britain and Ireland' and the creation of the Irish Free State.[9]

In April 1916 there were conflicts between Mr Asquith and Mr Lloyd

[1] Sir Austen Chamberlain, *Politics from Inside*, p. 617.

[2] Nicolson, *King George V*, p. 235.

[3] *Ibid.* p. 237.

[4] Sir Austen Chamberlain, *Politics from Inside*, p. 626.

[5] Nicolson, *King George V*, p. 240.

[6] *Ibid.* pp. 241–2.

[7] *Life of Lord Oxford and Asquith*, II, pp. 53–4.

[8] Oxford and Asquith, *Fifty Years of Parliament*, II, pp. 154–6.

[9] Above, pp. 373–4.

George, and it was suggested by the Lord Chief Justice that George V use his influence to secure agreement. Lord Stamfordham saw Mr Bonar Law and Mr Lloyd George, but agreement was reached in Cabinet without his mediation.[1]

It is, however, only in exceptional circumstances such as these that the Queen has a formal interview with Opposition leaders or that the private secretary can make less formal investigation of Opposition opinion. For the most part she must rely on their published speeches, on her knowledge of their views through their advice as ministers in previous Governments, and through the reading of Opposition newspapers. It is fairly obvious, for instance, that George V had very little knowledge of Labour party opinions before 1924. He met most of the leaders for the first time at a private dinner party in 1923.[2] Edward VII, on the other hand, had met some of the Liberal leaders privately before 1905, for they were 'in Society'.

§7. *The Queen as a Social Figure*

Finally, it must be remembered that the Queen is not merely part of the political machine. She is, too, an important part of the social structure. One would not emphasise this function so strongly as Walter Bagehot emphasised it.[3] The nature and importance of 'Society' have changed during the present century. It is no longer of political importance. In political matters, 'the City' has taken its place: and with this the Queen is not much in contact. The social importance of the royal family must nevertheless not be underestimated. Bagehot said that monarchy was an intelligible system. We should perhaps put it that the monarchy personifies that elusive entity, the State, far more easily than any legal fiction. It provides a focus for that patriotism which, even when it runs to extremes, is commonly regarded as a merit. This is of particular importance in a democracy, for the Government for the time being, though supported by a section of the people only, is the instrument of the whole. It is possible, therefore, for opposition to the Government to be attacked as opposition to the nation. The Government, too, does nothing to destroy the idea. It parades the national flag

[1] Nicolson, *King George V*, pp. 273–4.

[2] Snowden, *Autobiography*, II, pp. 661–2.

[3] *English Constitution*, ch. II.

and uses every opportunity to take to itself the title of 'National'. The ordinary individual appears to be on the horns of a dilemma. Either he must support the Government, or he must oppose the nation.

The monarchy provides a simple means of demonstrating that the dilemma does not exist. A person can be loyal to his Queen and yet oppose the Government. In 1914 the Liberal Government did not assert that, for reasons for which they were willing to explain, the Government had decided to send the army under its control to fight in France against an army under the control of the German Government, and that it desired recruits for that army. It simply said: 'Your King and Country need you.' Conservatives were able to 'serve the King' and yet oppose some aspects of the Liberal Government's policy. It is not to be suggested, of course, that British people in 1914 were more 'patriotic' than others. But patriotic fervour is more easily stimulated when the 'King' declares war and asks for recruits for the 'royal' forces. According to Mr Lloyd George, the King in 1917 enormously assisted the laying of industrial unrest by his visits to munition works and other places where suspicion of war motives was being aroused.[1]

In non-political matters the division between Queen and Government is even more obvious. The patronage of the Queen or of some other member of the royal family is an enormous asset to any charitable institution. It gives it a 'national appeal' which no other person, however eminent, could give. Her presence at ceremonies such as the laying of foundation stones, the launching of ships, and the opening of new works, enables people of opposing views to associate without suppressing their mutual opposition. In part, of course, she is asked to perform such ceremonies and to associate with charitable projects because of her 'publicity value'. A string of platitudes uttered by a prince commands more newspaper space than the most momentous pronouncement of a philosopher. Yet this too is a product of personal loyalty to the monarch. He is the national spokesman; and if he talks platitudes and not philosophy, it is because the nation talks platitudes and not philosophy.

The result is to make the office of Queen one of the most difficult in the world. She has to move in the constant glare of publicity, which

[1] Lloyd George, *War Memoirs*, IV, pp. 1961–3.

tends with some newspapers to go to the limit of vulgarity and sloppy stupidity. Croker records that when William IV drove to close Parliament in 1833, the mob observed that he spat out of the window, and remarked that George IV would not have done that. Croker commented: 'Kings are but mortals and must spit; but I agree with the mob, they had better not do so out of the window of the state coach.'[1] Nowadays, the press would have reporters and photographers on the spot to record the event. It is not divinity but publicity that hedges a king, as Edward VIII discovered.

Naturally, the Government is not averse from using the personal popularity of the Sovereign to strengthen its own popular appeal. It is certain that the Jubilee and Diamond Jubilee celebrations of 1887 and 1897 strengthened popular support for the imperialistic ideas of the Conservative Governments then in office.[2] It is certain, too, that the Silver Jubilee of 1935 strengthened the 'National' Government, whose popular support had until then been rapidly diminishing. According to his biographer, Mr Neville Chamberlain was 'cheered...by a belief that the decision to rearm and the Jubilee would both enrich the soil in which a Conservative Government may thrive'.[3]

Finally, one element in the personal position of the Sovereign must be mentioned, though it has little to do with the internal governmental system of Great Britain. The Queen is ruler not of the United Kingdom alone but of Canada, Australia, New Zealand, South Africa, Ceylon and Ghana also. She is, too, Head of a Commonwealth which includes not only these seven countries, but India, Pakistan and the Federation of Malaya also. The fact that she is not Queen of three of the ten countries, that her Headship of the Commonwealth is nominal, and that since 1948 the concept of 'British subject' or 'Commonwealth citizen' has borne no necessary relation to allegiance to the Crown, shows that the 'common allegiance' on which the Balfour Declaration of 1926 and the preamble to the Statute of Westminster lay emphasis is no longer of great importance. Nevertheless, in the Commonwealth countries which retain allegiance, the sentimental appeal is still important. The functions actually performed in relation to the overseas territories are

[1] *Croker Papers*, II, p. 212. [2] Cf. *Life of Joseph Chamberlain*, III, ch. LIV.

[3] *Life of Neville Chamberlain*, p. 242.

few, and they are always subject to limitation by local legislation. The Queen appoints Governors-General on the advice of her several Governments, but the Governors-General exercise most of her functions. Occasionally she has to issue formal documents for diplomatic representatives and consuls and for the making of treaties. Such powers, again, are exercised on the advice of the Governments concerned. Occasionally, too, she can find time to visit some of her other realms and territories. It is no longer possible for the Queen to ask, as George V once asked: 'How's the Empire?'[1] There is no Empire, though in some quarters Sir Winston Churchill's unhappy phrase, 'Commonwealth and Empire', is used. There is, however, a Commonwealth in which the number of independent members is growing apace. The Queen's services are shared by an increasing number of independent States.

[1] Sir Evelyn Wrench, *Geoffrey Dawson*, p. 329.

CHAPTER XIII

THE PERSONAL PREROGATIVES: DISMISSAL OF MINISTERS, DISSOLUTION OF PARLIAMENT, CREATION OF PEERS

§1. *The Personal Prerogatives in General*

The previous chapter shows that, while the Queen has in normal circumstances 'the right to be consulted, the right to encourage, the right to warn',[1] she must, in the last resort, give way to the advice of the Cabinet. There are, however, certain prerogative powers which she exercises on her own responsibility, and which may fitly be called 'the personal prerogatives'. Exactly what they are is by no means clear; for there are differences of opinion in respect of several of them. There is no controversy that she need not accept advice as to the appointment of a Prime Minister[2] or as to the creation of peers so as to override the opposition of the House of Lords. There is controversy as to whether she can dismiss a Government or dissolve Parliament without advice, or whether she can refuse to dissolve Parliament when advised to do so.

There have indeed been suggestions that other personal prerogatives survive. William IV seems to have suggested in 1834, after the burning of the Palace of Westminster, that he could summon Parliament to meet where he pleased. Lord Melbourne replied:

> There can be no question that, as your Majesty states, it is your Majesty's undoubted prerogative to appoint the meeting of your Parliament, but this place of meeting has been upon the present spot so unvariably for so many years—ever since the time of Charles II, who summoned one Parliament under very peculiar circumstances at Oxford—that, without adverting to the possibility of the House of Commons not sanctioning any arrangement made at present by voting the sums necessary to defray the expense of it, it appears

[1] Bagehot, *English Constitution* (World Classics edition, 1928), p. 67.
[2] Above, pp. 40–51.

to Viscount Melbourne that it would be highly inadvisable, and in some degree ungracious, to exercise this prerogative except after full consultation with the two Houses of Parliament.

He accordingly suggested that the Government should draw up a plan for submission to Parliament.[1] Lord Melbourne's reply was a polite and constitutionally correct intimation that the question was one between the Government and Parliament.

Mr Disraeli in 1852 considered that the Crown's right to refuse assent to legislation was still outstanding and was not 'an empty form'. 'It is not difficult to conceive the occasion when, supported by the sympathies of a loyal people, its exercise might defeat an unconstitutional ministry and a corrupt Parliament.'[2] Mr Disraeli had then had no experience of office and not very much experience of Parliament. The power had not, and has not, been exercised since the reign of Queen Anne. The Queen's pleasure is taken merely formally, in order that the letters patent creating the royal commission to assent to legislation may be sealed. Nevertheless, there were suggestions between 1912 and 1914 that George V could refuse his assent to the Home Rule Bill, which was then being put through Parliament under the Parliament Act of 1911.

The argument arose because the limitations of the power of the House of Lords by the Parliament Act destroyed the power of the Conservative party, subject to the threat of the creation of peers, to veto Liberal legislation. It could prevent the passing of the Home Rule Bill only if the King refused assent to it, or dismissed the ministers, or dissolved Parliament. Indeed, none of those remedies was available unless a further condition was satisfied. There would in any case be a general election, because if the King refused assent the Government would resign; and if the Government resigned or was dismissed the process of government could be obstructed by a combined Liberal, Labour and Irish Nationalist Opposition unless Parliament were dissolved. Hence the condition was that the electorate should, at a general election, produce a Unionist majority. This was, however, a reasonable gamble, particularly because the Unionists could ask the electorate to support not merely the Union but the King himself. Any action by the King would make him an ally of the Unionist party, in effect supporting

[1] *Lord Melbourne's Papers*, pp. 213–14. [2] Disraeli, *Life of Bentinck*, p. 45.

them in an appeal for the unity of the United Kingdom under the Union Jack.

The Unionists did not put the matter so plainly. Indeed, they put nothing very plainly because the issues were clouded with emotion. Their case was that the Liberals had removed one limb of the Constitution on a promise to replace it with an improved limb, a promise which they had not carried out. They were using the Constitution so dismembered to destroy the unity of the United Kingdom. Not only was their action unconstitutional but also they were carving up the King's dominions. It was therefore the duty of the King to preserve the Constitution and his own inheritance in accordance with his Coronation oath. Their ablest constitutional lawyers—and both Sir William Anson and Professor Dicey were active Unionists—were therefore brought out to prove that the King had the power to intervene, by refusal of assent or otherwise, and that that power had not become atrophied by disuse.

The King himself was a model of discretion, but it is evident from his correspondence with Mr Asquith that he was not in sympathy with Home Rule. What concerned him more, however, was the growing antagonism between the parties, which might have led to civil war in Ireland. He was not impressed by the Unionist argument because action by him would not solve the problem of Ireland but would on the other hand subject him to attack by Liberal, Labour and Nationalist politicians throughout the United Kingdom. The republicanism which had been so strong in Victorian Radicalism had diminished in strength, but it was still strong in Labour and Nationalist opinion, far stronger than it is today. What the Unionists were asking him to do, therefore, was to protect part of his inheritance by risking the whole. His solution to the whole problem was a compromise among the parties, and his efforts were directed to that end.

Though the Home Rule Bill was not introduced until April 1912, Mr Bonar Law raised the issue of the assent in January of that year.[1] At this stage, according to Lord Esher, the argument was based on the references to the royal assent in the Parliament Act itself. Lord Esher's comment was that the Liberal party could hardly have intended by

[1] *Esher Papers*, III, p. 117.

these references to restore the royal veto.[1] The real answer, though Lord Esher did not give it, is that the royal assent was in fact the enactment by the King in Parliament. The prior approval of the two Houses may or may not have been legally necessary—the question had never arisen for decision—but the draftsmen of the Parliament Bill had either to say that the Bill should be presented for the royal assent or that it should be presented for enactment by the King in Parliament.

Mr Bonar Law raised the point again at a dinner party at Buckingham Palace in May 1912. The Government had, he asserted, brought the Crown into the struggle. The King's only chance was that they should resign within two years. Otherwise the King would have either to accept the Home Rule Bill or dismiss ministers and choose others who would support him in vetoing it. 'In either case, half your subjects will think you have acted against them.' Mr Bonar Law added that the veto was dead only so long as there was a buffer between the King and the House of Commons; 'but they have destroyed the buffer'.[2] He repeated these views in a memorandum in September 1912, though he added that, if the point were put to the Prime Minister, 'he [i.e. the Prime Minister] would feel that it was his duty to extricate the King from so terrible a dilemma'.[3]

It will be seen that Mr Bonar Law assumed, no doubt, correctly, that the refusal of assent would necessarily lead to the resignation of ministers and an appeal to the country. Lord Esher, who was advising the King, denied the whole doctrine.[4] For reasons quoted in a previous section,[5] he insisted that it would be dangerous to the monarchy to refuse to accept the advice of ministers; and Sir William Harcourt, in a personal interview with the King, insisted that if there were a general election, Home Rule would not be mentioned, and the sole question would be—'Is the country governed by the King or by the people?'—and every minister, from Mr Asquith downwards, would attack the King personally.[6]

Lord Esher's view was that the King should ask for an answer in

[1] *Ibid.*
[2] Sir Austen Chamberlain, *Politics from Inside*, pp. 486–7.
[3] Nicolson, *King George V*, p. 201.
[4] *Esher Papers*, III, pp. 131–2.
[5] Above, pp. 373–8.
[6] *Esher Papers*, III, p. 132.

writing to a series of questions, of a tendentious nature (such as one might expect from an adviser of Lord Esher's opinions), and insist that these questions be laid before the Cabinet

together with a statement that although anxious to exercise his royal prerogative with every due regard to constitutional practice, he considers himself entitled to have from his ministers, in Cabinet assembled, categorical answers to these questions, which are prompted by a desire to adjust the position of the Sovereign to the novel Constitution created by the Parliament Act.

The King might advantageously point out that precedents which would have governed his action under our unwritten Constitution have doubtful authority now that a statute governs the relation to [among?] the three estates of the realm: and that having regard to the new conditions created for him by the Parliament Act, he thinks it is his duty to the Crown before assenting to any fresh alteration of the Constitution to see that the advice tendered by his ministers, is fully and frankly placed before him in a form which can be recorded for the use of his successors and possibly for the satisfaction of the people.[1]

The King did not accept Lord Esher's advice, but decided to await a memorandum promised by Mr Asquith.[2] The Prime Minister followed his usual practice of procrastination, and meanwhile the King made up his own mind. In principle, he agreed with the argument that there ought to be a general election before the Home Rule Bill became law. In practice, he foresaw that the Government would not agree to a dissolution, that if the King insisted the Government would resign, and that at the ensuing general election the King would be accused of political partisanship[3]. His solution, therefore, was a party compromise. In August 1913 he handed Mr Asquith a memorandum. It elaborated Mr Bonar Law's point ('Whatever I do I shall offend half the population') and went on to suggest a settlement by consent.[4] Mr Asquith, in his reply, pointed out that the royal veto had not been exercised since early in the reign of Queen Anne.

We have now a well-established tradition of 200 years, that, in the last resort, the occupant of the Throne accepts and acts upon the advice of his ministers. The Sovereign may have lost something of his personal power and authority, but the Crown has been thereby removed from the storms and

[1] *Esher Papers*, III, pp. 129–30.
[2] *Ibid.* p. 133.
[3] Nicolson, *King George V*, p. 222.
[4] *Ibid.* p. 223–4

vicissitudes of party politics, and the monarchy rests upon a solid foundation which is buttressed both by long tradition and by the general conviction that its personal status is an invaluable safeguard for the continuity of our national life.[1]

Mr Asquith went on to say that the Sovereign undoubtedly had power to change his advisers, though the power had not been exercised since 1834 and even then the authority of the Crown was disparaged. In Mr Asquith's view the Parliament Act was not intended to affect, and had not affected, the constitutional position of the Sovereign. If the King were to intervene on one side, which he could only do by dismissing ministers, he would be expected to do the same on another occasion. He would be dragged into the arena of party politics, and the Crown would become the football of contending factions. In a second memorandum[2] he rejected the demand for a general election, on the ground that an election would settle nothing, but expressed sympathy with the idea of a conference.

The King accepted the principle that he must act on advice, but pointed out that he would be blamed for accepting it. He questioned the thesis that he could never dismiss ministers or dissolve Parliament. He contested the view that the Parliament Act had not changed the situation, because there had been an organic change in one of the Estates of the Realm. He doubted whether the general election of December 1910 gave a verdict in favour of Home Rule and saw no objection to a new general election.[3]

Mr Balfour expressed no opinion on the question of assent, thought that there ought to be a general election, but appreciated that the Prime Minister would not advise one and the King would not be prepared to dismiss the ministers.[4] Meanwhile Lord Esher had changed his mind, and thought that the King ought to dismiss ministers.[5] In the end, the Prime Minister agreed to a conference and the idea of the refusal of assent was dropped. The King considered that that extreme course could not be adopted unless there was convincing evidence that it would avert a national disaster, or at least have a tranquillising effect on the

[1] *Life of Lord Oxford and Asquith*, II, pp. 29–31.
[2] *Ibid.* pp. 31–4.
[3] Nicolson, *King George V*, pp. 225–8.
[4] *Ibid.* p. 230.
[5] *Esher Papers*, III, p. 155.

distracting conditions of the time. In his view there was no such evidence. The letter in which these observations were made was never dispatched because of the imminence of war.[1]

It was assumed by the King throughout that he had not only the legal power but the constitutional right to refuse assent. On the other hand, he also recognised that his exercise of the power would involve the resignation of ministers, a dissolution of Parliament, and a general election in which the main issue would be the prerogatives of the Crown. There is something to be said for a power to dismiss an unconstitutional Ministry or to dissolve a corrupt Parliament, but nothing to be said for a power to refuse assent to a Bill because the King thinks it wrong. Nor can it properly be claimed that for the Lords' veto on behalf of the Conservative party there should be substituted a royal veto on behalf of that party. It must of course be admitted that the peers were less amenable to the Conservative whip than the Conservative members of the House of Commons and accordingly that there might have been remote contingencies in which the House of Lords would have rejected or severely amended Conservative legislation. Speaking generally, however, the claim based on the Parliament Act was a claim that there should be a veto on Liberal legislation. The conclusion seems to be that the Crown cannot refuse assent except on advice; but if there were such a power the Home Rule Bill was not an occasion for using it. Home Rule had been Liberal policy for a quarter of a century and Nationalist policy for even longer. Since the electorate of the United Kingdom had chosen a Home Rule majority, it was not the function of the King to reject the consequence. The constitutional issue was of course clouded by the remarkable and indeed incomprehensible depth of emotion that Home Rule produced.[2]

In 1855, on the resignation of Lord John Russell, the Cabinet at once decided to resign. Lord Aberdeen saw Queen Victoria, and at the next

[1] Nicolson, *King George V*, p. 234.

[2] Most of the lawyers who supported the Unionist party in 1913 agreed that the King could not 'veto' the Home Rule Bill. They agreed instead that he could exercise his prerogative of dissolution. See Appendix III, below, pp. 539–45. The veto would be, in the words of Mr George Cave (afterwards Lord Cave and Lord Chancellor), a 'challenge to democracy'. Professor Dicey, one of the most extreme Unionists at this time (he subscribed to the Ulster 'covenant'), appears to have disagreed, for he quoted with approval Burke's language on the veto: see below, p. 545.

meeting of the Cabinet (for surrendering seals) informed them that the Queen had 'peremptorily refused to accept the resignation of Aberdeen or of any of his colleagues. Her Majesty told Aberdeen, and commanded him to tell us, that our resignation under such conditions was unjust towards herself, injurious to our own character, and indefensible as regards the country.'[1] This does not tally with Prince Albert's account of Aberdeen's audience. He says that 'the Queen insisted...that Lord Aberdeen should make one appeal to the Cabinet to stand by her, which he promised to do to the best of his ability, but without hope of success'.[2] Nevertheless, it has sometimes been assumed that the events constitute a precedent for the principle that the Sovereign can refuse to accept a resignation. The Duke of Argyll commented: 'Although, of course, I was aware that it was part of the prerogative of the Crown to accept or refuse resignations, I had never realised it as a power likely to be brought into practical use.'[3] Actually, the Cabinet reconsidered the matter and came to the conclusion that resignation was bad policy. The case is thus no precedent. If it were, it would be a bad precedent. The question whether the Cabinet can or cannot continue to command a majority is not one which the Sovereign can decide. Here the Cabinet could not, as the events showed; at the same time its determination was probably in its own interest, for even in 1855 an accusation that the Cabinet had 'run away' would probably have been effective. In 1866 General Grey wrote to Mr Gladstone that the Queen 'considers it the bounden duty of her Ministers, in the present state of the Continent, not to abandon their posts, for she *knows* that it would be impossible at this moment to form another Government which would command the public confidence'.[4] The Government resigned, however, and a Conservative Government was formed and remained in office until 1868.

In 1881 Lord Beaconsfield, in his capacity of irresponsible and unconstitutional adviser, informed the Queen:

The principle of Sir W. Harcourt, that the Speech of the Sovereign [in Parliament] is only the Speech of the Ministers, is a principle not known to

[1] Duke of Argyll, *Autobiography and Memoirs*, I, pp. 517–18; see also Lady Frances Balfour, *Life of the Earl of Aberdeen*, II, pp. 281–9.

[2] *Letters of Queen Victoria*, 1st series, III, p. 93.

[3] Duke of Argyll, *Autobiography and Memoirs*, I, pp. 517–18.

[4] Guedalla, *The Queen and Mr Gladstone*, I, p. 43.

the British Constitution. It is only a piece of Parliamentary gossip. The speech from the Throne must be approved in Council[1] by the Sovereign, but to be so approved, it should be previously considered by the Sovereign. Ample time ought to be secured to the Sovereign for this purpose, so that suggestions may be made and explanations required and given.

The degree of resistance which the Crown may choose to make against any expressions which the Crown disapproves, must depend upon circumstances. If, for example, there was a proposal to surrender Malta under an alleged engagement of the Treaty of Amiens, the Sovereign would, in all probability, be supported by the nation in resisting such a counsel. The unfortunate state of parties at this moment[2] limits the power of the Crown, but that is no reason why the constitutional prerogative of the Crown should be treated as non-existing. Even under the present circumstances, your Majesty has a right, which it would be wise always to exercise, to express your Majesty's opinion on every point of policy of your Ministers and to require and receive explanations.[3]

This clearly suggests that the Sovereign could refuse to assent to an item in the Queen's Speech, even to the extent of accepting the resignation of the Government, provided that there is some prospect of securing an alternative Government. This is, in substance, the exercise of a power of dismissal. As to the Queen's Speech, it has been universally accepted since 1841 as the statement of ministerial policy, for which the Sovereign accepts no personal responsibility. In 1841, Lord John Russell said in the House of Commons: 'I thought that it was generally understood, that the Speech from the Throne was the Speech of Ministers....The Speech was the result of advice of Ministers, and Ministers alone are responsible for it.'[4] In 1881 the Queen objected to a paragraph in the Queen's Speech announcing the proposal to withdraw from Candahar. Lord Spencer and Sir William Harcourt, who were ministers in attendance, 'impressed upon Sir H. Ponsonby that the

[1] This is not so: the practice originated because it was convenient to hold a Council after a Cabinet meeting. Now that a Council meeting is rarely attended by more than two ministers, the argument no longer holds. Accordingly, though Queen Victoria regarded a proposal for a change as 'revolutionary', it was decided during the war of 1914–18 that the King could approve the speech under the sign manual. See Fitzroy, *Memoirs*, I, p. 31 and II, pp. 756–7.

[2] I.e. the heavy defeat of Lord Beaconsfield's Government at the election of 1880.

[3] *Letters of Queen Victoria*, 2nd series, III, pp. 181–2.

[4] *Annual Register*, 1841, p. 198. See also *Life of Lord Clarendon*, II, p. 138.

Speech from the Throne was in no sense an expression of her Majesty's individual sentiments but a declaration of policy made on the responsibility of her Ministers'.[1]

§2. *The Dismissal of a Government*

No Government has been dismissed by the Sovereign since 1783.[2] The general impression in 1834 was that Lord Melbourne's Government was, to use Palmerston's expression, 'turned out neck and crop'.[3] The facts now available do not substantiate this conclusion, though they do not deny that William IV might have dismissed his ministers if he had so pleased. The Whigs had already been weakened by the resignation of Lord Grey, Mr Stanley, and Sir James Graham, when the death of Earl Spencer transferred Lord Althorp to the House of Lords. Lord Melbourne had made Lord Althorp's adhesion a *sine qua non* to his acceptance of office on the resignation of Lord Grey, owing to the weakness of the Government in the House of Commons. The removal of the party leader in that House might be regarded as the removal of the foundation upon which the Government was built.[4]

Lord Melbourne therefore wrote to the King that 'in the new and altered circumstances it is for your Majesty to consider whether it is your pleasure to authorise Viscount Melbourne to make such fresh arrangements as may enable your Majesty's present servants to continue to conduct the affairs of the country, or whether your Majesty deems it advisable to adopt any other course'.[5] He added that he would never 'abandon' the King, and that his services would 'always be at your Majesty's disposal while they can be given honourably and conscientiously, and whilst your Majesty is pleased to deem them worthy of your acceptance'.[6] But he entreated that 'no personal consideration for him may prevent your Majesty from taking any measures or seek any

[1] *Life of Sir William Harcourt*, I, pp. 598–600. But the Queen's Speech is in the same position as any other act of ministers; i.e. the Queen's sanction is necessary, but she must assent if her ministers insist. There was therefore nothing unconstitutional in the Queen's original refusal to sanction, since she gave way in the end.

[2] Though the resignation of the Whigs in 1807 was in substance a dismissal.

[3] Lytton, *Life of Viscount Palmerston*, II, p. 207; for similar expressions by Lord Brougham, see *Peel Papers*, II, p. 255, and by Greville, see Greville, *Memoirs*, 1st series, III, p. 144.

[4] *Lord Melbourne's Papers*, p. 220.

[5] *Ibid.*

[6] *Ibid.*

other advice which your Majesty may think more likely to conduce to your Majesty's service and the advantage of the country'.[1]

The King mentioned, in his reply, that he could not help feeling that the Government existed only by the support of the House of Commons, and that the loss of Lord Althorp's services in that House had to be viewed with that consideration in mind.[2] Lord Melbourne had an audience next day. He suggested that Lord John Russell might lead the House, but the King objected that he would make a wretched figure when opposed by Sir Robert Peel and Mr Stanley and that he favoured certain policies with which the King did not agree. Further, the King stated that the conduct of Lord Brougham had tended to shake his confidence in the Government. As to the former objection, Lord Melbourne observed that the King 'would be at full liberty to refuse his assent to any measure submitted to him' and that Lord Melbourne and several of his colleagues had not committed themselves on the subject in question. Lord Melbourne did not, in any case, express any doubt as to his ability to carry on the Government. The King, however, believed that, in view of its resources in the House of Commons, the Government could not carry on satisfactorily, and that it would be broken up at a less convenient moment.[3] Accordingly, he wrote to Lord Melbourne 'that he conceives that the general weight and consideration of the present Government is so much diminished in the House of Commons, and in the country at large, as to render it impossible that they should continue to conduct the public affairs in the Commons, and particularly when it is considered that the King's confidential servants cannot derive any support from the House of Lords which can balance the want of success in the Commons'.[4] This communication was submitted to the Cabinet, whose members offered to remain in office until their successors were appointed. The King had already sent for the Duke of Wellington, who held the reins with Lord Lyndhurst while awaiting the arrival of Sir Robert Peel.

There are several peculiarities about these events which prevent them from being regarded as a precedent either for the dismissal of ministers

[1] *Lord Melbourne's Papers*, p. 220.
[2] *Ibid.* p. 222.
[3] The above is summarised from the King's own memorandum, printed in *Memoirs of Baron Stockmar*, I, pp. 329–35.
[4] *Lord Melbourne's Papers*, pp. 222–3.

or, indeed, for any principle at all. In the first place, the whole 'atmosphere' is that of the eighteenth century; the fundamental change effected by the Reform Act was ignored. The King assumed that a Government with strong support in the House of Lords could ignore the opposition of the House of Commons. The Reform Act made such a position impossible, there was no example after 1834, and it is inconceivable today. Both the King and Viscount Melbourne assumed that the King's opposition was sufficient to prevent legislation upon which the Cabinet was agreed. Though Disraeli made the same assumption later on, it is no longer tenable.[1] Also, the King believed that he could resist the appointment of Lord John Russell, even if Lord Melbourne pressed it; that, too, would not be possible today.[2]

In the second place, there was no 'dismissal'. Lord Melbourne raised the question and left it to the King to say whether the Government should continue. No Prime Minister would take such a step today without consulting the Cabinet; and the Cabinet would not leave the King to decide a question which depends essentially upon expert knowledge of the temper of the House of Commons. Even so, it was not a dismissal; it was the acceptance of a contingent resignation.

In the third place, Lord Melbourne stated that he believed that the Government would have a majority in the House of Commons. No Sovereign would accept the responsibility of asserting the contrary when advised by the Cabinet or Prime Minister.

In the fourth place, a general election became necessary, and the Tory Government was defeated as soon as the new House met. In modern conditions, the King's action would have been a matter of acute controversy during the election, and his relationship with a Government which had achieved success at the polls would be extremely difficult.

Sir Robert Peel is reported to have said that 'it was obvious that his Majesty's case was a bad one'.[3] Mr Gladstone said that 'the act was rash, and hard to justify'.[4] Whether the case was good or bad, justifiable or unjustifiable, the conditions cannot be repeated today, and it cannot be regarded as a precedent.

Prince Albert laid down the 'great axiom' that 'the Crown supports

[1] Above, p. 400.
[2] Above, pp. 61–70.
[3] *Croker Papers*, II, p. 165.
[4] *Gleanings*, I, p. 231.

frankly, honourably, and with all its might, the Ministry of the time, whatever it may be, so long as it commands a majority, and governs with integrity for the welfare of the country'.[1] The latter qualification is perhaps susceptible of interpretation. It was, no doubt, that qualification which justified in Queen Victoria's mind her efforts to overthrow the Liberal Government of 1886.[2] It is nevertheless worthy of remark that she never tried or, so far as is known, even suggested, that she might emulate her royal uncle.

In Canada, in 1873, a Royal Commission proved that there was corruption in Sir John MacDonald's Government. The Governor-General informed the Prime Minister that 'he did not consider it his duty to intervene until Parliament should have dealt with the matter, but that inasmuch as the decision of Parliament might itself be partially tainted by the corruption exposed, he should hold himself free to require the resignation of the Ministers in the event of their winning by anything short of a very commanding majority'. The Government thereupon resigned.[3] Lord Kimberley, the Colonial Secretary, appears to have thought that the Governor-General was bound to accept a vote of the Canadian House of Commons, but that he might have put a 'gentle pressure' on the Government. The Queen would not accept this view of constitutional monarchy, and Sir Henry Ponsonby wrote that 'Her Majesty... has always respected the obligations which exist between the Queen and her Ministry, but these obligations are mutual and honourable'.[4]

Mr Gladstone appears to have thought, in 1878, that the right to dismiss still existed.[5] Mr Disraeli, writing to the Queen in the same year, stated the power much more explicitly.

> If your Majesty's Government have from wilfulness, or even from weakness, deceived your Majesty, or not fulfilled their engagements to their Sovereign, they should experience the consequences of such misconduct, and the constitutional, and becoming, manner of their punishment is obvious. They cannot with their present Parliamentary majority in both Houses and the existing difficulties, as men of honour, resign, but your Majesty has the clear constitutional right to dismiss them.[6]

[1] *Life of the Prince Consort*, I, p. 110.
[2] Above, pp. 34–6.
[3] *Letters of Queen Victoria*, 2nd series, II, pp. 288–9.
[4] *Ibid.* 2nd series, II, pp. 291–2.
[5] Gladstone, *Gleanings*, I, pp. 230–2.
[6] *Life of Disraeli*, II, p. 1118.

This was mostly rhetorical flourish, and he did not explain what was to happen if, with 'their present Parliamentary majority', they were to be dismissed.

Disraeli's Colonial Secretary had some doubts on the subject when he had to take the responsibility for putting principles into practice. In the same year there was a dispute between the two Houses in Victoria. The Legislative Council rejected the Appropriation Bill, and the Government of Victoria retaliated by dismissing civil servants, an act in which the Governor acquiesced. Sir Michael Hicks Beach advised the Governor that he must follow his ministers' advice, though in case of necessity he should take legal opinion.[1] In the following year a similar problem arose in Canada. The Lieutenant-Governor of Quebec had dismissed his ministers. The Dominion ministers thereupon advised the Governor-General to dismiss the Lieutenant-Governor. The Governor-General asked the Colonial Secretary if he was bound to accept the advice. Sir Michael Hicks Beach replied that all he could do was 'to preach a constitutional homily for the benefit of the Dominion and tell Lord Lorne [the Governor-General] that he must follow the advice of his ministers, if, after my homily, they persist in their views'.[2]

The question did not become practical in England until 1913,[3] when the Conservatives, enraged by their impotence against a Government which was imposing the Home Rule Act on them under the Parliament Act, 1911, tried to find an ally in the Crown. Professor A. V. Dicey then wrote:

I entirely agree that the King can do nothing except on the advice of Ministers. I totally disagree with the doctrine drawn from this principle that he can never dismiss Ministers in order that he may ascertain the will of the nation. Of course, the incoming ministers must, like Sir Robert Peel, accept responsibility for the change of Ministry. No one need be ashamed of following the principle set by Pitt and Peel.[4]

[1] *Life of Sir Michael Hicks Beach*, I, p. 70.

[2] *Ibid.* I, p. 65.

[3] But Mr Balfour apparently thought that the King could have dismissed his ministers at the end of 1910, though it would have been 'imprudent and unwise'. *Esher Papers*, III, pp. 43–4.

[4] Colvin, *Life of Lord Carson*, II, p. 240.

In the course of his memorandum on the King's position in relation to the Home Rule Bill, Mr Asquith wrote:

The Sovereign undoubtedly has the power of changing his advisers, but it is relevant to point out that there has been, during the last 130 years, one occasion only on which the King has dismissed the Ministry which still possessed the confidence of the House of Commons. This was in 1834, when William IV (one of the least wise of British monarchs) called upon Lord Melbourne to resign. He took advantage (as we now know) of a hint improvidently given by Lord Melbourne himself, but the proceedings were neither well-advised nor fortunate. The dissolution which followed left Sir R. Peel in a minority, and Lord Melbourne and his friends in a few months returned to power, which they held for the next six years. The authority of the Crown was disparaged, and Queen Victoria, during her long reign, was careful never to repeat the mistake of her predecessor....

Nothing can be more important, in the best interests of the Crown and of the country, than that a practice, so long established and so well justified by experience, should remain unimpaired. It frees the occupant of the Throne from all personal responsibility for the acts of the Executive and the legislature. It gives force and meaning to the old maxim that 'the King can do no wrong'. So long as it prevails, however objectionable particular Acts may be to a large section of his subjects, they cannot hold him in any way accountable. If, on the other hand, the King were to intervene on one side, or in one case—which he could only do by dismissing ministers in *de facto* possession of a Parliamentary majority—he would be expected to do the same on another occasion, and perhaps for the other side. Every Act of Parliament of the first order of importance, and only passed after acute controversy, would be regarded as bearing the personal *imprimatur* of the Sovereign. He would, whether he wished it or not, be dragged into the arena of party politics; and at a dissolution following such a dismissal of ministers as has just been referred to, it is no exaggeration to say that the Crown would become the football of contending factions.

This is a constitutional catastrophe which it is the duty of every wise statesman to do the utmost in his power to avert.[1]

To these observations George V replied:

While you admit the Sovereign's undoubted power to change his advisers. I infer that you regard the exercise of that power as inexpedient and indeed dangerous.

[1] *Life of Lord Oxford and Asquith*, II, pp. 30–1.

Should the Sovereign *never* exercise that right, not even, to quote Sir Erskine May, 'in the interests of the State and on grounds which could be justified in Parliament'? Bagehot wrote, 'The Sovereign too possesses a power according to theory for extreme use on a critical occasion but which in law he can use on any occasion. He can *dissolve*....'[1]

Mr Asquith replied that for the King to dismiss ministers might entail consequences 'very injurious to the authority of the Crown'.[2] Lord Esher, while denying that the King could refuse assent, considered that 'the King still possesses the power of dismissing his Ministers, but not of dictating policy, whether in the form of a dissolution of Parliament or otherwise'.[3]

In February 1914 the King and Mr Asquith discussed the consequences of a failure in the negotiations proceeding among the parties. The King suggested that a general election would clear the air, would show whether the Government possessed a mandate, and would in any case relieve the King and the Prime Minister of responsibility for what followed. Mr Asquith replied that a general election would settle nothing and that, whatever the consequences, the responsibility would rest not with the King but with his ministers.

> The King replied that, although constitutionally he might not be responsible, still he could not allow bloodshed among his loyal subjects in any part of his Dominions without exerting every means in his power to avert it. Although at the present stage of the proceedings he could not rightly intervene he should feel it his duty to do what in his own judgment was best for his people generally.

Mr Asquith expressed his surprise and hoped that the King was not thinking of refusing assent, which would 'inevitably prove disastrous to the Monarchy'. The King could dismiss his ministers, but if so it should be done at once. The King replied that he had no intention of dismissing his ministers, though his future action must be guided by circumstances.[4]

Reasons have been given above for asserting that the precedent of 1834 is no precedent for the dismissal of ministers in modern conditions. Mr Asquith's memorandum, so far as it goes, is incontrovertible. It

[1] Nicolson, *King George V*, pp. 225–6.
[2] *Ibid.* p. 229.
[3] *Esher Papers*, III, p. 157.
[4] Nicolson, *op. cit.* pp. 233–4.

does not, however, meet the point which was made by Unionists in 1913 and mentioned by their most expert constitutional lawyer, that the King has the right to dismiss ministers if he has reason to believe that their policy, though approved by the House of Commons, has not the approval of the people. Such an argument, it must be confessed, is an argument for a dissolution and not for a dismissal of ministers. If the King believes that the Government has lost its majority, and if it is any concern of his, his obvious step is to ascertain whether his assumption is correct and to insist upon a dissolution. If ministers refused to 'advise' the dissolution in Council they would resign; and if they did not resign he could dismiss them.

But is it his duty to make such an assumption? Is he sufficiently in touch with public opinion to be able to form a judgment? It is suggested that the answer to the second question is in the negative. Though his 'splendid isolation' makes him more impartial than most, it also keeps him away from the movements of opinion. He can judge only from newspapers, from by-elections, and from his own entourage. Of the first, it is enough to say that even the unanimous opposition of London newspapers would be no criterion. Of the second it can be said that by-elections (as Mr Disraeli discovered) are apt to prove deceptive, especially to one far removed from them. Of the third it must be asserted that it is always more biased and less well-informed than the King himself.

Nor is it his business to anticipate the decision of the electorate. Every Government takes decisions which would not be approved by the electorate. It is neither practicable nor desirable that an election should be held whenever it is suspected that a particular decision is not approved.[1] The electorate is asked to approve not a particular decision but a course of policy. It is asked to approve such policy at intervals of four or five years, if not more frequently. If the King selects decisions which seem to him to be important, his selection must depend upon his subjective notions, which it is his duty, as an impartial Sovereign, to

[1] It is certain that the vast majority of the electorate disapproved of the 'peace proposals' made by the British and French Governments to Italy and Abyssinia in December 1935. Ought the King to have dismissed his ministers? Consider also the situation in the first half of 1957, when it seemed clear that neither the Eden nor the Macmillan Government had the support of a majority of the constituencies.

ignore. If he selects because of the vehemence of the Opposition, he invites all Oppositions to be vehement.

The Home Rule Bill differed from some other Government decisions in that, once accepted, its policy could hardly be reversed. It would not have been practicable for the Conservatives to have abolished Home Rule if the war had not intervened and they had taken office in 1915. In this it was not so exceptional as was sometimes argued. Nearly every decision of foreign policy or of Commonwealth or colonial policy, every constitutional change, and even such a matter of internal policy as the imposition of a general tariff or a fundamental modification of the system of taxation, is of a kind that cannot immediately be reversed. Home Rule had been a policy of the Liberal party from 1886 to 1910 even if, as the Conservatives alleged, it was not specifically submitted to the country in 1910. But, even if a fundamental change of policy is made without a 'mandate',[1] all the considerations urged by Mr Asquith suggest that it is not for the King to intervene, except by warnings and protests. It is inevitable that a Sovereign who dismisses ministers or compels them to resign should be regarded as the ally of the Opposition, and as such be made the subject of attack.[2]

George V did his very best in 1913–14 to exercise his functions impartially; but he was not impartial because, like everybody else in his kingdom, he was affected by the strong emotions prevailing. His principal advisers, Lord Stamfordham and Lord Esher, were in all essentials Conservatives and the latter quite openly. They agreed with Mr F. E. Smith that 'Ulster will fight', and they were by no means certain that he was wrong to add 'and Ulster will be right'. Both the King and Mr Asquith admitted the right to dismiss ministers and, as a matter of right, it cannot be denied: but if there had been neither agreement between the parties nor war and the King had dismissed ministers, there would probably have grown up a strong republican party.

The Queen's function is, it is suggested, to see that the Constitution functions in the normal manner. It functions in the normal manner so

[1] Below, pp. 503–9.

[2] As the Archbishop of Canterbury said, it would be 'gambling in the most dangerous manner, with the King as Stakes'. *Life of Randall Davidson*, I, pp. 626–7.

long as the electors are asked to decide between competing parties at intervals of reasonable length. She would be justified in refusing to assent to a policy which subverted the democratic basis of the Constitution, by unnecessary or indefinite prolongations of the life of Parliament, by a gerrymandering of the constituencies in the interests of one party, or by fundamental modification of the electoral system to the same end. She would not be justified in other circumstances; and certainly the King would not have been justified in 1913.[1]

§3. *The Dissolution of Parliament*

By the Septennial Act, 1715, as amended by section 7 of the Parliament Act, 1911, a Parliament 'shall and may...have continuance for five years and no longer, to be accounted from the day on which by the writ of summons...(such) Parliament shall be appointed to meet, unless...such Parliament...shall be sooner dissolved by His Majesty, his heirs or successors'. In practice a Parliament is dissolved by the Queen, on advice, before the five years elapse; and experience suggests that few Parliaments are likely to last much more than four years. In 1923, 1924, 1931 and 1951 Parliaments were dissolved, for political reasons, long before their normal periods expired. The Parliament elected at the end of 1910 was prolonged by legislation until 1918 owing to the undesirability of an election in time of war, and that elected in 1935 was prolonged, for the same reason, until 1945.

Three questions are raised by the exercise of this prerogative. The first relates to the advice upon which it is exercised. The second is whether the Queen is constitutionally bound to accept such advice. The third is whether the Queen can dissolve Parliament without advice. The

[1] In 1953 the Governor-General of Pakistan dismissed the Government of Khawaja Nazimuddin after the riots in Lahore. It was possible to form a Government without a dissolution, but there was always a minority, which on occasions became a majority, against the Governor-General, and in 1954 the Governor-General found it necessary to dissolve the Assembly. The consequential litigation involved taking four cases before the Federal Court: see Jennings, *Constitutional Problems in Pakistan*. The Governor-General justified the dismissal by asserting that the Government of India Act, 1935, as adapted for Pakistan, did not import British constitutional practice. The ministers held office at the pleasure of the Governor-General and the Governor-General took the view that 'the moment the Governor-General decides to withhold his pleasure in the interest of public order and tranquillity of the realm or in any national emergency, the Ministry ceases to hold office'.

last can be disposed of shortly. A dissolution involves the acquiescence of ministers. It necessitates an Order in Council, and the Lord President accepts responsibility for summoning the Council; and it necessitates a Proclamation and writs of summons under the Great Seal, for which the Lord Chancellor accepts responsibility. Consequently, the Queen cannot secure a dissolution without 'advice'; and if ministers refuse to give such advice, she can do no more than dismiss them.

Queen Victoria, in her anxiety to prevent the passing of a Home Rule Bill, seems to have ignored this obvious fact. In 1886 she made vague suggestions in her correspondence with Mr Goschen and Lord Salisbury that she might dissolve Parliament on her own responsibility. Lord Salisbury replied[1] that 'a dissolution, if resorted to, should take place on the advice of Mr Gladstone, according to the usual practice; for the present House of Commons was summoned on Lord Salisbury's advice'. In 1893 she asked the Duke of Argyll to

> see Lord Salisbury and the Duke of Devonshire upon some important points as to the future course of action, after the House of Lords have thrown out what I consider a foolish and terrible Bill. I thought that if Mr Gladstone did not resign, but wished to introduce it again, I ought to insist on a dissolution on the Home Rule Bill. This, the Duke of Argyll says, I should be quite justified in doing, though he was not sure of the prudence of doing so.[2]

Later, she said,

> on the particular point of my insisting on a dissolution he [the Duke of Argyll] said Lord Salisbury was of the opinion I had undoubted right to do so, and that it might come to this, but thought the time had not yet come for such a step. The Duke of Devonshire shared this opinion, but on the other hand Mr Chamberlain, to whom the Duke of Argyll had also spoken on the subject, was anxious for this very course—even suggesting it.[3]

Lord Salisbury put the matter in its proper perspective:

> A dissolution by the Queen, against the advice of her ministers, would, of course, involve their resignation. Their party could hardly help going to the country as the opponents of the royal authority; or, at least, as the severe critics of the mode in which it had been exerted.... There must be *some* hazard that, in the end, such a step would injure the authority of the Queen.

[1] *Letters of Queen Victoria*, 3rd series, I, p. 117.

[2] *Ibid.* 3rd series, II, p. 279.

[3] *Ibid.* 3rd series, II, p. 282.

It ought not, therefore, to be taken unless there is an urgent reason for taking it. No such reason exists at present. It *may* ultimately be necessary in order to escape from a deadlock.

He added what was probably with the Queen a more cogent argument, that a dissolution in the summer offered a better chance of success to the Conservative Party, and stated:

If, after the Bill has been rejected by the Lords a second time, a dissolution is still refused, the motives for approaching the Queen by petition to exercise her prerogative will become very cogent.[1]

The Liberal Government decided not to introduce the Bill a second time. In 1894 the Queen again raised the question when Lord Rosebery began attacking the House of Lords. She sent a copy of Lord Rosebery's letter to Lord Salisbury ('*very private*') without the Prime Minister's knowledge, and asked: 'Would it not be right to warn Lord Rosebery that she cannot let the Cabinet make such a proposal without ascertaining first whether the country would be in favour of it, which she does not believe?' She asked, also: 'Is the Unionist Party fit for dissolution *now*?'[2] Lord Salisbury replied that the Government had no right to announce a policy without the Queen's consent, that the Queen would be justified in requiring that the country should be consulted before a decision in so grave a matter was taken, and that the Unionist party was quite prepared for a dissolution.[3]

Lord Salisbury clearly contemplated that the Queen's insistence would certainly compel the resignation of the Government. It is in fact impossible that a dissolution should be carried out without their concurrence. What the Queen was really asking was whether she would be justified in dismissing her ministers, and whether the result would be a return to office for a substantial period of her own party. The question, in short, is one of dismissal and not of dissolution.[4]

Lord Esher says[5] that George V refused a dissolution in November

[1] *Letters of Queen Victoria*, 3rd series, II, pp. 297–9. [2] *Ibid.* 3rd series, II, p. 431.

[3] *Ibid.* 3rd series, II, p. 433; see also the opinions of Sir Henry James, the Duke of Devonshire, and Mr Joseph Chamberlain, *ibid.* pp. 442–5.

[4] As to which, see above, pp. 403–12.

[5] *Esher Papers*, III, p. 34. There is no reference to this matter in Nicolson, *King George V*. The question at issue was not whether there should be a dissolution, but whether the King should pledge himself to a creation of peers if the Liberals won the election.

1910 and that Mr Asquith and the Cabinet decided to resign. When the King came to London, however, he sent for Mr Asquith and Lord Crewe and agreed to a dissolution. Possibly Lord Esher meant only that the King refused, pending further consideration.

The above material was not available in 1913, when the question was hotly debated.[1] Nor, strange to say, did any of the eminent constitutional lawyers who contributed to the debate state the obvious fact that a dissolution without the intervention of ministers was impossible—though it was assumed by some that a decision to dissolve would in fact produce the resignation of the Government. The Home Rule Bill had been passed by the House of Commons in two successive sessions and had been rejected by the House of Lords in each of these sessions. The Unionists complained that the Government had received no mandate for the Bill in 1910 and therefore demanded a dissolution before the Bill was submitted to the House of Commons the third time and passed under the Parliament Act, 1911. In part, their plea was to Mr Asquith to advise a dissolution; but, realising that Mr Asquith was not likely to accept their advice, they also discussed the power of the King to dissolve without 'advice' for that purpose.

Mr George Cave started the argument by asserting that no reproach could be levelled against a decision of the Sovereign to satisfy himself that the House of Commons 'does indeed represent the democracy of today'. *The Times* replied that the prerogative of dissolution was 'atrophied by disuse', and that 'it is a first principle of our Constitution that the King acts solely on the advice of his Ministers'; and it further pointed out that, since the Government might secure a majority at the general election, the result might be 'an apparent disagreement between the occupant of the Throne and the majority of his people'.

Sir William Anson was not willing to admit that the prerogative was 'atrophied by disuse'; but he admitted that the advice of ministers was constitutionally necessary, and said that it would be necessary for the King to ascertain beforehand (*semble*, by communications with the Opposition if the Government would not consent) 'whether an alternative Ministry was willing to accept the responsibility for a dissolution'. Lord Hugh Cecil used the same argument, and reinforced it by

[1] See Appendix III, below, pp. 539–45.

a citation of precedents. Professor A. V. Dicey also agreed with Sir William Anson, and analysed the question in his usual methodical manner. Professor J. H. Morgan, however, emphasised that 'such an independent decision on [the King's] part would almost inevitably be equivalent to a dismissal of his ministers', that the conduct of an election under such circumstances and its effect on the position of the Sovereign 'would be such as no loyal subject could contemplate without misgiving', and that if once a dissolution were effected by the King's personal choice 'no dissolution would be free from ambiguity, and speculation as to the degree of responsibility of the Sovereign would be a feature of every election'.

There cannot be the least doubt that Professor Morgan was wholly in the right. Either the King 'persuades' his ministers to 'advise' a dissolution (in which case *cadit quæstio*) or ministers resign. In other words, the King cannot exercise his prerogative of dissolution without 'advice'; he can only dismiss his ministers. His power to do this has already been discussed;[1] and Professor Morgan's arguments against it are, it is submitted, entirely convincing.

The matter was discussed behind the scenes early in 1914. Lord Esher said that he was 'not at all sure it might not become the duty of the Sovereign, at any risk to himself, to insist upon a dissolution, and if it is refused by Asquith, to send for a neutral statesman, who would form a Government temporarily for the purpose of conducting an appeal to the country'. He said that this would have the advantage that in practically dismissing his ministers, the King would be 'keeping the ground until the country had determined which party was to govern'.[2] Lord Stamfordham seems to have replied pointing out the danger that the Liberals would appeal to the country against the King himself. Lord Esher retorted that he was thinking of 'what might be the duty of the King to do at the moment when armed conflict was recognised to be inevitable'.[3] It will be seen that Lord Esher recognised that a demand for dissolution was equivalent to a dismissal of ministers. What he implied, therefore, was that if the Conservatives, or some of them, stimulated rebellion in Ulster the King might dismiss his Liberal ministers in order to put in a 'neutral' politician who would hold an

[1] Above, pp. 403–12. [2] *Esher Papers*, III, p. 148. [3] *Ibid.* p. 149.

election in the midst of civil war. Meanwhile, presumably, no action would be taken against the rebels. Fortunately the King saw all the fallacies in this strange argument.[1] There was very little discussion about dissolution; the real questions were whether the King should refuse assent to the Home Rule Bill[2] or should dismiss ministers.[3]

'Advice', then, is necessary. The advice to dissolve was, at least until recently, submitted by the Prime Minister on the decision of the Cabinet. Lord Oxford and Asquith laid down the rule absolutely: 'Such a question as the dissolution of Parliament is always submitted to the Cabinet for ultimate decision.'[4] So far as can be ascertained, every decision to dissolve, from 1841 to 1910 inclusive, was taken by the Cabinet. In 1841 Lord Melbourne desired to resign but was overruled by the Cabinet, who wanted a dissolution.[5] 'In 1895, after the defeat of Lord Rosebery's Government on the Cordite Vote, the Prime Minister at once submitted to the Cabinet the alternatives of resignation and dissolution. There was much difference of opinion and prolonged debate, but the joint opinion of Lord Rosebery and Sir W. Harcourt in favour of resignation prevailed.'[6] In 1905 Mr Balfour desired to dissolve, but his colleagues insisted on resignation. With one exception, there appears to be no suggestion until very recent years that the Prime Minister could advise a dissolution without the consent of his Cabinet. Mr George Wyndham in 1905 wrote to Mr Balfour: 'It rests—as I understand the Constitution—with the Prime Minister *alone* to advise a dissolution. The sole responsibility is his and he must jealously preserve that power in its integrity.'[7] The obvious retort is that Mr Wyndham did *not* understand the Constitution. He had had no experience whatever in this connection, for he was only an Under-Secretary when the Cabinet decided to dissolve in 1900. The dissolutions in 1906 and 1910 (both) were advised after consultation with the Cabinet.[8]

In 1868 some ministers were very angry because Mr Disraeli asked

[1] Esher Papers, III, pp. 156–7. [2] See above, pp. 395–400.

[3] See above, pp. 403–12.

[4] Oxford and Asquith, *Fifty Years of Parliament*, II, p. 195.

[5] *Life of Lord John Russell*, I, pp. 372 *et seq.*

[6] Oxford and Asquith, *Fifty Years of Parliament*, II, p. 195.

[7] *Life and Letters of George Wyndham*, II, p. 505.

[8] Oxford and Asquith, *Fifty Years of Parliament*, II, p. 196.

for a dissolution without calling a Cabinet.[1] The Cabinet had given a general assent ten days before to a policy of dissolution, and Mr Disraeli probably wanted to present them with a *fait accompli* lest they changed their minds. He was in fact successful, for on the following day they endorsed his action, though with reluctance. It has also been said that Mr Gladstone 'dissolved in 1874 without consulting his Cabinet'.[2] In fact, however, he informed the Queen on 21 January that he would propose to the Cabinet that *they* should advise the Queen to dissolve Parliament.[3] The Queen agreed on the following day[4] and on the 23rd the Cabinet 'unanimously concurred'.[5]

The theory that the Prime Minister alone could advise a dissolution perhaps arose in 1916. When Mr Asquith resigned George V sent for Mr Bonar Law. He anticipated that, if Mr Bonar Law accepted the invitation to form a Government, he might make the condition that a dissolution be granted. He therefore consulted Lord Haldane, who advised: 'the only Minister who can properly give advice as to a dissolution of Parliament is the Prime Minister'.[6] This advice ignored the fact that, up to and including 1910, a dissolution had been advised by the Cabinet.

In any event, the practice was changed in 1918. In November of that year Mr Lloyd George wrote to Mr Bonar Law suggesting that the time had come for a dissolution. News of the suggestion leaked out, and the question being raised in the House of Commons, the following discussion took place:

Mr Bonar Law: If there is to be an election on the advice given to His Majesty by the Prime Minister, if that takes place, then we shall, I hope, be able as a Government to justify the decision which has been come to by the head of the Government....Nothing is more clearly recognised by our constitutional practice than that these things are the subject, not of any

[1] Malmesbury, *Memoirs of an Ex-Minister*, p. 639; *Life of Gathorne-Hardy*, I, pp. 276, 280.

[2] Laski, *The Crisis and the Constitution*, p. 12. Professor Laski informed the author that this statement was made on the authority of Lord Morley. Possibly Lord Morley confused 1868 and 1874.

[3] *Letters of Queen Victoria*, 2nd series, II, pp. 304–5.

[4] *Ibid.* 2nd series, II, p. 306.

[5] *Life of Gladstone*, II, p. 486.

[6] Nicolson, *King George V*, p. 289.

written rule, but they are governed by custom, and in my belief there is no custom more clearly defined than that what advice on this matter should be given to the Sovereign is a question not for the Cabinet but for the Prime Minister.

Mr Dillon: That is not a recognised practice, and I am amazed that the Right Hon. Gentleman should say that it is. I believe that the custom has always been that the advice should be given with the consent of the Cabinet.

Mr Bonar Law: And I am quite sure that the Hon. Member is quite wrong. I know of my own knowledge of recent cases where no intimation whatever was given to the Cabinet until the decision had been taken, and I believe that has always been the regular practice. At all events, the Hon. Member must recollect one instance very much complained of at the time, the instance in which Mr Gladstone dissolved Parliament in 1874, when his colleagues received, I believe, the intimation of the coming election from the public Press. At all events, it is an undoubted fact that he had sent the message to Her Majesty Queen Victoria before any one of his colleagues received any intimation.[1]

As the facts given above make clear, it was Mr Bonar Law who was quite wrong. Mr Lloyd George was anxious for a Khaki election in order to confirm himself in power, since his own (Liberal) party was in virtual Opposition. Mr Bonar Law was not so certain that there was advantage to the Conservative party in having a Coalition election. On balance he was prepared to leave it to the Prime Minister. Mr Balfour agreed: 'I think that whatever happens, the responsibility of a dissolution must rest with the Prime Minister. It always does so rest in fact; and on some previous occasions the Prime Minister of the day has not even gone through the form of consulting his colleagues'—thus erecting the so-called precedent of 1868 into 'some previous occasions'.[2] Nevertheless, the error has become the rule. No dissolution since 1918 has been brought before the Cabinet,[3] and all Prime Ministers since Mr Lloyd George have assumed a right to give the advice.

[1] 110 H.C.Deb. 5 s., 2425. [2] Blake, *The Unknown Prime Minister*, pp. 384–5.

[3] *Life of Arthur Henderson*, p. 25; Sir John Simon in *The Times*, 18 October 1935; in 1945 Mr Churchill announced a dissolution while the Labour ministers were at the Labour Party Conference. It is believed that the statement in Blake, *The Unknown Prime Minister*, p. 450, that the general election of 1922 was decided upon by the Cabinet, is incorrect. In 1935 Mr Baldwin took the decision personally against a volume of party opinion: A. W. Baldwin, *My Father*, p. 241.

It is sometimes suggested that the Queen has no choice but to accept the advice. This also is not in accordance with the precedents. Queen Victoria invariably considered whether she should grant or refuse a dissolution. The earlier precedents proceed upon the assumption that an appeal to the country was an appeal by the Sovereign, so that the failure of the Government was regarded as a personal rebuff to the Sovereign. Thus, in 1841, Lord Brougham wrote to the Queen that a dissolution was unjustifiable. 'For no one could ever think of such a proceeding as advising the Crown to dissolve Parliament in order to increase the force of the Opposition to its own future ministers, thus perverting to the mere purposes of party the exercise of by far the most eminent of the royal prerogatives.'[1] In 1846 Sir Robert Peel wrote:

> I think no minister ought to advise the Sovereign to dissolve Parliament without feeling a moral conviction that dissolution will enable them to carry on the Government of the country—will give them a Parliament with a decided working majority of supporters. The hope of getting a stronger minority is no justification of dissolution. Unsuccessful dissolutions are, generally speaking, injurious to the authority of the Crown. Following rapidly, one after the other, they blunt the edge of a great instrument given to the Crown for its protection. The dissolution of the Whigs in 1841 was, I think, an unjustifiable one. Dissolution now, if the result is likely to be the same, would be equally so.[2]

The Queen laid down the same doctrine:

> She considers the power of dissolving Parliament a most valuable and powerful instrument in the hands of the Crown, but which ought not to be used except in the extreme cases and with a certainty of success. To use this instrument and be defeated is a thing most lowering to the Crown and hurtful to the country. The Queen strongly feels that she made a mistake in allowing the dissolution in 1841; the result has been a majority returned against her of nearly one hundred votes; but suppose the result to have been nearly an equality of votes between the two contending parties, the Queen would have thrown away her last remedy, and it would have been impossible for her to get any Government which could have carried on public business with a chance of success.[3]

[1] *Letters of Queen Victoria*, 1st series, I, p. 369.
[2] Peel, *Memoirs*, II, p. 295.
[3] *Letters of Queen Victoria*, 1st series, II, p. 108.

This idea disappeared in the middle of the century, but the recognition of the Queen's complete freedom to reject advice did not. In discussing what should be done if the House of Lords rejected the Bill repealing the Navigation Acts, Lord John Russell said that if the Queen sent for Lord Stanley, 'I doubt whether the Queen would give him the power to dissolve'.[1] When Lord Stanley was sent for in 1851 he did not ask for a pledge:

> I hope I know my duty to my Sovereign too well to insist upon a pledge upon a question with respect to which no Sovereign ought to give a pledge. On the other hand, I am confident that her Majesty knows too well, and respects too highly, the mutual obligations, if I may venture to use the phrase, which subsist between a Constitutional Sovereign and her responsible advisers, to refuse...the ordinary powers entrusted to a minister, or to depart from the ordinary understanding of being guided by his advice.[2]

In 1851 there was discussion between the Queen and Lord John Russell as to her attitude if Lord Stanley accepted office on condition of being allowed to dissolve Parliament. Lord John Russell 'thought the responsibility too great for the Crown to refuse an appeal to the country to the new Government; he thought a decision on that point ought to depend on the peculiar circumstances of the case'.[3] When Lord Stanley was summoned he broached the question of dissolution, and said that 'if it was thought that the Queen would withhold from him the privilege of dissolving, he would not have the slightest chance in the House of Commons'. The Queen would not give him a 'contingent positive promise', but gave him permission to deny, if necessary, that the Queen would *not* consent to it.[4]

When it became likely that Lord Derby's Government would be defeated in 1858, the Queen sent Sir Charles Phipps to ask Lord Aberdeen's advice as to her action in the event of Lord Derby's asking for a dissolution. Lord Derby had asked permission to announce that, in the event of a defeat, he had her sanction to a dissolution. The Queen refused to give such sanction, or even to pledge herself to a dissolution. The Queen was in fact disinclined to grant a dissolution, and she

[1] *Later Correspondence of Lord John Russell*, I, p. 195.
[2] *Parl. Deb.* 3rd series, vol. 114, col. 1014.
[3] *Letters of Queen Victoria*, 1st series, II, p. 348.
[4] *Ibid.* 1st series, II, p. 366.

regarded a threat by Lord Derby to dissolve, with her sanction, as an unconstitutional biasing of the decision of Parliament. Lord Aberdeen thought that Lord Derby might reasonably threaten Parliament that he would advise a dissolution, but that he would have been quite wrong to have joined the Queen's name. As to the grant of a dissolution,

he said that he never entertained the slightest doubt that if the Minister advised the Queen to dissolve, she would, as a matter of course, do so. The Minister who advised the dissolution took upon himself the heavy responsibility of doing so, but that the Sovereign was bound to suppose that the person she had appointed as a Minister was a gentleman and an honest man, and that he would not advise her Majesty to take such a step unless he thought it was for the good of the country. There was no doubt of the power and prerogative of the Sovereign to refuse a dissolution—it was one of the very few acts which the Queen of England could do without responsible advice at the moment; but even in this case whoever was sent for to succeed, must, with his appointment, assume the responsibility of this act, and be prepared to defend it in Parliament. He could not remember a single instance in which the undoubted power of the Sovereign had been exercised upon this point, and the advice of the minister to dissolve Parliament had been rejected...and that the result of such refusal would be that the Queen would take upon herself the act of dismissing Lord Derby from office, instead of his resigning from being unable longer to carry on the Government. The Queen had during her reign, and throughout the numerous changes of Government, maintained an unassailable position of constitutional impartiality, and he had no hesitation in saying that he thought it would be more right, and certainly more safe, for her to follow the usual course, than to take this dangerous time for exercising an unusual and, he believed he might say, an unprecedented course, though the power to exercise the authority was undoubted. He said that he did not conceive that any reasons of expediency as to public business, or the possible effects of frequent general elections, would be sufficient grounds for refusing a dissolution (and reasons would have to be given by the new minister in Parliament), and, as he conceived, the only possible ground which could be maintained as foundation for such an exercise of authority would be the fearful danger to the existence of our power in India, which might arise from the intemperate discussion upon every hustings of the proceedings of the Government with respect to that country.[1]

The Queen accordingly granted permission to dissolve and, apparently, Lord Derby allowed this fact to 'become known' before the

[1] *Letters of Queen Victoria*, 1st series, III, pp. 363–5.

debate: for the Government was not defeated, and Lord Derby regarded as the primary reason 'the growing conviction' that in case of necessity the Queen would sanction a dissolution.[1] Lord Aberdeen's opinion is rather surprising for such an early date. It must obviously be related to the facts of the time. Lord Palmerston's Government had secured an enormous majority in 1857, but had been defeated on the Orsini Bill in 1858. Lord Derby's Government was thus in a substantial minority, and the alternatives were a dissolution and the return of Lord Palmerston. Seeing that Lord Palmerston had already been defeated by that House of Commons and that Mr Disraeli had led the House with some credit, the Queen's tentative decision not to allow Lord Derby to ask the electorate for a majority was rather absurd. A House of Commons which rejected both a Liberal and a Conservative Government would need to be dissolved.

It may be doubted, however, whether the wider propositions laid down by Lord Aberdeen could be defended. His own experience as Prime Minister was small, though his experience as Cabinet minister had been long. He had no experience of the reformed House of Commons, except at a distance; and he was not a statesman accustomed to examine constitutional principles, as Peel had been. It is not always true that a refusal of dissolution implies resignation. It is not always necessary that an incoming ministry should dissolve. Nor is it necessary that the new minister should give reasons for a refusal in the House of Commons.

It is clear that subsequent Prime Ministers did not consider the Queen's powers to be so limited as Lord Aberdeen suggested. In discussing the question as between dissolution and resignation in 1866, Lord Russell said: 'Should they [i.e. the Government] be of opinion that a dissolution is necessary...your Majesty would be entirely free, either to accept that advice, or to adopt the alternative, namely the resignation of your Majesty's ministers.'[2] Mr Disraeli stated the same proposition, in more courtly language, in 1868.[3] Lord Salisbury in 1886 was quite clear that Mr Gladstone might be refused leave to dissolve. But he advised the Queen to give leave because 'it is the natural

[1] *Ibid.* 1st series, III, p. 369.

[2] *Ibid.* 2nd series, I, p. 337; *Life of Lord John Russell*, II, p. 416.

[3] *Life of Disraeli*, II, p. 372.

and ordinary course; it will shield the Queen from any accusation of partisanship; it is likely to return a Parliament more opposed to Home Rule than the present; and it will adapt itself to the peculiar difficulties, as to the Queen's movements, which arise from the crisis coming at this particular date'.[1]

In 1905 King Edward was displeased by Mr Balfour's statement that the House of Commons could insist on a dissolution and that the Cabinet had dictated it.[2] In November 1910 George V actually refused a dissolution and the Liberal Government decided to resign. When the King came to London, however, he sent for Mr Asquith and Lord Crewe and agreed to a dissolution.[3] Apparently he wished to be assured that the Government could not carry on without a dissolution.[4] When Mr Asquith resigned in 1916, George V sent for Mr Bonar Law but assumed that Mr Bonar Law might ask for a dissolution. He had, therefore, asked Lord Haldane whether he would be constitutionally justified in refusing. In reply, Lord Haldane laid down the following propositions:

(1) The Sovereign ought at no time to act without the advice of a responsible Minister excepting when contemplating the exercise of his prerogative right to dismiss Ministers. The only Minister who can properly give advice as to a dissolution of Parliament is the Prime Minister.

(2) The Sovereign, before acting on advice to dissolve, ought to weigh that advice. His Majesty may, instead of accepting it, dismiss the Minister who gives it, or receive his resignation. This is the only alternative to taking his advice.

(3) It follows that the Sovereign cannot entertain any bargain for a dissolution merely with a possible Prime Minister before the latter is fully installed. The Sovereign cannot, before that event, properly weigh the general situation and the parliamentary position of the Ministry as formed.[5]

This opinion is perhaps too absolute. It does not necessarily follow that a Prime Minister who is refused a dissolution will resign. No doubt Lord Haldane had the conditions of 1913 in mind; but a wartime Prime Minister might conceivably think it his duty to acquiesce in the Sovereign's decision and carry on with the war. Nor does the third

[1] *Letters of Queen Victoria*, 3rd series, I, pp. 129–30.
[2] Lee, *King Edward VII*, II, pp. 43–4.
[3] *Esher Papers*, III, p. 34.
[4] Fitzroy, *Memoirs*, II, pp. 422–3.
[5] Nicolson, *King George V*, p. 289.

proposition follow from the second. If after the defeat of a Government in Parliament the Leader of the Opposition is sent for, the fundamental political fact is that his party has no majority, and he would be justified in refusing office unless he had the assurance of a dissolution. At his audience with Mr Bonar Law, the King himself raised the question of dissolution, but added that 'he would not give his consent, if asked'. Mr Bonar Law questioned the advisability of His Majesty refusing, and hoped the King would consider before adopting that attitude. Indeed he himself might succeed in forming a Government if he appealed to the country. Probably the King meant only that he would not pledge himself before a new Prime Minister was appointed.[1]

The dissolution of 1918 was granted by George V with considerable reluctance. It was an attempt, which proved successful, to exploit the winning of the war for the benefit of party, though as it happened the Conservative party and not Mr Lloyd George got most of the seats and was able to turn him out in 1922. George V realised that he was being asked to use his prerogative unwisely, and tried to persuade Mr Lloyd George to wait.[2] Sir Harold Nicolson says that the King had no alternative except Mr Lloyd George's resignation:[3] but the King never pushed the argument far enough to discover if Mr Lloyd George would resign; nor would Mr Lloyd George's resignation in 1918 (as we now know) have been a great national disaster. The King's decision was, in the circumstances, quite reasonable; but it was not the only possible decision.

Before his defeat at the Carlton Club in 1922, Mr Lloyd George toyed with the idea of asking for a dissolution.[4] This would have been a dissolution against his own supporters, rather like General Hertzog's attempt in 1939, and it would have raised difficult issues for George V. Evidently, however, the size of the vote at the Carlton Club convinced him that resignation was the only course. Mr Bonar Law's advice to dissolve was clearly reasonable and raised no constitutional issue. There is more doubt about the wisdom of the dissolution of 1923, and the King advised against it.[5] It could not be said, however, that it was an

[1] Blake, *The Unknown Prime Minister*, pp. 336–7.

[2] Nicolson, *op. cit.* pp. 328–9.

[3] *Ibid.* p. 329.   [4] *Ibid.* p. 370.   [5] *Ibid.* p. 380.

abuse of the prerogative. On the contrary, Mr Baldwin's advice was strictly constitutional. He considered it essential to meet the economic problem by tariffs but was bound by Mr Bonar Law's pledge not to make fundamental fiscal changes in that Parliament. The political wisdom of a dissolution was not the King's concern, since he was umpire and not captain.

The dissolution of 1924 was brought about by the decision of the Liberals to vote against the Labour Government on the Campbell case. It may be, as Sir Harold Nicolson suggests,[1] that 'the Liberals were beginning to fear that the success and moderation of the Government were attracting more and more votes to Labour and damaging the coherence and future of their own party'. They did not, however, want a dissolution, and Mr Asquith was at pains to point out that if Mr MacDonald asked for one the King could refuse.[2] On the other hand, when Lord Stamfordham made inquiries from Mr Baldwin and Mr Asquith, it became plain that neither was anxious to take office or to join a coalition.[3] When Mr MacDonald formally advised a dissolution, therefore, the King granted it with reluctance. In the circumstances there was nothing else he could do except, perhaps, to press Mr Baldwin to take office. If Mr Baldwin had accepted, he would probably have advised a dissolution; and then the King would have been in the uncomfortable position in which Lord Byng of Vimy found himself in 1926: having refused a dissolution to one party and granted it to another he would be accused of favouring one party at the expense of another, particularly in the conditions of 1924, when many Labour supporters still thought of 'Buckingham Palace' as the ally of 'the bosses'.

Lord Esher appears to have put the matter correctly:

According to my reading of constitutional usage the King can only accept, upon such a question as an appeal to the people, the advice of a Minister.

Of course His Majesty could dispense with the advice of Ramsay MacDonald, but only if he could find in Baldwin or Asquith another Prime Minister to take the responsibility.

And even then, under present circumstances, with parties balanced as they are in the existing Parliament, and in view of the real issues such as the Russian treaty, I think it would have been unwise to reject Ramsay's advice.[4]

[1] Nicolson, *King George V*, p 397.
[2] *The Times*, 19 December 1923.
[3] Nicolson, *op. cit.* p. 399.
[4] *Esher Papers*, IV, p. 296.

Lord Byng's case is a very strong one. At the Canadian general election of 1925 the Conservative party had a small majority over the Liberal party, but the Liberal Government believed that it could continue to govern with the aid of the smaller groups. Threatened with a vote of censure nine months later, the Liberal Prime Minister asked for a dissolution. Lord Byng, as Governor-General, refused on the ground that the Conservative party could form a Government. The Prime Minister thereupon resigned and the Conservative party took office but was defeated within a week and advised a dissolution, which was granted. At the general election the Liberals obtained a majority and again assumed office.[1]

It will be seen that for more than a hundred years there is no clear case in which the Sovereign has rejected advice to dissolve, though there have been examples in other Commonwealth countries. There has been, nevertheless, a persistent tradition that he could refuse if the necessary circumstances arose. It is difficult to see what those circumstances would be. An appeal to the electorate is an appeal to the supreme constitutional authority. It is true, as Lord Balfour said, that 'no constitution can stand a diet of dissolutions'; but dieting would be demanded only because the Constitution failed to carry on its proper function of providing a Government with a stable majority. If the electorate persists in returning a nicely balanced House, it will impel a coalition or compel one party to support another without coalition. But political forces alone can produce such a result. The Queen can suggest it but not compel it. If the Opposition coalesces, it is not unreasonable for a minority Government to challenge the coalition in the country. If the Government finds additional support, the question does not arise. If the major parties break up, the whole balance of the Constitution alters; and then, possibly, the Queen's prerogative becomes important.

It is true also that a Government desires a dissolution at a moment most favourable to itself. The Khaki elections of 1900 and 1918 are notorious. The Government in 1935 used a temporary agreement on an international problem to overcome its growing unpopularity. In 1945

[1] Nicolson, *King George V*, pp. 476–7; for other Commonwealth cases, see Evatt, *The King and his Dominion Governors*, ch. VIII; and for decisions about dissolution by the Federal Court of Pakistan, see Jennings, *Constitutional Problems in Pakistan*.

the Conservatives decided to have another Khaki election, on a stale register, in order to 'cash in' on Mr Winston Churchill's personal popularity and the nation's gratitude to him: they had, however, misjudged the mood of the electorate. In 1955 there was no need for a general election, but Sir Anthony Eden thought he was more likely to get a majority in 1955 than in 1956; and no doubt he was correct. It would, however, have been very difficult for the Sovereign to refuse in any of these cases, though some pressure for 'playing the game', as in 1918, would not be inappropriate.

Thus, while the Queen's personal prerogative is maintained in theory, it can hardly be exercised in practice. It is of course not true that the grant of a dissolution to Mr MacDonald in 1924 settled the issue. George V could have taken no other decision. The Labour Government could reasonably demand that it should ask the electors whether its record was not such as to warrant a majority. It could reasonably ask how many of the electors desired to continue to support the Liberal party, which first put it into office and then turned it out nine months later. The fact that its appeal was unsuccessful and that it appeared to detached observers that it would be unsuccessful is irrelevant. It was a reasonable exercise of the prerogative to ask the electors whether the three-party system was a success and, if the answer was in the negative, whether the Labour or the Conservative party should have the majority.

§4. *Compulsion of the House of Lords by the Creation of Peers*

Peers are created by the Queen on the advice of the Prime Minister.[1] Speaking generally, the prerogative raises no major constitutional issues. Before 1911, however, it was the only means by which a Government supported by a majority could overcome the opposition of the House of Lords, and even now it is not inconceivable that a Government might want to 'swamp' the Lords. It is, therefore, subject to special rules derived primarily from the precedents of 1832 and 1911, when the exercise of the prerogative for that purpose was threatened but, because of the success of the threat, not carried out.

The prerogative has actually been used for this purpose on one occasion only, in 1711–12. Queen Anne then agreed to the creation of

[1] See ch. XIV, below, pp. 462–71.

twelve peers in order to give the Tory Government a sufficient majority to secure the passage of the Treaty of Utrecht.[1] A precedent so old is no precedent, for the support of the House of Lords was then as necessary —if not more necessary—to a Government as the support of the House of Commons. An amendment to the Address, objecting to a peace which allotted Spain and the West Indies to the House of Bourbon, had been passed in the House of Lords, and the Government proceeded to obtain a majority in that House.

The support of the House of Lords is no longer necessary to any Government. But since, for the century before 1911, the House of Lords usually contained a Tory or Conservative majority, and since the support of that House was necessary to legislation, the absurd result followed that without the special creation of peers a Whig or Liberal Government and a Whig or Liberal House of Commons could be overruled by a Conservative Upper House. As Lord Grey said in 1832:

> I ask what would be the consequences if we were to suppose that such a prerogative did not exist, or could not be constitutionally exercised. The Commons have a control over the power of the Crown by the privilege in extreme cases of refusing supplies; and the Crown has, by reason of its power to dissolve the House of Commons, a control upon any violent or rash proceedings on the part of the Commons; but if a majority of this House [of Lords] is to have the power whenever they please of opposing the declared and decided wishes of the Crown and the people, without any means of modifying that power, then this country is placed entirely under the influence of an uncontrollable oligarchy.[2]

By 1911 some of these expressions needed modification, but the fundamental contention was sound. In modern language, the existence of an uncontrolled legislative power in the House of Lords was inconsistent with the principles of democracy upon which the Constitution was built.

It is true that, by 1911, the House of Lords had adopted the principle that its power was to be exercised only so as to secure that the House of Commons was supported by the electorate. On this principle it

[1] See a short account, from a Conservative point of view, in Esher, *Influence of King Edward*, pp. 68–72.

[2] Quoted Esher, *Influence of King Edward*, pp. 82–3.

rejected the Budget of 1909 and passed it after the first general election of 1910. But the history of its action from 1892 to 1895, and from 1906 to 1910, and its inaction when a Conservative Government was in power, can be brought into the principle only if it is assumed that everything which a Conservative Government proposed had the approval of the electorate and that very little which a Liberal Government proposed had that approval. The practical working of the principle, in other words, assumed that the electorate was always Conservative except at some general elections.

The precedent of 1911 was based upon that of 1832, though the action of the Liberal Government was in some respects more careful of the privileges of the House of Lords than that of the Whig Government. The Whig Government took office after a general election late in 1830. It is true, as Mr Asquith said,[1] that there was no Reform Bill before the country in 1830. But there had been a long period of agitation, there had been Bills suggesting modest reforms in the House of Commons, and Reform was the main issue of the election—in so far as any election before 1832 could be said to have an issue.[2] The Bill was introduced in March 1831; on 22 March it was given a second reading by a majority of one; on 19 April the Government was defeated in Committee; and Parliament was dissolved on 22 April by the King in person, in order to forestall an address from the House of Lords not to dissolve Parliament.

The Government secured an enormous majority, and the Bill passed the House of Commons at the end of September. On 8 October the House of Lords rejected the Bill on second reading by a majority of forty-one. The Cabinet decided to remain in office on condition of having the King's support for a new Bill of equal efficacy. The third Bill was introduced and read a second time on 12 December. On 2 January 1832 the Cabinet agreed to recommend an immediate creation of some peers, as evidence of the Government's intention to secure the passage of the Bill. The King did not immediately consent, but asked for the Cabinet's advice in writing. In the meantime, Lord Wharncliffe, who led the section of peers (called 'the Waverers') which

[1] *Life of Lord Oxford and Asquith*, I, p. 319.

[2] Butler, *The Passing of the Great Reform Bill*, chs. I–III, especially pp. 83 and 97.

was seeking a compromise, saw the King, and several other peers exercised their right of audience. On 13 January the Cabinet drafted a long formal minute of advice, setting out the Cabinet's view of the political situation, and emphasising that the power to create peers was the means available for preventing the House of Lords from 'continuing to place itself in opposition to the general wishes of the nation, and to the declared sense of the House of Commons'. This remedy could, however, only be used 'for the purpose of producing a change of conduct in the House of Lords, when the opinion of the people, strongly and generally expressed and identified with that of their representatives, leaves no other hope of terminating the existing division'. They accordingly advised that, as soon as it was evident that the Government was not able to secure the passage of the Bill, enough peers should be created to secure the success of the Bill.[1]

The King gave his consent, subject to the 'irrevocable condition' that the creations of new peers should not exceed three, the rest being heirs and Scottish and Irish peers.[2] The Bill was sent up to the House of Lords on 26 March. On the next day the Cabinet decided to recommend an immediate prorogation, followed by a creation of peers, if the Lords rejected the Bill. The King's reply showed that there were still reservations to his pledge to create peers. On 14 April the Bill passed its second reading by a majority of nine. But on going into Committee on 7 May the House agreed, by a majority of thirty-five, to postpone consideration of the disfranchising clauses.

The Cabinet met next day and drafted a minute advising the creation of such a number of peers 'as might ensure the success of the Bill in all its essential principles, and as might give to your Majesty's servants the strength which is necessary for conducting with effect the business of the country'.[3] On 9 May the King wrote that he 'cannot reconcile it to what he considers to be his duty, and to be the principles which should govern him in the exercise of his prerogative which the Constitution of this country has entrusted to him, to consent to so large an addition to the peerage as that which has been mentioned to him by Lord Grey

[1] Grey, *Correspondence with William IV and Sir Herbert Taylor*, II, pp. 96–102.
[2] *Ibid.* II, p. 113.
[3] *Ibid.* II, p. 394; *Taylor Papers*, p. 342.

and the Chancellor to be necessary'[1] and requesting the members of the Cabinet to remain in office until he had made other arrangements.[2]

The resignation of ministers was announced to Parliament, and the House of Commons proceeded to pass with a majority of eighty an address to the King praying him to 'call to his Council such persons only as will carry into effect, unimpaired in all its essential provisions, that Bill for Reforming the Representation of the People which has recently passed this House'. The King nevertheless sent for Lord Lyndhurst and asked him to consider whether an administration could be formed on the basis of moderate but extensive reform. The Duke of Wellington agreed to support the proposal, but Sir Robert Peel refused. The King then sent for the Duke, who was commissioned to form a Government, though not necessarily as Prime Minister. But Peel's opposition, and above all the attitude of the House of Commons, made the task impossible, and on 15 May the Duke resigned his commission.

The King at once proposed to Grey that the Bill should be passed by agreement, without the creation of peers. The old Cabinet met the same day and replied that 'they could not continue in their present situation ...except with a sufficient security that they will possess the power of passing the present Bill, unimpaired in its principles, and its essential provisions, and as nearly as possible in its present form'.[3] The King, however, drew attention to a statement by Mr Baring, the temporary Tory leader of the House of Commons, suggesting that an assurance might be given that the Bill would be allowed to pass. A Cabinet minute was drawn up in answer on 16 May, stating that the two possibilities were a cessation of opposition, and a creation of peers. They did not believe that the former was practicable, but as they wished to avoid the latter, they asked permission to hold over an answer until the 18th. On the morning of 17 May the King sent, through Sir Henry Taylor, a letter to the Duke and some of his followers, pointing out that a declaration in the House of Lords, by a sufficient number of peers, that they had resolved to drop opposition to the Bill, would remove all

[1] The minute was presented by Lords Grey and Brougham, who had mentioned the figure of fifty.

[2] Grey, *Correspondence with King William IV and Sir Henry Taylor*, II, p. 396; *Taylor Papers*, p. 343.

[3] Grey, *op. cit.* II, p. 411; *Taylor Papers*, pp. 347–8.

difficulties.[1] A copy was sent to Lord Grey. No such declarations were made, but the Duke and others informed the King that they would take no further part in the discussion of the Bill. The Cabinet, in a minute of 18 May, nevertheless asked for 'full and indisputable security' to carry the Bill.[2] The King at length gave his consent verbally. In a letter written the same evening he stated his willingness to give the necessary security.

With this view His Majesty authorises Lord Grey, if any obstacle should arise during the further progress of the Bill, to submit to him a creation of peers to such an extent as shall be necessary to enable him to carry the Bill, always bearing in mind that it has been, and still is, his Majesty's object to avoid any permanent increase in the peerage, and, therefore, that this addition to the House of Peers, if, unfortunately, it should become necessary, shall comprehend as large a proportion of the eldest sons of Peers and collateral heirs of childless Peers as can possibly be brought forward. In short, that the list of eldest sons and collaterals who can be brought forward shall be completely exhausted before any list be resorted to which can entail a permanent addition to the peerage.[3]

It was then announced in both Houses that, as the Government had the means to carry through the Bill unimpaired with efficiency, its members remained in office.

Sir Henry Taylor allowed it to be known that the King had consented to an unlimited creation of peers. Possibly as a result, the Bill passed through Committee, was read a third time on 4 June, and received the Royal assent on 7 June. It is pointed out by Lord Esher[4] that the King was 'well aware', when he gave his final promise, that no further obstacle would arise. The conclusion which Lord Esher desired to be drawn was, presumably, that the events of 1832 formed no precedent.[5] But, in truth, it is immaterial whether the King did or did not expect that his permission would need to be used. By giving his consent, he recognised that, if there proved to be no other way of securing the

[1] Grey, *Correspondence with King William IV and Sir Henry Taylor*, II, p. 420; *Taylor Papers*, pp. 351–2.

[2] Grey, *op. cit.* II, p. 432.

[3] *Ibid.* II, p. 434.

[4] *Influence of King Edward*, p. 78.

[5] The article in question appeared as letters in *The Times* between December 1909 and April 1910. As to its purpose, cf. *ibid.* p. 67.

passage of the Bill, peers would be created. Nor, indeed, was this last letter the first recognition. It was the last of a series; and the earlier sanctions differed from the last only in that the final permission was for an unspecified and therefore unlimited number. What is more, it is by no means certain that the famous letters of 17 May, in which the King asked the Duke and others to declare that they would allow the Bill to pass, were effective. They certainly obtained from the Duke a private promise to abstain from the further proceedings on the Bill. But it is by no means so certain that a sufficient number of peers would have followed his lead. What really secured the passage of the third Bill was the knowledge that the alternative was the creation of a substantial number of peers. Lord Brougham confessed to doubts, twelve years later, as to whether he would have assented to a creation of peers if the Lords had not given way.[1] Brougham's confessions are not to be taken too seriously. Nor is much attention to be paid to his recollection of his state of mind twelve years before. In any case, what matters is not what the Government would have done, but what it obtained authority to do.

Bagehot said that the Reform Act of 1867 completed the work of the Act of 1832 by giving the House of Commons preponderance over the House of Lords. Thus it was necessary 'to frame such tacit rules to establish such ruling but unenacted customs, as will make the House of Lords yield to the Commons when and as often as our new Constitution requires that it should yield'. This is 'whenever the opinion of the Commons is also the opinion of the nation, and when it is clear that the nation has made up its mind'. He did not suggest that the House of Lords, like a dog, was always entitled to two bites, for the fact that a Bill has been produced once or several times is an important factor, but not the only factor. 'The House of Lords ought, on a first-class subject, to be slow—very slow—in rejecting a Bill passed even once by a large majority of the House of Commons.'[2]

Such a doctrine would have compelled the House of Lords to have accepted the second Home Rule Bill (unless it could be asserted that the Irish people were not part of 'the nation'). Mr Gladstone denied the

[1] Brougham, *Political Philosophy* (2nd ed.), III, p. 308.

[2] Bagehot, *Parliamentary Reform*, pp. 201–3.

whole doctrine of the two bites. 'At no period of our history...has the House of Commons been dissolved at the call of the House of Lords, given through an adverse vote;...the establishment of such a principle would place the House of Commons in a position of inferiority, as a legislative chamber, to the House of Lords.'[1] Nevertheless, the House of Lords insisted on biting the Finance Bill of 1909 once before it swallowed it. In the view of the Liberal Government of the day, it became necessary to abolish the power of the House of Lords to compel a dissolution.[2]

The King's chief adviser at this time was Lord Esher, a former Conservative politician who had made himself useful about the court, especially as a constitutional adviser. He was in communication with Lord Haldane, who was, apparently, fishing for information as to the attitude of Edward VII. Lord Esher asserts that, before the first election of 1910, the Cabinet was discussing whether, instead of attempting to alter by statute the relations between the two Houses, they should advise the King to place permanently in the hands of the Prime Minister of the day the prerogative of creating peers. The alternative was a Bill introduced with the statement that the King had promised to create a sufficient number of peers to pass the measure. This information was passed on to the King's private secretary with the comment that either proposal was an 'outrage'. Queen Anne's precedent was only for the creation of twelve peers. The case of 1832 was no precedent 'as no peers were created, and it is by no means certain that the King would in the last resort have made them'.[3] This last statement is obviously based on Lord Brougham's subsequent comment. Apart from what was said above, it leads to the assumption that the precedent created in 1832 was that the King might promise to create peers and subsequently refuse to carry out his promise. Lord Esher further suggested that the grave aspect of Lord Haldane's information was the desire of the Government to secure a promise before the general election (the first of 1910). This Lord Esher regarded as a 'monstrous proposal', and he suggested that, if made, it should be met with a firm refusal.[4]

[1] *Letters of Queen Victoria*, 2nd series, III, p. 518.

[2] See Mr Asquith's subsequent comment, *Life of Lord Oxford and Asquith*, II, p. 33.

[3] *Esher Papers*, II, pp. 423–4.

[4] *Ibid.* II, pp. 424–5.

Lord Esher discussed the matter with Mr Balfour, though there is no evidence that it was done at the King's suggestion. Mr Balfour agreed that the King ought not under any circumstances to make a promise before the introduction of a Bill to deal with the House of Lords. He considered that if the suggestion were made a reasoned answer should be given pointing out that:

(*a*) there was no crisis necessitating urgency, because Lord Lansdowne pledged the House of Lords to pass the Budget if the Liberals were returned to power;
(*b*) it would be a breach of the King's duty, if not of his Coronation oath, to pledge himself to create peers to pass a Bill which he had never seen;
(*c*) there was no precedent for asking the Sovereign to use his prerogative to pass through the House of Lords a measure which had not even obtained the assent of the House of Commons;
(*d*) though there might be some justification for asking him to use his prerogative to pass a Bill which had already received the assent of an overwhelming majority of the House of Commons, there was none for asking him to promise to use it for the purpose of passing ultimately through the House of Lords a Bill which the House of Commons had not even seen;
(*e*) as regards the principle of the use of the prerogative, he must refuse to discuss it, as the principle was entirely dependent upon the circumstances.[1]

Mr Balfour added that Mr Asquith might resign in consequence, and the King would probably send for Mr Balfour and authorise him to state in Parliament the dilemma in which the ministers had placed the King. He felt confident that the King would be supported by the country.[2] Mr Balfour put his views into a memorandum.[3] When the election results were known, Lord Esher wrote a memorandum for the King and communicated Mr Balfour's views.[4] It is not clear whether Mr Balfour's memorandum was shown to the King, though it seems unlikely that Mr Balfour would write such a document merely for Lord Esher's edification.

In the meantime, Lord Knollys had already informed Mr Asquith during the dissolution, without his asking, that the King 'had come to

[1] *Esher Papers*, II, pp. 435–6.
[2] *Ibid.* II. p. 436.
[3] *Ibid.* II, p. 437.
[4] *Ibid.* II, pp. 441, 442.

the conclusion that he would not be justified in creating new peers (say 300) until after a second general election'. Further,

the King regards the policy of the Government as tantamount to the destruction of the House of Lords, and he thinks that before a large creation of peers is embarked upon or threatened the country should be acquainted with the particular project for accomplishing such destruction as well as with the general line of action as to which the country will be consulted at the forthcoming election.[1]

Language which Mr Asquith used in an election speech caused some to believe that the necessary 'guarantees' for the passing of a Bill to limit the powers of the House of Lords had been obtained. The King therefore asked to know the intention of the Government. The Cabinet drafted a formal minute:

His Majesty's ministers do not propose to advise or request any exercise of the Royal prerogative in existing circumstances, or until they have submitted their plan to Parliament. If in their judgment, it should become their duty to tender such advice, they would do so when—and not before—the actual necessity may arise.[2]

This was on 11 February 1910, after the Government had secured a substantial, though reduced, majority at the first general election of that year.

On 21 February as soon as possible after the meeting of Parliament, Mr Asquith made the position clear in the House of Commons.

I tell the House quite frankly that I have received no such guarantee, and that I have asked for no such guarantee. In my judgment it is the duty of statesmen and of responsible politicians in this country as long as possible and as far as possible to keep the name of the Sovereign and the prerogatives of the Crown outside the domain of party politics. If the occasion should arise, I should not hesitate to tender such advice to the Crown as in the circumstances the exigencies of the situation appear to warrant in the public interests. But to ask in advance for a blank authority for an indefinite exercise of the Royal prerogative in regard to a measure which has never been submitted to or approved by the House of Commons is a request which, in my judgment, no constitutional statesman can properly make, and it is a concession which the Sovereign cannot be expected to grant.[3]

[1] *Life of Lord Oxford and Asquith*, I, p. 261.
[2] *Ibid.* I, p. 273.
[3] 14 H.C.Deb. 5 s., 55–6.

Resolutions designed to form the basis of the Parliament Bill were introduced on 29 March and disposed of by 14 April, when the Parliament Bill was read a first time. On the latter date Mr Asquith explained the next step:

If the Lords fail to accept our policy, or decline to consider it as it is formally presented to the House, we shall feel it our duty immediately to tender advice to the Crown as to the steps which will have to be taken if that policy is to receive statutory effect in this Parliament. What the precise terms of that advice will be...it will, of course, not be right for me to say now; but if we do not find ourselves in a position to ensure that statutory effect shall be given to that policy in this Parliament, we shall then either resign our offices or recommend the dissolution of Parliament. Let me add this, that in no case will we recommend a dissolution except under such conditions as will secure that in the new Parliament the judgment of the people as expressed at the elections will be carried into law.[1]

On 27 April a meeting was held at Lambeth Palace which was clearly suggested by the King, since it was summoned by the Archbishop of Canterbury at the request of Lord Knollys. Besides the Archbishop and Lord Knollys there were present only Lord Esher and Mr Balfour. Thus, the purpose of the meeting was obviously to enable the King to find out Mr Balfour's views on the creation of peers. The Archbishop expressed the view that if the King was asked to create 500 peers to pass the Parliament Bill through the then Parliament his course seemed clear, but that it was not so clear what he should do if he were asked to grant a dissolution coupled with a promise to create peers in the event of a Liberal majority being returned after the election.[2]

Mr Balfour carefully refrained from expressing a positive opinion, but the bent of his mind was clearly in favour of the King's refusing a promise. He said that the refusal, if decided upon, should be in a carefully worded document. 'It would require care, but...a satisfactory document could be framed, and, if successfully framed, would add lustre to the position of the Sovereign.'[3] He pointed out that if the Government's proposal were refused the Government would resign, he, Mr Balfour, would then form a Government, and immediately ask the King to grant him a dissolution. There was some discussion on

[1] 16 H.C.Deb. 5 s., 1548. [2] *Esher Papers*, II, pp. 456–7. [3] *Ibid.* II, p. 457.

a possible compromise, and the precedent of 1884[1] was referred to. Mr Balfour said that he could see no objection to the King's proposing a compromise, but did not commit himself as to whether a compromise was possible.[2]

What the King would have done is an open question, though Lord Oxford's biographers express the view that King Edward would have done what his successor did.[3] King Edward died on 7 May. His death changed the situation, and with the consent of the new king Mr Asquith discussed with Mr Balfour the holding of a Conference to make some attempt to settle the problem by agreement. It met on 17 June, the Government being represented by Mr Asquith, Mr Lloyd George, Lord Crewe and Mr Birrell, and the Opposition by Mr Balfour, Lord Lansdowne, Mr Austen Chamberlain and Lord Cawdor. It failed, however, to reach agreement,[4] and the position was thus restored to that existing at the death of King Edward.

The last meeting of the Conference was held on 10 November. On the same day the Cabinet decided to ask the King for an immediate dissolution. On the following day Mr Asquith informed the King that it was necessary that, in the event of the Government obtaining an adequate majority in the new Parliament, the matter should be put in train for final settlement. In theory the Crown might withhold writs of summons to peers.

> But this has not been done for many centuries; it would be most invidious in practice; and it is at least doubtful whether it can be said to be constitutional. On the other hand the prerogative of creation [of Peers] is undoubted; it has never been recognised as having any constitutional limit; it was used for this very purpose in the 18th century, and agreed to be used on a large scale by King William IV in 1832. There could be, in Mr Asquith's opinion, no doubt that the knowledge that the Crown was ready to use the prerogative would be sufficient to bring about an agreement without any necessity for its actual exercise.[5]

[1] Above, pp. 383–4.
[2] *Esher Papers*, II, pp. 458–9.
[3] *Life of Lord Oxford and Asquith*, I, pp. 279–80. This opinion is based upon the King's statement quoted above, p. 437; but presumably the authors of the book were unaware of the Archbishop's informal conference.
[4] For the Constitutional Conference, see *Life of Lord Oxford and Asquith*, I, pp. 285–91; *Life of Lord Lansdowne*, pp. 396–403.
[5] *Life of Lord Oxford and Asquith*, I, p. 296; Nicolson, *King George V*, p. 134.

Mr Asquith did not ask for an immediate reply. It seems, however, that King George and his private secretary misunderstood the purport of the discussion. Mr Asquith intended to prepare the King for the advice which he would subsequently receive from the Cabinet, while the King thought that no guarantee for the creation of peers would be sought before the election. Three days later Lord Knollys discovered that the King was mistaken, and Sir Arthur Bigge was instructed to telegraph that it would be impossible for the King to give contingent guarantees.[1] The King 'much resented the implication' that in the event of a Liberal Government being returned he might fail to act constitutionally; and he considered that Mr Asquith was seeking to use his name to secure a Liberal victory.[2] On 15 November the Cabinet gave the following advice in a formal minute:

An immediate dissolution of Parliament—as soon as the necessary parts of the Budget, the provision of old age pensions, and one or two other matters have been disposed of. The House of Lords to have the opportunity, if they demand it,[3] at the same time, but not so as to postpone the date of the dissolution, to discuss the Government Resolution. H.M. Ministers cannot, however, take the responsibility of advising a dissolution unless they may understand that in the event of the policy of the Government being approved by an adequate majority in the new House of Commons, H.M. will be ready to exercise his constitutional powers (which may involve the prerogative of creating peers) if needed, to secure that effect shall be given to the decision of the country.

H.M. Ministers are fully alive to the importance of keeping the name of the King out of the sphere of party and electoral controversy. They take upon themselves, as is their duty, the entire and exclusive responsibility for the policy which they will place before the electorate. H.M. will doubtless agree that it would be inadvisable in the interest of the State that any communication of the intentions of the Crown should be made public unless and until the actual occasion should arise.[4]

[1] Nicolson, *op. cit.* p. 134.

[2] *Ibid.* p. 135.

[3] 'if they desired it' in Nicolson, *op. cit.* p. 136.

[4] This is the version in *Life of Lord Oxford and Asquith*, I, pp. 296–7. Apart from the alteration in the previous footnote, there are slight variations of punctuation, etc., in the version in Nicolson, *op. cit.* p. 136. For the controversy between Lord Knollys, advising the King's acceptance, and Sir Arthur Bigge, strongly objecting, see Nicolson, *op. cit.* pp. 137–8.

Mr Asquith and Lord Crewe (as leader of the House of Lords) saw the King on the following day. The King, after much discussion, 'agreed most reluctantly to give the Cabinet a secret understanding that, in the event of the Government being returned with a majority at the general election, I should use my prerogative to make peers if asked for. I disliked having to do this very much, but agreed that this was the only alternative to the Cabinet resigning, which at this moment would be disastrous.'[1]

The 'secret understanding' was due only to Mr Asquith's unfortunate speech of 14 April.[2] He was thought to have pledged himself to secure guarantees or resign. The 'secret understanding' was a compromise. It would enable Mr Asquith to say afterwards that they had not recommended a dissolution except on the conditions specified on 14 April. On the other hand the secrecy would meet the King's objection that the purpose of the guarantee was to make use of his name for catching votes. In other words, it was a device to save Mr Asquith's face.

The King insisted that the Parliament Bill should be submitted to the House of Lords before the election. To this Mr Asquith agreed, and the Bill was read a first time and discussed on second reading in the House of Lords before the dissolution. The elections then proceeded on the issue raised by the Bill, and the Government's position was substantially unchanged. At no time was any public announcement or private communication made that the King had consented to a creation of peers, if necessary.

On 12 December Lord Morley (who, of course, knew that the King had already consented) told Sir Almeric Fitzroy that he thought the position of the King was particularly difficult,

> as, if the demand should be made for him to create 500 peers, he thought he would have very good reason for refusing, doubtful as the consequences might be....He believed that Arthur Balfour would take office if, owing to the King's refusal, the Government would resign. Of course, another dissolution would follow, when he thought it likely that the country, in despair of any other expedient, would give the Unionists a majority.[3]

[1] Nicolson, *King George V*, p. 138; and see *Life of Lord Oxford and Asquith*, I, p. 398; and *Life of Lord Lansdowne*, p. 410.

[2] Above, p. 438.

[3] Fitzroy, *Memoirs*, II, p. 427.

Mr Balfour (who did not know of the King's promise) was of a different opinion. Writing to Lord Lansdowne on 27 December, he thought that no alternative to consent to create peers was possible. To change a Ministry without a dissolution was a confession of impotence, and in the absence of almost unthinkable provocation, a dissolution in February following on a dissolution in the preceding December, which itself followed on a dissolution in the preceding January, would be so unpopular that the Ministry which advised it could hardly expect to gain by it. The King would have to work with the present Government, and within rather wide limits they could compel him to take any course they pleased by threatening resignation.[1]

On 27 January the King saw Lord Lansdowne, and Lord Knollys had previously seen Mr Balfour. Mr Asquith had, apparently, at first objected, but the King said that he wanted not advice but the views of the Opposition. Mr Asquith had then reluctantly withdrawn his objection.[2] The King did not explain that he had already consented to a creation of peers, if necessary, but mentioned the possibility of his being asked. Lord Lansdowne said that he could conceive that the step might become inevitable, but it was one which had been universally condemned, as violently straining the Constitution. It was a step which, he felt sure, the King would be reluctant to take and ministers to advise; and he thought it not unfair to say that, up to a certain point, they would be justified in bearing this fact in mind when considering whether it was advisable to offer resistance to the Government proposals. The King then discussed the improbability of Mr Balfour's being able to form a Government and to go to the country, supposing that the King were to send for him. Lord Lansdowne agreed with the King and said that he did not see that Mr Balfour would stand a chance at an immediate election on the same issue.[3]

[1] *Life of Lord Lansdowne*, p. 407. On the other hand, Mr Balfour would have taken office if the King had refused to give the undertaking and the Government had resigned, and he would have had 'great hopes of carrying the country with me': Nicolson, *King George V*, p. 149. This shows the wisdom of the King in accepting the advice, for the Opposition would have played the King as their trump card. On the other hand, it also explains in part the emotion which Home Rule generated. The Opposition felt that the Government had played a dirty trick on the Sovereign in order to save Mr Asquith's face.

[2] *Life of Lord Lansdowne*, p. 409.

[3] This was, of course, on the facts as known to Mr Balfour and Lord Lansdowne.

But as the situation developed, it might undergo a change.[1] He warned the King not to take it for granted 'that in no circumstances might the House of Lords take a line which would render it impossible for him to overcome them except by the creation of peers'.[2]

The Parliament Bill went to the House of Lords on 23 May. It was read a second time without a division. It was in Committee from 28 June to 14 July, where it was completely transformed. As soon as this stage was over, a Cabinet minute was drafted, drawing the King's attention to the fact that the House of Commons could not be advised to accept the Bill as it now stood, that a deadlock between the two Houses would be created, and that a third dissolution was wholly out of the question. 'Hence, in the contingency contemplated, it will be the duty of ministers to advise the Crown to exercise its prerogative so as to get rid of the deadlock and secure the passing of the Bill. In such circumstances ministers cannot entertain any doubt that the Sovereign would feel it to be his constitutional duty to accept their advice.'[3] Three days later the King intimated that he would accept the advice.[4]

On 18 July Mr Lloyd George met Mr Balfour and Lord Lansdowne, and stated that a pledge to create peers had been obtained from the King in November. He also suggested that a formal notification should be made privately to the Opposition leaders. On the next day, as a result of communications between Mr Balfour and Lord Knollys, Lord Lansdowne asked Lord Knollys to call upon him. He suggested that the King's formal communication should be in writing, though it did not matter whether it was written by Lord Knollys or by the Prime Minister on the King's authority. Lord Knollys said that the King hoped that an intimation that peers would be created as a last resort would suffice for the purpose of passing the Bill without material amendments. It was ultimately agreed that Mr Asquith should communicate in writing the King's intention.[5] Mr Asquith insisted that the intimation should come from him, and as soon as the Bill was read a third time on 20 July, he sent formal notes to Mr Balfour and Lord Lansdowne stating that, should the necessity arise, the Government

[1] *Life of Lord Lansdowne*, p. 410.
[2] *Ibid.* p. 411.
[3] *Life of Lord Oxford and Asquith*, I, p. 310.
[4] *Ibid.* I, p. 310.
[5] *Life of Lord Lansdowne*, pp. 417–19.

would advise the King to exercise his prerogative to secure the enactment of the Bill in substantially the same form in which it left the House of Commons, and that the King had signified that he would accept and act upon that advice.[1]

On 21 July this information was communicated by Lord Lansdowne to a meeting of Unionist peers. A summary of its proceedings was, apparently, sent to the King by Lord Lansdowne. Lord Lansdowne and others agreed that the Bill ought to be allowed to pass, though there was a substantial section which disagreed. On 24 July the King saw Lord Lansdowne, but, though he mentioned that he and his advisers were anxious to avoid a large creation of peers, he did not, apparently, attempt to influence the action of the Unionist peers.[2]

On 24 July the Lords' amendments were considered by the House of Commons. Mr Asquith intended to announce publicly the Government's advice and its acceptance, but was shouted down.[3] He proposed to say that the precedent of 1832 was 'what the lawyers call a case precisely in point' and to give in some detail a history of that precedent.[4] On 7 and 8 August votes of censure were moved in the House of Commons and the House of Lords respectively on the double ground that the advice was a gross violation of constitutional liberty and that the people would be precluded from again pronouncing on the policy of Home Rule. In order to keep the King's action out of controversy as much as possible, Lord Crewe, with the King's leave, explained what had taken place at the interview of 16 November 1910.

On 8 August the House of Commons rejected the Lords' amendments, with one exception, and made a concession on another. On 9 August the Bill, as amended, was returned to the Lords. Lord Morley, with the King's sanction, informed the House that 'if the Bill should be defeated to-night his Majesty will assent to the creation of peers sufficient in numbers to guard against any possible combination of the different parties in opposition by which the Parliament Bill might be exposed a second time to defeat'.[5] The Government secured a majority of seventeen and the creation of peers then became unnecessary.

[1] *Life of Lord Oxford and Asquith*, I, pp. 212–13.

[2] *Life of Lord Lansdowne*, pp. 421–5. [3] *Life of Lord Oxford and Asquith*, I, p. 314.

[4] See the text of the undelivered speech, *ibid.* I, pp. 315–20.

[5] Morley, *Recollections*, II, p. 353.

The precedent of 1911 differs from that of 1832 in several respects:

(1) In 1831 the Government was defeated in the House of Commons and appealed to the country for that reason. In 1910 the Government was not defeated on the Parliament Bill in that House and was not defeated in the House of Lords until after the second election. The Bill was the consequence of the rejection of the Finance Bill, 1909. The first general election was primarily an appeal to the country on the latter Bill. A second general election became necessary to give the Government a 'mandate' for the Parliament Bill. Thus, in 1910 as in 1831 the Government had the approval of the electorate before the House of Lords was asked for a decision.

(2) In 1831 the (second) Reform Bill was defeated in the House of Lords. A third Bill was introduced in the House of Commons and the King's assent to the creation of peers was obtained before this Bill went to the Lords. In 1910–11 there were two Bills only, and the King's assent to the creation of peers, if necessary, was obtained before either the House of Lords or the electors had been specifically consulted on the principle of the Bill.[1]

(3) In 1831 the King's assent was conditional, the Government was defeated in the House of Lords on the third Bill, and when the advice was given to create peers the King refused. The Government then resigned and an attempt was made by the Opposition to form a Government. This failing, the Government resumed office, and then secured sanction for the creation of peers if necessary. In 1910 the King's assent was conditioned only by the return of the Liberal Government after the second general election, and by the necessity of the creation to pass the Bill. Consequently, when the Government was defeated in the House of Lords, the King's formal assent was given and the Government did not resign.

(4) In 1831–2 the King did not communicate with the Opposition until the resignation of the Government. In 1910 the King saw the leaders of the Opposition in order to obtain information as to their views.

(5) In 1832 the King actively intervened in an attempt to secure the acceptance of the Bill by the Opposition in the House of Lords. In 1910 an attempt was made by a constitutional conference to obtain a compromise. But the King himself did not intervene.

(6) In 1832 the King's final decision was made known by ministers in Parliament. In 1911 the King's decision was first communicated by ministers to the leaders of the Opposition.

(7) In neither case was the creation of peers necessary, since a sufficient number of peers abstained from voting.

[1] Lord Lansdowne considered that it was constitutional to ask for a creation of peers after the second election but not before: *Life of Randall Davidson*, I, p. 627.

The application of these precedents to any future dispute between the two Houses is complicated by the means now available for overcoming the opposition of the House of Lords under the Parliament Acts. A Money Bill so certified by the Speaker may become an Act of Parliament without the consent of the House of Lords if it is sent up at least one month before the end of the session and is not passed by the House of Lords within one month of its being sent up. A Public Bill (other than a Money Bill or a Bill extending the maximum duration of Parliament) may become an Act of Parliament without the consent of the House of Lords if it is passed in two successive sessions (whether of the same Parliament or not), and, having been sent up at least one month before the end of the session, is rejected by the House of Lords in each of those sessions, provided that one year has elapsed between the date of the second reading in the House of Commons in the first session and the date of its passing the House of Commons in the second session; and a Bill is to be deemed to be rejected if it is not passed either without amendment or with such amendments only as may be agreed to by both Houses.

It is clear that, in relation to Bills which come within the definition of 'Money Bill', no question of creating peers to overcome the opposition of the House of Lords can arise. The opposition will be ineffectual after the expiry of a month. 'Public Bills' are not, however, defined by the Act, except that it is provided that a Bill confirming a Provisional Order is not a Public Bill. Nor is there any other legal definition of Public Bill. Each House determines by its standing orders what Bills are to be termed private or hybrid. The Act speaks of a Public Bill which is 'passed by the House of Commons'. It seems, therefore, that a Bill is Public if it is passed by the House of Commons as a Public Bill. Since the House can always suspend standing orders so as to pass as Public a Bill which would otherwise be dealt with as a Private Bill or as a Hybrid Bill, it follows that the only Bills which cannot be passed under the Parliament Acts are (1) Bills to extend the maximum duration of Parliament, and (2) Bills to confirm Provisional Orders. A Bill to amend the Parliament Acts can be passed under those Acts.

With the two exceptions noticed, the House of Commons can secure the passing of any legislation it pleases within the space of little more than one year. It is unlikely that any question of creating peers would be raised in connection with the exceptions. It is therefore a question whether the power of creating peers could ever be used to overcome the opposition of the House of Lords.

It is not doubted that the prerogative remains. The only question is whether the Sovereign would be bound to assent to its use. It is clear that the power to refuse is extant. It was never suggested, either in 1832 or in 1910, that the King was bound to accept the advice of his ministers. In 1832, indeed, William IV accepted his ministers' resignations rather than consent to the creation of fifty peers. But that example also showed that he can in fact refuse only if an alternative Government is possible. He would be bound either to dissolve Parliament at the request of the Government with a majority, or to accept its resignation and to grant a dissolution to the new minority Government. It is true that a minority Government could remain in office for a time without a dissolution. It is commonly said that the House of Commons could 'refuse supplies'. But once the Appropriation Act has been passed the Government can remain in office until the resolutions under the Army and Air Force Acts have to be passed, assuming that it need not produce supplementary estimates or that it can meet additional expenditure out of the Civil Contingencies Fund or out of money borrowed under the Appropriation Act. This provides, however, a maximum period of only eight months. Moreover, if the Finance Act has not been passed, the levying of income tax and duties of customs and excise provided by annual votes becomes illegal under the Provisional Collection of Taxes Act, 1913.

A dissolution is thus inevitable. If the majority Government is compelled to resign, it is inevitable that the Sovereign's action should be the subject of controversy at the general election. If, however, a contingent promise to create peers is given, the action can be kept secret and thus preserved from controversy until the election is over, as in 1910. There was no justification for the 'secret understanding' in 1910; but, as we have seen, the King could not have refused without making his refusal the subject of party controversy. Thus, the Parliament Acts have altered the situation only in that (1) the question cannot arise in respect of a Money Bill, (2) the question is not likely to arise in respect of any other Bill unless the Government regards it as sufficiently urgent and fundamental to risk a general election, and (3) the House of Lords, knowing that its opposition can be overborne, is less likely to proceed to extreme opposition. The second point is particularly important, since many amendments can be forced upon the Government because of its reluctance to run the risk of a general election.

§5. *The Personal Prerogatives and Ministerial Responsibility*

It has frequently been asserted that for every act of the monarch some minister is responsible.[1] Undoubtedly the ordinary legal acts of the Queen, referred to in the last chapter, are in fact the acts of ministers, who are responsible for them to Parliament. It is a little difficult, however, to see what 'responsibility' means in relation to the personal prerogatives. The question arose over the dismissal of the Whigs in 1807. There were then discussions in both Houses as to whether the King's act was one for which he was personally responsible or whether the Tories, by taking office, became responsible.[2] In 1835 Peel admitted that by taking office he became technically responsible for the 'dismissal' of Lord Melbourne's Government.[3] The Duke of Wellington, on the other hand, denied that the new Government became responsible, and even Baron Stockmar thought the doctrine to be 'nonsense'.

Hearn[4] had some difficulty in understanding what the doctrine meant. 'No man can be criminally responsible for an act which he neither did nor advised, and to which he was not in any way privy'—and, it should be added, it is not in any event a criminal offence to dismiss ministers. 'It can hardly be contended that any person would be liable to impeachment or any other proceeding on the sole ground that at his Sovereign's command he had accepted office under the Crown, even though prior to his acceptance of such office the prerogative had been wrongly or even criminally exercised'—and, what is more, impeachment is as obsolete as the dodo and it is neither actionable nor criminal to dismiss ministers.

[1] Hearn, *Government of England*, p. 98; Todd, *Parliamentary Government in England* (Spencer Walpole's edition), I, pp. 73, 112.

[2] Erskine May, *Constitutional History* (5th ed.), I, pp. 109–16; Hans. Deb. 1st series, IX, 355–65. [3] Hans. Deb. 3rd series, XXVI, 216, 223; *Peel Memoirs*, II, pp. 31, 32.

[4] *Government of England*, p. 98.

But if criminal liability be thus impossible, the supposed responsibility of an incoming Minister can only mean that, in case of a difference between the Crown and Parliament respecting some exercise of the prerogative, the acceptance of office by a minister in circumstances unfavourable to the opinion of Parliament furnishes to Parliament a reasonable ground of objection to his appointment. If however there be a majority hostile to the Minister, it is not necessary to assign any reason or seek any excuse for advising the King to change his servants; and if there be not such a hostile majority, the disapprobation by either House of the dissolution or other exercise of the prerogative does not, according to modern practice, involve the necessity of resignation.

The truth is that the doctrine is a pure fiction. When it is said that a minister is responsible to Parliament, it is meant that the House of Commons has a right to demand an explanation. If that explanation is not considered satisfactory and the responsibility is collective, the House will vote against the Government and so compel a resignation or a dissolution. In fact, however, as will be explained more fully in a later chapter, such an event rarely happens. If the responsibility is not collective, but the act or advice was due to the negligence of or to an error of judgment by a minister, and the House disapproves, the minister will resign. But to suggest that the House can demand an explanation for a personal act of the monarch from a Government which had nothing to do with it, or that the House will censure a Government for an act which the Queen decided upon in the exercise of her personal prerogatives, is nonsense. If a Government acquiesces in a royal act of which it disapproves, it is answerable for its acquiescence. If it does not acquiesce but resigns, and a new Government is formed, the only question is whether that Government has a majority or can secure a majority at the next election.

Nor can the fiction protect the Queen from attack. A monarch who insists on a dissolution or, what is really the same thing, compels the resignations of ministers, will be attacked as a partisan in the House and in the country. No doubt the incoming Government will be attacked too. But all Governments are attacked, and it is the nature of our democratic system that they should be attacked. The impartial person —if such there be—would hold that the acceptance of office might in some circumstances be unconstitutional. But it could never be unconstitutional if the Government secured a majority in the House of Commons or in the country as the result of a personal act of the Queen. This does not mean, of course, that the Queen's act might not be unconstitutional; but it would not be unconstitutional to accept office with a majority merely because the Queen had compelled the resignation of the preceding Government.

CHAPTER XIV

PATRONAGE AND HONOURS

§1. *Appointments*

Lord Melbourne's famous remark, 'Damn it, another bishop dead', is succinct evidence of the difficulties attached to the comparatively unimportant function of administering the patronage vested in the Crown and exercised by ministers. Its importance was great so long as the House of Commons was 'managed' by the Crown or Government with the assistance of Treasury or Admiralty patronage. But Burke's Economy Act and other legislation and, above all, the passing of the Reform Act, immensely diminished its political value. Sir Robert Peel and Sir James Graham, too, established the system of paying more attention to merit than to political advantage.[1] 'The party interests of a Government', said Peel, 'are in the long run much better promoted by the honest exercise of patronage than by the *perversion* of it for the purpose of satisfying individual supporters.'[2] Similarly, speaking of honours, he said: 'I am resolved to consider the power of conferring them as a great public trust, to be administered on some public principle, such as, for instance, the strengthening of the Administration by rewarding those who do not hold office, or, in the case of those who do hold office, bestowing honours as the reward for public service, distinguished either by the length and fidelity of it, or by the eminence of it.'[3]

The acceptance of these principles did not imply a complete dissociation between party advantage and the exercise of powers of appointment and conferring honours. Mr Gladstone, as Member of Parliament for Oxford University, was particularly insistent in pressing the claims of his constituents on Lord Palmerston.[4] At least one bishopric was given because the person appointed had been Mr Gladstone's election agent.[5] Few Prime Ministers failed to consider the politics of

[1] See *Peel Papers*, III, ch. XV. [2] *Ibid.* III, p. 414. [3] *Ibid.* III, pp. 431–2.

[4] Guedalla, *Gladstone and Palmerston*, pp. 153–5, 187, 189, 232, 236–9, 338.

[5] *Ibid.* p. 338.

candidates for preferment, though none went so far in this direction as Mr Disraeli.[1]

The important patronage can be divided into three classes, relating respectively to public offices, the Church, and the Judiciary. Appointments of the first class are, strictly speaking, in the hands of the respective ministers. But all important posts are filled after consultation with the Prime Minister. In the most important cases of all, the Prime Minister, in substance, appoints. His consent is necessary to the appointment of the Permanent Secretaries or Permanent Under-Secretaries of State and other senior officials, acting for this purpose in consultation with the minister and the Permanent Head of the Civil Service.[2] But the relations between ministers and Prime Ministers are not strictly defined.

'The diplomatic appointments', said Sir Robert Peel in 1850, 'are disposed of immediately on the advice of the Secretary of State for Foreign Affairs, but the Secretary of State for Foreign Affairs would naturally confer on all important appointments with the First Lord of the Treasury; so, with regard to other offices, I apprehend that there is, or that there ought to be, that intimate concert and cordial union between the persons holding the highest offices in the State, that they would confer together upon every important appointment; I mean, that each head of a department would confer with the First Lord of the Treasury for example, that no colonial appointment would be made without previous communication between the Colonial Secretary and the First Lord of the Treasury. The First Lord of the Treasury would not make an appointment in any department but his own; officially and formally it would be made by the minister who presided over the department, but there would probably be communication between that minister and the First Lord of the Treasury in regard to important appointments.'[3]

[1] *Life of Disraeli*, II, pp. 397–413; *Letters of Queen Victoria*, 2nd series, I, pp. 536–7, 554–5. Todd's statement (Spencer Walpole's edition, I, p. 167), that 'as a rule the distribution of Church patronage by ministers of the Crown is not influenced by political considerations' is more nearly true today than it was when he wrote it. The reason is that the political importance of the Church has declined. Even now political considerations are not always absent. It was probably not entirely a coincidence that Bishop Barnes and Archbishop Temple were promoted on the recommendation of a Labour Prime Minister.

[2] See above, pp. 149–50.

[3] Report from the Select Committee on Official Salaries (B.P.P. 1850, XV), p. 35. For a case in which Lord Derby arbitrated between the Queen and the Secretary of State in respect of the appointment of an Ambassador to Berlin, see *Letters of Queen Victoria*, 2nd series, I, pp. 461–4.

Of the 970 or so[1] Church appointments in the gift of the Crown, some 700 are in the patronage of the Prime Minister. They are defined by the value in the King's books in the reign of Henry VIII, all those above £20 being in the gift of the Prime Minister.[2] These obviously include all bishoprics, deaneries and canonries.

The appointment of puisne judges of the High Court rests with the Lord Chancellor. But, at least up to 1850,

> The Lord Chancellor has always been in the habit of communicating to me [the Prime Minister], in case of a vacancy, who is the person that, upon inquiry, he thought fittest for the appointment; I take that rather as a piece of information and friendly concert on his part, and I should never think of interfering with his power in that respect, unless, which has never happened, his proposal was, to my mind, very objectionable; the Lord Chancellor takes the Queen's pleasure, and he swears in the new Judge; the First Lord of the Treasury has nothing to do with it.[3]

The practice which Lord Brougham followed was to take the King's pleasure and then to inform the Prime Minister.[4]

Other superior judges, including the Lords of Appeal, the Lords Justices, the Lord Chief Justice, the Master of the Rolls, the President of the Probate, Divorce and Admiralty Division, and the members of the Judicial Committee of the Privy Council, are appointed by the Prime Minister.[5] The Prime Minister usually consults the Lord Chancellor.[6] Political considerations are not, however, always excluded.[7] When the Coalition Government was formed in 1915, for instance, the Conservatives 'pegged claims' to certain judicial appointments.[8] Law Officers had had for many years 'a sort of claim' to the offices of Lord Chief Justice and Lord Chief Baron.[9] In 1873 the Cabinet recorded an opinion 'that, with the passing of the Judicature Act, all claims of either

[1] 309 H.C.Deb. 5 s., 1192.

[2] Report from the Select Committee on Official Salaries (B.P.P. 1850, xv), pp. 134–5 (Evidence of Lord John Russell).

[3] *Ibid.* p. 142.

[4] Brougham, *Life and Times*, III, pp. 86–8.

[5] Report from the Select Committee on Official Salaries (1850), p. 142.

[6] Cf. *Life of Lord Cave*, p. 263.

[7] Todd's statement to the contrary (Spencer Walpole's edition, I, p. 168), needs qualification.

[8] *Life of Lord Oxford and Asquith*, II, pp. 168–9. At least one more recent example could be quoted.

[9] Report from the Select Committee on Official Salaries (1850), p. 143.

or both Law Officers to a succession as of right to any particular judicial office (claims which were never adequately established) have naturally dropped; so that their promotion would henceforward rest on qualification and service only; not only on the possession of the post of Law Officer'.[1] Nevertheless, the Law Officers seem to have established 'a sort of claim' to the offices of Lord Chief Justice, Master of the Rolls, President of the Probate, Divorce and Admiralty Division, and Lord of Appeal in Ordinary.[2] In 1937, however, it was denied on behalf of the Prime Minister and the Law Officers that the claim had ever been made.[3]

Though, in the last resort, the Sovereign must accept advice as to the filling of such senior appointments, his capacity for resistance is, or may be, substantial. In 1893 Queen Victoria raised objections to the appointment of the Earl of Elgin as Viceroy of India, but Mr Gladstone insisted after consulting some of his colleagues.[4] In 1881 the Duke of Cambridge informed the Queen that if Sir Garnet Wolseley were appointed Adjutant-General he would resign his office as Commander-in-Chief. The Queen thereupon refused her approval. Sir William Harcourt, who was minister in attendance, refused to intervene, but wrote to Mr Gladstone to explain her views.[5] Wolseley was, nevertheless, appointed, the Duke withdrawing his opposition.

The Deanery of Windsor is, however, recognised to be in the gift of the Sovereign.[6] The Queen also claimed the canonries of Windsor,[7]

[1] *Letters of Queen Victoria*, 2nd series, II, p. 290.

[2] Mr Gladstone himself largely contributed to the establishment of the new 'claim', for in 1880–3 he seems to have assumed that his Attorney-General, Sir Henry James, was entitled to the offer of, successively, the posts of Lord of Appeal in Ordinary, and Master of the Rolls: *Life of Lord James of Hereford*, pp. 105–16.

[3] 324 H.C.Deb. 5 s., 1200.

[4] *Letters of Queen Victoria*, 3rd series, II, pp. 300–1, 304.

[5] *Life of Sir William Harcourt*, I, pp. 415–16.

[6] *Letters of Queen Victoria*, 2nd series, III, pp. 341–2; Guedalla, *The Queen and Mr Gladstone*, II, p. 235; *Life of Randall Davidson*, I, p. 64.

[7] *Letters of Queen Victoria*, 2nd series, II, p. 441; 3rd series, I, pp. 106–7. In 1821 George IV wanted to bestow a canonry of Windsor on the tutor of Lady Conyngham's children. Lord Liverpool refused to 'advise' accordingly. When the King told him that he had already promised the post and that his ministers could not allow him to be dishonoured, Lord Liverpool replied that, as the ministers were responsible, the King's honour would not be affected, and that it would be far more compromised if he persisted in trying to give posts to his mistress' protégés. The King gave way: *The Private Letters of Princess Lieven to Prince Metternich*, pp. 131–3.

though Mr Gladstone denied her title. The Queen explained that, while all submissions came formally from the Prime Minister, she had always mentioned the persons whom she wished to fill the appointments, and that her suggestions had invariably been complied with. Mr Gladstone denied that any suggestions had been made tending to exclude his own initiative.[1] This is one of those questions which can never be resolved, for it is clear that, even in the case of the Deanery, the appointment is 'submitted' to the Sovereign.[2] The degree to which the Prime Minister will conform to the Sovereign's wishes in the matter of canonries at Windsor must necessarily depend on the personality of both.

Queen Victoria insisted that her pleasure should be taken before steps were taken to ascertain whether the person recommended for appointment would accept it.[3] But this must obviously depend on the nature of the appointment. It is useless to recommend a queen's counsel for appointment as judge unless there is some prospect that he will accept it. In any case, no public announcement must be made until the Queen's pleasure has been taken.[4]

As in respect of other matters, the Sovereign may rely on 'irresponsible advisers'. Indeed, it was in connection with Church appointments that Lord Palmerston used the phrase. The Queen asked for more than one name to be submitted for a vacant canonry. Lord Palmerston said that this was 'a reference of a recommendation by one of your Majesty's responsible advisers to the judgment of your Majesty's irresponsible advisers in such matters'.[5] The Queen replied that she could consult whom she pleased.[6]

Dean Wellesley, Dean of Windsor, who died in 1882, had been cognisant of every Crown appointment in the Church for twenty-five years.[7] Sometimes the Dean's irresponsible advice overcame the Prime Minister's responsible advice. Thus, the Dean recommended Bishop Tait as Archbishop of Canterbury. The Queen thereupon wrote that

[1] *Letters of Queen Victoria*, 3rd series, I, pp. 109–10.

[2] Guedalla, *The Queen and Mr Gladstone*, II, p. 235; *Life of Randall Davidson*, I, p. 64.

[3] *Letters of Queen Victoria*, 1st series, I, p. 406; III, p. 242. But the offer of the Deanery to Connor in 1882 was made by Prince Leopold in the Queen's name, and not by Mr Gladstone: *Life of Randall Davidson*, I, p. 76.

[4] *Letters of Queen Victoria*, 1st series, II, p. 161.

[5] *Ibid.* 2nd series, I, p. 236.

[6] *Ibid.* 2nd series, I, p. 240.

[7] *Life of Gladstone*, III, p. 93.

everyone, except the extreme men, believed that the Bishop was the most suited to the post. Mr Disraeli replied that among other defects he possessed 'a strange fund of enthusiasm, a quality which ought never to be possessed by an Archbishop of Canterbury or a Prime Minister of England'. He was, nevertheless, appointed.[1] It should be added that Mr Disraeli's chief objection was that Tait was a Liberal, though 'all right on the Irish Church'.

For many years the Rev. Randall Davidson, afterwards Archbishop of Canterbury and Lord Davidson, was the Queen's confidential adviser in ecclesiastical matters. As Archbishop Temple's secretary and son-in-law he saw the Queen in connection with the Archbishop's successor.[2] He made a great impression on the Queen, and he was at once asked to find out the state of health of the Bishop of Winchester and the views of the bishops as to the Bishop of Truro.[3] Soon afterwards he was asked to advise about some deaneries,[4] and before very long he received a cipher so as to be able to communicate by telegraph.[5] Being thus in high favour, he was well on the way to promotion, and soon became Dean of Windsor, to Mr Gladstone's evident disgust.[6] As such, he exercised a commanding influence, though an influence largely personal to himself.

The method adopted by Queen Victoria when an important post fell vacant has been described by Davidson himself.[7] The Queen first asked Davidson for information as to the kind of man who ought to hold such a post. When the Prime Minister's informal advice reached her, she sent it to the Dean, by telegraph if necessary. The Dean then wrote a full memorandum, unless he thought he could say that the proposed appointment was the best possible. The Dean considered that the Queen should exercise her right to veto nominations, but should not make recommendations to fill any particular place. At the same time, he thought it suitable that she should occasionally put before the Prime Minister the names of men who ought to be considered when opportunities should arise. He believed that she was placed in a false position

[1] *Letters of Queen Victoria*, 2nd series, I, pp. 545–51.
[2] *Ibid.* 2nd series, III, pp. 365–6, 368–9.
[3] *Ibid.* 2nd series, III, pp. 375–8.
[4] *Ibid.* 2nd series, III, pp. 380–1.
[5] *Ibid.* 2nd series, III, p. 386.
[6] *Ibid.* 2nd series, III, p. 421.
[7] *Life of Randall Davidson*, I, pp. 164–5.

should she mention names for particular appointments and the Prime Minister did not approve of them.

The Dean's influence is obvious in many of the appointments of the period. The method is illustrated by the appointment of the Bishop of London in 1885. On the creation of the vacancy, General Ponsonby wrote to the Dean saying that he had already mentioned to the Queen the Bishop of Exeter. Shortly afterwards Ponsonby wrote again to the Dean to warn him that the Queen had expressed a wish to have the Bishop of Ripon translated. Accordingly, the Dean wrote to Ponsonby (for submission to the Queen) a letter in which he mentioned politely the claims of the Bishop of Ripon, but discussed in greater detail the claims of the Bishops of Durham, Exeter and Carlisle. Mr Gladstone had already written to the Archbishop of Canterbury to ask about the Bishop of Exeter. Letters then passed between the Archbishop and the Dean, the latter favouring the Bishop of Exeter. Presumably the Archbishop replied accordingly to Mr Gladstone. In the meantime the Dean wrote to Ponsonby suggesting that the Bishop of Exeter was the best candidate. Mr Gladstone then advised that the Bishop of Exeter be translated. The Queen asked the Dean for his opinion; that opinion was, naturally, favourable; and the Queen then approved Mr Gladstone's choice.[1]

Other examples of the Dean's influence may be quoted. On his advice, the Queen refused to appoint Liddon as Bishop of Oxford, the Queen pleading Liddon's ill-health as an excuse for not appointing a Puseyite.[2] In 1889 he recommended himself (probably at the Queen's suggestion) as Bishop of Durham,[3] but, though he was supported by the Archbishop and others, Lord Salisbury refused.[4] In the following year the Queen suggested his appointment as Bishop of Winchester, and was annoyed when Lord Salisbury hinted that her recommendation was due to personal friendship.[5] The Queen secured support from the Archbishop, but Lord Salisbury refused, and suggested that he should be given Rochester or Worcester.[6] The Queen advised the Dean to

[1] *Ibid.* I, pp. 166–70, 173–6.

[2] *Letters of Queen Victoria*, 3rd series, I, pp. 426–9; see also 3rd series, I, p. 536.

[3] *Ibid.* 3rd series, I, p. 539.

[4] *Ibid.* 3rd series, I, pp. 540–5, 553–6, 558–63.

[5] *Ibid.* 3rd series, I, pp. 631–4.

[6] *Ibid.* 3rd series, I, pp. 634–6, 639.

refuse.[1] Lord Salisbury's comment on the Dean's qualifications was sent to the Dean, who, to his credit, agreed with it.[2] He finally accepted Rochester.[3]

This recital shows, not merely the influence of 'irresponsible advisers' but also the advantages of friendship or acquaintance with the Sovereign. The Queen seems to have considered that minor appointments were especially suitable for persons who had assisted in the household of some member of the royal family. Thus, she recommended Mr E. in 1869 for appointment as Commissioner of Customs because Prince and Princess Christian 'found it necessary to make some alteration in the arrangement of their Household and consequently Mr E.'s services were no longer required'.[4] Mr Gladstone evaded the difficulty by pointing out that the position was to be abolished, and though in 1872 he was compelled to refuse him appointment as Charity Commissioner, he subsequently found him some kind of Secretaryship.[5]

In the previous year the Queen asked for a canonry for Charles Kingsley, on the grounds that his health was bad, he wanted the post, he was very fit for it, and he was a personal friend of the Queen.[6] Mr Disraeli refused, but Kingsley obtained his stall in 1873.[7] In 1868, also, the Queen asked for a less unhealthy living for Mr B., who had been tutor to the Prince of Wales, and later he received a canonry.[8] Mr D. was recommended for a canonry in 1874 because he had been governor to Prince Leopold and because, apart from other qualifications, it 'would gratify her poor sick boy and cheer him up so much'.[9] The Queen said that he would be 'very acceptable to the Dean of Westminster'—though in fact the Dean had said that 'his general qualifications are not quite equal to the occasion'.[10] Disraeli gave him the stall and thereby obtained 'no little odium'.[11] This gentleman had held the post of governor for two and a half years, and had already received

[1] *Letters of Queen Victoria*, 3rd series, I, pp. 639–42.
[2] *Ibid.* 3rd series, I, p. 645.
[3] *Ibid.* 3rd series, I, p. 648.
[4] Guedalla, *The Queen and Mr Gladstone*, I, p. 203.
[5] *Ibid.* I, pp. 341, 349.
[6] *Letters of Queen Victoria*, 2nd series, I, p. 519.
[7] *Ibid.* 2nd series, II, p. 248.
[8] *Ibid.* 2nd series, I, pp. 520, 531.
[9] *Ibid.* 2nd series, II, p. 373.
[10] *Ibid.* 2nd series, II, p. 375.
[11] *Ibid.* 2nd series, II, pp. 376–7, 423.

a benefice from Mr Gladstone.[1] Nor was King Edward, as Prince of Wales, less forward in urging the claims of his friends.[2]

The Queen's power was, however, used mainly to secure persons of 'moderate' views, especially in Church matters. This was especially the case after the beginning of the Oxford Movement. Thus, she expressed to Lord Derby in 1852 'her sense of the importance not to have Puseyites or Romanisers recommended for appointments in the Church'.[3] In 1868 she optimistically remarked that 'Mr Disraeli will, I think, make good Church appointments, as he sees the force of my arguments in favour of moderate and distinguished men'.[4] In truth, Mr Disraeli saw much stronger force in the argument that Conservative patronage ought to create Conservative prelates. Nevertheless, his inability to override his Sovereign except in extreme cases, together with his inability to meet the Queen's arguments (ably provided by her 'irresponsible advisers'), compelled him to give way frequently. With the acceptance of the principle of Disestablishment by many Liberals, the Queen's efforts were directed at the end of her reign to keeping out advocates of that principle. Thus, she objected to the appointment of Dr Percival to the see of Hereford because he favoured Welsh Disestablishment. Bishop Davidson pointed out that a refusal to accept Lord Rosebery's advice would lead people to believe that bishops must be of one kind of political opinion only; and Lord Rosebery pointed out that his nominee and he held the same opinions on Disestablishment.

Queen Victoria's influence on Church appointments was peculiar to herself. 'Her two successors on the Throne, King Edward and King George, were both alive to the importance of the best Church appointments, and careful to weigh the merits of alternative names before their formal submission; but, generally speaking, they had not the same individual interest in each particular case.'[5] Edward VII is said to have lost his interest in the appointment of bishops after 1906.[6] Moreover, no Dean of Windsor appears to have been such a 'power behind the Throne' after the appointment of Dr Davidson to the bishopric of

[1] Guedalla, *The Queen and Mr Gladstone*, I, pp. 222–3, 253.

[2] Lee, *King Edward VII*, I, pp. 208–14, 516–17.

[3] *Letters of Queen Victoria*, 1st series, II, p. 456.

[4] *Ibid.* 2nd series, I, p. 537.

[5] *Life of Randall Davidson*, II, p. 1236.

[6] Lee, *King Edward VII*, II, p. 53.

Rochester. The new bishop continued to act as adviser, especially after his translation to Winchester, when Osborne came within his diocese. Rather, the power of the Archbishop of Canterbury increased through the tendency of the Prime Ministers to rely on him. This was especially noticeable after Dr Davidson became Archbishop; for he was, primarily, an ecclesiastical politician, and he made a point of establishing personal contact with a new Prime Minister. We are told that none of the seven Prime Ministers from Mr Balfour to Mr Baldwin and Mr MacDonald made a single appointment which they knew to be fundamentally objectionable to the Archbishop, though they did not always follow his advice.[1] As soon as a vacancy occurred, the Archbishop wrote to the Prime Minister to explain the peculiar nature of the bishopric. He usually gave a list of three or four names of churchmen who might be regarded as candidates. He made inquiries of other persons as to suitable candidates; and he usually discussed the position both orally and by correspondence with the Prime Minister.[2] Under the present practice, the Archbishop of Canterbury as such has the greatest influence. Bishoprics are no longer of political importance and few Prime Ministers have the knowledge, time or inclination to take an active part in filling them. Since the Sovereign, though better informed, is usually equally disinterested, ecclesiastical patronage has for all practical purposes been transferred from the State to the Church.

It should be noted that the office of Governor-General, though still filled by the Queen, is filled on the advice of the Prime Minister of the country concerned. Before 1926 the practice had been for the Prime Minister of the United Kingdom to advise, after consultation with the Prime Minister of the country concerned. Lord Byng's refusal of a dissolution in 1926 led to the consideration of the question by the Imperial Conference of that year. The method of appointment was not settled, but some of the Commonwealth countries assumed that their choice must now be accepted. In 1929 General Hertzog, Prime Minister of South Africa, decided that Lord Clarendon should succeed Lord Athlone as Governor-General and proposed that he should appoint him direct. The King 'most strongly objects to anything being said to Lord Clarendon except by the Secretary of State'. In the end General Hertzog

[1] *Life of Randall Davidson*, II, p. 1237.

[2] *Ibid.* II, pp. 1237–8.

made a formal submission to the King, but the Prime Minister of the United Kingdom formally 'advised' General Hertzog's submission.[1]

In the following year Mr Scullin, Prime Minister of Australia, announced his intention of advising the King to appoint Sir Isaac Isaacs Governor-General of Australia. The King informed the Secretary of State that such an appointment could not be approved and that, since the 1926 resolutions precluded the Government of the United Kingdom from advising the Crown in a matter concerning the Dominion, it was for the Sovereign to act on his own initiative.[2] The Law Officers advised, somewhat perversely, that there was nobody who could constitutionally tender advice. Mr Scullin was, however, prevailed upon to leave the matter open until the Imperial Conference of 1930. The Conference passed a lengthy resolution,[3] the substance of which was that His Majesty's ministers in the Dominion concerned were to tender the formal advice after informal consultation with His Majesty. The King then saw Mr Scullin, who persisted in his recommendation of Sir Isaac Isaacs, whereupon the King concurred with great reluctance.[4]

The grant of uniforms to foreign monarchs is not, perhaps, of major importance. But occasionally difficulties have arisen. Thus, the Queen made William II of Germany an honorary Colonel-in-Chief in 1893 without ministerial consent.[5] In 1908 Edward VII made the Tsar of Russia an honorary Admiral of the Fleet without ministerial advice. Mr Asquith felt bound to point out that 'it would have been more in accordance with constitutional practice and with the accepted conditions of ministerial responsibility, if before his Majesty's departure, some intimation had been given to me and my colleagues that it was in contemplation....The Cabinet...is clearly entitled to a voice in such a matter.'[6] The King apologised; but Lord Esher suggested that it was 'trying the Constitution too high' to allow the King to depart without a minister of the highest rank in attendance.[7]

1 Nicolson, *King George V*, p. 478.

2 The position of the Governors-General was dealt with in Cmd. 2768, p. 16, but the reference to advice was on p. 17 and was a general proposition relating to the operation of Dominion legislation.

3 Cmd. 3717, pp. 26–7.

4 Nicolson, *King George V*, pp. 478–82.

5 *Life of Sir Henry Campbell-Bannerman*, I, p. 128.

6 *Life of Lord Oxford and Asquith*, I, pp. 249–50.

7 *Esher Papers*, II, p. 322.

§2. *Titles and Honours*

The King is the fountain of Honour, and all grants are made by him, but in the selection of the recipients of these grants, as in other things, he is in use not to act upon his own initiative but on the advice of his Ministers. The Minister responsible for the advising is the Prime Minister except in certain special cases, e.g., Order of St Michael and St George,[1] Naval, Military and Air Force honours, Orders of the Star of India and of the Indian Empire, where the Minister in charge tenders his advice direct. With these exceptions, and that of the Royal Victorian Order, which is a private Order and is bestowed by the King alone and upon his own selection, no grant of honour is ever made by the King except upon the recommendation of the Prime Minister. Even in the case in which the King might wish that an Order or a Peerage should be given to a member of his own Household, the recommendation would appear on the Prime Minister's list.[2]

The Royal Victorian Chain as well as the Royal Victorian Order is awarded by the Queen personally.[3] It was agreed between King Edward VII and Lord Salisbury in 1902 that appointments to the Order of Merit should 'as in the case of the Royal Victorian Order, be made on the initiative of the Sovereign and not on that of his advisers, but the Sovereign might, of course, receive unofficial assistance from the Prime Minister in choosing members'.[4] Lord Stamfordham stated in 1922 that the King never initiated honours. 'Of course this ruling does not apply to the Royal Victorian Order; also the Sovereign maintains the right of personally selecting members for the Order of Merit.'[5] It would seem, therefore, that either the Queen or the Prime Minister may initiate an award of the Order of Merit; and the same practice has applied to the Order of the Garter and the Order of the Thistle since 1946. In respect of all awards recommended to the Queen, she is consulted informally before formal advice is tendered, so that she may express her views before the individuals concerned are approached. In 1916 George V took strong exception to the procedure where a Conservative member holding a safe seat in Parliament was offered a peerage in order

[1] (Where the recommendations are made by the Foreign, Commonwealth Relations and Colonial Secretaries.)

[2] Royal Commission on Honours: Report, Cmd. 1789/1922, II, p. 99.

[3] Lee, *King Edward VII*, II, pp. 99, 100.

[4] *Ibid.* p. 99.

[5] Nicolson, *King George V*, pp. 511–12.

to free his seat for a minister. The King said he did not 'see his way' to approve because he did not consider that his services called for such special recognition. It was then disclosed that not only had the member been approached, but his impending elevation had been announced to his constituency association. The King approved the elevation, under protest, but insisted that in future he be consulted informally first. It seems, too, that even where some other minister recommends, the Prime Minister is consulted, and that the lists are collated.[1] Certainly the lists are published from Downing Street.

Mr Asquith once said that of all the onerous duties of the Prime Minister 'there is none, in my experience, more thankless, more irksome and more invidious than the recommendation of honours to the Crown —worse even than the nomination of bishops, which ranks high among the incongruous and inconvenient duties which our Constitution imposes upon the Prime Minister'.[2] But the grant is not entirely in the Prime Minister's discretion. The King is able to resist the grant of honours of which he does not approve. Thus, in 1859 Queen Victoria refused to consent to a Privy Councillorship for Mr Bright, because of his 'systematic attacks upon the institutions of the country'.[3] In 1886 she refused to create peers on the resignation of Lord Russell, pointing out that such proposals had not been made by Sir Robert Peel or Lord Aberdeen.[4] In 1869 she refused to sanction a peerage for Sir L. de Rothschild, chiefly because he was a Jew, but also because he was a banker engaged in financing foreign Governments.[5] In 1881 she firmly resisted Mr Gladstone's advice to make Sir Garnet Wolseley a peer.[6] In 1892 she objected to several peerages.[7] In 1906 King Edward VII objected to several peerages and privy councillorships, but gave way on being pressed.[8]

On the other hand, the Sovereign may press for the conferment of some honour. Thus Queen Victoria wanted Lord Lansdowne to be given a dukedom on his retirement from office as Viceroy of India.

[1] Royal Commission on Honours: Report, p. 6; but the statement is not definite.

[2] 156 H.C.Deb. 5 s., 1770–1.

[3] *Letters of Queen Victoria*, 1st series, III, p. 446.

[4] *Ibid.* 2nd series, I, p. 347. See also *ibid.* pp. 552–3.

[5] Guedalla, *The Queen and Mr Gladstone*, I, p. 207.

[6] *Ibid.* II, pp. 141–51, 158–61.

[7] *Letters of Queen Victoria*, 3rd series, II, p. 86.

[8] Lee, *King Edward VII*, II, p. 451.

Mr Gladstone suggested a G.C.B. The Queen objected to this, but Mr Gladstone, after consulting his colleagues, refused to advise a step in the peerage. Ultimately, it was agreed that the Garter should be offered.[1]

The chief problem of 'honours' arises from their use for party purposes. This is, indeed, no new problem. The distribution of honours was one of the more venial methods adopted by Walpole to keep his majority, and its use was continued throughout the eighteenth century. William Pitt, deprived by legislation of part of his patronage, used honours the more to keep his parliamentary majority. With the passing of the Reform Act the situation changed. 'Influence' became less important at parliamentary elections, and a party had to depend more on its policy than on the influence of its supporters. The consequence was, however, a tightening of party bonds and a desire for means of propaganda. Palmerston, Aberdeen and Disraeli had their 'organs' in the press. Disraeli and Joseph Chamberlain took the lead in the development of the great party organisations which gave not merely moral and vocal but also financial support. The first essential of a party is a party fund. It was easier to obtain contributions to that fund in the form of the thousands of pounds of the rich than of the pennies of the poor. But some at least of the rich desired a *quid pro quo*; and since 'honours' were prized by many, a promise of an 'honour' was sometimes alleged to be the consideration for financial support. It has indeed been said that there was a regular tariff—£50,000 for a barony, £25,000 for a baronetcy, and £15,000 for a knighthood. Certainly there have been 'touts' who claimed that, for a promise to pay a sum to party funds, an 'honour' could be arranged.

The procedure for making up the political list was thus explained by the Royal Commission on Honours in 1922:[2]

Those rewarded for political services may be divided into the two classes of those who are, and those who are not, members of the House of Commons. As regards the former, the person who would frame and put the list tentatively before the Prime Minister would always be his Patronage Secretary.[3] As

[1] *Letters of Queen Victoria*, 3rd series, II, pp. 340, 345–51, 357.

[2] Report, Cmd. 1789, p. 8.

[3] (I.e. the Parliamentary Secretary to the Treasury, otherwise known as the Chief Government Whip.)

regards the second, it would generally be the head of the party organisation, who might also be the Patronage Secretary. The practice seems to have varied as to how far the list of the party organiser would be submitted to the Patronage Secretary, if a separate officer, before it found its way to the Prime Minister. There have also been names of persons submitted to the Prime Minister which have not found their way to him through either of the lists mentioned.

It will, of course, be readily understood that this does not mean that the true initiative as to individual names rests with either the Patronage Secretary or the party manager. Suggestions and applications come from all quarters —sometimes from the candidate for honours himself, but more often from his friends. The friends, in the case of a member of the House of Commons, would probably be members of the House themselves, and in the case of other persons, either the members of the House representing the constituencies where the proposed recipient has had his sphere of activity or influential persons in the party in the same neighbourhood.

From the lists so submitted, and with such advice from either the framers of the lists or from other colleagues as he chooses, the Prime Minister makes his final selection. He naturally enquires from the makers of these lists the claims of each man that is put forward. He must obviously be dependent to a great extent on the information supplied to him, and it is too much to expect that he should be personally conversant with the services and position of every gentleman whose name is on the list. We put the question to each Prime Minister in turn,[1] whether he had ever been cognisant of any bargain or promise to the effect that an honour should be contingent on a contribution to Party funds. We received the answer that we expected, that they had not. Answers to the same effect were given by the Patronage Secretaries and party managers.

Allegations were made in Parliament in 1894 and 1906 that honours were 'purchased' by contributions to party funds. In February 1914 the House of Lords resolved unanimously:

That in the opinion of this House a contribution to party funds should not be a consideration to a Minister when he recommends any name for an honour to His Majesty; that it is desirable that effectual measures should be taken in order to assure the nation that Governments, from whatever political party they are drawn, will act according to this rule; and that this House requests the concurrence of the House of Commons in the foregoing Resolution.[2]

[1] (I.e. Mr Balfour, Mr Asquith and Mr Lloyd George.)

[2] 15 H.L.Deb. 5 s., 252–96.

The motion was communicated to the House of Commons, but no consequential action was taken by that House. In the House of Lords, the existence of the general belief that titles were bought and sold was acknowledged. It was not alleged that the Prime Minister, in recommending names, was aware whether or not there had been a contribution to his party funds. It was alleged only that the Chief Whip (then significantly known as the Patronage Secretary), or one of his subordinates, was so aware, and put forward names to the Prime Minister accordingly. The Marquess of Crewe gave a categorical assurance on behalf of the then Prime Minister (Mr Asquith), that 'a contribution to the party funds has not been a consideration to him when recommending names to His Majesty for honours'.[1]

The question was twice raised in the House of Lords in 1917.[2] On the second occasion it was resolved unanimously:

(1) That when any honour or dignity is conferred upon a British subject, other than a member of the Royal Family or the members of the Naval, Military, or permanent Civil Service under the Crown, a definite public statement of the reasons for which it has been recommended to the Crown shall accompany the notification of the grant;

(2) That the Prime Minister, before recommending any person for any such honour or dignity should satisfy himself that no payment or expectation of payment to any party or political fund is directly or indirectly associated with the grant or promise of such honour or dignity.

The motion as framed had a preamble which asserted that the House was 'convinced that ministers have in recent times advised His Majesty to confer honours and dignities on persons who have given or promised money to party funds as a consideration therefor'. This preamble was removed, but only by 48 votes to 34; and some at least of those who voted with the majority did so because the preamble appeared to be a censure on the four persons then living who had held the position of Prime Minister. Examples were in fact given which indicated, if not actual cases of buying and selling, at least a system of 'touts' or intermediaries who were believed to have the necessary influence.

Lord Selborne said:

I have been told by men who have actually had the offer made to them, who never for one moment thought of asking for an honour or thought that

[1] 15 H.L.Deb. 5 s., 284.

[2] 26 H.L.Deb. 5 s., 172–212; 835–86.

they deserved one, but to whom a person has come and said: 'If you will contribute so much to the party funds I can secure for you such and such an honour'; and the person who has given me that confidence certainly had no doubt whatever in his mind that, if he had agreed to the bargain, he would have received his payment in kind.[1]

He stated, again, that Sir James Gildea, the founder of the Soldiers' and Sailors' Families Association,

was offered £20,000 by one person, £10,000 by another, and £10,000 by a third for the Soldiers' and Sailors' Families Association if he would undertake to use any influence he possessed to obtain a baronetcy or a knighthood for the individual. Sir James Gildea said he would have nothing whatever to do with such a transaction; and the single-minded and disinterested philanthropists in question never gave a penny to the Soldiers' and Sailors' Families Association.[2]

Again

Dr Millard...authorises me to say that he had a friend who had done public service in many ways, and, unknown to that friend, he approached the local political association of the party to which the friend belonged, and asked whether an honour could be obtained for him in reward for his public service. The answer from the leader of the local political association came pat, and these were his words: 'Certainly we will consider your suggestion. But we must be quite frank with you. We know it is very objectionable, but we have got to do it. What is your friend prepared to pay?' The reply was that the suggestion had been made quite unknown to his friend, and that he knew his friend would in no circumstances pay anything; and then the matter dropped.[3]

The case following referred to Mr George Holman, seven times Mayor of Lewes. At the end of his seventh mayoralty some of his friends expressed a wish to secure an honour for him. He was willing; and 'one of his friends went straight to headquarters to the whip, and the whip said: "Yes, this is a clear case for an honour. What is he prepared to give to my party fund?" The friend returned to Mr Holman, who refused to give a penny. The friend went back once more to the whip, and the whip said on each occasion: "This is a very good case for an honour, but an honour he shall not have unless he contributes to my party fund."'[4]

[1] 26 H.L. Deb. 5 s., 180.
[2] *Ibid.* 845–6.
[3] *Ibid.* 846.
[4] *Ibid.* 846–7.

When Sir George Kekewich was in Parliament at the time of the Licensing Bill (1910),

> a friend of his, not unconnected with the trade, came to him and said he wanted a knighthood. He was introduced to the whip, and he was informed that there was no great difficulty about his request. He was a Liberal, and had been a benefactor of his Borough and Mayor of it. But he was told: 'There are two conditions you must fulfil. The first is that you should abandon opposition to the Licensing Bill; the second is that you should subscribe £5000 to the party funds.' He said: 'All right, I will do both.' His name appeared on the next list of honours.[1]

Lord Knutsford gave another example:

> I remember a gentleman, almost unknown, coming to me and asking, as the King was coming down to a certain hospital with which I happened to be connected, whether I thought if he gave £25,000 to the hospital he would be as likely to get a title as if he gave it to the party funds. Believing that honesty was the best policy, I told him he would be more likely to get a baronetcy if he gave the money to party funds. Within a short time of that date he came out as a baronet.[2]

Lord Loreburn said: 'A personal friend of mine told me that within a period which I will call five or six years he was three times approached with proposals that he should pay £25,000 for a baronetcy or £15,000 for a knighthood.' He refused, but a short time afterwards he was told (in his own words) that 'there was a chance of pulling it off if he would go to £10,000 for a knighthood', and that if he wanted a baronetcy later 'a full valuation for the first honour is allowed, and such candidate has a prior claim'.[3] Lord Loreburn added: 'Another friend of mine, who has been in a position of official authority...and whom no one could possibly suggest was what you call a "tout" said to me of the sale of titles, "Why, I have sold them myself"; and he gave two illustrations.'[4]

Earl Curzon of Kedleston, for the Government, apparently defended the practice, though he explained himself better later. Certainly, he defended the giving of titles for 'public munificence'. 'Just as the soldier gives his valour, or courage, or genius; just as the artist gives

[1] 26 H.L.Deb. 5 s., 847.
[2] *Ibid.* 190–1.
[3] *Ibid.* 837–8.
[4] *Ibid.* 838.

his talents; just as the captain of industry gives his energy or enterprise; just as the man of science gives his inventions to the service of the State, so the wealthy man gives, and in my view is rightly justified in giving, his wealth, which very often is his only asset, for the benefit of his country.'[1] So, a man who has no valour, courage, genius, talents, energy, enterprise, or power of invention ought to be ennobled if he has money and gives enough of it away.

The first part of the House of Lords resolution was adopted in subsequent honours lists. In March 1918 it was objected that inadequate information was furnished in the Honours List of 1 January 1918.[2] It was said, for instance, that a statement that X was 'Mayor of Bootle' was not sufficient, since there were many mayors, and some reason ought to be given for preferring one mayor to another. The reason was in fact given by the Lord President of the Council. This mayor was mayor of the Chancellor of the Exchequer's constituency and was recommended by him and by another minister.

The belief that honours were bought and sold did not disappear with the House of Lords resolution. In May 1919 the question was raised in the House of Commons.[3] It was pointed out, *inter alia*, that in the latest honours list, honours were granted to people connected with the *Daily Telegraph*, *Daily Mirror*, *Sunday Pictorial*, *Leeds Mercury*, *Glasgow Daily Record*, *People*, *Evening Standard*, *Daily Sketch*, *Daily Dispatch*, *Evening Chronicle*, *South Wales News*, *Cardiff Times*, and a press agency. Comparing this list with the list of honours granted to the fighting services, it was suggested that the pen was in truth mightier than the sword.[4] A motion that particulars of party funds should be made publishable by law was, however, defeated.

The matter came to a head with the offer of a peerage to Sir J. B. Robinson in 1922. He was resident in South Africa; he was recommended for 'National and Imperial Services'; he was stated to be 'Chairman of the Robinson South African Banking Corporation', when in fact that company was liquidated in 1905; and he had recently been condemned by the Supreme Court of South Africa to pay heavy damages for an act described by the Chief Justice as 'wholly incon-

[1] *Ibid.* 200.
[2] 29 H.L.Deb. 5 s., 513–33.
[3] 116 H.C.Deb. 5 s., 1334–82.
[4] *Ibid.* 1431.

sistent with the obligation of good faith'. It subsequently appeared that the Secretary of State for the Colonies had not been consulted; and as a result of the agitation Sir Joseph Robinson refused the peerage. Questions were raised in the House of Commons,[1] and debates took place in both Houses.[2] Though no corruption was alleged in this case, the general issue was necessarily raised.[3] The Government finally accepted a motion in the House of Lords for the appointment of a Royal Commission.[4]

This Royal Commission, presided over by Lord Dunedin, produced a report in 1922.[5] It recommended:

(i) That a committee of the Privy Council, of not more than three members, be appointed of persons not being members of the Government to serve for the period of the duration of office of the Government; the Committee to have a Secretary taken from the ranks of the Civil Service;

(ii) That before submission to His Majesty of the names of persons for appointment to any dignity or honour on account of political services, the names of such persons should be submitted to the Committee with, appended to each name, the following particulars:

(*a*) a statement of the service in respect of which, and the reason for which, the recommendation is proposed to be made;

(*b*) a statement by the Patronage Secretary or Party manager that no payment, or expectation of payment, to any Party or political fund is directly or indirectly associated with the recommendation;

(*c*) the name and address of the person who the Prime Minister considers was the original suggestor of the name of the proposed recipient.

[1] 155 H.C.Deb. 5 s., 1038, 1496, 1662, 1842–8, 2312–14; 156 H.C.Deb. 5 s., 23–4, 367–9.

[2] 50 H.L.Deb. 5 s., 1126–40; 51 H.L.Deb. 5 s., 103–38, 475–512; 156 H.C.Deb. 5 s., 1745–1862.

[3] The Duke of Northumberland gave four further examples of 'touting'. His figures were £10,000 to £12,000 for a knighthood and £35,000 to £40,000 for a baronetcy: 51 H.L.Deb. 5 s., 129. See also 51 H.L.Deb. 5 s., 507–10, for the text of letters addressed to persons who were believed to be likely recipients on payment being made. Lord Carson said: 'I have had more than once in my Chambers to advise on cases in which I have examined long correspondence which showed that there was a regular brokerage, however conducted, for the purpose of carrying out and obtaining honours': 51 H.L.Deb. 5 s., 136.

[4] It is significant that none of the whips spoke in the House of Commons, and that no former Chief Whip spoke in any House of Lords Debate.

[5] Royal Commission on Honours: Report, Cmd. 1789/1922.

(iii) That the Committee, after such enquiry as they think fit, should report to the Prime Minister whether, so far as they believe, the person is, in the whole circumstances, a fit and proper person to be recommended.

(iv) That in the event of the Committee reporting against any name and the Prime Minister determining still to recommend such name, the King should be informed of the report of the Committee.

(v) That an Act be passed imposing a penalty on anyone promising to secure, or to endeavour to secure, an honour in respect of any pecuniary payment or other valuable consideration, and on any person promising such payment or consideration in order to receive an honour.[1]

These recommendations were accepted by the Government. The Committee of Privy Councillors was constituted and is still in existence. The last recommendation was put into effect by the Honours (Prevention of Abuses) Act, 1923.

Lists are issued normally on 1 January and on the Queen's Birthday every year. But on any special occasion, such as a Coronation or a Jubilee, a special List is issued. On any such special occasion it is the practice of the Prime Minister to ask the Leader of the Opposition to make a few nominations.[2]

[1] Royal Commission on Honours: Report, Cmd. 1789/1922, pp. 11–12.
[2] 156 H.C.Deb. 5 s., 1771 (1922), per Mr Asquith.

CHAPTER XV

GOVERNMENT AND PARLIAMENT

§1. *The Strength of the Government*

It is not untrue to say that the most important part of Parliament is the Opposition in the House of Commons.[1] The function of Parliament is not to govern but to criticise. Its criticism, too, is directed not so much towards a fundamental modification of the Government's policy as towards the education of public opinion. The Government's majority exists to support the Government. The purpose of the Opposition is to secure a majority against the Government at the next general election and thus to replace the Government. This does not imply that a Government may not be defeated in the House of Commons. Nor does it imply that parliamentary criticism may not persuade the Government to modify, or even to withdraw, its proposals. These qualifications are important; but they do not destroy the truth of the principle that the Government governs and the Opposition criticises. Failure to understand this simple principle is one of the causes of the failure of so many of the progeny of the Mother of Parliaments and of the supersession of parliamentary government by dictatorships.

It is said that the House of Commons controls Parliament; and the lawyers point to the power of the House of Commons to refuse to legalise the Army and the Air Force and to refuse supplies, and thus to compel a Government to resign. It might perhaps be enough to point out that the House of Lords could similarly refuse to pass resolutions to keep the Army Act, 1955, and the Air Force Act, 1955, in operation,[2] that it could, before 1911, refuse supplies, and that it has not been suggested since 1832 that the Government is responsible for the House of Lords. But, in truth, the fundamental criticism of the proposition is that it ignores the party system and thus ignores the fact that, through

[1] On this chapter, see Jennings, *Parliament*.

[2] Formerly it was necessary to pass an annual Army and Air Force Bill. Now the Acts of 1955 are kept alive from year to year (for a period not exceeding five years unless Parliament otherwise provides) by Orders in Council; but the draft Orders must be approved by affirmative resolutions in both Houses.

the party system, it is the Government that controls the House of Commons.

Lord Palmerston once expressed the opinion that the life of the strongest Government was not worth more than three months' purchase.[1] His own Government of 1855 secured a great majority at the election of 1857 but was turned out in 1858. Yet his experience was wholly exceptional; and the life of a Government with a majority is really determined by the date fixed under the Parliament Act for the termination of Parliament. It is a very incompetent Government that cannot maintain its majority until, in due course, it appeals to the people.[2]

Burke's doctrine that the member of Parliament is returned to exercise his judgment on the facts and proposals put before him was probably not true of the Parliaments of George III and is certainly not true of the Parliaments of Elizabeth II. The successful candidate is almost invariably returned to Parliament not because of his personality nor because of his judgment and capacity, but because of his party label. His personality and his capacity are alike unknown to the great mass of his constituents. A good candidate can secure a number of votes because he is good; a bad candidate can lose a few because he is bad. Local party organisations therefore do their best to secure a candidate of force and character. But his appeal is an appeal on his party's policy. He asks his constituents to support the fundamental ideas which his party accepts. His own electioneering is far less important than the impression which his party creates in the minds of the electors. They vote for or against the Government or for or against the party to which he belongs. The 'national' speaker who comes into a constituency to urge electors to support the candidate probably knows nothing of him. He commends the candidate because he supports the party; he would condemn him with equal pleasure if he did not. Many of the posters are prepared and circulated by party headquarters. The candidate's own posters emphasise his party affiliation. He possesses an 'organisation' because the party supporters in the locality—stimulated, if necessary,

[1] *Life of W. H. Smith*, II, p. 180.

[2] Even when it appears to have nine-tenths of the people against it, as with respect to the peace proposals made by France and Great Britain to Abyssinia and Italy in December 1935.

by the party headquarters—believe in the party policy sufficiently strongly to give time and trouble to its work.

The member of Parliament is thus returned to support a party. He recognises his party obligations by receipt of the 'whip'; if he disagrees with the party policy on a particular matter, he may abstain from voting. Occasionally, perhaps, he votes against his party. If he does so too frequently, he loses the 'whip'; and this means, probably, the loss of party support at the next election. Without that support, he will probably not be elected. Also, his party loyalty as well as his self-interest will induce him normally to vote with the party. Sir Austen Chamberlain once referred to the 'almost incredible strength' of party loyalties; and John Bright is reported to have said that not thirty men outside the Irish would have voted for Home Rule in 1885 if any one but Mr Gladstone had proposed it.[1] Above all, a supporter of the Government is very unlikely to take any step which will defeat the Government. For, if it is defeated on a major issue, it will resign or dissolve Parliament. If it resigns, he has assisted the formation of a Government by the Opposition, which is *ex hypothesi* worse than that which he was elected to support. If Parliament is dissolved, he will have to undergo the trouble and possibly the expense of an election; and it may not be certain that he will be re-elected.

A Government which has a majority thus has the means for maintaining its majority. The energy of the whips' organisation is primarily directed to that end. The Government has, above all, the effective weapon of the dissolution. It can hold the threat above members' heads like a big stick. At a dissolution anything may happen. Lukewarm friends will almost certainly disappear. When the Conservatives were inclined to be rebellious in 1916, Mr Bonar Law threatened that the Government might advise a dissolution. Mr Winston Churchill declared that the suggestion was the most 'terribly immoral thing' he had ever heard.[2] A Government which is conducting a war can appeal to the 'patriotism' of the nation to save it from its friends. It can show the flag and beat the drum. It can complain that the 'nation' is in peril because it is not being adequately supported. It can assert that opposi-

[1] *Life and Letters of Sir Austen Chamberlain*, I, p. 271.

[2] Beaverbrook, *Politicians and the War*, II, pp. 106–7.

tion is treason. The result, as the khaki elections in 1900 and 1918 showed, and as was shown in the not very dissimilar conditions of 1931, is enormously to strengthen the Government and to decimate its opponents. In normal conditions the power is not so great, but it is nevertheless effective. 'I defy you on this motion and on all other motions which you may make; I defy your majorities. I stand by the Crown and shall appeal to the people.' So said Canning in 1807;[1] and so might say, in more diplomatic language, the Prime Minister of today.

A Government which possesses a real majority can thus be reasonably certain of maintaining itself in power as long as the Parliament lasts. It can secure the passage of its proposals. Even when it is defeated, it can ask the House to reverse its decision, like Peel in 1844.[2] 'I have great confidence', said Peel, 'in the effect of a steady declared intention of a Government to carry a particular measure, or to throw on others the responsibility of defeating it.'[3]

It does not follow, and it is not true, that a Government in possession of a majority forms a temporary dictatorship. It can, no doubt, press unpalatable measures upon the House. As Peel also said: 'Menaces of resignation if the House of Commons do not adopt certain measures are very unpalatable, and I think they should be reserved for very rare and very important occasions.'[4] The Government's majority is its authority; that majority rests upon popular support. If either disappears, the Government, too, will disappear in due course. The member's most precious possession is his party label; but the label is valueless unless the electors give it a value. If he desires to maintain his majority, he must keep in close touch with his constituency. He will soon become aware that the tide of the Government's popularity is receding. He will become more and more concerned as his electoral support falls away. It has been said that Governments, like men, no sooner begin to live than they begin to die. But if they manage well, they may be an

[1] Quoted by Dr Lushington, *Parl. Deb.* 3rd series, vol. 58, col. 1010.

[2] *Peel Papers*, III, pp. 147–53.

[3] *Ibid.* III, p. 175. For other examples of a reversal of a House of Commons decision, see *Letters of Queen Victoria*, 3rd series, II, pp. 382–3 (1894); Lee, *King Edward VII*, II, pp. 186–7 (1905); Ullswater, *A Speaker's Commentaries*, II, pp. 130–3 (1912); *Life and Letters of Sir Austen Chamberlain*, I, p. 323.

[4] *Peel Papers*, III, p. 354.

unconscionable time a-dying; and if they manage ill they will die young. In this sense a party leader may say with Carlyle: 'I am their leader, therefore I must follow them.' A Government must perpetually look over its shoulder to see whether it is being followed. If it is not, it must alter direction. For in this sense, and in this sense only, is it true that a democracy is government of the people by the people.

It follows that a Government, even with an enormous majority, cannot neglect the feeling of the House. The temperature of the party is, in large measure, the temperature of the electorate. A minute Opposition, like the Labour Opposition of 1931–5, uses its opportunities to appeal to public opinion. The House is its platform, the newspapers are its microphones, and the people is its audience.

Four examples may be cited. The National Government of 1934 had an unprecedented majority. It introduced what is called 'a very little Bill' to provide powers to protect the armed forces from propaganda.[1] As soon as the provisions of the Incitement to Disaffection Bill became known there was an immediate outcry. Opposition within the House of Commons made common cause with opposition without. The whole technique of propaganda—articles, pamphlets, letters to the press, meetings—was used to attack what was commonly called the 'Sedition Bill'. The Government soon realised, both directly and indirectly through the House of Commons, that it was gaining no credit and not a little discredit. Its prestige was implicated and the Bill was passed. On every vote it had a substantial and, indeed, overwhelming majority. But so great was the outcry that substantial amendments had to be accepted. The Bill as passed was very different from the Bill as presented; and public opinion had amended it.[2]

Even more noteworthy was the effect of public opinion on the Anglo-French proposals for a settlement of the Italo-Ethiopian dispute in December 1935.[3] These proposals were agreed upon by the Foreign Secretary and the French Prime Minister in Paris. They were communicated to the Prime Minister by messenger and were presented to the

[1] It has been suggested that the Bill was not referred to the Attorney-General before it came to the Home Affairs Committee, because it was regarded as uncontentious.

[2] See Jennings, 'The Technique of Opposition', *Political Quarterly*, VI, pp. 208–21.

[3] Lord Templewood, *Nine Troubled Years*, pp. 178–92; G. M. Young, *Baldwin*, pp. 216–18.

Cabinet. In the meantime they had become known to the press in Paris, and were reproduced in the London newspapers. There was an immediate outcry on what the Prime Minister called 'the ground of conscience and honour'.[1] 'I know that something has happened', said Mr Baldwin, 'that has appealed to the deepest feelings of our countrymen, that some note has been struck that brings back from them a response from the depths.'[2] Here there was no organisation of public opinion. The proposals produced a spontaneous outburst which led at once to protests among all sections of the population, and on both sides of the House of Commons.

The Cabinet was faced with the choice of approving the proposals or of publicly repudiating the action of the Foreign Secretary. It chose the former; but the opposition increased and the sense of outrage became more widespread. Only three weeks before, the Government had secured a majority of 250 as the result of the general election. That majority, faced with its election promises and the public outburst, could no longer be relied upon. The Opposition put down a motion which was, in substance, a vote of censure. A motion from the Government side sought to condemn the proposals. The Cabinet had not liked the proposals when first it saw them. Faced with the expressions of public concern, it reconsidered the situation. It felt that 'there could not be the support in this country behind these proposals even as terms of negotiation'.[3] It 'felt that there could not be that volume of public opinion which it is necessary to have in a democracy behind the Government in a matter so important as this'.[4] It decided to reverse its decision. The Foreign Secretary resigned. 'There is the hard ineluctable fact', he said, 'that I have not got the confidence of the great body of opinion in the country, and I feel that it is essential for the Foreign Secretary, more than any other minister in the country, to have behind him the general approval of his fellow-countrymen. I have not got that general approval behind me today, and as soon as I realised that fact, without any prompting, without any suggestion from anyone, I asked the Prime Minister to accept my resignation.'[5] 'It is perfectly obvious', said the Prime Minister, 'that the proposals are absolutely and com-

[1] 307 H.C.Deb. 5 s., 2030. [2] *Ibid.* [3] *Ibid.* 2030–1.
[4] *Ibid.* 2031. [5] *Ibid.* 2012.

pletely dead.'[1] Public opinion had killed them. An amendment to the Opposition motion was drafted by the Government and some of its supporters; it condemned the proposals only by implication and assured the Government of the full support of the House 'in pursuing the foreign policy outlined in the Government manifesto and endorsed by the country at the recent general election'—a policy with which, it was agreed by most, the proposals were not in accord. That amendment was carried as a substantive motion by a majority of 225. The Government remained in office, but the proposals had been killed.[2]

In the third case, that of 1940, public opinion compelled the Government to resign. The Labour and Liberal parties had supported Mr Neville Chamberlain's Conservative (or 'National') Government from September 1939 to May 1940. The futile attempt to defend Norway against German invasion and the imminent danger due to the progress of German arms in Western Europe led to a profound public dissatisfaction with the conduct of the Government. A vote of censure was moved in the House of Commons and was defeated, but so small was the majority, so vocal the opinions expressed, and so important the need for national unity that Mr Chamberlain, after ascertaining that the Labour and Liberal parties were not prepared to join any Government formed by him, resigned; and the King sent for Mr Winston Churchill.

The fourth example is more complicated and more controversial. In the 'Suez crisis' of 1956 not only British opinion but Commonwealth and world opinion played parts. Moreover, neither the Eden Government nor its successor admitted that public opinion had induced a change of policy, but offered a series of explanations to show that the policy had been correct and consistent. On 30 October 1956 'urgent communications' were addressed to Egypt and Israel calling for a cessation of warlike activity and the withdrawal of their forces from the Suez Canal. Further, in order to separate the belligerents and guarantee freedom of transit through the canal, the Governments of the United

[1] 307 H.C.Deb. 5 s., 2031.

[2] Mr G. M. Young in *Stanley Baldwin*, p. 217, asserts that if the Opposition had not 'overplayed its hand' the Government might have been defeated. The assertion is quite incredible because of the public loyalty of the Conservative party under Opposition attacks. Conservatives may change leaders in private; they always support them in public, except when there is no risk of defeat.

Kingdom and France asked the Egyptian Government to agree that Anglo-French forces should move temporarily into key positions at Port Said, Ismailia and Suez. If there was no such undertaking within twelve hours British and French forces would intervene. There were immediate protests from the Opposition and a strongly adverse public opinion developed outside. That opinion was by no means unanimous, and indeed if a referendum had been taken the Government might have had a majority. The adverse opinions were, however, strongly held and firmly expressed because, as with the Hoare–Laval proposals, the Government's action raised questions of right and wrong. Equally important was an almost unanimous adverse opinion in the United States, Canada, India, Pakistan, Ceylon and indeed the United Nations. In the Security Council a resolution was carried against Britain and France (as well as Israel) but was defeated by reason of the British and French veto. In the House of Commons the Government was again attacked on 31 October, and on the following day a vote of censure was moved but defeated by 320 votes to 257. On the same day the General Assembly of the United Nations met and defeated by 62 votes to 2 (Britain and France) a motion challenging the Assembly's jurisdiction and adopted by 64 votes to 5 (Australia, France, Israel, New Zealand and the United Kingdom) a motion for an immediate cease-fire. An emergency session of the House of Commons was summoned for Saturday, 3 November, when it was announced that Britain and France would accept a cease-fire on certain conditions. On 4 November the Assembly adopted other resolutions by 57 votes to nil, 59 votes to 5, 57 votes to nil, 64 votes to nil and 65 votes to 1 (Israel). On 5 November the Government announced that there would be a cease-fire as soon as Egypt and Israel accepted the Canadian resolution (the first of those passed by the Assembly on 5 November). On 6 November it was announced that a cease-fire had been ordered, and on 3 December, after the arrival of the United Nations force, it was announced that the Anglo-French forces would be withdrawn.

As mentioned above, the British Government never accepted the view that its actions had been dictated by pressure of opinion, but it is clear that parliamentary questions and debates and an active public opinion, as well as the pressure of world opinion expressed through the

Security Council and the General Assembly of the United Nations, had diverted British policy—to the evident disappointment of the French Government. The effect of public opinion on a democratic Government was made more evident by the contemporary inability of opinion, national or international, to interfere with the intervention of the Soviet Union in the internal affairs of Hungary.

'The possession of power', as Sir James Graham remarked, 'is the sole object of political warfare.'[1] But Governments must so conduct their side of the political war that they maintain themselves in power. This compels a sensitiveness to public opinion that no other form of government provides. Political power rests on public opinion; and such opinion is expressed not merely at a general election but by all the instruments which a free people possesses.

These considerations are important because they qualify the power of a Government. It is nevertheless true that the Government controls the House of Commons. No Government with a majority has been overthrown by the House of Commons since 1895—and then the Government resigned because of its internal dissensions and used the defeat as an excuse. The Government of 1886 was defeated because of the defection of a section of its party on a major issue. In 1885 the Government was breaking up. Not since 1866 has there been any real 'control' of the Government by the House of Commons. A majority Government can be defeated only by reason of a party split. So long as the party holds, it is the Government that controls the House, and not the House that controls the Government.

The House possesses the instruments necessary to determine the fate of Governments. If it fails to approve the Government's policy the Government must resign or dissolve Parliament. If a Government has really lost the confidence of the House of Commons, the House can make the Army and Air Force illegal by refusing to pass the resolutions necessary for keeping the Army Act and the Air Force Act in existence; it can make the levying of income tax and surtax unlawful by failing to pass the Finance Bill; it can prevent the expenditure of money on the Supply Services by failing to pass the Appropriation Bill. These powers are mentioned in all the books. They are important elements in

[1] *Life of Sir James Graham*, I, p. 289.

strengthening the constitutional conventions that govern Cabinet Government, but their practical importance is small.

The 'confidence' of the House of Commons has a more complex connotation. If the Government has a majority, it is merely the confidence of the party in its leaders. It becomes important only when no party has a majority, for then the simplicity of Cabinet government breaks down and new considerations become important.

Minority Governments are more common than is generally supposed.[1] They are undoubtedly weaker than majority Governments. Gladstone rightly regarded the existence of the Peelites as a source of weakness in the Constitution.[2] The Irish until 1914, the Labour party from 1910 to 1914, and the Liberal party between 1924 and 1929, have similarly obstructed the normal working of the party system. A system of proportional representation—whether desirable or not on other grounds—would certainly weaken the Government and so provide an argument for the enemies of democracy.

Yet a Government without a majority is not entirely disarmed. It still possesses the weapon of dissolution. It is, it is true, a double-edged weapon. The major party in opposition can always point to the weakness of the Government as if the Government itself was at fault. It can always assert that since the Government cannot obtain a majority, it is better to give the Opposition a majority. But, as against the third party, it is effective. For both logic and experience suggest that the third party risks decimation in a dissolution. Its supporters will be critical whether it supports the one party or the other—and it cannot continue to give support to neither. Discriminating support tends to appear in practice to be mere wavering, however logical it be in theory. One at least of the other parties, if not both, tends to advance upon its terrain in order to catch some of its votes. It offers no career to ambitious men: it causes electors to ask whether they need cast their votes into the void. The young electors tend to see their choice as one of alternatives, not of three different courses. These reasons explain the gradual weakening of the Liberal party in recent years, and not defects of personnel or lack of constructive thought.

Thus, a dissolution is a greater menace to the third party than to the

[1] See above, p. 31.

[2] *Life of Gladstone*, I, pp. 540, 552, 558.

Government supporters. Though it can modify the Government's policy, it must accept much that it cannot approve. The Liberal party learned the lesson of 1924, gave the Labour Government of 1929 two years of office, and had no hand in its fall. Moreover, the existence of the third party is itself a menace to the Government's supporters. Rebellion is less possible because its consequences are more obvious. The member of a huge majority can exercise some discrimination in his support; the support of a minority Government must be unwavering. Minority Governments are weaker than majority Governments, but they are not so weak that they cannot govern.

British Governments are in fact expected to govern. If necessary, they are expected to act even when they have no legal powers. They can rely on their majorities and on the common sense of the House to ratify their acts. There is and can be no limitation on retroactive legislation. A Government can act first and ask for approval afterwards. It can declare war though it has not the power to place the forces on a war footing—though it is the duty of the Government to summon Parliament at once.[1] It can take precautionary measures in case war breaks out: in 1870 the Cabinet authorised the War Office to exceed the vote for ammunition.[2] It can enter into treaties without parliamentary sanction and accept obligations even when legislation is necessary. Secret treaties were made in 1898 and 1900 and not published until after 1918.[3] It can authorise the Bank of England to break the law—as when the Bank Charter Act was suspended in 1847 and 1857 and when the Bank was authorised to suspend payments in gold in 1931—though again the immediate summoning of Parliament is necessary. The Government of 1847 spent a million pounds a month on the relief of destitution in Ireland without prior parliamentary sanction.[4] These are examples only of the great emergency powers which the British Government possesses because it has behind it the support of a majority of the House of Commons.

[1] *Life of Lord John Russell*, II, p. 285; *Letters of Queen Victoria*, 2nd series, II, p. 38; Fitzroy, *Memoirs*, pp. 495, 560. See also Winston Churchill, *Second World War*, II, p. 543.

[2] *Letters of Queen Victoria*, 2nd series, II, p. 47.

[3] *Life of Joseph Chamberlain*, III, pp. 319–20.

[4] Disraeli, *Life of Bentinck*, p. 258.

Yet that majority must be treated with respect. It expects full information on all matters which can reasonably be made public. Treaties, for instance, must usually be laid before Parliament. As Lord Palmerston said in 1841:

All formal engagements of the Crown, which involve the question of peace and war, must be submitted to Parliament....It would scarcely be consistent with the spirit of the British Constitution for the Crown to enter into a binding engagement of such a nature, without formally placing it on record, so that Parliament might have an opportunity of expressing its opinions thereupon....But if the engagement was merely verbal, though it would bind the Ministers who made it, it might be disavowed by their successors.[1]

Nor could a British Government undertake to declare war, unless it had or expected the authority of Parliament. As Lord Salisbury said in 1901:

The British Government cannot undertake to declare war, for any purpose, unless it is a purpose of which the electors of this country would approve. If the Government promised to declare war for an object which did not commend itself to public opinion, the promise would be repudiated, and the Government would be turned out....We might, to some extent, divest ourselves of the full responsibility of such a step, by *laying an Agreement with the Triple Alliance before Parliament* as soon as it is concluded. But there are very grave objections to such a course....Several times during the last sixteen years Count Hatzfeldt has tried to elicit from me, in conversation, some opinion as to the probable conduct of England, if Germany or Italy were involved in war with France. I have always replied that an English minister could not venture on such a forecast. The course of the English Government in such a crisis must depend on the view taken by public opinion in this country, and public opinion would be largely, if not exclusively, governed by the nature of the *casus belli*.[2]

There are, however, matters on which Parliament allows a measure of reticence. Though questions can be asked on all questions of policy or administration, they will usually not be asked if the questioner is advised beforehand that an answer would not be in the public interest. If they are asked, Parliament would always accept a statement, *prima facie* justified, that the disclosure of information would not be in the

[1] Quoted Joll, *Britain and Europe*, pp. 102–3. [2] Quoted *ibid.* pp. 199–200.

public interest. Parliament supports the Government in refusing to disclose the use of secret-service money, the operation of the security services, or the operations of the Exchange Equalisation Fund.[1] It did not know that from 1783 to 1886 a sum of £10,000 a year of the secret-service money was used for political purposes.[1] It does not ask—or, if it asks for it, it supports the minister in refusing—information as to the plans of the Defence Committee, the amount and kinds of ammunition available,[2] or the efficacy of new engines of war.[3] The fact that most Opposition leaders are members of the Privy Council, bound by an oath of secrecy, enables the Government to satisfy the Opposition, without disclosing information in public, that its reticence is reasonable. If a committee of Privy Councillors, including members from Opposition parties, reports on security precautions, or the limits within which information about nuclear fission or fusion can be disclosed, the Opposition will accept their recommendation. Reticence may sometimes have doubtful consequences. The country was pledged in honour by the military 'conversations' between the military experts of Great Britain and France before 1914 when Parliament knew nothing of them. When a question was asked in the House of Commons, Sir Edward Grey was deliberately evasive. 'Parliament has', he wrote years later, 'an unqualified right to know of any agreements or arrangements that bind the country to action or restrain its freedom. But it cannot be told of military and naval measures to meet possible contingencies. So long as Governments are compelled to contemplate the possibility of war, they are under a necessity to take precautionary measures, the object of which would be defeated if they were made public.'[4] This explanation may be held by some to understate the nature of the 'conversations'; but the Government alone can judge.

It is, in short, the function of the Government to govern and of the House of Commons to criticise; but there are limits to the scope of criticism; and if the Government asserts that discussion is not in the

[1] *Life of Lord Randolph Churchill*, II, p. 186.

[2] Cf. Campbell-Bannerman's attitude on the cordite vote of 1895: *Life of Sir William Harcourt*, II, p. 363.

[3] As to other military matters, see Todd, *Parliamentary Government in England* (Spencer Walpole's edition), I, pp. 162–4.

[4] Grey, *Twenty-five Years*, I, pp. 289–90.

public interest the House can do no more than accept the decision. Even where publication of information is not inimical, the powers of the House are limited in fact. It is a deliberative assembly, not a governing body. In discussing Mr Roebuck's motion on the conduct of the Crimean War, Mr Gladstone said: 'Your business is not to govern the country, but it is, if you think fit, to call to account those who do govern it.'[1] 'Those powers which this House undeniably possesses', he said later, 'are powers that, if used without stint or guard, would enable it to throw the whole country into confusion; but it is the wise and prudent limitation which the House has itself put upon its own powers that enables it to emit and to wield its enormous force without crushing to atoms the other bodies which exercise power or are charged with power in this country.'[2]

His conclusion, that an inquiry into the conduct of the Crimean War was an abuse of the powers of the House, was perhaps not the necessary consequence of his premises. Mr Disraeli[3] and Lord John Russell,[4] at least, thought so. Nor do serious results appear to have followed from Lord Palmerston's subsequent acceptance of an inquiry or from the Dardanelles and Mesopotamia Reports during the war of 1914–18. It is recognised that where the exercise of the royal prerogative is in dispute, the House ought not to appoint a Select Committee.[5] It can, however, address the Crown to appoint a Royal Commission. The former method is technically an inquiry by Parliament, the latter an inquiry by the Crown; but the result is the same, an examination and public report of the conduct of ministers. Even so, the Government has its majority. It accepts a motion for an inquiry only because it thinks there is a good answer to accusations, or because it believes that there have been defects of administration not due to its own members, or because the state of public opinion renders politic the acceptance of the demand for inquiry. If it insists on objecting to an inquiry, as when General Sir Frederick Maurice accused Mr Lloyd George of making false statements in 1918,

[1] *Parl. Deb.* 3rd series, vol. 136, col. 1202.

[2] *Ibid.* 1840. See also *Life of Sir James Graham*, II, pp. 268–9.

[3] *Ibid.* col. 1208.

[4] *Life of Lord John Russell*, II, p. 238.

[5] See the debates on the 'sale' of honours in 1922. 51 H.L.Deb. 5 s., 103–38; 156 H.C.Deb. 5 s., 1745–1862; and above, pp. 431–6.

the House has the option of 'white-washing' the Government or of breaking it up.[1]

At the same time, few would be disposed to agree with Sir James Graham's statement: 'the House of Commons, although a good judge of the merits of an Administration and of their merits as a whole, is bewildered in a labyrinth of details and miscarries in its judgment when it attempts to deal with minute particulars. It is safer and easier to displace a Ministry than to change and direct its policy by the active intervention of Parliament.'[2] A Government will not give way on a major question of policy. Parliamentary criticism of details compels the Government, by an appeal to public opinion, and its reaction in the House, to modify its attitude, and to qualify the application of its principles, without overthrowing the principles themselves. It is only by an attack on details that 'concessions' can be secured.

One may suspect, too, that Queen Victoria's constant attempts to limit parliamentary interference[3] were due primarily to her antipathy to democratic government. It would be impossible to strengthen parliamentary control of administration without appreciably weakening the Government,[4] for the power of the Government rests on its majority, not on any abnegation of control by the House of Commons. The suggestion to the contrary in the Report of the Joint Select Committee on Indian Constitutional Reform[5] is a confusion of thought. The tradition of Parliament that 'Her Majesty's Opposition' shall not be oppressed is not a tradition merely; it rests on policy. Given free elections, an Opposition that is not allowed to oppose in Parliament is by that fact supplied with arguments for opposition in the country. If it can be asserted that the Government fears criticism, it can be suggested with considerable force that there is ground for criticism. The Opposition is given a forum in Parliament because if it were not it would be given a convincing argument in the forum of the country.

[1] See 105 H.C.Deb. 5 s., 2347–402. [2] *Life of Sir James Graham*, II, p. 316.

[3] See, for example, *Letters of Queen Victoria*, 1st series, III, p. 218; *ibid.* 1st series, III, p. 221; *ibid.* 2nd series, III, pp. 107–14; Guedalla, *The Queen and Mr Gladstone*, I, pp. 341–2.

[4] See Jennings, *Parliamentary Reform*, pp. 140–61.

[5] Report of the Joint Select Committee on Indian Constitutional Reform, vol. I, part I, p. 62.

It follows that much must be brought under the cognisance of Parliament even when new legal powers are unnecessary. Secret treaties for instance, can be made, but there are limits to the effective powers of the Government. When suggestions for a formal alliance with France were made in 1906 Sir Edward Grey told the British Ambassador in Paris that 'it was too serious a matter to be kept secret from Parliament. The Government could conclude it without the consent of Parliament, but it would have to be published afterwards. No British Government could commit the country to such a serious thing and keep the engagement secret.'[1] It would be impolitic for the Government and it would fail of its effect; for British Governments may fall by the operation of the electoral system, and no incoming Government would uphold a secret engagement made without the consent of Parliament. Mr Gladstone's dictum, that 'an incoming Government must recognise existing obligations'[2] would not apply to such an undertaking. It is well settled that important treaties must be laid before Parliament.[3] The alienation of territory needs parliamentary sanction by resolution, though legislation is perhaps not necessary.[4] This need for parliamentary approval has the advantage, as Lord Palmerston pointed out, that it compels the Government to give its engagements precise form.[5] It cannot, however, prevent 'obligations of honour' similar to that which arose about the military 'conversations' of 1905 to 1914.[6] In 1924 the Labour Government announced that it would submit all treaties to Parliament and lay them on the table for twenty-one days before proceeding to ratification.[7] The succeeding Government refused to follow this practice.[8] It was restored by the Labour Government in 1929,[9] but has presumably not been followed by its successors, though no formal announcement to that effect appears to have been made. The practice is in any event not binding on Governments which desire not to follow it.

[1] *Life of Sir Henry Campbell-Bannerman*, II, p. 255.

[2] *Life of Gladstone*, II, p. 627.

[3] Cf. the Russian Treaty of 1924; Snowden, *Autobiography*, II, p. 685.

[4] See the precedents of 1890: *Life of Robert, Marquis of Salisbury*, IV, p. 300; and of 1904: Lee, *King Edward VII*, II, pp. 251–3.

[5] Ashley, *Life of Lord Palmerston*, II, p. 103.

[6] See above, pp. 292–3.

[7] 171 H.C.Deb. 5 s., 2001–6.

[8] 179 H.C.Deb. 5 s., 565.

[9] 230 H.C.Deb. 5 s., 408.

It must not be thought, however, that parliamentary control weakens the Government. The Government that dares to make its policy open and secures the support of the elected representatives of the people is strengthened in the international arena. A Government which has secured a majority at an election speaks for a nation. Even if twelve million people have voted against it, it has the support of that twelve million in all reasonable actions, for those twelve million people admit the right of the majority to determine national policy; and in so admitting they acquiesce in the policy that is followed. They know that they can criticise; they are aware that their criticism will have effect on a Government whose whole basis is popular support; they know that a comparatively small change of opinion will, in the near future, alter both Government and policy; and they know, above all, that the Government knows it, and will act accordingly. The Government has to be sure that it is being followed; but, if it is, its support rests on willing consent. A consent which is obtained by force or 'spoils' or propaganda can always be undermined. It may be destroyed by a bullet or a bomb. The power that creates a dictator may destroy him. Responsible ministers die in bed.

It is, indeed, an advantage to be openly attacked because attack implies defence. An attack that appeals to reason can be met by a defence that also appeals to reason. Writing of 1914, Mr Winston Churchill has said: 'No parliamentary attack gave me an opportunity of defending myself.'[1] In that statement lies the fundamental principle of Cabinet government. Mr Neville Chamberlain has given similar testimony. When he was Lord Mayor of Birmingham he was invited by Mr Lloyd George to become Minister of National Service without a seat in the House of Commons. His efforts in that office did not meet with public approval, and Mr Chamberlain believed that this was because he could not defend himself in the House. 'My recent experiences', he said, 'have impressed very strongly upon my mind the difficulties of attempting to carry on administration without being in the House. The Cabinet is highly sensitive of party [*sic*] opinion, and a Minister outside the House not only cannot exert influence upon that opinion, he actually excites it against him.'[2] The history of the Poor Law Commissioners

[1] Churchill, *World Crisis*, I, p. 398.

[2] *Life of Neville Chamberlain*, p. 74.

of 1843–47 supplies an instructive lesson. They had substantial powers of government in respect of a service which profoundly affected the lives of many people (not, however, electors). They were, nevertheless, freed from parliamentary control and they had no representative in Parliament. They were the subject of constant attack and they had no means of public defence. In 1847 they were superseded by a Poor Law Board with a responsible minister. Sir George Cornewall Lewis, himself a Commissioner, had some doubts about the result.

If it should be found in experience that the direct representation of the Poor Law Commission in Parliament leads to the abandonment of some wholesome regulations which are in force, and renders the administration less impartial, this change must be imputed to our parliamentary constitution, and not to the Poor Law Department or the existing administration. Parliament is supreme, and we cannot be better governed than Parliament is willing to govern us. It is vain for a body of subordinate functionaries to attempt to enforce, on such a subject as the Poor Laws, opinions which are repudiated by the majority of the sovereign legislature.[1]

He himself supplied the answer. The immediate result of the Act was that 'the horrors of workhouses, and the blessings of out-door relief, are now as much forgotten in the House of Commons as if they had not been mentioned'.[2] A modern historian has commented, 'from an official point of view, the great merit of this beautiful machinery for enabling the ordinary citizen[3] to make his voice heard effectively was that it was even more effective in keeping him silent'.[4] An attack is dangerous only to those who have not the means for defence.

§2. *The Government, the House of Lords and the Electorate*

'With a majority in the House of Commons all things are possible; without it, nothing is safe',[5] said Sir James Graham. A Conservative politician may be excused for forgetting the House of Lords; members of other parties cannot forget. Until 1911 the House of Lords possessed, at least in theory, an equal power of rejecting legislation, subject only

[1] *Letters of Sir George Cornewall Lewis*, p. 151.
[2] *Ibid.* p. 186.
[3] *Sic.* He meant that small section of the citizens to whom the vote was given under the Reform Act of 1832.
[4] G. Slater in Laski, Jennings and Robson, *A Century of Municipal Progress*, p. 343.
[5] *Peel Papers*, II, p. 428.

to the remote possibility of the creation of peers[1] or the stopping of supplies. Nor did it hesitate overmuch to use that power. Yet it has never been assumed since 1832 that the House of Lords could, by its vote, overthrow a Government. 'The day is gone when a conclave of Dukes could sway a Parliament', said Sir James Graham in a completely different connection in 1859.[2] In 1839 the House of Lords voted for a Select Committee on Ireland. The Government then asked the House of Commons for a vote of confidence.[3] Sir Robert Peel objected, not because the confidence of the House of Commons could not override the lack of confidence of the House of Lords, but because 'the opinions of one branch of the Legislature ought to be inferred from its general proceedings—from the support or opposition it may give to measures of the Government—than from abstract declarations'.[4] Again in 1850 the Government was defeated in the House of Lords, this time in a debate on the Don Pacifico dispute. A resolution of confidence was moved and passed in the House of Commons.[5] Since then, Governments have often been defeated in the Upper House, but a resolution of confidence in the Commons is no longer regarded as necessary.

The explanation is, not that the House of Commons can stop supplies—for the House of Lords could before 1911 stop supplies as it rejected the Finance Bill in 1909—but that the power of the Government rests on the support of the electorate. The electorate chooses the party complexion of the Government. It votes in effect for a Prime Minister.[6] Given that support, the Prime Minister dissents respectfully from the Sovereign and snaps his fingers at the peers. So certain is it that the electorate is the basis of all governmental power, that a Government which is defeated at the poll resigns at once, without going through the formality of a vote of no-confidence in the House of Commons.

Lord John Russell admitted in 1841 that the election had decided the fate of the Government, and the Tory newspapers unanimously condemned the Whigs for meeting Parliament before resigning.[7] But the

[1] Above, pp. 428–48. [2] *Life of Sir James Graham*, II, p. 366.

[3] *Life of Viscount Melbourne*, p. 472. See also *Parl. Deb.* 3rd series, vol. 47, cols. 5, 7, 9, 10.

[4] *Peel Papers*, II, p. 386.

[5] *Life of Lord John Russell*, II, p. 12; Greville, *Memoirs*, 2nd series, III, pp. 342–4.

[6] Above, pp. 200–3. [7] *Later Correspondence of Lord John Russell*, I, p. 40.

precedent was not created until 1868, when Mr Disraeli, having appealed to the country in vain, decided with his usual realism that it was useless to meet Parliament again. Queen Victoria and the Cabinet agreed with him. 'The result of the appeal to the country', said the former, 'is too evident to require its being proved by a vote in Parliament, and the Queen entirely agrees with Mr Disraeli and his followers in thinking that the most dignified course for them to pursue, as also the best for the public interests, was immediate resignation.'[1]

Mr Gladstone in 1874 hesitated to follow suit. 'It is Parliament, not the constituencies,' he said, 'that ought to dismiss the Government, and the proper function of the House of Commons cannot be taken away from it without diminishing somewhat its dignity and authority.'[2] He told the Queen that to receive its sentence from Parliament was the course 'most agreeable to usage, and to the rules of parliamentary government' and that any departure from it could only be justified upon exceptional grounds.[3] But some of his colleagues, as well as the Queen, thought differently. The Queen answered flatly that 'whatever advantage there may be in adhering to usage and precedent, it is counterbalanced by the disadvantage of nearly three weeks' delay for the country and the public service'.[4] Finally, Mr Gladstone agreed with his colleagues that his was an exceptional case—though indeed there was nothing to differentiate it from 1841—and the Government resigned. Lord Beaconsfield in 1880, Mr Gladstone in 1886, Mr MacDonald in 1924, Mr Winston Churchill in 1945, and Mr Attlee in 1951 followed the example. Where the Government is defeated and another party has a majority, there is every reason in favour of resignation and none for meeting Parliament. That the Government is to die is evident; it can do nothing in the interval; it is futile to draft a Queen's speech when nothing in it can be carried out; it is a waste of time for Parliament to debate a no-confidence amendment when the consequence is plain.

The position is different when no party obtains a majority. Lord Salisbury in 1885 and 1892 and Mr Baldwin in 1923 decided to meet

[1] *Life of Gladstone*, II, pp. 252–3. [2] *Ibid.* II, pp. 492–3.

[3] *Letters of Queen Victoria*, 2nd series, II, p. 316.

[4] *Ibid.* 2nd series, II, p. 317.

Parliament, for in none of the cases was it clear that the Opposition parties would coalesce or support each other. In 1885, indeed, the Liberals deliberately did not vote on the general question of confidence, but supported an amendment for the 'three acres and a cow' policy.[1] In 1892 the Liberals had a majority only if they were supported by the Irish,[2] and a no-confidence amendment to the Address was moved by Mr Asquith. In 1923 it was not certain that the Liberals would support the Labour party, and only the vote on a no-confidence amendment to the Address determined the question. Mr Baldwin's instinct was to resign at once, but George V thought this procedure incorrect, since the Conservative party was still the largest party and 'the Sovereign ought not to accept the verdict of the polls, except as expressed by the representatives of the electorate across the floor of the House of Commons'. Mr Baldwin then acquiesced.[3]

In 1929, however, Mr Baldwin resigned at once. His party was no longer the strongest party, as it had been in 1923. It was unlikely that it would secure Liberal support. Some took the view that the Government ought to meet Parliament. 'I took the view, that whatever had been the constitutional position, under universal suffrage the situation had altered; that the people of this country had shown plainly that whether they wanted Hon. Members opposite or not, they certainly did not want me, and I was going to get out as soon as I could. My colleagues agreed with me.'[4]

It is a further result of the fact that the strength of the Government rests on the electorate that it can, if defeated in the House of Commons, appeal to the people by advising a dissolution of Parliament. It is a question of tactics whether it will resign or dissolve. Its resignation almost invariably involves a dissolution. It depends on the political temper of the moment whether it is likely to gain or lose if it allows its opponents to dissolve. Since elections are open and free, and Crown

[1] For Lord Salisbury's decision to await defeat in Parliament, see *Letters of Queen Victoria*, 2nd series, III, p. 707.

[2] Lord Salisbury desired to make plain to the people that the Liberals governed by consent of the Irish.

[3] Nicolson, *King George V*, pp. 382–4.

[4] 261 H.C.Deb. 5 s., 535 (1932). Mr Baldwin thought he would be regarded as 'unsporting' if he did not resign: Nicolson, *op. cit.* p. 434. The King did not reply that he could appeal to the umpire.

'patronage' or 'influence' no longer exists, the Government in power has not the advantage which persists even in some democratic countries and which is evident in all countries where terrorism exists. The Government has no control over returning officers. It can in no way control the result of an election. It has only the weapons which the Opposition also possesses, the weapons of justification and criticism. A Government that is strong in its belief in its own opinion will not be satisfied until it has appealed to the people; a Government that is divided against itself will seize the opportunity of a parliamentary defeat, as in 1885 and 1895, to resign.

It must not be thought, however, that a single defeat necessarily demands either resignation or dissolution. Such a result follows only where the defeat implies loss of confidence. Tactically, it is desirable for the Government not to accept defeat readily. If a Government allows itself to be overridden it encourages independence in its members. It is the fear of defeat and the threat of dissolution that supply the most effective elements of the Government's power over its majority. Consequently, modern Governments tend to treat most questions as questions of confidence; yet there are many examples of defeats that have been accepted.

Sir Robert Peel's Government was defeated in 1834 on an amendment to the Address. It did not resign then, but resigned on a subsequent defeat on an appropriation resolution.[1] From 1834 to March 1840, the Whig Government was defeated fifty-eight times in the Commons and forty-nine times in the Lords.[2] In 1841 it was defeated on the sugar duties, but did not resign. Sir Robert Peel then moved 'That Her Majesty's Ministers do not sufficiently possess the confidence of the House of Commons to enable them to carry through that House measures which they deem of essential importance to the public welfare, and that their continuance in office, under such circumstances, is at variance with the spirit of the Constitution.' Lord John Russell replied that members could not be expected to approve of every measure in detail. But the Government was defeated by one vote and decided to

[1] *Lord Melbourne's Papers*, p. 264.

[2] *Parl. Deb.* 3rd series, vol. 53, col. 551. This statement was made by a Tory in the House of Lords, but was not contradicted by Lord Melbourne.

dissolve. First, however, it took credits for six months, and cleared up the legislative programme.[1]

The Coalition Government was in 1853 defeated three times in one week.[2] Lord Rosebery's Government was defeated on a 'snap vote' in 1894 but did not resign.[3] Mr Balfour's Government was defeated in Committee of Supply on an Irish Question in 1905, but neither resigned nor dissolved Parliament.[4]

A minority Government is especially liable to defeat. In 1886 Lord Salisbury wrote to Lord Randolph Churchill suggesting that he should inform the House of Commons that

> we will be responsible for the guidance of Parliament only on the questions which we ourselves submit to it. All questions submitted by independent members, unless they affect our executive action on the measures we have proposed, we shall treat as open questions, taking no collective responsibility for the decision of Parliament upon them.... Open questions were much more common when I entered Parliament than they are now, but as we are entering again upon the period of precarious majorities the system will have to be resumed.[5]

Private members' motions no longer play the part in parliamentary procedure which they played in 1886. The question now is not as to private members' proposals but as to the extent to which the Government can suffer defeat on its own proposals. In 1924 Mr MacDonald announced:

> The Labour Government will go out if it is defeated upon substantial issues, issues of principle, issues which really matter. It will go out if the responsible leaders of either party or any party move a direct vote of no confidence, and carry that vote. But I propose to introduce my business, knowing that I am in a minority, accepting the responsibilities of a minority, and claiming the privileges that attach to those responsibilities. If the House on matters non-essential, matters of mere opinion, matters that do not strike at the root of the proposals that we make, and do not destroy fundamentally the general intentions of the Government in introducing legislation—if the

[1] *Parl. Deb.* 3rd series, vol. 58, cols. 805–1196.

[2] *Life of Disraeli*, I, p. 1322.

[3] *Life of Lord Rosebery*, II, p. 445.

[4] *Life of Sir Henry Campbell-Bannerman*, II, pp. 173–4.

[5] *Life of Lord Randolph Churchill*, II, p. 136.

House wish to vary our propositions, the House must take the responsibility for that variation—then a division on such amendments and questions as those will not be regarded as a vote of no confidence.[1]

The Government was in fact defeated ten times between January and August 1924.[2] This statement was not, apparently, repeated in 1929.

What the Government will treat as a matter of sufficient importance to demand resignation or dissolution is, primarily, a question for the Government. The Opposition can always test the opinion of the House by a vote of no-confidence. No Government since 1832 has failed to regard such a motion, if carried, as decisive. A House whose opinion was rejected has always at hand the ultimate remedy of the refusal of supply. A Government always finds time for a vote of censure upon itself; and, if it did not, there would again be available the sanction of refusal of supply. The Government of 1841 was defeated on a no-confidence amendment to the Address. That of 1846 resigned after a defeat on an Irish Coercion Bill. The Whig Government of 1851 was defeated on a franchise motion in a thin House and resigned, but continued in office when an alternative Government proved impossible. The Whig Government of 1852 resigned after a defeat on the Militia Bill. The Conservative Government of the same year failed to secure a majority at a general election and resigned after defeat on the Budget. The Coalition Government resigned in 1855 after a defeat on Roebuck's motion for an inquiry into the conduct of the Crimean War. Lord Palmerston's Government was defeated in 1857 on its China policy, but advised a dissolution and secured a majority. It was, however, defeated on a Conspiracy Bill in 1858 and resigned. The Conservative Government which succeeded it failed to obtain a majority at a general election and resigned after a no-confidence amendment to the Address. The Liberal Government of 1866 was defeated on the Reform Bill and resigned. The Conservative Government of 1868 was defeated on an Irish Church motion and advised a dissolution; being defeated at the general election it resigned without meeting Parliament. The Liberal Government was defeated in 1873 on the Irish University Bill and resigned, but continued in office on Mr Disraeli's refusal to form a Government. It was defeated at the general election of 1874 and resigned without meeting Parliament.

[1] 169 H.C.Deb. 5 s., 749–50.

[2] Snowden, *Autobiography*, II, p. 680.

The Liberal Government of 1885 was defeated on the Budget and resigned. The Conservative Government which followed was unable to secure a majority at the general election and was defeated on an amendment to the Address. The Liberal Government of 1886 was defeated on the Home Rule Bill and advised a dissolution; being defeated at the general election it resigned without meeting Parliament. The Liberal Government of 1895 was defeated in supply on the cordite vote and resigned. The Conservative Government of 1923, having failed to secure a majority at a general election, was defeated on a no-confidence amendment to the Address. The Labour Government of 1924 was defeated on a motion on the Campbell case and advised a dissolution; being defeated at the general election it resigned without meeting Parliament.[1] It is significant that resignations and dissolutions due to the defeat of the Government in the House of Commons have been rare in the present century.[2]

Four factors really determine the attitude of a Government to a parliamentary defeat. The first is its loss of prestige. A weak Government is a bad Government. Defeat is a sign of weakness which can be overcome only by resignation or dissolution. The second is the strength of its own cohesion. A Government on the verge of disintegration, as in 1885 and 1895, will seize an opportunity to resign. The third is the nature of the issue on which it has been defeated. It is ill-advised to risk a dissolution on a matter which can be made a point of attack on political platforms unless it feels that it has a good defence with a wide popular appeal. The fourth is the importance of the proposal or matter on which it was defeated. A defeat on an important part of the Budget, as in 1852 and 1885, is obviously too important to be passed over.[3] An amendment to the Address in answer to the Queen's Speech is, in substance, a vote of no-confidence.[4] A definite statement that the Government would resign if a proposal is not accepted is a notice that the Government treats the motion as one of confidence, as in 1873.[5] In other cases,

[1] See Appendix I, below, pp. 511–33.

[2] See above, pp. 472–89.

[3] *Life of Gladstone*, II, p. 203; *Letters of Queen Victoria*, 2nd series, III, p. 661.

[4] See Lord Salisbury's positive statement, *Letters of Queen Victoria*, 3rd series, I, p. 22: 'An amendment to the Address is one of the well-known forms of ejecting a Ministry.'

[5] Guedalla, *The Queen and Mr Gladstone*, I, pp. 399–402.

as in 1852 and 1858, the circumstances may suggest that the defeat is in substance a vote of censure.[1]

§3. *Collective Responsibility in Practice*

The defeat of a minister on any issue is a defeat of the Government. The proposals made by a minister, whether or not they have been approved by the Cabinet, are the proposals of the Government. An attack on a minister is an attack on the Government. This is the parliamentary aspect of that collective responsibility which has been studied elsewhere.[2] Yet the principle must be accepted subject to qualifications. Though the Government accepts responsibility for a minister's proposal, there is nothing to prevent it from bowing to that 'feeling of the House' to which experienced politicians are sensitive and withdrawing the proposal, as in December 1935. If the minister feels that his credit has thereby been impaired, he will resign. Again, a Government does not accept responsibility for a personal mistake by a minister. Lord Ellenborough in 1858 published a despatch to the Viceroy of India which ought not to have been made public, and he resigned in anticipation of a parliamentary vote of censure. The vote was moved against the Government, which did not attempt to defend the action, but merely excused it.[3] Lord Ellenborough 'took upon himself the whole and sole responsibility for having authorised the publication of the despatch'.[4]

In 1864 the House of Commons censured the Education Department for suppressing parts of the inspectors' reports. The Cabinet was prepared to support Mr Lowe, the Vice-President of the Council, but he insisted on resigning. He demanded an inquiry by a Select Committee, and when this exonerated him the vote was rescinded.[5] In 1865 the House of Commons resolved that there had been 'a laxity of practice and a want of caution' in dealing with an appointment to the Leeds Bankruptcy Court. Lord Westbury, who, as Lord Chancellor, was responsible, thereupon resigned.[6] In 1873 there were accounting irregularities in the practice of the Post Office which were not checked

[1] *Letters of Queen Victoria*, 1st series, II, p. 444; *ibid.* 1st series, III, p. 337.

[2] Above, pp. 277–89.

[3] *Letters of Queen Victoria*, 1st series, III, pp. 356–61.

[4] *Ibid.* III, p. 361.

[5] *Life and Letters of Viscount Sherburne*, II, p. 226.

[6] *Life of Lord Granville*, I, pp. 479 *et seq.*

by the Treasury. None of the ministers concerned had had their minds directed to the question, though the Postmaster-General was the accounting officer and was thus technically as well as ministerially responsible. Mr Gladstone effected a change of offices for the three ministers concerned.[1] In 1914 the Secretary of State for War resigned because he had allowed an 'interpretation' to be added to a Cabinet memorandum on the duties of officers in Ulster.[2] In 1917 Mr Austen Chamberlain resigned because he considered himself to be ministerially responsible, as Secretary of State, for the inefficiency of the Government of India disclosed by the report of the Royal Commission on Mesopotamia.[3] In 1922 Mr E. S. Montagu, as Secretary of State for India, permitted the Government of India to publish a telegram involving major policy without Cabinet sanction.[4] In 1935 Sir Samuel Hoare resigned when the Cabinet withdrew its sanction to the Italo-Ethiopian proposals.

Some of these examples disclose a rather high sense of obligation in the ministers concerned. But they show, also, that the Government does not accept responsibility for an error of judgment or bad administration by one of its members. The process of government compels a delegation of authority. The Cabinet must leave to each minister a substantial discretion as to what matters he will bring before it. If he makes a mistake, then he must accept the personal responsibility. On

[1] *Life of Gladstone*, II, pp. 460–1; *Epitome of the Reports from the Select Committee of Public Accounts*, pp. 36–46.

[2] *Life of Lord Oxford and Asquith*, II, p. 46.

[3] The Commission reported: 'We have included the War Committee of the Cabinet and the Secretary of State for India among those upon whom responsibility for this misadventure rests. It is true that the War Committee and the Secretary of State acted upon the opinions of their expert military advisers, and that the Secretary of State gave his assent to the advance after he had received an assurance from the General on the spot that he had an available force sufficient for his purpose. But so long as the system of responsible departmental administration exists in this country, those who are political heads of departments in time of war, whether they be civilian or military, cannot be entirely immune from the consequences of their own actions. They have the option and power of accepting or rejecting the advice of their expert subordinates. The acceptance by a chief of wrong advice from expert subordinates cannot secure complete immunity from the responsibility for the evils which may ensue.' Quoted, *Life and Letters of Sir Austen Chamberlain*, II, pp. 82–3; and see *ibid.* pp. 87–8 for Mr Chamberlain's views on his resignation.

[4] *Life of Lord Curzon*, III, pp. 285–6

the other hand, a minister cannot hide behind the error of a subordinate. Within a department there must be substantial delegation of power, but the most essential characteristic of the civil service is the responsibility of the minister for every act done in his department. In practice, the minister can hardly avoid saying that the mistake was that of a subordinate, but Parliament censures the minister and not the subordinate.

§4. *The Function of the Opposition*

Attacks upon the Government and upon individual ministers are the function of the Opposition. The duty of the Opposition is to oppose. It adopts Sir Toby's advice, 'So soon as ever thou seest him, draw; and, as thou drawest, swear horrible.' That duty is the major check which the Constitution provides upon corruption and defective administration. It is, too, the means by which individual injustices are prevented. The House of Commons is at its best when it debates those individual acts of oppression or bad faith which can never completely be overcome in a system of government which places responsibility on such minor officials as police officers. It is the public duty of the Opposition to raise such questions. It is a duty hardly less important than that of government. 'Her Majesty's Opposition' is second in importance to 'Her Majesty's Government'. The apparent absurdity that the Opposition asks for parliamentary time to be set aside by the Government in order that the Opposition may censure the Government, or that the Government is asked to move a vote of supplies for the Ministry of Labour in order that the Opposition may attack the Minister of Labour, is not an absurdity at all. It is the recognition by both sides of the House that the Government governs openly and honestly and that it is prepared to meet criticism not by secret police and concentration camps but by rational argument.

There is a duty to oppose in another sense; perhaps it may be described as a duty to accept defeat. It is so obvious a duty, so much an ordinary part of parliamentary democracy, that we are apt to forget its importance. The parties believe, with a fervour which ordinary 'cross-bench' people find puzzling, in the rightness of their respective causes, though they do not always believe what they put into speeches and election addresses. When they are defeated ignorance or malevolence or fraud has triumphed and the truth has been trampled on by mass prejudice. Nevertheless, there they are every day, sitting on the Opposition benches, asking their questions, making their speeches, pretending that it is all such fun; and before they catch the late buses home they tramp through the lobbies, knowing that the vote is a foregone conclusion. There are countries in which there are no minorities because they might become majorities; and there are countries where the minorities have taken to the barricades because they could not win votes. Only once since 1832 has such action been threatened in the United Kingdom, when Ulster started arming against Home Rule. That occasion was unique, and no doubt it had unusual causes. Even then the rebels were not the Conservative party, but only some of the least worthy of the Unionists. The Conservative party as such remained to act as His Majesty's Opposition, though it did once shout down the Prime Minister.

The best example, however, is the Labour Opposition of 1931. Defeated at an election in which defeat was inevitable, and by methods which were unnecessarily offensive—though it cannot be alleged that the Labour candidates themselves treated their 'renegades' with studied politeness—a small band of fifty-two survivors took their seats on the Opposition benches, led by two relics of the former Labour Government, neither of whom was very experienced or very able. They kept the machinery of Opposition working, and their principal opponent recognized it: 'They might have sulked, they might have seceded, and they never thought of it. When the history of Parliament is written, see that Lansbury gets his due.' So said Mr Baldwin.[1]

Opposition and government are carried on alike by agreement. The minority agrees that the majority must govern, and the majority agrees that the minority should criticise. The process of parliamentary government would break down if there were not mutual forbearance. The most important elements in parliamentary procedure are the discussions 'behind the Speaker's Chair' or 'through the usual channels'. The Prime Minister meets the convenience of the leader of the Opposition and the leader of the Opposition meets the convenience of the Government. The respective whips, in consultation with the respective leaders,

[1] G. M. Young, *Stanley Baldwin*, p. 203.

settle the subjects to be debated, the time to be allowed and, sometimes, the information to be provided and the line of attack. The Government agrees that a vote of censure be moved on Monday provided that a Bill be given a second reading on Tuesday. The Opposition assents to its inevitable defeat at 6.30 p.m. in order that it may move a resolution for the rest of the evening and suffer its inevitable defeat at 10 p.m.

Sometimes, indeed, it agrees not to oppose. This is particularly true of foreign affairs. For the enmity within is as nothing compared with the enmity without. The suggestion that the nation is divided gives encouragement to enemies abroad. From the outbreak of war in 1914 until the formation of the Coalition Government in 1915 the Opposition did not oppose in public but made representations in private. The Government in its turn communicated paraphrases of secret cables—paraphrases in case the documents should fall into enemy hands and so disclose the ciphers—to the Opposition 'Shadow Cabinet'.[1] Mr Austen Chamberlain, as the former Conservative Chancellor of the Exchequer, assisted the Liberal Chancellor of the Exchequer on the financial questions of the war.[2] Agreement was especially necessary where secret promises were made which might have to be carried out by a subsequent Government, as with the promise to allot Constantinople to Russia.[3] In January 1918 the Liberal leaders were informed of the Government's peace proposals.[4] Throughout the period of crisis from early 1938 to the fall of his Government in 1940 Mr Neville Chamberlain kept the Opposition leaders informed of his actions, though they did not always agree with him. The notion that it is 'unpatriotic' to oppose a foreign policy or a 'little war' is, however, a perversion of this doctrine. It is always difficult for Government supporters, especially Conservatives, to distinguish between what is right and what they think to be right. There are, unfortunately, no agreed criteria of right and wrong, except under dictatorships. If the Opposition considers a policy to be wrong it must say so, within whatever discretionary limits that the national interest seems to them to require. In the Suez crisis of 1956 the Labour

[1] Beaverbrook, *Politicians and the War*, I, p. 51.

[2] Lloyd George, *War Memoirs*, I, pp. 105–6, 119.

[3] Beaverbrook, *Politicians and the War*, I, p. 59; Churchill, *World Crisis*, II, pp. 198–9.

[4] Lloyd George, *The Truth about the Peace Treaties*, I, p. 69.

party were not the 'friends of Nasser' but the critics of Sir Anthony Eden.

Nor is this process necessarily limited to foreign affairs. In 1929 Mr Baldwin as leader of the Opposition agreed on the announcement of Dominion status for India.[1] In 1930 the Labour Government set up a committee including Liberals and Conservatives 'to advise as to the policy to be adopted at the forthcoming Disarmament Conference'[2] and in 1931 it consulted the Opposition on the financial crisis of that year.[3] Where there is opposition between the two Houses, compromise is the obvious solution, as on the Irish Church Bill of 1868–9,[4] the Education Bill of 1870,[5] the Ballot Bill of 1872,[6] the Franchise Bill of 1884,[7] the Education Bill of 1906,[8] the Parliament Bill of 1910–11,[9] and the Home Rule Bill of 1913–14. The influence of the Sovereign can obviously be used to secure the first steps towards consultation.[10]

Further, agreement may be made with the Opposition to secure the settlement of a question which has so long divided political parties that an agreed solution becomes necessary. Lord Morley pointed out that the repeal of the Test Act in 1828, Catholic Emancipation in 1829, the repeal of the Corn Laws in 1846, and the extension of the franchise in 1867 were secured by party co-operation,[11] though these are examples of co-operation on the floor of the House rather than 'behind the Speaker's Chair'. Mr Gladstone's hope that the Conservatives would deal with Home Rule in 1886 in the same way was doomed to disappointment. The Liberals were compelled to wait thirty-five years for Conservative conversion. A more unusual arrangement was that whereby Lord Palmerston governed the country with the secret acquiescence of Lord Derby from 1860 to 1866 'en société anonyme'.[12] It was

[1] *Life of Neville Chamberlain*, p. 172.

[2] Lord Templewood, *Nine Troubled Years*, pp. 117–18.

[3] J. H. Thomas, *My Story*, p. 195.

[4] See above, pp. 382–3.

[5] *Life of Lord Ripon*, I, pp. 226–8.

[6] *Letters of Queen Victoria*, 2nd series, II, p. 223.

[7] *Life of Gladstone*, III, pp. 135 *et seq.*; above, p. 383.

[8] *Life of Sir Henry Campbell-Bannerman*, II, pp. 307–11; *Life of Lord Lansdowne*, p. 356; *Life of Randall Davidson*, I, pp. 726–9.

[9] *Life of Lord Oxford and Asquith*, I, pp. 285–93.

[10] See above, pp. 382–90.

[11] *Life of Gladstone*, III, p. 257.

[12] G. Saintsbury, *Lord Derby*, ch. VIII.

unusual because Lord Derby did not desire to form a Government and Lord Palmerston was the main bulwark against Radicalism. Even so, it had to be kept secret for fear of 'mutiny in Lord Derby's camp'.[1] Unusual, also, was the agreement between the Government, the Opposition and the Speaker to bring to an end the famous long sitting of 31 January–2 February 1881, and the agreement between Government and Opposition for proposals to reduce Irish obstruction.[2]

Sometimes, the attempt of the Government to secure collaboration does not succeed. The Education Bill of 1906 did not pass. The Constitutional Conference of 1910 could not reach agreement. Attempts in 1917 and 1948 to secure agreement on the reform of the House of Lords proved abortive. The attempts of Mr Disraeli to minimise opposition to his Eastern policy in 1877 did not succeed.[3] Sir Henry Campbell-Bannerman refused to assist Mr Joseph Chamberlain in his attempts to 'bluff' President Kruger by waving a big stick.[4] The reform of the House of Lords still awaits an agreed solution after more than half a century. But a Government that does not make outrageous demands will not be met by outrageous demands. Where there is a desire to compromise on one side, it will usually be met by a similar desire on the other. Where no acceptance of policy is involved, the collaboration of Opposition leaders can readily be secured. Mr Balfour assisted the Committee of Imperial Defence in 1908.[5] The Labour Government of 1929 to 1931 similarly invited Opposition leaders to take part in some aspects of the Committee's work.[6] Discussions by a minority Government with the third party are not of the same character, but they help to make the machine work even under difficulties, as in 1886–92 and 1929–31.[7]

§5. *The Electors' Mandate*

In the last resort, a Government which has a majority in the House of Commons and does not fear the House of Lords can pass through

[1] Guedalla, *Gladstone and Palmerston*, p. 150.

[2] *Letters of Queen Victoria*, 2nd series, II, pp. 532, 534, 538.

[3] *Ibid.* III, pp. 187–95.

[4] *Life of Sir Henry Campbell-Bannerman*, I, pp. 233–5. (It is immaterial whether he in fact did or did not use the word 'Bluff'.)

[5] *Life of Lord Oxford and Asquith*, I, pp. 243–7; *Esher Papers*, II, pp. 316–17, 364.

[6] Above, p. 304.

[7] Snowden, *Autobiography*, II, pp. 879–89.

Parliament any proposals which it considers politic to put forward: this is subject to the doctrine of the 'mandate'. This doctrine appears to have been invented by the Conservatives to justify the opposition of the House of Lords to Liberal measures.[1] It is, however, based upon an important principle. A Government exists only because it has secured a majority at an election, or is likely to secure such a majority when an election takes place: but it secures that majority by appealing to the electorate to support a policy. The electorate expects that that policy will be carried to fruition. It does not expect that radical changes will be made unless they were part of the party policy or are the necessary consequences of that policy. The Government must, of course, meet emergencies if and when they arise, but, emergencies apart, major developments of policy should not be entered upon without that approval of the electorate which is secured by the return of a party to power.

The principle was well put by Lord Hartington in opposing the Home Rule Bill in 1886.

> Although no principle of a 'mandate' may exist, there are certain limits which Parliament is morally bound to observe, and beyond which Parliament has, morally, not the right to go in its relations with the constituents. The constituencies of Great Britain[2] are the source of the power at all events of this branch of Parliament, and I maintain that, in the absence of an emergency that could not be foreseen, the House of Commons has no right to initiate legislation, especially immediately upon its first meeting, of which the constituencies were not informed, and of which the constituencies might have been informed, and of which if they had been informed, there is, at all events, the very greatest doubt as to what their decision might be.[3]

Whether a mandate has been given, and of what a mandate consists, are matters of argument. Lord Salisbury announced before the election

[1] Cf. *Life of Robert, Marquis of Salisbury*, II, pp. 23–8. As early as 1869, however, Lord Derby justified his opposition to the Irish Church Bill by asserting that though the subject was before the electorate at the general election of 1868, the electorate had had no opportunity of judging the merits of the Bill itself: *Letters of Queen Victoria*, 2nd series, I, p. 607. Lord Randolph Churchill said in 1883 that the proposal to enable a person to affirm instead of taking an oath was 'a change in the Constitution of such vital and momentous importance that the people of this country will not hastily ratify it and that the opinion of the country must be ascertained before the Parliament can assent to it': *Life of Randolph Churchill*, I, p. 253.

[2] Unionists affected to ignore the opinion of Ireland on its own destiny.

[3] *Life of the Duke of Devonshire*, II, pp. 141–2.

of 1892 that the Opposition had put so many matters before the electors that he would not regard a Liberal majority as giving a mandate for Home Rule.[1] Lord Hartington moved the rejection of the Home Rule Bill in the following year on the ground that in a case so serious not only the principle but the form of the measure should be before the country before the election before a mandate could be said to have been given.[2] Other Unionists pointed out that if the electors of Ireland were not counted, the Government had not a mandate at all. Similarly the Unionists demanded that the Government receive a mandate for the land taxes of 1909. When that had been given, they demanded that it receive a mandate for the Parliament Bill; and, because, having asked for a mandate for that purpose, the Liberals could not be said to have obtained a mandate for Home Rule, they demanded another election in 1913.[3] In short, the doctrine of the mandate is part of the political cant. It is a stick used by the Opposition to beat the Government. It could hardly be said in 1918 that Mr Lloyd George had a mandate for the extension of the suffrage, especially to women. In 1921 he had no mandate for the settlement of the Irish question which had dominated politics from 1885 to 1914. Mr Baldwin in 1928 had no mandate for giving women an equal franchise with men.

The doctrine is, however, of importance. Though it must necessarily be vague and its operation a matter of dispute, it is recognised to exist. Mr Joseph Chamberlain raised the tariff question in 1903 in order that a mandate might be obtained at the next election.[4] The official Liberal policy in 1905 accepted Home Rule in principle but asserted that no mandate for it was being sought and no measure for this purpose would be proposed without a fresh reference to the electors.[5] Mr Baldwin dissolved Parliament in 1923 because he wanted a mandate for tariff reform.[6] He did not introduce a general tariff between 1924 and 1929 because, as he admitted, he had no mandate for it. The National

[1] *Life of Robert, Marquis of Salisbury*, IV, p. 403.

[2] *Life of the Duke of Devonshire*, II, p. 254.

[3] See Appendix III.

[4] *Life of the Duke of Devonshire*, II, p. 303.

[5] *Life of Lord Oxford and Asquith*, I, p. 176.

[6] 'My Ministry recently laid before the country proposals which, in their judgment, would have contributed substantially to a solution of this problem [of unemployment] ...but these proposals were not accepted by the country.' (The King's Speech, 15 January 1924.) 169 H.C.Deb. 5 s., 79.

Government was able to introduce it in 1932 because, at least as the Conservatives insisted, they had secured a 'doctor's mandate' to do what seemed best, after inquiry, to redress something called 'the adverse balance of trade'. The National Government asked for a renewal of its mandate in 1935 because, as it alleged, the causes which had called the first National Government into existence had not disappeared. Because it is a stick to beat the Government it is important, for its plausibility is obvious. It is a useful argument that the Government has used its majority to effect changes to which the electorate has not been asked to consent. It suggests that the Government cannot be trusted and ought to be turned out. Honesty apart, it is politic for the Government to consider whether or not the argument can, in future, be used against it with effect.

There may indeed be circumstances in which it is the duty of the Government to ignore its lack of mandate and even to act counter to the mandate which it has received. From 1919 to 1935 the policy of His Majesty's Government, whatever party was in power, was based upon the principle of 'collective security' through the League of Nations. This principle was affirmed by the Conservative party at every general election and was stated even more emphatically by the Liberal and Labour parties. What is more, a powerful non-political, or at least all-party, organisation, the League of Nations Union, had an efficient and active propaganda machine which had helped to convince the electorate that this was the policy to follow. Nor indeed did the electorate need much convincing, for collective security seemed to offer a means of avoiding the repetition of the sort of war from which every family in the country had suffered from 1914 to 1918. The opposite policy, of reliance on armaments and alliances, was believed to lead and to have led in 1914 to war. In retrospect it will generally be agreed that the thesis became untenable in 1931, when the League of Nations failed to prevent the Japanese attack on Manchuria, though it will not be agreed whether this was due to the defects of the League organisation, as the Conservatives would contend, or to the failure of the National Government to use the League machinery properly, as the Opposition contended. On this point public opinion seemed to be with the Opposition, not only in 1931 but even after the accession of Hitler in 1933.

In the autumn of 1933 the Government lost a by-election at East Fulham at which the successful Labour candidate had placed unusual emphasis on collective security and had attacked the Government for failing to support it by its actions. Nor did opinion change when Hitler began rearming Germany contrary to the Treaty of Versailles, withdrew from the League of Nations, and reoccupied the Rhineland, nor when the League of Nations failed to prevent Mussolini from attacking Abyssinia. In fact, the Opposition continued to vote against the Service Estimates until 1937.

Members of the Government, on the other hand, had apparently reached the conclusion in the winter of 1933–4 that a policy of re-armament was necessary because collective security had failed and was bound to fail. Mr Neville Chamberlain has said that the whole of 1934 was occupied in examining the deficiencies of the defence system and drawing up a new programme, and that it was not until 1935 that the Government knew what it wanted to do.[1]

Owing to the force of public opinion, nothing was said about this in public, and even at the general election of 1935 the need for rearmament was not stressed. Indeed, the Conservative party manifesto asked for a mandate for 'the establishment of a settled peace' and stated the Government's intention 'to continue to do all in our power to uphold the Covenant and to maintain and increase the efficiency of the League'.[2] Mr Neville Chamberlain wanted to fight the election on Defence—to 'substitute for the hope of fresh benefits (in social services, etc.) a fear in the public mind—always the strongest motive to induce people to vote'. He mentioned the danger of attempting to keep rearmament secret—an accusation 'that we had deliberately deceived the people'. The election agents thought otherwise and Mr Chamberlain's view did not prevail. The need for rearmament was mentioned in the Conservative party manifesto but it was not given the emphasis which it was clearly receiving in the Cabinet.[3]

In November 1936, in reply to accusations by Mr Churchill that the national defences were inadequate, Mr Baldwin pointed out that Britain

[1] *Life of Neville Chamberlain*, pp. 312–13.
[2] *House of Commons* (*The Times*, 1935), p. 23.
[3] *Life of Neville Chamberlain*, pp. 266–9.

started late and said he wanted to say a word about 'the years the locusts have eaten'. Mr Churchill had mentioned the anxieties caused after the events in January 1933 and the urgent need of the Government to make preparations in 1933–4. He (Mr Baldwin) had said that a democracy was always two years behind a dictator, and it was so in this case. He put his view before the House 'with an appalling frankness'. From 1933 he and his friends were worried about events in Europe. A Disarmament Conference was sitting and in 1933 and 1934 a more strongly pacifist feeling was running through the country than at any time since the war—as witness the East Fulham by-election.

My position as the leader of a great party was not altogether a comfortable one. I asked myself what chance was there—when that feeling that was given expression to in Fulham was common throughout the country—what chance was there within the next year or two of that feeling being so changed that the country would give a mandate for rearmament? Supposing I had gone to the country and said that Germany was rearming and that we must rearm, does anybody think that this pacific democracy would have rallied to that cry at that moment? I cannot think of anything that would have made the loss of the election from my point of view more certain. I think the country itself learned by certain events that took place during the winter of 1934–5 what the perils might be to it. All I did was to take a moment perhaps less unfortunate than another might have been, and we won the election with a large majority; but frankly I could conceive that we should at that time, by advocating certain courses, have been a great deal less successful. We got from the country—with a large majority—a mandate for doing a thing that no one, 12 months before, would have believed possible. It is my firm conviction that had the Government, with this great majority, used that majority to do anything that might be described as arming without a mandate —and they did not do anything, except the slightly increased air programme for which they gave their reasons—had I taken such action as my Right Hon. Friend desired me to take, it would have defeated entirely the end I had in view.[1]

Mr Chamberlain's comment was that the statement had a good deal of truth in it but not the whole truth. Working out the programme took nearly the whole of 1934 and it was not until 1935 that they knew what they wanted to do. 'To the best of my recollection we then

[1] 317 H.C.Deb. 5 s., 1144–5 (12 November 1936).

started on the programme, but we did not tell the public except in the most general terms until after the election.'[1]

It is clear enough that in the winter of 1933–4 the MacDonald Government had no 'mandate' for a rearmament programme which would assure the failure of collective security. It is equally clear that if a general election had been held at that time on such issues the National Government would have lost many seats. Mr Baldwin's view apparently,[2] was that an election fought on this issue would have been lost at any time 'within the next year or two' (presumably up to the autumn of 1935), though opinion began to change in the winter of 1934–5. Mr Baldwin became Prime Minister in June 1935 and dissolved Parliament in October 1935. Though the need for better armaments was mentioned in the manifesto the election was not fought on that issue, as Mr Neville Chamberlain had suggested, and equal prominence was given to collective security. Nevertheless, the election was taken to have given a 'mandate' for a large rearmament programme.

The incident thus bears witness to the weakness as well as the strength of the doctrine of the mandate. It is strong enough to prevent a Government from doing what it believes to be necessary in the interests of the country, but it is weak enough to enable that Government—to use an understatement—to put the best construction on its actions and to wrap up its request for a 'mandate' in sufficiently vague language.

* * * * *

[1] *Life of Neville Chamberlain*, pp. 312–13.

[2] In R. Bassett, 'Telling the Truth to the People: The Myth of the Baldwin Confession', *Cambridge Journal*, vol. II, pp. 84–95, it is argued that Mr Baldwin referred not to the election of 1935 but to a hypothetical election in 1933–4. This was not the impression when the general election of 1935 and the subsequent rearmament programme were fresh in our minds, and Mr Chamberlain's papers seem to support the contemporary opinion. The Government did not 'tell the public until after the election'. Besides, Mr Baldwin was not Prime Minister in 1933–4. Mr A. W. Baldwin has a better defence in his biography, *My Father*, pp. 267–87. The first defence, that Mr Baldwin did not mean what he said, but was merely musing aloud, is unconvincing; the second, that it is the duty of a statesman to carry the country with him, makes the question one of ethics. A statesman has to persuade, and that takes time. How long ought he to dissemble between elections, and to what extent is it permissible to dissemble at a general election? See also Lord Templewood, *Nine Troubled Years*, pp. 192–6. Lord Templewood considers that Mr Baldwin referred to a hypothetical election in 1933, and not to the general election of 1935, but does not quote the 'mandate' which the Conservative party sought in 1935, nor the material in Mr Neville Chamberlain's papers.

Cromwell said that when he forcibly dissolved the Long Parliament 'not a dog barked'. Government can be carried on quite successfully without a Parliament. It is indeed a dilatory and inefficient talking machine. Yet speed and efficiency are not the only requirements of government. Justice is the supreme political virtue. Nor is ability to act first and think afterwards, if at all, a quality which commends itself. The British governmental machine is, in spite of its many defects, one of the most efficient, if not the most efficient, constitutional structures of the world. It is reasonably efficient because it can be criticised. It is reasonably just because its actions are proclaimed to the people by those who have no cause to praise it. It is, in short, a good system because it rests upon Parliament and, through Parliament, upon the willing consent of those who are governed. The dogs bark *in* Parliament; if there were no Parliament, they might bite.

APPENDIX I

GOVERNMENTS SINCE 1835

1. *Whig Government, 1835–1841*

Prime Minister: Viscount Melbourne.

Leader of the House of Commons: Lord John Russell.

The Government was formed in 1835 after the defeat of Sir Robert Peel's Government at the general election. It was maintained in office by Queen Victoria. It resigned in 1839 because it secured an inadequate majority on the Jamaica Bill. Melbourne advised the Queen to send for the Duke of Wellington; but the latter advised her to send for Sir Robert Peel. Peel accepted the commission but resigned it owing to the 'Bedchamber Question'. The Whig Cabinet accepted responsibility for the Queen's refusal to change her Ladies, and continued in office, without an effective majority, until 1841. Being then defeated on a no-confidence resolution, it advised a dissolution. The Conservatives secured a majority, but the Government met Parliament, was defeated on amendments to the Address in both Houses, and resigned.

BIBLIOGRAPHY

For the resignation of 1839 and the 'Bedchamber Question', see *Letters of Queen Victoria*, 1st series, I, pp. 198–218; *Peel Papers*, II, pp. 387–407; *Memoirs of Lord Melbourne*, pp. 480–4; *Melbourne Papers*, pp. 396–8; Clark, *Peel and the Conservative Party*, pp. 415–25.

2. *Conservative Government, 1841–1846*

Prime Minister: Sir Robert Peel.

On the defeat of his Government, Lord Melbourne advised the Queen to send for Sir Robert Peel. Negotiations between the Prince Consort and Peel, through the former's secretary, had removed the difficulty of the Ladies. Accordingly, Peel formed his Government and remained in office with a majority until 1845. In 1845 the Government resigned owing to differences of opinion about the Corn Laws. In informal discussions with the Queen, Peel suggested that she should send for Lord John Russell. Russell occupied a week in discussing with his friends and trying to secure a definite promise of support from Sir Robert Peel. Finally he refused to take office, on the ground that Lord Grey would not accept office if Lord Palmerston was at the

Foreign Office, and the support of both was necessary. Peel therefore continued in office and repealed the Corn Laws, but was defeated on a Coercion Bill in 1846 by a combination of Whigs and Protectionists, and resigned.

BIBLIOGRAPHY

For the formation of Peel's Government, see *Letters of Queen Victoria*, 1st series, I, pp. 337–90; *Peel Papers*, II, pp. 455–80; *Life of the Prince Consort*, I, pp. 105–11. For the crisis of 1845, see *Letters of Queen Victoria*, 1st series, II, pp. 55–74; *Peel Papers*, III, pp. 229–55 and 283–5; *Memoirs of Sir Robert Peel*, II, pp. 97–235; *Life of Lord John Russell*, I, pp. 409–19; *Later Correspondence of Lord John Russell*, I, pp. 87–99.

3. *Whig Government, 1846–1852*

Prime Minister: Lord John Russell.

Peel was defeated in 1846 by the Protectionists supporting the Whigs. The Queen sent for Lord John Russell who, after seeing Peel, undertook to form a Government, though in a minority in the House of Commons. It remained without an effective majority even after the general election of 1847, but could rely on Peelite support. In 1851 a Franchise motion which was opposed by the Government was passed in the House of Commons, and the Government resigned. In informal discussion, it was agreed that the Queen ought to send for Lord Stanley, as the leader of the Protectionist Opposition. The Protectionists had not, however, been responsible for the defeat, and Lord Stanley considered that it ought first to be seen whether some other Government was not possible. He suggested a coalition of Whigs and Peelites; but if it was clear that no other Government could be formed, he would accept the obligation of forming a Protectionist Government. The Queen then sent for Lord John Russell and Sir James Graham (as a prominent Peelite) to put the case before them. The Duke of Wellington, Lord Aberdeen, and Russell and Graham again were consulted in ensuing discussions. Ultimately, the Peelites refused to serve with Russell, and Lord Stanley was again asked to form a Government. Stanley attempted to obtain Peelite support; and, this failing, a Protectionist party meeting decided that he could not take office owing to the refusal of some of his prominent supporters to join a Government. Lord John Russell was then sent for and he agreed to resume office. He being unable to obtain Peelite support, the Whig Government was restored. After the dismissal of Lord Palmerston from the Foreign Office, however, the Government was defeated in 1852 on the Militia Bill, and resigned.

BIBLIOGRAPHY

On the resignation of Peel and the formation of the Whig Government, see *Letters of Queen Victoria*, 1st series, II, pp. 94–100; *Memoirs of Sir Robert Peel*, II, pp. 288–325; *Life of Lord John Russell*, I, pp. 420–8.

For the crisis of 1851, see *Letters of Queen Victoria*, 1st series, II, pp. 345–81; *Life of Lord John Russell*, II, pp. 123–8; *Life of Sir James Graham*, II, pp. 126–31; *Life of Disraeli*, I, pp. 1101–12.

4. *Conservative Government, 1852*

Prime Minister: Earl of Derby.

Leader of the House of Commons: Mr Disraeli.

The events of 1851 had indicated that on the defeat of the Whig Government the Queen should send for Lord Derby (formerly Lord Stanley). Lord Derby accepted the Commission, though he had no majority in the House of Commons. After vainly seeking the collaboration of Lord Palmerston he formed a Conservative Government consisting of persons nearly all of whom had had no previous ministerial experience (the 'who-who' Ministry). At the general election five months later the Government's strength in the House of Commons was increased, and theirs was by far the largest party. Opposition, however, brought together the Opposition groups and the Government was defeated on the Budget and resigned.

BIBLIOGRAPHY

For the formation of the Government, see *Letters of Queen Victoria*, 1st series, II, pp. 444–53; *Life of Disraeli*, I, pp. 1147–62.

5. *Coalition Government, 1852–1855*

Prime Minister: Earl of Aberdeen.

Leader of the House of Commons: Lord John Russell.

The Whigs and Peelites in opposition had come to an agreement to serve under the Earl of Aberdeen. This information becoming known to Lord Derby, he informed the Queen. He advised the Queen, however, to send for Lord Lansdowne, though the Prince Consort pointed out that it did not lie with him to give advice. The Queen sent for both Lansdowne and Aberdeen but Lansdowne was unable to come, and Aberdeen consulted him before seeing the Queen and had come to an understanding with him. The Queen commissioned Lord Aberdeen to form a Government, and he accepted. The allocation of offices between Whigs and Peelites, and the position of Lord John Russell as the Whig leader, caused difficulties which were overcome. In spite of the testimony of the Duke of Argyll, the coalition was not a success. On the resignation of Lord John Russell in 1855, owing to his alleged inability to oppose Roebuck's motion for a Select Committee on the Crimean War, the Government decided to resign, but on the Queen's insistence decided to meet the motion. Being defeated, it then resigned.

BIBLIOGRAPHY

For the formation of the Government, see *Letters of Queen Victoria*, 1st series, II, pp. 499–516; *Life of Lord John Russell*, pp. 154–69; *Life of Sir James Graham*, II, pp. 165–200; Stanhope, *Lord Aberdeen*, ch. VIII; Balfour, *Life of the Earl of Aberdeen*, II, pp. 171–7.

6. *Liberal Government, 1855–1858*

Prime Minister: Viscount Palmerston.

On the resignation of Lord Aberdeen's Government, informal discussions took place, at which it was agreed that the Queen should send for Lord Derby. He refused unless he could get support. Failing to get support from any Peelites or from Lord Palmerston, he refused office. The Queen then saw Lord Lansdowne as an 'elder statesman'. He refused to consider becoming Prime Minister, and suggested Lord Clarendon. This suggestion being scouted by the Queen, he agreed to see Lord Palmerston, the leading Peelites, and Lord John Russell. As a result of these discussions, he suggested that the Queen should send for Lord John Russell, though he did not believe that Russell could form a Government. The Queen accepted this suggestion, and Lord John Russell thought that he could form a Government. On making the attempt, he thought differently. The Queen then saw Lord Palmerston and Lord Clarendon and, subsequently, Lord Lansdowne again. As a result of these discussions, she asked Lord Palmerston if he could form a Government. He was able to reform the coalition but, when it was decided to accept Roebuck's motion, three leading Peelites resigned. The Government thus became almost wholly Liberal and brought the war to a conclusion. For a time, there appeared to be some prospect of the reabsorption of the Peelites in the Conservative party, and the Government was defeated in 1857 on its China policy. It advised the Queen to dissolve Parliament, and was returned with a triumphant majority. It was, nevertheless, defeated on the (Orsini) Conspiracy Bill in 1858, and resigned.

BIBLIOGRAPHY

On the resignation of Lord Aberdeen's Government and the formation of Palmerston's Government, see *Letters of Queen Victoria*, 1st series, III, pp. 93–131; *Life of Lord John Russell*, II, pp. 237–41; Ashley, *Life of Viscount Palmerston*, II, pp. 70–80; Guedalla, *Gladstone and Palmerston*, pp. 100–7; Stanhope, *Lord Aberdeen*, chs. X and XI; Balfour, *Life of the Earl of Aberdeen*, II, pp. 288–96; *Life of Disraeli*, I, pp. 1372–80; *Life of Gladstone*, I, pp. 521–39.

7. *Conservative Government, 1858–1859*

Prime Minister: Earl of Derby.

Leader of the House of Commons: Mr Disraeli.

On the resignation of Lord Palmerston, the Queen sent for Lord Derby, who asked for time for consideration, seeing that (as he said with some exaggeration) he had a majority of two to one against him in the House of Commons. The Prince Consort saw Lord Clarendon, and, as a result, came to the conclusion that Palmerston's resignation was to be taken seriously. Accordingly, the Queen asked Derby to form a Government. He approached Lord Grey and Mr Gladstone, but they refused to join. He therefore formed a wholly Conservative Government. By adroit management in the House of Commons, the Government continued until the spring of 1859, when it was defeated on the Reform Bill and advised a dissolution. As a result of the election the Conservative force in the House of Commons was increased, but not by enough to give the Government a clear majority over a united Opposition. As in 1852, Opposition created union, and attempts by the Government to take in Palmerston or Gladstone were unsuccessful. An agreed amendment to the Address was proposed and carried, and the Government resigned.

BIBLIOGRAPHY

For the formation of Derby's second Government, see *Letters of Queen Victoria*, 1st series, III, pp. 335–45; *Life of Disraeli*, I, pp. 1513–19; *Life of Gladstone*, I, pp. 574–91.

8. *Liberal Government, 1859–1865*

Prime Minister: Viscount Palmerston.

Lord Palmerston and Lord John Russell had agreed, before the defeat of Lord Derby's Government, that if either of them was sent for by the Queen, the other would serve under him. The Queen had, however, already informed Lord Granville that she regarded him as the leader of the Liberal party. When

Derby resigned, therefore, she asked Granville to form a Government. He replied that he regarded either Lord Palmerston or Lord John Russell as the prospective Prime Minister. The Queen replied that it was invidious to choose between them, that each led a section only of the Liberal party, and that Granville had been selected as the leader of the Party in the House of Lords. Granville then accepted the task of making the attempt. Lord Palmerston was willing to serve under Lord Granville, but Lord John Russell was not willing, and Granville therefore declined the post. The Queen thereupon commissioned Lord Palmerston to form a Government. He was able to secure the adhesion of Lord John Russell and Mr Gladstone, and so created a united Liberal Party. The Government continued in office until the death of Lord Palmerston in 1865.

BIBLIOGRAPHY

For the formation of Lord Palmerston's second Government, see *Letters of Queen Victoria*, 1st series, III, pp. 436–45; *Life of Lord Granville*, I, pp. 324–6; Ashley, *Life of Viscount Palmerston*, II, pp. 154–7; *Life of Lord John Russell*, II, pp. 304–9.

9. *Liberal Government, 1865–1866*

Prime Minister: Earl Russell.

Leader of the House of Commons: Mr Gladstone.

On the death of Lord Palmerston, Earl Russell (formerly Lord John Russell) was appointed Prime Minister and re-formed the Government with a considerable reshuffling of offices. It was, however, defeated in the following year on the Reform Bill, Mr Lowe leading a section of Liberals (known as the 'Cave of Adullam') to vote against the Government, and the Government resigned.

BIBLIOGRAPHY

On the formation of Earl Russell's second Government, see *Letters of Queen Victoria*, 2nd series, I, pp. 279–83; *Life of Gladstone*, II, pp. 151–7.

10. *Conservative Government, 1866–1868*

Prime Minister: Earl of Derby.

Leader of the House of Commons: Mr Disraeli.

On the resignation of Earl Russell's Government, the Queen urged them to continue. After reconsideration, however, they decided upon resignation, and the Queen sent for Lord Derby. Since there had recently been a general election at which the Liberals had obtained a majority, his position was again difficult. A party meeting agreed that he should form a Government if he could find sufficient support, and overtures were made to Lord Clarendon, the Duke of Somerset, and some of the Adullamite leaders, but without success. Derby then formed a wholly Conservative Government. This remained in office, though in a minority, until 1868, and even passed the second Reform Act. Derby resigned, owing to ill-health, in 1868.

BIBLIOGRAPHY

For the formation of Derby's third Government, see *Letters of Queen Victoria*, 2nd series, I, pp. 333–54; *Life of Disraeli*, II, pp. 173–9; *Life of Lord John Russell*, II, pp. 414–17.

11. *Conservative Government, 1868*

Prime Minister: Mr Disraeli.

On his retirement, Lord Derby advised the Queen to send for Mr Disraeli. This was done, and Disraeli formed a Government differing but little from that of Lord Derby. The Government was, however, defeated within a couple of months on a motion by Mr Gladstone on the Irish Church. Disraeli, with the Queen's strong support, refused to resign, but decided to expedite the making of the new register of electors and to appeal to the country when that was done. At the general election six months later, the Government was decisively defeated, and it then resigned without meeting Parliament.

BIBLIOGRAPHY

For the appointment of Mr Disraeli, see *Letters of Queen Victoria*, 2nd series, I, pp. 495–509; *Life of Disraeli*, II, pp. 316–34.

For the controversy on Mr Disraeli's refusal to resign, see *Letters of Queen Victoria*, 2nd series, I, pp. 521–8; *Life of Disraeli*, II, pp. 366–79; *Life of Gladstone*, II, pp. 247–8.

12. *Liberal Government, 1868–1874*

Prime Minister: Mr Gladstone.

On the resignation of Mr Disraeli's Government, the Queen passed over Earl Russell and sent for Mr Gladstone, who formed a Government. In 1873 it was defeated on the Irish University Bill, and resigned. The Queen sent for Mr Disraeli, who was prepared to take office, but not with the then House of Commons; i.e. he wanted Gladstone to dissolve, and would be prepared to take office if the Conservatives obtained a majority. The Liberal

Government therefore continued in office until it was defeated at the general election in 1874, when it resigned without meeting Parliament.

BIBLIOGRAPHY

For the formation of Mr Gladstone's Government, see *Letters of Queen Victoria*, 2nd series, I, pp. 559–68; *Life of Gladstone*, II, pp. 249–56.

For the controversy of 1873, see Guedalla, *The Queen and Mr Gladstone*, I, pp. 385—410; *Life of Gladstone*, II, pp. 446–56; *Life of Disraeli*, II, pp. 546–60; *Life of Gathorne-Hardy*, I, pp. 319–25.

13. *Conservative Government, 1874–1880*

Prime Minister: Mr Disraeli (raised to the peerage as Earl of Beaconsfield while in office).

On the resignation of the Liberal Government, the Queen sent for Mr Disraeli, who made no difficulty about forming a Government. No essential change was made when the Prime Minister became Earl of Beaconsfield in 1876, and the Government remained in office until, being defeated at the general election of 1880, it resigned without meeting Parliament.

BIBLIOGRAPHY

For the formation of Mr Disraeli's second Government, see *Letters of Queen Victoria*, 2nd series, II, pp. 315–21; *Life of Disraeli*, II, pp. 621–8.

14. *Liberal Government, 1880–1885*

Prime Minister: Mr Gladstone.

The choice of a successor to the Earl of Beaconsfield was by no means easy. Mr Gladstone had retired from the leadership of the Liberal Party after its defeat in 1874. In accordance with the usual practice he had not been replaced, but the Marquis of Hartington had led the Opposition in the House of Commons and Earl Granville in the House of Lords. Lord Beaconsfield, the Prince of Wales, and others advised the Queen to send for Lord Hartington, and this was her first step. But the lead in the attack on Lord Beaconsfield had in fact been taken by Mr Gladstone, both in the House of Commons and in the constituencies. The election was viewed in the constituencies as a personal duel between Beaconsfield and Gladstone. Hartington and Granville agreed that Gladstone must become Prime Minister, and so informed the Queen. Nevertheless, Hartington agreed to form a Government if Gladstone would consent to serve. This Gladstone refused to do, whereupon the Queen, on Hartington's advice, sent for

Mr Gladstone, who formed a Government. There were many attendant personal difficulties, not only between the Queen and the new Prime Minister, but also between the Prime Minister and the Radical section of his party.

The Government was defeated on the Budget in 1885. An immediate dissolution was not possible, since the Redistribution Bill consequent upon the third Reform Act was not yet through Parliament. The Government therefore resigned.

BIBLIOGRAPHY

For the formation of Mr Gladstone's second Government, see *Letters of Queen Victoria*, 2nd series, III, pp. 73–90; *Life of Disraeli*, II, pp. 1396–1413; *Life of Gladstone*, II, pp. 616–31; *Life of the Duke of Devonshire*, I, pp. 255–81; *Life of Lord Granville*, II, pp. 193–4; *Life of Sir Charles Dilke*, I, pp. 303–12; *Life of Joseph Chamberlain*, I, pp. 285–303.

15. *Conservative Government, 1885–1886*

Prime Minister: Marquis of Salisbury.

Leader of the House of Commons: Sir Michael Hicks Beach.

Since the death of the Earl of Beaconsfield there had been no leader of the Conservative party. The Marquis of Salisbury led the party in the House of Lords, and Sir Stafford Northcote in the House of Commons. Theoretically, therefore, the Queen had a choice between them. But in effect the leadership had been vested in Lord Salisbury, and on the resignation of Gladstone's Government she entrusted him with the task of forming a Government. Salisbury considered that the Government ought not to have resigned. He asked for pledges of support from the Liberal party while the steps preliminary to a dissolution were being taken. At first Gladstone refused, and Salisbury asked the Queen to make a formal statement in writing; this the Queen, on Sir Henry Ponsonby's advice, refused to do. Ultimately a formula was agreed between the two leaders, and Lord Salisbury formed a Government. At the ensuing general election, the Conservatives did not secure a majority. But as it was by no means clear that the Liberals could form a Government with a majority, owing to internal dissensions, the Government met Parliament and was defeated on a 'three acres and a cow' amendment to the Address, whereupon the Government resigned.

BIBLIOGRAPHY

For the formation of Lord Salisbury's first Government, see *Letters of Queen Victoria*, 2nd series, III, pp. 657–80; *Life of Lord Randolph Churchill*, I, pp. 397–422; *Life of Gladstone*, III, pp. 200–8; Guedalla, *The Queen and Mr Gladstone*, II, pp. 361–75; *Life of Robert, Marquis of Salisbury*, III, pp. 133–43; *Life of Sir Michael Hicks Beach*, I, pp. 232–7; *Lord John Manners and his Friends*, II, pp. 307–13.

16. *Liberal Government, 1886*

Prime Minister: Mr Gladstone.

The defeat of Mr Gladstone's second Government was due to serious differences of opinion on the subject of the government of Ireland, though the actual occasion was a defeat on the Budget. The general election of 1885 did not solve the difficulties, and though the great body of the party supported the amendment which compelled Lord Salisbury to resign, they did so primarily because it had nothing to do with Ireland. The formation of a Liberal Government was therefore attended with considerable difficulties. The Queen's views by this time were in fundamental opposition to Gladstone's policies. Before Lord Salisbury's resignation, she communicated with Mr Goschen with the intention of persuading the Whigs not to join with Mr Gladstone in turning out the Government. Mr Goschen, Lord Hartington and Sir Henry James in fact voted with the Government on the 'three acres and a cow' amendment. On the resignation of Lord Salisbury, the Queen, on Lord Salisbury's formal advice sent for Mr Goschen. He asked leave not to obey the command, and Sir Henry Ponsonby saw him on the Queen's behalf. Mr Goschen advised the Queen to send for Mr Gladstone, as Lord Salisbury had already done. Mr Gladstone accepted, but was unable to secure the support of the Whigs, and obtained Mr Joseph Chamberlain's support only until the Irish policy was declared. The defection of these leaders and their supporters left the Government without a majority, and it was defeated on the Home Rule Bill. Parliament was dissolved, but an anti-Home Rule majority was returned, and the Government resigned without meeting Parliament.

BIBLIOGRAPHY

For the formation of Mr Gladstone's third Government, see *Letters of Queen Victoria*, 2nd series, III, pp. 706–18; 3rd series, I, pp. 5–46; *Life of Robert, Marquis of Salisbury*, III, pp. 272–92; *Life of Gladstone*, III, pp. 277–97; *Life of Lord Goschen*, I, pp. 312–21; II, pp. 1–24; *Life of Lord Randolph Churchill*, II, pp. 1–47; *Life of Joseph Chamberlain*, II, pp. 159–73; Joseph Chamberlain, *A Memoir*, pp. 185–9.

17. *Conservative Government, 1886–1892*

Prime Minister: Marquis of Salisbury.

Leaders of the House of Commons: Lord Randolph Churchill (1886); Mr W. H. Smith (1886–1892).

On the resignation of Mr Gladstone's third Government, the Queen asked Mr Goschen if she should send for Lord Salisbury. His answer was in the affirmative, and Lord Salisbury formed his second Government. There was no Conservative majority, but the Government had an effective majority so long as it could rely on the support of the Liberal-Unionists. Lord Salisbury tried to form a coalition with the Liberal-Unionists, but failed, though Mr Goschen became Chancellor of the Exchequer on the resignation of Lord Randolph Churchill at the end of 1886. The Government had no difficulty in maintaining itself in office so long as the Parliament lasted, but at the general election of 1892 the Liberals gained enough votes to be able to out-vote the Government whenever they could secure the support of the Irish Nationalist Party. The Government met Parliament, but was defeated on a no-confidence amendment to the Address, and resigned.

BIBLIOGRAPHY

For the formation of Lord Salisbury's second Government, see *Letters of Queen Victoria*, 3rd series, I, pp. 161–71; *Life of Robert, Marquis of Salisbury*, III, pp. 307–12; *Life of Lord Goschen*, II, pp. 81–96; *Life of the Duke of Devonshire*, II, pp. 162–74; *Life of Lord Randolph Churchill*, II, pp. 116–27.

18. *Liberal Government, 1892–1894*

Prime Minister: Mr Gladstone.

Before the election of 1892, the Queen had decided to send for Lord Rosebery in the event of a Liberal victory. But Sir Henry Ponsonby went round collecting views, and the Queen was convinced that she had no alternative but to send for Mr Gladstone. Mr Gladstone's fourth Government remained in office until his personal resignation in 1894, though the strength of the Liberal party in the House of Commons was less than the combined Unionist Opposition.

BIBLIOGRAPHY

For the formation of Mr Gladstone's fourth Government, see *Letters of Queen Victoria*, 3rd series, II, pp. 103–46; *Life of Gladstone*, III, pp. 490–5; Guedalla, *The Queen and Mr Gladstone*, II, pp. 436–40; *Life of Lord Rosebery*, II, pp. 399–403.

19. *Liberal Government, 1894–1895*

Prime Minister: Earl of Rosebery.

Leader of the House of Commons: Sir William Harcourt.

Mr Gladstone's resignation was stated to be due to ill-health, but was in fact due to differences of opinion as to the Estimates. He was not asked formally to give his opinion as to his successor, and he refused to answer informal questions by Sir Henry Ponsonby except at the Queen's request.

He told Lord Acton that, if asked, he would advise her to send for Lord Kimberley, but later he told Mr Morley that he would advise her to send for Lord Spencer. In fact, however, the choice lay between Lord Rosebery and Sir William Harcourt. Sir Henry Ponsonby suggested the former, and it was clear that Rosebery was more likely to keep the party together than was Sir William Harcourt. Accordingly, the Queen sent for Lord Rosebery, who continued Mr Gladstone's Government without much alteration. He found leadership no easy matter, and the Cabinet seized the opportunity of a defeat on the cordite vote to resign in 1895.

BIBLIOGRAPHY

For the formation of Lord Rosebery's Government, see *Letters of Queen Victoria*, 3rd series, II, pp. 364–77; *Life of Gladstone*, III, pp. 507–16; *Life of Lord Rosebery*, II, pp. 437–44; *Life of Sir William Harcourt*, II, pp. 258–76; Morley, *Recollections*, II, pp. 11–16; Lord Gladstone, *After Thirty Years*, pp. 342–6.

20. *Unionist Government, 1895–1902*

Prime Minister: Marquis of Salisbury.

Leader of the House of Commons: Mr Balfour.

Lord Salisbury considered that the Liberal Government ought to have advised a dissolution. Nevertheless, he accepted office and formed a Government, which included the Liberal Unionist leaders. He advised a dissolution almost at once, and secured a substantial majority. It was further increased at the 'Khaki' election of 1900, and only Lord Salisbury's ill-health brought his Government to an end, in 1902.

BIBLIOGRAPHY

For the formation of Lord Salisbury's third Government, see *Letters of Queen Victoria*, 3rd series, II, 321–31; *Life of the Duke of Devonshire*, II, pp. 216–63; *Life of Joseph Chamberlain*, III, pp. 4–7

21. *Unionist Government, 1902–1905*

Prime Minister: Mr Balfour.

On the resignation of Lord Salisbury the King, apparently on his own initiative, sent for Mr Balfour, who continued Lord Salisbury's Government without substantial change. It was gradually weakened by internal dissensions and a change in public opinion. A defeat on the Irish Land Bill in July 1905 was not followed by resignation or dissolution, but the Government suddenly resigned in December of that year.

BIBLIOGRAPHY

For the formation of Mr Balfour's Government, see Lee, *King Edward VII*, II, pp. 158–60; *Life of the Duke of Devonshire*, II, pp. 279–80.

For the discussions on the defeat of 1905, see *Esher Papers*, II, pp. 91–2.

22. *Liberal Government, 1905–1908*

Prime Minister: Sir Henry Campbell-Bannerman.

The weakness of Mr Balfour's Government had made it clear in 1905 that a change of Government could not be long delayed. Sir Henry Campbell-Bannerman had been leader of the Liberal Opposition in the House of Commons since the resignation of Sir William Harcourt in 1899. The split in the party between the 'Pro-Boers' and the 'Liberal Imperialists' had, however, made his leadership little more than nominal so far as some of the important members of the party were concerned. Nevertheless, Mr Balfour in 1904 expressed the view to Lord Esher (which was doubtless passed on to the King) that Campbell-Bannerman should be sent for. Lord Rosebery expressed the same view in conversation with Lord Knollys. The King came to the same conclusion in 1905. On his resignation, Mr Balfour provided the King with information on the papers of 1873–4, and Lord Esher wrote a memorandum based on the precedents of 1880 and 1895. The King sent for Campbell-Bannerman, who considered the question of refusing so as to compel Mr Balfour to advise a dissolution. Finally, however, he accepted; and after some difficulties with the Liberal Imperialists formed a Government which obtained a majority at the ensuing general election and lasted until his resignation on the ground of ill-health in 1908.

BIBLIOGRAPHY

For the formation of the Liberal Government, see Lee, *King Edward VII*, II, pp. 441–3; *Esher Papers*, II, pp. 56, 78, 119, 123; *Life of Sir Henry Campbell-Bannerman*, II, pp. 188–94; *Life of Lord Ripon*, II, pp. 272–7.

23. *Liberal Government, 1908–1915*

Prime Minister: Mr Asquith.

The illness of Campbell-Bannerman made discussion as to his successor necessary in 1907. The King saw Mr Asquith in 1908 before the Prime Minister resigned, and expressed his intention of appointing him to the office.

Mr Asquith presided over the Cabinet during the period of Campbell-Bannerman's illness while in office, and was sent for by the King as soon as the resignation was communicated. Mr Asquith to some extent remodelled the Cabinet. A conflict with the House of Lords reached its climax by the rejection by that House of the Budget of 1909. A dissolution followed in 1910, at which the Conservatives gained substantially, but not enough to defeat the Government if it was supported by the Irish Nationalists. The introduction of the Parliament Bill compelled a second dissolution in 1910, in spite of the accession of George V. There was no substantial change in the parliamentary position, and the Government continued with its programme. The outbreak of war in 1914 involved some changes, but secured for the Government the discriminating support of the Conservative party, until the restiveness of the 'Opposition' compelled the formation of a coalition Government in 1915.

BIBLIOGRAPHY

For the formation of Mr Asquith's Government, see Lee, *King Edward VII*, II, pp. 578–82; *Esher Papers*, II, pp. 256, 272–3; *Life of Lord Oxford and Asquith*, I, pp. 194–8.

For the Constitutional crisis of 1909–11, see Lee, *King Edward VII*, II, pp. 664–71 and 695–714; Nicolson, *King George V*, pp. 123–55; *Life of Lord Oxford and Asquith*, I, pp. 252–342; *Life of Lord Lansdowne*, pp. 373–431; *Life of John Redmond*, pp. 161–90.

24. *Coalition Government, 1915–1916*

Prime Minister: Mr Asquith.

The Conservative 'Opposition' gave support to the Liberal Government during the early months of the war. During the early months of 1915, however, they became increasingly restive. Sir John French endeavoured to blame the Government for his failure in the second Battle of Ypres by suggesting that the cause was the shortage of high-explosive. Communications to the effect were made to the Conservative leaders. A dispute between Mr Winston Churchill and Lord Fisher at the Admiralty resulted in the resignation of the latter. The Conservatives supported Lord Fisher, and Mr Bonar Law informed Mr Asquith, through Mr Lloyd George, that some change in the Government was necessary for Conservative support. Mr Asquith then secured the King's assent to the formation of a coalition Government, containing Liberal, Unionist and Labour Members.

BIBLIOGRAPHY

For the formation of the first wartime Coalition Government, see Nicolson, *King George V*, pp. 263–4; Blake, *The Unknown Prime Minister*, pp. 241–56; *Life of Lord Oxford and Asquith*, II, pp. 164–72; *Memoirs of David Lloyd George*, I, pp. 223–35; Beaverbrook, *Politicians and the War*, I, pp. 90–115; Churchill, *The World Crisis*.

25. *Coalition Government, 1916–1921*

Prime Minister: Mr Lloyd George.

Late in 1916, the lack of military success led to a growing public feeling against the Coalition Government, and especially against the Prime Minister. Mr Lloyd George, within the Government, urged the formation of an effective War Committee, of which the Prime Minister should not be a member, to take day-to-day decisions on the conduct of the war. Mr Bonar Law was gradually brought to the same conclusion. The Prime Minister, however, insisted that he should be chairman. Apart from Bonar Law, the Unionist members of the Government were against Lloyd George; and they requested Mr Asquith to resign, in the belief, apparently, that Mr Lloyd George would be asked to form a Government and would then find himself without support. Mr Bonar Law omitted to show the document to the Prime Minister, who understood that the Unionists were supporting Mr Lloyd George against him. After some communication with Mr Lloyd George, Mr Asquith received the King's commission to form a new Government. Mr Bonar Law refused to serve in a new Government if the War Committee (without Asquith) was not set up, and Mr Lloyd George resigned. Mr Asquith then resigned and advised the King to send for Mr Bonar Law. Mr Bonar Law found that Mr Asquith would not serve under him or under Mr Balfour, a refusal which he maintained at a conference between the King and the party leaders. He then advised the King to send for Mr Lloyd George, who was able to form a Government without Mr Asquith. The effective conduct of the war now passed to a War Cabinet of five members, which continued, with changes of personnel, in 1919. At the 'Khaki' election of 1918, the first since 1911, its opponents were overwhelmed. The ordinary Cabinet system was restored in 1919, and the Coalition continued until 1921.

BIBLIOGRAPHY

Accounts of the formation of the second Coalition do not entirely agree. See Nicolson, *King George V*, pp. 285–93; Blake, *The Unknown Prime Minister*, pp. 278–325; Beaverbrook, *Politicians and the War*, II, pp. 208–325; *Life of Lord Oxford and Asquith*, II, pp. 248–78; *Memoirs of David Lloyd George*, II, pp. 997–1000; Addison, *Four-and-a-Half Years*, I, pp. 271–8; A. Chamberlain, *Down the Years*; Viscount Samuel, *Memoirs*, pp. 119–27.

26. *Conservative Government, 1922–1923*

Prime Minister: Mr Bonar Law.

The Conservative party outside the Government in 1921 became increasingly dissatisfied with the conduct of public affairs. At a party meeting there was an overwhelming majority in favour of breaking up the Coalition. Mr Bonar Law, who had resigned in 1920 on account of ill-health, expressed strong views to that effect. Mr Lloyd George immediately resigned, without meeting Parliament, and Mr Bonar Law formed a wholly Conservative Government. At the ensuing general election the Government secured a majority. But ill-health soon compelled the Prime Minister to resign.

BIBLIOGRAPHY

For the formation of the Government of 1922, see Nicolson, *King George V*, pp. 366–71; Blake, *The Unknown Prime Minister*, pp. 436–58; G. M. Young, *Stanley Baldwin*, pp. 36–43; A. W. Baldwin, *My Father*, pp. 112–17; *Life of Lord Curzon*, III, pp. 309–21; Nicolson, *Curzon, The Last Phase*, pp. 276–80; *Life of Lord Birkenhead*, II, pp. 175–9; Salvidge, *Salvidge of Liverpool*, pp. 235–49; *Life and Letters of Sir Austen Chamberlain.*

27. *Conservative Government, 1923*

Prime Minister: Mr Baldwin.

Mr Bonar Law's resignation created a serious problem. Lord Curzon was the most experienced of the ministers. But he was in the House of Lords, and the official 'Opposition' was provided by the Labour party, who were unrepresented in the House of Lords. It is said that Lord Balfour, Lord Long, Lord Salisbury, and Mr Amery were consulted by the King, who, in the end, sent for Mr Baldwin to reconstitute the Government. Mr Baldwin came to the conclusion that the problem of unemployment could not be met except by a system of tariffs, but as he was precluded from introducing this remedy because of the pledges of his predecessor, the Government advised a dissolution. The Conservatives remained the strongest party after the election, but they could be out-voted by a combination of Liberal and Labour members. The Government met Parliament, was defeated on a no-confidence amendment to the Address, and resigned.

BIBLIOGRAPHY

For the appointment of Mr Baldwin, see Nicolson, *King George V*, pp. 375–9; Blake, *The Unknown Prime Minister*, pp. 516–27; G. M. Young, *Stanley Baldwin*, pp. 48–9; *Life of Lord Curzon*, III, pp. 349–54; Nicolson, *Curzon, The Last Phase*, pp. 352–6.

28. *Labour Government, 1923–1924*

Prime Minister: Mr MacDonald.

On the resignation of the Conservative Government the King sent for Mr MacDonald, as leader of the Opposition, who formed a Labour Government. The Government could count on only one-third of the votes in the House of Commons, but was able to secure Liberal support for most of its measures until it was defeated on the Campbell case. The Government advised a dissolution, but, as the Conservatives obtained a clear majority, resigned without meeting the new Parliament.

BIBLIOGRAPHY

For the formation of the first Labour Government, see Nicolson, *King George V*, pp. 382–7; G. M. Young, *Stanley Baldwin*, pp. 64–71; Snowden, *Autobiography*, II, pp. 589–612; Bibesco, *Lord Thomson of Cardington*, pp. 149–53.

29. *Conservative Government, 1924–1929*

Prime Minister: Mr Baldwin.

Mr Baldwin formed a Conservative Government which remained in office throughout that Parliament. At the general election of 1929 it lost its majority, and the Labour party became the strongest party, though also without a majority. The Government therefore resigned without meeting Parliament.

BIBLIOGRAPHY

For the formation of Mr Baldwin's second Government, see Nicolson, *King George V*, pp. 397–403; G. M. Young, *Stanley Baldwin*, pp. 81–8; *Life of Neville Chamberlain*, p. 60.

30. *Labour Government, 1929–1931*

Prime Minister: Mr MacDonald.

Mr MacDonald formed a Labour Government which secured Liberal support for its main measures. In 1931, serious deflationary measures were demanded in order to meet currency difficulties. The Cabinet could not agree on the measures for the purpose, and resigned.

APPENDIX I

BIBLIOGRAPHY

For the formation of the second Labour Government, see Nicolson, *King George V*, pp. 434–6; G. M. Young, *Stanley Baldwin*, pp. 138–41; Snowden, *Autobiography*, II, pp. 754–69.

31. *Coalition (National) Government, 1931*

Prime Minister: Mr MacDonald.

In August 1931 the committee of the Labour Cabinet which had been discussing the financial situation decided to consult the Opposition leaders. Mr MacDonald and Mr Snowden saw Mr Baldwin and Mr Neville Chamberlain and then Sir Herbert Samuel; the proposals to be reported to the Cabinet were disclosed. These proposals were, however, supported by only a minority in the Cabinet. As no agreement could be reached, Mr MacDonald and Mr Snowden saw Mr Neville Chamberlain, Sir Samuel Hoare, Sir Herbert Samuel and Sir Donald Maclean, and the Opposition leaders agreed to support the proposals of the Prime Minister and Mr Snowden. There were three other meetings of the same group, while the Cabinet went on disagreeing and eventually agreed to resign. Mr MacDonald offered the resignation of his Government and advised the King to consult the Opposition leaders as to the course to be taken. Mr Baldwin and Sir Herbert Samuel advised that an all-party Government should be formed, and Mr MacDonald agreed. The King then held a conference consisting of Mr MacDonald, Mr Baldwin, and Sir Herbert Samuel. He first presided and then withdrew. Agreement being reached, Mr MacDonald accepted the task of forming a Coalition ('National') Government. It was announced that it would not be a Coalition Government in the ordinary sense, but a Government of co-operation for the one pupose of dealing with the national emergency. 'When that purpose is achieved the political parties will resume their respective positions.' The action of their leaders was supported at meetings of the Conservative and Liberal parties, but no meeting of the Parliamentary Labour party was summoned and nearly all the Labour members followed Mr Henderson into Opposition. When a vote of confidence was proposed in the House of Commons in September there voted for the Government 243 Conservatives, 53 Liberals, 12 Labour and 3 Independents; and against the Government 243 Labour and 8 Independents, the Government thus had a majority of 60.

BIBLIOGRAPHY

The establishment of the so-called 'National' Government has been the subject of much controversy. See Nicolson, *King George V*, pp. 453–69; G. M. Young, *Stanley Baldwin*, pp. 164–8; Viscount Samuel, *Memoirs*, pp. 202–5; Snowden, *Autobiography*, II, pp. 929–61; Hamilton, *Arthur Henderson*, pp. 371–401; Webb, 'What Happened in 1931: A Record', *Political Quarterly* iii, pp. 1–17.

32. *Coalition (National) Government, 1931–1935*

Prime Minister: Mr MacDonald.

The first National Government was a temporary Government formed 'to deal with the national emergency that now exists' and when that purpose was accomplished the political parties would resume their respective positions. A Cabinet of ten persons (four Labour, four Conservatives and two Liberals) was formed. The Prime Minister stated in his broadcast that the general election which would follow the completion of the task would not be fought by the Government. The Conservatives, however, pressed for a general election, the Liberals opposing strongly. The Prime Minister and the other Labour members eventually giving way, however, a dissolution was decided upon. An enormous majority was obtained and the Government reconstituted. The Liberals (but not the Liberal Nationals) resigned over the Ottawa Agreements of 1932 and Mr Snowden with them: but the Government remained in office until the resignation of Mr MacDonald in 1935.

BIBLIOGRAPHY

For the formation of the second 'National' Government, see Nicolson, *King George V*, pp. 491–6; Viscount Samuel, *Memoirs*, pp. 207–13; Snowden, *Autobiography*, II, pp. 950–61.

33. *Coalition (National) Government, 1935–1937*

Prime Minister: Mr Baldwin.

In 1935 Mr MacDonald resigned on the ground of ill-health, though he had actually ceased to be in command of the situation since 1933. The change was made in 1935 because the Conservative party, which controlled the Government, preferred to fight the election of 1935 under its own banner. Mr Baldwin became Prime Minister but the fiction that the Government was 'National' was (rather shamefacedly) maintained, and Mr MacDonald remained in office as Lord President of the Council.

BIBLIOGRAPHY

This change of Government being merely nominal, the bibliography is small: see Nicolson, *King George V*, p. 527; G. M. Young, *Stanley Baldwin*, p. 204; *Life of Neville Chamberlain*, p. 260.

34. *Coalition (National) Government, 1937–1939*

Prime Minister: Mr Neville Chamberlain.

Mr Baldwin resigned in May 1937 on account of advancing age and ill-health. Mr Neville Chamberlain had been Mr Baldwin's principal lieutenant in the Conservative party since 1931 and had in effect (though not in form) been Deputy Prime Minister since 1935. Mr Chamberlain was thus the inevitable Prime Minister.

BIBLIOGRAPHY

This was another easy transition. See G. M. Young, *Stanley Baldwin*, pp. 245–8; A. W. Baldwin, *My Father*, pp. 302–5; *Life of Neville Chamberlain*, pp. 303–6.

35. *War Government, 1939–1940*

Prime Minister: Mr Neville Chamberlain.

On the outbreak of war Mr Chamberlain 'invited his colleagues... collectively to place their resignations in his hands' and reconstituted the Government with a Cabinet of nine members. Mr Winston Churchill and Mr Anthony Eden, who had been out of office, joined the Government, the former being a member of the War Cabinet. The Government remained fundamentally Conservative (or 'National') and neither the Liberal party nor the Labour party was represented.

BIBLIOGRAPHY

For the formation of the first War Government, see *Life of Neville Chamberlain*, pp. 420–2; Winston Churchill, *Second World War*, I, pp. 361–5.

36. *Coalition Government, 1940–1945*

Prime Minister: Mr Winston Churchill.

In consequence of the withdrawal from Norway in May 1940, the Labour party decided to end its 'discriminating support' of the Chamberlain Government and moved a vote of censure. The Government secured a majority of

81 only; 33 Conservatives voted for the motion and some 60 abstained. Mr Chamberlain decided that a Government of all parties should be formed. At a conference the Labour leaders made it plain that they were not prepared to serve under Mr Chamberlain or Lord Halifax. Mr Chamberlain then resigned and (apparently) advised the King to send for Mr Churchill, under whom the Labour and Liberal leaders agreed to serve.

BIBLIOGRAPHY

Report of the Forty-Third Annual Conference of the Labour Party, 1944, pp. 112–13; *Life of Neville Chamberlain*, pp. 437–42; Dalton, *The Fateful Years*, pp. 304–21; Winston Churchill, *Second World War*, pp. 593–601; Jennings, 'The Formation of the Truly National Government', *American Political Science Review*, 1940.

37. *Conservative Government, 1945*

Prime Minister: Mr Churchill.

In May 1945, ten days after the unconditional surrender of the German forces, and two days before the annual Conference of the Labour party, Mr Churchill wrote to the leaders of the Labour, Liberal and Liberal National parties, suggesting that their parties should remain in the Government until the termination of the war against Japan or else withdraw at once so that there might be a general election in July. Mr Attlee, having consulted the National Executive and the Conference of the Labour party, rejected the suggestion that the Labour ministers should remain in the Government until the end of the war against Japan. He considered that there must be an election in 1945, that the parties were divided on the issues of post-war policy, and accordingly that the Labour ministers must withdraw before the general election. He urged, however, that the election should be held on the new register in the autumn. Sir Archibald Sinclair considered that there ought to be a general election, preferably in the autumn, but was willing to consult about continuing the Coalition. Mr Churchill rejected the idea of an autumn election and on 23 May tendered his resignation and was commissioned to form a new Government. At the same time he asked for a dissolution of Parliament, which was granted. The reconstructed Government was wholly Conservative (and Liberal National) and, its task being to govern the country until the result of the general election was known, it was described as a 'Caretaker Government'. The Conservative party was heavily defeated at the general election and Mr Churchill resigned without meeting Parliament.

BIBLIOGRAPHY

This was a 'Caretaker Government': see R. B. McCallum and Alison Readman, *The British General Election of 1945*, ch. 1; Winston Churchill, *Second World War*, VI, pp. 508–19; Dalton, *The Fateful Years*, pp. 455–61; Attlee, *As it Happened*, pp. 132–8.

38. *Labour Government, 1945–1951*

Prime Minister: Mr Attlee.

As soon as it became clear that the Labour party had obtained a definite majority, Mr Churchill tendered his resignation and five minutes later Mr Attlee was received in audience and commissioned to form a Government, all of whose members were drawn from the Labour party. The Labour party won the general election of 1950 with a majority of six only. It was weakened in the following year by the resignations of Sir Stafford Cripps and Mr Bevin because of ill-health and that of Mr Bevan through disagreement. Parliament was dissolved in September 1951, a Conservative majority was produced by the general election, and Mr Attlee resigned.

BIBLIOGRAPHY

For the general election of 1945, see R. B. McCallum and Alison Readman, *The British General Election of 1945*, pp. 245–6; for that of 1950 see H. G. Nicholas, *The British General Election of 1950*; and for that of 1951 see D. E. Butler, *The British General Election of 1951*.

39. *Conservative Government, 1951–1955*

Prime Minister: Sir Winston Churchill.

On the defeat of the Labour party in 1951 Mr Attlee resigned without meeting Parliament and Sir Winston Churchill became Prime Minister. He resigned because of advancing age in April, 1955, but retained his seat and won it again at the general election of 1955.

BIBLIOGRAPHY

For the general election of 1951, see D. E. Butler, *The British General Election of 1951*.

40. *Conservative Government, 1955–1957*

Prime Minister: Sir Anthony Eden.

Sir Anthony Eden had been designated as Sir Winston Churchill's successor during the war and had been Deputy Prime Minister since 1951. There was accordingly no doubt about the succession. For some unexplained reason, Sir Anthony Eden decided to hold an election forthwith in summer and on a stale register. The manœuvre succeeded and his Government increased its majority.

BIBLIOGRAPHY

For the general election of 1955, see D. E. Butler, *The British General Election of 1955*.

41. *Conservative Government, 1957–*

Prime Minister: Mr MacMillan

Sir Anthony Eden resigned because of ill-health in January 1957. There was no obvious successor, though it was generally thought that the choice lay between Mr R. A. Butler and Mr Harold Macmillan. The Queen consulted Sir Winston Churchill and the Marquis of Salisbury and chose Mr Macmillan.

SUMMARY

Causes of Changes of Government, 1835–1957

Cause	Years	No.
Defeat at general election	1835, 1841, 1868 (2), 1874, 1880, 1886 (2), 1892, 1923, 1924, 1929, 1945 (2), 1951	12
Defeat in House of Commons	1846, 1852, 1852 (2), 1855, 1858, 1859, 1866, 1885, 1886, 1895	10
Death of Prime Minister	1865	1
Resignation of Prime Minister (ill-health or advancing years)	1868, 1894, 1902, 1908, 1923, 1935, 1937, 1955, 1957	9
Resignation of Prime Minister (loss of support without defeat)	1940	1
Internal Dissension	1905, 1916, 1922, 1931	4
Formation of Coalition	1915, 1931, 1939	3
End of Coalition	1945	1
Reconstruction of Government	1931 (2)	1

APPENDIX II

EXAMPLES OF GOVERNMENTS

(Members of the House of Lords are marked with an asterisk: Under-Secretaries, etc., are omitted, and so are Household Officers and Law Officers).

SIR ROBERT PEEL'S GOVERNMENT OF 1841

The Cabinet

First Lord of the Treasury
*Lord Chancellor
*President of the Council
*First Lord of the Admiralty
*Lord Privy Seal
Home Secretary
*Foreign Secretary
Colonial Secretary
*President of the Board of Control
Secretary-at-War
*President of the Board of Trade
Chancellor of the Exchequer
Paymaster-General
*Without Office

Not of the Cabinet

*Postmaster-General
*Chancellor of the Duchy of Lancaster
*First Commissioner of Land Revenue
Vice-President of the Board of Trade and Master of the Mint
Master-General of the Ordnance

Ireland

*Lord Lieutenant
Lord Chancellor
*Chief Secretary

MR DISRAELI'S GOVERNMENT OF 1874

The Cabinet

First Lord of the Treasury
*Lord Chancellor
*President of the Council

*Lord Privy Seal
Chancellor of the Exchequer
Secretary of State, Home Department
*Secretary of State, Foreign Department
*Secretary of State for the Colonies
Secretary of State for War
*Secretary of State for India
First Lord of the Admiralty
Postmaster-General

Not of the Cabinet

*Field Marshal Commanding in Chief
Chief Commissioner of Works and Public Buildings
Chancellor of the Duchy of Lancaster
Vice-President of the Committee of Council for Education
President of the Board of Trade
President of the Local Government Board

Ireland

*Lord Lieutenant
Lord Chancellor
Chief Secretary to the Lord Lieutenant

SIR HENRY CAMPBELL-BANNERMAN'S GOVERNMENT OF 1905

The Cabinet

Prime Minister and First Lord of the Treasury
*Lord President of the Council
*Lord Chancellor
Chancellor of the Exchequer
Secretary of State, Home Department
Secretary of State, Foreign Affairs
*Secretary of State, Colonial Office
Secretary of State, War Office
Secretary of State, India Office
*First Lord of the Admiralty
Chief Secretary for Ireland
*Lord Privy Seal
President of the Board of Education
President of the Board of Trade
President of the Local Government Board

*President of the Board of Agriculture
Postmaster-General
Chancellor of the Duchy of Lancaster

Not of the Cabinet

*Lord Lieutenant of Ireland
Paymaster-General

Coalition (National) Government, 1935

The Cabinet

Prime Minister, First Lord of the Treasury, and Leader of the House of Commons
Lord President of the Council
Chancellor of the Exchequer
*Lord Chancellor
Secretary of State for the Home Department and Deputy Leader of the House of Commons
Secretary of State for Foreign Affairs
*Lord Privy Seal and Leader of the House of Lords
Secretary of State for War
Secretary of State for the Dominions
*Secretary of State for Air
*Secretary of State for India
Secretary of State for Scotland
Secretary of State for the Colonies
President of the Board of Trade
*First Lord of the Admiralty
Minister Without Portfolio
Minister of Agriculture and Fisheries
President of the Board of Education
Minister of Health
Minister of Labour
First Commissioner of Works
Minister for the Co-ordination of Defence

Not of the Cabinet

Minister of Transport
Minister of Pensions
Chancellor of the Duchy of Lancaster
Postmaster-General
*Paymaster-General

Labour Government, January 1949

The Cabinet

Prime Minister and First Lord of the Treasury
Lord President of the Council and Leader of the House of Commons
Secretary of State for Foreign Affairs
Chancellor of the Exchequer
Minister of Defence
Chancellor of the Duchy of Lancaster
*Lord Privy Seal, Paymaster-General and Leader of the House of Lords
*Lord Chancellor
Secretary of State for the Home Department
Secretary of State for the Colonies
Secretary of State for Commonwealth Relations
Secretary of State for Scotland
Minister of Labour and National Service
Minister of Health
Minister of Agriculture and Fisheries
Minister of Education
President of the Board of Trade

Ministers not in the Cabinet

*First Lord of the Admiralty
Secretary of State for War
Secretary of State for Air
Minister of Transport
Minister of Food
Minister of Town and Country Planning
Minister of National Insurance
Minister of Supply
Minister of Fuel and Power
*Minister of Civil Aviation
Postmaster-General
Minister of Works
*Minister of State for Colonial Affairs
Minister of State
Minister of Pensions

Conservative Government, 1957

The Cabinet

Prime Minister and First Lord of the Treasury
*Lord President of the Council
Secretary of State for the Home Department and Lord Privy Seal and Leader of the House of Commons
*Lord Chancellor
Chancellor of the Exchequer
Secretary of State for Foreign Affairs
*Secretary of State for Commonwealth Relations
Secretary of State for the Colonies
Secretary of State for Scotland
Minister of Defence
President of the Board of Trade
Minister of Agriculture, Fisheries and Food
Minister of Labour and National Service
Minister of Housing and Local Government and Minister for Welsh Affairs
*Minister of Education
*Minister of Power
Minister of Transport and Civil Aviation
Chancellor of the Duchy of Lancaster

Ministers not in the Cabinet

*First Lord of the Admiralty
Secretary of State for War
Secretary of State for Air
Minister of Pensions and National Insurance
Minister of Supply
Minister of Health
Minister of Works
Postmaster-General
Paymaster-General
*Minister without Portfolio
*Minister of State Scottish Office
Ministers of State for Foreign Affairs (two)
*Minister of State for Colonial Affairs

APPENDIX III

THE PREROGATIVE OF DISSOLUTION

DISCUSSIONS ON THE HOME RULE BILL, 1913

The following material is taken from *The Times* for September 1913. The Home Rule Bill had been passed by the House of Commons in two successive Sessions and rejected by the House of Lords in each of those Sessions. The discussions below took place before the beginning of the third Session, during which the Home Rule Bill became law under the Parliament Act, 1911.

1. *Mr George Cave to* The Times

The passage of the Home Rule Bill in its present form means the division of the kingdom, the impoverishment of Ireland, the use of British troops to dragoon a part of that country into submission to a new authority, the probability of that most bitter and lamentable of all forms of conflict—civil war. It must profoundly affect the future of Great Britain as well as of every part of Ireland. Is it so foolish to suggest that, before action such as this is taken in the name of the people of England and Scotland, they should be asked whether they assent to it or not? I confess that, founding myself on my estimate of the character of the Prime Minister and some of his colleagues rather than on any spoken word, I have hitherto inclined to the belief that before making themselves answerable to the country and to history for consequences so tremendous they would themselves desire to have the plain sanction of a direct popular vote.

Mr Birrell seems to suggest that an election is now unnecessary because Home Rule was a 'live' issue at the election of December 1910....I am convinced that in every British constituency such consideration as any elector may then have given to Home Rule was clouded, and in most cases overshadowed, by his views on the question of the House of Lords. Why then should we not make sure?

But if Ministers prove obdurate, what is the prospect? It is not a pleasant one for those who desire a constitutional solution of the crisis; but may we not hope that in that event the Sovereign will exercise his undoubted right and dissolve Parliament before the commencement of the next Session? A refusal of Royal Assent to the Home Rule Bill after its third passing might no doubt be represented as a challenge to the democracy; but no such reproach could be levelled against a decision of the Sovereign to satisfy himself, before the House of Commons is finally committed to a decision which must change the history of his kingdom, that that House does indeed represent the democracy of to-day. (*The Times*, 6 September 1913.)

2. The Times *leading article*, 8 *September 1913*

(After quoting Mr Cave's letter.) A section of the Unionist Party are advocating this very 'challenge to democracy' by canvassing a proposal for petitioning the King to refuse his assent to the Home Rule Bill after its third passage under the Parliament Act.

Such a proposal does not bear analysis. It originated in irresponsible quarters and it betrays its amateur origin in a complete ignorance of our legal and constitutional usage. But it at least serves to show the un-wisdom of the Government in remaining silent in face of the unswerving attitude of Ulster. The alternative suggestion put forward by Mr Cave, coming as it does from a politician of influence and standing, will receive more consideration. The author of the suggestion admits that his proposal is hardly constitutional; but he falls back on the 'undoubted right' of the Sovereign to dissolve Parliament before the next Session begins. Legally there is no question that under the Constitution there are certain reserved rights of the Crown; but they are atrophied by long disuse. In spite of this, Mr Cave thinks that the policy of the Government justifies their reassertion after the lapse of centuries. It is, however, in our judgment, inconceivable that the Sovereign should contemplate a step which might lead to an apparent disagreement between the occupant of the Throne and the majority of his people. Unionists must face the possibility, however remote they believe it to be, of another reverse at the next general election. A dissolution of Parliament by an exercise of the Royal Prerogative, *proprio motu regis*, might be followed by a vindication at the polls of those very Ministers whose advice had been set aside. The proposal, in fact, has only to be stated with its implications for its constitutional absurdity to be revealed. It is a first principle of our Constitution that the King acts solely on the advice of his Ministers. Ministers, therefore, must bear on their own shoulders complete responsibility for the advice they give. It is their duty to give the Sovereign certain assurances, on which he acts, and for which he is justified in asking before giving the Royal Assent. If Mr Asquith, whose knowledge of constitutional practice is perhaps unrivalled, is unable to give such assurances, His Majesty will no doubt dissolve Parliament on the advice of his Ministers.

3. *Sir William R. Anson to* The Times

I do not think that those who tell us what, in their opinion and under existing circumstances, the King should or can do always bear in mind the twofold consideration of present facts and constitutional principles.

The facts are these. The Government have taken advantage of a combination of groups in the House of Commons to deprive the Second Chamber of its constitutional right to bring about an appeal to the people on measures of high importance which have never been submitted to the consideration of the electorate. While this part of our Constitution is in abeyance they are pressing on legislation which will shortly lead to civil war.

Our only safeguard against such disaster is to be found in the exercise of the prerogatives of the Crown. I am not ready to admit that, under such circumstances, these prerogatives have been atrophied by disuse: but, on the other hand, they can be exercised only under certain conditions which those who write on the subject are apt to ignore.

For every public act of the King his Ministers must accept responsibility. If, therefore, the King should desire to dissolve Parliament before the Irish and Welsh Bills enter upon their third session, and if the Government are of the same opinion, the prerogative of dissolution would be exercised in the ordinary course. If not, it would be necessary to ascertain beforehand whether an alternative Ministry was prepared to accept the responsibility of a dissolution.

Mr Cave is doubtless right in holding that a dissolution would be a milder exercise of the prerogative than the refusal of the Royal Assent to a Bill: but he might have gone on to note that it might be easier to find Ministers who would accept responsibility for the one than for the other.

It really comes to this, that if the King should determine, in the interests of the people, to take a course which his Ministers disapprove, he must either convert his Ministers to his point of view, or, before taking action, must find other Ministers who agree with him. (*The Times*, 10 September 1913.)

4. *Lord Hugh Cecil to* The Times

There is surely some confusion of thought in your comments on Mr Cave's letter. It is certainly an undisputed rule of our Constitution that the Sovereign must never act upon his own responsibility—that is, he must always have advisers who will bear the responsibility of his acts. But this does not mean that he must always automatically accept the advice of those who are his Ministers at a given moment. What is constitutional is determined in our country by precedent and by authority; and the theory that the Sovereign must act automatically will find no support in precedent, nor, I think, from any authority of acknowledged weight. The doctrine—sustained, I believe, both by precedent and authority—is that the Sovereign may refuse the advice of his Ministers, though that refusal should involve their resignation, and may even (in an extreme case) dismiss his Ministers; but that these powers are in practice closely restricted by the condition that he must find advisers to bear the responsibility of his action who have the confidence of the House of Commons; or can obtain that confidence after a general election.

This doctrine was acted upon in 1784, 1801, 1807, 1832, 1834, and 1839; and it was also fully and generally recognized in 1831, for no one doubted that King William might, if he had pleased, have refused the famous dissolution of that year. It is said, too, that at a late period of Queen Victoria's reign she contemplated dissent from her Ministers, but was otherwise advised by the then leader of the Opposition. Precedent therefore clearly upholds as constitutional the right of the Sovereign to reject the advice of his Ministers if he can find other advisers who will bear the responsibility of that rejection, and if those other advisers have or can obtain the confidence of the House of Commons....

This relates to the constitutional right of the Sovereign. In what circumstances it may be wise for the Sovereign to exercise his constitutional right is quite another question. What is constitutional is not always judicious, as reference to the precedents of 1801 and 1834 sufficiently proves. But what may briefly be called the 'automatic' theory is a serious misrepresentation of the Constitution calling for protest quite apart from what may or may not be expedient at the present time. For that theory mistakes the underlying principle of which the conventions of the Constitution are the expressions. That principle is that there must be no conflict between the King and his people, nor consequently between the King and a House of Commons which correctly represents his people. But there is nothing unconstitutional in a disagreement between the King and his Ministers except in so far as it implies a disagreement with the House of Commons and ultimately with the people. The constitutional rules which I have endeavoured to state do three things: they absolutely prevent a conflict between the King and the people; they prevent a conflict between the King and the House of Commons except in the case where both he and experienced advisers see reason to doubt that the House of Commons really represents the people; and in the event of such a conflict they require the King to protect the dignity of his office from all controversy or censure by interposing a ministry to bear the whole responsibility for what has been done. But they do not prevent, because there is no object in preventing, a disagreement between the King and his Ministers, apart from the House of Commons or the people. The 'automatic' theory would invest the Ministry as such with a sanctity which is as useless and unrelated to any constitutional principle as it is unsupported by precedent or authority.

(*The Times*, 10 September 1913.)

5. *Professor J. H. Morgan to* The Times

Any proposal coming from Mr Cave is entitled to respectful consideration. But I do not see how anyone who considers impartially his suggestion that the Sovereign should dissolve Parliament before the commencement of next Session can question the weighty arguments which you advance against it in your issue of to-day. And there are others. Such a course would raise greater difficulties than the one solved—if, indeed, it did solve it. His Majesty's decision would first have to be communicated to his Ministers, and they might then regard themselves as confronted with the painful duty of resigning as a protest against it. The Sovereign cannot act alone, and such an independent decision on his part would almost inevitably be equivalent to a dismissal of his Ministers, who surely could not be expected to go to the country under circumstances which made it plain to the electorate that they did not accept responsibility for the dissolution. The conduct of an election held under these circumstances and its effect on the position of the Sovereign would be such as no loyal subject could contemplate without misgiving. Moreover, such a claim, once exercised by the Sovereign, however exceptional or imperative the circumstances might seem to be, would seriously compromise any future exercise of the right of dissolution by a Ministry under quite normal circumstances. No dissolution in future would be free from ambiguity, and speculation as to the degree of responsibility of the Sovereign would be a feature of every election. The right of dissolution, regarded as a Ministerial right, owes its existence to a general recognition of the Sovereign's immunity from responsibility for its exercise; until that immunity was achieved any dissolution was a source of grave anxiety to the Sovereign as carrying with it the implication that not only was the Ministry defeated, but the Crown compromised or, to use the language of Queen Victoria in the early days of her reign, 'affronted'.

Moreover, it seems extremely doubtful whether either party could if it would—or, indeed, would if it could—confine the issue to Home Rule. Would there not be a considerable danger of a presumption—even if Unionist candidates scrupulously refused to raise it—that the Sovereign disapproved of the Parliament Act, and if of the Parliament Act, why not of the measures already passed into law under its ultimate sanction—measures for which, be it remembered, the House of Lords, by declining (deplorably, as I think) to amend them, had repudiated all responsibility as passed under a 'suspended Constitution' or a 'revolutionary interregnum'? In that case there would be no limits to the implication of the Sovereign in the current political controversies. (*The Times*, 10 September 1913.)

6. *Professor A. V. Dicey to* The Times

Allow me to express my complete agreement with Sir William Anson's masterly exposition of the principles regulating the exercise of the prerogative of dissolution. On this matter I write with some little confidence. My 'Law of the Constitution' (7th edition), pp. 428–434, contains an examination of the constitutional doctrine as to the dissolution of Parliament. This doctrine has been repeated and defended during the last 28 years in every edition of my book. My opinion as to the occasions on which a dissolution may rightly take place has, as far as I know, never been assailed and assuredly has never been controverted by any writer of authority. Let me add to the lucid statement of constitutional law by my friend Sir William Anson the following observations which at the present moment deserve attention:

1. A dissolution of Parliament before the beginning of the next Session by the King in conformity with the advice of a Minister ready to assume the responsibility for this course of action, would be amply justified by the precedents of 1784 and 1834. No statesman need be ashamed to follow the example of Pitt or of Peel. One may add that the whole current of modern constitutional custom involves the admission that the final decision of every grave political question now belongs, not to the House of Commons, but to the electors as the representatives of the nation.

2. A dissolution before the commencement of the next Session, which will be the third Session of the Home Rule Bill, may take place, and ought to take place, with the assent of Mr Asquith and his colleagues. Such a dissolution will not be the sacrifice of the policy of Home Rule; it will not even be the sacrifice of the present Home Rule Bill. If the Government obtain after the dissolution a substantial majority in the House of Commons they will still, under the Parliament Act, be able to present the Bill to the King for his acceptance without obtaining the consent of the House of Lords (see Parliament Act, section 2).

3. A dissolution after the beginning of the next Session, but before the Home Rule Bill has become the Home Rule Act, will be fatal to the existing Home Rule Bill, and this for a perfectly plain reason. In order that the

Parliament Act may apply to the Bill the Bill must be passed by the House of Commons and rejected by the House of Lords in each of three 'successive' Sessions. But if a dissolution takes place during the third Session, but before the Bill has become an Act, it can never be passed and rejected in three such successive Sessions. If a dissolution does not take place before the beginning of the next Session the destruction of the Home Rule Bill by a dissolution which may take place during the next Session will be due to the obstinacy of Ministers who will have refused to give ear in due time to the demand of the nation that the union between England and Ireland shall not be in effect repealed until the policy of Home Rule shall have obtained the direct and indubitable sanction of the electorate.

4. Rumour imputes to the Premier the intention of passing the Home Rule Act, 1914, say in June next, and advising a dissolution during the months which must elapse before the Act will have come into full operation. The recklessness and fatuity of such a policy renders its adoption all but incredible. This sham appeal to the people will, in the eyes of Unionists, whether in England or in Ireland, involve the addition of insult to injustice. A man of Mr Asquith's calmness and sense cannot wish to redouble the chance of civil war; he has apparently rejected the idea of submitting the Home Rule Bill to a Referendum; he surely cannot think that Englishmen or Irishmen will tolerate that parody of a Referendum which, under the name of a plebiscite, has been invented by French Jacobinism and has been performed again and again by French Imperialism.

5. The question is sometimes now raised whether during the present political crisis the King could rightly or wisely refuse assent to the Home Rule Bill after it should for a third time have been passed by the House of Commons and rejected by the House of Lords. This is happily a purely academic inquiry on which I decline now to enter. Every advantage by way of appeal to the electors, in consequence of the exercise of the so-called Royal veto, can be far better and more regularly obtained by a dissolution of Parliament. Mr Balfour has struck the right note. The safety and the prosperity of the United Kingdom absolutely demand a speedy dissolution. As regards the Veto itself, I am well content to adopt the language of Burke:

'The King's negative to Bills is one of the most undisputed of the Royal prerogatives, and it extends to all cases whatsoever. I am far from certain that if several laws which I know had fallen under the stroke of that sceptre the public would have had a very heavy loss. But it is not the propriety of the exercise which is in question. Its repose may be the preservation of its existence, and its existence may be the means of saving the Constitution itself on an occasion worthy of bringing it forth.' (*The Times*, 15 September 1913.)

APPENDIX IV

BIOGRAPHICAL AND BIBLIOGRAPHICAL NOTES

ABERDEEN, George Hamilton-Gordon, fourth Earl of (1784–1860); Scottish representative peer, 1806–14; ambassador-extraordinary at Vienna, 1813; cr. Viscount Gordon, 1814; Chancellor of the Duchy of Lancaster in Wellington's Cabinet and afterwards Foreign Secretary, 1828–30; Secretary of State for War and the Colonies in Peel's Cabinet, 1834–5; Foreign Secretary in Peel's Cabinet, 1841–6; Prime Minister, 1852–5.

The Life of George, Fourth Earl of Aberdeen, by Lady Frances Balfour, 2 vols. (1922).

The Earl of Aberdeen, by Lord Stanmore (1893).

ADDERLEY, Sir Charles Bowyer, *see* NORTON

ADDISON, Christopher, first Viscount (b. 1869); Liberal M.P., 1910–22; Labour M.P., 1929–31 and 1934–5; Parliamentary Secretary to the Board of Education in Asquith's Government, 1914–15; Parliamentary Secretary to the Ministry of Munitions in Asquith's Coalition Government, 1915–16; Minister of Munitions, 1916–17, Minister of Reconstruction, 1917–19, President of the Local Government Board, 1919, Minister of Health, 1919–21, and Minister without Portfolio, all in Lloyd George's Government; Parliamentary Secretary to the Ministry of Agriculture in MacDonald's Government, 1929–30; Minister of Agriculture and Fisheries in MacDonald's Cabinet, 1930–1; Secretary of State for Commonwealth Relations, 1945–7 and Lord Privy Seal in Attlee's Cabinet.

Four-and-a-half Years, by the Rt. Hon. Christopher Addison, 2 vols. (1934).

ALBERT, Francis Charles Augustus Emmanuel, Prince Consort (1819–1861); m. Queen Victoria, 1840.

The Life of His Royal Highness the Prince Consort, by Theodore Martin, 5 vols. (1877–80).

The Prince Consort and His Brother, edited by Hector Bolitho (1933).

ALTHORP, Viscount, *see* SPENCER, John Charles, Earl

AMERY, Leopold Stennett (1873–1955), Conservative M.P., 1911–45; Parliamentary Under-Secretary, Colonial Office, 1919–21, and Parliamentary and Financial Secretary to the Admiralty, 1921–2, in Lloyd George's

Government; First Lord of the Admiralty, 1922–4, in Bonar Law's and Baldwin's Cabinets; Secretary of State for the Colonies, 1924–9, in Baldwin's Cabinet; Secretary of State for India, 1940–1944, in Mr Churchill's War Government.

My Political Life, by L. S. Amery, 3 vols. (1953–55).

ARGYLL, George Douglas Campbell, eighth Duke of (1823–1900); succeeded as Marquess of Lorne, 1837; succeeded to Dukedom, 1847; Lord Privy Seal in Aberdeen's Cabinet, 1853–5; Postmaster-General in Palmerston's Cabinet, 1855–8; Lord Privy Seal in the same Cabinet, 1859–60; Postmaster-General, 1860; Lord Privy Seal, 1860–6; Secretary of State for India in Gladstone's Cabinet, 1868–74; Lord Privy Seal, 1880–1; Liberal Unionist after 1886.

Autobiography and Memoirs, by George Douglas, Eighth Duke of Argyll, 2 vols. (1906).

ARNOLD-FORSTER, Hugh Oakeley (1855–1909); Unionist M.P., 1892–1909; Parliamentary Secretary at the Admiralty in Lord Salisbury's Government, 1901–3; Secretary of State for War in Balfour's Cabinet, 1903–5.

The Right Honourable Hugh Oakeley Arnold-Forster, A Memoir, by his Wife (1910).

ASQUITH, Herbert Henry, *see* OXFORD AND ASQUITH, Earl of

ATTLEE, Clement Richard, first Earl (b. 1883); Labour M.P., 1922–55; Parliamentary Under-Secretary of State for War in MacDonald's Government, 1924; Chancellor of the Duchy of Lancaster, 1930–1 and Postmaster-General, 1931, in MacDonald's Government; Leader of the Opposition, 1935–40 and 1951–5; Lord Privy Seal, 1940–2, Secretary of State for the Dominions, 1942–3, Lord President of the Council, 1943–5, and Deputy Prime Minister, 1942–5, in Churchill's War Cabinet; Prime Minister 1945–50.

As It Happened, by Earl Attlee (1954).

BALDWIN, Stanley, first Earl (1867–1947); Conservative M.P., 1908–37; Financial Secretary to the Treasury in Lloyd George's Government, 1917–21; President of the Board of Trade in Lloyd George's Cabinet, 1921–2; Chancellor of the Exchequer in Bonar Law's Cabinet, 1922–3; Prime Minister, 1923–4 and 1924–9; Lord President of the Council in MacDonald's Cabinet, 1931–5; Prime Minister, 1935–7; cr. Earl, 1937.

Stanley Baldwin, by G. M. Young (1952).
My Father, by A. W. Baldwin (1955).

BALFOUR, Arthur James, first Earl (1848–1930); Conservative M.P., 1874–1922; Private Secretary to Lord Salisbury, 1878–80; President of Local

Government Board, 1885–6, Secretary for Scotland, 1886–7, Chief Secretary for Ireland, 1887–91, and First Lord of the Treasury and Leader of the House of Commons, 1891–2 and 1895–1902, in Lord Salisbury's Cabinets; Prime Minister, 1902–6; First Lord of the Admiralty in Asquith's Cabinet, 1915–16; Foreign Secretary in Lloyd George's Government, 1916–19; Lord President of the Council in Lloyd George's Cabinet, 1919–22, and in Baldwin's Cabinet, 1925–9; cr. Earl, 1922.

Chapters of Autobiography, by Arthur James, first Earl Balfour (1930).
Life of Arthur James Balfour, by Blanche E. C. Dugdale, 2 vols. (1936).

BEACH, Sir Michael Edward Hicks, *see* ST ALDWYN, first Earl

BEACONSFIELD, Benjamin Disraeli, first Earl of (1804–1881); Conservative M.P., 1837–76; a leader of the Protectionists, 1845–50; Chancellor of the Exchequer and Leader of the House of Commons in Derby's Cabinet, 1852; led Conservative Opposition in House of Commons, 1852–8; Chancellor of the Exchequer and Leader of the House of Commons in Derby's Cabinet, 1858–9; in Opposition, 1859–66; Chancellor of the Exchequer and Leader of the House of Commons in Derby's Cabinet, 1866–8; Prime Minister, 1868; in Opposition, 1868–73; Prime Minister, 1874–80; cr. Earl of Beaconsfield, 1876.

The Life of Benjamin Disraeli, Earl of Beaconsfield, by W. F. Monypenny and O. E. Buckle, 6 vols. (1910–20). [The references are to the new edition in 2 vols. (1929).]
Lord Beaconsfield's Correspondence with his Sister, 1832–1852, 2nd ed. (1886).
The Letters of Disraeli to Lady Bradford and Lady Chesterfield, edited by the Marquess of Zetland, 2 vols. (1929).
Lord George Bentinck: A Political Biography, by the Rt. Hon. B. Disraeli, M.P., new edition (1858).

BEAVERBROOK, William Maxwell Aitken, first Baron (b. 1879); Conservative M.P., 1910–16; close friend of Mr Bonar Law; cr. Baron, 1917; Chancellor of the Duchy of Lancaster and Minister of Information in Lloyd George's Government, 1917; Minister of Aircraft Production in Churchill's Government, 1940.

Politicians and the War, by Lord Beaverbrook, 2 vols. (1928, 1932).

BENTINCK, Lord George (1802–1848); Tory M.P., 1826–48; led Protectionists in opposition to Peel, 1846–7.

Lord George Bentinck: A Political Biography, by the Rt. Hon. B. Disraeli, M.P., new edition (1858).

BIGGE, *see* STAMFORDHAM

BIRKENHEAD, Frederick Edwin Smith, first Earl of (1872–1930); Conservative M.P., 1906–19; Solicitor-General, 1915, and Attorney-General, 1915–19, in Asquith's and Lloyd George's Governments; Lord Chancellor in Lloyd George's Cabinet, 1919–22; Secretary of State for India in Baldwin's Cabinet, 1924–8; cr. Baron, 1919, Viscount, 1921, Earl, 1922.

Frederick Edwin, Earl of Birkenhead, by his son, the Earl of Birkenhead, 2 vols. (1933, 1934).

BRENTFORD, William Joynson-Hicks, first Viscount (1865–1932); Conservative M.P., 1908–29; Parliamentary Secretary, Overseas Trade Department, in Bonar Law's Government, 1922–3; Postmaster-General in Baldwin's Government, 1923; Financial Secretary to the Treasury in Baldwin's Cabinet, 1923, and Minister of Health, 1923–4; Home Secretary in Baldwin's Cabinet, 1924–9; cr. Viscount, 1929.

Jix—Viscount Brentford, by H. A. Taylor (1933).

BROUGHAM of Vaux, Henry Peter, first Baron (1778–1868); Whig M.P., 1810–30; Lord Chancellor in Melbourne's Cabinet, 1830–4; cr. Lord Brougham of Vaux, 1830.

The Life and Times of Henry, Lord Brougham, written by himself, 3 vols. 2nd ed. (1871).

Lord Brougham and the Whig Party, by A. Aspinall (1927).

BRYCE, James, first Viscount (1838–1922); Liberal M.P., 1880–1907; Under-Secretary of State for Foreign Affairs in Gladstone's Government, 1886; Chancellor of the Duchy of Lancaster, 1892–4, and President of the Board of Trade, 1894–5, in Gladstone's and Rosebery's Cabinets; Chief Secretary for Ireland in Campbell-Bannerman's Cabinet, 1905–7; Ambassador at Washington, 1907–13; cr. Viscount, 1914.

James Bryce, by H. A. L. Fisher, 2 vols. (1927).

CAMPBELL-BANNERMAN, Sir Henry (1836–1908), Liberal M.P., 1868–1908; Financial Secretary to the War Office in Gladstone's Governments, 1871–4 and 1880–2; Parliamentary Secretary to the Admiralty, 1882–4; Chief Secretary for Ireland, 1884–5; Secretary of State for War in Gladstone's Cabinet, 1886, and in Gladstone's and Rosebery's Cabinets, 1892–5; Leader of the Liberal Party in the House of Commons, 1899–1908; Prime Minister, 1905–8.

The Life of The Right Hon. Sir Henry Campbell-Bannerman, by J. A. Spender, 2 vols. (1923).

CARSON, Sir Edward Henry, Baron (Life Peer), (1854–1935); Conservative M.P., 1892–1921; Solicitor-General for Ireland, 1892; Solicitor-General in Salisbury's and Balfour's Governments, 1900–6; Attorney-General in Asquith's Coalition Government, 1915; First Lord of the Admiralty, 1917; Minister without Portfolio in the War Cabinet, 1917–18; Lord of Appeal in Ordinary, 1921–9.

The Life of Lord Carson, vol. II, by Ian Colvin (1934).

CAVE, George, first Viscount (1856–1928); Conservative M.P., 1906–18; Solicitor-General in Asquith's Coalition Government, 1915–16; Home Secretary in Lloyd George's Government, 1916–19; Lord of Appeal in Ordinary, 1919–22; Lord Chancellor in Bonar Law's and Baldwin's Cabinets, 1922–4, and Baldwin's Cabinet, 1924–8.

Lord Cave: A Memoir, by Sir Charles Mallet (1931).

CHAMBERLAIN, Sir Joseph Austen (1863–1937); Conservative M.P., 1892–1937; Civil Lord of the Admiralty, 1895 and 1900, Financial Secretary to the Treasury, 1900–2, and Postmaster-General, 1902–3, in Salisbury's Government; Chancellor of the Exchequer in Balfour's Cabinet, 1903–6; Secretary of State for India in Asquith's Cabinet, 1915–17; Member of the War Cabinet, 1918; Chancellor of the Exchequer, 1919–21, and Lord Privy Seal and Leader of the House of Commons, 1921–2, in Lloyd George's Cabinet; Secretary of State for Foreign Affairs in Baldwin's Cabinet, 1924–9; First Lord of the Admiralty in MacDonald's National Cabinet, 1931.

Down the Years, by the Rt. Hon. Sir Austen Chamberlain (1935).
Politics from Inside, by the Rt. Hon. Sir Austen Chamberlain (1936).
Life and Letters of Sir Austen Chamberlain, by Sir Charles Petre, 2 vols. (1939).

CHAMBERLAIN, Joseph (1836–1914); Liberal M.P., 1876–86; Liberal Unionist M.P., 1886–1906; President of the Board of Trade in Gladstone's Cabinet, 1880–5; President of Local Government Board in Gladstone's Cabinet, 1886, but resigned in consequence of Home Rule Bill and went into opposition; Secretary of State for the Colonies in Salisbury's and Balfour's Cabinets, 1895–1903; resigned office to conduct tariff reform agitation, 1903.

The Life of Joseph Chamberlain, by J. L. Garvin, 3 vols. (1932–5), continued by Julian Amery (1951).

CHAMBERLAIN, Arthur Neville (1869–1940); Conservative M.P., 1918–40; Director-General of National Service in Lloyd George's War Government, 1916–17; Postmaster-General in Bonar Law's Government,

1922–3; Minister of Health in Baldwin's Cabinets of 1923, and 1924–9; Chancellor of the Exchequer, 1931–7, in MacDonald's and Baldwin's Cabinets; Prime Minister, 1937–40; Lord President of the Council in Churchill's War Cabinet, 1940.

The Life of Neville Chamberlain, by Keith Feiling (1946).

CHILDERS, Hugh Culling Eardley (1827–1896); Liberal M.P., 1860–86; Financial Secretary to the Treasury in Russell's Government, 1865–6; First Lord of the Admiralty in Gladstone's Cabinet, 1868–71; Chancellor of the Duchy of Lancaster, 1872–3; Secretary of State for War in Gladstone's Cabinet, 1880–2; Chancellor of the Exchequer, 1882–5; Home Secretary, 1886.

The Life and Correspondence of the Rt. Hon. Hugh C. E. Childers, by Lieut.-Col. Spencer Childers, 2 vols. (1901).

CHURCHILL, Lord Randolph Henry Spencer (1849–1894); Conservative M.P., 1874–94; member of 'Fourth Party'; Secretary of State for India in Salisbury's Cabinet, 1885–6; Chancellor of the Exchequer and Leader of the House of Commons in Salisbury's Cabinet, 1886; resigned over Estimates, 1886.

Lord Randolph Churchill, by Winston Spencer Churchill, M.P., 2 vols. (1906).
Lord Randolph Churchill, by the Earl of Rosebery [in *Miscellanies*, vol. 1].

CHURCHILL, Sir Winston Leonard Spencer (b. 1874); Conservative M.P., 1900–3; Liberal M.P., 1903–22; Conservative M.P., since 1924; Under-Secretary of State for the Colonies in Campbell-Bannerman's Government, 1906–8; President of the Board of Trade, 1908–10, Home Secretary, 1910–11, First Lord of the Admiralty, 1911–15, and Chancellor of the Duchy of Lancaster, 1915, in Asquith's Cabinets; Secretary of State for War and for Air, 1918–21, and for the Colonies, 1921–2, in Lloyd George's Cabinet; Chancellor of the Exchequer in Baldwin's Cabinet, 1924–9; First Lord of the Admiralty, 1939–40, in Chamberlain's War Cabinet; Prime Minister and Minister of Defence, 1940–5 and 1951–5; Leader of the Opposition, 1945–51.

The World Crisis, by Winston S. Churchill, 5 vols. (1923–8).
The Second World War, by Winston Churchill, 6 vols. (1948–54).

CLARENDON, George William Frederick Villiers, fourth Earl of (1800–1870); diplomatic service, 1820–39; succeeded to Earldom, 1839; Lord Privy Seal in Melbourne's Cabinet, 1839–41; President of the Board of Trade, 1846, and Lord-Lieutenant of Ireland, 1847–52, in Russell's Cabinet;

Foreign Secretary in Aberdeen's and Palmerston's Cabinets, 1853–8; Chancellor of the Duchy of Lancaster, 1864; Foreign Secretary in Russell's Cabinet, 1865–6; Foreign Secretary in Gladstone's Cabinet, 1868–70.

The Life and Letters of George William Frederick, Fourth Earl of Clarendon, by the Rt. Hon. Sir Herbert Maxwell, Bart., 2 vols. (1913).

CLARKE, Sir Edward George (1841–1931); Conservative M.P., 1880–1906; Solicitor-General in Salisbury's Government, 1886–92.

The Story of My Life, by Sir Edward Clarke (1923).

COBDEN, Richard (1804–1865); Liberal M.P., 1841–57, 1859–64; a leader of the Anti-Corn-Law League, negotiated commercial treaty with France, 1859–60.

The Life of Richard Cobden, by John Morley, 2 vols. (1879).
Richard Cobden: the International Man, by J. A. Hobson (1918).

CONSORT, Prince, *see* ALBERT

COOK, Sir Edward Tyas (1857–1919); editor, *Pall Mall Gazette*, 1890–2; editor, *Westminster Gazette*, 1893–6; editor, *Daily News*, 1895–1901; author of *Life of Delane* (q.v.).

Sir Edward Cook, K.B.E.: A Biography, by J. Saxon Mills (1921).

CRANBROOK, Gathorne Gathorne-Hardy, first Earl of (1814–1906); Conservative M.P., 1856–78; Parliamentary Under-Secretary of State for Home Affairs in Derby's Government, 1858–9; President of the Poor Law Board and afterwards Home Secretary in the Derby–Disraeli Cabinet, 1866–8; Secretary of State for War in Disraeli's Cabinet, 1874–8; cr. Viscount Cranbrook, 1878; Secretary of State for India in Disraeli's Cabinet, 1878–80; Lord President of the Council in Salisbury's Governments, 1885–92; cr. Earl of Cranbrook, 1892.

Gathorne Hardy, First Earl of Cranbrook, A Memoir, edited by the Hon. Alfred E. Gathorne-Hardy, 2 vols. (1910).

CROMER, Evelyn Baring, first Earl of (1841–1917); Army, 1855–67; first Commissioner in Egypt, 1877–9; British controller in Egypt, 1879; Financial Member of Viceroy's Council in India, 1880–3; British Agent and Consul-General in Egypt, 1883–1907; cr. Baron Cromer, 1892; Viscount, 1899; Earl, 1901.

Lord Cromer, by the Marquess of Zetland (1932).

CURZON of Kedleston, George Nathaniel Curzon, first Marquess (1859–1925); Conservative M.P., 1886–98; Under-Secretary of State for India in Salisbury's Government, 1891–2; Under-Secretary of State for Foreign Affairs in Salisbury's Government, 1895–8; Viceroy and Governor-General of India, 1899–1905; succeeded as Baron Scarsdale, 1898; Viscount Scarsdale, 1911, and Earl Curzon of Kedleston, 1911; Lord Privy Seal in Asquith's Cabinet, 1915–16; President of the Air Board, 1916, Lord President of the Council, 1916–19, and member of the War Cabinet, 1916, in Lloyd George's Government; Leader of the House of Lords, 1916–24; cr. Marquess, 1921.

The Life of Lord Curzon, by the Rt. Hon. the Earl of Ronaldshay, 3 vols. (1928). *Curzon: The Last Phase*, by Harold Nicolson (1934).

DE GREY, *see* RIPON, first Marquess of

DELANE, John Thadeus (1817–1879); editor of *The Times*, 1841–77.

John Thadeus Delane, Editor of The Times: *His Life and Correspondence*, by Arthur Irwin Dasent, 2 vols. (1908).

DERBY, Edward George Geoffrey Smith Stanley, fourteenth Earl of (1799–1869); Whig M.P., 1822–35; Conservative M.P., 1835–44; Under-Secretary of State for the Colonies under Canning and Goderich; Chief Secretary for Ireland in Grey's Government, 1830–3; Secretary of State for the Colonies in Grey's Cabinet, 1833–4; resigned over Irish Church, 1834; joined Conservative Opposition, 1835; Colonial Secretary in Peel's Cabinet, 1841–5; cr. Lord Stanley of Bickerstaffe, 1844; resigned over Corn Laws, 1845, and became leader of Protectionists; attempted to form Conservative Government, 1851; succeeded to Earldom, 1851; Prime Minister, 1852, 1858–9, and 1866–8.

The Earl of Derby, by George Saintsbury (1892).

DEVONSHIRE, Spencer Compton Cavendish, eighth Duke of (1833–1908); Liberal M.P., 1857–86; Liberal Unionist M.P., 1886–91; became Marquess of Hartington, 1858; Under-Secretary of State for War in Palmerston's Government, 1863–6; Secretary of State for War in Russell's Cabinet, 1866; Postmaster-General in Gladstone's Cabinet, 1869–70; Chief Secretary for Ireland, 1870–4; led Liberal Party in House of Commons, 1875–80; Secretary of State for India, 1880–2, and for War, 1882–5, in Gladstone's Cabinet; refused to join Gladstone's third Government on account of Home Rule; leader of Liberal Unionist Party after 1886, in opposition to Gladstone, 1886, and in support of Salisbury, 1886–92; succeeded to Dukedom, 1891; Lord President of the Council in Salisbury's and Balfour's Cabinets, 1895–1903; resigned over free trade, 1903.

The Life of Spencer Compton, Eighth Duke of Devonshire, by Bernard Holland, C.B., 2 vols. (1911).

DILKE, Sir Charles Wentworth, second baronet (1843–1911); Radical M.P., 1868–86, 1892–1911; Under-Secretary of State for Foreign Affairs in Gladstone's Government, 1880–2; President of the Local Government Board in Gladstone's Cabinet, 1882–5; out of Parliament and public life, owing to divorce court proceedings in 1886.

The Life of the Rt. Hon. Sir Charles W. Dilke, Bart., M.P., by Stephen Gwynn, M.P., and Gertrude M. Tuckwell, 2 vols. (1917).

DISRAELI, Benjamin, *see* BEACONSFIELD, first Earl of

EDEN, Sir Anthony (b. 1897); Conservative M.P., 1923–57; Parliamentary Under-Secretary, Foreign Office, 1931–3, and Lord Privy Seal, 1934–5, in MacDonald's 'National' Government; Secretary of State for Foreign Affairs, 1935–8, in Baldwin's and Chamberlain's Governments; Secretary of State for the Dominions in Chamberlain's War Government, 1939–40; Secretary of State for Foreign Affairs, 1940–5, and Leader of the House of Commons, 1942–5, in Churchill's War Government, and Secretary of State for Foreign Affairs and Deputy Prime Minister, 1951–5, in Churchill's last Government; Prime Minister, 1955–7.

EDWARD VII, King (1841–1910); Prince of Wales, 1841–1901; King, 1901–10.

King Edward VII: A Biography, by Sir Sidney Lee, 2 vols. (1925–7).
The Influence of King Edward and Essays on Other Subjects, by the Viscount Esher (1915).

EDWARD VIII, King (b. 1894); Prince of Wales, 1910–36; succeeded his father January 1936; abdicated December 1936; cr. first Duke of Windsor.

ESHER, Reginald Baliol Brett, second Viscount (1852–1930); Liberal M.P., 1880–5; Secretary to the Office of Works, 1895–1902; Lieutenant and Deputy-Governor of Windsor Castle, 1901–28; Chairman of War Office Reconstitution Committee, 1904; Permanent Member of the Committee of Imperial Defence, 1905; Governor of Windsor Castle, 1928–30; private adviser to Edward VII and George V; co-editor of *Queen Victoria's Letters*, 1st series.

Journals and Letters of Reginald, Viscount Esher, edited by Maurice V. Brett, 4 vols. (1934–8). [Quoted as *Esher Papers*.]

FAWCETT, Henry (1833–1884); Liberal M.P., 1865–8
in Gladstone's Government, 1880–4.

Life of Henry Fawcett, by Leslie Stephen (1885).

FITZROY, Sir Almeric William (1851–1934); Clerk o
1898–1923.

Memoirs, by Sir Almeric Fitzroy, 2 vols. (1925).

FORSTER, William Edward (1818–1886); Liberal M.P., 1861–86; Under-Secretary of State for the Colonies in Palmerston's and Russell's Governments, 1865–6; Vice-President of the Council in Gladstone's Government, 1868–74; Chief Secretary for Ireland in Gladstone's Government, 1880–2; resigned over Irish policy, 1882.

Life of the Rt. Hon. William Edward Forster, by T. Wemyss Reid, 2 vols. (1888).

FOWLER, Henry Hartley, *see* WOLVERHAMPTON, first Viscount

FRENCH, Sir John, *see* YPRES

GATHORNE-HARDY, Gathorne, *see* CRANBROOK, first Viscount

GEORGE, David Lloyd, first Earl Lloyd George (1863–1945); Liberal M.P., 1890–1945; President of the Board of Trade in Campbell-Bannerman's Cabinet, 1905–8; Chancellor of the Exchequer, 1908–15, Minister of Munitions, 1915–16, and Secretary of State for War, 1916, in Asquith's Cabinets; Prime Minister, 1916–22.

War Memoirs of David Lloyd George, 4 vols. (1933).
The Truth about the Peace Treaties, 2 vols.
The Real Lloyd George, by A. J. Sylvester.
Lloyd George, by Thomas Jones (1952).

GEORGE V, King (1866–1936); Prince of Wales, 1901–10; King, 1910–36, succeeding Edward VII.

King George V, His Life and Reign, by Sir Harold Nicolson (1952).

GEORGE VI, King (1895–1952); succeeded as King on the abdication of his brother, Edward VIII, in 1936; died 1952.

GLADSTONE, Herbert John, first Viscount (1854–1930); Liberal M.P., 1880–1910; Private Secretary to W. E. Gladstone, 1880–1; Lord of the Treasury in Gladstone's Government, 1881–5; Financial Secretary at the War Office in Gladstone's Government, 1886; Under-Secretary of State for Home Affairs, 1892–4, and First Commissioner of Works,

1894–5, in Gladstone's and Rosebery's Governments; Chief Whip to Liberal party, 1899–1906; Secretary of State for Home Affairs in Campbell-Bannerman's and Asquith's Cabinets, 1905–10; cr. Viscount, 1910; Governor-General of South Africa, 1910–14.

After Thirty Years, by Lord Gladstone (1930).

GLADSTONE, William Ewart (1809–1898); Conservative M.P., 1832–45; Peelite M.P., 1847–65; Liberal M.P., 1865–95; Junior Lord of the Treasury and afterwards Under-Secretary of State for War in Peel's Government, 1834–5; Vice-President of the Board of Trade in Peel's Government, 1841–3; President of the Board of Trade in Peel's Cabinet, 1843–4; resigned over Maynooth grant, 1844; Secretary of State for the Colonies, 1845–6; Chancellor of the Exchequer in Aberdeen's Government, 1852–5; reappointed by Palmerston but resigned over Roebuck's motion, 1855; Chancellor of the Exchequer in Palmerston's Cabinet, 1859–66; Chancellor of the Exchequer and Leader of the House of Commons in Russell's Cabinet, 1866; Leader of Liberal party, 1867–8; Prime Minister, 1868–74; resigned leadership of the Liberal party, 1875; Prime Minister, 1880–5, 1886, and 1892–4; resigned over Estimates, 1894.

The Life of William Ewart Gladstone, by John Morley, 3 vols. (1903).
Gleanings of Past Years, by the Rt. Hon. W. E. Gladstone, M.P., 6 vols. (1879).
Mr Gladstone at the Board of Trade, by Francis Edwin Hyde (1934).
Gladstone, by Francis Birrell (1933).
The Queen and Mr Gladstone, by Philip Guedalla, 2 vols. (1933).
Gladstone and Palmerston, edited by Philip Guedalla (1928).

GOSCHEN, George Joachim, first Viscount (1831–1907); Liberal M.P., 1863–85; Conservative M.P., 1886–1900; Vice-President of the Board of Trade in Russell's Government, 1865–6; Chancellor of the Duchy of Lancaster in Russell's Cabinet, 1866; President of the Poor Law Board in Gladstone's Cabinet, 1868–71; First Lord of the Admiralty in the same Cabinet, 1871–4; joined with Marquess of Hartington to form Liberal Unionist party; Chancellor of the Exchequer in Salisbury's Cabinet after resignation of Lord Randolph Churchill, 1886–92; First Lord of the Admiralty in Salisbury's Cabinet, 1895–1900; cr. Viscount Goschen, 1900.

The Life of George Joachim Goschen, first Viscount Goschen, 1831–1907, by the Hon. Arthur D. Elliott, 2 vols. (1911).

GRAHAM, Sir James, second Baronet (1792–1861); Whig M.P., 1818–21, 1826–41; Conservative M.P., 1841–6; Peelite M.P., 1846–59; Liberal

M.P., 1859–61; First Lord of the Admiralty in Grey's Cabinet, 1830–4; resigned with Stanley, 1834, and in opposition, 1834–41; Secretary of State for Home Affairs in Peel's Cabinet, 1841–6; First Lord of the Admiralty in Aberdeen's Cabinet, 1852–5; resigned from Palmerston's Government with other Peelites, 1855.

Life and Letters of Sir James Graham, by C. S. Parker, 2 vols. (1907).

GRANVILLE, Granville George Leveson-Gower, second Earl (1815–1891); Whig M.P., 1836–46; Under-Secretary of State for Foreign Affairs in Melbourne's Government, 1840–1; succeeded to Earldom, 1846; Vice-President of the Board of Trade, 1848, Paymaster of the Forces, 1848–51, and Secretary of State for Foreign Affairs, 1851–2, in Russell's Cabinet; Lord President of the Council, 1852–4, and Chancellor of the Duchy of Lancaster, 1854–8, in Aberdeen's and Palmerston's Cabinets; Leader of the Liberal Party in the House of Lords from 1855 to 1891; Lord President of the Council in Palmerston's and Russell's Cabinets, 1859–66; Secretary of State for the Colonies, 1868–70, and for Foreign Affairs, 1870–4 and 1880–5, in Gladstone's Cabinets; Secretary of State for the Colonies in Gladstone's Cabinet of 1886.

The Life of Granville George Leveson-Gower, Second Earl Granville, K.G., by Lord Edmond Fitzmaurice, 2 vols. (1905).

GREVILLE, Charles Cavendish Fulke (1794–1865); Clerk of the Council, 1821–59.

The Greville Memoirs: A Journal of the Reigns of King George IV and King William IV, by the late C. F. Greville. Edited by Henry Reeve, 3 vols. (1874).
The Greville Memoirs (Second Part). A Journal of the Reign of Queen Victoria from 1837 to 1852, by the late Charles C. F. Greville, 3 vols. (1885).
The Greville Memoirs (Third Part). A Journal of the Reign of Queen Victoria, 1853 to 1859, by the late Charles C. F. Greville, 2 vols. (1887).
The Letters of Charles Grey and Henry Reeve, edited by A. H. Johnson (1924).

GREY, Charles, second Earl (1764–1845); Whig M.P., 1786–1807; First Lord of the Admiralty, 1806; Secretary of State for Foreign Affairs, 1806–7; Prime Minister, 1830–4.

Lord Grey of the Reform Bill, by G. M. Trevelyan (1920).

GREY, Lieutenant-General the Hon. Charles, son of the above; Private Secretary to Prince Albert, 1849–61; Acting Private Secretary to Queen Victoria, 1862–7; Private Secretary to the Queen, 1867–70.

GREY OF FALLODON, Edward, first Viscount (1862–1932); Liberal M.P., 1885–1916; Under-Secretary of State for Foreign Affairs in Gladstone's and Rosebery's Governments, 1892–5; Secretary of State for Foreign Affairs in Campbell-Bannerman's and Asquith's Cabinets, 1905–16.

Twenty-Five Years, by Viscount Grey of Fallodon, 2 vols. (1925).
Grey of Fallodon, by G. M. Trevelyan (1937).

HAIG of Bemersyde, Field-Marshal Douglas Haig, first Earl (1861–1928); commanded First Army, British Expeditionary Force, France, 1914–15; Commander-in-Chief, British Forces in France, 1915–18. Cr. Earl, 1919.

The Private Papers of Douglas Haig, 1914–19, edited by Robert Blake (1952).

HAMILTON, Lord George Francis (1845–1927); Conservative M.P., 1868–1906; Under-Secretary of State for India, 1874–8, and Vice-President of the Council, 1878–80, in Disraeli's Government; First Lord of the Admiralty, 1885–6 and 1886–92, and Secretary of State for India, 1895–1903, in Salisbury's Cabinets.

Parliamentary Reminiscences and Reflections, by the Rt. Hon. Lord George Hamilton, 2 vols. (1917, 1922).

HARCOURT, Sir William George Granville Venables Vernon (1827–1904); Liberal M.P., 1868–1904; Solicitor-General in Gladstone's Government, 1873–4; Home Secretary in Gladstone's Cabinet, 1880–5; Chancellor of the Exchequer in Gladstone's Cabinets, 1886 and 1892–4; Chancellor of the Exchequer and Leader of the House of Commons in Rosebery's Cabinet, 1894–5; resigned leadership of Liberal party in House of Commons, 1898.

The Life of Sir William Harcourt, by A. G. Gardiner, 2 vols. (1923).

HARDY, Gathorne Gathorne-, *see* CRANBROOK, first Earl of

HARTINGTON, Marquess of, *see* DEVONSHIRE, eighth Duke of

HICKS BEACH, Sir Michael, *see* ST ALDWYN, first Viscount

HOARE, Sir Samuel, *see* TEMPLEWOOD, first Viscount.

HODGE, John (1855–1937); Labour M.P., 1906–23; trade union leader; Minister for Labour, 1916–17, and Minister of Pensions, 1917–19, in Lloyd George's Government.

Workman's Cottage to Windsor Castle, by the Rt. Hon. J. Hodge (n.d.).

JAMES OF HEREFORD, Henry, first Baron (1828–1911); Liberal M.P., 1869–85; Liberal Unionist M.P., 1886–95; Solicitor-General in Gladstone's

Government, 1873; Attorney-General in Gladstone's Governments, 1873–4 and 1880–5; joined Liberal Unionist party in 1886; Chancellor of the Duchy of Lancaster in Salisbury's Cabinet, 1895–1903.

Lord James of Hereford, by Lord Askwith (1930).

JOYNSON-HICKS, Sir William, *see* BRENTFORD, first Viscount

KILBRACKEN, of Killegar, Sir Arthur Godley, first Baron (1847–1935); Private Secretary to Mr Gladstone, 1872–4 and 1880–2; Commissioner of Inland Revenue, 1882–3; Permanent Under-Secretary of State for India, 1883–1909.

Reminiscences of Lord Kilbracken (1931).

LABOUCHERE, Henry du Pré (1831–1912); diplomatic service, 1854–64; founder and editor of *Truth*, from 1876; Liberal M.P., 1876–1905.

The Life of Henry Labouchere, by Algar Labouchere Thorold (1913).

LANSDOWNE, Henry Charles Keith Petty-Fitzmaurice, fifth Marquess of (1845–1927); Lord of the Treasury, 1869–72, and Under-Secretary of State for War, 1872–4, in Gladstone's Government; Under-Secretary for India in Gladstone's Government, 1880; Governor-General of Canada, 1883–8; Governor-General of India, 1888–93; Secretary of State for War, 1895–1900, and for Foreign Affairs, 1900–5, in Salisbury's and Balfour's Cabinets; Minister without Portfolio in Asquith's Cabinet, 1915–16.

Lord Lansdowne: A Biography, by Lord Newton (1929).

LANSDOWNE, Henry Petty-Fitzmaurice, third Marquess of (1780–1863); Whig M.P., 1803–9; Chancellor of the Exchequer, 1806–7; Minister without Portfolio, 1827–8; Lord President of the Council in Whig Cabinets, 1830–41, and in Russell's Cabinet, 1846–52; Minister without Portfolio in Aberdeen's and Palmerston's Cabinets, 1852–63.

LAW, Andrew Bonar (1858–1923); Conservative M.P., 1900–23; Parliamentary Secretary to the Board of Trade in Balfour's Government, 1902–6; Leader of the Opposition, 1911–15; Secretary of State for the Colonies in Asquith's Cabinet, 1915–16; Chancellor of the Exchequer in Lloyd George's War Cabinet, 1916–18; Lord Privy Seal and Leader of the House of Commons in Lloyd George's Cabinet, 1919–21; Prime Minister, 1922–3.

The Strange Case of Andrew Bonar Law, by H. A. Taylor (n.d.).
The Unknown Prime Minister, by Robert Blake (1955).

LLOYD GEORGE, Earl, *see* GEORGE, David Lloyd

LONG OF WRAXALL, Walter Hume, first Viscount (1854–1917), Conservative M.P., 1880–1921; Parliamentary Secretary to the Local Government Board in Salisbury's Government, 1886–92; President of the Board of Agriculture, 1895–1900, and of the Local Government Board, 1900–5, in Salisbury's and Balfour's Cabinets; Chief Secretary for Ireland, 1905–6; President of the Local Government Board in Asquith's Cabinet, 1915–16; Secretary of State for the Colonies in Lloyd George's Government, 1916–18; First Lord of the Admiralty in Lloyd George's Cabinet, 1919–21; cr. Viscount, 1921.

Memoirs, by Viscount Long of Wraxall (1923).

LOWE, Robert, *see* SHERBROOKE, first Viscount

MACAULAY, Thomas Babington, first Baron (1800–1859); Liberal M.P., 1830–2; various administrative offices in England and India, 1832–8; Liberal M.P., 1839–47 and 1852–6; Secretary at War in Melbourne's Government, 1839–41; cr. Lord Macaulay, 1857; the historian.

The Life and Letters of Lord Macaulay, by George Otto Trevelyan, M.P., 2 vols., new edition (1878).

MACDONALD, James Ramsay (1866–1937); Labour M.P., 1906–18 and 1922–31; National Labour M.P., 1931–5, and 1936–7; Prime Minister and Secretary of State for Foreign Affairs, 1924; Prime Minister, 1929–35; Lord President of the Council, 1935–7.

The Life of James Ramsay MacDonald, by Lord Elton (1939).

MACMILLAN, Harold (b. 1894); Conservative M.P., 1924–9 and since 1931; Parliamentary Secretary, Ministry of Supply, 1940–2, Parliamentary Under-Secretary of State, Colonial Office, 1942, and Minister Resident at Allied H.Q. in North-West Africa, 1942–5, in Churchill's War Government, Secretary of State for Air, 1945, in Churchill's Caretaker Government; Minister of Housing and Local Government, 1951–4, and Minister of Defence, 1954–5, in Churchill's last Government; Secretary of State for Foreign Affairs, 1955, and Chancellor of the Exchequer, 1955–7, in Eden's Government; Prime Minister since 1957.

MAGEE, William Connor (1821–1891); Dean of Cork, 1864–8; Bishop of Peterborough, 1868–91; Archbishop of York, 1891.

The Life and Correspondence of William Connor Magee, Archbishop of York, by John Cotter MacDonnell, D.D., 2 vols. (1896).

MALMESBURY, James Howard Harris, third Earl of (1807–1899); Conservative M.P., 1841; succeeded to Earldom, 1841; Protectionist Whip in House of Lords; Secretary of State for Foreign Affairs in Derby's Cabinets, 1852 and 1858–9; Lord Privy Seal in Derby's and Disraeli's Cabinets, 1866–8 and 1874–6.

Memoirs of an Ex-Minister: An Autobiography, by the Rt. Hon the Earl of Malmesbury, K.G., 2 vols. (1884), new edition (1885). [References are to the new edition.]

MANNERS, Lord John, *see* RUTLAND, seventh Duke of

MELBOURNE, William Lamb, second Viscount (1779–1848); Whig M.P., 1806–12, 1816–29; Chief Secretary for Ireland, 1827–30; succeeded to Viscounty, 1829; Home Secretary in Grey's Cabinet, 1830–4; Prime Minister, 1834; 'dismissed', 1834; Prime Minister, 1835–41.

Memoirs of William Lamb, Second Viscount Melbourne, by W. M. Torrens, new edition, revised by the author (1890).

Lord Melbourne's Papers, edited by Lloyd C. Sanders, 2nd ed. (1890).

MELCHETT, Alfred Moritz Mond, first Baron (1868–1930); Liberal M.P., 1906–28; First Commissioner of Works, 1916–21, and Minister of Health, 1921–2, in Lloyd George's Cabinet; cr. Baron, 1928.

Alfred Mond, first Lord Melchett, by Hector Bolitho (1932).

MILNER, Sir Alfred, first Viscount (1854–1925); Private Secretary to Mr Goschen (Chancellor of the Exchequer), 1887–9; Chairman, Board of Inland Revenue, 1892–7; Governor of the Cape of Good Hope, 1897–1901; Governor of Transvaal and Orange River Colony, 1901–5, and High Commissioner for South Africa, 1897–1905; Minister without Portfolio in Lloyd George's War Cabinet, 1916–18; Secretary of State for War in Lloyd George's Government, 1918–19; Secretary of State for the Colonies in Lloyd George's Cabinet, 1919–21; cr. Baron, 1901; Viscount, 1902.

The Milner Papers, edited by Cecil Headlam, 2 vols. (1932, 1933).

MOND, Sir Alfred, *see* MELCHETT, first Baron

MORLEY of Blackburn, John, first Viscount (1838–1923); Liberal M.P., 1883–1908; Chief Secretary for Ireland in Gladstone's and Rosebery's Cabinets, 1886 and 1892–5; Secretary of State for India in Campbell-Bannerman's and Asquith's Cabinets, 1905–10; Lord President of the

Council in Asquith's Cabinet, 1910–14; resigned on declaration of war; cr. Viscount, 1908.

Recollections, by John, Viscount Morley, 2 vols. (1917).

NORTON, Charles Bowyer Adderley, first Baron (1814–1905); Conservative M.P., 1841–78; became protectionist in 1846; Vice-President of the Council in Derby's Government, 1858–9; Under-Secretary of State for the Colonies in the Derby–Disraeli Government, 1866–8; President of the Board of Trade in Disraeli's Government, 1874–8; cr. Baron, 1878.

Life of Lord Norton, by William S. Childe-Pemberton (1909).

O'CONNELL, Daniel (1775–1847); 'the Liberator'; Nationalist M.P., 1828–47; founded the 'Order of Liberator'.

The Life and Letters of Daniel O'Connell, M.P., edited by his son, John O'Connell, M.P., 2 vols. (1846).

O'CONNOR, Thomas Power (1848–1929); Nationalist M.P., 1885–1929; journalist.

Memoirs of an Old Parliamentarian, by the Rt. Hon. T. P. O'Connor, 2 vols. (1929).

OXFORD AND ASQUITH, Herbert Henry Asquith, first Earl of (1852–1928); Liberal M.P., 1886–1918 and 1920–4; Secretary of State for Home Affairs in Gladstone's and Rosebery's Cabinets, 1892–5; Chancellor of the Exchequer in Campbell-Bannerman's Cabinet, 1905–8; Prime Minister, 1908–16; cr. Earl, 1925.

Memories and Reflections, by the Earl of Oxford and Asquith, 2 vols. (1926).
Fifty Years of Parliament, by the Earl of Oxford and Asquith, 2 vols. (1928).
Life of Herbert Henry Asquith, Lord Oxford and Asquith, by J. A. Spender and Cyril Asquith, 2 vols. (1932).

PALMERSTON, Henry John Temple, third Viscount, in the peerage of Ireland (1784–1865); succeeded to Viscounty, 1802; Tory M.P., 1807–30; Whig and Liberal M.P., 1830–65; Junior Lord of the Admiralty, 1808–9; Secretary at War, 1809–28; Secretary of State for Foreign Affairs in Grey's, Melbourne's and Russell's Cabinets, 1830–4, 1835–41, 1846–51; dismissed by Russell, 1851, and had his 'tit-for-tat'; Home Secretary in Aberdeen's Cabinet, 1852–5; Prime Minister, 1855–8, 1858–65.

The Life of Henry John Temple, Viscount Palmerston, by the Rt Hon. Sir Henry Lytton Bulwer, G.C.B., M.P. (Lord Dalling), 3 vols. (1870–4).
The Life of Henry John Temple, Viscount Palmerston, 1846–1865, by the Hon. Evelyn Ashley, M.P., 2 vols. (1876).
Gladstone and Palmerston, by Philip Guedalla (1928).
Palmerston, by Philip Guedalla (1926).

PANMURE, Fox Maule, second Baron, subsequently eleventh Earl of Dalhousie in the peerage of Scotland; Liberal M.P., 1835–52; Under-Secretary of State in Melbourne's Government, 1835–41; Secretary at War in Russell's Government, 1846–52; Secretary of State for War in Palmerston's Government, 1855–8; succeeded to Barony, 1852; and to Earldom, 1860.

The Panmure Papers, edited by Sir George Douglas, Bart., M.A., and Sir George Dalhousie Ramsay, C.B., 2 vols. (1908).

PEEL, Sir Robert, second Baronet (1788–1850); Tory M.P., 1809–50; Under-Secretary of State for War and Colonies, 1810–12; Chief Secretary for Ireland, 1812–18; Home Secretary, 1822–7; Home Secretary and Leader of the House of Commons in Wellington's Cabinet, 1828–30; Prime Minister, 1834 and 1841–6.

Memoirs of the Rt Hon. Sir Robert Peel, Bart., M.P., published by the Trustees of his Papers, Lord Mahon (Earl Stanhope) and the Rt Hon. Edward Cardwell, M.P., 2 vols. (1856).
Sir Robert Peel from his Private Papers, edited by Charles Stuart Parker, 3 vols. (1891). [Quoted as *Peel Papers.*]
Peel and the Conservative Party, by George Kitson Clark (1929).
Sir Robert Peel, by the Earl of Rosebery [in *Miscellanies*, vol. 1].

PONSONBY, General Sir Henry (1825–1895); Private Secretary to Queen Victoria, 1870–95.

Henry Ponsonby, by A. Ponsonby (1947).

REDMOND, John Edward (1856–1918); Nationalist M.P., 1881–1918; supported Parnell, 1890, and led Parnellite group after 1891; Leader of reunited Nationalist party, 1900–18.

The Life of John Redmond, by Denis Gwynn (1932).

REEVE, Henry (1813–1895); staff of *The Times*, 1840–55; editor, *Edinburgh Review*, 1855–95; editor of Greville's *Memoirs* (q.v.); Registrar of the Privy Council.

Memoirs of the Life and Correspondence of Henry Reeve, C.B., D.C.L., by John Knox Laughton, 2nd edition, 2 vols. (1893).
The Letters of Charles Greville and Henry Reeve, 1836–1865, edited by the Rev. A. H. Johnson, M.A. (1924).

RIPON, George Frederick Samuel Robinson, first Marquess of (1827–1909); son of the first Viscount Goderich (afterwards Earl of Ripon), the Prime Minister; known as Viscount Goderich, 1833–59; Liberal M.P., 1853–9; succeeded as Earl de Grey and Earl of Ripon, 1859; Under-Secretary of

State for War, for India, and for War again, in Palmerston's Government, 1859–63; Secretary of State for War in Palmerston's and Russell's Cabinets, 1863–6; Secretary of State for India in Russell's Cabinet, 1866; Lord President of the Council in Gladstone's Cabinet, 1868–73; cr. Marquess, 1871; Governor-General of India, 1880–4; First Lord of the Admiralty in Gladstone's Cabinet, 1886; Secretary of State for the Colonies in Gladstone's and Rosebery's Cabinets, 1892–5; Lord Privy Seal and Leader of the House of Lords in Campbell-Bannerman's Cabinet, 1905–8.

Life of the first Marquess of Ripon, by Lucien Wolf, 2 vols. (1921).

ROSEBERY, Archibald Philip Primrose, fifth Earl of (1847–1929); succeeded to Earldom, 1868; Under-Secretary of State for Home Affairs in Gladstone's Government, 1881–3; Lord Privy Seal and First Commissioner of Works in Gladstone's Cabinet, 1885; Secretary of State for Foreign Affairs in Gladstone's Cabinets, 1886 and 1892–4; Prime Minister, 1894–5.

Lord Rosebery, by the Marquess of Crewe, 2 vols. (1931).
Miscellanies, Literary and Historical, by Lord Rosebery, 2 vols. (1921).

RUSSELL, John, first Earl (1792–1878); known as Lord John Russell for most of his political career; Whig M.P., 1813–61; Paymaster-General of the Forces in Grey's Cabinet, 1831–4; Home Secretary and Leader of the House of Commons in Melbourne's Cabinet, 1835–9; Secretary of State for the Colonies, 1839–41; Prime Minister, 1846–52; Foreign Secretary and Leader of the House of Commons in Aberdeen's Cabinet, 1852–3, continuing as Minister without Portfolio until 1854, when he became Lord President of the Council; resigned 1855 on Roebuck's motion; Secretary of State for the Colonies in Palmerston's Cabinet, 1855; Foreign Secretary in Palmerston's Cabinet, 1859–65; cr. Earl Russell, 1861; Prime Minister on death of Palmerston, 1865–6.

The Life of Lord John Russell, by Spencer Walpole, 2 vols. (1889).
The Later Correspondence of Lord John Russell, edited by G. P. Gooch, 2 vols. (1925).
Selections from Speeches of Earl Russell and from Despatches, 2 vols. (1870).
An Essay on the History of the English Government and Constitution, by John, Earl Russell (1865).

RUTLAND, [Lord] John James Robert Manners, seventh Duke of Rutland (1818–1906); Conservative M.P., 1841–88; succeeded to the Dukedom, 1888; one of Disraeli's 'Young England Party'; First Commissioner of Works in Derby's Cabinets, 1852, 1858, and 1866–8; Postmaster-

General in Disraeli's Cabinet, 1874–80; Chancellor of the Duchy of Lancaster in Salisbury's Cabinet, 1886–92.

Lord John Manners and His Friends, by Charles Whibley, 2 vols. (1925).

ST ALDWYN, Sir Michael Edward Hicks Beach, first Earl (1837–1916); Conservative M.P., 1864–1906; Parliamentary Secretary to the Poor Law Board and afterwards Under-Secretary of State for Home Affairs in Disraeli's Government, 1868; Chief Secretary for Ireland in Disraeli's Government, 1874–8, entering Cabinet in 1876; Secretary of State for the Colonies in Lord Beaconsfield's Cabinet, 1878–80; Chancellor of the Exchequer and Leader of the House of Commons in Salisbury's Cabinet, 1885; Chief Secretary for Ireland, 1886–7, and President of the Board of Trade, 1888–92, in Salisbury's Cabinet; Chancellor of the Exchequer in Salisbury's Cabinet, 1895–1902; cr. Viscount, 1906, and Earl, 1915.

Life of Sir Michael Hicks Beach, by Lady Victoria Hicks Beach, 2 vols. (1932).

SALISBURY, Robert Arthur Talbot Gascoyne-Cecil, third Marquess of (1830–1903); Conservative M.P., 1853–68 (as Lord Robert Cecil until 1865 and as Viscount Cranborne, 1865–8); succeeded to Marquisate, 1868; Secretary of State for India in Derby's Cabinet, 1866–7, resigning over Reform Bill; Secretary of State for India, 1874–8, and for Foreign Affairs, 1878–80, in Disraeli's Cabinet; Leader of Conservative party in House of Lords after death of Beaconsfield; Prime Minister and Foreign Secretary, 1885–6, 1886–92, and 1895–1900; Prime Minister and Lord Privy Seal, 1900–2.

Life of Robert, Marquis of Salisbury, by his daughter, Lady Gwendolen Cecil, 5 vols. (1921).

SALISBURY, Robert Arthur James Gascoyne-Cecil, fifth Marquess of, (b. 1893); Conservative M.P., 1929–41 (as Viscount Cranborne); Parliamentary Under-Secretary of State, Foreign Office, 1935–8, in Baldwin's and Chamberlain's Governments; Paymaster-General, 1940, Secretary of State for the Dominions, 1940–2; Secretary of State for the Colonies, 1942, Lord Privy Seal, 1942–3, and Secretary of State for the Dominions, 1943–5, in Churchill's War Government; Lord Privy Seal, 1951–2, and Secretary of State for Commonwealth Relations, 1952, in Churchill's last Government; Lord President of the Council, 1952–7, in Churchill's, Eden's and Macmillan's Governments. Cr. Lord Cecil of Essendon, 1941; succeeded fourth Marquess, 1947.

SAMUEL, Herbert Louis Samuel, first Viscount (b. 1870); Liberal M.P., 1902–18 and 1929–35; Parliamentary Under-Secretary of State for Home Affairs, 1905–9, in Campbell-Bannerman's and Asquith's Governments; Chancellor of the Duchy of Lancaster, 1909–10, Postmaster-General, 1910–14 and 1915–16, in Asquith's Cabinet; Leader of the Liberal Parliamentary party, 1931–5; Secretary of State for Home Affairs, 1931–2, in MacDonald's Cabinet.

Memoirs, by Viscount Samuel (1945).

SELBORNE, Sir Roundell Palmer, first Earl of (1812–1895); Conservative M.P., 1847, but gradually became Liberal, and Liberal M.P. until 1872; Solicitor-General, 1861–3, and Attorney-General, 1863–6, in Palmerston's and Russell's Governments; Lord Chancellor in Gladstone's Cabinets, 1872–4 and 1880–5; cr. Baron, 1872, and Earl, 1882; opposed Home Rule in 1886.

Memorials, by Roundell Palmer, Earl of Selborne, 4 vols. (1896–8).

SHERBROOKE, Robert Lowe, first Viscount (1811–1892); Liberal M.P., 1852–80; Joint Secretary of the Board of Control in Aberdeen's Government, 1852–5; Vice-President of the Board of Trade and Paymaster-General, 1855–8, and Vice-President of the Council, 1859–64, in Palmerston's Governments; led the 'Cave of Adullam' against the Reform Bill of 1866; Chancellor of the Exchequer in Gladstone's Cabinet, 1868–73, and Home Secretary, 1873–4; cr. Viscount, 1880.

Life and Letters of the Rt. Hon. Robert Lowe, Viscount Sherbrooke, by A. Patchett Martin, 2 vols. (1893).

SIMON, John Allsebrooke, first Viscount (1873–1954); Liberal M.P., 1906–18 and 1922–31; Liberal National M.P. and Leader of the Liberal National party, 1931–40; Solicitor-General in Asquith's Government, 1910–13; Attorney-General, 1913–15, and Secretary of State for Home Affairs in Asquith's Cabinets; Secretary of State for Foreign Affairs in MacDonald's Cabinet, 1931–5; Secretary of State for Home Affairs in Baldwin's Cabinet, 1935–7; Chancellor of the Exchequer in Chamberlain's Cabinet, 1937–40; Lord Chancellor in Churchill's Government, 1940–5.

Retrospect: the Memoirs of Viscount Simon (1953).

SMITH, Frederick Edwin, *see* BIRKENHEAD, first Earl of

SMITH, William Henry (1825–1891); Conservative M.P., 1868–91; First Lord of the Admiralty in Disraeli's Cabinet, 1877–80; First Lord of the

Treasury and Leader of the House of Commons in Salisbury's Cabinet, 1886–91.

Life and Times of the Rt. Hon. William Henry Smith, M.P., by Sir Herbert Maxwell, Bart., M.P., 2 vols. (1893).

SNOWDEN, Philip, first Viscount (1864–1937); Labour M.P., 1906–18 and 1922–31; Chancellor of the Exchequer in MacDonald's Cabinets, 1924, and 1929–32; cr. Viscount, 1931.

An Autobiography, by Philip, Viscount Snowden, 2 vols. (1934).

SOMERSET, Edward Adolphus Seymour, twelfth Duke of (1804–1885); Whig M.P., 1830–55; Junior Lord of the Treasury, 1835–9, Secretary to Board of Control, 1839–41, and Under-Secretary of State for Home Affairs, 1841, in Melbourne's Government; First Commissioner of Works in Russell's Cabinet, 1851–2; succeeded to Dukedom, 1855; First Lord of the Admiralty in Palmerston's and Russell's Cabinets, 1859–66.

Letters, Remains, and Memoirs of Edward Adolphus Seymour, twelfth Duke of Somerset, edited by W. H. Matlock and Lady Gwendolen Ramsden (1893).

SPENCER, John Charles, third Earl (1782–1845); known for much of his public life as Viscount Althorp; Whig M.P., 1806–34; Leader of the Whigs in the House of Commons, 1830, and Chancellor of the Exchequer and Leader of the House of Commons in Grey's Cabinet, 1830–4; succeeded to Earldom, 1834, with the result that the Government was 'dismissed' by William IV.

Memoirs of John Charles, Viscount Althorp, third Earl Spencer, by Sir Denis le Marchant, Bart. (1876).

STAMFORDHAM, Lieutenant-Colonel Sir Arthur John Bigge, first Baron (1849–1931); Assistant Private Secretary to Queen Victoria, 1880–95; Private Secretary to the Queen, 1895–1900; Private Secretary to King George V as Prince of Wales and King, 1901–30.

STANLEY, Arthur Penrhyn (1815–1881); Dean of Westminster, 1864–81.

The Life and Correspondence of Arthur Penrhyn Stanley, by Rowland E. Prothero, 2 vols. (1893).

STANLEY, Edward George Geoffrey Smith, known as Lord Stanley, *see* DERBY, fourteenth Earl of

STOCKMAR, Christian Friedrich, Baron von (1787–1863); adviser to Coburg family.

Memoirs of Baron Stockmar, by his son, Baron E. von Stockmar, 2 vols. (1872).

TAIT, Archibald Campbell (1811–1882); Dean of Carlisle, 1849–56; Bishop of London, 1856–69; Archbishop of Canterbury, 1869–82.

Life of Archbishop Campbell Tait, Archbishop of Canterbury, by Randall T. Davidson and William Benham, 3rd ed, 2 vols. (1891).

TAYLOR, Sir Herbert (1775–1839); Private Secretary to the Duke of York, George III, Queen Charlotte, and William IV.

The Taylor Papers, arranged by Ernest Taylor (1913).

TEMPLE, Frederick (1821–1902); Bishop of Exeter, 1869–85; Bishop of London, 1885–96; Archbishop of Canterbury, 1896–1902.

Memoirs of Archbishop Temple, by seven friends, 2 vols. (1906).

TEMPLEWOOD, (Sir) Samuel John Gurney Hoare, first Viscount; Conservative M.P., 1910–44; Secretary of State for Air, 1922–4 and 1924–9, in Baldwin's Cabinets; Secretary of State for India, 1931–5, in 'National' Government; Secretary of State for Foreign Affairs, 1935, and First Lord of the Admiralty, 1936–7, in Baldwin's Cabinet; Secretary of State for Home Affairs, 1937–9, in Chamberlain's Cabinet; Lord Privy Seal in Chamberlain's War Cabinet, 1939–40; H.M. Ambassador to Spain, 1940–4; cr. Viscount, 1944.

Nine Troubled Years, by Viscount Templewood (1955).

THOMAS, James Henry (1874–1947); Labour M.P., 1910–31; National Labour M.P., 1931–6; Secretary of State for the Colonies in MacDonald's Cabinet, 1923; Lord Privy Seal, 1929–30, and Secretary of State for the Dominions, 1930–5, in MacDonald's Cabinets.

My Story, by J. H. Thomas (1937).

THOMSON of Cardington, Christopher Birdwood, first Baron (1875–1930); cr. 1924; Secretary of State for Air in MacDonald's Cabinets, 1924 and 1929–30.

Lord Thomson of Cardington, by Princess Marthe Bibesco (1932).

TREVELYAN, Sir George Otto (1838–1928); Liberal M.P., 1865–97; Civil Lord of the Admiralty in Gladstone's Government, 1868–74; Secretary of the Admiralty, 1880–2, and Chief Secretary for Ireland, 1882–4, in

Gladstone's Government; Chancellor of the Duchy of Lancaster, 1884–5, and Secretary for Scotland, 1886 and 1892–5, in Gladstone's and Rosebery's Cabinets.

Sir George Otto Trevelyan, by his son, George Macaulay Trevelyan (1932).

VICTORIA, Queen (1819–1901); succeeded, 1837.

The Letters of Queen Victoria, 1st series, edited by Arthur Christopher Benson and Viscount Esher, 3 vols. (1907).
The Letters of Queen Victoria, 2nd series, edited by George Earl Buckle, 3 vols. (1926, 1928).
The Letters of Queen Victoria, 3rd series, edited by George Earl Buckle, 3 vols. (1930–2).
[See also under GLADSTONE and PALMERSTON.]

WELLINGTON, Arthur Wellesley, first Duke of (1769–1852); Tory M.P., 1790–5, 1806–9; Chief Secretary for Ireland, 1807–9; cr. Viscount, 1809, Marquess, 1812; Field-Marshal, 1813; cr. Duke, 1814; Master General of the Ordnance in the Cabinet, 1818–27; Prime Minister, 1828–30, Prime Minister and Home Secretary, 1834, on 'dismissal' of Melbourne and while Peel was posting home from Rome; Foreign Secretary in Peel's Cabinet, 1834; Leader of Conservative Opposition in House of Lords, 1835–41; Minister without Portfolio in Peel's Cabinet, 1841–6; Commander-in-Chief, 1827–8, and 1842–52.

The Duke, by Philip Guedalla (1931).
The Life of Wellington, by W. H. Maxwell, 2 vols. (1839).

WEST, Sir Algernon Edward (1832–1921); Private Secretary to Gladstone, 1868–72; Commissioner of Inland Revenue, 1872–92, being Chairman of the Board, 1881–92.

Recollections, by the Rt. Hon. Sir Algernon West, 2nd ed., 2 vols. (1899).
Private Diaries of the Rt. Hon. Sir Algernon West, edited by H. G. Hutchinson (1922).

WILSON, Field-Marshal Sir Henry Hughes, Bt. (1864–1922); Director of Military Operations, 1910–14; Assistant Chief of General Staff to General French, 1914; Chief of Imperial General Staff, 1918–22.

Field-Marshal Sir Henry Wilson, His Life and Diaries, by Major-General Sir C. E. Callwell, 2 vols. (1927).

WOLVERHAMPTON, Henry Hartley Fowler, first Viscount (1830–1911); Liberal M.P., 1880–1908; Under-Secretary of State for Home Affairs, 1884–5, and Financial Secretary to the Treasury, 1886, in Gladstone's Governments; President of the Board of Trade in Gladstone's Cabinet,

1892–4, and Secretary of State for India in Rosebery's Cabinet, 1894–5; Chancellor of the Duchy of Lancaster in Campbell-Bannerman's Cabinet, 1905–8; cr. Viscount, 1908; Lord President of the Council in Asquith's Cabinet, 1908.

The Life of Henry Hartley Fowler, first Viscount Wolverhampton, by his daughter, Edith Henrietta Fowler (1912).

WYNDHAM, George (1863–1913); Private Secretary to Mr Balfour, 1887; Conservative M.P., 1889–1913; Under-Secretary of State for War in Salisbury's Government, 1898–1900; Chief Secretary for Ireland in Salisbury's and Balfour's Cabinets, 1900–5.

Life and Letters of George Wyndham, by G. W. Mackail and Guy Wyndham, 2 vols. (n.d.).

YPRES, Field-Marshal John Denton Pinkstone French, first Earl of (1852–1925); Chief of Imperial General Staff, 1911–14; Commander-in-Chief in France, 1914–15; Commander-in-Chief in the United Kingdom, 1915–18; Lord-Lieutenant of Ireland, 1918–21; cr. Viscount, 1915; Earl, 1921.

The Life of Field-Marshal Sir John French, by his son, Major the Hon. Gerald French (1931).

Index